FORD ESCORT/TRACER
1991-02 REPAIR MANUAL

Covers all U.S. and Canadian models of Ford Escort and Mercury Tracer 1991 through 2002

by Alan Ahlstrand

CHILTON Automotive Books

PUBLISHED BY **HAYNES NORTH AMERICA, Inc.**

Manufactured in USA
©2009, 2010 Haynes North America, Inc.
ISBN-13: 978-1-56392-893-2
ISBN-10: 1-56392-893-0
Library of Congress Control Number 2010939034

Haynes Publishing Group
Sparkford Nr Yeovil
Somerset BA22 7JJ England

Haynes North America, Inc
861 Lawrence Drive
Newbury Park
California 91320 USA

ABCDE
FGHIJ
KLMNO
PQRST
2

10N4

Contents

Mechanic, author and photographer with Escort

ACKNOWLEDGEMENTS

Wiring diagrams originated exclusively for Haynes North America, Inc. by Valley Forge Technical Information Services.

113719622

About this manual

ITS PURPOSE

The purpose of this manual is to help you get the best value from your vehicle. It can do so in several ways. It can help you decide what work must be done, even if you choose to have it done by a dealer service department or a repair shop; it provides information and procedures for routine maintenance and servicing; and it offers diagnostic and repair procedures to follow when trouble occurs.

We hope you use the manual to tackle the work yourself. For many simpler jobs, doing it yourself may be quicker than arranging an appointment to get the vehicle into a shop and making the trips to leave it and pick it up. More importantly, a lot of money can be saved by avoiding the expense the shop must pass on to you to cover its labor and overhead costs. An added benefit is the sense of satisfaction and accomplishment that you feel after doing the job yourself.

USING THE MANUAL

The manual is divided into Chapters. Each Chapter is divided into numbered Sections, which are headed in bold type between horizontal lines. Each Section consists of consecutively numbered paragraphs.

At the beginning of each numbered Section you will be referred to any illustrations which apply to the procedures in that Section. The reference numbers used in illustration captions pinpoint the pertinent Section and the Step within that Section. That is, illustration 3.2 means the illustration refers to Section 3 and Step (or paragraph) 2 within that Section.

Procedures, once described in the text, are not normally repeated. When it's necessary to refer to another Chapter, the reference will be given as Chapter and Section number. Cross references given without use of the word "Chapter" apply to Sections and/or paragraphs in the same Chapter. For example, "see Section 8" means in the same Chapter.

References to the left or right side of the vehicle assume you are sitting in the driver's seat, facing forward.

Even though we have prepared this manual with extreme care, neither the publisher nor the author can accept responsibility for any errors in, or omissions from, the information given.

➡NOTE

A *Note* provides information necessary to properly complete a procedure or information which will make the procedure easier to understand.

✳ CAUTION

A *Caution* provides a special procedure or special steps which must be taken while completing the procedure where the Caution is found. Not heeding a Caution can result in damage to the assembly being worked on.

✳ WARNING

A *Warning* provides a special procedure or special steps which must be taken while completing the procedure where the Warning is found. Not heeding a Warning can result in personal injury.

Introduction

The front-drive design features unitized construction and 4-wheel independent suspension. Models are available in 2-door, 4-door and station wagon body styles.

The transversely mounted four-cylinder engine drives the front wheels through a five-speed manual or four-speed automatic transaxle by way of unequal length driveaxles. The rack-and-pinion steering gear is mounted behind the engine and is available with power assist. Brakes are discs at the front and drum-type at the rear with vacuum assist. Rear disc brakes are optional.

Vehicle identification numbers

Modifications are a continuing and unpublicized process in vehicle manufacturing. Since spare parts lists and manuals are compiled on a numerical basis, the individual vehicle numbers are necessary to correctly identify the component required.

VEHICLE IDENTIFICATION NUMBER (VIN)

This very important identification number is stamped on a plate attached to the dashboard inside the windshield on the driver's side of the vehicle (see illustration). The VIN also appears on the Vehicle Certificate of Title and Registration. It contains information such as where and when the vehicle was manufactured, the model year and the body style.

VEHICLE CERTIFICATION LABEL

The Vehicle Certification Label is attached to the driver's side door pillar (see illustration). Information on this label includes the name of the manufacturer, the month and year of production, the Gross Vehicle Weight Rating (GVWR), the Gross Axle Weight Rating (GAWR) and the certification statement.

ENGINE NUMBER

The engine number is stamped onto a machined pad on the external surface of the engine block. There's also an identification label that's usually on the timing belt cover.

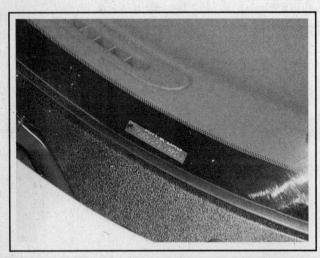

The Vehicle Identification Number (VIN) is visible from outside the vehicle through the driver's side of the windshield

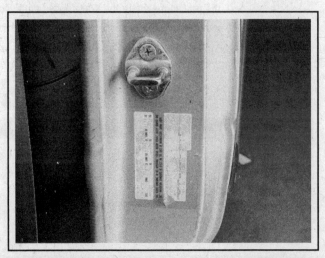

The Certification label is located on the left front door post

Buying parts

Replacement parts are available from many sources, which generally fall into one of two categories - authorized dealer parts departments and independent retail auto parts stores. Our advice concerning these parts is as follows:

Retail auto parts stores: Good auto parts stores will stock frequently needed components which wear out relatively fast, such as clutch components, exhaust systems, brake parts, tune-up parts, etc. These stores often supply new or reconditioned parts on an exchange basis, which can save a considerable amount of money. Discount auto parts stores are often very good places to buy materials and parts needed for general vehicle maintenance such as oil, grease, filters, spark plugs, belts, touch-up paint, bulbs, etc. They also usually sell tools and general accessories, have convenient hours, charge lower prices and can often be found not far from home.

Authorized dealer parts department: This is the best source for parts which are unique to the vehicle and not generally available elsewhere (such as major engine parts, transmission parts, trim pieces, etc.).

Warranty information: If the vehicle is still covered under warranty, be sure that any replacement parts purchased - regardless of the source - do not invalidate the warranty!

To be sure of obtaining the correct parts, have engine and chassis numbers available and, if possible, take the old parts along for positive identification.

MAINTENANCE TECHNIQUES

There are a number of techniques involved in maintenance and repair that will be referred to throughout this manual. Application of these techniques will enable the home mechanic to be more efficient, better organized and capable of performing the various tasks properly, which will ensure that the repair job is thorough and complete.

Fasteners

Fasteners are nuts, bolts, studs and screws used to hold two or more parts together. There are a few things to keep in mind when working with fasteners. Almost all of them use a locking device of some type, either a lockwasher, locknut, locking tab or thread adhesive. All threaded fasteners should be clean and straight, with undamaged threads and undamaged corners on the hex head where the wrench fits. Develop the habit of replacing all damaged nuts and bolts with new ones. Special locknuts with nylon or fiber inserts can only be used once. If they are removed, they lose their locking ability and must be replaced with new ones.

Rusted nuts and bolts should be treated with a penetrating fluid to ease removal and prevent breakage. Some mechanics use turpentine in a spout-type oil can, which works quite well. After applying the rust penetrant, let it work for a few minutes before trying to loosen the nut or bolt. Badly rusted fasteners may have to be chiseled or sawed off or removed with a special nut breaker, available at tool stores.

If a bolt or stud breaks off in an assembly, it can be drilled and removed with a special tool commonly available for this purpose. Most automotive machine shops can perform this task, as well as other repair procedures, such as the repair of threaded holes that have been stripped out.

Flat washers and lockwashers, when removed from an assembly, should always be replaced exactly as removed. Replace any damaged washers with new ones. Never use a lockwasher on any soft metal surface (such as aluminum), thin sheet metal or plastic.

Fastener sizes

For a number of reasons, automobile manufacturers are making wider and wider use of metric fasteners. Therefore, it is important to be able to tell the difference between standard (sometimes called U.S. or SAE) and metric hardware, since they cannot be interchanged.

All bolts, whether standard or metric, are sized according to diameter, thread pitch and length. For example, a standard 1/2 - 13 x 1 bolt is 1/2 inch in diameter, has 13 threads per inch and is 1 inch long. An M12 - 1.75 x 25 metric bolt is 12 mm in diameter, has a thread pitch of 1.75 mm (the distance between threads) and is 25 mm long. The two bolts are nearly identical, and easily confused, but they are not interchangeable.

In addition to the differences in diameter, thread pitch and length, metric and standard bolts can also be distinguished by examining the bolt heads. To begin with, the distance across the flats on a standard bolt head is measured in inches, while the same dimension on a metric bolt is sized in millimeters (the same is true for nuts). As a result, a standard wrench should not be used on a metric bolt and a metric wrench should not be used on a standard bolt. Also, most standard bolts have slashes

radiating out from the center of the head to denote the grade or strength of the bolt, which is an indication of the amount of torque that can be applied to it. The greater the number of slashes, the greater the strength of the bolt. Grades 0 through 5 are commonly used on automobiles. Metric bolts have a property class (grade) number, rather than a slash, molded into their heads to indicate bolt strength. In this case, the higher the number, the stronger the bolt. Property class numbers 8.8, 9.8 and 10.9 are commonly used on automobiles.

Strength markings can also be used to distinguish standard hex nuts from metric hex nuts. Many standard nuts have dots stamped into one side, while metric nuts are marked with a number. The greater the number of dots, or the higher the number, the greater the strength of the nut.

Metric studs are also marked on their ends according to property class (grade). Larger studs are numbered (the same as metric bolts), while smaller studs carry a geometric code to denote grade.

It should be noted that many fasteners, especially Grades 0 through 2, have no distinguishing marks on them. When such is the case, the only way to determine whether it is standard or metric is to measure the thread pitch or compare it to a known fastener of the same size.

Standard fasteners are often referred to as SAE, as opposed to metric. However, it should be noted that SAE technically refers to a non-metric fine thread fastener only. Coarse thread non-metric fasteners are referred to as USS sizes.

Since fasteners of the same size (both standard and metric) may have different strength ratings, be sure to reinstall any bolts, studs or nuts removed from your vehicle in their original locations. Also, when replacing a fastener with a new one, make sure that the new one has a strength rating equal to or greater than the original.

Tightening sequences and procedures

Most threaded fasteners should be tightened to a specific torque value (torque is the twisting force applied to a threaded component such as a nut or bolt). Overtightening the fastener can weaken it and cause it to break, while undertightening can cause it to eventually come loose. Bolts, screws and studs, depending on the material they are made of and their thread diameters, have specific torque values, many of which are noted in the Specifications at the end of each Chapter. Be sure to follow the torque recommendations closely. For fasteners not assigned a specific torque, a general torque value chart is presented here as a guide. These torque values are for dry (unlubricated) fasteners threaded into steel or cast iron (not aluminum). As was previously mentioned, the size and grade of a fastener determine the amount of torque that can safely be applied to it. The figures listed here are approximate for Grade 2 and Grade 3 fasteners. Higher grades can tolerate higher torque values.

Fasteners laid out in a pattern, such as cylinder head bolts, oil pan bolts, differential cover bolts, etc., must be loosened or tightened in sequence to avoid warping the component. This sequence will normally be shown in the appropriate Chapter. If a specific pattern is not given, the following procedures can be used to prevent warping.

Initially, the bolts or nuts should be assembled finger-tight only. Next, they should be tightened one full turn each, in a criss-cross or diagonal pattern. After each one has been tightened one full turn, return to the first one and tighten them all one-half turn, following the same

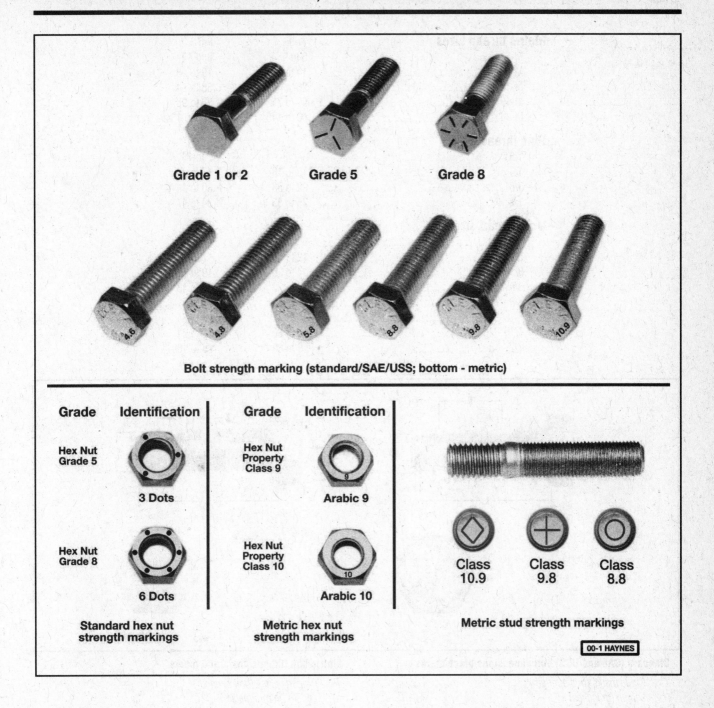

Grade 1 or 2   Grade 5   Grade 8

Bolt strength marking (standard/SAE/USS; bottom - metric)

Grade	Identification	Grade	Identification
Hex Nut Grade 5	3 Dots	Hex Nut Property Class 9	Arabic 9
Hex Nut Grade 8	6 Dots	Hex Nut Property Class 10	Arabic 10

Standard hex nut strength markings

Metric hex nut strength markings

Class 10.9   Class 9.8   Class 8.8

Metric stud strength markings

00-1 HAYNES

pattern. Finally, tighten each of them one-quarter turn at a time until each fastener has been tightened to the proper torque. To loosen and remove the fasteners, the procedure would be reversed.

Component disassembly

Component disassembly should be done with care and purpose to help ensure that the parts go back together properly. Always keep track of the sequence in which parts are removed. Make note of special characteristics or marks on parts that can be installed more than one way, such as a grooved thrust washer on a shaft. It is a good idea to lay the disassembled parts out on a clean surface in the order that they were removed. It may also be helpful to make sketches or take instant photos of components before removal.

When removing fasteners from a component, keep track of their locations. Sometimes threading a bolt back in a part, or putting the washers and nut back on a stud, can prevent mix-ups later. If nuts and bolts cannot be returned to their original locations, they should be kept in a compartmented box or a series of small boxes. A cupcake or muffin tin is ideal for this purpose, since each cavity can hold the bolts and nuts from a particular area (i.e. oil pan bolts, valve cover bolts, engine

Metric thread sizes

	Ft-lbs	Nm
M-6	6 to 9	9 to 12
M-8	14 to 21	19 to 28
M-10	28 to 40	38 to 54
M-12	50 to 71	68 to 96
M-14	80 to 140	109 to 154

Pipe thread sizes

1/8	5 to 8	7 to 10
1/4	12 to 18	17 to 24
3/8	22 to 33	30 to 44
1/2	25 to 35	34 to 47

U.S. thread sizes

1/4 - 20	6 to 9	9 to 12
5/16 - 18	12 to 18	17 to 24
5/16 - 24	14 to 20	19 to 27
3/8 - 16	22 to 32	30 to 43
3/8 - 24	27 to 38	37 to 51
7/16 - 14	40 to 55	55 to 74
7/16 - 20	40 to 60	55 to 81
1/2 - 13	55 to 80	75 to 108

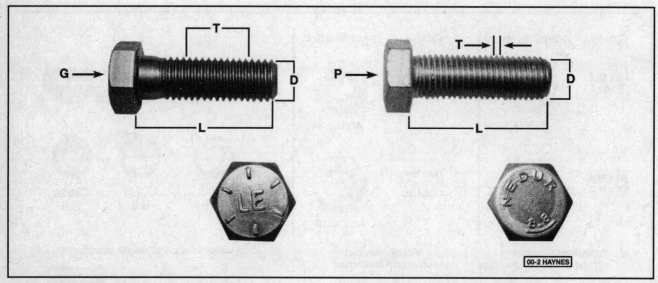

00-2 HAYNES

Standard (SAE and USS) bolt dimensions/grade marks
G   Grade marks (bolt strength)
L   Length (in inches)
T   Thread pitch (number of threads per inch)
D   Nominal diameter (in inches)

Metric bolt dimensions/grade marks
P   Property class (bolt strength)
L   Length (in millimeters)
T   Thread pitch (distance between threads in millimeters)
D   Diameter

mount bolts, etc.). A pan of this type is especially helpful when working on assemblies with very small parts, such as the carburetor, alternator, valve train or interior dash and trim pieces. The cavities can be marked with paint or tape to identify the contents.

Whenever wiring looms, harnesses or connectors are separated, it is a good idea to identify the two halves with numbered pieces of masking tape so they can be easily reconnected.

Gasket sealing surfaces

Throughout any vehicle, gaskets are used to seal the mating surfaces between two parts and keep lubricants, fluids, vacuum or pressure contained in an assembly.

Many times these gaskets are coated with a liquid or paste-type gasket sealing compound before assembly. Age, heat and pressure can sometimes cause the two parts to stick together so tightly that they are very difficult to separate. Often, the assembly can be loosened by striking it with a soft-face hammer near the mating surfaces. A regular hammer can be used if a block of wood is placed between the hammer and the part. Do not hammer on cast parts or parts that could be easily damaged. With any particularly stubborn part, always recheck to make sure that every fastener has been removed.

Avoid using a screwdriver or bar to pry apart an assembly, as they

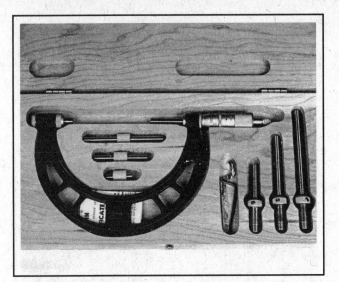

Micrometer set

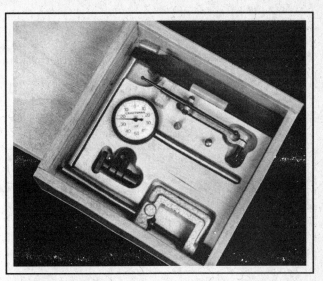

Dial indicator set

can easily mar the gasket sealing surfaces of the parts, which must remain smooth. If prying is absolutely necessary, use an old broom handle, but keep in mind that extra clean up will be necessary if the wood splinters.

After the parts are separated, the old gasket must be carefully scraped off and the gasket surfaces cleaned. Stubborn gasket material can be soaked with rust penetrant or treated with a special chemical to soften it so it can be easily scraped off.

❈❈ CAUTION:

Never use gasket removal solutions or caustic chemicals on plastic or other composite components.

A scraper can be fashioned from a piece of copper tubing by flattening and sharpening one end. Copper is recommended because it is usually softer than the surfaces to be scraped, which reduces the chance of gouging the part. Some gaskets can be removed with a wire brush, but regardless of the method used, the mating surfaces must be left clean and smooth. If for some reason the gasket surface is gouged, then a gasket sealer thick enough to fill scratches will have to be used during reassembly of the components. For most applications, a non-drying (or semi-drying) gasket sealer should be used.

Hose removal tips

❈❈ WARNING:

If the vehicle is equipped with air conditioning, do not disconnect any of the A/C hoses without first having the system depressurized by a dealer service department or a service station.

Hose removal precautions closely parallel gasket removal precautions. Avoid scratching or gouging the surface that the hose mates against or the connection may leak. This is especially true for radiator hoses. Because of various chemical reactions, the rubber in hoses can bond itself to the metal spigot that the hose fits over. To remove a hose, first loosen the hose clamps that secure it to the spigot. Then, with slip-joint pliers, grab the hose at the clamp and rotate it around the spigot. Work it back and forth until it is completely free, then pull it off. Silicone or other lubricants will ease removal if they can be applied between the hose and the outside of the spigot. Apply the same lubricant to the inside of the hose and the outside of the spigot to simplify installation.

As a last resort (and if the hose is to be replaced with a new one anyway), the rubber can be slit with a knife and the hose peeled from the spigot. If this must be done, be careful that the metal connection is not damaged.

If a hose clamp is broken or damaged, do not reuse it. Wire-type clamps usually weaken with age, so it is a good idea to replace them with screw-type clamps whenever a hose is removed.

TOOLS

A selection of good tools is a basic requirement for anyone who plans to maintain and repair his or her own vehicle. For the owner who has few tools, the initial investment might seem high, but when compared to the spiraling costs of professional auto maintenance and repair, it is a wise one.

To help the owner decide which tools are needed to perform the tasks detailed in this manual, the following tool lists are offered: *Maintenance and minor repair, Repair/overhaul and Special.*

The newcomer to practical mechanics should start off with the *maintenance and minor repair* tool kit, which is adequate for the simpler jobs performed on a vehicle. Then, as confidence and experience grow, the owner can tackle more difficult tasks, buying additional tools as they are needed. Eventually the basic kit will be expanded into the *repair and overhaul* tool set. Over a period of time, the experienced do-it-yourselfer will assemble a tool set complete enough for most repair and overhaul procedures and will add tools from the special category when it is felt that the expense is justified by the frequency of use.

Maintenance and minor repair tool kit

The tools in this list should be considered the minimum required for performance of routine maintenance, servicing and minor repair work. We recommend the purchase of combination wrenches (box-end and open-end combined in one wrench). While more expensive than open end wrenches, they offer the advantages of both types of wrench.

Combination wrench set (1/4-inch to 1 inch or 6 mm to 19 mm)
Adjustable wrench, 8 inch
Spark plug wrench with rubber insert

Spark plug gap adjusting tool
Feeler gauge set
Brake bleeder wrench
Standard screwdriver (5/16-inch x 6 inch)
Phillips screwdriver (No. 2 x 6 inch)
Combination pliers - 6 inch
Hacksaw and assortment of blades
Tire pressure gauge
Grease gun

Oil can
Fine emery cloth
Wire brush
Battery post and cable cleaning tool
Oil filter wrench
Funnel (medium size)
Safety goggles
Jackstands (2)
Drain pan

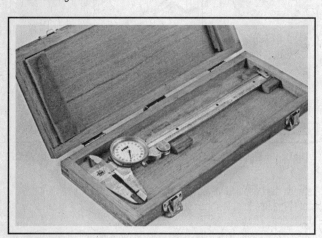

Dial caliper

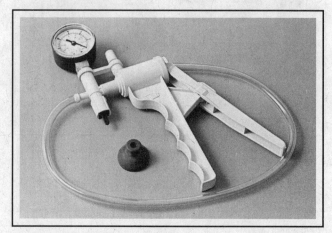

Hand-operated vacuum pump

Timing light

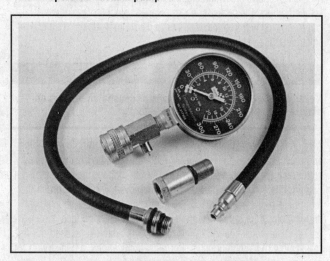

Compression gauge with spark plug hole adapter

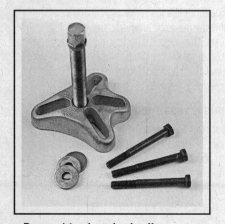

Damper/steering wheel puller

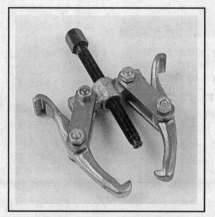

General purpose puller

Hydraulic lifter removal tool

→**Note: If basic tune-ups are going to be part of routine maintenance, it will be necessary to purchase a good quality stroboscopic timing light and combination tachometer/dwell meter. Although they are included in the list of special tools, it is mentioned here because they are absolutely necessary for tuning most vehicles properly.**

Repair and overhaul tool set

These tools are essential for anyone who plans to perform major repairs and are in addition to those in the maintenance and minor repair tool kit. Included is a comprehensive set of sockets which, though expensive, are invaluable because of their versatility, especially when various extensions and drives are available. We recommend the 1/2-inch drive over the 3/8-inch drive. Although the larger drive is bulky and more expensive, it has the capacity of accepting a very wide range of large sockets. Ideally, however, the mechanic should have a 3/8-inch drive set and a 1/2-inch drive set.

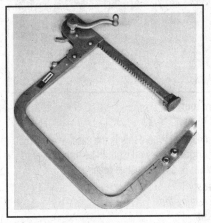
Valve spring compressor

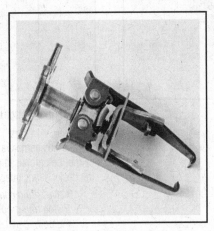
Valve spring compressor

Ridge reamer

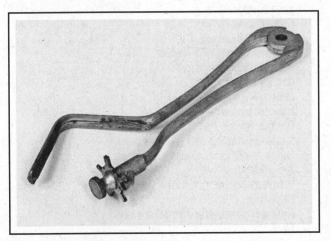
Piston ring groove cleaning tool

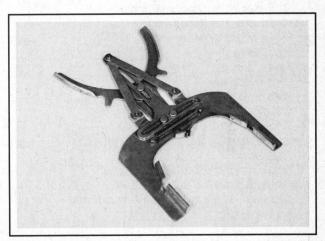
Ring removal/installation tool

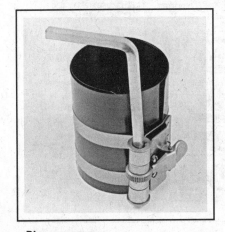
Ring compressor

Cylinder hone

Brake hold-down spring tool

Torque angle gauge

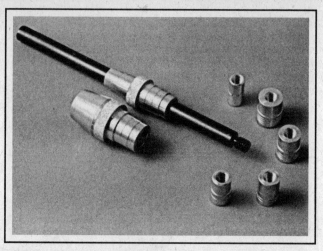

Clutch plate alignment tool

Socket set(s)
Reversible ratchet
Extension - 10 inch
Universal joint
Torque wrench (same size drive as sockets)
Ball peen hammer - 8 ounce
Soft-face hammer (plastic/rubber)
Standard screwdriver (1/4-inch x 6 inch)
Standard screwdriver (stubby - 5/16-inch)
Phillips screwdriver (No. 3 x 8 inch)
Phillips screwdriver (stubby - No. 2)
Pliers - vise grip
Pliers - lineman's
Pliers - needle nose
Pliers - snap-ring (internal and external)
Cold chisel - 1/2-inch
Scribe
Scraper (made from flattened copper tubing)
Centerpunch
Pin punches (1/16, 1/8, 3/16-inch)
Steel rule/straightedge - 12 inch
Allen wrench set (1/8 to 3/8-inch or 4 mm to 10 mm)
A selection of files
Wire brush (large)
Jackstands (second set)
Jack (scissor or hydraulic type)

➡**Note: Another tool which is often useful is an electric drill with a chuck capacity of 3/8-inch and a set of good quality drill bits.**

Special tools

The tools in this list include those which are not used regularly, are expensive to buy, or which need to be used in accordance with their manufacturer's instructions. Unless these tools will be used frequently, it is not very economical to purchase many of them. A consideration would be to split the cost and use between yourself and a friend or friends. In addition, most of these tools can be obtained from a tool rental shop on a temporary basis.

This list primarily contains only those tools and instruments widely available to the public, and not those special tools produced by the vehicle manufacturer for distribution to dealer service departments. Occasionally, references to the manufacturer's special tools are included in the text of this manual. Generally, an alternative method of doing the job without the special tool is offered. However, sometimes there is no alternative to their use. Where this is the case, and the tool cannot be purchased or borrowed, the work should be turned over to the dealer service department or an automotive repair shop.

Valve spring compressor
Piston ring groove cleaning tool
Piston ring compressor
Piston ring installation tool
Cylinder compression gauge
Cylinder ridge reamer
Cylinder surfacing hone
Cylinder bore gauge
Micrometers and/or dial calipers
Hydraulic lifter removal tool
Balljoint separator
Universal-type puller
Impact screwdriver
Dial indicator set
Stroboscopic timing light (inductive pick-up)
Hand operated vacuum/pressure pump
Tachometer/dwell meter
Universal electrical multimeter
Cable hoist
Brake spring removal and installation tools
Floor jack

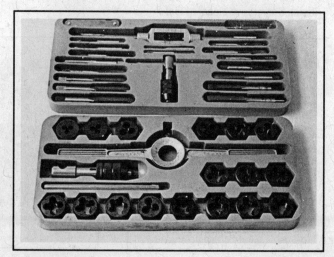

Tap and die set

Buying tools

For the do-it-yourselfer who is just starting to get involved in vehicle maintenance and repair, there are a number of options available when purchasing tools. If maintenance and minor repair is the extent of the work to be done, the purchase of individual tools is satisfactory. If, on the other hand, extensive work is planned, it would be a good idea to purchase a modest tool set from one of the large retail chain stores. A set can usually be bought at a substantial savings over the individual tool prices, and they often come with a tool box. As additional tools are needed, add-on sets, individual tools and a larger tool box can be purchased to expand the tool selection. Building a tool set gradually allows the cost of the tools to be spread over a longer period of time and gives the mechanic the freedom to choose only those tools that will actually be used.

Tool stores will often be the only source of some of the special tools that are needed, but regardless of where tools are bought, try to avoid cheap ones, especially when buying screwdrivers and sockets, because they won't last very long. The expense involved in replacing cheap tools will eventually be greater than the initial cost of quality tools.

Care and maintenance of tools

Good tools are expensive, so it makes sense to treat them with respect. Keep them clean and in usable condition and store them properly when not in use. Always wipe off any dirt, grease or metal chips before putting them away. Never leave tools lying around in the work area. Upon completion of a job, always check closely under the hood for tools that may have been left there so they won't get lost during a test drive.

Some tools, such as screwdrivers, pliers, wrenches and sockets, can be hung on a panel mounted on the garage or workshop wall, while others should be kept in a tool box or tray. Measuring instruments, gauges, meters, etc. must be carefully stored where they cannot be damaged by weather or impact from other tools.

When tools are used with care and stored properly, they will last a very long time. Even with the best of care, though, tools will wear out if used frequently. When a tool is damaged or worn out, replace it. Subsequent jobs will be safer and more enjoyable if you do.

HOW TO REPAIR DAMAGED THREADS

Sometimes, the internal threads of a nut or bolt hole can become stripped, usually from overtightening. Stripping threads is an all-too-common occurrence, especially when working with aluminum parts, because aluminum is so soft that it easily strips out.

Usually, external or internal threads are only partially stripped. After they've been cleaned up with a tap or die, they'll still work. Sometimes, however, threads are badly damaged. When this happens, you've got three choices:

1) *Drill and tap the hole to the next suitable oversize and install a larger diameter bolt, screw or stud.*

2) *Drill and tap the hole to accept a threaded plug, then drill and tap the plug to the original screw size. You can also buy a plug already threaded to the original size. Then you simply drill a hole to the specified size, then run the threaded plug into the hole with a bolt and jam nut. Once the plug is fully seated, remove the jam nut and bolt.*

3) *The third method uses a patented thread repair kit like Heli-Coil or Slimsert. These easy-to-use kits are designed to repair damaged threads in straight-through holes and blind holes. Both are available as kits which can handle a variety of sizes and thread patterns. Drill the hole, then tap it with the special included tap. Install the Heli-Coil and the hole is back to its original diameter and thread pitch.*

Regardless of which method you use, be sure to proceed calmly and carefully. A little impatience or carelessness during one of these relatively simple procedures can ruin your whole day's work and cost you a bundle if you wreck an expensive part.

WORKING FACILITIES

Not to be overlooked when discussing tools is the workshop. If anything more than routine maintenance is to be carried out, some sort of suitable work area is essential.

It is understood, and appreciated, that many home mechanics do not have a good workshop or garage available, and end up removing an engine or doing major repairs outside. It is recommended, however, that the overhaul or repair be completed under the cover of a roof.

A clean, flat workbench or table of comfortable working height is an absolute necessity. The workbench should be equipped with a vise that has a jaw opening of at least four inches.

As mentioned previously, some clean, dry storage space is also required for tools, as well as the lubricants, fluids, cleaning solvents, etc. which soon become necessary.

Sometimes waste oil and fluids, drained from the engine or cooling system during normal maintenance or repairs, present a disposal problem. To avoid pouring them on the ground or into a sewage system, pour the used fluids into large containers, seal them with caps and take them to an authorized disposal site or recycling center. Plastic jugs, such as old antifreeze containers, are ideal for this purpose.

Always keep a supply of old newspapers and clean rags available. Old towels are excellent for mopping up spills. Many mechanics use rolls of paper towels for most work because they are readily available and disposable. To help keep the area under the vehicle clean, a large cardboard box can be cut open and flattened to protect the garage or shop floor.

Whenever working over a painted surface, such as when leaning over a fender to service something under the hood, always cover it with an old blanket or bedspread to protect the finish. Vinyl covered pads, made especially for this purpose, are available at auto parts stores.

Booster battery (jump) starting

Observe these precautions when using a booster battery to start a vehicle:

a) Before connecting the booster battery, make sure the ignition switch is in the Off position.
b) Turn off the lights, heater and other electrical loads.
c) Your eyes should be shielded. Safety goggles are a good idea.
d) Make sure the booster battery is the same voltage as the dead one in the vehicle.
e) The two vehicles MUST NOT TOUCH each other!
f) Make sure the transaxle is in Neutral (manual) or Park (automatic).
g) If the booster battery is not a maintenance-free type, remove the vent caps and lay a cloth over the vent holes.

Connect the red jumper cable to the positive (+) terminals of each battery (see illustration).

Connect one end of the black jumper cable to the negative (-) terminal of the booster battery. The other end of this cable should be connected to a good ground on the vehicle to be started, such as a bolt or bracket on the body.

Start the engine using the booster battery, then, with the engine running at idle speed, disconnect the jumper cables in the reverse order of connection.

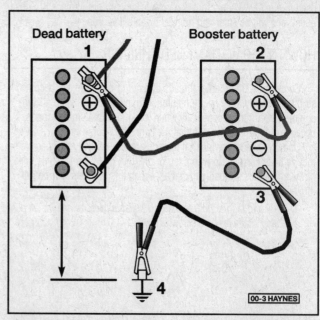

Make the booster battery cable connections in the numerical order shown (note that the negative cable of the booster battery is NOT attached to the negative terminal of the dead battery)

Jacking and towing

JACKING

The jack supplied with the vehicle should be used only for raising the vehicle when changing a tire or placing jackstands under the frame.

✳✳ WARNING:

Never work under the vehicle or start the engine when this jack is being used as the only means of support.

The vehicle should be on level ground with the wheels blocked and the transaxle in Park (automatic) or Neutral (manual). If a tire is being changed, loosen the lug nuts one-half turn and leave them in place until the wheel is raised off the ground. Make sure no one is in the vehicle as it's being raised off the ground.

Place the jack under the side of the vehicle at the jacking point nearest the wheel to be changed (see illustration).

✳✳ CAUTION:

Never place the jack under the rear trailing arms.

If you're using a floor jack, place it beneath the crossmember at the front or rear (see illustrations). Operate the jack with a slow, smooth motion until the wheel is raised off the ground. If you're using jackstands, position them beneath the support points along the front or rear side sills. Remove the lug nuts, pull off the wheel, install the spare and thread the lug nuts back on with the beveled sides facing in. Tighten snugly, but wait until the vehicle is lowered to tighten completely.

Lower the vehicle, remove the jack and tighten the lug nuts (if loosened or removed) in a criss-cross pattern. If possible, tighten them with a torque wrench (see Chapter 1 for the torque figures). If you don't have access to a torque wrench, have the nuts checked by a service station or repair shop as soon as possible. Retighten the lug nuts after 500 miles.

If the vehicle is equipped with a temporary spare tire, remember that it is intended only for temporary use until the regular tire can be repaired. Do not exceed the maximum speed that the tire is rated for.

The jack supplied with the vehicle fits over the rocker panel flange

Front floor jack jacking point

Rear floor jack jacking point

Place jackstands beneath the unibody rails at the front of the vehicle, then lower the jack until the jackstands support the weight of the vehicle

Place jackstands beneath the unibody rails at the rear of the vehicle, then lower the jack until the vehicle rests securely on the jackstands

TOWING

The vehicle must be towed with the front (drive) wheels off the ground to prevent damage to the transaxle. If the vehicle must be towed backward, place the front wheels on a dolly.

✳✳ CAUTION:

Don't use the hook loops under the vehicle for towing (they're intended only for use as tie-downs).

A wheel lift is recommended. A flatbed truck can also be used. In this case, pull the vehicle onto the truck towards the front, using J-hooks at the front suspension control arms with the points turned down.

While towing, the parking brake must be released and the transaxle must be in Neutral. The steering must be unlocked (ignition switch in the OFF position). Don't exceed 50 mph (35 mph on rough roads).

Safety is a major consideration while towing and all applicable state and local laws must be obeyed. A safety chain system must be used at all times. Remember that power steering and power brakes will not work with the engine off.

Automotive chemicals and lubricants

A number of automotive chemicals and lubricants are available for use during vehicle maintenance and repair. They include a wide variety of products ranging from cleaning solvents and degreasers to lubricants and protective sprays for rubber, plastic and vinyl.

CLEANERS

Carburetor cleaner and choke cleaner is a strong solvent for gum, varnish and carbon. Most carburetor cleaners leave a dry-type lubricant film which will not harden or gum up. Because of this film it is not recommended for use on electrical components.

Brake system cleaner is used to remove brake dust, grease and brake fluid from the brake system, where clean surfaces are absolutely necessary. It leaves no residue and often eliminates brake squeal caused by contaminants.

Electrical cleaner removes oxidation, corrosion and carbon deposits from electrical contacts, restoring full current flow. It can also be used to clean spark plugs, carburetor jets, voltage regulators and other parts where an oil-free surface is desired.

Demoisturants remove water and moisture from electrical components such as alternators, voltage regulators, electrical connectors and fuse blocks. They are non-conductive and non-corrosive.

Degreasers are heavy-duty solvents used to remove grease from the outside of the engine and from chassis components. They can be sprayed or brushed on and, depending on the type, are rinsed off either with water or solvent.

LUBRICANTS

Motor oil is the lubricant formulated for use in engines. It normally contains a wide variety of additives to prevent corrosion and reduce foaming and wear. Motor oil comes in various weights (viscosity ratings) from 0 to 50. The recommended weight of the oil depends on the season, temperature and the demands on the engine. Light oil is used in cold climates and under light load conditions. Heavy oil is used in hot climates and where high loads are encountered. Multi-viscosity oils are designed to have characteristics of both light and heavy oils and are available in a number of weights from 0W-20 to 20W-50.

Gear oil is designed to be used in differentials, manual transmissions and other areas where high-temperature lubrication is required.

Chassis and wheel bearing grease is a heavy grease used where increased loads and friction are encountered, such as for wheel bearings, ball-joints, tie-rod ends and universal joints.

High-temperature wheel bearing grease is designed to withstand the extreme temperatures encountered by wheel bearings in disc brake equipped vehicles. It usually contains molybdenum disulfide (moly), which is a dry-type lubricant.

White grease is a heavy grease for metal-to-metal applications where water is a problem. White grease stays soft under both low and high temperatures (usually from -100 to +190-degrees F), and will not wash off or dilute in the presence of water.

Assembly lube is a special extreme pressure lubricant, usually containing moly, used to lubricate high-load parts (such as main and rod bearings and cam lobes) for initial start-up of a new engine. The assembly lube lubricates the parts without being squeezed out or washed away until the engine oiling system begins to function.

Silicone lubricants are used to protect rubber, plastic, vinyl and nylon parts.

Graphite lubricants are used where oils cannot be used due to contamination problems, such as in locks. The dry graphite will lubricate metal parts while remaining uncontaminated by dirt, water, oil or acids. It is electrically conductive and will not foul electrical contacts in locks such as the ignition switch.

Moly penetrants loosen and lubricate frozen, rusted and corroded fasteners and prevent future rusting or freezing.

Heat-sink grease is a special electrically non-conductive grease that is used for mounting electronic ignition modules where it is essential that heat is transferred away from the module.

SEALANTS

RTV sealant is one of the most widely used gasket compounds. Made from silicone, RTV is air curing, it seals, bonds, waterproofs, fills surface irregularities, remains flexible, doesn't shrink, is relatively easy to remove, and is used as a supplementary sealer with almost all low and medium temperature gaskets.

Anaerobic sealant is much like RTV in that it can be used either to seal gaskets or to form gaskets by itself. It remains flexible, is solvent resistant and fills surface imperfections. The difference between an anaerobic sealant and an RTV-type sealant is in the curing. RTV cures when exposed to air, while an anaerobic sealant cures only in the absence of air. This means that an anaerobic sealant cures only after the assembly of parts, sealing them together.

Thread and pipe sealant is used for sealing hydraulic and pneumatic fittings and vacuum lines. It is usually made from a Teflon compound, and comes in a spray, a paint-on liquid and as a wrap-around tape.

CHEMICALS

Anti-seize compound prevents seizing, galling, cold welding, rust and corrosion in fasteners. High-temperature anti-seize, usually made with copper and graphite lubricants, is used for exhaust system and exhaust manifold bolts.

Anaerobic locking compounds are used to keep fasteners from vibrating or working loose and cure only after installation, in the absence of air. Medium strength locking compound is used for small nuts, bolts and screws that may be removed later. High-strength locking compound is for large nuts, bolts and studs which aren't removed on a regular basis.

Oil additives range from viscosity index improvers to chemical treatments that claim to reduce internal engine friction. It should be noted that most oil manufacturers caution against using additives with their oils.

Gas additives perform several functions, depending on their chemical makeup. They usually contain solvents that help dissolve gum and varnish that build up on carburetor, fuel injection and intake parts. They also serve to break down carbon deposits that form on the inside surfaces of the combustion chambers. Some additives contain upper cylinder lubricants for valves and piston rings, and others contain chemicals to remove condensation from the gas tank.

MISCELLANEOUS

Brake fluid is specially formulated hydraulic fluid that can withstand the heat and pressure encountered in brake systems. Care must be taken so this fluid does not come in contact with painted surfaces or plastics. An opened container should always be resealed to prevent contamination by water or dirt.

Weatherstrip adhesive is used to bond weatherstripping around doors, windows and trunk lids. It is sometimes used to attach trim pieces.

Undercoating is a petroleum-based, tar-like substance that is designed to protect metal surfaces on the underside of the vehicle from corrosion. It also acts as a sound-deadening agent by insulating the bottom of the vehicle.

Waxes and polishes are used to help protect painted and plated surfaces from the weather. Different types of paint may require the use of different types of wax and polish. Some polishes utilize a chemical or abrasive cleaner to help remove the top layer of oxidized (dull) paint on older vehicles. In recent years many non-wax polishes that contain a wide variety of chemicals such as polymers and silicones have been introduced. These non-wax polishes are usually easier to apply and last longer than conventional waxes and polishes.

CONVERSION FACTORS

LENGTH (distance)

Inches (in)	X	25.4	= Millimeters (mm)	X 0.0394	= Inches (in)
Feet (ft)	X	0.305	= Meters (m)	X 3.281	= Feet (ft)
Miles	X	1.609	= Kilometers (km)	X 0.621	= Miles

VOLUME (capacity)

Cubic inches (cu in; in³)	X	16.387	= Cubic centimeters (cc; cm³)	X 0.061	= Cubic inches (cu in; in³)
Imperial pints (Imp pt)	X	0.568	= Liters (l)	X 1.76	= Imperial pints (Imp pt)
Imperial quarts (Imp qt)	X	1.137	= Liters (l)	X 0.88	= Imperial quarts (Imp qt)
Imperial quarts (Imp qt)	X	1.201	= US quarts (US qt)	X 0.833	= Imperial quarts (Imp qt)
US quarts (US qt)	X	0.946	= Liters (l)	X 1.057	= US quarts (US qt)
Imperial gallons (Imp gal)	X	4.546	= Liters (l)	X 0.22	= Imperial gallons (Imp gal)
Imperial gallons (Imp gal)	X	1.201	= US gallons (US gal)	X 0.833	= Imperial gallons (Imp gal)
US gallons (US gal)	X	3.785	= Liters (l)	X 0.264	= US gallons (US gal)

MASS (weight)

Ounces (oz)	X	28.35	= Grams (g)	X 0.035	= Ounces (oz)
Pounds (lb)	X	0.454	= Kilograms (kg)	X 2.205	= Pounds (lb)

FORCE

Ounces-force (ozf; oz)	X	0.278	= Newtons (N)	X 3.6	= Ounces-force (ozf; oz)
Pounds-force (lbf; lb)	X	4.448	= Newtons (N)	X 0.225	= Pounds-force (lbf; lb)
Newtons (N)	X	0.1	= Kilograms-force (kgf; kg)	X 9.81	= Newtons (N)

PRESSURE

Pounds-force per square inch (psi; lbf/in²; lb/in²)	X	0.070	= Kilograms-force per square centimeter (kgf/cm²; kg/cm²)	X 14.223	= Pounds-force per square inch (psi; lbf/in²; lb/in²)
Pounds-force per square inch (psi; lbf/in²; lb/in²)	X	0.068	= Atmospheres (atm)	X 14.696	= Pounds-force per square inch (psi; lbf/in²; lb/in²)
Pounds-force per square inch (psi; lbf/in²; lb/in²)	X	0.069	= Bars	X 14.5	= Pounds-force per square inch (psi; lbf/in²; lb/in²)
Pounds-force per square inch (psi; lbf/in²; lb/in²)	X	6.895	= Kilopascals (kPa)	X 0.145	= Pounds-force per square inch (psi; lbf/in²; lb/in²)
Kilopascals (kPa)	X	0.01	= Kilograms-force per square centimeter (kgf/cm²; kg/cm²)	X 98.1	= Kilopascals (kPa)

TORQUE (moment of force)

Pounds-force inches (lbf in; lb in)	X	1.152	= Kilograms-force centimeter (kgf cm; kg cm)	X 0.868	= Pounds-force inches (lbf in; lb in)
Pounds-force inches (lbf in; lb in)	X	0.113	= Newton meters (Nm)	X 8.85	= Pounds-force inches (lbf in; lb in)
Pounds-force inches (lbf in; lb in)	X	0.083	= Pounds-force feet (lbf ft; lb ft)	X 12	= Pounds-force inches (lbf in; lb in)
Pounds-force feet (lbf ft; lb ft)	X	0.138	= Kilograms-force meters (kgf m; kg m)	X 7.233	= Pounds-force feet (lbf ft; lb ft)
Pounds-force feet (lbf ft; lb ft)	X	1.356	= Newton meters (Nm)	X 0.738	= Pounds-force feet (lbf ft; lb ft)
Newton meters (Nm)	X	0.102	= Kilograms-force meters (kgf m; kg m)	X 9.804	= Newton meters (Nm)

VACUUM

Inches mercury (in. Hg)	X	3.377	= Kilopascals (kPa)	X 0.2961	= Inches mercury
Inches mercury (in. Hg)	X	25.4	= Millimeters mercury (mm Hg)	X 0.0394	= Inches mercury

POWER

Horsepower (hp)	X	745.7	= Watts (W)	X 0.0013	= Horsepower (hp)

VELOCITY (speed)

Miles per hour (miles/hr; mph)	X	1.609	= Kilometers per hour (km/hr; kph)	X 0.621	= Miles per hour (miles/hr; mph)

FUEL CONSUMPTION *

Miles per gallon, Imperial (mpg)	X	0.354	= Kilometers per liter (km/l)	X 2.825	= Miles per gallon, Imperial (mpg)
Miles per gallon, US (mpg)	X	0.425	= Kilometers per liter (km/l)	X 2.352	= Miles per gallon, US (mpg)

TEMPERATURE

Degrees Fahrenheit = (°C x 1.8) + 32   Degrees Celsius (Degrees Centigrade; °C) = (°F - 32) x 0.56

*It is common practice to convert from miles per gallon (mpg) to liters/100 kilometers (l/100km), where mpg (Imperial) x l/100 km = 282 and mpg (US) x l/100 km = 235

FRACTION/DECIMAL/MILLIMETER EQUIVALENTS

DECIMALS to MILLIMETERS

Decimal	mm	Decimal	mm
0.001	0.0254	0.500	12.7000
0.002	0.0508	0.510	12.9540
0.003	0.0762	0.520	13.2080
0.004	0.1016	0.530	13.4620
0.005	0.1270	0.540	13.7160
0.006	0.1524	0.550	13.9700
0.007	0.1778	0.560	14.2240
0.008	0.2032	0.570	14.4780
0.009	0.2286	0.580	14.7320
		0.590	14.9860
0.010	0.2540		
0.020	0.5080		
0.030	0.7620		
0.040	1.0160	0.600	15.2400
0.050	1.2700	0.610	15.4940
0.060	1.5240	0.620	15.7480
0.070	1.7780	0.630	16.0020
0.080	2.0320	0.640	16.2560
0.090	2.2860	0.650	16.5100
		0.660	16.7640
0.100	2.5400	0.670	17.0180
0.110	2.7940	0.680	17.2720
0.120	3.0480	0.690	17.5260
0.130	3.3020		
0.140	3.5560		
0.150	3.8100		
0.160	4.0640	0.700	17.7800
0.170	4.3180	0.710	18.0340
0.180	4.5720	0.720	18.2880
0.190	4.8260	0.730	18.5420
		0.740	18.7960
0.200	5.0800	0.750	19.0500
0.210	5.3340	0.760	19.3040
0.220	5.5880	0.770	19.5580
0.230	5.8420	0.780	19.8120
0.240	6.0960	0.790	20.0660
0.250	6.3500		
0.260	6.6040		
0.270	6.8580	0.800	20.3200
0.280	7.1120	0.810	20.5740
0.290	7.3660	0.820	20.8280
		0.830	21.0820
0.300	7.6200	0.840	21.3360
0.310	7.8740	0.850	21.5900
0.320	8.1280	0.860	21.8440
0.330	8.3820	0.870	22.0980
0.340	8.6360	0.880	22.3520
0.350	8.8900	0.890	22.6060
0.360	9.1440		
0.370	9.3980		
0.380	9.6520		
0.390	9.9060	0.900	22.8600
0.400	10.1600	0.910	23.1140
0.410	10.4140	0.920	23.3680
0.420	10.6680	0.930	23.6220
0.430	10.9220	0.940	23.8760
0.440	11.1760	0.950	24.1300
0.450	11.4300	0.960	24.3840
0.460	11.6840	0.970	24.6380
0.470	11.9380	0.980	24.8920
0.480	12.1920	0.990	25.1460
0.490	12.4460	1.000	25.4000

FRACTIONS to DECIMALS to MILLIMETERS

Fraction	Decimal	mm	Fraction	Decimal	mm
1/64	0.0156	0.3969	33/64	0.5156	13.0969
1/32	0.0312	0.7938	17/32	0.5312	13.4938
3/64	0.0469	1.1906	35/64	0.5469	13.8906
1/16	0.0625	1.5875	9/16	0.5625	14.2875
5/64	0.0781	1.9844	37/64	0.5781	14.6844
3/32	0.0938	2.3812	19/32	0.5938	15.0812
7/64	0.1094	2.7781	39/64	0.6094	15.4781
1/8	0.1250	3.1750	5/8	0.6250	15.8750
9/64	0.1406	3.5719	41/64	0.6406	16.2719
5/32	0.1562	3.9688	21/32	0.6562	16.6688
11/64	0.1719	4.3656	43/64	0.6719	17.0656
3/16	0.1875	4.7625	11/16	0.6875	17.4625
13/64	0.2031	5.1594	45/64	0.7031	17.8594
7/32	0.2188	5.5562	23/32	0.7188	18.2562
15/64	0.2344	5.9531	47/64	0.7344	18.6531
1/4	0.2500	6.3500	3/4	0.7500	19.0500
17/64	0.2656	6.7469	49/64	0.7656	19.4469
9/32	0.2812	7.1438	25/32	0.7812	19.8438
19/64	0.2969	7.5406	51/64	0.7969	20.2406
5/16	0.3125	7.9375	13/16	0.8125	20.6375
21/64	0.3281	8.3344	53/64	0.8281	21.0344
11/32	0.3438	8.7312	27/32	0.8438	21.4312
23/64	0.3594	9.1281	55/64	0.8594	21.8281
3/8	0.3750	9.5250	7/8	0.8750	22.2250
25/64	0.3906	9.9219	57/64	0.8906	22.6219
13/32	0.4062	10.3188	29/32	0.9062	23.0188
27/64	0.4219	10.7156	59/64	0.9219	23.4156
7/16	0.4375	11.1125	15/16	0.9375	23.8125
29/64	0.4531	11.5094	61/64	0.9531	24.2094
15/32	0.4688	11.9062	31/32	0.9688	24.6062
31/64	0.4844	12.3031	63/64	0.9844	25.0031
1/2	0.5000	12.7000	1	1.0000	25.4000

Safety first!

Regardless of how enthusiastic you may be about getting on with the job at hand, take the time to ensure that your safety is not jeopardized. A moment's lack of attention can result in an accident, as can failure to observe certain simple safety precautions. The possibility of an accident will always exist, and the following points should not be considered a comprehensive list of all dangers. Rather, they are intended to make you aware of the risks and to encourage a safety conscious approach to all work you carry out on your vehicle.

ESSENTIAL DOS AND DON'TS

DON'T rely on a jack when working under the vehicle. Always use approved jackstands to support the weight of the vehicle and place them under the recommended lift or support points.

DON'T attempt to loosen extremely tight fasteners (i.e. wheel lug nuts) while the vehicle is on a jack - it may fall.

DON'T start the engine without first making sure that the transmission is in Neutral (or Park where applicable) and the parking brake is set.

DON'T remove the radiator cap from a hot cooling system - let it cool or cover it with a cloth and release the pressure gradually.

DON'T attempt to drain the engine oil until you are sure it has cooled to the point that it will not burn you.

DON'T touch any part of the engine or exhaust system until it has cooled sufficiently to avoid burns.

DON'T siphon toxic liquids such as gasoline, antifreeze and brake fluid by mouth, or allow them to remain on your skin.

DON'T inhale brake lining dust - it is potentially hazardous (see Asbestos below).

DON'T allow spilled oil or grease to remain on the floor - wipe it up before someone slips on it.

DON'T use loose fitting wrenches or other tools which may slip and cause injury.

DON'T push on wrenches when loosening or tightening nuts or bolts. Always try to pull the wrench toward you. If the situation calls for pushing the wrench away, push with an open hand to avoid scraped knuckles if the wrench should slip.

DON'T attempt to lift a heavy component alone - get someone to help you.

DON'T rush or take unsafe shortcuts to finish a job.

DON'T allow children or animals in or around the vehicle while you are working on it.

DO wear eye protection when using power tools such as a drill, sander, bench grinder, etc. and when working under a vehicle.

DO keep loose clothing and long hair well out of the way of moving parts.

DO make sure that any hoist used has a safe working load rating adequate for the job.

DO get someone to check on you periodically when working alone on a vehicle.

DO carry out work in a logical sequence and make sure that everything is correctly assembled and tightened.

DO keep chemicals and fluids tightly capped and out of the reach of children and pets.

DO remember that your vehicle's safety affects that of yourself and others. If in doubt on any point, get professional advice.

STEERING, SUSPENSION AND BRAKES

These systems are essential to driving safety, so make sure you have a qualified shop or individual check your work. Also, compressed suspension springs can cause injury if released suddenly - be sure to use a spring compressor.

AIRBAGS

Airbags are explosive devices that can CAUSE injury if they deploy while you're working on the vehicle. Follow the manufacturer's instructions to disable the airbag whenever you're working in the vicinity of airbag components.

ASBESTOS

Certain friction, insulating, sealing, and other products - such as brake linings, brake bands, clutch linings, torque converters, gaskets, etc. - may contain asbestos or other hazardous friction material. Extreme care must be taken to avoid inhalation of dust from such products, since it is hazardous to health. If in doubt, assume that they do contain asbestos.

FIRE

Remember at all times that gasoline is highly flammable. Never smoke or have any kind of open flame around when working on a vehicle. But the risk does not end there. A spark caused by an electrical short circuit, by two metal surfaces contacting each other, or even by static electricity built up in your body under certain conditions, can ignite gasoline vapors, which in a confined space are highly explosive. Do not, under any circumstances, use gasoline for cleaning parts. Use an approved safety solvent.

Always disconnect the battery ground (-) cable at the battery before working on any part of the fuel system or electrical system. Never risk spilling fuel on a hot engine or exhaust component. It is strongly recommended that a fire extinguisher suitable for use on fuel and electrical fires be kept handy in the garage or workshop at all times. Never try to extinguish a fuel or electrical fire with water.

FUMES

Certain fumes are highly toxic and can quickly cause unconsciousness and even death if inhaled to any extent. Gasoline vapor falls into this category, as do the vapors from some cleaning solvents. Any draining or pouring of such volatile fluids should be done in a well ventilated area.

When using cleaning fluids and solvents, read the instructions on the container carefully. Never use materials from unmarked containers.

Never run the engine in an enclosed space, such as a garage. Exhaust fumes contain carbon monoxide, which is extremely poisonous. If you need to run the engine, always do so in the open air, or at least have the rear of the vehicle outside the work area.

THE BATTERY

Never create a spark or allow a bare light bulb near a battery. They normally give off a certain amount of hydrogen gas, which is highly explosive.

Always disconnect the battery ground (-) cable at the battery before working on the fuel or electrical systems.

If possible, loosen the filler caps or cover when charging the battery from an external source (this does not apply to sealed or maintenance-free batteries). Do not charge at an excessive rate or the battery may burst.

Take care when adding water to a non maintenance-free battery and when carrying a battery. The electrolyte, even when diluted, is very corrosive and should not be allowed to contact clothing or skin.

Always wear eye protection when cleaning the battery to prevent the caustic deposits from entering your eyes.

HOUSEHOLD CURRENT

When using an electric power tool, inspection light, etc., which operates on household current, always make sure that the tool is correctly connected to its plug and that, where necessary, it is properly grounded. Do not use such items in damp conditions and, again, do not create a spark or apply excessive heat in the vicinity of fuel or fuel vapor.

SECONDARY IGNITION SYSTEM VOLTAGE

A severe electric shock can result from touching certain parts of the ignition system (such as the spark plug wires) when the engine is running or being cranked, particularly if components are damp or the insulation is defective. In the case of an electronic ignition system, the secondary system voltage is much higher and could prove fatal.

HYDROFLUORIC ACID

This extremely corrosive acid is formed when certain types of synthetic rubber, found in some O-rings, oil seals, fuel hoses, etc. are exposed to temperatures above 750-degrees F (400-degrees C). The rubber changes into a charred or sticky substance containing the acid. *Once formed, the acid remains dangerous for years. If it gets onto the skin, it may be necessary to amputate the limb concerned.*

When dealing with a vehicle which has suffered a fire, or with components salvaged from such a vehicle, wear protective gloves and discard them after use.

Troubleshooting

CONTENTS

This section provides an easy reference guide to the more common problems which may occur during the operation of your vehicle. These problems and possible causes are grouped under various components or systems; i.e. Engine, Cooling System, etc., and also refer to the Chapter and/or Section which deals with the problem.

Remember that successful troubleshooting is not a mysterious black art practiced only by professional mechanics. It's simply the result of a bit of knowledge combined with an intelligent, systematic approach to the problem. Always work by a process of elimination, starting with the simplest solution and working through to the most complex - and never overlook the obvious. Anyone can forget to fill the gas tank or leave the lights on overnight, so don't assume that you are above such oversights.

Finally, always get clear in your mind why a problem has occurred and take steps to ensure that it doesn't happen again. If the electrical system fails because of a poor connection, check all other connections in the system to make sure that they don't fail as well. If a particular fuse continues to blow, find out why - don't just go on replacing fuses. Remember, failure of a small component can often be indicative of potential failure or incorrect functioning of a more important component or system.

ENGINE

1 Engine will not rotate when attempting to start

1 Battery terminal connections loose or corroded. Check the cable terminals at the battery. Tighten the cable or remove corrosion as necessary.
2 Battery discharged or faulty. If the cable connections are clean and tight on the battery posts, turn the key to the On position and switch on the headlights and/or windshield wipers. If they fail to function, the battery is discharged.
3 Automatic transaxle not completely engaged in Park or Neutral or clutch pedal not completely depressed.
4 Broken, loose or disconnected wiring in the starting circuit. Inspect all wiring and connectors at the battery, starter solenoid and ignition switch.
5 Starter motor pinion jammed in flywheel ring gear. If manual transaxle, place transaxle in gear and rock the vehicle to manually turn the engine. Remove starter (Chapter 5) and inspect pinion and flywheel at earliest convenience.
6 Starter solenoid faulty (Chapter 5).
7 Starter motor faulty (Chapter 5).
8 Ignition switch faulty (Chapter 12).

2 Engine rotates but will not start

1 Fuel tank empty.
2 Fault in the fuel injection system (Chapter 4).
3 Battery discharged (engine rotates slowly). Check the operation of electrical components as described in the previous Section.
4 Battery terminal connections loose or corroded (see previous Section).
5 Fuel pump inertia switch disabled (frequently occurs after a collision - even a minor one) or fuel pump faulty (Chapter 4).
6 Excessive moisture on, or damage to, ignition components (see Chapter 5).
7 Worn, faulty or incorrectly gapped spark plugs (Chapter 1).
8 Broken, loose or disconnected wiring in the starting circuit (see previous Section).
9 Distributor loose (1.8L only), causing ignition timing to change. Turn the distributor as necessary to start the engine, then set the ignition timing as soon as possible (Chapter 5).
10 Broken, loose or disconnected wires at the ignition coil or faulty coil (Chapter 5).

3 Starter motor operates without rotating engine

1 Starter pinion sticking. Remove the starter (Chapter 5) and inspect.
2 Starter pinion or flywheel teeth worn or broken. Remove the flywheel/driveplate access cover and inspect.

4 Engine hard to start when cold

1 Battery discharged or low. Check as described in Section 1.
2 Fault in the fuel or electrical systems (Chapters 4 and 5).
3 Distributor rotor (1.8L only) carbon tracked and/or damaged (Chapters 1 and 5).

5 Engine hard to start when hot

1 Air filter clogged (Chapter 1).
2 Fault in the fuel or electrical systems (Chapters 4 and 5).
3 Corroded battery connections, especially ground (see Chapter 1).

6 Starter motor noisy or excessively rough in engagement

1 Pinion or flywheel gear teeth worn or broken. Remove the cover at the rear of the engine (if so equipped) and inspect.
2 Starter motor mounting bolts loose or missing.

7 Engine starts but stops immediately

1 Loose or faulty electrical connections at distributor (1.8L only), coil or alternator.
2 Low fuel pressure. Check the fuel pump (see Chapter 4).
3 Fault in the ignition system RUN circuit or ignition switch (see Chapter 12).
4 Vacuum leak at the gasket surfaces of the intake manifold. Make sure all mounting bolts/nuts are tightened securely and all vacuum hoses connected to the manifold are positioned properly and in good condition.

8 Engine lopes while idling or idles erratically

1 Vacuum leakage. Check the mounting bolts/nuts at the intake manifold for tightness. Make sure all vacuum hoses are connected and in good condition. Use a stethoscope or a length of fuel hose held against your ear to listen for vacuum leaks while the engine is running.

A hissing sound will be heard. A soapy water solution will also detect leaks.

2 Fault in the fuel or electrical systems (Chapters 4 and 5).
3 Leaking EGR valve or plugged PCV valve (see Chapters 1 and 6).
4 Air filter clogged (Chapter 1).
5 Fuel pump not delivering sufficient fuel to the fuel injection system (see Chapter 4).
6 Leaking head gasket. Perform a compression check (Chapter 2).
7 Camshaft lobes worn (see Chapter 2).

9 Engine misses at idle speed

1 Spark plugs worn, fouled, or not gapped properly (Chapter 1).
2 Fault in the fuel or electrical systems (Chapters 4 and 5).
3 Faulty spark plug wires (Chapter 1).

10 Engine misses throughout driving speed range

1 Fuel filter clogged and/or impurities in the fuel system (Chapter 1).
2 Faulty or incorrectly gapped spark plugs (Chapter 1).
3 Fault in the fuel or electrical systems (Chapters 4 and 5).
4 Incorrect ignition timing (Chapter 5).
5 Cracked distributor cap, disconnected distributor wires and damaged distributor components (1.8L only) (Chapter 1).
6 Defective spark plug wires (Chapter 1).
7 Faulty emissions system components (Chapter 6).
8 Low or uneven cylinder compression pressures. Perform a compression test (Chapter 2).
9 Weak or faulty ignition system (Chapter 5).
10 Vacuum leaks at the intake manifold or vacuum hoses (see Section 8).

11 Engine stalls

1 Idle speed incorrect. Refer to the VECI label and Chapter 1.
2 Fuel filter clogged and/or water and impurities in the fuel system (Chapter 1).
3 Distributor components damp or damaged (1.8L only) (Chapter 5).
4 Fault in the fuel system or sensors (Chapters 4 and 6).
5 Faulty emissions system components (Chapter 6).
6 Faulty or incorrectly gapped spark plugs (Chapter 1). Also check the spark plug wires (Chapter 1).
7 Vacuum leak at the intake manifold or vacuum hoses. Check as described in Section 8.

12 Engine lacks power

1 Incorrect ignition timing (Chapter 1).
2 Fault in the fuel or electrical systems (Chapters 4 and 5).
3 Excessive play in the distributor shaft (1.8L only). At the same time, check for a damaged rotor, faulty distributor cap, wires, etc. (Chapters 1 and 5).
4 Faulty or incorrectly gapped spark plugs (Chapter 1).
5 Faulty coil (Chapter 5).
6 Brakes binding (Chapter 1 and Chapter 9).
7 Automatic transaxle fluid level incorrect (Chapter 1).
8 Clutch slipping (Chapter 8).
9 Fuel filter clogged and/or impurities in the fuel system (Chapter 1).
10 Emissions control system not functioning properly (Chapter 6).

11 Use of substandard fuel. Fill the tank with the proper octane fuel.
12 Low or uneven cylinder compression pressures. Perform a compression test (Chapter 2).

13 Engine backfires

1 Emissions system not functioning properly (Chapter 6).
2 Fault in the fuel or electrical systems (Chapters 4 and 5).
3 Ignition timing incorrect (Chapter 1).
4 Faulty secondary ignition system (cracked spark plug insulator, faulty plug wires, distributor cap and/or rotor (1.8L only) (Chapters 1 and 5).
5 Fault in the engine control system (Chapter 6).
6 Vacuum leak at the intake manifold or vacuum hoses. Check as described in Section 8.
7 Valves sticking (Chapter 2)

14 Pinging or knocking engine sounds during acceleration or uphill

1 Incorrect grade of fuel. Fill the tank with fuel of the proper octane rating.
2 Fault in the fuel or electrical systems (Chapters 4 and 5).
3 Ignition timing incorrect (Chapter 5).
4 Improper spark plugs. Check the plug type. Also check the plugs and wires for damage (Chapter 1).
5 Worn or damaged distributor components (1.8L only) (Chapter 5).
6 Faulty emissions system (Chapter 6).
7 Vacuum leak. Check as described in Section 8.

15 Engine diesels (continues to run) after switching off

1 Idle speed too high. Refer to Chapter 1.
2 Fault in the fuel or electrical systems (Chapters 4 and 5).
3 Ignition timing incorrectly adjusted (Chapter 5).
4 Excessive engine operating temperature. Probable causes of this are a malfunctioning thermostat, clogged radiator, faulty water pump (see Chapter 3).

ENGINE ELECTRICAL SYSTEM

16 Battery will not hold a charge

1 Alternator drivebelt defective or not adjusted properly (Chapter 1).
2 Electrolyte level low or battery discharged (Chapter 1).
3 Battery terminals loose or corroded (Chapter 1).
4 Alternator not charging properly (Chapter 5).
5 Loose, broken or faulty wiring in the charging circuit (Chapter 5).
6 Short in the vehicle wiring causing a continuous drain on battery (refer to Chapter 12 and the Wiring Diagrams).
7 Battery defective internally.

17 Ignition light fails to go out

1 Fault in the alternator or charging circuit (Chapter 5).
2 Alternator drivebelt defective or not properly adjusted (Chapter 1).

18 Ignition light fails to come on when key is turned on

1 Instrument cluster warning light bulb defective (Chapter 12).
2 Alternator faulty (Chapter 5).
3 Fault in the instrument cluster printed circuit, dashboard wiring or bulb holder (Chapter 12).

FUEL SYSTEM

19 Excessive fuel consumption

1 Dirty or clogged air filter element (Chapter 1).
2 Incorrect ignition timing (Chapter 1).
3 Emissions system not functioning properly (Chapter 6).
4 Fault in the fuel or electrical systems (Chapters 4 and 5).
5 Fault in the engine control system (Chapter 6).
6 Low tire pressure or incorrect tire size (Chapter 1).

20 Fuel leakage and/or fuel odor

1 Leak in a fuel feed or vent line (Chapter 4).
2 Tank overfilled. Fill only to automatic shut-off.
3 Evaporative emissions system canister clogged (Chapter 6).
4 Vapor leaks from system lines (Chapter 4).
5 Fault in the engine control system (Chapter 6).

COOLING SYSTEM

21 Overheating

1 Insufficient coolant in the system (Chapter 1).
2 Water pump drivebelt defective or not adjusted properly (Chapter 1).
3 Radiator core blocked or radiator grille dirty and restricted (see Chapter 3).
4 Thermostat faulty (Chapter 3).
5 Fan blades broken or cracked (Chapter 3).
6 Fault in electric fan motor or wiring (see Chapter 3).
7 Radiator cap not maintaining proper pressure. Have the cap pressure tested by gas station or repair shop.
8 Ignition timing incorrect (Chapter 1).

22 Overcooling

1 Thermostat faulty (Chapter 3).
2 Inaccurate temperature gauge (Chapter 12).

23 External coolant leakage

1 Deteriorated or damaged hoses or loose clamps. Replace hoses and/or tighten the clamps at the hose connections (Chapter 1).
2 Water pump seals defective. If this is the case, water will drip from the weep hole in the water pump body (Chapter 3).
3 Leakage from radiator core or header tank. This will require the radiator to be professionally repaired (see Chapter 3 for removal procedures).
4 Engine drain plug leaking (Chapter 1) or water jacket core plugs leaking (see Chapter 2).

24 Internal coolant leakage

→Note: Internal coolant leaks can usually be detected by examining the oil. Check the dipstick and inside of the cylinder head cover for water deposits and an oil consistency like that of a milkshake.

1 Leaking cylinder head gasket. Have the cooling system pressure tested.
2 Cracked cylinder bore or cylinder head. Dismantle the engine and inspect (Chapter 2).

25 Coolant loss

1 Too much coolant in the system (Chapter 1).
2 Coolant boiling away due to overheating (see Section 15).
3 External or internal leakage (see Sections 23 and 24).
4 Faulty radiator cap. Have the cap pressure tested.

26 Poor coolant circulation

1 Inoperative water pump. A quick test is to pinch the top radiator hose closed with your hand while the engine is idling, then let it loose. You should feel the surge of coolant if the pump is working properly (see Chapter 3).
2 Restriction in the cooling system. Drain, flush and refill the system (Chapter 1). If necessary, remove the radiator (Chapter 3) and have it reverse flushed.
3 Water pump drivebelt defective or not adjusted properly (Chapter 1).
4 Thermostat sticking (Chapter 3).

CLUTCH

27 Fails to release (pedal pressed to the floor - shift lever does not move freely in and out of Reverse)

1 Leak in the clutch hydraulic system. Check the master cylinder, slave cylinder and lines (see Chapter 8).
2 Clutch plate warped or damaged (Chapter 8).

28 Clutch slips (engine speed increases with no increase in vehicle speed)

1 Clutch plate oil soaked or lining worn. Remove clutch (Chapter 8) and inspect (check for a leaking rear main oil seal or transaxle input shaft seal).
2 Clutch plate not seated. It may take 30 or 40 normal starts for a new one to seat.

29 Grabbing (chattering) as clutch is engaged

1 Oil on clutch plate lining. Remove (Chapter 8) and inspect. Correct any leakage source.
2 Worn or loose engine or transaxle mounts. These units move slightly when the clutch is released. Inspect the mounts and bolts (Chapter 2).
3 Worn splines on clutch plate hub. Remove the clutch components (Chapter 8) and inspect.
4 Warped pressure plate or flywheel. Remove the clutch components and inspect.

30 Squeal or rumble with clutch fully disengaged (pedal depressed)

1 Worn, defective or broken release bearing (Chapter 8).
2 Worn or broken diaphragm fingers (Chapter 8).

31 Clutch pedal stays on floor

1 Linkage or release bearing binding. Inspect the linkage or remove the clutch components as necessary.
2 Make sure proper pedal stop (bumper) is installed.

MANUAL TRANSAXLE

32 Knocking noise at low speeds

1 Worn driveaxle constant velocity (CV) joints (see Chapter 8).
2 Worn side gear shaft counterbore in differential case (see Chapter 7A).

33 Noise most pronounced when turning

Differential gear noise (see Chapter 7A).

34 Clunk on acceleration or deceleration

1 Loose engine or transaxle mounts (see Chapters 2 and 7A).
2 Worn differential pinion shaft in case.
3 Worn side gear shaft counterbore in differential case (see Chapter 7A).
4 Worn or damaged driveaxle inner CV joints (see Chapter 8).

35 Noisy in Neutral with engine running

1 Input shaft bearing worn.
2 Damaged main drive gear bearing.
3 Worn countershaft bearings.
4 Worn or damaged countershaft end play shims.

36 Noisy in all gears

1 Any of the above causes, and/or:
2 Insufficient lubricant (see the checking procedures in Chapter 1).

37 Noisy in one particular gear

1 Worn, damaged or chipped gear teeth for that particular gear.
2 Worn or damaged synchronizer for that particular gear.

38 Slips out of gear

1 Damaged shift linkage.
2 Interference between the floor shift handle and console.
3 Broken or loose engine mounts.
4 Shift mechanism stabilizer bar loose.
5 Improperly installed shifter boot.
6 Damaged or worn transaxle internal components.

39 Difficulty in engaging gears

1 Clutch not releasing completely (see clutch adjustment in Chapter 1).
2 Loose, damaged or out-of-adjustment shift linkage. Make a thorough inspection, replacing parts as necessary (Chapter 7).

40 Leaks lubricant

1 Excessive amount of lubricant in the transaxle (see Chapter 1 for correct checking procedures). Drain lubricant as required.
2 Side cover loose or gasket damaged.
3 Driveaxle oil seal or speedometer oil seal in need of replacement (Chapter 7).

AUTOMATIC TRANSAXLE

➡Note: Due to the complexity of the automatic transaxle, it's difficult for the home mechanic to properly diagnose and service this component. For problems other than the following, the vehicle should be taken to a dealer service department or a transmission shop.

41 General shift mechanism problems

1 Chapter 7 deals with checking and adjusting the shift linkage on automatic transaxles. Common problems which may be attributed to poorly adjusted linkage are:
>   Engine starting in gears other than Park or Neutral.
>   Indicator on shifter pointing to a gear other than the one actually being selected.
>   Vehicle moves when in Park.
2 Refer to Chapter 7 to adjust the linkage.

42 Transaxle will not downshift with accelerator pedal pressed to the floor

Chapter 7 deals with adjusting the throttle cable to enable the transaxle to downshift properly. This requires special equipment and should be done by professionals.

43 Transaxle slips, shifts roughly, is noisy or has no drive in forward or reverse gears

1 There are many probable causes for the above problems, but the home mechanic should be concerned with only one possibility - fluid level.
2 Before taking the vehicle to a repair shop, check the level and condition of the fluid as described in Chapter 1. Correct fluid level as necessary or change the fluid and filter if needed. If the problem persists, have a professional diagnose the probable cause.

44 Fluid leakage

1 Automatic transaxle fluid is a deep red color when new, but it can darken with age. Fluid leaks should not be confused with engine oil, which can easily be blown by air flow to the transaxle. A good way to tell the difference is to place a drop of transaxle fluid from the dipstick on a clean, lint-free paper towel, then do the same thing with a drop of

engine oil. This will enable you to compare the two.

2   To pinpoint a leak, first remove all built-up dirt and grime from around the transaxle. Degreasing agents and/or steam cleaning will achieve this. With the underside clean, drive the vehicle at low speeds so air flow will not blow the leak far from its source. Raise the vehicle and determine where the leak is coming from. Common areas of leakage are:

a) *Pan:* Tighten the mounting bolts and/or replace the pan gasket as necessary (see Chapter 7).
b) *Filler pipe:* Replace the rubber seal where the pipe enters the transaxle case.
c) *Transaxle lubricant lines:* Tighten the connectors where the lines enter the transaxle case and/or replace the lines.
d) *Vent pipe:* Transaxle overfilled and/or water in lubricant (see checking procedures, Chapter 1).
e) *Speedometer connector:* Replace the O-ring where the speedometer cable enters the transaxle case (Chapter 7).

45   Transaxle lubricant brown or has a burned smell

Transaxle lubricant burned (see Chapter 1).

DRIVEAXLES

46   Clicking noise in turns

Worn or damaged outer joint. Check for cut or damaged seals. Repair as necessary (Chapter 8).

47   Knock or clunk when accelerating after coasting

Worn or damaged inner joint. Check for cut or damaged seals. Repair as necessary (Chapter 8).

48   Shudder or vibration during acceleration

1   Worn or damaged CV joints. Repair or replace as necessary (see Chapter 8).
2   Sticking CV joint assembly. Correct or replace as necessary (see Chapter 8).

49   Vibration at highway speeds

1   Out-of-balance front wheels or tires (see Chapters 1 and 10).
2   Out-of-round front tires (see Chapters 1 and 10).
3   Worn CV joints (see Chapter 8).

REAR AXLE

50   Noise

1   Road noise. No corrective procedures available.
2   Tire noise. Inspect tires and check tire pressures (Chapter 1).
3   Rear wheel bearings loose, worn or damaged (Chapter 1).

BRAKES

→Note: **Before assuming that a brake problem exists, make sure that the tires are in good condition and inflated properly (see Chapter 1), that the front end alignment is correct and that the vehicle is not loaded with weight in an unequal manner.**

51   Vehicle pulls to one side during braking

1   Incorrect tire pressures (see Chapter 1).
2   Front end out of alignment (have the front end aligned).
3   Front or rear tires not matched to one another.
4   Restricted brake lines or hoses (see Chapter 9).
5   Defective, damaged or oil contaminated disc brake pads on one side. Inspect as described in Chapter 9.
6   Excessive wear of brake pad material or disc on one side. Inspect and correct as necessary.
7   Loose or disconnected front suspension components. Inspect and tighten all bolts to the specified torque (Chapter 10).
8   Defective caliper assembly. Remove the caliper and inspect for a stuck piston or other damage (Chapter 9).

52   Noise (high-pitched squeal with the brakes applied)

Disc brake pads worn out. The noise comes from the wear sensor (if equipped) rubbing against the disc or the actual pad backing plate itself if the material is completely worn away. Replace the pads with new ones immediately (Chapter 9). If the pad material has worn completely away, the brake discs should be inspected for damage as described in Chapter 9.

53   Excessive brake pedal travel

1   Partial brake system failure. Inspect the entire system (Chapter 9) and correct as required.
2   Insufficient fluid in the master cylinder. Check (Chapter 1), add fluid and bleed the system if necessary (Chapter 9).
3   Rear brakes not adjusting properly. Make a series of starts and stops while the vehicle is in Reverse. If this does not correct the situation, remove the drums and inspect the self-adjusters (Chapter 9).

54   Brake pedal feels spongy when depressed

1   Air in the hydraulic lines. Bleed the brake system (Chapter 9).
2   Faulty flexible hoses. Inspect all system hoses and lines. Replace parts as necessary.
3   Master cylinder mounting bolts/nuts loose.
4   Master cylinder defective (Chapter 9).

55   Excessive effort required to stop vehicle

1   Power brake booster not operating properly (Chapter 9).
2   Excessively worn linings or pads. Inspect and replace if necessary (Chapter 9).
3   One or more caliper pistons or wheel cylinders seized or sticking. Inspect and rebuild as required (Chapter 9).
4   Brake linings or pads contaminated with oil or grease. Inspect and replace as required (Chapter 9).

5 New pads or shoes installed and not yet seated. It will take a while for the new material to seat against the drum (or rotor).

56 Pedal travels to the floor with little resistance

1 Little or no fluid in the master cylinder reservoir caused by leaking wheel cylinder(s), leaking caliper piston(s), loose, damaged or disconnected brake lines. Inspect the entire system and correct as necessary.
2 Worn master cylinder (see Chapter 9).
3 Loose, damaged or disconnected brake lines (see Chapter 9).

57 Brake pedal pulsates during brake application

1 Caliper improperly installed. Remove and inspect (Chapter 9).
2 Disc or drum defective. Remove (Chapter 9) and check for excessive lateral runout and parallelism (disc) or out-of-roundness (drum). Have the disc or drum resurfaced or replace it with a new one.

58 Dragging brakes

1 Incorrect adjustment of brake light switch (see Chapter 9).
2 Master cylinder pistons not returning correctly (see Chapter 9).
3 Restricted brake lines or hoses (see Chapters 1 and 9).
4 Incorrect parking brake adjustment (see Chapter 9).

59 Grabbing or uneven braking action

1 Malfunction or proportioning valve (see Chapter 9).
2 Contaminated brake linings (see Chapter 9).
3 Binding brake pedal mechanism (see Chapter 9).

60 Parking brake does not hold

Parking brake linkage improperly adjusted (see Chapters 1 and 9).

SUSPENSION AND STEERING SYSTEMS

61 Vehicle pulls to one side

1 Tire pressures uneven (Chapter 1).
2 Defective tire (Chapter 1).
3 Excessive wear in suspension or steering components (Chapter 10).
4 Front end in need of alignment.
5 Front brakes dragging. Check the calipers for binding (see Chapter 9).

62 Shimmy, shake or vibration

1 Tire or wheel out-of-balance or out-of-round. Have professionally balanced.
2 Loose, worn or out-of-adjustment rear wheel bearings (Chapter 1).
3 Strut dampers and/or suspension components worn or damaged (Chapter 10).
4 Excessive wheel runout (see Chapter 10).
5 Blister or bump on tire (see Chapter 10).

63 Excessive pitching and/or rolling around corners or during braking

1 Worn strut dampers (see Chapter 10).
2 Broken or weak springs and/or suspension components. Inspect as described in Chapter 10.
3 Loose stabilizer bar (see Chapter 10).

64 Excessively stiff steering

1 Lack of fluid in power steering fluid reservoir (Chapter 1).
2 Incorrect tire pressures (Chapter 1).
3 Front end out of alignment.

65 Excessive play in steering

1 Wheel bearing(s) worn (see Chapter 1).
2 Tie-rod end loose (see Chapter 10).
3 Rack and pinion loose (see Chapter 10).
4 Worn or loose steering intermediate shaft (see Chapter 10).

66 Lack of power assistance

1 Steering pump drivebelt faulty or not adjusted properly (Chapter 1).
2 Fluid level low (Chapter 1).
3 Hoses or lines restricted. Inspect and replace parts as necessary.
4 Air in power steering system. Bleed the system (Chapter 10).

67 Excessive tire wear (not specific to one area)

1 Incorrect tire pressures (Chapter 1).
2 Tires out-of-balance. Have professionally balanced.
3 Wheels damaged. Inspect and replace as necessary.
4 Suspension or steering components excessively worn (Chapter 10).
5 Overloaded vehicle.
6 Tires not rotated regularly.

68 Excessive tire wear on outside edge

1 Inflation pressures incorrect (Chapter 1).
2 Excessive speed in turns.
3 Front end alignment incorrect (excessive toe-in). Have professionally aligned.
4 Suspension arm bent or twisted (Chapter 10).

69 Excessive tire wear on inside edge

1 Inflation pressures incorrect (Chapter 1).
2 Front end alignment incorrect. Have professionally aligned.
3 Loose or damaged steering components (Chapter 10).

70 Tire tread worn in one place

1 Tires out-of-balance.
2 Damaged or buckled wheel. Inspect and replace if necessary.
3 Defective tire (Chapter 1).

71   Wheel makes a thumping noise

1   Blister or bump on tire (see Chapter 10).
2   Improper strut damper action (see Chapter 10).

72   Steering wheel does not return to the straight-ahead position

1   Lack of lubrication at balljoints and tie-rod ends (see Chapter 10).
2   Binding in balljoints (see Chapter 10).
3   Binding in steering column (see Chapter 10).
4   Lack of lubricant in rack and pinion assembly (see Chapter 10).
5   Front wheel alignment (see Chapter 10).

73   Abnormal noise at the front end

1   Loose wheel nuts (see Chapter 1 for torque specifications).
2   Lack of lubrication at balljoints and tie-rod ends (see Chapters 1 and 10).
3   Damaged strut mounting (see Chapter 10).
4   Worn control arm bushings or tie-rod ends (see Chapter 10).
5   Loose stabilizer bar (see Chapter 10).
6   Loose suspension bolts (see Chapter 10).

74   Wander or poor steering stability

1   Mismatched or uneven tires (see Chapter 10).
2   Wheel alignment (see Chapter 10).
3   Worn strut assemblies (see Chapter 10).
4   Loose stabilizer bar (see Chapter 10).
5   Broken or sagging springs (see Chapter 10).
6   Wheel alignment (see Chapter 10).

75   Erratic steering when braking

1   Wheel bearings worn (see Chapter 1).
2   Broken or sagging springs (see Chapter 10).
3   Leaking caliper (see Chapter 9).
4   Warped rotors or drums (see Chapter 9).

76   Suspension bottoms

1   Overloaded vehicle.
2   Worn strut dampers (see Chapter 10).
3   Incorrect, broken or sagging springs (see Chapter 10).

77   Cupped tires

1   Wheels out of alignment (see Chapter 10).
2   Worn strut dampers (see Chapter 10).
3   Worn wheel bearings (see Chapter 1).
4   Excessive tire or wheel runout (see Chapter 10).
5   Worn balljoints (see Chapter 10).

78   Rattling or clicking noise in rack and pinion

1   Insufficient or improper lubricant in rack and pinion assembly (see Chapter 10).
2   Rack and pinion attachment loose (see Chapter 10).

1

TUNE-UP AND MAINTENANCE

Section

Reference to other Chapters

1 Maintenance schedule

The following maintenance intervals are based on the assumption that the vehicle owner will be doing the maintenance or service work, as opposed to having a dealer service department do the work. Although the time/mileage intervals are loosely based on factory recommendations, most have been shortened to ensure, for example, that such items as lubricants and fluids are checked/changed at intervals that promote maximum engine/driveline service life. Also, subject to the preference of the individual owner interested in keeping his or her vehicle in peak condition at all times, and with the vehicle's ultimate resale in mind, many of the maintenance procedures may be performed more often than recommended in the following schedule. We encourage such owner initiative.

When the vehicle is new it should be serviced initially by a factory authorized dealer service department to protect the factory warranty. In many cases the initial maintenance check is done at no cost to the owner.

EVERY 250 MILES OR WEEKLY, WHICHEVER COMES FIRST

Check the engine oil level (see Section 4)
Check the engine coolant level (see Section 4)
Check the windshield washer fluid level (see Section 4)
Check the brake fluid level (see Section 4)
Check the tires and tire pressures (see Section 5)

EVERY 3000 MILES OR 3 MONTHS, WHICHEVER COMES FIRST

All items listed above plus . . .
Check the power steering fluid level (see Section 6)
Check the automatic transaxle fluid level (see Section 7)
Change the engine oil and oil filter (see Section 8)

EVERY 6000 MILES OR 6 MONTHS, WHICHEVER COMES FIRST

All items listed above plus . . .
Adjust the clutch pedal (see Section 9)

Inspect and, if necessary, replace the underhood hoses (see Section 10)
Check/adjust the drivebelts (see Section 11)
Check/service the battery (see Section 12)

EVERY 12,000 MILES OR 12 MONTHS, WHICHEVER COMES FIRST

All items listed above plus . . .
Inspect/replace the windshield wiper blades (see Section 13)
Replace the air filter (see Section 14)
Replace the crankcase emission filter (models so equipped) (see Section 14)
Check the PCV valve (see Section 15)
Check the fuel system (see Section 16)
Inspect the cooling system (see Section 17)
Inspect the exhaust system (see Section 18)
Rotate the tires (see Section 19)
Inspect the steering and suspension components (see Section 20)
Inspect the brake system (see Section 21)
Check the parking brake linkage (see Section 21)
Inspect the clutch hydraulic linkage (see Section 22)
Check/replenish the manual transaxle lubricant (see Section 23)

EVERY 30,000 MILES OR 30 MONTHS, WHICHEVER COMES FIRST

Replace the spark plugs (except models with platinum spark plugs) (see Section 24)
Check/replace the spark plug wires and, if equipped, the distributor cap and rotor (see Section 25)
Service the cooling system (drain, flush and refill) (see Section 26)
Change the automatic transaxle fluid and filter (see Section 27)

EVERY 60,000 MILES

Inspect and, if necessary, replace the timing belt (see Chapter 2A)
Replace the PCV valve (see Section 15)
Replace the spark plugs (models with platinum spark plugs) (see Section 24)

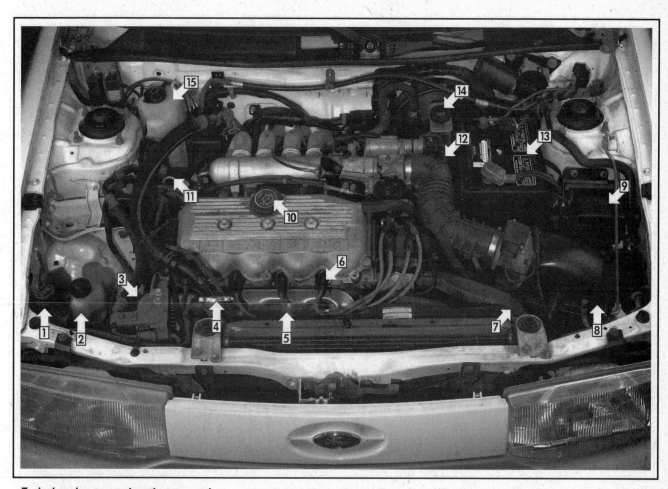

Typical engine compartment components

1	Coolant reservoir	6	Spark plug
2	Power steering fluid reservoir	7	Upper radiator hose
3	Drivebelt	8	Air filter housing
4	Radiator cap	9	Fuse panel
5	Spark plug wire	10	Engine oil filler cap

11	Engine oil dipstick
12	Automatic transaxle fluid dipstick
13	Battery
14	Brake fluid reservoir
15	Windshield washer fluid reservoir

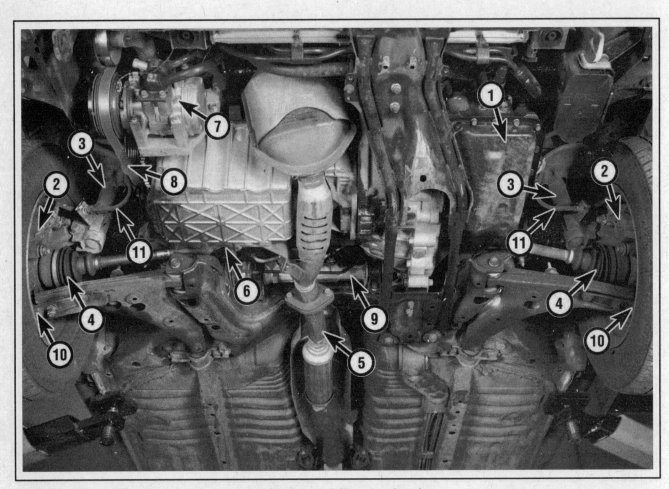

Typical engine compartment underside components (model with 1.9L engine shown)

1	Automatic transaxle fluid pan	5	Exhaust pipe	9	Power steering gear (rack and pinion)
2	Disc brake calipers	6	Engine oil drain plug	10	Balljoints
3	Front suspension strut assemblies	7	Air conditioning compressor	11	Brake hoses
4	Outer driveaxle boots	8	Drivebelt		

Typical rear underside components

1	*Rear suspension strut assemblies*	*3*	*Exhaust system hangers*	*5*	*Brake hoses*
2	*Muffler*	*4*	*Fuel tank*		

2   Introduction

✳✳ WARNING:

The electric cooling fan on these models can activate at any time, even when the ignition is in the Off position. Disconnect the fan motor or negative battery cable when working in the vicinity of the fan.

This Chapter is designed to help the home mechanic maintain the Escort and Tracer with the goals of maximum performance, economy, safety and reliability in mind.

Included is a master maintenance schedule, followed by procedures dealing specifically with each item on the schedule. Visual checks, adjustments, component replacement and other helpful items are included. Refer to the accompanying illustrations of the engine compartment and the underside of the vehicle for the locations of various components.

Servicing your vehicle in accordance with the mileage/time maintenance schedule and the step-by-step procedures will result in a planned maintenance program that should produce a long and reliable service life. Keep in mind that it is a comprehensive plan, so maintaining some items but not others at the specified intervals will not produce the same results.

As you service your vehicle, you will discover that many of the procedures can - and should - be grouped together because of the nature of the particular procedure you're performing or because of the close proximity of two otherwise unrelated components to one another.

For example, if the vehicle is raised for chassis lubrication, you should inspect the exhaust, suspension, steering and fuel systems while you're under the vehicle. When you're rotating the tires, it makes good sense to check the brakes since the wheels are already removed. Finally, let's suppose you have to borrow or rent a torque wrench. Even if you only need it to tighten the spark plugs, you might as well check the torque of as many critical fasteners as time allows.

The first step in this maintenance program is to prepare yourself before the actual work begins. Read through all the procedures you're planning to do, then gather up all the parts and tools needed. If it looks as if you might run into problems during a particular job, seek advice from a mechanic or an experienced do-it-yourselfer.

3   Tune-up general information

The term tune-up is used in this manual to represent a combination of individual operations rather than one specific procedure.

If, from the time the vehicle is new, the routine maintenance schedule is followed closely and frequent checks are made of fluid levels and high wear items, as suggested throughout this manual, the engine will be kept in relatively good running condition and the need for additional work will be minimized.

More likely than not, however, there will be times when the engine is running poorly. This is even more likely if a used vehicle, which has not received regular and frequent maintenance checks, is purchased. In such cases, an engine tune-up will be needed outside of the regular routine maintenance intervals.

The first step in any tune-up or diagnostic procedure to help correct a poor running engine is a cylinder compression check. A compression check (see Chapter 2B) will help determine the condition of internal engine components and should be used as a guide for tune-up and repair procedures. If, for instance, a compression check indicates serious internal engine wear, a conventional tune-up will not improve the performance of the engine and would be a waste of time and money. Because of its importance, the compression check should be done by someone with the right equipment and the knowledge to use it properly.

The following procedures are those most often needed to bring a generally poor running engine back into a proper state of tune.

MINOR TUNE-UP

Clean, inspect and test the battery (see Section 12)

Check all engine related fluids (see Section 4)
Check and adjust the drivebelts (see Section 11)
Replace the spark plugs (see Section 24)
Inspect the distributor cap and rotor (models so equipped) (see Section 25)
Inspect the spark plug and coil wires (see Section 25)
Check the PCV valve (models so equipped) (see Section 15)
Check the air filter (see Section 14)
Check the crankcase ventilation filter (models so equipped) (see Section 15)
Check the cooling system (see Section 17)
Check all underhood hoses (see Section 10)

MAJOR TUNE-UP

All items listed under Minor tune-up, plus . . .
Check the EGR system (see Chapter 6)
Check the ignition system (see Chapter 5)
Check the charging system (see Chapter 5)
Check the fuel system (see Chapter 4)
Replace the fuel filter (see Chapter 4)
Replace the air and crankcase ventilation filters (see Sections 14 and 15)
Replace the distributor cap and rotor (models so equipped) (see Section 25)
Replace the spark plug wires (see Section 24)

4 Fluid level checks (every 250 miles or weekly)

1   Fluids are an essential part of the lubrication, cooling, brake and windshield washer systems. Because the fluids gradually become depleted and/or contaminated during normal operation of the vehicle, they must be periodically replenished. See *Recommended lubricants, fluids and capacities* at the end of this Chapter before adding fluid to any of the following components.

➡**Note: The vehicle must be on level ground when fluid levels are checked. Fluid level checking points are shown in the accompanying illustrations and the illustrations near the beginning of this Chapter.**

ENGINE OIL

▸ **Refer to illustrations 4.2, 4.4 and 4.6**

2   The oil level is checked with a dipstick, which is attached to the engine block (see illustration). The dipstick handle may be near the windshield washer and power steering fluid reservoirs, at the back of the engine or at the timing belt end of the engine. The dipstick extends through a metal tube down into the oil pan.

3   The oil level should be checked before the vehicle has been driven, or about 5 minutes after the engine has been shut off. If the oil is checked immediately after driving the vehicle, some of the oil will remain in the upper part of the engine, resulting in an inaccurate reading on the dipstick.

4   Pull the dipstick from the tube and wipe all the oil from the end with a clean rag or paper towel. Insert the clean dipstick all the way back into the tube and pull it out again. Note the oil at the end of the dipstick. At its highest point, the level should be above the L or ADD mark, in the SAFE range (see illustration).

5   It takes one quart of oil to raise the level from the L or ADD mark to the F or FULL mark. Do not allow the level to drop below the L or ADD mark, or oil starvation may cause engine damage. Conversely, overfilling the engine (adding oil above the F or FULL mark) may cause oil fouled spark plugs, oil leaks or oil seal failures.

6   To add oil, remove the filler cap located on the valve cover (see illustration). After adding oil, wait a few minutes to allow the level to stabilize, then pull out the dipstick and check the level again. Add more oil if required. Install the filler cap and tighten it by hand only.

7   Checking the oil level is an important preventive maintenance step. A consistently low oil level indicates oil leakage through damaged seals, defective gaskets or worn rings or valve guides. The condition of the oil should also be checked. If the oil looks milky in color or has water droplets in it, the cylinder head gasket may be blown or the head or block may be cracked. The engine should be checked immediately. Whenever you check the oil level, slide your thumb and index finger up the dipstick before wiping off the oil. If you see small dirt or metal particles clinging to the dipstick, the oil should be changed (see Section 8).

4.2 The engine oil level is checked with a dipstick - the dipstick handle location varies according to model (early model shown)

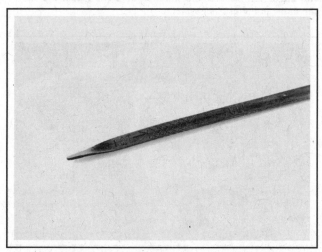

4.4 The oil level should be in the Safe range - if it's below the L or ADD line, add enough oil to bring it up to or near the F or FULL line

4.6 Turn the oil filter cap counterclockwise to remove it (1.9L engine shown) - always make sure the area around the opening is clean before unscrewing the cap (to prevent dirt from contaminating the engine)

ENGINE COOLANT

♦ **Refer to illustration 4.8**

❄❄ **WARNING:**

Do not allow antifreeze to come in contact with your skin or painted surfaces of the vehicle. Flush contaminated areas immediately with plenty of water. Do not store new coolant or leave old coolant lying around where it's accessible to children or pets - they are attracted by its sweet smell. Ingestion of even a small amount of coolant can be fatal! Wipe up garage floor and drip pan coolant spills immediately. Keep antifreeze containers covered and repair leaks in your cooling system immediately. Antifreeze is also flammable, so keep it away from open flames and other heat sources.

8 All vehicles covered by this manual are equipped with a pressurized coolant recovery system. A plastic coolant reservoir located in the right front or left front corner of the engine compartment is connected by a hose to the radiator filler neck. The filler cap is clearly marked (see illustration). If the engine overheats, coolant escapes through a valve in the radiator cap and travels through the hose into the reservoir. As the engine cools, the coolant is automatically drawn back into the cooling system to maintain the correct level.

9 The coolant level in the reservoir should be checked regularly.

❄❄ **WARNING:**

Do not remove the radiator cap to check the coolant level when the engine is warm. The level in the reservoir varies with the temperature of the engine. When the engine is cold, the coolant level should be at or slightly above the ADD mark on the reservoir. Once the engine has warmed up, the level should be at or near the FULL HOT mark. If it isn't, allow the engine to cool, then remove the cap from the reservoir and add a 50/50 mixture of ethylene glycol based antifreeze and water.

10 Drive the vehicle and recheck the coolant level. Do not use rust inhibitors or additives. If only a small amount of coolant is required to bring the system up to the proper level, water can be used. However, repeated additions of water will dilute the antifreeze and water solution. In order to maintain the proper ratio of antifreeze and water, always top up the coolant level with the correct mixture. An empty plastic milk jug or bleach bottle makes an excellent container for mixing coolant.

11 If the coolant level drops consistently, there may be a leak in the system. Inspect the radiator, hoses, filler cap, drain plugs and water pump (see Section 17). If no leaks are noted, have the radiator cap pressure tested by a service station.

12 If you have to remove the radiator cap, wait until the engine has cooled completely, then wrap a thick cloth around the cap and turn it to the first stop. If coolant or steam escapes, let the engine cool down longer, then remove the cap.

13 Check the condition of the coolant as well. It should be relatively clear. If it is brown or rust colored, the system should be drained, flushed and refilled. Even if the coolant appears to be normal, the corrosion inhibitors wear out, so it must be replaced at the specified intervals.

BRAKE/CLUTCH FLUID

♦ **Refer to illustration 4.15**

14 The master cylinder is mounted in the left rear corner of the engine compartment. On manual transaxle models, the same reservoir is used for the brake and clutch hydraulic systems.

15 The fluid level should be between the MAX and MIN lines on the side of the reservoir (see illustration). If the fluid level is low, wipe the top of the reservoir and the cap with a clean rag to prevent contamination of the system as the cap is unscrewed.

16 Add only the specified brake fluid to the reservoir (see *Recommended lubricants, fluids and capacities* at the end of this Chapter or your owner's manual). Mixing different types of brake fluid can damage the system. Fill the reservoir to the MAX line.

❄❄ **WARNING:**

Brake fluid can harm your eyes and damage painted surfaces, so use extreme caution when handling or pouring it. Do not use brake fluid that has been standing open or is more than one year old. Brake fluid absorbs moisture from the air. Excess moisture can damage the braking system.

4.8 The coolant reservoir is clearly marked with LOW and FULL marks - make sure the level is slightly above the LOW mark when the engine is cold and at or near the FULL mark when the engine is warmed up

4.15 The brake fluid level should be kept between the MIN and MAX marks on the translucent plastic reservoir - unscrew the cap to add fluid; on manual transaxle models, the same reservoir contains the clutch fluid and is connected to the clutch master cylinder by a hose

17 While the reservoir cap is off, check the master cylinder reservoir for contamination. If rust deposits, dirt particles or water droplets are present, the system should be drained and refilled by a dealer service department or repair shop.

18 After filling the reservoir to the proper level, make sure the cap is seated to prevent fluid leakage and/or contamination.

19 The fluid level in the master cylinder will drop slightly as the brake shoes or pads at each wheel wear down during normal operation. If the brake fluid level drops significantly, check the entire system for leaks immediately. Examine all brake lines, hoses and connections, along with the calipers, wheel cylinders and master cylinder (see Section 21).

20 When checking the fluid level, if you discover one or both reservoirs empty or nearly empty, the brake system should be bled (see Chapter 9).

WINDSHIELD WASHER FLUID

▶ **Refer to illustration 4.21**

21 The front windshield washer fluid reservoir is mounted in the engine compartment. On 1.8L engine models, it's in the right front-corner, between the power steering fluid reservoir and the fender. On 1.9L and 2.0L engine models, it's in the right rear corner, behind the strut tower (see illustration).

22 The rear windshield washer reservoir on four-door station wagons is in the right rear corner of the luggage area. Add fluid when necessary through the filler hole.

23 In milder climates, plain water can be used in the reservoir, but it should be kept no more than 2/3 full to allow for expansion if the water freezes. In colder climates, use windshield washer system antifreeze, available at any auto parts store, to lower the freezing point of the fluid. Mix the antifreeze with water in accordance with the manufacturer's directions on the container.

❊❊ CAUTION:

Do not use cooling system antifreeze - it will damage the vehicle's paint.

4.21 The windshield washer fluid reservoir on 1.9L and 2.0L engine models is at the rear of the engine compartment

5 Tire and tire pressure checks (every 250 miles or weekly)

▶ **Refer to illustrations 5.2, 5.3, 5.4a, 5.4b and 5.8**

1 Periodic inspection of the tires may spare you the inconvenience of being stranded with a flat tire. It can also provide you with vital information regarding possible problems in the steering and suspension systems before major damage occurs.

2 The original tires on this vehicle are equipped with 1/2-inch wide bands that will appear when tread depth reaches 1/16-inch, at which point the tires can be considered worn out. Tread wear can be monitored with a simple, inexpensive device known as a tread depth indicator (see illustration).

3 Note any abnormal tread wear (see illustration). Tread pattern irregularities such as cupping, flat spots and more wear on one side than the other are indications of front end alignment and/or balance problems. If any of these conditions are noted, take the vehicle to a tire shop or service station to correct the problem.

4 Look closely for cuts, punctures and embedded nails or tacks. Sometimes a tire will hold air pressure for a short time or leak down very slowly after a nail has embedded itself in the tread. If a slow leak

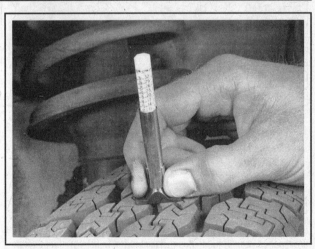

5.2 Use a tire tread depth indicator to monitor tire wear - they are available at auto parts stores and service stations and cost very little

UNDERINFLATION

CUPPING

Cupping may be caused by:
- Underinflation and/or mechanical irregularities such as out-of-balance condition of wheel and/or tire, and bent or damaged wheel.
- Loose or worn steering tie-rod or steering idler arm.
- Loose, damaged or worn front suspension parts.

OVERINFLATION

INCORRECT TOE-IN
OR EXTREME CAMBER

FEATHERING DUE
TO MISALIGNMENT

5.3 This chart will help you determine the condition of the tires, the probable cause(s) of abnormal wear and the corrective action necessary

5.4a If a tire loses air on a steady basis, check the valve core first to make sure it's snug (special inexpensive wrenches are commonly available at auto parts stores)

5.4b If the valve core is tight, raise the corner of the vehicle with the low tire and spray a soapy water solution onto the tread as the tire is turned slowly - leaks will cause small bubbles to appear

persists, check the valve stem core to make sure it is tight (see illustration). Examine the tread for an object that may have embedded itself in the tire or for a "plug" that may have begun to leak (radial tire punctures are repaired with a plug that is installed in the puncture). If a puncture is suspected, it can be easily verified by spraying a solution of soapy water onto the puncture area (see illustration). The soapy solution will bubble if there is a leak. Unless the puncture is unusually large, a tire

shop or service station can normally repair the tire.

5   Carefully inspect the inner sidewall of each tire for evidence of brake fluid leakage. If you see any, inspect the brakes immediately.

6   Correct air pressure adds miles to the lifespan of the tires, improves mileage and enhances overall ride quality. Tire pressure cannot be accurately estimated by looking at a tire, especially if it's a radial. A tire pressure gauge is essential. Keep an accurate gauge in the glove-

box. The pressure gauges attached to the nozzles of air hoses at gas stations are often inaccurate.

7   Always check tire pressure when the tires are cold. Cold, in this case, means the vehicle has not been driven over a mile in the three hours preceding a tire pressure check. A pressure rise of four to eight pounds is not uncommon once the tires are warm.

8   Unscrew the valve cap protruding from the wheel or hubcap and push the gauge firmly onto the valve stem (see illustration). Note the reading on the gauge and compare the figure to the recommended tire pressure shown on the tire placard on the driver's side door. Be sure to reinstall the valve cap to keep dirt and moisture out of the valve stem mechanism. Check all four tires and, if necessary, add enough air to bring them up to the recommended pressure.

9   Don't forget to keep the spare tire inflated to the specified pressure (see your owner's manual or the tire sidewall). Note that the pressure recommended for the compact spare is higher than for the tires on the vehicle.

5.8 To extend the life of the tires, check the air pressure at least once a week with an accurate gauge (don't forget the spare!)

6   Power steering fluid level check (every 3000 miles or 3 months)

♦ **Refer to illustration 6.2**

1   Check the power steering fluid level periodically to avoid steering system problems, such as damage to the pump.

❋❋ CAUTION:

DO NOT hold the steering wheel against either stop (extreme left or right turn) for more than five seconds. If you do, the power steering pump could be damaged.

2   The power steering reservoir, located at the right rear corner of the engine compartment, has LOW and FULL fluid level marks on the side (see illustration). The fluid level can be seen without removing the reservoir cap.

3   Park the vehicle on level ground and apply the parking brake.

4   Run the engine until it has reached normal operating temperature. With the engine at idle, turn the steering wheel back and forth about 10 times to get any air out of the steering system. Shut the engine off with the wheels in the straight ahead position.

5   Note the fluid level on the side of the reservoir. It should be between the two marks.

6   Add small amounts of fluid until the level is correct.

❋❋ CAUTION:

Do not overfill the reservoir. If too much fluid is added, remove the excess with a clean syringe or suction pump.

7   Check the power steering hoses and connections for leaks and wear.

8   Check the condition and tension of the power steering pump drivebelt (see Section 11).

6.2 The fluid level in the power steering reservoir must be between the LOW and FULL marks

7 Automatic transaxle fluid level check (every 3000 miles or 3 months)

◆ Refer to illustrations 7.4 and 7.6

1 The automatic transaxle fluid level should be carefully maintained. Low fluid level can lead to slipping of loss of drive, while overfilling can cause foaming and loss of fluid. Either condition can cause transaxle damage.

2 Since transmission fluid expands as it heats up, the fluid level should only be checked when the transaxle is warm (at normal operating temperature). If the vehicle has just been driven over 20 miles the transaxle can be considered warm.

❋❋ CAUTION:

If the vehicle has just been driven for a long time at high speed or in city traffic in hot weather, or if it has been pulling a trailer, an accurate fluid level reading cannot be obtained. Allow the transaxle to cool down for about 30 minutes. You can also check the transaxle fluid level when the transaxle is cold. If the vehicle has not been driven for over five hours and the fluid is about room temperature (70 to 95-degrees F), the transaxle is cold. However, the cold temperature scale on the dipstick should be used only for reference; recheck its reading with the transaxle warm as soon as possible.

3 Immediately after driving the vehicle, park it on a level surface, set the parking brake and start the engine. While the engine is idling, depress the brake pedal and move the selector lever through all the gear ranges, beginning and ending in P.

4 Locate the automatic transaxle dipstick in the engine compartment near the master cylinder reservoir (see illustration).

5 With the engine still idling, pull the dipstick from the tube, wipe it off with a clean rag, push it all the way back into the tube and withdraw it again, then note the fluid level.

6 The fluid level should be between the low and full notches of the high temperature scale (hot range) (see illustration). If the level is low, add the specified automatic transmission fluid through the dipstick tube. Use a funnel to prevent spills.

7 Add just enough of the recommended fluid to fill the transaxle to the proper level. It takes about one pint to raise the level from the lower notch to the upper notch when the fluid is hot, so add the fluid a little at a time and keep checking the level until it's correct.

8 The condition of the fluid should also be checked along with the level. If the fluid is black or a dark reddish-brown color, or if it smells burned, it should be changed (see Section 27). If you are in doubt about its condition, purchase some new fluid and compare the two for color and smell.

7.4 The automatic transaxle dipstick is located in a tube near the brake/clutch master cylinder

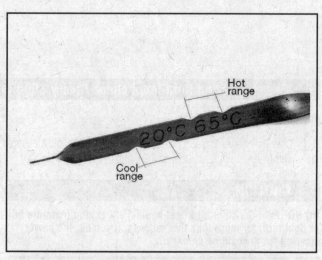

7.6 The fluid level should be between the notches of the high-temperature range; the low-temperature range should be used only for reference

8 Engine oil and filter change (every 3000 miles or 3 months)

◆ Refer to illustrations 8.2, 8. 7, 8.11 and 8.16

1 Frequent oil changes are among the most important preventive maintenance procedures that can be done by the home mechanic. As engine oil ages, it becomes diluted and contaminated, which leads to premature engine wear. Although some sources recommend oil filter changes every other oil change, a new filter should be installed every time the oil is changed.

2 Make sure that you have all the necessary tools before you begin this procedure (see illustration). You should also have plenty of rags or

newspapers handy for mopping up oil spills.

3 Access to the oil drain plug and filter will be improved if the vehicle can be lifted on a hoist, driven onto ramps or supported by jackstands.

❋❋ WARNING:

Do not work under a vehicle that's supported only by a bumper, hydraulic or scissors-type jack - always use jackstands!

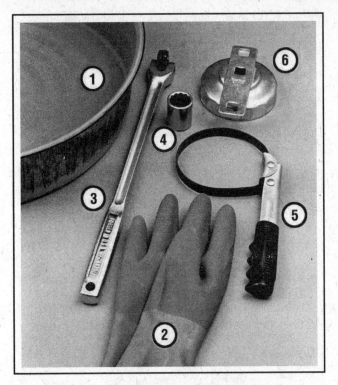

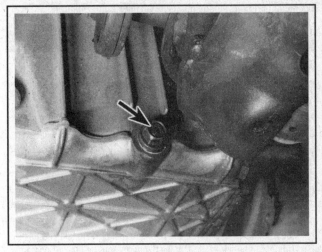

8.7 **Use a box-end wrench or six-point socket to remove the oil drain plug without rounding it off (1.9L engine shown)**

8.2 **These tools are required when changing the engine oil and filter**

1   **Drain pan** - *It should be fairly shallow in depth, but wide to prevent spills*
2   **Rubber gloves** - *When removing the drain plug and filter, you will get oil on your hands (the gloves will prevent burns)*
3   **Breaker bar** - *Sometimes the oil drain plug is tight, and a long breaker bar is needed to loosen it*
4   **Socket** - *To be used with the breaker bar or a ratchet (must be the correct size to fit the drain plug - six-point preferred)*
5   **Filter wrench** - *This is a metal band-type wrench, which requires clearance around the filter to be effective*
6   **Filter wrench** - *This type fits on the bottom of the filter and can be turned with a ratchet or breaker bar (different-size wrenches are available for different types of filters)*

8.11 **The oil filter (1.9L engine shown) is usually on very tight and will require a special wrench for removal - DO NOT use the wrench to tighten the new filter!**

4   If you haven't changed the oil on this vehicle before, get under it and locate the Oil drain plug and the oil filter. The exhaust components will be warm as you work, so note how they are routed to avoid touching them when you are under the vehicle.

5   Start the engine and allow it to reach normal operating temperature - oil and sludge will flow out more easily when warm. Park on a level surface and shut off the engine when it's warmed up. Remove the oil filler cap.

6   Raise the vehicle and support it on jackstands. Make sure it is safely supported!

7   Being careful not to touch the hot exhaust components, position a drain pan under the plug in the bottom of the engine oil pan (see illustration), then remove the plug. It's a good idea to wear an old glove while unscrewing the plug the final few turns to avoid being scalded by hot oil.

8   It may be necessary to move the drain pan slightly as oil flow slows to a trickle. Inspect the old oil for the presence of metal particles.

9   After all the oil has drained, wipe off the drain plug with a clean rag. Any small metal particles clinging to the plug would immediately contaminate the new oil.

10   Clean the area around the drain plug opening, reinstall the plug and tighten it securely, being careful not to strip the threads.

11   Move the drain pan into position under the oil filter, located on the rear firewall side) of the engine (see illustration).

12   Loosen the oil filter by turning it counterclockwise with a filter wrench. Any standard filter wrench will work.

13   Sometimes the oil filter is screwed on so tightly that it cannot be loosened. If it is, punch a metal bar or long screwdriver directly through it, as close to the engine as possible, and use it as a lever to turn the filter. Be prepared for oil to spurt out of the canister as it is punctured.

14   Once the filter is loose, use your hands to unscrew it from the block. Just as the filter is detached from the block, immediately tilt the

open end up to prevent the oil inside the filter from spilling out.

15 Using a clean rag, wipe off the mounting surface on the block. Make sure the old gasket does not remain stuck to the mounting surface.

16 Compare the old filter with the new one to make sure they are the same type. Smear some engine oil on the rubber gasket of the new filter and screw it into place (see illustration). Overtightening the filter will damage the gasket, so don't use a filter wrench. Most filter manufacturers recommend tightening the filter by hand only. If you're using an original equipment filter, the factory recommends tightening 1-1/6 turns for 1.8L engines or 3/4-turn for 1.9L engines after the gasket contacts the engine, but be sure to follow the directions on the filter or container.

17 Remove all tools and materials from under the vehicle, being careful not to spill the oil in the drain pan, then lower the vehicle.

18 Add 3-1/2 quarts of new oil to the engine (see Section 4 if necessary). Use a funnel to prevent oil from spilling onto the top of the engine. Wait a few minutes to allow the oil to drain into the pan, then check the level on the dipstick. If the oil level is in the Safe range, install the filler cap.

19 Start the engine and run it for about a minute. While the engine is running, look under the vehicle and check for leaks at the oil pan drain plug and around the oil filter. If either one is leaking, stop the engine and tighten the plug or filter slightly.

20 Stop the engine, wait a few minutes, then recheck the level on the dipstick. Add oil as necessary to bring the level into the SAFE range.

21 During the first few trips after an oil change, make it a point to check frequently for leaks and proper oil level.

22 The old oil drained from the engine cannot be reused in its present state and should be discarded. Check with your local auto parts store, disposal facility or environmental agency to see if they will accept the oil for recycling. After the oil has cooled it can be drained into a container (capped plastic jugs, topped bottles, milk cartons, etc.) for transport to one of these disposal sites. Don't dispose of the oil by pouring it on the ground or down a drain.

8.16 Lubricate the oil filter gasket with clean engine oil before installing the filter on the engine

9 Clutch pedal adjustment (every 6000 miles or 6 months)

⬧ **Refer to illustration 9.4**

1 Measure pedal height from the floorboard to the top center of the pedal pad. Compare the measurement with that listed in this Chapter's Specifications.

2 If pedal height is incorrect, disconnect the electrical connector from the clutch switch. Loosen the switch lock nut and turn the switch to adjust pedal height.

3 Once pedal height is correct, tighten the locknut and connect the electrical connector.

4 Press the pedal by hand until resistance is felt. Measure the distance the pedal traveled without resistance (this distance is known as "freeplay") and compare it to that listed in this Chapter's Specifications (see illustration).

5 If pedal freeplay is incorrect, loosen the pushrod locknut. Turn the pushrod to adjust the freeplay, then retighten the locknut.

6 Press the pedal until the clutch disengages, then measure pedal height at that point and compare with the Specifications.

7 When pedal height and disengagement height are within specifications, tighten the pushrod lock nut.

8 If you can't adjust the pedal to the correct specifications, check for worn hydraulic linkage or pedal components (see Chapter 8).

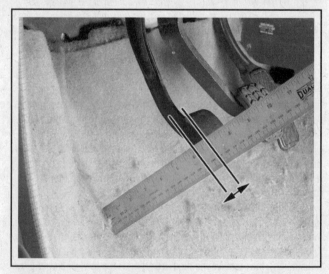

9.4 Pedal freeplay is the distance from the natural resting point of the pedal to the point at which resistance is felt

10 Underhood hose check and replacement (every 6000 miles or 6 months)

✳✳ WARNING:

Replacement of air conditioning hoses must be left to a dealer service department or air conditioning shop that has the equipment to depressurize the system safely. Never remove air conditioning components or hoses until the system has been depressurized.

GENERAL

1   High temperatures under the hood can cause the deterioration of the rubber and plastic hoses used for engine, accessory and emission systems operation. Inspect the hoses periodically for cracks, loose clamps, material hardening and leaks.

2   Information specific to the cooling system hoses can be found in Section 17.

3   Most (but not all) hoses are secured to the fittings with clamps. Where clamps are used, check to be sure they haven't lost their tension, allowing the hose to leak. If clamps aren't used, make sure the hose has not expanded and/or hardened where it slips over the fitting, allowing it to leak.

PCV SYSTEM HOSE

4   To reduce hydrocarbon emissions, crankcase blow-by gas is vented through the PCV valve in the valve cover to the intake manifold via a rubber hose. The blow-by gases mix with incoming air in the intake manifold before being burned in the combustion chambers.

5   Check the PCV hose for cracks, leaks and other damage. Disconnect it from the cylinder head cover and the intake manifold and check the inside for obstructions. If it's clogged, clean it out with solvent.

Vacuum hoses

6   It is quite common for vacuum hoses, especially those in the emissions system, to be color coded or identified by colored stripes molded into each hose. Various systems require hoses with different wall thicknesses, collapse resistance and temperature resistance. When replacing hoses, be sure the new ones are made of the same material.

7   Often the only effective way to check a hose is to remove it completely from the vehicle. If more than one hose is removed, be sure to label the hoses and fittings to ensure correct installation.

8   When checking vacuum hoses, be sure to include any plastic T-fittings in the check. Inspect the fittings for cracks and the hose where it fits over each fitting for distortion, which could cause leakage.

9   A small piece of vacuum hose (1/4-inch inside diameter) can be used as a stethoscope to detect vacuum leaks. Hold one end of the hose to your ear and probe around vacuum hoses and fittings, listening for the "hissing" sound characteristic of a vacuum leak.

✳✳ WARNING:

When probing with the vacuum hose stethoscope, be careful not to allow your body or the hose to come into contact with moving engine components such as drivebelts, the cooling fan, etc.

Fuel hose

✳✳ WARNING:

Gasoline is extremely flammable, so take extra precautions when you work on any part of the fuel system. Don't smoke or allow open flames or bare light bulbs near the work area, and don't work in a garage where a gas-type appliance (such as a water heater or clothes dryer) is present. If you spill any fuel on your skin, rinse it off immediately with soap and water. When you perform any kind of work on the fuel tank, wear safety glasses and have a Class B type fire extinguisher on hand. The fuel system on these vehicles is under pressure. You must relieve this pressure before servicing the fuel lines. Refer to Chapter 4 for the fuel pressure relief procedure.

10 Check all rubber fuel lines for deterioration and chafing. Check especially for cracks in areas where the hose bends and just before fittings, such as where a hose attaches to the fuel tank, fuel filter or a fuel injection component.

11 If any fuel lines show damage, deterioration or wear, they should be replaced (see Chapter 4). Be sure to use fuel line that is designed for use in fuel injection systems and is an exact duplicate of the original.

12 Spring-type clamps are commonly used on fuel lines. These clamps often lose their tension over a period of time, and can be "sprung" during the removal process. As a result, it is recommended that all spring-type clamps be replaced with screw clamps whenever a hose is replaced.

Metal lines

13 Sections of metal line are often used for fuel line between the fuel pump and fuel injection unit. Check carefully to be sure the line has not been bent and crimped and that cracks have not started in the line, particularly where bends occur.

14 If a section of metal fuel line must be replaced, use original equipment replacement line only, since other types of tubing do not have the strength necessary to withstand vibration caused by the engine.

✳✳ WARNING:

The fuel system pressure must be relieved before any fuel lines can be replaced (see Chapter 4).

15 Check the metal brake lines where they enter the master cylinder and brake proportioning unit (if used) for cracks in the lines and loose fittings. Any sign of brake fluid leakage calls for an immediate thorough inspection of the brake system.

11 Drivebelt check, adjustment and replacement (every 6000 miles or 6 months)

1 Vehicles equipped with the 1.8L engine use a pair of V-belts, mounted on the timing belt end of the engine. The 1.9L engine uses a single serpentine belt. The condition and tension of the drivebelts are critical to the operation of the engine and accessories. Excessive tension causes bearing wear, while insufficient tension produces slippage, noise, component vibration and belt failure. Because of their composition and the high stresses to which they are subjected, drivebelts stretch and deteriorate as they get older. As a result, they must be periodically checked and adjusted.

CHECK

▶ Refer to illustrations 11.3a and 11.3b

2 The number and type of belts used on a particular vehicle depends on the accessories installed.

3 With the engine off, open the hood and locate the drivebelts at the right end of the engine. With a flashlight, check each belt for separation of the rubber plies from each side of the core, a severed core, separation of the ribs from the rubber, cracks, torn or worn ribs and cracks in the inner ridges of the ribs. Also check for fraying and glazing, which give belts a shiny appearance (see illustrations). Both sides of the belt(s) should be inspected, which means you'll have to twist them to check the undersides. Use your fingers to feel a belt where you can't see it. If any of the above conditions are evident, replace the belt as described below.

Belt tension (1.8L engine)

▶ Refer to illustration 11.4

4 To check the tension of each belt, press firmly on the belt midway between pulleys and measure how much it deflects (see illustration). Compare your measurement to the figure listed in this Chapter's Specifications for a used belt.

➡ Note: A "new" belt is defined as any belt which has not been run; a "used" belt is one that has been run for more than ten minutes.

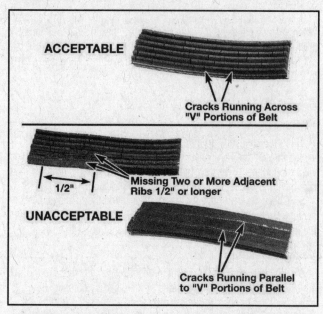

11.3b Check V-ribbed belts for signs of wear like these - if it looks worn, replace it

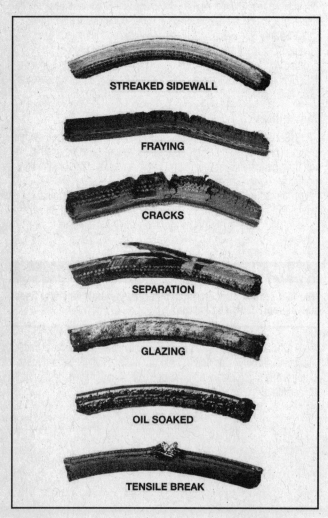

11.3a Here are some of the common problems associated with drivebelts (check the belts very carefully to prevent an untimely breakdown)

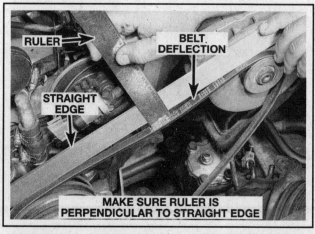

11.4 Measuring drivebelt deflection with a straightedge and ruler (typical)

5   To adjust the alternator belt, loosen the mounting and adjusting bolts. The mounting bolt is accessible from under the vehicle. Pry against an alternator case bolt (don't pry against the stator frame) while pushing on the belt to measure its deflection. When belt deflection is correct, tighten the adjusting bolt, then the mounting bolt.

6   To adjust the power steering and air conditioning belt, loosen the power steering pump mounting bolt and nut. Turn the adjusting bolt while you measure belt deflection. Once it's correct, tighten the mounting bolt and nut.

Belt tension (1.9L and 2.0L engines)

7   Belt tension on these engines is controlled automatically by the belt tensioner. There's no provision for manual adjustment.

REPLACEMENT (1.8L ENGINE)

8   To replace a belt, follow the above procedures for drivebelt adjustment, but slip the belt off the pulleys and remove it. Since belts tend to wear out more or less at the same time, it's a good idea to replace both of them at the same time. Mark each belt and the corresponding pulley grooves so the replacement belts can be installed properly.

9   Take the old belts with you when purchasing new ones in order to make a direct comparison for length, width and design.

REPLACEMENT (1.9L AND 2.0L ENGINES)

▸ **Refer to illustration 11.10**

10 On 1.9L and 2.0L SPI engines, place a 3/8-inch drive ratchet or breaker bar in the tensioner hole. On 2.0L Zetec engines, use a ratchet and socket on the center bolt of the tensioner. Pull the handle toward the front of the vehicle to loosen the belt and slip the belt off the pulleys (see illustration).

11 Make sure that the new belt fits properly into the pulley grooves; it must be completely engaged and ride in the center of each pulley.

11.10 To loosen the belt tensioner on a 1.9L or 2.0L SPI engine, insert a 3/8-inch drive ratchet or breaker bar into the tensioner hole and pull the handle toward the front of the vehicle

---

12 Battery check, maintenance and charging (every 6000 miles or 6 months)

CHECK AND MAINTENANCE

▸ **Refer to illustrations 12.1, 12.4, 12.8a, 12.8b, 12.8c and 12.8d**

✳✳ WARNING:

Certain precautions must be followed when checking and servicing the battery. Hydrogen gas, which is highly flammable, is always present in the battery cells, so keep lighted tobacco and all other flames and sparks away from it. The electrolyte inside the battery is actually dilute sulfuric acid, which will cause injury if splashed on your skin or in your eyes. It will also ruin clothes and painted surfaces. When removing the battery cables, always detach the negative cable first and hook it up last!

1   Battery maintenance is an important procedure which will help ensure that you are not stranded because of a dead battery. Several tools are required for this procedure (see illustration).

2   Before servicing the battery, always turn the engine and all accessories off and disconnect the cable from the negative terminal of the battery.

3   A sealed (sometimes called maintenance free battery is standard equipment. The cell caps cannot be removed, no electrolyte checks are required and water cannot be added to the cells. However, if an after-market battery has been installed and it is a type that requires regular maintenance, the following procedures can be used.

12.1 Tools and materials required for battery maintenance

1   **Face shield/safety goggles** - *When removing corrosion with a brush, the acidic particles can easily fly up into your eyes*

2   **Baking soda** - *A solution of baking soda and water can be used to neutralize corrosion*

3   **Petroleum jelly** - *A layer of this on the battery posts will help prevent corrosion*

4   **Battery post/cable cleaner** - *This wire brush cleaning tool will remove all traces of corrosion from the battery posts and cable clamps*

5   **Treated felt washers** - *Placing one of these on each post, directly under the cable clamps, will help prevent corrosion*

6   **Puller** - *Sometimes the cable clamps are very difficult to pull off the posts, even after the nut/bolt has been completely loosened. This tool pulls the clamp straight up and off the post without damage*

7   **Battery post/cable cleaner** - *Here is another cleaning tool which is a slightly different version of Number 4 above, but it does the same thing*

8   **Rubber gloves** - *Another safety item to consider when servicing the battery; remember that's acid inside the battery!*

4   Check the electrolyte level in each of the battery cells (see illustration). It must be above the plates. There's usually a split-ring indicator in each cell to indicate the correct level. If the level is low, add distilled water only, then install the cell caps.

⁕⁕ CAUTION:

Overfilling the cells may cause electrolyte to spill over during periods of heavy charging, causing corrosion and damage to nearby components.

12.4 Remove the cell caps to check the water level in the battery - if the level is low, add distilled water only

5   If the positive terminal and cable clamp on your vehicle's battery is equipped with a rubber protector, make sure that it's not torn or damaged. It should completely cover the terminal.

6   The external condition of the battery should be checked periodically. Look for damage such as a cracked case.

7   Check the tightness of the battery cable clamps to ensure good electrical connections and inspect the entire length of each cable, looking for cracked or abraded insulation and frayed conductors.

8   If corrosion (visible as white, fluffy deposits) is evident, remove the cables from the terminals, clean them with a battery brush and reinstall them (see illustrations). Corrosion can be kept to a minimum by installing specially treated washers available at auto parts stores or by applying a layer of petroleum jelly or grease to the terminals and cable clamps after they are assembled.

9   Make sure that the battery carrier is in good condition and that the hold-down clamp bolt is tight. If the battery is removed (see Chapter 5 for the removal and installation procedure), make sure that no parts remain in the bottom of the carrier when it's reinstalled. When reinstalling the hold-down clamp, don't overtighten the bolt.

10   Corrosion on the carrier, battery case and surrounding areas can be removed with a solution of water and baking soda. Apply the mixture with a small brush. Let it work, then rinse it off with plenty of clean water.

11   Any metal parts of the vehicle damaged by corrosion should be coated with a zinc-based primer, then painted.

12   Additional information on the battery, charging and jump starting can be found in Chapter 5 and the front of this manual.

CHARGING

13   Remove all of the cell caps (if equipped) and cover the holes with a clean cloth to prevent spattering electrolyte. Disconnect the negative battery cable and hook the battery charger leads to the battery posts (positive to positive, negative to negative), then plug in the charger. Make sure it is set at 12 volts if it has a selector switch.

14   If you're using a charger with a rate higher than two amps, check the battery regularly during charging to make sure it doesn't overheat. If you're using a trickle charger, you can safely let the battery charge

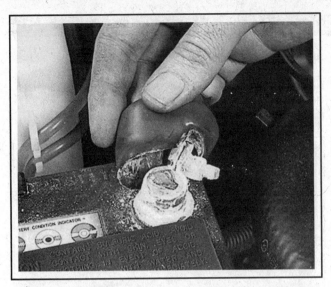

12.8a Battery terminal corrosion usually appears as light, fluffy powder

12.8b Removing the cable from a battery post with a wrench - sometimes special battery pliers are required for this procedure if corrosion has caused deterioration of the nut hex (always remove the ground cable first and hook it up last!)

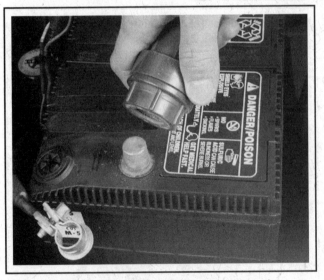

12.8c Regardless of the type of tool used on the battery posts, a clean, shiny surface should be the result

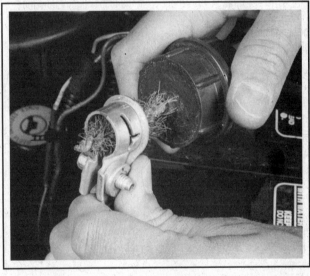

12.8d When cleaning the cable clamps, all corrosion must be removed (the inside of the clamp is tapered to match the taper on the post, so don't remove toomuch material)

overnight after you've checked it regularly for the first couple of hours.

15 If the battery has removable cell caps, measure the specific gravity with a hydrometer every hour during the last few hours of the charging cycle. Hydrometers are available inexpensively from auto parts stores - follow the instructions that come with the hydrometer. Consider the battery charged when there's no change in the specific gravity reading for two hours and the electrolyte in the cells is gassing (bubbling) freely. The specific gravity reading from each cell should be very close to the others. If not, the battery probably has a bad cell(s).

16 Some batteries with sealed tops have built-in hydrometers on the top that indicate the state of charge by the color displayed in the hydrometer window. Normally, a bright-colored hydrometer indicates a full charge and a dark hydrometer indicates the battery still needs charging. Check the battery manufacturer's instructions to be sure you know what the colors mean.

17 If the battery has a sealed top and no built-in hydrometer, you can hook up a digital voltmeter across the battery terminals to check the charge. A fully charged battery should read 12.6 volts or higher.

18 Further information on the battery and jump starting can be found in Chapter 5 and at the front of this manual.

13 Windshield wiper blade check and replacement (every 12,000 miles or 12 months)

1   Road film can build up on the wiper blades and affect their efficiency, so they should be washed regularly with a mild detergent solution.

CHECK

2   The windshield wiper and blade assembly should be inspected periodically for damage, loose components and cracked or worn blade elements. The action of the wiping mechanism can loosen bolts, nuts and fasteners, so they should be checked and tightened, as necessary, at the same time the wiper blades are checked.

3   If the wiper blade elements are cracked, worn or warped, or no longer clean adequately, they should be replaced with new ones.

REPLACEMENT

▶ **Refer to illustrations 13.5, 13.6a and 13.6b**

4   Park the wiper blades in a convenient position to be worked on. To do this, run the wipers then turn the ignition key to Off when the wiper blades reach the desired position.

5   On 1991 through 1995 models, lift the blade slightly from the windshield. Press on the coil spring retainer with a small screwdriver to release the blade (see illustration). Move the blade back and forth and take it off. Push the new blade assembly onto the arm pivot pin. Make sure the spring retainer secures the blade to the pin.

6   On 1996 and later models, push the release pin to release the blade, unhook the wiper arm from the blade (see illustrations) and take the blade off. Slide the new blade onto the wiper arm until the blade locks. Make sure the spring lock secures the blade to the pin.

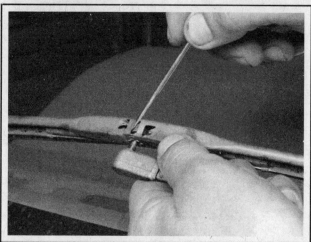

13.5 Press on the coil spring retainer with a small screwdriver to release the blade

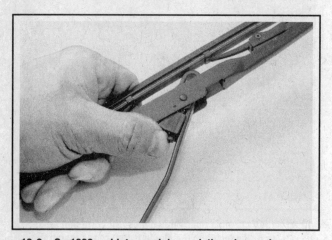

13.6a On 1996 and later models, push the release pin . . .

13.6b . . . and pull the wiper blade in the direction of the arrow to separate it from the arm

14 Air filter replacement (every 12,000 miles or 12 months)

1   The air filter cannot be cleaned. If it's dirty, replace it.

REMOVAL

1.8L engine models

2   Loosen the resonance chamber clamp and detach the resonance chamber from the vane air flow meter.

3   Disconnect the electrical connector from the vane air flow meter.

4   Remove the screws that secure the air cleaner upper cover.

5   Lift off the vane air flow meter and the air cleaner upper cover as an assembly.

6   Lift out the filter element.

14.7 On 1.9L engines, release the cover clips . . .

14.8 . . . then lift the cover off to remove the air filter

14.9 On 2.0L engine models, loosen the filter band . . .

14.10 . . . then separate the MAF sensor from the housing and pull out the filter element

1.9L engine models

▶ Refer to illustrations 14.7 and 14.8

7   Release the four clips that secure the air cleaner cover (see illustration).
8   Lift the cover off and lift out the filter element (see illustration).

2.0L engine models

▶ Refer to illustrations 14.9 and 14.10

9   Loosen the band that secures the filter housing to the outlet tube (see illustration).
10 Separate the Mass Air Flow (MAF) sensor from the filter housing and pull out the filter element (see illustration).
11 Installation is the reverse of the removal steps.

INSPECTION AND INSTALLATION (ALL MODELS)

12 Inspect the rubber seal on the air cleaner element. Replace the element if the seal is worn or damaged. Also replace the filter if replacement is indicated on the maintenance schedule or if it is so dirty that you can't clearly see the light from a flashlight held against the opposite side.
13 Clean the inner sealing surface between the air cleaner housing and cover.
14 Before installing the new air filter, check it for deformed seals and holes in the paper. If the filter is marked TOP, be sure the marked side faces up.
15 The remainder of installation is the reverse of the removal steps.

15 PCV valve and filter replacement (every 12,000 miles or 12 months)

PCV VALVE REPLACEMENT (ALL MODELS)

▶ **Refer to illustration 15.1**

1   Pull the PCV valve out of the valve cover (1.8L engine models) or crankcase vent tube (1.9L and 2.0L engine models) (see illustration).

2   Shake the valve; it should rattle. If not, replace it.

3   Check the valve for built-up deposits. If these are present, the PCV hoses should be removed and cleaned.

4   Disconnect the PCV valve and elbow from the hose. If the new valve comes with an elbow, install it. If not, reuse the old one.

❋❋ CAUTION:

Do not force the elbow onto the valve or you'll break it. If it is difficult to install, soak it in warm water; you may have to soak it for an hour.

15.1 The PCV valve on 1.9L (shown) and 2.0L engine models is mounted in the crankcase vent tube; the PCV valve on 1.8L engine models is mounted in the valve cover

5   Connect the PCV system hose(s).

PCV FILTER REPLACEMENT (1.9L ENGINE MODELS)

▶ **Refer to illustration 15.7**

6   Remove the air cleaner cover (refer to Section 14).

7   Pull the PCV filter out of its pocket in the air cleaner housing (see illustration). Inspect the filter and replace it if it's clogged or damaged.

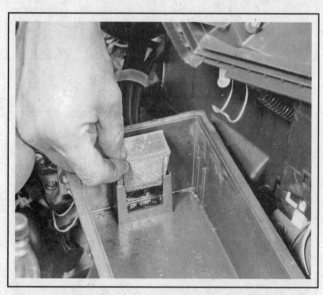

15.7 On 1.9L engine models, there's a PCV filter mounted in the air cleaner housing

16 Fuel system check (every 12,000 miles or 12 months)

❋❋ WARNING:

Gasoline is extremely flammable, so take extra precautions when you work on any part of the fuel system. Don't smoke or allow open flames or bare light bulbs near the work area, and don't work in a garage where a gas-type appliance (such as a water heater or clothes dryer) is present. If you spill any fuel on your skin, rinse it off immediately with soap and water. When you perform any kind of work on the fuel system, wear safety glasses and have a Class B type fire extinguisher on hand.

1   If you smell gasoline while driving or after the vehicle has been sitting in the sun, inspect the fuel system immediately.

2   Remove the gas filler cap and inspect if for damage and corro-sion. The gasket should have an unbroken sealing imprint. If the gasket is damaged or corroded, install a new cap.

3   Inspect the fuel feed and return lines for cracks. Make sure that the connections between the fuel lines and fuel injection system and between the fuel lines and the in-line fuel filter are tight.

❋❋ WARNING:

You must relieve fuel system pressure before servicing fuel injection system components. The fuel system pressure relief procedure is outlined in Chapter 4.

4   Since some components of the fuel system - the fuel tank and

part of the fuel feed and return lines, for example - are underneath the vehicle, they can be inspected more easily with the vehicle raised on a hoist. If a hoist is unavailable, raise the vehicle and support it on jackstands.

5   With the vehicle raised and safely supported, inspect the gas tank and filler neck for punctures, cracks and other damage. The connection between the filler neck and the tank is particularly critical. Sometimes a rubber filler neck will leak because of loose clamps or deteriorated rubber. Inspect all fuel tank mounting brackets and straps to be sure that the tank is securely attached to the vehicle.

✳✳ WARNING:

Do not, under any circumstances, try to repair a fuel tank (except rubber components). A welding torch or any open flame can easily cause fuel vapors inside the tank to explode.

6   Carefully check all rubber hoses and metal lines leading away from the fuel tank. Check for loose connections, deteriorated hoses, crimped lines and other damage. Repair or replace damaged sections as necessary (see Chapter 4).

17 Cooling system check (every 12,000 miles or 12 months)

▶ **Refer to illustration 17.4**

1   Many major engine failures can be attributed to a faulty cooling system. If the vehicle is equipped with an automatic transaxle, the cooling system also plays an important role in prolonging transaxle life because it cools the transmission fluid.

2   The engine should be cold for the cooling system check, so perform the following procedure before the vehicle is driven for the day or after it has been shut off for at least three hours.

3   Remove the radiator cap and clean it thoroughly, inside and out, with clean water. Also clean the filler neck on the radiator. The presence of rust or corrosion in the filler neck means the coolant should be changed (see Section 26). The coolant inside the radiator should be relatively clean and transparent. If it's rust colored, drain the system and refill it with new coolant.

4   Carefully check the radiator hoses and the smaller diameter heater hoses (see illustrations in Chapter 3). Inspect each coolant hose along its entire length, replacing any hose which is cracked, swollen or deteriorated (see illustration). Cracks will show up better if the hose is squeezed. Pay close attention to hose clamps that secure the hoses to cooling system components. Hose clamps can pinch and puncture hoses, resulting in coolant leaks.

5   Make sure that all hose connections are tight. A leak in the cooling system will usually show up as white or rust colored deposits on the area adjoining the leak. If wire-type clamps are used on the hoses, it may be a good idea to replace them with screw-type clamps.

6   Clean the front of the radiator and air conditioning condenser with compressed air, if available, or a soft brush. Remove all bugs, leaves, etc. embedded in the radiator fins. Be extremely careful not to damage the cooling fins or cut your fingers on them.

7   If the coolant level has been dropping consistently and no leaks are detectable, have the radiator cap and cooling system pressure checked at a service station.

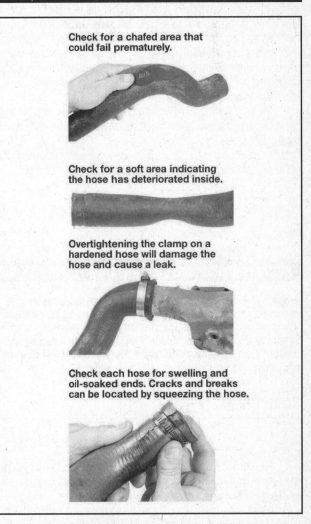

Check for a chafed area that could fail prematurely.

Check for a soft area indicating the hose has deteriorated inside.

Overtightening the clamp on a hardened hose will damage the hose and cause a leak.

Check each hose for swelling and oil-soaked ends. Cracks and breaks can be located by squeezing the hose.

17.4 Hoses, like drivebelts, have a habit of failing at the worst possible time - to prevent the inconvenience of a blown radiator or heater hose, inspect them carefully as shown here

18 Exhaust system check (every 12,000 miles or 12 months)

1   With the engine cold (at least three hours after the vehicle has been driven), check the complete exhaust system from the engine to the end of the tailpipe. Ideally, the inspection should be done with the vehicle on a hoist to permit unrestricted access. If a hoist is not available, raise the vehicle and support it securely on jackstands.

2   Check the exhaust pipes and connections for evidence of leaks, severe corrosion and damage. Make sure that all brackets and hangers are in good condition and tight.

3   At the same time, inspect the underside of the body for holes, corrosion, open seams, etc. which may allow exhaust gases to enter the passenger compartment. Seal all body openings with silicone sealant or body putty.

4   Rattles and other noises can often be traced to the exhaust system, especially the mounts and hangers. Try to move the pipes, muffler and catalytic converter. If the components can come in contact with the body or suspension parts, secure the exhaust system with new mounts.

5   Check the running condition of the engine by inspecting inside the end of the tailpipe. The exhaust deposits here are an indication of engine state-of-tune. If the pipe is black and sooty or coated with white deposits, the engine is in need of a tune-up, including a thorough fuel system inspection and adjustment. Also, the catalytic converter may be malfunctioning (see Chapter 6).

19 Tire rotation (every 12.000 miles or 12 months)

▶ **Refer to illustration 19.2**

1   The tires should be rotated at the specified intervals and whenever uneven wear is noticed. Since the vehicle will be raised and the tires removed anyway, check the brakes also (see Section 21).

2   Radial tires must be rotated in a specific pattern (see illustration).

3   Refer to the information in *Jacking and towing* at the front of this manual for the proper procedure to follow when raising the vehicle and changing a tire. If the brakes are to be checked, do not apply the parking brake, as stated.

4   The vehicle must be raised on a hoist or supported on jackstands to get two wheels at a time off the ground. Make sure the vehicle is safely supported!

5   After the rotation procedure is finished, check and adjust the tire pressures as necessary and be sure to check the lug nut tightness.

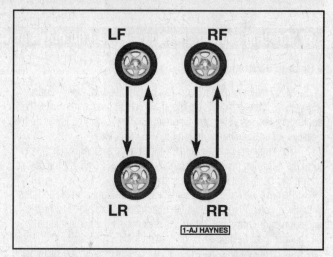

19.2 The recommended rotation pattern for radial tires

20 Suspension and steering check (every 12,000 miles or 12 months)

➡**Note: The steering linkage and suspension components should be checked periodically. Worn or damaged suspension and steering linkage components can result in excessive and abnormal tire wear, poor ride quality and vehicle handling and reduced fuel economy. For detailed illustrations of the steering and suspension components, refer to Chapter 10.**

STRUT CHECK

1   Park the vehicle on level ground, turn the engine off and set the parking brake. Check the tire pressures.

2   Push down at one corner of the vehicle, then release it while noting the movement of the body. It should stop moving and come to rest in a level position within one or two bounces.

3   If the vehicle continues to move up and down or if it fails to return to its original position, a worn or weak strut is probably the reason.

4   Repeat the above check at each of the three remaining corners of the vehicle.

5   Raise the vehicle and support it securely on jackstands.

6   Check the shock struts for evidence of fluid leakage. A light film of fluid on the shaft is no cause for concern. Make sure that any fluid noted is from the shocks and not from some other source. If leakage is noted, replace both struts at that end of the vehicle (front or rear).

7   Check the struts to be sure that they are securely mounted and undamaged. Check the upper mounts for damage and wear. If damage or wear is noted, replace both struts on that end of the vehicle.

8   If struts must be replaced, refer to Chapter 10 for the procedure.

FRONT SUSPENSION AND STEERING CHECK

▶ **Refer to illustrations 20.10a, 20.10b and 20.11**

9   Visually inspect the steering system components for damage and distortion. Look for leaks and damaged seals, boots and fittings.

10 Wipe off the lower end of the steering knuckle and control arm assembly. Have an assistant grasp the lower edge of the tire and move the wheel in and out while you look for movement at the balljoint-to-steering knuckle joint (see illustrations). If there is any

movement, the balljoints must be replaced (see Chapter 10).

11 Grasp each front tire at the front and rear edges, push in at the rear, pull out at the front and feel for play in the steering system components (see illustration). If any freeplay is noted, check the steering gear mounts and the tie-rod ends for looseness. If the steering gear mounts are loose, tighten them. If the tie-rod ends are loose, they will probably need to be replaced (see Chapter 10).

FRONT WHEEL BEARING CHECK

➡**Note: The front wheel bearings are a "cartridge" design and are permanently lubricated and sealed at the factory. They require no scheduled maintenance or adjustment. They can, however, be checked for excessive play. If the following check indicates that either of the front bearings is faulty, replace both bearings.**

12 Grasp each front tire at the front and rear edges, then push in and out on the wheel and feel for play. There should be no noticeable movement. Turn the wheel and listen for noise from the bearings. If either of

these conditions is noted, refer to Chapter 10 for the bearing replacement procedure.

DRIVEAXLE CONSTANT VELOCITY (CV) JOINT BOOT CHECK

♦ **Refer to illustration 20.14**

13 If the driveaxle rubber boots are damaged or deteriorated, serious and costly damage can occur to the CV joints.

14 It is very important that the boots be kept clean, so wipe them off before inspection. Check the four boots (two on each driveaxle) for cracks, tears, holes, deteriorated rubber and loose or missing clamps. Also check for grease flung around the CV joint boot area, which also indicates a hole in the boot (the grease leaks out through the hole). Pushing on the boot surface can reveal cracks not ordinarily visible (see illustration).

15 If damage or deterioration is evident check the CV joints for damage (see Chapter 8) and replace the boot(s) with new ones.

20.10a To check the balljoints, try to move the lower edge of each front wheel in and out while watching or feeling for movement at the top of the tire . . .

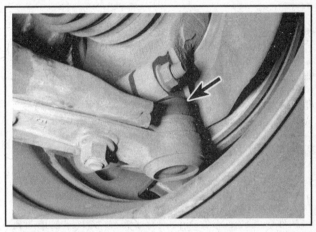

20.10b . . . and at the balljoint-to-steering knuckle joint (arrow)

20.11 To check the steering gear mounts and tie-rod connections for play, grasp each front tire like this and try to move it back and forth - if play is noted, check the steering gear mounts and make sure they're tight; if either tie-rod is worn or bent, replace it

20.14 Flex the driveaxle boots by hand to check for cracks and/or leaking grease

21 Brake check (every 12,000 miles or 12 months)

➡Note: In addition to the specified intervals, the brake system should be inspected each time the wheels are removed or a malfunction is indicated. Because of the obvious safety considerations, the following brake system checks are some of the most important maintenance procedures you can perform on your vehicle.

SYMPTOMS OF BRAKE SYSTEM PROBLEMS

1   If you hear a squealing or scraping noise when the brakes are applied, inspect the pads immediately or expensive damage to the rotors could result.

2   Any of the following symptoms could indicate a brake system defect: the vehicle pulls to one side when the brake pedal is depressed, the brakes make squealing or dragging noises when applied, brake pedal travel is excessive, the pedal pulsates or brake fluid leaks are noted (usually on the inner side of the tire or wheel). If any of these conditions are noted inspect the brake system immediately.

BRAKE LINES AND HOSES

➡Note: Steel tubing is used throughout the brake system, with the exception of flexible, reinforced hoses at the front and rear wheels. Periodic inspection of these hoses and lines is very important.

3   Park the vehicle on level ground and turn the engine off.

4   Remove the wheel covers. Loosen, but do not remove, the lug nuts.

5   Raise the vehicle and support it securely on jackstands.

6   Remove the wheels (see *Jacking and towing* at the front of this manual, or refer to your owner's manual, if necessary).

7   Check all brake hoses and lines for cracks, chafing of the outer cover, leaks, blisters and distortion. Check all threaded fittings for leaks and make sure the brake hose mounting bolts and clips are secure.

8   If leaks or damage are discovered they must be fixed immediately. Refer to Chapter 9 for detailed information on brake system repair procedures.

21.11 The front disc brake pads can be checked easily through the inspection hole in each caliper - position a ruler or tape measure against the pads and measure the lining thickness

FRONT AND REAR DISC BRAKES

▸ **Refer to illustration 21.11**

➡Note: All models are equipped with front disc brakes. Some models, notably the Escort GT, Escort coupe and Tracer LTS, are equipped with rear disc brakes. Other models are equipped with rear drum brakes.

9   If it hasn't already been done, raise the front (or rear) of the vehicle and support it securely on jackstands. Apply the parking brake and remove the front wheels.

10 The disc brake calipers, which contain the pads, are now visible. Each caliper has an outer and an inner pad - all pads should be checked.

11 Note the pad thickness by looking through the inspection hole in the caliper (see illustration). If the lining material is less than listed in this Chapter's Specifications, or if it is tapered from end to end, the pads should be replaced (see Chapter 9). Keep in mind that the lining material is riveted or bonded to a metal plate or shoe - the metal portion is not included in this measurement.

12 Check the condition of the brake disc. Look for score marks, deep scratches and overheated areas (they will appear blue or discolored). If damage or wear is noted, the disc can be removed and resurfaced by an automotive machine shop or replaced with a new one. Refer to Chapter 9 for more detailed inspection and repair procedures.

REAR DRUM BRAKES

▸ **Refer to illustrations 21.14 and 21.16**

13 Refer to Chapter 9 and remove the rear brake drums.

❋❋ WARNING:

Brake dust produced by lining wear and deposited on brake components is hazardous to your health. DO NOT blow it out with compressed air and DO NOT inhale! DO NOT use gasoline or solvents to remove the dust. Brake system cleaner should be used to flush the dust into a drain pan. After the brake components are wiped clean with a damp rag, dispose of the contaminated rag(s) and solvent in a covered and labeled container.

14 Note the thickness of the lining material on the rear brake shoes (see illustration) and look for signs of contamination by brake fluid and grease. If the lining material is within 1/16-inch of the recessed rivets or metal shoes, replace the brake shoes with new ones. The shoes should also be replaced if they are cracked, glazed (shiny lining surfaces) or contaminated with brake fluid or grease. See Chapter 9 for the replacement procedure.

15 Check the shoe return and hold-down springs and the adjusting mechanism to make sure they are installed correctly and in good condition. Deteriorated or distorted springs, if not replaced, could allow the linings to drag and wear prematurely.

16 Check the wheel cylinders for leakage by carefully peeling back the rubber boots (see illustration). If brake fluid is noted behind the boots, the wheel cylinders must be replaced (see Chapter 9).

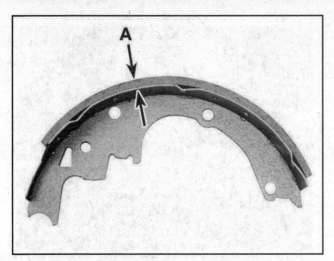

21.14 If the lining is bonded to the brake shoe, measure the lining thickness from the outer surface to the metal shoe, as shown here; if the lining is riveted to the shoe, measure from the lining outer surface to the rivet head

21.16 Carefully peel back the rubber boots on each end of the wheel cylinder - if the exposed area is covered with brake fluid, the wheel cylinder is leaking and must be replaced

17 Check the drums for cracks, score marks, deep scratches and hard spots, which will appear as small discolored areas. If imperfections cannot be removed with emery cloth, the drums must be resurfaced by an automotive machine shop (see Chapter 9 for more detailed information).

18 Refer to Chapter 9 and install the brake drums.

19 Install the wheels, remove the jackstands, lower the vehicle and tighten the lug nuts.

PARKING BRAKE CHECK

20 The parking brake cable and linkage should be periodically checked for damage and for wear caused by rubbing on the vehicle.

21 The easiest, and perhaps most obvious, method of checking the parking brake is to park the vehicle on a steep hill with the parking brake set and the transaxle in Neutral. If the parking brake cannot prevent the vehicle from rolling, refer to Chapter 9 and adjust it.

22 Clutch hydraulic linkage inspection (every 12,000 milesor 12 months)

1 Check the line running from the brake and clutch fluid reservoir to the master cylinder for leaks. Replace the line and bleed the hydraulic system if there's any sign of fluid leakage (see Chapter 8).

2 Pull back the rubber boot from the slave cylinder on the side of the clutch hydraulic line and check for fluid leaks. Slight moisture inside the boot is acceptable, but if fluid runs out, refer to Chapter 8 and overhaul or replace the slave cylinder.

23 Manual transaxle lubricant level check and change (every 12,000 miles or 12 months)

▶ **Refer to illustration 23.8**

LUBRICANT LEVEL CHECK

➡**Note: The transaxle lubricant should not deteriorate under normal driving conditions. However, it is recommended that you check the level occasionally. The most convenient time is when the vehicle is raised for another reason, such as an engine oil change.**

1 Park the vehicle on a level surface. Turn the engine off, apply the parking brake and block the wheels. Open the hood and locate the vehicle speed sensor at the transaxle.

2 To protect the transaxle from contamination, wipe off any dirt or grease in the area around the speed sensor.

3 Disconnect the electrical connector from the speed sensor. Remove the retaining clip and disconnect the speedometer cable.

4 Pry the speed sensor out of the transaxle and check the lubricant level - the lubricant level should be between the FULL and LOW ridges (1.8L engine model) or between the top and bottom edge of the gear

(1.9L and 2.0L engine models). If necessary, add the specified fluid, a little at a time, through the speed sensor hole. A funnel will help prevent spills.

5   Inspect the speed sensor O-ring and replace it if it's cut, cracked or broken.

6   Install the speed sensor and tighten the retaining bolt securely.

7   Connect the speedometer cable and electrical connector to the speed sensor.

LUBRICANT CHANGE

8   Changing the manual transaxle lubricant shouldn't be necessary under normal circumstances. To change the lubricant, remove the speed sensor (see Steps 3 and 4). Remove the transaxle drain plug (see illustration) and drain the fluid into a suitable container. After the fluid has drained completely, install the drain plug and tighten it securely. Fill the transaxle to the correct level with the specified lubricant.

23.8 Typical manual transaxle drain plug (arrow)

24 Spark plug replacement (see the maintenance schedule for service intervals)

♦ **Refer to illustrations 24.2, 24.5a, 24.5b, 24.6, 24.9 and 24.10**

➡**Note 1: Every time a spark plug wire is detached from a spark plug, the distributor cap or the coil, silicone dielectric compound (a special grease available at auto parts stores) must be applied to the inside of each spark plug wire boot and terminal before reconnection. Use a small standard screwdriver to coat the entire inside surface of each boot with a thin layer of the compound.**

➡**Note 2: If you are reinstalling the old spark plugs, make sure that each one is placed in its original position.**

1   The spark plugs are located in the center of the cylinder head on 1.8L and 2.0L Zetec engines and on the front (radiator) side of the cylinder head on 1.9L engines and 2.0L SPI.

2   In most cases, the tools necessary for spark plug replacement include a spark plug socket which fits onto a ratchet (spark plug sockets are padded inside to prevent damage to the porcelain insulators on the new plugs), various extensions and a gap gauge to check and adjust the gaps on the new plugs (see illustration on next page). A special plug wire removal tool is available for separating the wire boots from the spark plugs, but it isn't absolutely necessary. A torque wrench should be used to tighten the new plugs.

3   The best approach when replacing the spark plugs is to purchase the new ones in advance, adjust them to the proper gap and replace the plugs one at a time. When buying the new spark plugs, be sure to obtain the correct plug type for your particular engine. This information can be found on the Vehicle Emission Control Information label located under the hood and in this Chapter's Specifications. If differences exist between the plug specified on the emissions label and in the Specifications, assume that the emissions label is correct.

4   Allow the engine to cool completely before attempting to remove any of the plugs. While you are waiting for the engine to cool, check the new plugs for defects and adjust the gaps.

5   The gap is checked by inserting the proper thickness gauge between the electrodes at the tip of the plug (see illustration). The gap between the electrodes should be the same as the one specified on the Vehicle Emissions Control Information label or the Specifications at the

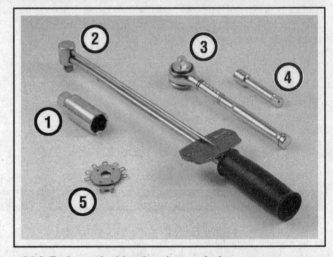

24.2 Tools required for changing spark plugs

1   ***Spark plug socket*** - *This will have special padding inside to protect the spark plug's porcelain insulator*

2   ***Torque wrench*** - *Although not mandatory, using this tool is the best way to ensure the plugs are tightened properly*

3   ***Ratchet*** - *Standard hand tool to fit the spark plug socket*

4   ***Extension*** - *Depending on model and accessories, you may need special extensions and universal joints to reach one or more of the plugs*

5   ***Spark plug gap gauge*** - *This gauge for checking the gap comes in a variety of styles. Make sure the gap for your engine is included*

end of this Chapter. The wire should just slide between the electrodes with a slight amount of drag. If the gap is incorrect, use the adjuster on the gauge body to bend the curved side electrode slightly until the proper gap is obtained (see illustration). If the side electrode is not exactly over the center electrode, bend it with the adjuster until it is. Check for cracks in the porcelain insulator (if any are found, the plug

24.5a Spark plug manufacturers recommend using a wire-type gauge when checking the gap - if the wire does not slide between the electrodes with a slight drag, adjustment is required

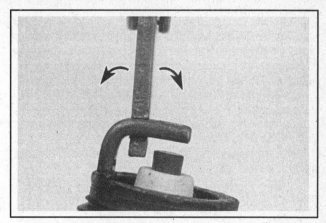

24.5b To change the gap, bend the side electrode only, as indicated by the arrows, and be very careful not to crack or chip the porcelain insulator surrounding the center electrode

should not be used).

6   With the engine cool, remove the spark plug wire from one spark plug. Pull only on the boot at the end of the wire - do not pull on the wire. A plug wire removal tool should be used if available (see illustration).

7   If compressed air is available, use it to blow any dirt or foreign material away from the spark plug hole. A common bicycle pump will also work. The idea here is to eliminate the possibility of debris falling into the cylinder as the spark plug is removed.

8   Place the spark plug socket over the plug and remove it from the engine by turning it in a counterclockwise direction.

9   Compare the spark plug to those shown in the photos (see illustration) to get an indication of the general running condition of the engine.

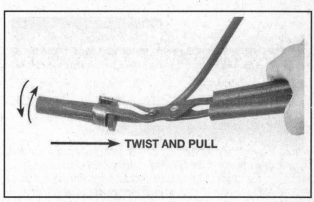

TWIST AND PULL

24.6 When removing the spark plug wires, pull only on the boot and twist it back-and-forth

A normally worn spark plug should have light tan or gray deposits on the firing tip.

A carbon fouled plug, identified by soft, sooty, black deposits, may indicate an improperly tuned vehicle. Check the air cleaner, ignition components and engine control system.

An oil fouled spark plug indicates an engine with worn piston rings and/or bad valve seals allowing excessive oil to enter the chamber.

This spark plug has been left in the engine too long, as evidenced by the extreme gap- Plugs with such an extreme gap can cause misfiring and stumbling accompanied by a noticeable lack of power.

A physically damaged spark plug may be evidence of severe detonation in that cylinder. Watch that cylinder carefully between services, as a continued detonation will not only damage the plug, but could also damage the engine.

A bridged or almost bridged spark plug, identified by a build-up between the electrodes caused by excessive carbon or oil build-up on the plug.

24.9 Inspect the spark plug to determine engine running conditions

10 Thread one of the new plugs into the hole until you can no longer turn it with your fingers, then tighten it with a torque wrench (if available) or the ratchet. It's a good idea to slip a short length of rubber hose over the end of the plug to use as a tool to thread it into place (see illustration). The hose will grip the plug well enough to turn it, but will start to slip if the plug begins to cross-thread in the hole this will prevent damaged threads and the accompanying repair costs.

11 Before pushing the spark plug wire onto the end of the plug, inspect it following the procedures outlined in Section 25.

12 Attach the plug wire to the new spark plug, again using a twisting motion on the boot until it is seated on the spark plug.

13 Repeat the procedure for the remaining spark plugs, replacing them one at a time to prevent mixing up the spark plug wires.

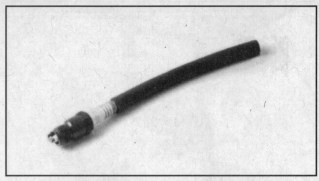

24.10 A length of snug-fitting rubber hose will save time and prevent damaged threads when installing the spark plugs

25 Spark plug wire, distributor cap and rotor check and replacement (every 30,000 miles or 30 months)

SPARK PLUG WIRES

▶ **Refer to illustration 25.9**

➡**Note: Every time a spark plug wire is detached from a spark plug, the distributor cap or the coil, silicone dielectric compound (a special grease available at auto parts stores) must be applied to the inside of each boot before reconnection. Use a small standard screwdriver to coat the entire inside surface of each boot with a thin layer of the compound.**

1 The spark plug wires should be checked and, if necessary, replaced at the same time the new spark plugs are installed.

✳✳ WARNING:

Don't touch the spark plug or coil wires with the engine running. The moisture on your skin can conduct high ignition voltage even through good wires, causing serious electrical shocks.

2 The easiest way to identify bad wires is to make a visual check while the engine is running. In a dark, well-ventilated garage, start the engine and look at each plug wire. Be careful not to come into contact with any moving engine parts. If there is a break in the wire, you will see arcing or a small spark at the damaged area. If arcing is noticed, make a note to obtain new wires.

3 The spark plug wires should be in-spected one at a time, beginning with the spark plug for the number one cylinder (the one nearest the right end of the engine), to prevent confusion. Clearly label each original plug wire with a piece of tape marked with the correct number. The plug wires must be reinstalled in the correct order to ensure proper engine operation.

4 Disconnect the plug wire from the first spark plug. A removal tool can be used (see illustration 24.6), or you can grab the wire boot, twist it slightly and pull the wire free. Do not pull on the wire itself, only on the rubber boot.

5 Push the wire and boot back onto the end of the spark plug. It should fit snugly. If it doesn't, detach the wire and boot once more and use a pair of pliers to carefully crimp the metal connector inside the wire boot until it does.

6 Using a clean rag that's damp with solvent, wipe the entire length of the wire to remove built-up dirt and grease.

7 Once the wire is clean, check for burns, cracks and other damage. Do not bend the wire sharply or you might break the conductor.

8 On 1.8L engines, disconnect the wire from the distributor. Again, pull only on the rubber boot. Check for corrosion and a tight fit. Reinstall the wire in the distributor. Be sure the wires are connected to the proper terminals.

9 On 1.9L engines, squeeze the locking tabs on the plug wire retainer to free the wire from the coil pack (see illustration).

✳✳ CAUTION:

Don't pull on the wire. Inspect the wire, then reinstall it. Be sure the wires are connected to the proper terminals.

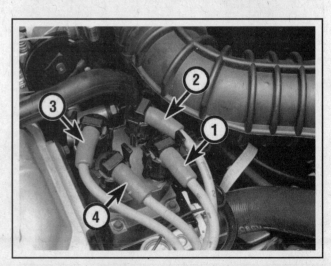

25.9 Coil pack terminal numbers (1.9L and 2.0L engines)

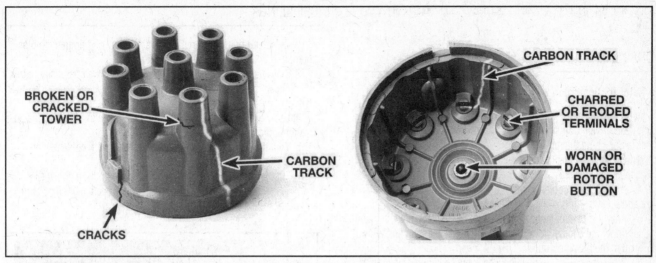

25.12 Shown here are some of the common defects to look for when inspecting the distributor cap (if in doubt about its condition, install a new one)

10 Inspect each of the remaining spark plug wires, making sure that each one is securely fastened at the distributor or coil pack and spark plug when the check is complete.

11 If new spark plug wires are required, purchase a set for your specific engine model. Pre-cut wire sets with the boots already installed are available. Remove and replace the wires one at a time to avoid mixups in the firing order.

DISTRIBUTOR CAP AND ROTOR (1.8L ENGINE MODELS)

♦ Refer to illustrations 25.12 and 25.13

➡Note: It is common practice to install a new distributor cap and rotor each time new spark plug wires are installed. If you're planning to install new wires, install a new cap and rotor also. But if you are planning to reuse the existing wires, be sure to inspect the cap and rotor to make sure that they are in good condition.

12 Remove the mounting screws and detach the cap from the distributor. Check it for cracks, carbon tracks and worn, burned or loose terminals (see illustration).

13 Check the rotor for cracks and carbon tracks. Make sure the center terminal spring tension is adequate and look for corrosion and wear on the rotor tip (see illustration).

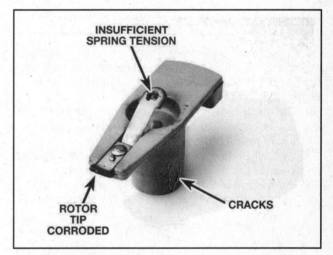

25.13 The ignition rotor should be checked for wear and corrosion as indicated here (if in doubt about its condition, buy a new one)

14 Replace the cap and rotor if damage or defects are found.

15 When installing a new cap, remove the wires from the old cap one at a time and attach them to the new cap in the exact same location - do not simultaneously remove all the wires from the old cap or firing order mix-ups may occur.

26 Cooling system servicing (draining, flushing and refilling) (every 30,000 miles or 30 months)

❋❋ WARNING:

Do not allow antifreeze to come in contact with your skin or painted surfaces of the vehicle. Rinse off spills immediately with plenty of water. Antifreeze is highly toxic if ingested. Never leave antifreeze lying around in an open container or in puddles on the floor; children and pets are attracted by it's sweet smell and may drink it. Check with local authorities about disposing of used antifreeze. Many communities have collection centers which will see that antifreeze is disposed of safely.

1 Periodically, the cooling system should be drained, flushed and refilled to replenish the antifreeze mixture and prevent formation of rust and corrosion, which can impair the performance of the cooling system and cause engine damage. When the cooling system is serviced, all

hoses and the radiator cap should be checked and replaced if necessary.

DRAINING

▶ **Refer to illustration 26.4**

2   Apply the parking brake and block the wheels. If the vehicle has just been driven, wait several hours to allow the engine to cool down before beginning this procedure.

3   Once the engine is completely cool, remove the radiator cap to vent the cooling system.

4   Move a large container under the radiator drain to catch the coolant and open the drain fitting (see illustration).

5   After the coolant stops flowing out of the radiator, move the container under the engine block drain plug. Remove the plug and allow the coolant in the block to drain.

6   While the coolant is draining, check the condition of the radiator hoses, heater hoses and clamps (see Section 17 if necessary).

7   Replace any damaged clamps or hoses.

FLUSHING

8   Once the system is completely drained, reinstall the block drain plug and close the radiator drain. Fill the radiator with fresh water from a garden hose, let the water settle, then fill the radiator again. Repeat this procedure until the radiator stays full.

9   Start the engine and let it idle for 3 to 5 minutes. Shut the engine off and open the radiator drain. Repeat this procedure until clear water flows from the radiator drain.

10 If the radiator is severely corroded, damaged or leaking, it should be removed (see Chapter 3) and taken to a radiator repair shop.

11 Remove the overflow hose from the coolant recovery reservoir. Drain the reservoir and flush it with clean water, then reconnect the hose.

REFILLING

12 Close and tighten the radiator drain. Install and tighten the block drain plug.

13 Slowly add new coolant (a 50/50 mixture of water and antifreeze) to the radiator until it is full. Add coolant to the reservoir up to the lower mark.

14 Leave the radiator cap off and run the engine in a well-ventilated area for approximately 12 minutes.

15 With the engine running, refill the radiator with coolant, then install the radiator cap.

16 Fill the coolant reservoir to the Full Hot mark with coolant.

17 Start the engine, allow it to reach normal operating temperature and check for leaks.

26.4 The radiator drain fitting is located at the lower left corner of the radiator and is accessible from beneath the vehicle - unscrew it to drain the coolant - it may be helpful to attach a short length of hose to the drain hole (arrow) to direct the coolant into the drain pan

---

27   Automatic transaxle fluid and filter change (every 30,000 miles or 30 months

▶ **Refer to illustrations 27.5a, 27.5b, 27.6, 27.7, 27.8, 27.10 and 27.11**

1   Before beginning work, purchase the specified transmission fluid (see *Recommended lubricants and fluids* at the end of this Chapter) and a new filter. The filter will come with a new pan gasket and seal.

2   The fluid should be drained immediately after the vehicle has been driven. More sediment and contaminants will be removed with the fluid if it's hot.

✳✳ WARNING:

Fluid temperature can exceed 350-degrees F in a hot transaxle, so wear gloves when draining the fluid.

3   After the vehicle has been driven to warm up the fluid, raise it and support it on jackstands.

4   Position a drain pan capable of holding six quarts under the transaxle. Be careful not to touch any of the hot exhaust components. If you're working on a 1997 or later model, remove the transaxle drain

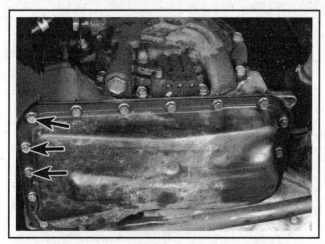

27.5a Remove all the pan bolts except the three at the driver's side front corner (arrows) - after removing the other bolts, loosen the three bolts two turns each

27.5b To reach some of the bolts, you'll need a 10 mm socket and universal adapter like the one shown here or a 10 mm swivel socket

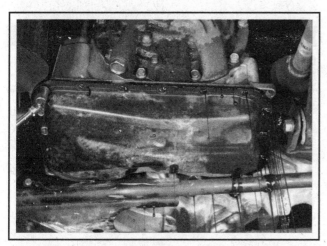

27.6 Once you've removed all but the three front bolts, carefully pry the pan loose from the transaxle case and let the fluid drain - be careful; too much force could damage the flange and cause leaks

27.7 After the fluid has drained, remove the three bolts and take the pan out; if it hangs up on the crossmember, lift the transaxle slightly with a jack and block of wood (arrow)

plug (it's similar to the manual transaxle drain plug shown in illustration 23.8). Let the fluid drain into the pan.

5   Remove all of the pan bolts except for the three at the driver's side corner (see illustration). You'll need a 10 mm wrench for the bolt at the front corner on the passenger side and a 10 mm universal socket or 10 mm socket and universal adapter for the bolts above the crossmember (see illustration). Unscrew the three remaining bolts two turns, but leave them in place to support the pan.

6   Carefully separate the pan from the transaxle case and allow the fluid to drain out (see illustration). Try not to splash fluid as the gasket seal is broken and the pan is detached.

7   Once the fluid has drained, remove the three bolts and detach the pan (see illustration). It may be necessary to place a jack beneath the transaxle at the point shown in the illustration and raise it slightly so the pan will clear the crossmember.

8   Inspect the magnets inside the pan (see illustration). Fine powdery material on the magnets is normal, but if there are fragments of metal, the transaxle should be inspected by a dealer or qualified transmission shop.

27.8 If there are a lot of metal fragments clinging to the magnets inside the case, the transaxle should be inspected by a dealer service department of transmission shop (some small shavings, like the ones seen here, are normal)

27.10 The filter is held in place by three bolts (arrows)

27.11 Slip the seal onto the filter and make sure it's securely engaged

9   Scrape all traces of the old gasket from the pan and the transaxle case, then clean the pan with solvent and dry it with compressed air. DO NOT use a rag to wipe out the pan (lint from the pan could contaminate the transaxle).

10   Remove the filter bolts and detach the filter (see illustration). You'll need a 10 mm universal socket or 10 mm socket and universal adapter to remove the bolt directly below the crossmember. Note that the bolt on the driver's side and to the rear secures a wiring harness retainer. Discard the filter and the seal.

11   Attach the new seal to the new filter, then bolt the filter to the transaxle (see illustration).

12   Position the new gasket on the pan, then hold the pan against the transaxle case and install the bolts.

13   Tighten the pan bolts to the torque listed in this Chapter's Specifications in a criss-cross pattern. Work up to the final torque in three steps.

❋❋ CAUTION:

Don't overtighten the bolts or the pan flange could be distorted and leaks could result.

14   Lower the vehicle. With the engine off, fill the transaxle with fluid (see Section 7 if necessary. Use a funnel to prevent spills. It is best to add a little fluid at a time, continually checking the level with the dipstick. Allow the fluid time to drain into the pan.

15   Start the engine and shift the selector into all positions from Park through Low, then shift into Park and apply the parking brake.

16   With the engine idling, check the fluid level. Lower the vehicle, drive it for several miles, then recheck the fluid level and look for leaks at the transaxle pan.

Specifications

Recommended lubricants, fluids and capacities

➡Note: Listed here are manufacturer recommendations at the time this manual was written. Manufacturers occasionally upgrade their fluid and lubricant specifications, so check with your local auto parts store for current recommendations.

Type	API "certified for gasoline engines"
Viscosity	
1991 through 2000	
1.8L and 1.9L engines	See accompanying chart
2.0L engines	5W-30
2001 and 2002	5W-20
Capacity (with filter change)	
1991 through 1997	4.0 qts
1998 on	4.5 qts
1999 through 2000	
Sedan	4.0 qts
ZX2	4.5 qts
2001 and 2002	4.0 qts
Brake fluid type	DOT 3 heavy-duty brake fluid
Power steering fluid type	MERCON automatic transmission fluid
Automatic transaxle fluid	
Type	MERCON automatic transmission fluid
Approximate capacity (drain and refill)*	
1991 through 1996	2.5 qts
1997 and 1998	5.7 qts
1999 and 2000	4.1 qts
2001 and 2002	5.4 qts

Measure the amount drained and add approximately the same amount. Use dipstick to determine the exact amount (see text).

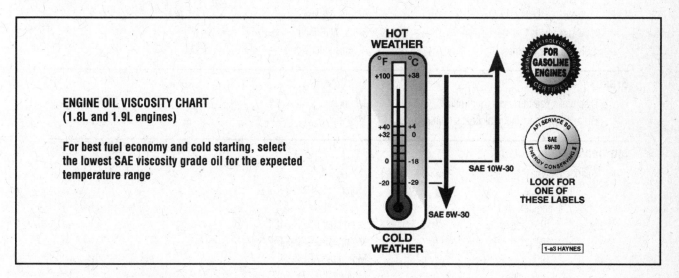

**ENGINE OIL VISCOSITY CHART
(1.8L and 1.9L engines)**

For best fuel economy and cold starting, select the lowest SAE viscosity grade oil for the expected temperature range

HOT WEATHER

COLD WEATHER

SAE 10W-30

SAE 5W-30

FOR GASOLINE ENGINES

LOOK FOR ONE OF THESE LABELS

1-a3 HAYNES

Manual transaxle lubricant	
Type	MERCON automatic transmission fluid
Capacity (approximate)	
1991 through 1998	2.9 qts
1999 and later	3.6 qts

Recommended lubricants, fluids and capacities (continued)

➡Note: Listed here are manufacturer recommendations at the time this manual was written. Manufacturers occasionally upgrade their fluid and lubricant specifications, so check with your local auto parts store for current recommendations.

Coolant
    Type   50/50 mixture of ethylene glycol-based antifreeze and water

Coolant Capacity (approximate)	
1.8L and 1.9L engines	
Manual transaxle	5.3 qts
Automatic transaxle	6.3 qts
1991 through 1998	
2.0L SPI engine	
Manual transaxle	5.8 qts
Automatic transaxle	7.9 qts
2.0L Zetec engine	
Manual transaxle	7.0 qts
Automatic transaxle	7.5 qts
1999 and 2000	
Manual transaxle	5.3 qts
Automatic transaxle	6.3 qts
2001 and 2002	
2.0L Zetec engine	
Automatic transaxle	7.5 qts
Manual transaxle	7.0 qts
2.0L SPI engine	
Automatic transaxle	7.9 qts
Manual transaxle	5.8 qts

Drivebelt deflection

1.8L engine	
New belt	5/16 to 3/8 inch
Used belt**	3/8 to 7/16 inch
1.9L and 2.0L engines	Automatic tensioner

Brakes

Disc brake pad thickness (minimum)	1/8 inch
Drum brake shoe lining thickness (minimum)	1/16 inch

Ignition system

Spark plug type***	
1.8L engine	Motorcraft AGSP-32C
1.9L engine	
1994 and earlier	Motorcraft AGSF-34C
1995	Motorcraft AGSF-34PP
1996	Motorcraft AGSF-34EE
2.0L SPI engine	Motorcraft AGSF-34EE
2.0L Zetec engine	
Through 1998	Motorcraft AZFS-ZZF
1999 and later	AZFS-32FE
Spark plug gap	
1.8L engine	0.039 to 0.043 inch
1.9L engine	0.054 inch

2.0L engines
    SPI engines through 2000   0.052 to 0.056 in
    SPI engines, 2001 and 2002   0.044 in
    Zetec engines, 1999 and 2000   0.048 to 0.052 in
    Zetec engines, 2001 and 2002   0.044 in
Firing order   1-3-4-2

Clutch pedal

1991 through 1996 models
    Height   7-3/4 to 8 inches
    Freeplay   1/4 to 1/2 inch
    Disengagement height   1-5/8 inches
1997 and later models
    Height   8-3/8 to 8 inches
    Freeplay   1/4 to 1/2 inch
    Disengagement height   2-3/8 inches

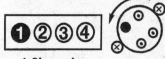

1.9L & 2.0L engines

1.8L engine

FRONT

2046.01-Haynes

Cylinder/coil terminal locations and distributor rotation

The blackened terminal shown on the distributor cap indicates the Number One spark plug wire position

Torque specifications   Ft-lbs (unless otherwise indicated)

➡Note: One foot-pound (ft-lb) of torque is equivalent to 12 inch-pounds (in-lbs) of torque. Torque values below approximately 15 ft-lbs are expressed in inch-pounds, since most foot-pound torque wrenches are not accurate at these smaller values.

Wheel lug nuts   65 to 87
Spark plugs
    1.8 engine   11 to 17
    1.9L engine   96 to 180 in-lbs
    2.0L engines   80 to 177 in-lbs
Oil pan drain plug
    1.8L engine   22 to 30
    1.9L and 2.0L SPI engines   15 to 22
    2.0L Zetec engine   29 to 41
Manual transaxle drain plug   29 to 39
Manual transaxle speed sensor bolt   70 to 99 in-lbs
Automatic transaxle drain plug   29 to 39
Automatic transaxle pan bolts
    1991   74 to 95 in-lbs
    1992 on   69 to 95 in-lbs

Notes

Section

Reference to other Chapters

CHECK ENGINE light on - See Chapter 6

2A

ENGINES

1   General information

This Part of Chapter 2 is devoted to in-vehicle repair procedures for the engine. All information concerning engine removal and installation and engine block and cylinder head overhaul can be found in Chapter 2B.

The following repair procedures are based on the assumption that the engine is installed in the vehicle. If the engine has been removed from the vehicle and mounted on a stand, many of the steps outlined in this Part of Chapter 2 will not apply.

The Specifications included in this Part of Chapter 2 apply only to the procedures contained in this Part. Chapter 2B contains the Specifications necessary for cylinder head and engine block rebuilding.

2   Repair operations possible with the engine in the vehicle

Many major repair operations can be accomplished without removing the engine from the vehicle.

Clean the engine compartment and the exterior of the engine with some type of degreaser before any work is done. It will make the job easier and help keep dirt out of the internal areas of the engine.

Depending on the components involved, it may be helpful to remove the hood to improve access to the engine as repairs are performed (see Chapter 11 if necessary). Cover the fenders to prevent damage to the paint. Special pads are available, but an old bedspread or blanket will also work.

If vacuum, exhaust, oil or coolant leaks develop, indicating a need for gasket or seal replacement, the repairs can generally be made with the engine in the vehicle. The intake and exhaust manifold gaskets, timing cover gasket, oil pan gasket, crankshaft oil seals and cylinder head gasket are all accessible with the engine in place.

Exterior engine components, such as the intake and exhaust manifolds, the oil pan, the water pump, the starter motor, the alternator, the distributor (if equipped) and the fuel system components can be removed for repair with the engine in place.

Since the cylinder head can be removed without pulling the engine, valve component servicing can also be accomplished with the engine in the vehicle. Replacement of the timing belt is also possible with the engine in the vehicle.

In extreme cases caused by a lack of necessary equipment, repair or replacement of piston rings, pistons, connecting rods and rod bearings is possible with the engine in the vehicle. However, this practice is not recommended because of the cleaning and preparation work that must be done to the components involved.

3   Top Dead Center (TDC) for number one piston - locating

1   Top Dead Center (TDC) is the highest point in the cylinder that each piston reaches as it travels up-and-down when the crankshaft turns. Each piston reaches TDC on the compression stroke and again on the exhaust stroke, but TDC generally refers to piston position on the compression stroke.

2   Positioning the piston(s) at TDC is an essential part of many procedures such as rocker arm removal, camshaft and timing belt removal and distributor removal.

3   Before beginning this procedure, be sure to place the transaxle in Neutral and apply the parking brake or block the rear wheels. Also, disable the ignition system by detaching the coil wire from the center terminal of the distributor cap and grounding it on the block with a jumper wire (1.8L engine models) or disconnecting all four spark plug wires from the plugs and grounding them on the engine using jumper wires with alligator clips (1.9L engine models). On all models, remove the spark plugs (see Chapter 1).

4   In order to bring any piston to TDC, the crankshaft must be turned using one of the methods outlined below. When looking at the drivebelt end of the engine, normal crankshaft rotation is clockwise.

   a) *The preferred method is to turn the crankshaft with a socket and ratchet attached to the bolt threaded into the front of the crankshaft.*

   b) *A remote starter switch, which may save some time, can also be used. Follow the instructions included with the switch. Once the piston is close to TDC, use a socket and ratchet as described in the previous paragraph.*

   c) *If an assistant is available to turn the ignition switch to the Start position in short bursts, you can get the piston close to TDC without a remote starter switch. Make sure your assistant is out of the vehicle, away from the ignition switch, then use a socket and ratchet as described above to complete the procedure.*

1.8L ENGINE

♦ **Refer to illustration 3.8**

➡**Note: The following procedure is based on the assumption that the distributor is correctly installed. If you are trying to locate TDC to install the distributor correctly, piston position must be determined by feeling for compression at the number one spark plug hole, then aligning the ignition timing marks as described in Step 8.**

5   Note the position of the terminal for the number one spark plug wire on the distributor cap.

3.8 On 1.8L engines, align the timing mark with the "T" on the timing plate

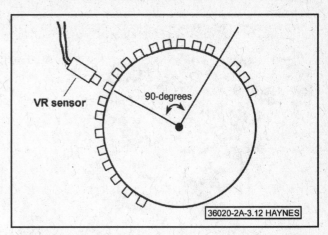

3.12 On 1.9L engines, align the ninth tooth from the missing tooth with the VR sensor

6   Use a felt-tip pen or chalk to make a mark on the distributor body directly under the terminal.

7   Detach the cap from the distributor and set it aside (see Chapter 1 if necessary).

8   Turn the crankshaft (see Step 4) until the notch in the crankshaft pulley is aligned with the "T" on the timing plate (located at the front of the engine) (see illustration).

9   Look at the distributor rotor - it should be pointing directly at the mark you made on the distributor body.

10   If the rotor is 180-degrees off, the number one piston is at TDC on the exhaust stroke.

11   To get the piston to TDC on the compression stroke, turn the crankshaft one complete turn (360-degrees) clockwise. The rotor should now be pointing at the mark on the distributor. When the rotor is pointing at the number one spark plug wire terminal in the distributor cap and the ignition timing marks are aligned, the number one piston is at TDC on the compression stroke.

1.9L AND 2.0L SPI ENGINES

▶ **Refer to illustration 3.12**

➡**Note: The 1.9L and 2.0L SPI engines are not equipped with a distributor. Piston position must be determined by feeling for compression at the number one spark plug hole, then aligning the ignition timing marks as described in Step 12.**

12   The crankshaft pulley has 35 teeth, evenly spaced every 10-degrees around the pulley, and a gap where a 36th tooth would be. The gap is located at 90-degrees before top dead center (BTDC) (see illustration). Turn the crankshaft (see Step 4) until you feel compression at the number one spark plug hole, then turn it slowly until the ninth tooth from the missing tooth is aligned with the variable reluctance (VR) sensor.

➡**Note: If the valve cover is removed, you can verify the number one piston is at TDC by checking the number one cylinder rocker arms - they should feel slightly loose and not be putting any pressure on the valves (the valve springs should not be compressed).**

2.0L ZETEC ENGINE

▶ **Refer to illustrations 3.16 and 3.17**

➡**Note: The 2.0L Zetec engine is not equipped with a distributor. Piston position must be determined by inserting a compression gauge in the number one spark plug hole, turning the crankshaft until compression registers on the gauge, then aligning the ignition timing marks as described in Step 12.**

13   Remove the spark plugs (see Chapter 1).

14   Remove the catalytic converter (see Chapter 4).

15   Remove the splash shield from under the right front corner of the engine compartment.

16   Note the notches in the outer rim of the crankshaft pulley. In the normal direction of crankshaft rotation (clockwise, viewed from the passenger side of the vehicle) the second notch indicates TDC when aligned with the raised mark on the oil pan. Rotate the crankshaft clockwise until the second notch aligns with the edge of the oil pan mark (see illustration). Install a compression gauge in the No. 1 spark plug hole as you turn the crankshaft. If compression doesn't build-up on the gauge as the piston nears TDC, No. 4 piston is on the compression stroke and No. 1 piston is on the exhaust stroke. Rotate the crankshaft

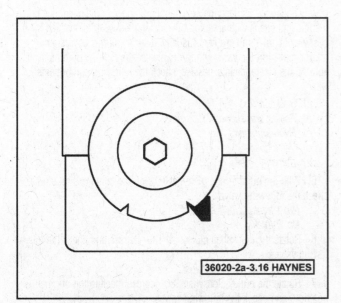

3.16 TDC notch in crankshaft damper (2.0L Zetec engine)

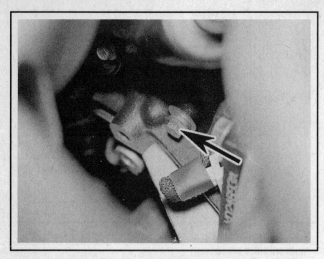

3.17 TDC timing hole plug (2.0L Zetec engine)

one full turn and align the marks again; this will position No. 1 cylinder at TDC compression.

17 There's a TDC timing hole on the front of the cylinder block which is used to position the crankshaft precisely at TDC (see illustration). With the marks aligned as described in Step 16, unscrew the timing hole plug and insert a timing peg (available from a specialty tool sup-plier). It may be necessary to turn the crankshaft slightly to insert the peg all the way. Turn the crankshaft clockwise against the peg.

> ❋ **CAUTION:**
>
> **Be sure to remove the peg before turning the engine again.**

ALL MODELS

18 After the number one piston has been positioned at TDC on the compression stroke, TDC for any of the remaining pistons can be located by turning the crankshaft and following the firing order. On 1.8L engines only, mark the remaining spark plug wire terminal locations on the distributor body just like you did for the number one terminal, then number the marks to correspond with the cylinder numbers. As you turn the crankshaft, the rotor will also turn. When it's pointing directly at one of the marks on the distributor, the piston for that particular cylinder is at TDC on the compression stroke. On 1.9L and 2.0L engines, make a mark 180-degrees (18 teeth on the crankshaft pulley) from the TDC position. Rotate the crankshaft 180-degrees to set the next cylinder in the firing order (1-3-4-2) at TDC. For example, rotating the crankshaft 180-degrees clockwise from the number one TDC position will set the number three piston at TDC. Rotating the crankshaft another 180-degrees clockwise (back to where it was for number one) will set the number four piston at TDC, etc.

4   Valve lifter clearance (1.9L and 2.0L engines) - checking

HYDRAULIC LIFTER CLEARANCE (1.9L AND 2.0L SPI ENGINES)

> ❋ **CAUTION:**
>
> **Be sure to perform this procedure after a valve job or whenever the camshaft, rocker arms or rocker arm supports (fulcrums) are replaced. Insufficient clearance can cause the valves to remain open all the time, resulting in rough running and expensive engine damage. Also, excessive clearance (usually caused by worn components) can result in noise in the valve cover area (clattering) and reduced engine performance.**

1   The valve stem-to-rocker arm clearance must be within specification with the valve lifter completely collapsed.

2   To check the clearance, crank the engine with the ignition off until the number one cylinder is at Top Dead Center (TDC) on the compression stoke. With the spark plug removed and your finger over the hole, the compression can be felt.

3   Mark the crankshaft pulley with chalk or white paint at TDC and 180 degrees opposite (see Section 3).

4   The hydraulic lifter should be slowly bled down until it is com-pletely collapsed as described in Steps 5, 6 and 7. If the clearance is insufficient, check with an automotive machine shop to determine the best way to solve the problem (usually, resurfacing the valve stem(s) and/or replacing the valve(s) and/or valve seat(s) are the options available). If the clearance is excessive, check the following components for wear:

  a) Rocker arms
  b) Rocker arm supports (fulcrums)
  c) Hydraulic lifters
  d) Valve tips
  e) Camshaft lobes

5   With the number one piston at TDC on the compression stroke, check the following valves:

  No. 1 intake, No. 1 exhaust
  No. 2 intake

6   Rotate the crankshaft clockwise 180-degrees and check the fol-lowing valves:

  No. 3 intake, No. 3 exhaust

7   Rotate the pulley clockwise 180-degrees (back to the original position) and check the following valves:

  No. 4 intake No. 4 exhaust
  No. 2 exhaust

MECHANICAL LIFTER CLEARANCE (2.0L ZETEC ENGINE)

Checking

♦ **Refer to illustration 4.10**

8   Place the engine at TDC compression for the number one cylinder (Section 3).

9   Remove the valve cover (Sections 5 and 6).

10 Measure the clearance between the lifters and cam lobes on No. 1 cylinder (see illustration). Compare the measurements to the values listed in this Chapter's Specifications. If the measurements are not within the specified range, write them down for later use. Note the cylinder number and whether the valve is an intake or exhaust.

11 Turn the engine to place the remaining cylinder at TDC compression (see Section 3) and measure the remaining valves in the same way. Again, write down any clearances that are not within the specified range.

12 Out-of-range clearances are adjusted by replacing the shim that's installed on top of each valve lifter with a shim of a different thickness. If the clearance is too large, you need a thicker shim. If the clearance is too small, you need a thinner shim. Thicknesses are marked on the shims, but if the markings are worn away you'll need a micrometer to measure the thickness.

13 The manufacturer recommends removing the camshafts for access to the shims. For some engines of similar design, special tools are available that allow removal of the valve adjusting shim without removing the camshafts. At the time of printing, there was no special tool available for the Zetec engine, but it would be a good idea to check with local auto parts stores to see if a tool has become available before going to the trouble of removing the camshafts.

14 Before you remove the shims from the valves that need them, calculate the thickness of the new shims as follows:

4.10 Measure between the cam lobe and adjusting shim with a feeler gauge (2.0L Zetec engine)

Sample calculation – clearance too small

Desired clearance (A)	= 0.004 inch
Measured clearance (B)	= 0.003 inch
Shim thickness found (C)	= 0.100 inch
Thickness required (D)	= C + B − A = 0.099 inch

Sample calculation – clearance too large

Desired clearance (A)	= 0.004 inch
Measured clearance (B)	= 0.005 inch
Shim thickness found (C)	= 0.100 inch
Thickness required (D)	= C + B − A = 0.101 inch

15 Install the new shims and recheck the valve clearances.

16 Once all clearances are within the Specifications, install all parts removed for access.

---

5   Timing belt - removal, inspection and installation

1.8L ENGINE

♦ **Refer to illustrations 5.10, 5.13, 5.19 and 5.22**

Removal

> **✳✳ CAUTION ✳✳**
>
> The timing system is complex. Severe engine damage will occur if you make any mistakes. Do not attempt this procedure unless you are highly experienced with this type of repair. If you are at all unsure of your abilities, consult an expert. Double-check all your work and be sure everything is correct before you attempt to start the engine.

1   Remove the timing belt upper cover screws, then lift off the cover and gasket.

2   Loosen the water pump pulley bolts, but don't remove them yet.

3   Remove the alternator/water pump drivebelt (see Chapter 1).

4   Unbolt and remove the water pump pulley.

5   Securely block the rear wheels so the vehicle can't roll. Loosen the lug nuts on the right front wheel. Jack up the front end and place it securely on jackstands, then remove the lug nuts and the right front wheel.

6   Remove the upper and lower splash shield on the passenger side.

7   Remove the air conditioning and power steering drivebelt (models so equipped) (see Chapter 1).

8   Unbolt the crankshaft pulley. Remove the pulley, its guide plate, and the timing belt guide plates.

9   Unbolt the middle and lower timing belt covers, then lift off the covers and gaskets.

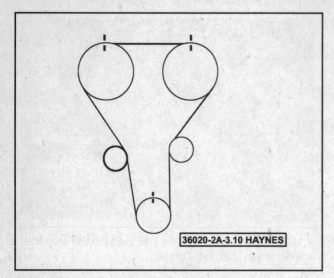

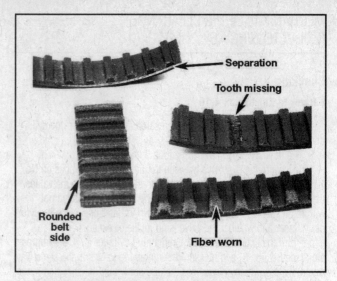

5.10 Camshaft and crankshaft sprocket timing mark alignment

5.13 Check the timing belt for cracked or missing teeth. If the belt is cracked or worn, check the pulleys for nicks and burrs. Wear on one side of the belt indicates pulley misalignment problems

10 Turn the crankshaft pulley as described in Section 3 to align the timing marks on the camshaft pulleys with the marks on the seal plates and the mark on the crankshaft pulley with the mark on the engine block (see illustration).

11 If you're planning to reuse the timing belt, use chalk or paint to mark an arrow on the belt indicating direction of rotation (clockwise, viewed from the timing belt end of the engine). Also make match marks on the belt and the camshaft pulleys. If you're going to install a new belt, note whether the teeth on the old one are squared off or rounded. Be sure the new belt has the same type of teeth (see illustration 5.34).

12 Loosen the timing belt tensioner lock-bolt to release tension on the belt. Lift the belt off the pulleys and remove it.

Inspection

13 Rotate the tensioner and idler pulleys by hand and move them side-to-side, checking for bearing play and rough rotation. Next, inspect the timing belt for wear (especially on the thrust side of the teeth), cracks, splits, fraying and oil contamination (see illustration). Replace the belt if any of these conditions exist.

➡Note: Considering the amount of work required to remove the timing belt, and also considering the expensive engine damage that may occur if the timing belt breaks, we recommend replacing the timing belt whenever it is removed, even if it looks to be in fairly good condition.

Installation

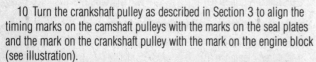

❊❊ **CAUTION** ❊❊

Before starting the engine, carefully rotate the crankshaft by hand through at least two full revolutions (use a socket and breaker bar on the crankshaft pulley centerbolt). If you feel any resistance, STOP! There is something wrong - most likely, valves are contacting the pistons. You must find the problem before proceeding. Check your work and see if any updated repair information is available.

14 Push or pry the timing belt tensioner all the way to the left so the spring is extended, then tighten its lock-bolt.

15 Make sure the crankshaft and camshaft pulley alignment marks are aligned correctly.

16 Install the timing belt on the pulleys. If you're reusing the old belt, align the match marks on the belt and pulleys and make sure the directional arrow made in Step 11 points in the proper direction.

17 Loosen the tensioner lock-bolt, push the tensioner against the belt to tighten it and tighten the lock-bolt.

18 Turn the crankshaft exactly two full turns clockwise and make sure the timing marks on the camshaft and crankshaft pulleys still align. If they don't, remove the timing belt and start the procedure over.

❊❊ **CAUTION:**

If you feel resistance while turning the crankshaft, the valves are probably hitting the pistons because the timing is not correct. Do not force the crankshaft or you'll bend the valves. Remove the timing belt and go back to Step 14.

19 Turn the crankshaft 1-5/6 turns clockwise, so the tension setting mark aligns with the crankshaft timing belt pulley mark (see illustration).

20 Loosen the tensioner lock-bolt, press the tensioner against the timing belt so it is taut, then tighten the lock-bolt to the torque listed in this Chapter's Specifications.

21 Turn the crankshaft 2-1/6 turns clockwise, so the camshaft pulley marks align with those on the seal plates and the crankshaft pulley mark aligns with the mark cylinder block.

22 Press on the timing belt midway between the camshaft pulleys with 22 lb force and measure how far the belt deflects (see illustration). If not within the range listed in this Chapter's Specifications, loosen the tensioner lock-bolt and move the tensioner to adjust it.

23 Once timing belt tension is correctly set, turn the crankshaft exactly two full turns clockwise and make sure the camshaft and crankshaft pulley marks still align.

24 The remainder of installation is the reverse of the removal steps.

5.19 Align the timing belt pulley mark with the tension set mark (at the 10 o'clock position) (1.8L engine)

1.9L AND 2.0L SPI ENGINES

◆ Refer to illustrations 5.26, 5.27a through 5.27f, 5.28a, 5.28b, 5.28c, 5.29a, 5.29b, 5.29c, 5.32 and 5.34

Removal and inspection

> ※※ **CAUTION** ※※
>
> The timing system is complex. Severe engine damage will occur if you make any mistakes. Do not attempt this procedure unless you are highly experienced with this type of repair. If you are at all unsure of your abilities, consult an expert. Double-check all your work and be sure everything is correct before you attempt to start the engine.

25 Disconnect the cable from the negative terminal of the battery.

26 Remove the accessory drivebelt (see Chapter 1). Remove the drivebelt tensioner center bolt and remove the tensioner (see illustration).

27 Remove the timing belt cover (see illustrations).

➡Note: If you're working on a 1.9L engine model, it may be necessary to remove the engine mount to get the cover out. If so, support the engine under the oil pan with a jack and block of wood and refer to Section 19 for engine mount details.

5.22 Check timing belt deflection midway between the camshaft pulleys (1.8L engine)

5.26 The drivebelt tensioner is secured by a single mounting bolt and comes off as an assembly (1.9L engine)

5.27a Remove the bolts (arrows) that secure the air conditioning hose retainers to the alternator bracket . . .

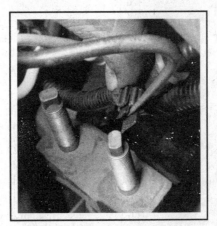

5.27b . . . then, with a pointed tool, undo the tie wraps that secure the wiring harness and air conditioning hose together . . .

5.27c . . . remove the timing belt cover nuts (arrows) . . .

5.27d . . . pull back the air conditioning hose, slide the cover off the studs and lift it out (1.9L engine)

5.27e Remove the upper nuts and bolt (2.0L SPI engine) . . .

5.27f . . . and the lower nut and bolt (one bolt hidden) (2.0L SPI engine)

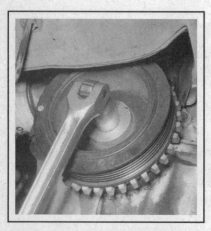

5.28a Turn the crankshaft with a socket and breaker bar on the pulley bolt

5.28b Align the mark on the crankshaft sprocket with the notch in the oil pump housing . . .

5.28c . . . and the mark on the camshaft sprocket with the mark on the cylinder head (1.9L engine)

5.29a On 1.9L engines, loosen the tensioner bolt (arrow) . . .

28 Use a socket and breaker bar on the crankshaft damper bolt (see illustration) and rotate the engine clockwise until the timing mark on the camshaft pulley is aligned with the one on the cylinder head and the crankshaft pulley mark is aligned with the TDC mark on the oil pump housing (see illustrations).

29 Loosen the belt tensioner bolt, pry the tensioner to one side and retighten the bolt to hold the tensioner in position (see illustrations).

30 Remove the spark plugs (see Chapter 1).

31 Securely block the rear wheels so the vehicle can't roll. Jack up the front end and place it securely on jackstands, then remove the splash shield from the passenger's side of the vehicle.

32 Hold the crankshaft from turning with a chain wrench or strap wrench. Remove the crankshaft damper bolt (see illustration), then remove the damper.

33 Remove the timing belt.

34 If you're installing a new belt, be sure it's the correct type. Belts with squared or rounded teeth are used in production (see illustration). The two types are not interchangeable. Inspect the belt and idler pulley, as described in Step 13. Also, check the water pump (see Chapter 3) and replace it, if necessary.

5.29b . . . pry the tensioner to the left to loosen the belt, then retighten the bolt (if you plan to reuse the belt, be sure to pad it at the points where the prybar or screwdriver contacts it) (arrows)

5.29c On 2.0L SPI engines, pry the tensioner to the left with an 8mm Allen wrench (left arrow), then slip a 1/8-inch drill bit into the hole (right arrow) to lock the tensioner in the released position

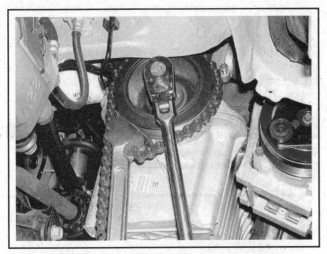

5.32 Hold the crankshaft damper with a chain wrench or strap wrench and unscrew the bolt (if a chain wrench is used, wrap a section of old drivebelt around the damper to protect it)

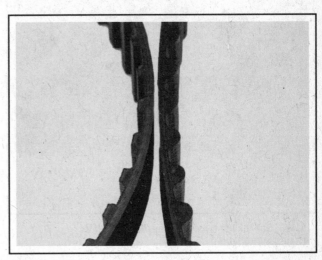

5.34 The timing belt may have squared or rounded teeth - if you replace the belt, be sure to use the same type that's on the engine

Installation

> **✳✳ CAUTION ✳✳**
>
> Before starting the engine, carefully rotate the crankshaft by hand through at least two full revolutions (use a socket and breaker bar on the crankshaft pulley centerbolt). If you feel any resistance, STOP! There is something wrong - most likely, valves are contacting the pistons. You must find the problem before proceeding. Check your work and see if any updated repair information is available.

35 Starting at the crankshaft, install a new belt in a counterclockwise direction over the pulleys. Be sure to keep the belt span from the crank-shaft to the camshaft tight while installing it over the remaining pulleys.

36 Loosen the belt tensioner attaching bolt so the tensioner snaps into place against the belt.

37 Install the crankshaft damper and bolt and tighten it to the torque listed in this Chapter's Specifications.

38 Rotate the crankshaft two complete revolutions clockwise and stop on the second revolution at the point where the crankshaft sprocket returns to the TDC position (see illustration 5.28b). Verify that the camshaft sprocket is also at TDC (see illustration 5.28c). If it isn't, the belt has jumped a tooth and the installation procedure will have to be repeated.

39 Tighten the tensioner attaching bolt to the torque listed in this Chapter's Specifications.

40 The remainder of installation is the reverse of the removal steps.

5.47 Use a camshaft aligning tool to hold the camshafts in the TDC position

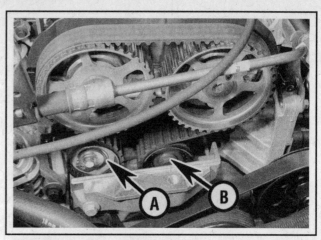

5.48a The 2.0L Zetec timing belt tensioner (A) and timing belt idler pulley (B)

➡**Note:** If you're planning to reuse the belt, mark an arrow mark indicating the direction of engine rotation.

45 Remove the accessory drivebelt (see Chapter 1), then remove the drivebelt idler pulley.

46 Remove the water pump pulley (see Chapter 3).

47 Install a camshaft alignment tool to hold the camshafts in the proper position (see illustration). This is a bar that fits in the slots at the rear ends of the camshafts. You can make a similar tool from flat bar stock or angle iron; just be sure it fits exactly in the camshaft grooves.

✳✳ **CAUTION:**

Don't use the alignment tool to hold the camshafts while you tighten or loosen the sprocket bolts or the camshafts may be damaged.

48 Loosen the timing belt tensioner bolt and detach the tensioner tab from the timing belt backplate (see illustrations).

49 Slip the timing belt off the sprockets.

Installation

✳✳ **CAUTION** ✳✳

Before starting the engine, carefully rotate the crankshaft by hand through at least two full revolutions (use a socket and breaker bar on the crankshaft pulley centerbolt). If you feel any resistance, STOP! There is something wrong - most likely, valves are contacting the pistons. You must find the problem before proceeding. Check your work and see if any updated repair information is available.

50 Make sure No. 1 cylinder is still at TDC compression. Align the camshafts and install the camshaft alignment tool (see Step 47).

51 If the timing belt tensioner was removed, install it loosely, then slip the timing belt onto the sprockets. If you're reinstalling a used belt, make sure the directional arrow points in the direction of rotation.

52 Reattach the timing belt tensioner tab to the backplate (see illustration 5.48b). Using a 6mm Allen wrench, turn the tensioner counterclockwise to align the tensioner pointer with the index mark. Hold the marks aligned and tighten the tensioner bolt.

53 The remainder of installation is the reverse of the removal steps.

5.48b Unhook the tensioner from the backplate (2.0L Zetec engine)

2.0L ZETEC ENGINE

Removal and inspection

✳✳ **CAUTION** ✳✳

The timing system is complex. Severe engine damage will occur if you make any mistakes. Do not attempt this procedure unless you are highly experienced with this type of repair. If you are at all unsure of your abilities, consult an expert. Double-check all your work and be sure everything is correct before you attempt to start the engine.

♦ **Refer to illustrations 5.47, 5.48a and 5.48b**

41 Disconnect the cable from the negative terminal of the battery.

42 Place No. 1 cylinder at TDC compression (see Section 3).

43 Remove the valve cover (see Section 6).

44 Remove the three bolts that secure the upper timing belt cover and take the cover off.

6 Valve cover - removal and installation

1.8L ENGINE

▶ **Refer to illustration 6.3**

1 Detach the spark plug wires from the wire loom and position them out of the way.

2 Disconnect the vacuum hoses from the valve cover.

3 Remove the valve cover bolts, then lift off the cover and gasket (see illustration). If the cover is stuck, bump it lightly with a rubber mallet to break the gasket seal.

4 Installation is the reverse of the removal steps. Clean the gasket surfaces on the cylinder head and valve cover carefully using a scraper, if necessary.

※※ CAUTION:

Be extremely careful when scraping, since the cylinder head and valve cover are made of aluminum that can easily be gouged or scratched, which will lead to oil leaks. Aerosol gasket removal compounds are available at many auto parts stores and may be helpful.

After all gasket material is removed, wipe the gasket surfaces with lacquer thinner or acetone. Use a new gasket and tighten the cover bolts evenly to the torque listed in this Chapter's Specifications.

1.9L AND 2.0L SPI ENGINES

▶ **Refer to illustration 6.7**

5 Disconnect the PCV hose from the valve cover.

6 Detach both spark plug wire looms from the valve cover and position them out of the way.

7 Remove the valve cover bolts, then lift off the cover and gasket (see illustration). If the cover is stuck, bump it lightly with a rubber mallet to break the gasket seal.

8 Installation is the reverse of the removal steps. Make sure the gasket surfaces on the cylinder head and valve cover are perfectly clean (wiping them with a rag soaked in lacquer thinner or acetone may help).

Press the new gasket firmly into the groove in the valve cover (don't use any sealant on the gasket). Tighten the cover bolts evenly to the torque listed in this Chapter's Specifications.

2.0L ZETEC ENGINE

▶ **Refer to illustrations 6.13, 6.14a and 6.14b**

9 Disconnect the oil solenoid electrical connector and PCV hose from the valve cover.

10 If you're working on an early production model, unbolt the trim cover from the center of the valve cover.

11 Disconnect the throttle and cruise control cables from the throttle body and lay them out of the way (see Chapter 4).

12 Remove the upper timing belt cover (see Section 5).

13 Remove four bolts from the center of the valve cover and three along each outer edge, then lift off the cover and gasket (see illustration). If the cover is stuck, bump it lightly with a rubber mallet to break the gasket seal.

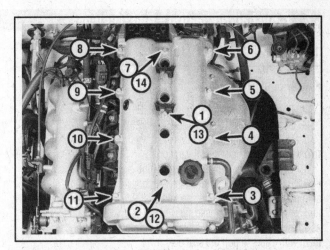

6.3 Valve cover details (1.8L engine) - tightening sequence shown

6.7 Three bolts (arrows) secure the valve cover on 1.9L and 2.0L SPI engines

6.13 Loosen the valve cover bolts evenly, then remove them (2.0L Zetec engine)

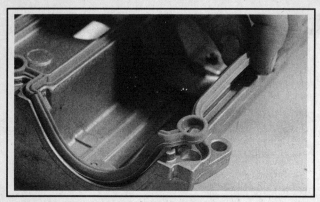

6.14a **Place the gasket completely into the cover groove**

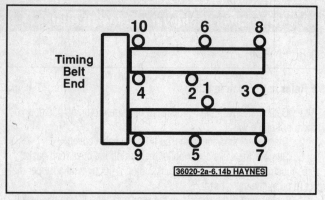

6.14b **Valve cover bolt tightening sequence - 2.0L Zetec engine**

14 Installation is the reverse of the removal steps. Make sure the gasket surfaces on the cylinder head and valve cover are perfectly clean (wiping them with a rag soaked in lacquer thinner or acetone may help). Press the new gasket firmly into the groove in the valve cover (don't use any sealant on the gasket) (see illustration). Tighten the cover bolts in sequence to the torque listed in this Chapter's Specifications (see illustration).

7 Camshaft oil seal(s) - replacement

1.8L ENGINE MODELS

▶ **Refer to illustration 7.3**

1 Remove the timing belt (see Section 5).
2 Remove the valve cover (see Section 6).
3 Hold each camshaft in turn with a wrench on the flat section and remove the pulley bolt (see illustration).
4 Unbolt the seal plate from the engine and take it off.
5 Remove the seals with a small slide hammer, available at most auto parts stores that handle special tools. If you don't have the special tool, punch holes in opposite sides of the seal with a sharp tool, such as an awl, then thread sheet metal screws into the holes and pull on them with pliers to pull the seal out.
6 Clean all residue from the seal mounting area.
7 Coat the lip of a new seal with clean engine oil. Install the seal with a special installation too, available at most auto parts stores. If you don't have the special tools, carefully drive the seal into position with a socket with the same outside diameter as the outer edge of the seal.
8 The remainder of installation is the reverse of the removal steps.

1.9L AND 2.0L SPI ENGINE MODELS

9 Disconnect the negative cable from the battery.
10 Remove the accessory drivebelt (see Chapter 1).
11 Remove the engine timing belt (see Section 5).
12 Insert a suitable bar through the camshaft pulley to lock it, remove the retaining bolt and withdraw the sprocket.
13 Using a suitable hooked tool, pry the seal out.
14 Apply a light coat of clean engine oil to the lip of the new seal. Place the seal in place and draw it into position, using a long bolt the same thread size as the pulley bolt and a suitable spacer piece such as a large socket.
15 Reinstall the sprocket and tighten the bolt to the torque listed in this Chapter's Specifications.

16 The remainder of installation is the reverse of the removal steps.

2.0L ZETEC ENGINE MODELS

17 Remove the timing belt and valve cover (see Sections 5 and 6).
18 Remove the camshaft sprocket and the front camshaft bearing cap (see Section 8).
19 Remove the camshaft seals from their bores.
20 Reinstall the camshaft bearing cap and tighten its bolts to the torque listed in this Chapter's Specifications.
21 Install the new camshaft seals, using a tool similar to the one used for the 1.8L engine. A large socket and a bolt of the same diameter and thread pitch as the sprocket bolt will work if you don't have the special tool.
22 The remainder of installation is the reverse of the removal steps.

7.3 **Hold each camshaft in turn with a wrench on the flat designed for the purpose and remove the camshaft pulley bolt with a socket and breaker bar (1.8L engine)**

8 Camshaft(s), lifters and rocker arms - removal, inspection and installation

1.8L ENGINE

♦ **Refer to illustrations 8.7, 8.13, 8.14, 8.15 and 8.20**

Removal

1 Disconnect the negative cable from the battery.
2 Remove the drivebelts (see Chapter 1).
3 Remove the distributor (see Chapter 5).
4 Remove the timing belt (see Section 5).
5 Remove the valve cover (see Section 6).
6 Remove the camshaft seal plate (see Section 7).
7 Loosen the camshaft bearing cap bolts evenly in the specified sequence (see illustration). Lift the caps off and arrange them in order on a clean surface. The caps are numbered and have arrows to indicate the correct direction of installation.
8 Lift out the camshafts and oil seals. Be sure to mark the camshafts so they can be reinstalled in their original locations.
9 Make alignment marks on the lifters and cylinder head so the lifters can be reinstalled in their original orientation. Pull the lifters out of the head and place them in a holder to keep them in order so they can be returned to their original bores.

Inspection

10 Hold the lifter in one hand and try to press in on the plunger. If it moves, replace the lifter.
11 Check each lifter for wear on the camshaft contact surface and cylinder head contact surface. Replace worn lifters.
12 Inspect the camshaft for wear, particularly on the lobes. Look for places where the hardened surface of the lobe is flaking off, scored or showing excessive wear. Replace the camshaft if any of these conditions exist. Pitting isn't cause for replacement unless it occurs at the toe (the highest point of the cam lobe).

13 Using a micrometer, measure the camshaft bearing journals (the raised round areas). Compare your measurements with this Chapter's Specifications. If the measurements are out of specification, replace the camshaft. Also measure the cam lobe heights on the camshafts and compare them to this Chapter's Specifications (see illustration).
14 Lay the camshaft in its journals and set up a dial indicator to measure endplay (see illustration). Move the camshaft back and forth against the indicator pointer and compare the reading with that listed in this Chapter's Specifications. If it's excessive, replace the cylinder head or camshaft, whichever is worn.

8.7 Camshaft bearing cap LOOSENING sequence (1.8L engine)

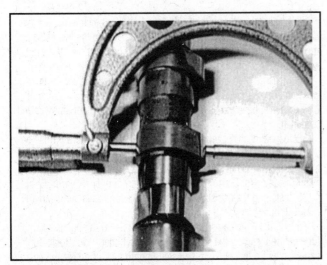

8.13 Measuring the cam lobe height - on 1.8L engines, compare this measurement to this Chapter's Specifications - on 1.9L engines, you must subtract the base circle measurement from this measurement before comparing it to the specifications (see Step 36)

8.14 Measure camshaft endplay with a dial indicator (1.8L engine)

8.15 Camshaft bearing cap TIGHTENING sequence (1.8L engine)

8.20 Apply a thin layer of silicone sealant to the points shown (1.8L engine)

15 Place both camshafts in their journals. Cut a piece of plastigage the length of each journal and lay it along the journal top surface (parallel to the centerline of the camshaft). Install the bearing caps and tighten evenly in sequence (see illustration) to the torque listed in this Chapter's Specifications.

16 Loosen the caps evenly in sequence (see illustration 8.7) and lift them off.

17 Measure the width of the plastigage to determine camshaft bearing clearance, then compare it with that listed in this Chapter's Specifications. If it's beyond specifications and the camshaft journals were within specifications in Step 13, replace the cylinder head.

Installation

18 Lubricate the lifters with clean engine oil and install them in their bores. If you're reusing the old lifters, return them to their original bores and align the marks made during removal.

19 Coat the camshaft journals, cam lobes and bearing surfaces in the cylinder head with engine assembly lube.

20 Lay the camshafts in position. Apply a thin layer of silicone sealant to the mating surfaces of the front bearing caps and cylinder head (see illustration).

21 Install the camshaft bearing caps. Refer to the numbers and arrow marks on the caps to make sure they are installed in the correct positions and point in the proper direction.

22 Tighten the bearing caps evenly in sequence (see illustration 8.15) to the torque listed in this Chapter's Specifications.

23 The remainder of installation is the reverse of the removal steps.

1.9L AND 2.0L SPI ENGINES

♦ **Refer to illustrations 8.28a, 8.28b, 8.36, 8.38a, 8.38b and 8.38c**

24 Disconnect the negative cable from the battery.

25 Remove the air cleaner intake duct (see Chapter 4).

26 Remove the valve cover (see Section 6).

27 Remove the drivebelt (see Chapter 1).

28 Remove the flange bolts and remove the fulcrums, rocker arms, lifter guide retainer, lifter guides and lifters (see illustrations). Keep the components in their originally installed sequence by marking them with

a piece of numbered tape or by using a suitable sub-divided box (such as an egg carton). If the lifters are not marked with color codes, be sure to mark each lifter so you know which end faces the front of the engine, since you must reinstall the lifters so they rotate in the same direction they originally did.

29 Remove the ignition coil pack (see Chapter 5).

30 Remove the timing belt (see Section 5).

31 Pass a rod or large screwdriver through one of the holes in the camshaft pulley to lock it and unscrew the sprocket bolt. Remove the sprocket.

32 Remove the two bolts and pull out the camshaft thrust plate.

33 Remove the cup plug from the transaxle end of the cylinder head.

34 Carefully withdraw the camshaft from the transaxle end of the cylinder head.

35 Perform Steps 11 through 13 above to inspect the lifters and camshaft.

36 Measure each cam lobe at points A and B shown in the accompanying illustration. Compare the difference between the two measurements to the lobe lift listed in this Chapter's Specifications. If it's not within specification, replace the camshaft.

37 Measure the camshaft bearing bore diameter in the cylinder head and compare with that listed in this Chapter's Specifications. If it's excessive, have the bearing bores machined to accept an oversized camshaft.

38 Inspect each rocker arm for wear at the points where it rides on the lifter, fulcrum and valve stem (see illustrations). Replace any rocker arms or fulcrums that show excessive wear. Replace rocker arms and fulcrums as pairs. Do not replace just a fulcrum or rocker arm.

39 Installing the camshaft, lifters and rocker arms is the reverse of removal, but observe the following points.

40 Lubricate the camshaft bearings and lobes with engine assembly lube before inserting the camshaft into the cylinder head. Rotate the camshaft as it's inserted and be careful not to nick or gouge the bearing surfaces.

41 A new oil seal should always be installed after the camshaft has been installed (see Section 7). Apply thread locking compound to the pulley bolt threads. Reinstall the pulley and tighten the bolt to the torque listed in this Chapter's Specifications.

42 Install and adjust the timing belt as described in Section 5.

43 Lubricate the hydraulic lifters with engine oil before inserting

8.28a The rocker arms are mounted diagonally, in parallel rows

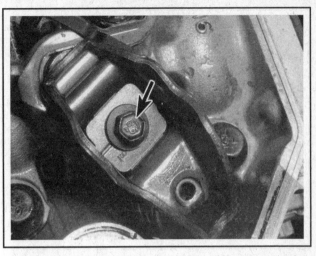

8.28b Remove the bolt (arrow), then lift out the fulcrum and rocker arm

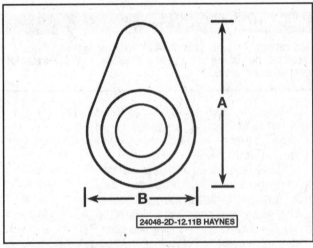

24048-2D-12.11B HAYNES

8.36 Subtract the base circle measurement (B) from the lobe height (A) to get the camshaft lobe lift

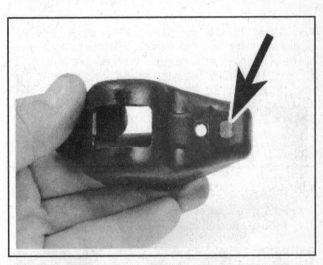

8.38a Check the rocker arm surfaces that contact the valve stem and lifter . . .

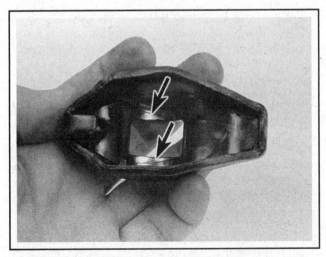

8.38b . . . the fulcrum seats in the rocker arms . . .

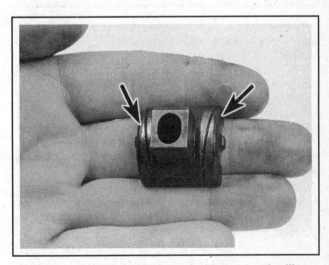

8.38c . . . and the fulcrums themselves for wear and galling

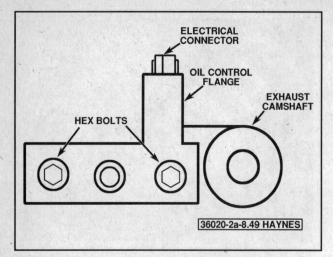

8.49 Unscrew the oil control solenoid flange bolts and rotate the flange 1/4-turn; be sure not to lose the triple O-ring

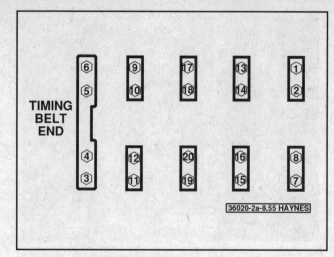

8.55 Camshaft bolt TIGHTENING sequence (2.0L Zetec engine)

them into their original bores. Position the lifters with their guide flats parallel to the centerline of the camshaft and the color code dots opposite the oil feed holes. Install the guides, retainers, rocker arms and fulcrums in their original positions, then install the bolts and tighten them to the torque listed in this Chapter's Specifications.

44 If any components are being replaced, check the collapsed tappet clearance, as described in Section 4.

2.0L ZETEC ENGINE

▶ **Refer to illustrations 8.49 and 8.55**

45 Remove the timing belt and valve cover (see Sections 5 and 6).

46 Hold each camshaft from turning with an open-end wrench.

✳✳ CAUTION:

Do not use a camshaft alignment tool to hold the camshaft while you loosen the bolts or the camshafts may be damaged.

47 Unscrew the oil plug from the front of the exhaust camshaft and remove the plug, together with its O-ring. Unscrew the sprocket bolt, then pull the sprocket and oil control solenoid off the camshaft.

48 Remove the bolt from the front of the intake camshaft sprocket, then pull the sprocket off the camshaft.

49 Remove the two hex bolts that secure the oil control solenoid flange to the cylinder head (see illustration). As you face the engine from the timing belt end, they're located to the left of the exhaust camshaft. Don't remove the center Torx bolt. Rotate the flange up and away from the head 1/4-turn. Be careful not to lose the three-loop flange O-ring.

50 Check the camshaft bearing caps for arrow marks pointing to the timing belt end of the engine and for cap numbers. If you don't see the marks, make your own.

✳✳ CAUTION:

The camshaft bearing caps must be installed in their original locations, and facing in the proper direction, or the camshaft(s) may seize and break.

51 Loosen the camshaft bolts two turns at a time, in the reverse of the tightening sequence (see illustration 8.55). Go through the loosening sequence until all of the bolts are completely loose, then pull them out and remove the bearing caps.

52 Lift the camshafts out of the head. Pull the oil control solenoid and its flange off the front end of the exhaust camshaft. Note that the end of the solenoid with three ribs goes toward the camshaft.

53 Make alignment marks on the lifters and cylinder head so the lifters can be reinstalled in their original orientation. Pull the lifters and the valve adjustment shims out of the head, making sure to keep each shim with its lifter. Store the lifters and shims in a numbered container so they can be returned to their original positions in the cylinder head.

54 Refer to Steps 11 through 17 in this Section to inspect the lifters and camshaft.

55 Installation is the reverse of the removal steps, with the following additions:

a) Make sure the tab on the back of the exhaust sprocket engages the hole in the oil control solenoid.

b) Be sure to install the O-rings between the oil control flange and cylinder head.

c) Apply sealant to the sealing surface of the front camshaft bearing cap, then tighten the bearing cap within four minutes or the sealer may allow oil leaks.

d) Tighten the bearing cap bolts in sequence, two turns at a time, until they're all snug, then tighten them in sequence to the torque listed in this Chapter's Specifications (see illustration).

e) Tighten the oil control solenoid flange bolts, exhaust side bolt first, to the torque listed in this Chapter's Specifications.

f) Once the bolts are tight, rotate the camshafts slowly through one full turn and make sure they don't bind.

g) Tighten the sprocket bolts and oil plug to the torques listed in this Chapter's Specifications.

9 Valve springs, retainers and seals - replacement

ALL ENGINES

▶ **Refer to illustration 9.4**

➡**Note: Broken valve springs and defective valve stem seals can be replaced without removing the cylinder head. Special tools and a compressed air source are normally required to perform this operation, so read through this Section carefully and rent or buy the tools before beginning the job.**

1 Refer to Section 6 and remove the valve cover from the cylinder head.

2 Remove the spark plug from the cylinder which has the defective component. If all of the valve stem seals are being replaced, all of the spark plugs should be removed.

3 Turn the crankshaft until the piston in the affected cylinder is at top dead center on the compression stroke (see Section 3 for instructions). If you're replacing all of the valve stem seals, begin with cylinder number one and work on the valves for one cylinder at a time. Move from cylinder-to-cylinder following the firing order sequence (see this Chapter's Specifications).

4 Thread an adapter into the spark plug hole (see illustration) and connect an air hose from a compressed air source to it. Most auto parts stores can supply the air hose adapter.

➡**Note: Many cylinder compression gauges utilize a screw-in fitting that may work with your air hose quick-disconnect fitting.**

5 Apply compressed air to the cylinder.

✳✳ WARNING:

The piston may be forced down by compressed air, causing the crankshaft to turn suddenly. If the wrench used when positioning the number one piston at TDC is still attached to the bolt in the crankshaft nose, it could cause damage or injury when the crankshaft moves.

✳✳ CAUTION:

Expensive engine damage may occur if the crankshaft is turned separately from the camshaft. If the timing belt is not installed, be careful not to let air pressure turn the crankshaft.

6 The valves should be held in place by air pressure. If they aren't, the valves and faces are in such poor condition that the cylinder head should be removed so they can be inspected.

1.8L AND 2.0L ZETEC ENGINES

7 Remove the camshaft and lifters on the side of the engine with the defective part (intake or exhaust) (see Section 8). If all of the valve stem seals are being removed, remove both camshafts and all of the lifters.

8 Install a valve spring compressor bar and brackets, available at most auto parts stores, on the cylinder head. Install a 1/2-inch drive ratchet handle in the compressor.

9 Line up the compressor directly over the valve spring seat, then compress the spring and remove the keepers with a magnet.

10 Release the spring tension and remove the upper spring seat, spring and lower seat.

➡**Note: If air pressure fails to hold the valve in the closed position during this operation, the valve face or seat is probably damaged. If so, the cylinder head will have to be removed for additional repair operations.**

11 Remove the valve stem seal with a slide hammer and remover adapter, available at most auto parts stores.

1.9L AND 2.0L SPI ENGINES

▶ **Refer to illustrations 9.13a and 9.13b**

12 Remove the bolt, fulcrum and rocker arm for the valve with the defective part. If all of the valve stem seals are being replaced, all of the rocker arms should be removed (see Section 8).

13 Compress the valve spring with a lever-type compressor, pivoting on the fulcrum nut or bolt head (see illustration). Remove the keepers (see illustration), spring retainer and valve spring, then remove the guide seal.

➡**Note: If air pressure fails to hold the valve in the closed position during this operation, the valve face or seat is probably damaged. If so, the cylinder head will have to be removed for additional repair operations.**

9.4 This is what the air hose adapter that threads into the spark plug hole looks like - they're commonly available from auto parts stores

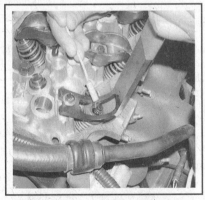

9.13a The recommended valve spring compressor for 1.9L and 2.0L SPI engines is a lever type that pivots on the rocker arm fulcrum nut or bolt head

9.13b Use a valve spring compressor to compress the springs, then remove the keepers from the valve stem with a magnet or small needle-nose pliers

ALL ENGINES

▶ **Refer to illustration 9.20**

14 Wrap a rubber band or tape around the top of the valve stem so the valve won't fall into the combustion chamber, then release the air pressure.

15 Inspect the valve stem for damage. Rotate the valve in the guide and check the end for eccentric movement, which would indicate that the valve is bent.

16 Move the valve up-and-down in the guide and make sure it doesn't bind. If the valve stem binds, either the valve is bent or the guide is damaged. In either case, the head will have to be removed for repair.

17 Reapply air pressure to the cylinder to retain the valve in the closed position, then remove the tape or rubber band from the valve stem.

18 Lubricate the valve stem with engine oil and install a new guide seal. On 1.9L and 2.0L SPI engines, use the installation tool provided with the new seal to prevent damage to the seal.

19 Install the lower seat and valve spring in position over the valve.

20 Install the valve spring retainer. Compress the valve spring and carefully position the keepers in the groove. Apply a small dab of grease to the inside of each keeper to hold it in place (see illustration).

21 Remove the pressure from the spring tool and make sure the keepers are seated.

22 The remainder of installation is the reverse of the removal steps.

23 Start and run the engine, then check for oil leaks and unusual sounds coming from the valve cover area.

9.20 Apply a small dab of grease to each keeper as shown here before installation - it'll hold them in place on the valve stem as the spring is released

---

10 Intake manifold - removal and installation

1.8L ENGINE

1 Disconnect the negative cable from the battery.

2 Depressurize the fuel system (see Chapter 4).

3 Label and disconnect the vacuum hoses, idle speed control hose and bypass air hose from the intake manifold and plenum.

4 Remove the vacuum chamber canister from the plenum (see Chapter 4).

5 Disconnect the accelerator cable (and kickdown cable on automatic transaxle models) from the throttle cam. Remove the throttle cam bracket from the plenum.

6 Disconnect the electrical connector(s) from the throttle body.

7 Remove the fuel rail (see Chapter 4).

8 Remove two bolts and detach the transaxle vent tube from the plenum.

9 Remove the upper nuts from the intake manifold.

10 Securely block the rear wheels so the vehicle can't roll. Jack up the front end and place it securely on jackstands. DO NOT get under a vehicle that's supported only by a jack!

11 Remove the intake plenum support bracket.

12 Remove the jackstands and lower the vehicle.

13 Remove the lower intake manifold nuts, then remove the manifold together with the intake plenum and throttle body.

14 Remove the intake manifold gasket from the engine.

15 If necessary, detach the intake plenum and throttle body from the manifold (see Chapter 4).

16 Using a scraper, clean all traces of old gasket and sealant from the manifold and its mounting surface on the cylinder head.

✳✳ CAUTION:

The cylinder head and manifold are made of aluminum, which can easily be scratched or gouged. Be very careful when using the scraper. Aerosol gasket removal solvents are commonly available from auto parts stores and may prove helpful.

17 If the throttle body or plenum was removed from the manifold, install it.

18 Position a new intake manifold gasket on the cylinder head. Install the manifold and tighten the mounting nuts evenly, working from the center outwards, to the torque listed in this Chapter's Specifications.

19 The remainder of installation is the reverse of the removal steps.

1.9L AND 2.0L SPI ENGINES

▶ **Refer to illustrations 10.26, 10.27, 10.28a through 10.28d and 10.29**

20 Relieve fuel system pressure (see Chapter 4).

21 Drain the cooling system below the level of the intake manifold (see Chapter 1).

22 Disconnect the negative cable from the battery.

23 Remove the air cleaner intake tube (see Chapter 4).

24 Disconnect the electrical connectors for the crankshaft position sensor and camshaft position sensor (see Chapter 5) and the fuel injector harness (located at the passenger's side strut tower).

25 Disconnect the fuel lines (see Chapter 4).

10.26 Rotate the cable drum to slacken the throttle cable and slip it out of the drum (do the same thing with the kickdown cable if you're working on an automatic transaxle model), then remove the bolts (arrows) that secure the cable bracket to the manifold (1.9L engine)

10.27 Several vacuum lines are connected to a fitting on top of the intake manifold (arrow) (1.9L engine)

10.28a Remove one manifold nut at the driver's side lower corner . . .

10.28b . . . one nut at the driver's side upper corner . . .

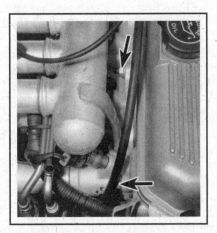

10.28c . . . two nuts along the top (arrows) . . .

10.28d . . . and three hidden below the manifold (a socket and long extension, as shown here, will probably be necessary) (1.9L engine)

26 Detach the accelerator cable (and kickdown cable on automatic transaxle models) from the throttle lever (see illustration). Remove the cable bracket from the intake manifold.

1.9L engine

27 Disconnect the vacuum lines from the fitting on top of the manifold (see illustration) as well as the vacuum hose from the bottom of the throttle body.

28 Remove seven nuts that secure the intake manifold (see illustrations).

29 Slide the manifold off the studs (see illustration). Remove the gasket (see illustration).

2.0L SPI engine

30 Disconnect the vacuum hose from the fuel pressure sensor and intake manifold.

31 Unscrew the EGR tube from the EGR valve at the fitting below the valve, and remove the engine oil dipstick tube from the engine.

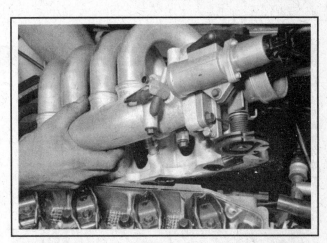

10.29 You may need to pivot the manifold to remove it (1.9L engine shown)

32 Remove one bolt and eight nuts that secure the manifold. Slide the manifold off the studs and remove the gasket.

33 To remove the intake manifold runner control, depressurize the fuel system and disconnect the fuel line from the fuel rail (see Chapter 4). Disconnect the electrical connectors from the IMRC actuator and all four fuel injectors.

34 Slide the IMRC off the studs and remove the gasket.

35 Using a scraper, clean all traces of old gasket and sealant from the mating surfaces of the IMRC (2.0L SPI engine only), intake manifold and cylinder head.

☀☀ CAUTION:

The cylinder head and manifold are made of aluminum, which can easily be scratched or gouged. Be very careful when using the scraper. Aerosol gasket removal solvents are commonly available from auto parts stores and may prove helpful.

36 Clean the intake manifold studs, then apply a light coat of clean engine oil to the threads.

37 If you removed the IMRC on a 2.0L SPI engine, slip a new gasket over the studs and install the IMRC. On all models, slip a new intake manifold gasket over the studs. Install the manifold and tighten the nuts evenly to the torque listed in this Chapter's Specifications.

38 The remainder of installation is the reverse of the removal steps.

2.0L ZETEC ENGINE

▶ **Refer to illustration 10.50**

39 Depressurize the fuel system and disconnect the fuel line at the intake manifold (see Chapter 4).

40 Disconnect the negative cable from the battery.

41 Disconnect the electrical connector from the throttle position sensor and the two main engine control connectors.

42 Remove the accessory drivebelt and drain the cooling system (see Chapter 1).

43 Remove the coolant hose retaining bolt below the crankshaft pulley. Disconnect the coolant hoses from the heater core (see Chapter 3).

44 Disconnect the vacuum hoses from the intake manifold and the PCV hose from the valve cover.

45 Unbolt the alternator mounting bracket and position it and the alternator out of the way.

46 Remove two bolts and seven nuts that secure the intake manifold. Loosen them in several stages, in the opposite of the tightening sequence (see illustration 10.50).

47 Slip the intake manifold off the studs and remove the gasket.

☀☀ CAUTION:

The intake manifold is made of fiberglass-reinforced plastic. If it won't come off easily, don't force it or it may break. Check to make sure all fasteners have been removed.

48 Using a scraper, clean all traces of old gasket and sealant from the mating surfaces of the intake manifold and cylinder head.

☀☀ CAUTION:

The cylinder head and manifold can easily be scratched or gouged. Be very careful when using the scraper. Aerosol gasket removal solvents are commonly available from auto parts stores and may prove helpful.

49 Clean the intake manifold studs, then apply a light coat of clean engine oil to the threads.

50 Slip a new intake manifold gasket over the studs. Install the manifold and tighten the nuts evenly to the torque listed in this Chapter's Specifications, following the tightening sequence (see illustration).

51 The remainder of installation is the reverse of the removal steps.

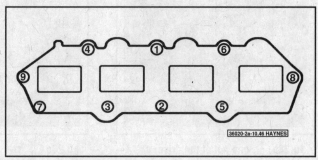

10.50 Intake manifold TIGHTENING sequence (2.0L Zetec engine)

11 Exhaust manifold - removal and installation

➡**Note: Because of the heating and cooling cycles exhaust components (particularly exhaust manifolds) are subjected to, fasteners frequently become frozen and are difficult to remove. Apply penetrating oil to the threads and allow it to soak in before removal. Tapping lightly on the fastener head may help the oil penetrate. When installing the exhaust manifold, apply anti-seize compound to the fasteners so they'll be easier to remove next time.**

1.8L ENGINE

1 Disconnect the negative cable from the battery.

2 Remove the air cleaner resonance duct (see Chapter 4).

3 Disconnect the upper hose from the radiator and remove the cooling fan (see Chapter 3).

4 Securely block the rear wheels so the vehicle won't roll, then jack up the front and place it securely on jackstands. DO NOT get under a vehicle that's supported only by a jack!

5 Disconnect the exhaust pipe from the manifold and remove the gasket between the pipe and manifold.

6 Remove both bolts that secure the exhaust pipe bracket.

7 Remove the lower splash shield on the driver's side.

8 Remove the jackstands and lower the vehicle.

9 Disconnect the electrical connector from the exhaust gas oxygen (EGO) sensor.

10 Unbolt and remove the exhaust manifold heat shield.

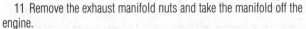

11.20 The exhaust manifold heat shield on 1.9L and 2.0L Zetec engines is secured by three nuts (arrows); on 2.0L SPI engines it's secured by five nuts

11 Remove the exhaust manifold nuts and take the manifold off the engine.

12 Using a scraper, clean all traces of old gasket and carbon from the manifold and its mounting surface on the cylinder head.

> ❈❈ **CAUTION:**
>
> **The cylinder head is made of aluminum, which can easily be scratched or gouged. Be very careful when using the scraper. Aerosol gasket removal solvents are commonly available from auto parts stores and may prove helpful.**

13 Position a new gasket on the studs. Install the manifold and tighten its mounting nuts evenly to the torque listed in this Chapter's Specifications.

14 Install the heat shield and tighten its bolts to the torque listed in this Chapter's Specifications.

15 The remainder of installation is the reverse of the removal steps.

1.9L AND 2.0L ENGINES

▶ **Refer to illustrations 11.20, 11.24a and 11.24b**

16 Disconnect the negative cable from the battery. If you're working on a 2.0L SPI engine, follow the wiring harness from the upstream oxygen sensor to the electrical connector and disconnect it.

17 Remove the drivebelt (see Chapter 1).

18 If you're working on a 1.9L or 2.0L SPI engine, remove the alternator (see Chapter 5). If you're working on a 2.0L Zetec engine, remove the bolt that secures the engine oil dipstick tube to the engine.

19 Remove the cooling fan and shroud (see Chapter 3).

➡ **Note: While not absolutely necessary, it's a good idea to remove the radiator as well; the core can easily be damaged if it's bumped by the manifold during removal.**

20 Remove the heat shield nuts and lift the heat shield off (see illustration).

21 Securely block the rear wheels so the vehicle won't roll, then jack up the front and place it securely on jackstands. DO NOT get under a vehicle that's supported only by a jack!

22 Disconnect the catalytic converter inlet pipe from the exhaust manifold. If you're working on a 2.0L SPI engine, remove the nuts and

11.24a Remove the exhaust manifold nuts (the studs may come out with the nuts) . . .

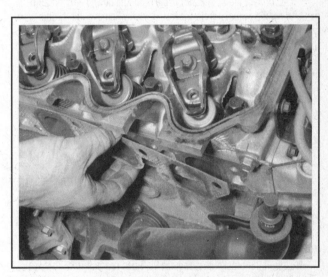

11.24b . . . then lift off the manifold and remove the gasket

studs that secure the EGR tube to the exhaust manifold.

23 Remove the jackstands and lower the vehicle.

24 Remove the exhaust manifold attaching nuts and slip the manifold off the studs (see illustrations). Remove the gasket.

25 Using a scraper, clean all traces of old gasket and carbon from the manifold and its mounting surface on the cylinder head.

> ❈❈ **CAUTION:**
>
> **The cylinder head is made of aluminum, which can easily be scratched or gouged. Be very careful when using the scraper. Aerosol gasket removal solvents are commonly available from auto parts stores and may prove helpful.**

26 Position a new gasket on the studs. Install the manifold and tighten its mounting nuts evenly to the torque listed in this Chapter's Specifications.

27 Install the heat shield and tighten its nuts to the torque listed in this Chapter's Specifications.

28 The remainder of installation is the reverse of the removal steps.

12 Cylinder head - removal and installation

1.8L ENGINE

▶ **Refer to illustrations 12.20 and 12.26**

1   Relieve fuel system pressure (see Chapter 4).

2   Disconnect the negative cable from the battery.

3   Drain the cooling system (see Chapter 1).

4   Remove the upper and middle timing belt covers and gaskets. Align the camshaft timing marks as you would for timing belt removal (see Section 5). Secure the timing belt tensioner in the slack position, slip the timing belt off the camshaft pulleys and tie it out of the way, maintaining tension on the belt so it remains engaged with the crankshaft pulley.

5   Remove the valve cover (see Section 6).

6   Remove the air duct that runs between the resonance chamber and throttle body (see Chapter 4).

7   Disconnect the accelerator cable (and kickdown cable on automatic transaxle models) from the throttle cam. Remove the throttle cam bracket from the plenum.

8   Label and disconnect the vacuum lines, electrical connectors and hoses attaching the cylinder head, throttle body and intake plenum to the engine and vehicle.

9   Disconnect the ground straps from the head.

10   Remove the radiator top hose (see Chapter 3).

11   Remove the upper right bolt that secures the transaxle to the engine block.

12   Disconnect and plug the fuel pressure and return lines (see Chapter 4).

13   Disconnect the ignition coil and primary wires from the distributor.

14   Remove the two bolts that secure the transaxle vent tube brackets.

15   Securely block the rear wheels so the vehicle won't roll, then jack up the front and place it securely on jackstands. DO NOT get under a vehicle that's supported only by a jack!

16   Unbolt the bracket that secures the hose running from the water pump to cylinder head (see Chapter 3).

17   Detach the exhaust pipe from the manifold and unbolt the exhaust pipe support bracket (see Section 11).

18   Remove the intake plenum support bracket (see Section 10).

19   Remove the jackstands and lower the vehicle.

20   Loosen the cylinder head bolts in several stages, following the specified sequence (see illustration). Discard the bolts. You'll need to obtain new ones for reassembly.

21   Lift the head off the engine with the intake and exhaust manifolds attached. If the head is stuck to the block, use the manifolds as levers to rock it free. If you need to service the cylinder head, remove the manifolds (see Sections 10 and 11).

22   Use a scraper to clean all old gasket material from the mating surfaces of cylinder head and engine block. Clean the surfaces with a rag soaked in lacquer thinner or acetone.

❊❊ CAUTION:

The cylinder head is made of aluminum and can easily be scratched or gouged, so scrape carefully. Gasket removal solvents are commonly available at auto parts stores and may prove helpful.

➡**Note: It's a good idea to check the cylinder head gasket surface for warpage while the head is off the vehicle. Additional information on cylinder head servicing is in Chapter 2B.**

23   Install a new head gasket on the block. Use the block dowels to position the gasket properly. The upper surface of most gaskets is marked "UP" or "TOP". Be sure this side faces up.

24   Position the head on the engine block.

25   Lubricate the threads of the new head bolts with clean engine oil.

26   Install the head bolts. Tighten in several stages to the torque listed in this Chapter's Specifications. Follow the specified sequence (see illustration).

27   The remainder of installation is the reverse of the removal steps with the following additions:

   a) *Align the yellow timing mark on the crankshaft pulley with the TDC mark on the timing belt cover.*

   b) *Be sure to follow all of the timing belt installation steps in Section 5.*

12.20 Cylinder head bolt LOOSENING sequence (1.8L engine)

12.26 Cylinder head bolt TIGHTENING sequence (1.8L engine)

1.9L ENGINE

➡**Note: The following procedure describes removing the cylinder head with the intake and exhaust manifolds attached, which may be easier if all you need to do is replace the head gasket. However, if you're planning to do any cylinder head servicing (such as a valve job), it will probably be easier to first disconnect the intake and exhaust manifolds from the cylinder head, tying them out of the way so the head can be removed separately (see Sections 10 and 11).**

Removal

➤ **Refer to illustrations 12.34, 12.36, 12.48, 12.50a, 12.50b, 12.53, 12.54 and 12.55**

28 Place the No. 1 piston at top dead center (TDC) (see Section 3).

29 Relieve the fuel system pressure (see Chapter 4).

30 Disconnect the negative cable from the battery.

31 Drain the cooling system (see Chapter 3).

32 Remove the air intake duct (see Chapter 4).

33 Disconnect the power brake hose from the intake manifold, the PCV hose from the valve cover and the vacuum hose from the bottom of the throttle body.

34 Label and disconnect all electrical connectors, including the ground strap, attaching the cylinder head to the engine and vehicle (see illustration).

35 Disconnect the throttle cable (and kickdown cable on automatic transaxle models) from the throttle lever. Detach the cable bracket from the manifold (see illustration 10.26).

36 Disconnect the heater hose that runs to the coolant temperature switches at the firewall (see illustration). Disconnect the radiator upper hose (see Chapter 3).

37 Remove the dipstick tube nut from the stud on the cylinder head.

38 Unbolt the power steering and air conditioner hose brackets from the alternator bracket.

39 Remove the drivebelt and its tensioner (see Chapter 1).

40 Remove the alternator (see Chapter 5).

41 Remove the catalytic converter inlet pipe (see Chapter 4).

42 Detach the starter motor wiring harness from its clip beneath the intake manifold.

43 Remove the timing belt (see Section 5).

44 Remove the starter motor bolt that secures the heater hose support bracket.

1991 models only

45 Securely block the rear wheels so the vehicle won't roll, then jack up the front and place it securely on jackstands. DO NOT get under a vehicle that's supported only by a jack!

46 Place a jack beneath the engine to support it. Use a block of wood between the jack and oil pan so the oil pan won't be damaged.

47 Remove the passenger's side engine mount damper (see Section 19). Unbolt the right-hand engine mount from the engine. Loosen the engine mount through-bolt, then roll the mount away from the engine.

All 1.9L engine models

48 Remove the bolt that secures the alternator bracket to the cylinder head (see illustration).

49 Remove the valve cover (see Section 6).

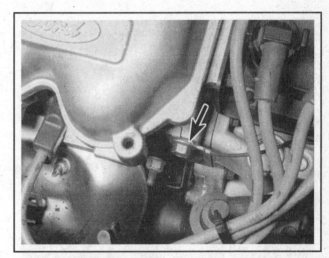

12.34 Detach the ground wire at the corner of the cylinder head near the ignition coil pack (arrow) (1.9L engine)

12.36 The hose that runs to the coolant temperature switch assembly is secured to the firewall fitting by a spring-type clamp (arrow) (1.9L engine)

12.48 After the alternator is removed, remove the one bolt that secures the alternator bracket to the cylinder head (1.9L engine)

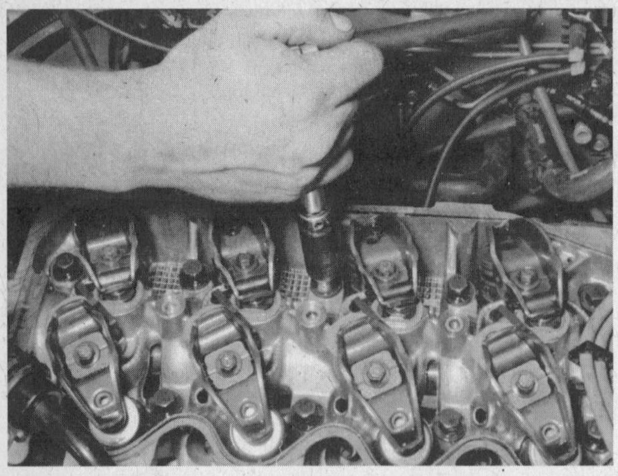

12.50a Loosen the head bolts in several stages (1.9L engine)

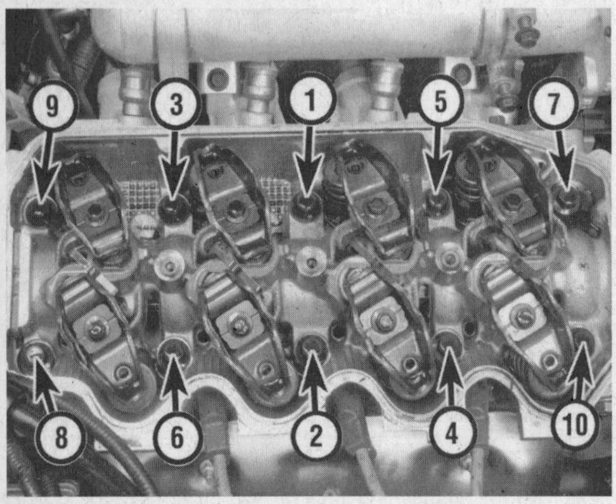

12.50b Cylinder head bolt TIGHTENING sequence (1.9L engine)

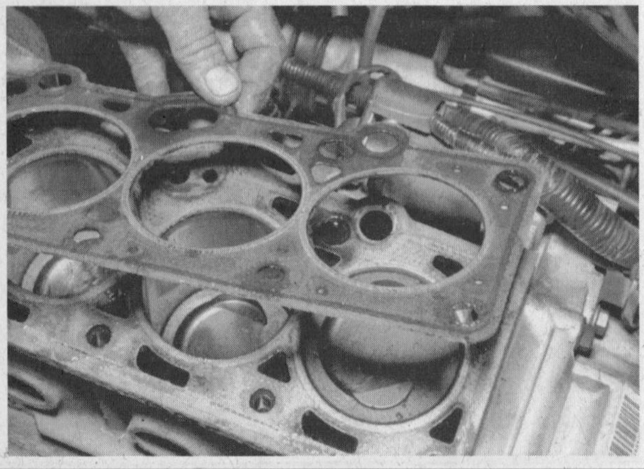

12.53 Try not to damage the gasket when you remove it - a used gasket is best for measuring piston squish height (1.9L engine)

50 Loosen the cylinder head bolts in the opposite order of the tightening sequence (see illustrations). Loosen in several stages.

51 Remove the cylinder head bolts.

➡Note: Keep the head bolts for use in measuring piston squish height. However, the bolts must not be reused for final installation of the cylinder head. Use new ones.

52 Remove the cylinder head with the intake and exhaust manifolds attached.

53 Remove the old gasket (see illustration).

54 Note the locations of the cylinder head dowels, then remove them (see illustration).

55 Remove all traces of old gasket material from the head and cylinder block mating surfaces (see illustration). Clean the surfaces with a rag soaked in lacquer thinner or acetone.

✲✲ CAUTION:

The cylinder head is made of aluminum and can easily be scratched or gouged, so scrape carefully. Gasket removal solvents are commonly available at auto parts stores and may prove helpful.

➡Note 1: Before installing the cylinder head, the piston "squish" height must be checked (see Steps 56 through 60). Try to keep the head gasket in good condition during removal, as a used head gasket is preferred for the squish height measurement.

➡Note 2: It's a good idea to check the cylinder head gasket surface for warpage while the head is off the vehicle. This procedure, as well as other information on cylinder head servicing, is in Chapter 2B.

Piston "squish" height - checking

➡Note: If only the head gasket is being replaced, and the same thickness head gasket is being reinstalled, the squish height should be within specification. If the cylinder head gasket surface has been resurfaced, the block has been decked, the crankshaft, connecting rods or pistons are being replaced or a thinner head gasket is being installed, the squish height may be out of specification.

56 Place small pieces of solder around the top of each piston.

57 Rotate the crankshaft to lower the piston and install the head gasket and the cylinder head.

➡Note: A compressed (used) head gasket is preferred.

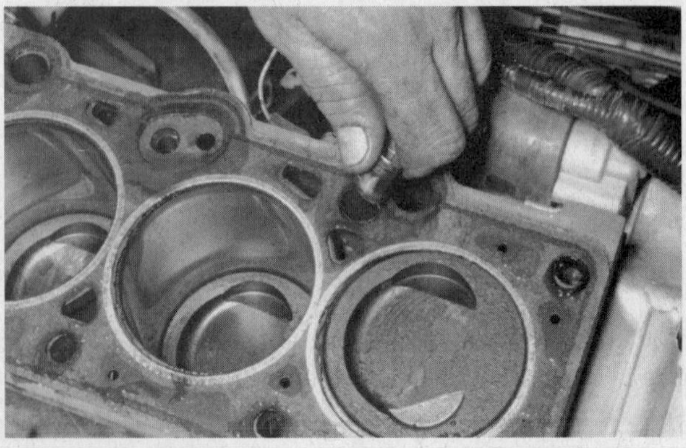

12.54 Remove the cylinder head locating dowels from the block (1.9L engine)

58 Install the locating dowels and the original head bolts (not new ones) and tighten them to 30-44 ft-lbs in the proper tightening sequence (see illustration 12.50b).

➡**Note: This specification is solely for the purpose of checking the piston squish height. When reinstalling the cylinder head, be sure to use the torque values listed in this Chapter's Specifications.**

Rotate the engine until the piston returns to TDC, and continue to turn the crankshaft until the piston begins its downward travel.

59 Loosen the cylinder head bolts in the opposite order of the tightening sequence and remove the cylinder head.

60 Measure the thickness of the compressed solder and compare with that listed in this Chapter's Specifications. If the thickness is not within specification, double-check to make sure that any new parts installed which might affect "squish" height, such as the head gasket or pistons, are the parts specified for this engine. If you have the correct parts and the "squish" height is still not within this Chapter's Specifications, consult your local service facility or dealer service department.

Installation

61 Place a new head gasket on the cylinder block and then locate the cylinder head on the dowels.

❊❊ CAUTION:

If you've replaced any dowels, make sure they're completely seated in the block. Also make sure they don't protrude as high as the combined height of the head gasket and the recess in the cylinder head. If the dowels protrude too far, the head will not seat properly against the gasket.

62 Apply a thin coat of clean engine oil to the threads of new cylinder head bolts. Install the bolts and tighten them in the stages listed in this Chapter's Specifications, following the proper tightening sequence (see illustration 12.50b).

63 The remainder of installation is the reverse of the removal steps.

64 Run the engine and check for leaks.

2.0L SPI ENGINE

➡**Note: The following procedure describes removing the cylinder head with the intake and exhaust manifolds attached, which may be easier if all you need to do is replace the head gasket. However, if you're planning to do any cylinder head servicing (such as a valve job), it will probably be easier to first disconnect the intake and exhaust manifolds from the cylinder head, tying them out of the way so the head can be removed separately (see Sections 10 and 11).**

Removal

65 Place the No. 1 piston at top dead center (TDC) (see Section 3).

66 Relieve the fuel system pressure and disconnect the fuel supply line at the fuel rail (see Chapter 4).

67 Disconnect the negative cable from the battery. Drain the cooling system (see Chapter 3).

68 Remove the air cleaner and its outlet tube (see Chapter 4).

69 Disconnect the vacuum hoses from the fitting on the intake manifold, and at the fuel pressure regulator, EGR valve, PCV valve and idle air control valve.

70 Label and disconnect all electrical connectors attaching the cylinder head to the engine and vehicle.

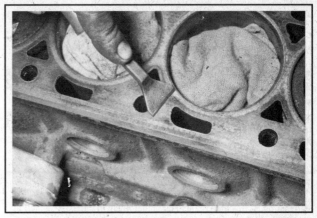

12.55 Stuff rags into the cylinder bores to keep debris from falling down where you can't retrieve it, then carefully scrape all old gasket material from the mating surface on the block (clean the cylinder head surface as well)

71 Disconnect the throttle cable (and cruise control cable if equipped) from the throttle lever. Detach the cable bracket from the manifold.

72 Disconnect the oxygen sensor electrical connector at the cooling fan shroud.

73 Remove the engine oil dipstick tube from the engine.

74 Remove the accessory drivebelt, alternator and air conditioning compressor (see Chapters 1, 5 and 3). Loosen the single nut and four lower bolts that secure the accessory bracket to the engine by four turns each. Remove the bracket's front uppermost bolt.

75 Detach the exhaust manifold from the catalytic converter (see Chapter 4).

76 Detach the starter motor wiring harness from its clip beneath the intake manifold.

77 Remove the timing belt and valve cover (see Sections 5 and 6).

78 Disconnect the coolant hoses from the thermostat housing (see Chapter 3).

79 Loosen the cylinder head bolts in the opposite order of the tightening sequence (see illustration 12.50b). Loosen in several stages.

80 Remove and discard the cylinder head bolts. The bolts are a stretch type that must be replaced with new ones whenever they're removed.

81 Remove the cylinder head with the intake and exhaust manifolds attached.

82 Remove the old gasket.

83 Note the locations of the cylinder head dowels, then remove them (see illustration 12.54).

84 Remove all traces of old gasket material from the head and cylinder block mating surfaces (see illustration 12.55). Clean the surfaces with a rag soaked in lacquer thinner or acetone.

❊❊ CAUTION:

The cylinder head is made of aluminum and can easily be scratched or gouged, so scrape carefully. Gasket removal solvents are commonly available at auto parts stores and may prove helpful.

➡**Note: It's a good idea to check the cylinder head gasket surface for warpage while the head is off the vehicle. This procedure, as well as other information on cylinder head servicing, is in Chapter 2B.**

Installation

85 Place a new head gasket on the cylinder block and then locate the cylinder head on the dowels.

※※ CAUTION:

If you've replaced any dowels, make sure they're completely seated in the block. Also make sure they don't protrude as high as the combined height of the head gasket and the recess in the cylinder head. If the dowels protrude too far, the head will not seat properly against the gasket.

86 Apply a thin coat of clean engine oil to the threads of new cylinder head bolts. Install the bolts and tighten them in the stages listed in this Chapter's Specifications, following the proper tightening sequence (see illustration 12.50b).

87 The remainder of installation is the reverse of the removal steps.

88 Run the engine and check for leaks.

2.0L ZETEC ENGINE

▶ Refer to illustration 12.110

→Note: The following procedure describes removing the cylinder head with the intake and exhaust manifolds attached, which may be easier if all you need to do is replace the head gasket. However, if you're planning to do any cylinder head servicing (such as a valve job), it will probably be easier to first disconnect the intake and exhaust manifolds from the cylinder head, tying them out of the way so the head can be removed separately (see Sections 10 and 11).

Removal

89 Place the No. 1 piston at top dead center (TDC) (see Section 3).

90 Relieve the fuel system pressure and disconnect the fuel supply line at the fuel rail (see Chapter 4).

91 Disconnect the negative cable from the battery.

92 Drain the cooling system (see Chapter 3).

93 Remove the air cleaner and its outlet tube (see Chapter 4).

94 Disconnect the vacuum hoses from the fitting on the intake manifold, and at the fuel pressure regulator, PCV valve and throttle body.

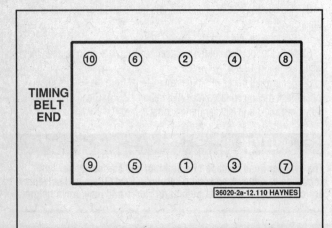

12.110 Cylinder head bolt TIGHTENING sequence - 2.0L Zetec engine

95 Label and disconnect all electrical connectors attaching the cylinder head to the engine and vehicle.

→Note: Disconnect the fuel injection wiring at the main engine connector. Follow the oxygen sensor harness to the connector and disconnect it.

96 Disconnect the throttle cable (and cruise control cable if equipped) from the throttle lever. Detach the cable bracket from the manifold.

97 Remove the engine oil dipstick tube from the engine.

98 Remove the accessory drivebelt, alternator and air conditioning compressor (see Chapters 1, 5 and 3).

99 Detach the exhaust manifold from the catalytic converter (see Chapter 4).

100 Remove the timing belt, valve cover and camshafts (see Sections 5, 6 and 8).

101 Disconnect the coolant hoses from the thermostat housing and remove the thermostat housing from the engine (see Chapter 3).

102 Remove the ignition coil pack (see Chapter 5).

103 Loosen the cylinder head bolts in the opposite order of the tightening sequence (see illustration 12.110). Loosen in several stages.

104 Remove and discard the cylinder head bolts. The bolts are a stretch type that must be replaced with new ones whenever they're removed.

105 Remove the cylinder head.

106 Remove the old gasket.

107 Note the locations of the cylinder head dowels, then remove them.

108 Remove all traces of old gasket material from the head and cylinder block mating surfaces (see illustration 12.55). Clean the surfaces with a rag soaked in lacquer thinner or acetone.

※※ CAUTION:

The cylinder head is made of aluminum and can easily be scratched or gouged, so scrape carefully. Gasket removal solvents are commonly available at auto parts stores and may prove helpful.

→Note: It's a good idea to check the cylinder head gasket surface for warpage while the head is off the vehicle. This procedure, as well as other information on cylinder head servicing, is in Chapter 2B.

Installation

109 Place a new head gasket on the cylinder block and then locate the cylinder head on the dowels.

※※ CAUTION:

If you've replaced any dowels, make sure they're completely seated in the block. Also make sure they don't protrude as high as the combined height of the head gasket and the recess in the cylinder head. If the dowels protrude too far, the head will not seat properly against the gasket.

110 Apply a thin coat of clean engine oil to the threads of new cylinder head bolts. Install the bolts and tighten them in the stages listed in this Chapter's Specifications, following the proper tightening sequence (see illustration).

111 The remainder of installation is the reverse of the removal steps.

112 Run the engine and check for leaks.

13 Oil pan - removal and installation

1.8L ENGINE

1 Securely block the rear wheels so the vehicle won't roll, then jack up the front and place it securely on jackstands. DO NOT get under a vehicle that's supported only by a jack!

2 Drain the engine oil (see Chapter 1).

3 Remove the upper splash shield on the passenger's side of the vehicle.

4 Remove the lower splash shield from both sides of the vehicle.

5 Detach the exhaust pipe from the manifold and unbolt the exhaust pipe support bracket (see Section 11).

6 Unbolt the oil pan from the transaxle.

7 Place a jackstand under the oil pan to support it so it won't fall during removal.

8 Unbolt the oil pan from the engine block.

9 Lower the pan away from the engine. If it's stuck, pry only at the rear of the pan, by the transaxle. Don't pry anywhere else or the sealing surfaces may be damaged.

10 If the crankcase stiffeners are stuck to the block or oil pan, carefully pry them loose without bending them.

11 Remove the pan gaskets (if equipped) and end seals.

12 If necessary, unbolt the oil strainer and remove its gasket.

13 Using a scraper, clean all traces of old gasket from the mating surfaces of the oil pan, engine block and stiffeners. Be extremely careful not to scratch or gouge the gasket surfaces or oil leaks will develop. Gasket removal solvents are available at auto parts stores and may prove helpful. Wipe the gasket surfaces clean with a rag soaked in lacquer thinner or acetone. Thoroughly clean the threads of the oil pan bolts.

14 Install the oil strainer (if removed), using a new gasket. Tighten its bolts to the torque listed in this Chapter's Specifications.

15 Apply silicone sealant to the crankcase stiffeners in a continuous bead along the insides of the bolt holes. Stick the crankcase stiffeners to the oil pan.

16 Apply sealant to the end seals. Install the seals on the oil pan with their projections in the notches.

17 Apply silicone sealant to the tops of the crankcase stiffeners, again routing it inside of the oil pan bolt holes. Make sure the sealant overlaps the ends of the end seals.

18 Place the oil pan on the engine and install the mounting bolts. Tighten the bolts evenly in a criss-cross pattern to the torque listed in this Chapter's Specifications.

19 The remainder of installation is the reverse of the removal steps.

1.9L AND 2.0L SPI ENGINES

▶ **Refer to illustration 13.24**

20 Disconnect the negative cable from the battery.

21 Securely block the rear wheels so the vehicle won't roll, then jack up the front and place it securely on jackstands. DO NOT get under a vehicle that's supported only by a jack!

22 Drain the engine oil (see Chapter 1).

23 Remove the catalytic converter (see Chapter 4). Note that the bracket which supports the rear end of the converter outlet pipe bolts to the oil pan.

24 If you're working on a 1.9L engine, remove both bolts that secure

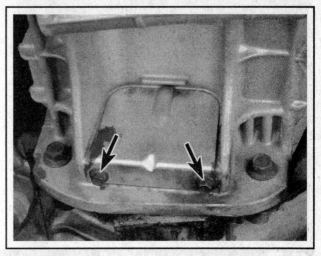

13.24 Remove the oil pan-to-transaxle bolts (arrows) (1.9L engine)

the oil pan to the transaxle (see illustration).

25 Unbolt the oil pan from the engine and lower it clear. If it's stuck, bump it gently with a rubber mallet. Don't pry between the pan and engine block or the mating surfaces may be damaged. Also, don't lose the oil pan-to-transaxle spacers.

26 Remove the gasket from the oil pan.

27 Unbolt the oil strainer from the block. If you're working on a 2.0L SPI engine, remove the four nuts and detach the oil baffle from the cylinder block.

28 Using a scraper, clean all traces of old gasket from the mating surfaces of the oil pan and engine block. Be extremely careful not to scratch or gouge the delicate aluminum gasket surfaces on the oil pan. Gasket removal solvents are available at auto parts stores and may prove helpful. Wipe the gasket surfaces clean with a rag soaked in lacquer thinner or acetone. Thoroughly clean the threads of the oil pan bolts.

29 Install the oil strainer, using a new gasket. Tighten the bolts securely.

30 Install a new oil pan gasket in the pan. Be sure the tabs are pressed all the way into the gasket channel in the pan.

31 Apply a 1/8-inch bead of silicone sealant to the corners of the block and to the points where the oil pump meets the crankshaft rear seal retainer.

➡**Note: The oil pan must be installed within 10 minutes after the sealant is installed.**

32 Position the oil pan on the engine. Install the pan-to-engine bolts and tighten them slightly to align the holes for the oil pan-to-transaxle bolts.

➡**Note: If the engine is out of the vehicle, bolt the transaxle to the engine to align the oil pan-to-transaxle bolt holes. In all cases, be sure the spacers are installed between the transaxle and oil pan.**

33 Install the oil pan-to-transaxle bolts. Tighten to the torque listed in this Chapter's Specifications, then loosen them 1/2-turn.

34 Tighten the oil pan-to-engine bolts to the torque listed in this Chapter's Specifications.

35 Retighten the oil pan to transaxle bolts to the torque listed in this Chapter's Specifications.

36 The remainder of installation is the reverse of the removal steps.

37 Check oil level on the dipstick (see Chapter 1). Run the engine and check for leaks.

2.0L ZETEC ENGINE

38 Securely block both rear wheels so the vehicle won't roll, then jack up the front and place it securely on jackstands. DO NOT get under a vehicle that's supported only by a jack!

39 Drain the engine oil (see Chapter 1).

40 Remove the catalytic converter (see Chapter 4).

41 Remove the oil pan bolts evenly. Tap the pan loose from the lower cylinder block and remove it from beneath the vehicle.

42 Clean all traces of sealant from the mating surfaces of the oil pan and lower cylinder block, then clean them with solvent and let them dry.

43 Coat the sealing surface on the oil pan with a continuous 1/8-inch bead of RTV sealant.

➡**Note: The oil pan must be installed within four minutes after the sealant has been applied to prevent oil leaks.**

44 Install the oil pan on the engine, then tighten the bolts evenly, starting from the center and working outward. Tighten to the torque listed in this Chapter's Specifications.

14 Oil pump - removal and installation

1.8L ENGINE

▶ **Refer to illustration 14.9**

1   Disconnect the negative cable from the battery.

2   Remove the timing belt (see Section 5).

3   Remove the timing belt pulley bolt with a socket and breaker bar. To hold the crankshaft while removing the bolt, remove the inspection cover from the transaxle bellhousing and wedge a screwdriver into the flywheel ring gear teeth.

4   Remove the timing belt pulley from the crankshaft. If it won't come off easily, use a steering wheel puller.

5   Remove the oil pan and strainer (see Section 13).

6   Unbolt the air conditioning compressor (if equipped) and set the compressor aside (see Chapter 3). DO NOT disconnect the compressor lines! Also remove the alternator.

7   Unbolt the compressor mounting bracket from the engine.

8   Remove the dipstick tube bracket bolt and the alternator lower mounting bolt.

9   Remove the oil pump bolts (see illustration). Take the pump off.

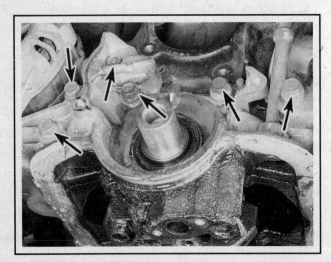

14.9 Oil pump mounting bolts (1.8L engine)

10 Using a gasket scraper, carefully clean all traces of old gasket from the pump and engine. Be very careful not to scratch or gouge the gasket mating surfaces. Gasket removal solvents are available from auto parts stores and may prove helpful. Wipe the mating surfaces clean with a rag soaked in lacquer thinner or acetone.

11 Place a new gasket on the oil pump, then place the pump on the engine. Tighten the oil pump bolts to the torque listed in this Chapter's Specifications.

12 The remainder of installation is the reverse of the removal steps.

1.9L AND 2.0L SPI ENGINES

13 Disconnect the negative cable from the battery.

14 Place the number one cylinder at top dead center (TDC) on the compression stroke (see Section 3).

15 Remove the drivebelt (see Chapter 1). Remove the drivebelt tensioner.

16 Place a jack beneath the engine to support it. Use a block of wood between the jack and oil pan to protect the pan.

17 Remove the damper from the right engine mount. Unbolt the mount from the bracket, loosen the mount through-bolt and pivot the mount away from the engine.

18 Remove the timing belt cover (see Section 5).

19 Pivot the engine mount back into position and reattach it to the engine. Remove the jack from beneath the engine.

20 Loosen the timing belt tensioner bolt, pry the tensioner toward the rear of the engine and tighten the bolt to hold the tensioner in this position.

21 Securely block the rear wheels so the vehicle won't roll, then jack up the front and place it securely on jackstands. DO NOT get under a vehicle that's supported only by a jack!

22 Remove the splash shield from the passenger's side of the vehicle.

23 Remove the catalytic converter (see Chapter 4).

24 Remove the oil pan (see Section 13).

25 Remove the oil filter (see Chapter 1).

26 Remove the crankshaft damper and timing belt (see Section 5). Remove the timing belt pulley and guide from the crankshaft.

27 Remove the crank angle sensor (see Chapter 5).

28 Unbolt the oil pump from the engine. Take off the oil pump and gasket.

29 Unbolt the screen and cover assembly from the pump.

30 Remove and discard the crankshaft front oil seal from the pump.

31 Using a gasket scraper, carefully clean all traces of old gasket from the pump, screen and engine. Be very careful not to scratch or gouge the gasket mating surfaces. Gasket removal solvents are available from auto parts stores and may prove helpful. Wipe the mating surfaces clean with a rag soaked in lacquer thinner or acetone.

32 Lubricate the outer edge of a new crankshaft seal with light engine oil, then install the seal. Lubricate the seal lip with light engine oil. To install the seal, place the oil pump on wood blocks, and drive the new seal into place with a hammer and socket that's slightly smaller in diameter than the outer edge of the seal.

33 Place the oil pump gasket on the pump. Pour oil into the pump and rotate its shaft to prime it, then position the pump on the engine. Use a small screwdriver, inserted through the oil pick-up hole, to guide the pump drive gear onto the crankshaft and make sure the pump seats securely against the block. Don't install the oil strainer until the pump is correctly installed on the engine.

34 Install the oil pump mounting bolts and tighten them evenly to the torque listed in this Chapter's Specifications. Make sure the oil pump gasket doesn't extend below the sealing surface on the cylinder block.

35 Install the oil screen, using a new gasket. then tighten its bolts to the torque listed in this Chapter's Specifications.

36 Install the timing belt guide on the crankshaft with its flanged side away from the timing belt.

37 The remainder of installation is the reverse of the removal steps. Be sure to follow the timing belt installation and alignment mark checking procedures in Section 5.

38 Fill the engine with oil and check its level (see Chapter 1). Run the engine and check for oil leaks.

2.0L ZETEC ENGINE

39 Removal of the 2.0L Zetec oil pump requires removing the lower cylinder block, which in turn requires removing the engine from the vehicle.

40 Remove the engine from the vehicle (see Chapter 2B).

41 Remove the oil pan (Section 13) and the lower cylinder block (see Chapter 2B).

42 Unbolt the oil pump from the crankshaft damper end of the engine.

43 Installation is the reverse of the removal steps. Use a new gasket and tighten the bolts to the torque listed in this Chapter's Specifications.

15 Flywheel/driveplate - removal and installation

1   Raise the vehicle and support it securely on jackstands, then refer to Chapter 7 and remove the transaxle. If it's leaking, now would be a very good time to replace the transaxle input shaft or torque converter-to-transaxle seal.

2   Remove the pressure plate and clutch disc (see Chapter 8) (manual transaxle equipped vehicles). Now is a good time to check/replace the clutch components and pilot bearing.

3   Use a center-punch to make alignment marks on the flywheel/driveplate and crankshaft to ensure correct alignment during reinstallation.

4   Remove the bolts that secure the flywheel/driveplate to the crankshaft. If the crankshaft turns, wedge a screwdriver through the starter opening to jam the flywheel.

5   Remove the flywheel/driveplate (and adapter on 1.8L engine models equipped with automatic transaxle) from the crankshaft. Since the flywheel is fairly heavy, be sure to support it while removing the last bolt.

6   Clean the flywheel to remove grease and oil. Inspect the surface

for cracks, rivet grooves, burned areas and score marks. Light scoring can be removed with emery cloth. Check for cracked and broken ring gear teeth. Lay the flywheel on a flat surface and use a straightedge to check for warpage.

7   Clean and inspect the mating surfaces of the flywheel/driveplate and the crankshaft. If the crankshaft rear seal is leaking, replace it before reinstalling the flywheel/driveplate.

8   Position the flywheel/driveplate against the crankshaft. Be sure to align the marks made during removal. Note that some engines have an alignment dowel or staggered bolt holes to ensure correct installation. Before installing the bolts, apply thread locking compound to the threads.

9   Wedge a screwdriver through the starter motor opening to keep the flywheel/driveplate from turning as you tighten the bolts to the torque listed in this Chapter's Specifications. Tighten the bolts in a criss-cross pattern.

10   The remainder of installation is the reverse of the removal procedure.

16 Crankshaft front oil seal - replacement

1.8L ENGINE

▶ **Refer to illustrations 16.4 and 16.6**

1 Remove the timing belt (see Section 5).
2 Remove the timing belt pulley (see Section 14).
3 Cut the lip of the seal with a razor blade so it will come out easily.
4 Wrap a rag around a screwdriver to prevent scratching the sealing surfaces and pry the seal out (see illustration).
5 Coat the lip of a new seal with clean engine oil.
6 Install the seal. Use a seal replacer tool, available at most auto parts stores (see illustration). If not, drive the seal in with a socket the same diameter as the seal. The seal should be flush with the oil pump body when installed.

1.9L AND 2.0L ENGINES

7 Disconnect the negative cable from the battery.
8 Remove the drivebelt (see Chapter 1).
9 Securely block the rear wheels so the vehicle won't roll, then jack up the front and place it securely on jackstands. DO NOT get under a vehicle that's supported only by a jack!
10 Remove the splash shield from the passenger's side of the vehicle.
11 Remove the crankshaft damper and timing belt (see Section 5).
12 Remove the timing belt pulley and guide from the crankshaft.
13 Using a suitable hooked tool, pry out the oil seal from the oil pump housing.
14 Apply a coat of light engine oil to the lip of the new seal and press it into position using a seal replacer tool. if available. If not, tap the seal into position with a socket with an outside diameter slightly smaller than the outside diameter of the seal.
15 The remainder of installation is the reverse of the removal steps. Be sure to follow the timing belt installation procedures in Section 5.

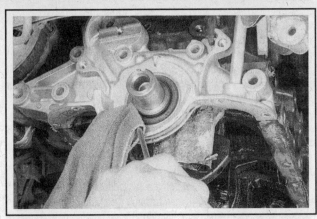

16.4 Pry the oil seal out with a screwdriver wrapped in a rag (1.8L engine)

16.6 Install the seal with a replacer tool, if available; if not, use a socket the same diameter as the seal - be sure the seal is flush with the oil pump body when installed (1.8L engine)

17 Crankshaft rear oil seal - replacement

▶ **Refer to illustrations 17.6 and 17.8**

1 Disconnect the battery negative cable.
2 Remove the transaxle (see Chapter 7).
3 On automatic transaxle models, remove the driveplate (see Section 16).
4 On manual transaxle models, remove the flywheel (see Section 16).
5 On 1.9L engine models, professionals recommend removing the oil pan (see Section 13), then unbolting the seal retainer from the rear of the block and prying or driving the seal out from the back side. However, if you want to try removing the seal without going through the trouble of removing the pan and retainer, you might try punching a hole in the seal with an awl or other sharp tool. Then, if you have a slide

hammer with a seal remover adapter, thread it into the hole and pull out the seal. If not, thread a sheet metal screw into the hole and pull on it with pliers to remove the seal.

✳✳ CAUTION:

If you attempt this method, be extremely careful not to scratch or otherwise damage the crankshaft or the bore in the seal retainer.

6 On 1.8L and 2.0L engine models, pry the old seal out of the seal retainer using a screwdriver (see illustration).
7 On all models, coat the lip of the new seal with clean engine oil

17.6 Pry the seal out with a screwdriver (1.8L and 2.0L engines)

17.8 Install the seal with a special tool, if available; if not, drive the seal in with a punch, but be careful not to damage it (1.8L engine)

8   Press the new seal into position. If the seal retainer is removed from the engine, use a block of wood and a hammer. If the retainer is still on the engine, use a special tool, available at most auto parts stores. If the special tool is unavailable, you may be able to tap the seal into position squarely with a hammer and a short, large-diameter piece of pipe (slightly smaller than the outside diameter of the seal) or a blunt

punch and hammer (see illustration). If you must use this method, be very careful not to damage the seal or crankshaft. On 1.8L engines, the seal should be flush with the rear cover when installed.

9   The remainder of installation is the reverse of the removal steps.

10 Run the engine and check for oil leaks.

18 Oil cooler (1.8L engine) - removal and installation

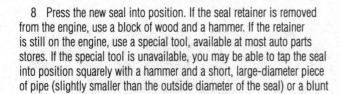

1   Drain the engine oil and remove the oil filter (see Chapter 1).
2   Drain the engine coolant (see Chapter 3).
3   Disconnect the two coolant hoses at the oil cooler.
4   Remove the mounting nut and detach the oil cooler.
5   Attach the cooler to the engine and tighten its mounting nut to the

torque listed in this Chapter's Specifications.

6   The remainder of installation is the reverse of the removal steps. Use a new oil cooler gasket and refill the cooling system with the proper mixture of water and coolant (see Chapter 1).

19 Engine mounts - check and replacement

▶ **Refer to illustrations 19.3, 19.5a through 19.5g and 19.11**

1   Engine mounts seldom require attention, but broken or deteriorated mounts should be replaced immediately or the added strain placed on the driveline components may cause damage or wear.

CHECK

2   During the check, the engine must be raised slightly to remove the weight from the mounts.

19.3 Support the engine with a jack and block of wood whenever you undo the mount fasteners

19.5a The engine mount has a vibration damper (arrow) . . .

19.5b . . . to remove it, remove the bolt and damper nut with a deep socket . . .

19.5c . . . and lift the damper off . . .

3   Raise the vehicle and support it securely on jackstands, then position a jack under the engine oil pan. Place a large block of wood between the jack head and the oil pan, then carefully raise the engine just enough to take the weight off the mounts.

※※ WARNING:

DO NOT place any part of your body under the engine when it's supported only by a jack!

4   Check the mounts to see if the rubber is cracked, hardened or separated from the metal.
5   Check for relative movement between the mount and the engine or frame. Use a large screwdriver or prybar to attempt to move the mounts (see illustrations). If movement is noted, lower the engine and tighten the mount fasteners.

6   Rubber preservative should be applied to the mounts to slow deterioration.

REPLACEMENT

7   Disconnect the negative battery cable from the battery.
8   Support the engine with a jack (see illustration 19.3).
9   Remove the fasteners and detach the mount from the engine and chassis (see illustrations 19.5a through 19.5g).
10 Installation is the reverse of the removal procedures with the following additions.
11 The cone washers on the engine mounts are installed tapered side down (see illustration).
12 Use thread locking compound on the mount bolts and tighten the bolts to the torque listed in this Chapter's Specifications.

19.5d . . . remove the mount nuts with a deep socket . . .

19.5e . . . and the through bolt with a box wrench and socket . . .

19.5f . . . then lift the mount off the studs (arrows)

19.5g The front transaxle mount is bolted to the transaxle and chassis (arrows)

19.11 Install the engine mount cone washers tapered side down

Specifications

1.8L engine

General

Type	Inline four-cylinder
Displacement	1.8 liter (112.2 cubic inches)
Bore	3.27 inches
Stroke	3.35 inches
Firing order	1-3-4-2
Timing belt deflection	0.35 to 0.45 inch

1.9L & 2.0L engines

1.8L engine

FRONT

2046.01-Haynes

Cylinder location and distributor rotation/coil terminal arrangement

The blackened terminal shown on the distributor cap indicates the Number One spark plug wire position

Camshaft

Lobe height	
Standard	
Intake	1.736 inches
Exhaust	1.756 inches
Minimum	
Intake	1.7281 inches
Exhaust	1.748 inches
Endplay	0.0028 to 0.0075 inch
Journal-to-bearing (oil) clearance	0.0014 to 0.0032 inch
Journal diameter	1.0213 to 1.022 inches
Journal out-of-round limit	0.002 inch

1.9L engine

General

Type	Inline four-cylinder
Displacement	1.9 liters (113.4 cubic inches)
Bore	3.23 inches
Stroke	3.46 inches
Firing order	1-3-4-2

Cylinder head and valve train

Piston "squish" height dimension	0.039 to 0.070 inch
Rocker arm ratio	1.65:1
Valve lifters	
Diameter (standard)	0.8740 to 0.8745 inch
Clearance in bore	
Standard	0.0009 to 0.0026 inch
Service limit	0.005 inch
Roundness	0.0005 inch
Collapsed lifter gap	0 to 0.177 inch
Lifter bore diameter	0.8676 +/- 0.0006 inch

Camshaft

Camshaft bore inside diameter	
Standard	1.8030 to 1.8040 inch
Oversize	1.8179 to 1.8189 inch
Lobe lift	
1991	0.240 inch
1992 and later	0.245 inch

1.9L engine (continued)

Camshaft (continued)

Allowable lobe lift loss (all years)	0.005 inch
Theoretical valve lift (measured at valve end of rocker arm)	
1991	0:468 inch
1992 and later	0.405 inch
Endplay	
Standard	0.0018 to 0.006 inch
Service limit	0.0078 inch
Journal-to-bearing (oil) clearance	0.0335 to 0.0835 inch
Runout limit	0.005 inch (runout of center bearing relative to No. 1 and No. 5)
Out-of-round limit	0.003 inch
Assembled gear face runout	
Crankshaft	0.026 inch
Camshaft	0.011 inch

2.0L SPI engine

General

Type	Inline four-cylinder
Displacement	2.0 liters (121 cubic inches)
Bore	3.34 inches
Stroke	3.46 inches
Firing order	1-3-4-2

Cylinder head and valve train

Rocker arm ratio	1.65:1
Valve lifters	
Diameter (standard)	0.8740 to 0.8745 inch
Clearance in bore	
Standard	0.0009 to 0.0026 inch
Service limit	0.005 inch
Roundness	0.0005 inch
Collapsed lifter gap	0 to 0.177 inch
Lifter bore diameter	0.8676 +/- 0.0006 inch

Camshaft

Camshaft bore inside diameter	1.8030 to 1.8040 inch
Camshaft journal diameter	1.8007 to 1.8017 inch
Lobe lift	0.245 inch
Allowable lobe lift loss	0.005 inch
Theoretical valve lift (measured at valve end of rocker arm)	0.405 inch
Endplay	
Standard	0.0008 to 0.0078 inch
Service limit	0.0078 inch
Journal-to-bearing (oil) clearance	0.0013 to 0.0033 inch
Runout limit	0.005 inch (runout of center bearing relative to No. 1 and No. 5)
Out-of-round limit	0.003 inch
Assembled gear face runout	
Crankshaft	0.026 inch
Camshaft	0.011 inch

2.0L Zetec engine

General

Type	Inline four-cylinder
Displacement	2.0 liters (121 cubic inches)
Bore	3.34 inches
Stroke	3.46 inches
Firing order	1-3-4-2

Cylinder head and valve train

Valve clearance	
Intake	0.004 to 0.007 inch
Exhaust	0.010 to 0.013 inch
Valve lifters	
Diameter (standard)	1.116 to 1.117 inch
Clearance in bore	0.001 to 0.003 inch

Camshaft

Camshaft bore inside diameter	Not specified
Theoretical valve maximum lift	
Intake	0.364 inch
Exhaust	0.338 inch
Lobe lift	Same as valve maximum lift
Endplay	0.0031 to 0.0086 inch
Journal-to-bearing (oil) clearance	0.0008 to 0.0027 inch
Bearing journal diameter	1.022 to 1.023 inch

Torque specifications   Ft-lbs (unless otherwise indicated)

➡**Note: One foot-pound (ft-lb) of torque is equivalent to 12 inch-pounds (in-lbs) of torque. Torque values below approximately 15 ft-lbs are expressed in inch-pounds, since most foot-pound torque wrenches are not accurate at these smaller values.**

1.8L engine

Camshaft seal plate bolts	69 to 95 in-lbs
Camshaft bearing cap bolts	100 to 126 in-lbs
Camshaft pulley bolt	36 to 45
Crankshaft pulley bolts	109 to 152 in-lbs
Crankshaft rear cover bolts	69 to 95 in-lbs
Cylinder head bolts	56 to 60
Dipstick bracket bolt	69 to 95 in-lbs
Engine mount fasteners	
Through-bolt and nut	49 to 69
Mount-to-engine nuts	54 to 76
Transaxle support bracket bolts	41 to 59
Transaxle upper mount bolts	32 to 45
Transaxle upper mount nuts	49 to 69
Exhaust manifold head shield bolts	69 to 95 in-lbs
Exhaust manifold nuts	28 to 34
Flywheel/driveplate bolts	71 to 76
Intake manifold nuts	14 to 19
Oil pan drain plug	See Chapter 1
Oil pump bolts	14 to 19

1.8L engine (continued)

Oil screen bolts	69 to 95 in-lbs
Oil pan-to-block bolts	69 to 95 in-lbs
Oil pan-to-transaxle bolts	27 to 38
Oil cooler mounting nut	22 to 29
Timing belt pulley lock-bolt	80 to 87
Timing belt cover bolts	69 to 95 in-lbs
Timing belt tensioner lock-bolt	27 to 38
Valve cover bolts	43 to 78 in-lbs

1.9L engine

Camshaft sprocket bolt	70 to 85
Camshaft thrust plate-to-head bolts	6 to 9
Crankshaft damper bolt	81 to 96
Cylinder head bolts*	
Step 1	30 to 44
Step 2	Loosen two turns
Step 3	44
Step 4	Tighten 1/4 turn from Step 3
Step 5	Tighten 1/4 turn from Step 4
Exhaust manifold bolts/nuts	16 to 19
Flywheel/driveplate bolts	54 to 67
Intake manifold nuts	12 to 15
Oil pan drain plug	See Chapter 1
Oil pan to block bolts	15 to 22
Oil pan to transaxle bolts	30 to 40
Oil pump to block bolts	150 in-lbs
Oil screen bolts	100 in-lbs
Rocker arm bolt	17 to 22
Valve cover bolts	50 to 100 in-lbs
Timing belt tensioner attaching bolt	17 to 22
Timing belt cover bolts	80 in-lbs

2.0L SPI engine

Camshaft sprocket bolt	70 to 85
Camshaft thrust plate-to-head bolts	71 to 115 in-lbs
Crankshaft damper bolt	81 to 96
Cylinder head bolts*	
Step 1	30 to 44
Step 2	Loosen 1/2 turn
Step 3	30 to 44
Step 4	Tighten 1/4 turn from Step 3
Step 5	Tighten 1/4 turn from Step 4
Exhaust manifold nuts	15 to 17
Flywheel/driveplate bolts	54 to 67
Intake manifold nuts	15 to 22
Oil pan drain plug	See Chapter 1
Oil pan baffle bolts	15 to 22
Oil pan to block bolts	15 to 22
Oil pump to block bolts	96 to 144 in-lbs
Oil screen bolts	71 to 97 in-lbs

Torque specifications (continued)　　　Ft-lbs (unless otherwise indicated)

➡**Note: One foot-pound (ft-lb) of torque is equivalent to 12 inch-pounds (in-lbs) of torque. Torque values below approximately 15 ft-lbs are expressed in inch-pounds, since most foot-pound torque wrenches are not accurate at these smaller values.**

2.0L SPI engine (continued)

Rocker arm bolt	17 to 22
Valve cover bolts	71 to 97 in-lbs
Timing belt tensioner attaching bolt	15 to 22

2.0L Zetec engine

Camshaft bearing cap bolts	120 to 144 in-lbs
Camshaft sprocket bolt	
Intake camshaft	50
Exhaust camshaft	88
Camshaft sprocket plug (exhaust camshaft)	27
Crankshaft pulley bolt	81 to 89
Cylinder head bolts*	
Through 1998	
Step 1	15 to 25
Step 2	35 to 45
Step 3	Tighten an additional 105 degrees
1999 and later	
Step 1	12 to 18
Step 2	26 to 33
Step 3	Tighten an additional 105 degrees
Dipstick tube nut	71 to 97 in-lbs
Engine mount fasteners	
Transaxle to engine bolts (automatic)	28 to 38
Transaxle to engine bolts (manual)	41 to 59
Front engine isolator bolts/nuts	50 to 68
Front roll restrictor bolts/nuts	48 to 65
Rear roll restrictor bolts/nuts	28 to 38
Transaxle upper mount nuts	49 to 69
Exhaust manifold head shield nuts	71 to 79 in-lbs
Exhaust manifold nuts	120 to 144 in-lbs
Flywheel/driveplate bolts	75 to 85
Intake manifold nuts	144 to 180 in-lbs
Oil pan drain plug	See Chapter 1
Oil control solenoid flange bolts	88 in-lbs
Oil pump bolts	88 to 97 in-lbs
Oil screen bolts	71 to 97 in-lbs
Oil separator	71 to 97 in-lbs
Oil pan-to-block bolts	15 to 22
Timing belt idler pulley bolt	35
Timing belt cover bolts	
Lower cover	61 in-lbs
Middle cover	120 in -lbs
Valve cover bolts	54 to 70 in-lbs
Valve cover trim cover bolts (early models only)	62 in-lbs

Cylinder head bolts are torque-to-yield design. Always replace them with new ones whenever they are removed.

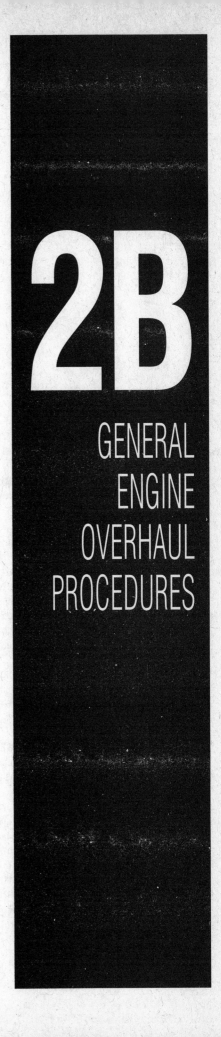

2B

GENERAL
ENGINE
OVERHAUL
PROCEDURES

1 General information

Included in this portion of Chapter 2 are the general overhaul procedures for the cylinder head and internal engine components.

The information ranges from advice concerning preparation for an overhaul and the purchase of replacement parts to detailed, step-by-step procedures covering removal and installation of internal engine components and the inspection of parts.

The following Sections have been written based on the assumption that the engine has been removed from the vehicle. For information concerning in-vehicle engine repair, as well as removal and installation of the external components necessary for the overhaul, see Chapter 2A and Section 7 of this Chapter.

The Specifications included in this Part are only those necessary for the inspection and overhaul procedures which follow. Refer to Part A for additional Specifications.

2 Engine overhaul - general information

▶ Refer to illustration 2.4

It's not always easy to determine when, or if, an engine should be completely overhauled, as a number of factors must be considered.

High mileage is not necessarily an indication that an overhaul is needed, while low mileage doesn't preclude the need for an overhaul. Frequency of servicing is probably the most important consideration. An engine that's had regular and frequent oil and filter changes, as well as other required maintenance, will most likely give many thousands of miles of reliable service. Conversely, a neglected engine may require an overhaul very early in its life.

Excessive oil consumption is an indication that piston rings, valve seals and/or valve guides are in need of attention. Make sure that oil leaks aren't responsible before deciding that the rings and/or guides are bad. Perform a compression check to determine the extent of the work required (see Section 3).

Check the oil pressure with a gauge installed in place of the oil pressure sending unit (see illustration) and compare it to this Chapter's Specifications. If it's extremely low, the bearings and/or oil pump are probably worn out.

Loss of power, rough running, knocking or metallic engine noises, excessive valve train noise and high fuel consumption rates may also point to the need for an overhaul, especially if they're all present at the same time. If a complete tune-up doesn't remedy the situation, major mechanical work is the only solution.

An engine overhaul involves restoring the internal parts to the specifications of a new engine. During an overhaul, the piston rings are replaced and the cylinder walls are reconditioned (rebored and/or honed). If a rebore is done by an automotive machine shop, new oversize pistons will also be installed. The main bearings, connecting rod bearings and camshaft bearings are generally replaced with new ones and, if necessary, the crankshaft may be reground to restore the journals. Generally, the valves are serviced as well, since they're usually in less-than-perfect condition at this point.

While the engine is being overhauled, other components, such as the distributor (if equipped), starter and alternator, can be rebuilt as well. The end result should be a like-new engine that will give many trouble-free miles.

➡Note: Critical cooling system components such as the hoses, drivebelts, thermostat and water pump MUST be replaced with new parts when an engine is overhauled. The radiator should be checked carefully to ensure that it isn't clogged or leaking (see Chapter 3). Also, we don't recommend overhauling the oil pump - always install a new one when an engine is rebuilt.

2.4 The 1.9L oil pressure sending unit (arrow) is mounted on the firewall side of the engine, near the starter

Before beginning the engine overhaul, read through the entire procedure to familiarize yourself with the scope and requirements of the job. Overhauling an engine isn't difficult if you follow all of the instructions carefully, have the necessary tools and equipment and pay close attention to all specifications; however, it is time consuming. Plan on the vehicle being tied up for a minimum of two weeks, especially if parts must be taken to an automotive machine shop for repair or reconditioning. Check on availability of parts and make sure that any necessary special tools and equipment are obtained in advance. Most work can be done with typical hand tools, although a number of precision measuring tools are required for inspecting parts to determine if they must be replaced. Often an automotive machine shop will handle the inspection of parts and offer advice concerning reconditioning and replacement.

➡Note: Always wait until the engine has been completely disassembled and all components, especially the engine block, have been inspected before deciding what service and repair operations must be performed by an automotive machine shop. Since the block's condition will be the major factor to consider when determining whether to overhaul the original engine or buy a rebuilt one, never purchase parts or have machine work done on other components until the block has been thoroughly inspected. As a general rule, time is the primary cost of an overhaul, so it doesn't pay to install worn or substandard parts.

As a final note, to ensure maximum life and minimum trouble from a rebuilt engine, everything must be assembled with care in a spotlessly clean environment.

3 Compression check and vacuum gauge diagnostic checks

COMPRESSION CHECK

1   A compression check will tell you what mechanical condition the upper end (pistons, rings, valves, head gaskets) of your engine is in. Specifically, it can tell you if the compression is down due to leakage caused by worn piston rings, defective valves and seats or a blown head gasket.

➡Note: The engine must be at normal operating temperature and the battery must be fully charged for this check.

2   Begin by cleaning the area around the spark plugs before you remove them (compressed air should be used, if available). The idea is to prevent dirt from getting into the cylinders as the compression check is being done.

3   Remove all of the spark plugs from the engine (see Chapter 1).

4   Block the throttle wide open.

5   On 1.8L engines, detach the coil wire from the center of the distributor cap and ground it on the engine block. Use a jumper wire with alligator clips on each end to ensure a good ground. On all other engines, unplug the primary (low voltage) electrical connector from the ignition coil pack (see Chapter 5). Also, disable the fuel pump by lifting the button on the fuel pump inertia switch (see the fuel pressure relief procedure in Chapter 4).

6   Install the compression gauge in the number one spark plug hole.

7   Crank the engine over at least seven compression strokes and watch the gauge. The compression should build up quickly in a healthy engine. Low compression on the first stroke, followed by gradually increasing pressure on successive strokes, indicates worn piston rings. A low compression reading on the first stroke, which doesn't build up during successive strokes, indicates leaking valves or a blown head gasket (a cracked head could also be the cause). Deposits on the undersides of the valve heads can also cause low compression. Record the highest gauge reading obtained.

8   Repeat the procedure for the remaining cylinders and compare the results to this Chapter's Specifications.

9   Add some engine oil (about three squirts from a plunger-type oil can) to each cylinder, through the spark plug hole, and repeat the test.

10   If the compression increases after the oil is added, the piston rings are definitely worn. If the compression doesn't increase significantly, the leakage is occurring at the valves or head gasket. Leakage past the valves may be caused by burned valve seats and/or faces or warped, cracked or bent valves.

11   If two adjacent cylinders have equally low compression, there's a strong possibility that the head gasket between them is blown. The appearance of coolant in the combustion chambers or the crankcase would verify this condition.

12   If one cylinder is 20 percent lower than the others, and the engine has a slightly rough idle, a worn exhaust lobe on the camshaft could be the cause.

13   If the compression is unusually high, the combustion chambers are probably coated with carbon deposits. If that's the case, the cylinder head should be removed and decarbonized.

14   If compression is way down or varies greatly between cylinders, it would be a good idea to have a leak-down test performed by an automotive repair shop. This test will pinpoint exactly where the leakage is occurring and how severe it is.

VACUUM GAUGE DIAGNOSTIC CHECKS

◆ Refer to illustration 3.20

15   A vacuum gauge provides inexpensive but valuable information about what is going on in the engine. You can check for worn rings or cylinder walls, leaking head or intake manifold gaskets, incorrect carburetor adjustments, restricted exhaust, stuck or burned valves, weak valve springs, improper ignition or valve timing and ignition problems.

16   Unfortunately, vacuum gauge readings are easy to misinterpret, so they should be used in conjunction with other tests to confirm the diagnosis.

17   Both the absolute readings and the rate of needle movement are important for accurate interpretation. Most gauges measure vacuum in inches of mercury (in-Hg). The following references to vacuum assume the diagnosis is being performed at sea level. As elevation increases (or atmospheric pressure decreases), the reading will decrease. For every 1,000 foot increase in elevation above approximately 2000 feet, the gauge readings will decrease about one inch of mercury.

18   Connect the vacuum gauge directly to the intake manifold vacuum, not to ported (throttle body) vacuum. Be sure no hoses are left disconnected during the test or false readings will result.

19 Before you begin the test, allow the engine to warm up completely. Block the wheels and set the parking brake. With the transmission in Park, start the engine and allow it to run at normal idle speed.

✳✳ WARNING:

Keep your hands and the vacuum gauge clear of the fans.

20 Read the vacuum gauge; an average, healthy engine should normally produce about 17 to 22 in-Hg with a fairly steady needle (see illustration). Refer to the following vacuum gauge readings and what they indicate about the engine's condition:

21 A low steady reading usually indicates a leaking gasket between the intake manifold and cylinder head(s) or throttle body, a leaky vacuum hose, late ignition timing or incorrect camshaft timing. Check ignition timing with a timing light and eliminate all other possible causes, utilizing the tests provided in this Chapter before you remove the timing chain cover to check the timing marks.

22 If the reading is three to eight inches below normal and it fluctuates at that low reading, suspect an intake manifold gasket leak at an intake port or a faulty fuel injector.

23 If the needle has regular drops of about two-to-four inches at a steady rate, the valves are probably leaking. Perform a compression check or leak-down test to confirm this.

24 An irregular drop or down-flick of the needle can be caused by a sticking valve or an ignition misfire. Perform a compression check or leak-down test and read the spark plugs.

25 A rapid vibration of about four in-Hg vibration at idle combined with exhaust smoke indicates worn valve guides. Perform a leak-down test to confirm this. If the rapid vibration occurs with an increase in engine speed, check for a leaking intake manifold gasket or head gasket, weak valve springs, burned valves or ignition misfire.

26 A slight fluctuation, say one inch up and down, may mean ignition problems. Check all the usual tune-up items and, if necessary, run the engine on an ignition analyzer.

27 If there is a large fluctuation, perform a compression or leak-down test to look for a weak or dead cylinder or a blown head gasket.

28 If the needle moves slowly through a wide range, check for a clogged PCV system, incorrect idle fuel mixture, carburetor/throttle body or intake manifold gasket leaks.

29 Check for a slow return after revving the engine by quickly snapping the throttle open until the engine reaches about 2,500 rpm and let it shut. Normally the reading should drop to near zero, rise above normal idle reading (about 5 in-Hg over) and then return to the previous idle reading. If the vacuum returns slowly and doesn't peak when the throttle is snapped shut, the rings may be worn. If there is a long delay, look for a restricted exhaust system (often the muffler or catalytic converter). An easy way to check this is to temporarily disconnect the exhaust ahead of the suspected part and redo the test.

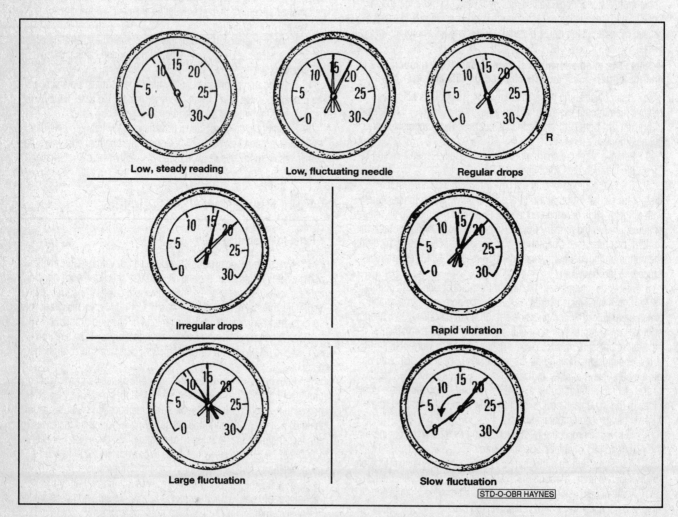

Low, steady reading   Low, fluctuating needle   Regular drops

Irregular drops   Rapid vibration

Large fluctuation   Slow fluctuation

STD-O-OBR HAYNES

3.20 Typical vacuum gauge readings

4 Engine removal - methods and precautions

If you've decided that an engine must be removed for overhaul or major repair work, several preliminary steps should be taken.

Locating a suitable place to work is extremely important.

Adequate work space, along with storage space for the vehicle, will be needed. If a shop or garage isn't available, at the very least a flat, level, clean work surface made of concrete or asphalt is required.

Cleaning the engine compartment and engine before beginning the removal procedure will help keep tools clean and organized.

An engine hoist or A-frame will also be necessary. Make sure the equipment is rated in excess of the combined weight of the engine and accessories. Safety is of primary importance, considering the potential hazards involved in lifting the engine out of the vehicle.

If the engine is being removed by a novice, a helper should be available. Advice and aid from someone more experienced would also be helpful. There are many instances when one person cannot simultaneously perform all of the operations required when lifting the engine out of the vehicle.

Plan the operation ahead of time. Arrange for or obtain all of the tools and equipment you'll need prior to beginning the job. Some of the equipment necessary to perform engine removal and installation safely and with relative ease are (in addition to an engine hoist) a heavy duty floor jack, complete sets of wrenches and sockets as described in the front of this manual, wooden blocks and plenty of rags and cleaning solvent for mopping up spilled oil, coolant and gasoline. If the hoist must be rented, make sure that you arrange for it in advance and perform all of the operations possible without it beforehand. This will save you money and time.

Plan for the vehicle to be out of use for quite a while. A machine shop will be required to perform some of the work which the do-it-yourselfer can't accomplish without special equipment. These shops often have a busy schedule, so it would be a good idea to consult them before removing the engine in order to accurately estimate the amount of time required to rebuild or repair components that may need work.

Always be extremely careful when removing and installing the engine. Serious injury can result from careless actions. Plan ahead, take your time and a job of this nature, although major, can be accomplished successfully.

5 Engine - removal and installation

▶ **Refer to illustration 5.6**

✷✷ WARNING:

The air conditioning system is under high pressure! Have a dealer service department or service station depressurize the system before disconnecting any air conditioning system hoses or fittings.

REMOVAL

1.8L engine models

➡**Note: If the vehicle has a manual transaxle, the engine and transaxle are removed as a unit. If it has an automatic transaxle, the engine is removed separately from the transaxle.**

1   On automatic transaxle models, have the air conditioning system depressurized by a dealer or other qualified shop. DO NOT depressurize the system yourself!

2   Refer to Chapter 4 and relieve the fuel system pressure, then disconnect the negative cable from the battery. On manual transaxle models, remove the battery, battery tray and battery duct (see Chapter 5).

3   Cover the fenders and cowl and remove the hood (see Chapter 11). Special pads are available to protect the fenders, but an old bedspread or blanket will also work.

4   Remove the air cleaner assembly (see Chapter 4).

5   Drain the cooling system and engine oil (see Chapter 1).

6   Label the vacuum lines, emissions system hoses, wiring connectors, ground straps and fuel lines, to ensure correct reinstallation, then detach them. Pieces of masking tape with numbers or letters written on them work well (see illustration). If there's any possibility of confusion, make a sketch of the engine compartment and clearly label the lines, hoses and wires.

7   Label and detach all coolant hoses from the engine. Disconnect the heater hoses at the firewall.

8   Remove the cooling fan, shroud and radiator (see Chapter 3).

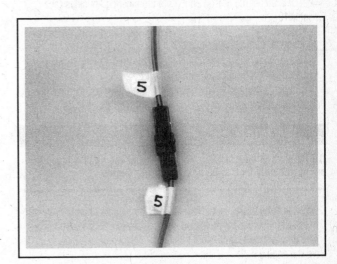

5.6 Label each wire before unplugging the connector

9   Remove the drivebelts (see Chapter 1).

Disconnect the fuel lines running from the engine to the chassis and detach their clips (see Chapter 4). Plug or cap all open fittings/lines.

10 Disconnect the accelerator cable (and kickdown cable, if equipped) from the throttle cam.

11 Disconnect the cable bracket from the intake plenum (see Chapter 4).

12 On power-steering-equipped models, unbolt the power steering pump and bracket (see Chapter 10). Leave the lines/hoses attached and make sure the pump is kept in an upright position in the engine compartment (use wire or rope to restrain it out of the way).

13 On air-conditioned models, unbolt the compressor (see Chapter 3). On automatic transaxle models, remove the compressor from the engine compartment. On manual transaxle models, set the compressor aside without disconnecting the hoses.

14 On automatic transaxle models, remove the starter motor. On manual transaxle models, disconnect the starter motor wires (see Chapter 5).

15 On automatic transaxle models, remove the alternator (see Chapter 5).

16 Securely block the rear wheels so the vehicle can't roll. Jack up the front and position it securely on jackstands. DO NOT get under a vehicle that's supported only by a jack!

17 Detach the exhaust system from the engine (see Chapter 4).

18 Remove the upper and lower splash shields from the passenger's side of the vehicle.

Manual transaxle models

19 Detach the clutch release (slave) cylinder line bracket from the transaxle and place the release cylinder aside without disconnecting the line (see Chapter 8).

20 Disconnect the extension bar, shift control rod and speedometer cable from the transaxle (see Chapter 7A).

21 Remove the stabilizer bar (see Chapter 10).

22 Disconnect the tie-rod ends from the steering knuckles (see Chapter 10).

23 Remove the inner ends of the driveaxles from the transaxle (see Chapter 8).

24 Remove the transaxle mounting nuts from the crossmember.

25 Remove the jackstands and lower the vehicle.

26 Attach a lifting sling to the engine lifting brackets. Connect a hoist to the sling.

27 Raise the hoist just until it supports the engine, then remove the crankshaft pulley (see *Timing belt replacement* in Chapter 2A).

28 Remove the engine mount though-bolt, then detach the mount from the engine.

29 Remove the transaxle upper mount and support bracket.

30 Recheck to be sure nothing is still connecting the engine to the transmission or vehicle. Disconnect anything still remaining.

31 Carefully lift the engine and transaxle out of the engine compartment. They should come out easily. Stop lifting if the engine seems to be caught. Find and fix the problem before you continue lifting.

32 Once the engine is out, remove the intake support bracket from the plenum.

33 Remove the starter motor (see Chapter 5).

34 Remove the transaxle front mount and lower the engine/transaxle assembly to the floor.

35 Unbolt the engine (including the oil pan) from the transaxle, then take the transaxle off the engine.

36 Remove the clutch from the flywheel (see Chapter 8).

37 Remove the flywheel (see Chapter 2A).

38 Raise the engine and bolt it to an engine stand.

➡Note: Engine stands are available inexpensively from most automotive equipment suppliers.

Automatic transaxle models

39 Remove the driveaxle bearing support (see Chapter 8).

40 Remove the inspection plate and remove the torque converter-to-driveplate fasteners (see Chapter 7).

41 Remove the crankshaft pulley (see *Timing belt replacement* in Chapter 2A).

42 Remove all of the transaxle-to-engine bolts that can be reached from beneath the vehicle.

43 Remove the vacuum chamber canister, fuel pressure regulator and bracket (see Chapter 4).

44 Remove the shutter valve actuator and bracket.

45 Attach a lifting sling to the engine lifting brackets. Connect a hoist to the sling.

46 Raise the hoist just enough to support the engine.

47 Remove the remaining bolts that secure the transaxle to the engine, including the oil pan-to-transaxle bolts.

48 Remove the crankshaft pulley and engine mount (see *Timing belt replacement* in Chapter 2A).

49 Ease the engine away from the transaxle, then lift it out of the engine compartment. It should come out easily. Stop lifting if the engine seems to be caught. Find and fix the problem before you continue lifting.

50 Remove the driveplate (see *Flywheel driveplate - removal and installation* in Chapter 2A).

51 Bolt the engine to an engine stand.

➡Note: Engine stands are available inexpensively from most automotive equipment suppliers.

1.9L engine models

➡Note: If the vehicle has a manual transaxle, the engine and transaxle are removed as a unit. If it has an automatic transaxle, the engine is removed separately from the transaxle.

52 Have the air conditioning system discharged by a dealer or other qualified shop. DO NOT discharge the system yourself!

53 Refer to Chapter 4 and relieve the fuel system pressure, then disconnect the negative cable from the battery. On manual transaxle 1.9L models, remove the battery, battery tray and battery duct (see Chapter 5).

54 Cover the fenders and cowl and remove the hood (see Chapter 11). Special pads are available to protect the fenders, but an old bedspread or blanket will also work.

55 Remove the air cleaner assembly (see Chapter 4).

56 Drain the cooling system and engine oil (see Chapter 1).

57 Label the vacuum lines, emissions system hoses, wiring connectors, ground straps and fuel lines, to ensure correct reinstallation, then detach them. Pieces of masking tape with numbers or letters written on them work well (see illustration 5.6). If there's any possibility of confusion, make a sketch of the engine compartment and clearly label the lines, hoses and wires. Remove any retainers or brackets that will interfere with engine removal.

58 Remove the idle air bypass valve (see Chapter 4).

59 Label and detach all coolant hoses from the engine. Disconnect the heater hoses at the firewall.

60 Remove the cooling fan, shroud and radiator (see Chapter 3).

61 Remove the drivebelt (see Chapter 1). On automatic transaxle models, remove the drivebelt tensioner and idler pulley.

❋❋ WARNING:

Gasoline is extremely flammable, so extra precautions must be taken when working on any part of the fuel system. DO NOT smoke or allow open flames or bare light bulbs near the vehicle. Also, don't work in a garage if a natural gas appliance with a pilot light is present.

Disconnect the fuel lines running from the engine to the chassis and detach their clips (see Chapter 4). Plug or cap all open fittings/lines.

62 Disconnect the accelerator cable (and the cruise control and kickdown cables, if equipped) from the throttle lever.

63 Disconnect the cable bracket from the intake plenum (see Chapter 4).

64 On power steering equipped vehicles, disconnect the return hose from the pump reservoir and the pressure hose from the pump (see Chapter 10). Detach the bracket that secures the power steering and air conditioning lines to the alternator bracket, then position the power steering hoses out of the way. Cap or plug the hoses and fittings to keep out contamination.

65 On air-conditioned models, disconnect the suction line at the accumulator/drier. Unbolt and remove the compressor (see Chapter 3). Set the compressor aside without disconnecting the hoses and tie it out of the way.

66 Remove the splash shield from the driver's side and both splash shields from the passenger side of the vehicle.

67 Remove the catalytic converter (see Chapter 4).

68 Remove the starter motor (see Chapter 5).

69 If you're working on a vehicle with an automatic transaxle, detach the kickdown cable bracket (if equipped) from the back side of the engine block and place it out of the way.

70 Remove the crankshaft damper (see *Timing belt - removal, inspection and installation* in Chapter 2A).

71 If you're working on a vehicle with a manual transaxle, loosen the front wheel lug nuts.

72 Securely block the rear wheels so the vehicle can't roll. Jack up the front and position it securely on jackstands. DO NOT get under a vehicle that's supported only by a jack!

Manual transaxle models

73 Remove the shift control rod and extension bar (see Chapter 7A).

74 Remove the driveaxles (see Chapter 8).

❋❋ CAUTION:

Be sure to place plugs in the differential side gears or they may fall out of position.

75 Disconnect the speedometer cable or the speed sensor electrical connector.

76 Detach the slave cylinder and its hydraulic line from the transaxle and set them aside without disconnecting the line.

77 Remove the transaxle mounting bolts.

78 Install the front wheels, lower the vehicle and tighten the wheel lug nuts.

79 Attach a lifting sling to the engine lifting brackets. Connect a hoist to the sling.

❋❋ WARNING:

DO NOT place any part of your body under the engine when it's supported only by a hoist or other lifting device.

80 Lift the hoist just enough to support the engine, then remove the right-hand engine mount and damper.

81 Remove the transaxle upper mount.

82 Recheck to be sure nothing is still connecting the engine to the transaxle or vehicle. Disconnect anything still remaining.

83 Carefully lift the engine and transaxle out of the engine compartment. They should come out easily. Stop lifting if the engine seems to be caught. Find and fix the problem before you continue lifting.

84 Lower the engine/transaxle assembly to the floor. Unbolt the engine (including the oil pan) from the transaxle, then take the transaxle off the engine.

85 Remove the clutch from the flywheel (see Chapter 8).

86 Remove the flywheel (see *Flywheel/driveplate* in Chapter 2A).

87 Raise the engine and bolt it to an engine stand.

➡**Note: Engine stands are available inexpensively from most automotive equipment suppliers.**

Automatic transaxle models

88 Remove the driveplate inspection shield.

89 Remove the torque converter-to-driveplate nuts.

90 Remove the engine-to-transaxle bolts that can be reached from below.

91 Remove the jackstands and lower the vehicle.

92 Remove the transaxle-to-engine bolts that are accessible from above. Remove the engine mounts.

93 Recheck to be sure nothing is still connecting the engine to the transmission or vehicle. Disconnect anything still remaining.

94 Ease the engine away from the transaxle and carefully lift it out of the engine compartment. It should come out easily. Stop lifting if the engine seems to be caught. Find and fix the problem before you continue lifting. Remove the driveplate and bolt the engine to an engine stand.

➡**Note: Engine stands are commonly available from automotive equipment suppliers.**

2.0L engine models

➡**Note: The engine and transaxle are removed as a unit.**

95 Have the air conditioning system discharged by a dealer or other qualified shop. DO NOT discharge the system yourself!

96 Refer to Chapter 4 and relieve the fuel system pressure, then

disconnect the negative cable from the battery. Remove the battery and battery tray.

97 Cover the fenders and cowl and remove the hood (see Chapter 11). Special pads are available to protect the fenders, but an old bedspread or blanket will also work.

98 Remove the air cleaner outlet duct (see Chapter 4).

99 Drain the cooling system and engine oil (see Chapter 1).

100 Label the vacuum lines, emissions system hoses, wiring connectors, ground straps and fuel lines, to ensure correct reinstallation, then detach them. Pieces of masking tape with numbers or letters written on them work well (see illustration 5.6). If there's any possibility of confusion, make a sketch of the engine compartment and clearly label the lines, hoses and wires. Remove any retainers or brackets that will interfere with engine removal.

101 Remove the Constant Control Relay Module (CCRM).

102 Label and detach all coolant hoses from the engine. Disconnect the heater hoses at the firewall.

103 Remove the cooling fan, shroud and radiator (see Chapter 3). On 2.0L Zetec manual transaxle models, remove the coolant reservoir.

104 Remove the drivebelt (see Chapter 1). On automatic transaxle models, remove the drivebelt tensioner and idler pulley.

✳✳ WARNING:

Gasoline is extremely flammable, so extra precautions must be taken when working on any part of the fuel system. DO NOT smoke or allow open flames or bare light bulbs near the vehicle. Also, don't work in a garage if a natural gas appliance with a pilot light is present.

Disconnect the fuel lines running from the engine to the chassis and detach their clips (see Chapter 4). Plug or cap all open fittings/lines.

105 Disconnect the accelerator cable (and the cruise control and kickdown cables, if equipped) from the throttle lever (see Chapter 4). On manual transaxle 2.0L Zetec engine models, remove the throttle return spring from the throttle cable. On all 2.0L Zetec engine models, remove the cable brackets from the engine.

106 On power steering equipped vehicles, disconnect the return and pressure hoses from the pump (see Chapter 10).

107 Detach the bracket that secures the power steering pressure hose to the alternator bracket, then position the power steering hoses out of the way. Cap or plug the hoses and fittings to keep out contamination.

108 Remove the air conditioning hose bracket bolt, then disconnect the suction line at the accumulator/drier and at the condenser. Remove the compressor from the vehicle (see Chapter 3).

109 Remove the splash shield from the driver's side and remove both splash shields from the passenger side of the vehicle.

110 Remove the catalytic converter (see Chapter 4).

111 Remove the starter motor (see Chapter 5).

112 Loosen the front wheel lug nuts. Securely block the rear wheels so the vehicle can't roll. Jack up the front and position it securely on jackstands. DO NOT get under a vehicle that's supported only by a jack!

Manual transaxle models

113 Remove the shift control rod and extension bar (see Chapter 7A).

114 Detach the slave cylinder and its hydraulic line from the transaxle and set them aside without disconnecting the line.

Automatic transaxle models

115 Disconnect the transmission shift cable and fluid cooler lines.

All 2.0L engine models

116 Remove the driveaxles (see Chapter 8).

✳✳ CAUTION:

Be sure to place plugs in the differential side gears or they may fall out of position.

117 Install the front wheels, lower the vehicle and tighten the wheel lug nuts.

118 Disconnect the speed sensor electrical connector.

119 Attach a lifting sling to the engine lifting brackets. Connect a hoist to the sling.

✳✳ WARNING:

DO NOT place any part of your body under the engine when it's supported only by a hoist or other lifting device.

120 Lift the hoist just enough to support the engine, then remove the right-hand engine mount and damper.

121 Remove the transaxle mounts.

122 Recheck to be sure nothing is still connecting the engine to the transaxle or vehicle. Disconnect anything still remaining.

123 Carefully lift the engine and transaxle out of the engine compartment. They should come out easily. Stop lifting if the engine seems to be caught. Find and fix the problem before you continue lifting.

124 On automatic transaxle models, remove the driveplate inspection shield and torque converter-to-driveplate nuts.

125 Lower the engine/transaxle assembly to the floor. Unbolt the engine from the transaxle, then take the transaxle off the engine.

126 On manual transaxle models, remove the clutch from the flywheel (see Chapter 8).

127 Remove the flywheel or driveplate (see *Flywheel/driveplate* in Chapter 2A).

128 Raise the engine and bolt it to an engine stand.

➡Note: Engine stands are available inexpensively from most automotive equipment suppliers.

INSTALLATION (ALL MODELS)

129 Check the engine and transmission mounts. If they're worn or damaged, replace them.

130 If you're working on a manual transmission equipped vehicle, install the clutch and pressure plate (see Chapter 8). Now is a good time to install a new clutch. Reinstall the transaxle on the engine (see Chapter 7).

131 Carefully lower the engine into the engine compartment - make sure the engine mounts line up.

132 If you're working on an automatic transaxle equipped vehicle, guide the torque converter into the crankshaft following the procedure outlined in Chapter 7. Install the transmission-to-engine bolts and tighten them securely.

✳✳ CAUTION:

DO NOT use the bolts to force the transmission and engine together!

133 Reinstall the remaining components in the reverse order of removal.

134 Add coolant, oil, power steering and transmission fluid as needed.

135 Run the engine and check for leaks and proper operation of all accessories, then install the hood and test drive the vehicle.

136 Have the air conditioning system recharged (if it was discharged) and leak tested.

6 Engine rebuilding alternatives

The do-it-yourselfer is faced with a number of options when performing an engine overhaul. The decision to replace the engine block, piston/connecting rod assemblies and crankshaft depends on a number of factors, with the number one consideration being the condition of the block. Other considerations are cost, access to machine shop facilities, parts availability, time required to complete the project and the extent of prior mechanical experience on the part of the do-it-yourselfer.

Some of the rebuilding alternatives include:

Individual parts - If the inspection procedures reveal that the engine block and most engine components are in reusable condition, purchasing individual parts may be the most economical alternative. The block, crankshaft and piston/connecting rod assemblies should all be inspected carefully. Even if the block shows little wear, the cylinder bores should be surface honed.

Short block - A short block consists of an engine block with a crankshaft and piston/connecting rod assemblies already installed. All new bearings are incorporated and all clearances will be correct. The existing camshaft, valve train components, cylinder head and external parts can be bolted to the short block with little or no machine shop work necessary.

Long block - A long block consists of a short block plus an oil pump, oil pan, cylinder head, valve cover, camshaft and valve train components, timing sprockets and chain or gears and timing cover. All components are installed with new bearings, seals and gaskets incorporated throughout. The installation of manifolds and external parts is all that's necessary.

Give careful thought to which alternative is best for you and discuss the situation with local automotive machine shops, auto parts dealers and experienced rebuilders before ordering or purchasing replacement parts.

7 Engine overhaul - disassembly sequence

1 It's much easier to disassemble and work on the engine if it's mounted on a portable engine stand. A stand can often be rented quite cheaply from an equipment rental yard. Before the engine is mounted on a stand, the flywheel/driveplate should be removed from the engine.

2 If a stand isn't available, it's possible to disassemble the engine with it blocked up on the floor. Be extra careful not to tip or drop the engine when working without a stand.

3 If you're going to obtain a rebuilt engine, all external components must come off first, to be transferred to the replacement engine, just as they will if you're doing a complete engine overhaul yourself. These include:

Alternator and brackets
Emissions control components
Distributor (1.8L engine), coil pack (1.9L and 2.0L engines)
Spark plug wires and spark plugs
Thermostat and housing cover
Water pump
EFI components
Intake/exhaust manifolds
Oil filter
Engine mounts
Clutch and flywheel/driveplate
Engine rear plate

➡**Note: When removing the external components from the engine, pay close attention to details that may be helpful or important during installation. Note the installed position of gaskets, seals, spacers, pins, brackets, washers, bolts and other small items.**

4 If you're obtaining a short block, which consists of the engine block, crankshaft, pistons and connecting rods all assembled, then the cylinder head, oil pan and oil pump will have to be removed as well. See *Engine rebuilding alternatives* for additional information regarding the different possibilities to be considered.

5 If you're planning a complete overhaul, the engine must be disassembled and the internal components removed in the following order:

Timing belt cover(s)
Timing belt
Valve cover
Intake and exhaust manifolds
Rocker arms (1.9L and 2.0L SPI engines) and camshaft(s)
Valve lifters
Cylinder head
Lower cylinder block (2.0L Zetec engines)
Oil pan
Oil pump
Piston/connecting rod assemblies
Crankshaft and main bearings

6 Before beginning the disassembly and overhaul procedures, make sure the following items are available. Also, refer to *Engine overhaul - reassembly sequence* for a list of tools and materials needed for engine reassembly.

Common hand tools
Small cardboard boxes or plastic bags for storing parts
Gasket scraper
Ridge reamer
Vibration damper puller
Micrometers
Telescoping gauges
Dial indicator set
Valve spring compressor
Cylinder surfacing hone
Piston ring groove cleaning tool
Electric drill motor
Tap and die set
Wire brushes
Oil gallery brushes
Cleaning solvent

8 Cylinder head - disassembly

▸ **Refer to illustrations 8.2, 8.3 and 8.4**

➡**Note: New and rebuilt cylinder heads are commonly available for most engines at dealerships and auto parts stores. Due to the fact that some specialized tools are necessary for the disassembly and inspection procedures, and replacement parts may not be readily available, it may be more practical and economical for the home mechanic to purchase replacement head rather than taking the time to disassemble, inspect and recondition the original(s).**

1 Cylinder head disassembly involves removal of the intake and exhaust valves and related components. If they're still in place, remove the rocker arms, lifters and fulcrums (1.9L and 2.0L SPI engines) from the cylinder head. Label the parts or store them separately so they can be reinstalled in their original locations.

2 Before the valves are removed, arrange to label and store them, along with their related components, so they can be kept separate and reinstalled in the same valve guides they are removed from (see illustration).

3 Compress the springs on the first valve with a spring compressor and remove the keepers (see illustration). Refer to *Valve springs* in Chapter 2A for details of valve spring compressor use. Carefully release the valve spring compressor and remove the retainer, the spring and the spring seat (if used).

4 Pull the valve out of the head, then remove the oil seal from the guide. If the valve binds in the guide (won't pull through), push it back into the head and deburr the area around the keeper groove with a fine file or whetstone (see illustration).

5 Repeat the procedure for the remaining valves. Remember to keep all the parts for each valve together so they can be reinstalled in the same locations.

6 Once the valves and related components have been removed and stored in an organized manner, the head should be thoroughly cleaned and inspected. If a complete engine overhaul is being done, finish the engine disassembly procedures before beginning the cylinder head cleaning and inspection process.

8.2 A small plastic bag, with an appropriate label, can be used to store the valve train components so they can be kept together and reinstalled in the original position

8.3 Use a valve spring compressor to compress the spring, then remove the keepers from the valve stem

8.4 If the valve won't pull through the guide, deburr the edge of the stem end and the area around the top of the keeper groove with a file or whetstone

9 Cylinder head - cleaning and inspection

▸ **Refer to illustrations 9.12, 9.14, 9.15, 9.16, 9.17 and 9.18**

1 Thorough cleaning of the cylinder head and related valve train components, followed by a detailed inspection, will enable you to decide how much valve service work must be done during the engine overhaul.

➡**Note: If the engine was severely overheated, the cylinder head is probably warped (see Step 12).**

CLEANING

2 Scrape all traces of old gasket material and sealing compound off the head gasket, intake manifold and exhaust manifold sealing surfaces. Be very careful not to gouge the cylinder head. Special gasket removal solvents that soften gaskets and make removal much easier are available at auto parts stores.

3 Remove all built-up scale from the coolant passages.

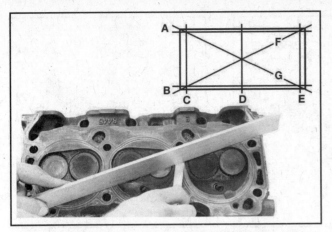

9.12 Check the cylinder head gasket surface for warpage by trying to slip a feeler gauge under the straightedge (see this Chapter's Specifications for the maximum warpage allowed and use a feeler gauge of that thickness)

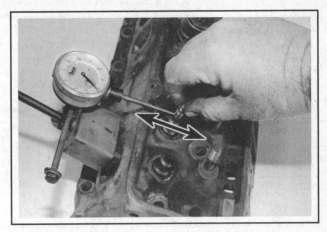

9.14 A dial indicator can be used to determine the valve stem-to-guide clearance (move the valve stem as indicated by the arrows)

4   Run a stiff wire brush through the various holes to remove deposits that may have formed in them.

5   Run an appropriate size tap into each of the threaded holes to remove corrosion and thread sealant that may be present. If compressed air is available, use it to clear the holes of debris produced by this operation.

✳✳ WARNING:

Wear eye protection when using compressed air!

6   Clean the rocker arm bolts (1.9L engines) with a wire brush.

7   Clean the cylinder head with solvent and dry it thoroughly. Compressed air will speed the drying process and ensure that all holes and recessed areas are clean.

→Note: Decarbonizing chemicals are available and may prove very useful when cleaning cylinder heads and valve train components. They are very caustic and should be used with caution. Be sure to follow the instructions on the container.

8   Clean the rocker arms and fulcrums (1.9L engines) with solvent and dry them thoroughly (don't mix them up during the cleaning process). Compressed air will speed the drying process and can be used to clean out the oil passages.

9   Clean all the valve springs, spring seats, keepers and retainers (or rotators) with solvent and dry them thoroughly. Do the components from one valve at a time to avoid mixing up the parts.

10   Scrape off any heavy deposits that may have formed on the valves, then use a motorized wire brush to remove deposits from the valve heads and stems. Again, make sure the valves don't get mixed up.

INSPECTION

→Note: Be sure to perform all of the following inspection procedures before concluding that machine shop work is required. Make a list of the items that need attention.

Cylinder head

11   Inspect the head very carefully for cracks, evidence of coolant leakage and other damage. If cracks are found, check with an automotive machine shop concerning repair. If repair isn't possible, a new

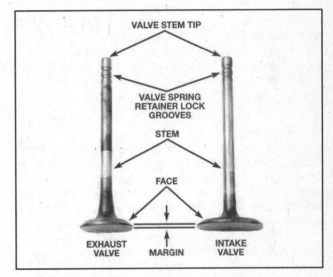

9.15 Check for valve wear at the points shown here

cylinder head should be obtained.

12   Using a straightedge and feeler gauge, check the head gasket mating surface for warpage (see illustration). If the warpage exceeds the limit listed in this Chapter's Specifications, it can be resurfaced at an automotive machine shop.

13   Examine the valve seats in each of the combustion chambers. If they're pitted, cracked or burned, the head will require valve service that's beyond the scope of the home mechanic.

14   Check the valve stem-to-guide clearance by measuring the lateral movement of the valve stem with a dial indicator attached securely to the head (see illustration). The valve must be in the guide and approximately 1/16-inch off the seat. The total valve stem movement indicated by the gauge needle must be divided by two to obtain the actual clearance. After this is done, if there's still some doubt regarding the condition of the valve guides they should be checked by an automotive machine shop (the cost should be minimal).

Valves

15   Carefully inspect each valve face for uneven wear, deformation, cracks, pits and burned areas (see illustration). Check the valve stem for

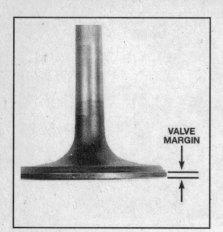

9.16 The margin width on each valve must be as specified (if no margin exists, the valve cannot be reused)

9.17 Measure the free length of each valve spring with a dial or vernier caliper

9.18 Check each valve spring for squareness

scuffing and galling and the neck for cracks. Rotate the valve and check for any obvious indication that it's bent. Look for pits and excessive wear on the end of the stem. The presence of any of these conditions indicates the need for valve service by an automotive machine shop.

16 Measure the margin width on each valve (see illustration). Any valve with a margin narrower than specified will have to be replaced with a new one.

Valve components

17 Check each valve spring for wear (on the ends) and pits. Measure the free length and compare it to the Specifications (see illustration). Any springs that are shorter than specified have sagged and should not be reused. The tension of all springs should be checked with a special fixture before deciding that they're suitable for use in a rebuilt engine (take the springs to an automotive machine shop for this check).

18 Stand each spring on a flat surface and check it for squareness (see illustration). If any of the springs are distorted or sagged, replace

all of them with new parts.

19 Check the spring retainers and keepers for obvious wear and cracks. Any questionable parts should be replaced with new ones, as extensive damage will occur if they fail during engine operation.

Rocker arm components (1.9L and 2.0L SPI engines only)

20 Check the rocker arm faces (the areas that contact the lifters and valve stems) for pits, wear, galling, score marks and rough spots. Check the rocker arm pivot contact areas and fulcrums as well. Look for cracks in each rocker arm and bolt.

21 Any damaged or excessively worn parts must be replaced with new ones.

22 If the inspection process indicates that the valve components are in generally poor condition and worn beyond the limits specified, which is usually the case in an engine that's being overhauled, reassemble the valves in the cylinder head and refer to Section 10 for valve servicing recommendations.

10 Valves - servicing

1 Because of the complex nature of the job and the special tools and equipment needed, servicing of the valves, the valve seats and the valve guides, commonly known as a valve job, should be done by a professional.

2 The home mechanic can remove and disassemble the head, do the initial cleaning and inspection, then reassemble and deliver it to a dealer service department or an automotive machine shop for the actual service work. Doing the inspection will enable you to see what condition the head and valvetrain components are in and will ensure that you know what work and new parts are required when dealing with an automotive machine shop.

3 The dealer service department, or automotive machine shop, will

remove the valves and springs, recondition or replace the valves and valve seats, recondition the valve guides, check and replace the valve springs, spring retainers and keepers (as necessary), replace the valve seals with new ones, reassemble the valve components and make sure the installed spring height is correct. The cylinder head gasket surfaces will also be resurfaced if they're warped.

4 After the valve job has been performed by a professional, the head will be in like-new condition. When the head is returned, be sure to clean it again before installation on the engine to remove any metal particles and abrasive grit that may still be present from the valve service or head resurfacing operations. Use compressed air, if available, to blow out all the oil holes and passages.

11 Cylinder head - reassembly

1   Regardless of whether or not the head was sent to an automotive repair shop for valve servicing, make sure it's clean before beginning reassembly.

2   If the head was sent out for valve servicing, the valves and related components will already be in place.

3   If you disassembled the head yourself, refer to *Valve springs* in Chapter 2A for instructions on installing the valves and related components.

4   If you're working on a 1.9L engine, apply moly-base grease to the rocker arm faces and the fulcrums, then install the rocker arms and pivots on the cylinder head studs.

12 Pistons/connecting rods - removal

▶ **Refer to illustrations 12.2, 12.4, 12.5 and 12.7**

➡**Note: Prior to removing the piston/connecting rod assemblies, remove the cylinder head, the oil pan and the oil pump by referring to the appropriate Sections in Chapter 2A.**

1   If you're working on a 2.0L Zetec engine, unbolt the lower cylinder block from the bottom of the cylinder block. Tap carefully around the periphery of the lower cylinder block to break the seal, then remove it from the cylinder block.

2   Use your fingernail to feel if a ridge has formed at the upper limit of ring travel (about 1/4-inch down from the top of each cylinder). If carbon deposits or cylinder wear have produced ridges, they must be completely removed with a special tool (see illustration). Follow the manufacturer's instructions provided with the tool. Failure to remove the ridges before attempting to remove the piston/connecting rod assemblies may result in piston breakage.

3   After the cylinder ridges have been removed, turn the engine upside-down so the crankshaft is facing up.

4   Before the connecting rods are removed, check the endplay with feeler gauges. Slide them between the first connecting rod and the crankshaft throw until the play is removed (see illustration). The endplay is equal to the thickness of the feeler gauge(s). If the endplay exceeds the service limit, new connecting rods will be required. If new rods (or a new crankshaft) are installed, the endplay may fall under the specified minimum (if it does, the rods will have to be machined to restore it - consult an automotive machine shop for advice if necessary). Repeat the procedure for the remaining connecting rods.

5   Check the connecting rods and caps for identification marks. If they aren't plainly marked, use a small center-punch to make the appropriate number of indentations on each rod and cap (1, 2, 3, etc., depending on the engine type and cylinder they're associated with) (see illustration).

12.2 A ridge reamer is required to remove the ridge from the top of each cylinder - do this before removing the pistons!

12.4 Check the connecting rod side clearance with a feeler gauge as shown

12.5 Mark the rod bearing caps in order from the front of the engine to the rear (one mark for the front cap, two for the second one and so on)

6   Loosen each of the connecting rod cap nuts 1/2-turn at a time until they can be removed by hand. Remove the number one connecting rod cap and bearing insert. Don't drop the bearing insert out of the cap.

7   Slip a short length of plastic or rubber hose over each connecting rod cap bolt to protect the crankshaft journal and cylinder wall as the piston is removed (see illustration).

8   Remove the bearing insert and push the connecting rod/piston assembly out through the top of the engine. Use a wooden hammer handle to push on the upper bearing surface in the connecting rod. If resistance is felt, double-check to make sure that all of the ridge was removed from the cylinder.

9   Repeat the procedure for the remaining cylinders.

10 After removal, reassemble the connecting rod caps and bearing inserts in their respective connecting rods and install the cap nuts finger tight. Leaving the old bearing inserts in place until reassembly will help prevent the connecting rod bearing surfaces from being accidentally nicked or gouged.

11 Don't separate the pistons from the connecting rods (see Section 17 for additional information).

12.7 To prevent damage to the crankshaft journals and cylinder walls, slip sections of rubber or plastic hose over the rod bolts before removing the pistons

13 Crankshaft - removal

▸ Refer to illustrations 13.1, 13.3 and 13.4

➡Note: The crankshaft can be removed only after the engine has been removed from the vehicle. It's assumed that the flywheel or driveplate, vibration damper, timing belt, oil pan, oil pump and piston/connecting rod assemblies have already been removed. The rear main oil seal housing must be unbolted and separated from the block before proceeding with crankshaft removal. If you're working on a 2.0L Zetec engine, the lower cylinder block must be unbolted from the cylinder block.

1   Before the crankshaft is removed, check the endplay. Mount a dial indicator with the stem in line with the crankshaft and just touching one of the crank throws (see illustration).

2   Push the crankshaft all the way to the rear and zero the dial indicator. Next, pry the crankshaft to the front as far as possible and check the reading on the dial indicator. The distance that it moves is the endplay. If it's greater than the limit listed in this Chapter's Specifications, check the crankshaft thrust surfaces for wear. If no wear is evident, new main bearings should correct the endplay.

3   If a dial indicator isn't available, feeler gauges can be used. Gently pry or push the crankshaft all the way to the front of the engine. Slip feeler gauges between the crankshaft and the front face of the thrust main bearing to determine the clearance (see illustration).

13.1 Checking crankshaft endplay with a dial indicator

13.3 Checking the crankshaft endplay with a feeler gauge

4   Check the main bearing caps to see if they're marked to indicate their locations (see illustration). They should be numbered consecutively from the front of the engine to the rear. If they aren't, mark them with number stamping dies or a center-punch. Main bearing caps generally have a cast-in arrow, which points to the front of the engine. Loosen the main bearing cap bolts 1/4-turn at a time each, until they can be removed by hand. Note if any stud bolts are used and make sure they're returned to their original locations when the crankshaft is reinstalled.

5   Gently tap the caps with a soft-face hammer, then separate them from the engine block. If necessary, use the bolts as levers to remove the caps. Try not to drop the bearing inserts if they come out with the caps.

6   Carefully lift the crankshaft out of the engine. It may be a good idea to have an assistant available, since the crankshaft is quite heavy. With the bearing inserts in place in the engine block and main bearing caps, return the caps to their respective locations on the engine block and tighten the bolts finger tight.

13.4 The main bearing caps are marked with arrows that point to the timing belt end of the engine and numbers that indicate position (counting from the timing belt end of the engine)

14   Engine block - cleaning

▶ **Refer to illustrations 14.2a, 14.2b, 14.9 and 14.11**

1   On 1.8L engines, remove the oil jet from the block (see illustration 1.1c).

✳✳ CAUTION:

The core plugs (also known as freeze plugs or soft plugs) may be difficult or impossible to retrieve if they're driven into the block coolant passages.

2   Remove the core plugs from the engine block. To do this, knock one side of each plug into the block with a hammer and punch, then grasp it with large pliers and pull it out (see illustrations).

3   Using a gasket scraper, remove all traces of gasket material from the engine block. Be very careful not to nick or gouge the gasket sealing surfaces.

4   Remove the main bearing caps and separate the bearing inserts from the caps and the engine block. Tag the bearings, indicating which cylinder they were removed from and whether they were in the cap or the block, then set them aside.

5   Remove all of the threaded oil gallery plugs from the block. The plugs are usually very tight - they may have to be drilled out and the holes retapped. Use new plugs when the engine is reassembled.

6   If the engine is extremely dirty it should be taken to an automotive machine shop to be steam cleaned or hot tanked.

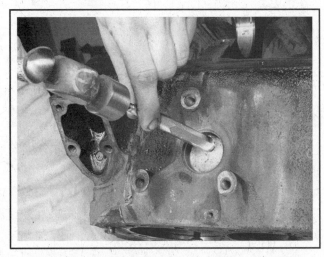

14.2a A hammer and large punch can be used to knock the core plugs sideways in their bores

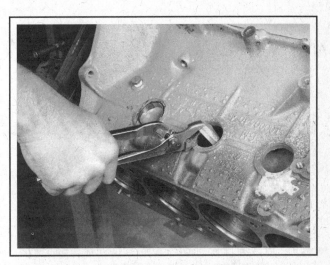

14.2b Pull the core plugs from the block with pliers

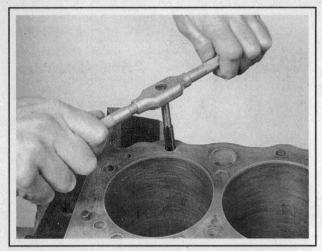

14.9 All bolt holes in the block - particularly the main bearing cap and head bolt holes - should be cleaned and restored with a tap (be sure to remove debris from the holes after this is done)

14.11 A large socket on an extension can be used to drive the new core plugs into the bores

7   After the block is returned, clean all oil holes and oil galleries one more time. Brushes specifically designed for this purpose are available at most auto parts stores. Flush the passages with warm water until the water runs clear, dry the block thoroughly and wipe all machined surfaces with a light, rust preventive oil. If you have access to compressed air, use it to speed the drying process and to blow out all the oil holes and galleries.

✳✳ WARNING:

Wear eye protection when using compressed air!

8   If the block isn't extremely dirty or sludged up, you can do an adequate cleaning job with hot soapy water and a stiff brush. Take plenty of time and do a thorough job. Regardless of the cleaning method used, be sure to clean all oil holes and galleries very thoroughly, dry the block completely and coat all machined surfaces with light oil.

9   The threaded holes in the block must be clean to ensure accurate torque readings during reassembly. Run the proper size tap into each of the holes to remove rust, corrosion, thread sealant or sludge and restore damaged threads (see illustration). If possible, use compressed air to clear the holes of debris produced by this operation. Now is a good time to clean the threads on the head bolts and the main bearing cap bolts as well.

10   Reinstall the main bearing caps and tighten the bolts finger tight.

11   After coating the sealing surfaces of the new core plugs with Permatex no. 2 sealant, install them in the engine block (see illustration). Make sure they're driven in straight and seated properly or leakage could result. Special tools are available for this purpose, but a large socket, with an outside diameter that will just slip into the core plug, a 1/2-inch drive extension and a hammer will work just as well.

12   Apply non-hardening sealant (such as Permatex no. 2 or Teflon pipe sealant) to the new oil gallery plugs and thread them into the holes in the block. Make sure they're tightened securely.

13   If the engine isn't going to be reassembled right away, cover it with a large plastic trash bag to keep it clean.

15 Engine block - inspection

▶ **Refer to illustrations 15.4a, 15.4b and 15.4c**

1   Before the block is inspected, it should be cleaned as described in Section 14.

2   Visually check the block for cracks, rust and corrosion. Look for stripped threads in the threaded holes. It's also a good idea to have the block checked for hidden cracks by an automotive machine shop that has the special equipment to do this type of work. If defects are found, have the block repaired, if possible, or replaced.

3   Check the cylinder bores for scuffing and scoring.

4   Measure the diameter of each cylinder at the top (just under the ridge area), center and bottom of the cylinder bore, parallel to the crankshaft axis (see illustrations).

5   Next, measure each cylinder's diameter at the same three locations across the crankshaft axis. Compare the results to this Chapter's Specifications.

6   If the required precision measuring tools aren't available, the piston-to-cylinder clearances can be obtained, though not quite as accurately, using feeler gauge stock. Feeler gauge stock comes in 12-inch lengths and various thicknesses and is generally available at auto parts stores.

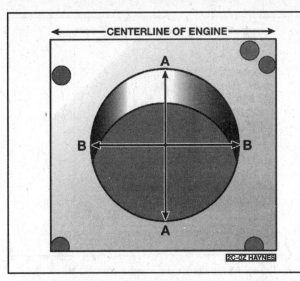

15.4a Measure the diameter of each cylinder at a right angle to the engine centerline (A), and parallel to engine centerline (B) - out-of-round is the difference between A and B; taper is the difference between A and B at the top of the cylinder and A and B at the bottom of the cylinder

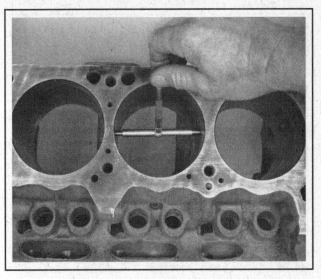

15.4b The ability to "feel" when the telescoping gauge is at the correct point will be developed over time, so work slowly and repeat the check until you're satisfied the bore measurement is accurate

7   To check the clearance, select a feeler gauge and slip it into the cylinder along with the matching piston. The piston must be positioned exactly as it normally would be. The feeler gauge must be between the piston and cylinder on one of the thrust faces (90-degrees to the piston pin bore).

8   The piston should slip through the cylinder (with the feeler gauge in place) with moderate pressure.

9   If it falls through or slides through easily, the clearance is excessive and a new piston will be required. If the piston binds at the lower end of the cylinder and is loose toward the top, the cylinder is tapered. If tight spots are encountered as the piston/feeler gauge is rotated in the cylinder, the cylinder is out-of-round.

10 Repeat the procedure for the remaining pistons and cylinders.

11 If the cylinder walls are badly scuffed or scored, or if they're out-of-round or tapered beyond the limits given in this Chapter's Specifications, have the engine block rebored and honed at an automotive machine shop. If a rebore is done, oversize pistons and rings will be required.

12 If the cylinders are in reasonably good condition and not worn to the outside of the limits, and if the piston-to-cylinder clearances can be maintained properly, then they don't have to be rebored. Honing is all that's necessary (see Section 16).

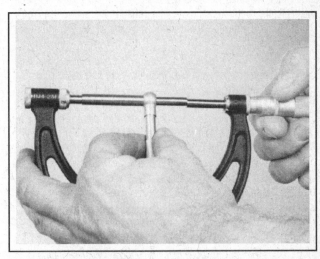

15.4c The gauge is then measured with a micrometer to determine the bore size

16 Cylinder honing

♦ Refer to illustrations 16.3a and 16.3b

1   Prior to engine reassembly, the cylinder bores must be honed so the new piston rings will seat correctly and provide the best possible combustion chamber seal.

➡Note: If you don't have the tools or don't want to tackle the honing operation, most automotive machine shops will do it for a reasonable fee.

2   Before honing the cylinders, install the main bearing caps and tighten the bolts to the torque listed in this Chapter's Specifications.

16.3a A "bottle brush" hone is the easiest type of hone to use

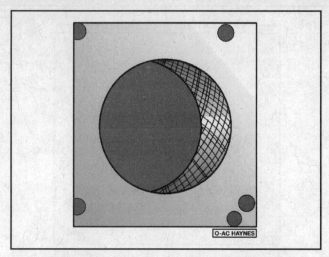

16.3b The cylinder hone should leave a smooth, crosshatch pattern with the lines intersecting at approximately a 60-degree angle

3   Two types of cylinder hones are commonly available - the flex hone or "bottle brush" type and the more traditional surfacing hone with spring-loaded stones. Both will do the job, but for the less experienced mechanic, the "bottle brush" hone will probably be easier to use. You'll also need some kerosene or honing oil, rags and an electric drill motor. Proceed as follows:

a) *Mount the hone in the drill motor, compress the stones and slip it into the first cylinder (see illustration). Be sure to wear safety goggles or a face shield!*

b) *Lubricate the cylinder with plenty of honing oil, turn on the drill and move the hone up-and-down in the cylinder at a pace that will produce a fine crosshatch pattern on the cylinder walls. Ideally, the crosshatch lines should intersect at approximately a 60-degree angle (see illustration). Be sure to use plenty of lubricant and don't take off any more material than is absolutely necessary to produce the desired finish.*

➡**Note: Piston ring manufacturers may specify a smaller crosshatch angle than the traditional 60-degrees - read and follow any instructions included with the new rings.**

c) *Don't withdraw the hone from the cylinder while it's running. Instead, shut off the drill and continue moving the hone up-and-down in the cylinder until it comes to a complete stop, then compress the stones and withdraw the hone. If you're using a "bottle brush" type hone, stop the drill motor, then turn the chuck in the normal direction of rotation while withdrawing the hone from the cylinder.*

d) *Wipe the oil out of the cylinder and repeat the procedure for the remaining cylinders.*

4   After the honing job is complete, chamfer the top edges of the cylinder bores with a small file so the rings won't catch when the pistons are installed. Be very careful not to nick the cylinder walls with the end of the file.

5   The entire engine block must be washed again very thoroughly with warm, soapy water to remove all traces of the abrasive grit produced during the honing operation.

➡**Note: The bores can be considered clean when a lint-free white cloth - dampened with clean engine oil- used to wipe them out doesn't pick up any more honing residue, which will show up as gray areas on the cloth. Be sure to run a brush through all oil holes and galleries and flush them with running water.**

6   After rinsing, dry the block and apply a coat of light rust preventive oil to all machined surfaces. Wrap the block in a plastic trash bag to keep it clean and set it aside until reassembly.

17 Pistons/connecting rods - inspection

▶ **Refer to illustrations 17.4a, 17.4b, 17.10 and 17.11**

1   Before the inspection process can be carried out, the piston/connecting rod assemblies must be cleaned and the original piston rings removed from the pistons.

➡**Note: Always use new piston rings when the engine is reassembled.**

2   Using a piston ring installation tool, carefully remove the rings from the pistons. Be careful not to nick or gouge the pistons in the process.

3   Scrape all traces of carbon from the top of the piston. A hand-held wire brush or a piece of fine emery cloth can be used once most of the deposits have been scraped away. Do not, under any circumstances, use a wire brush mounted in a drill motor to remove deposits from the pistons. The piston material is soft and may be eroded away by the wire brush.

4   Use a piston ring groove cleaning tool to remove carbon deposits from the ring grooves. If a tool isn't available, a piece broken off the old ring will do the job. Be very careful to remove only the carbon deposits - don't remove any metal and do not nick or scratch the sides of the ring grooves (see illustrations).

17.4a The piston ring grooves can be cleaned with a special tool, as shown here . . .

17.4b . . . or a section of a broken ring

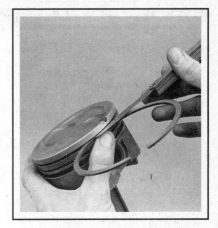

17.10 Check the ring side clearance with a feeler gauge at several points around the groove

5   Once the deposits have been removed, clean the piston/rod assemblies with solvent and dry them with compressed air (if available). Make sure the oil return holes in the back sides of the ring grooves are clear.

6   If the pistons and cylinder walls aren't damaged or worn excessively, and if the engine block is not rebored, new pistons won't be necessary. Normal piston wear appears as even vertical wear on the piston thrust surfaces and slight looseness of the top ring in its groove. New piston rings, however, should always be used when an engine is rebuilt.

7   Carefully inspect each piston for cracks around the skirt, at the pin bosses and at the ring lands.

8   Look for scoring and scuffing on the thrust faces of the skirt, holes in the piston crown and burned areas at the edge of the crown. If the skirt is scored or scuffed, the engine may have been suffering from overheating and/or abnormal combustion, which caused excessively high operating temperatures. The cooling and lubrication systems should be checked thoroughly. A hole in the piston crown is an indication that abnormal combustion (preignition) was occurring. Burned areas at the edge of the piston crown are usually evidence of spark knock (detonation). If any of the above problems exist, the causes must be corrected or the damage will occur again. The causes may include intake air leaks, incorrect fuel/air mixture, incorrect ignition timing and EGR system malfunctions.

9   Corrosion of the piston, in the form of small pits, indicates that coolant is leaking into the combustion chamber and/or the crankcase. Again, the cause must be corrected or the problem may persist in the rebuilt engine.

10 Measure the piston ring side clearance by laying a new piston ring in each ring groove and slipping a feeler gauge in beside it (see illustration). Check the clearance at three or four locations around each groove. Be sure to use the correct ring for each groove - they are different. If the side clearance is greater than the figure listed in this Chapter's Specifications, new pistons will have to be used.

11 Check the piston-to-bore clearance by measuring the bore (see Section 15) and the piston diameter. Make sure the pistons and bores are correctly matched. Measure the piston across the skirt, at a 90-degree angle to and in line with the piston pin (see illustration). Subtract the piston diameter from the bore diameter to obtain the clearance. If it's greater than specified, the block will have to be rebored and new pistons and rings installed.

12 Check the piston-to-rod clearance by twisting the piston and rod in opposite directions. Any noticeable play indicates excessive wear, which must be corrected. The piston/connecting rod assemblies should be taken to an automotive machine shop to have the pistons and rods resized and new pins installed.

13 If the pistons must be removed from the connecting rods for any reason, they should be taken to an automotive machine shop. While they are there have the connecting rods checked for bend and twist, since automotive machine shops have special equipment for this purpose.

➡Note: Unless new pistons and/or connecting rods must be installed, do not disassemble the pistons and connecting rods.

14 Check the connecting rods for cracks and other damage. Temporarily remove the rod caps, lift out the old bearing inserts, wipe the rod and cap bearing surfaces clean and inspect them for nicks, gouges and scratches. After checking the rods, replace the old bearings, slip the caps into place and tighten the nuts finger tight.

➡Note: If the engine is being rebuilt because of a connecting rod knock, be sure to install new rods.

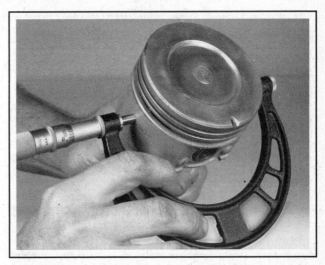

17.11 Measure the piston diameter at a 90-degree angle to the piston pin and in line with it

18 Crankshaft - inspection

▶ **Refer to illustrations 18.1, 18.2, 18.4, 18.6 and 18.8**

1 Remove all burrs from the crankshaft oil holes with a stone, file or scraper (see illustration).

2 Clean the crankshaft with solvent and dry it with compressed air (if available). Be sure to clean the oil holes with a stiff brush (see illustration) and flush them with solvent.

3 Check the main and connecting rod bearing journals for uneven wear, scoring, pits and cracks.

4 Rub a penny across each journal several times (see illustration). If a journal picks up copper from the penny, it's too rough and must be reground.

5 Check the rest of the crankshaft for cracks and other damage. It should be magnafluxed to reveal hidden cracks - an automotive machine shop will handle the procedure.

6 Using a micrometer, measure the diameter of the main and connecting rod journals and compare the results to this Chapter's Speci-fications (see illustration). By measuring the diameter at a number of points around each journal's circumference, you'll be able to determine whether or not the journal is out-of-round. Take the measurement at each end of the journal, near the crank throws, to determine if the journal is tapered.

7 If the crankshaft journals are damaged, tapered, out-of-round or worn beyond the limits given in the Specifications, have the crankshaft reground by an automotive machine shop. Be sure to use the correct size bearing inserts if the crankshaft is reconditioned.

8 Check the oil seal journals at each end of the crankshaft for wear and damage. If the seal has worn a groove in the journal, or if it's nicked or scratched (see illustration), the new seal may leak when the engine is reassembled. In some cases, an automotive machine shop may be able to repair the journal by pressing on a thin sleeve. If repair isn't feasible, a new or different crankshaft should be installed.

9 Refer to Section 19 and examine the main and rod bearing inserts.

18.1 The oil holes should be chamfered so sharp edges don't gouge or scratch the new bearings

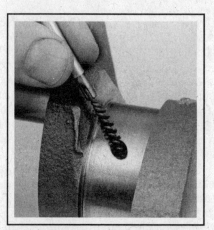

18.2 Use a wire or stiff plastic bristle brush to clean the oil passages in the crankshaft

18.4 Rubbing a penny lengthwise on each journal will reveal its condition - if copper rubs off and is embedded in the crankshaft, the journals should be reground

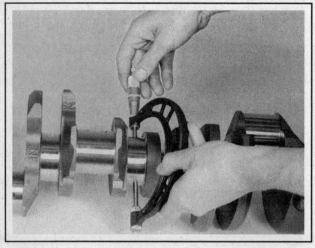

18.6 Measure the diameter of each crankshaft journal at several points to detect taper and out-of-round conditions

18.8 If the seals have worn grooves in the crankshaft journals, or if the seal contact surfaces are nicked or scratched, the new seals will leak

19 Main and connecting rod bearings - inspection

Refer to illustration 19.1

1   Even though the main and connecting rod bearings should be replaced with new ones during the engine overhaul, the old bearings should be retained for close examination, as they may reveal valuable information about the condition of the engine (see illustration).

2   Bearing failure occurs because of lack of lubrication, the presence of dirt or other foreign particles, overloading the engine and corrosion. Regardless of the cause of bearing failure, it must be corrected before the engine is reassembled to prevent it from happening again.

3   When examining the bearings, remove them from the engine block, the main bearing caps, the connecting rods and the rod caps and lay them out on a clean surface in the same general position as their location in the engine. This will enable you to match any bearing problems with the corresponding crankshaft journal.

4   Dirt and other foreign particles get into the engine in a variety of ways. It may be left in the engine during assembly, or it may pass through filters or the PCV system. It may get into the oil, and from there into the bearings. Metal chips from machining operations and normal engine wear are often present. Abrasives are sometimes left in engine components after reconditioning, especially when parts are not thoroughly cleaned using the proper cleaning methods. Whatever the source, these foreign objects often end up embedded in the soft bearing material and are easily recognized. Large particles will not embed in the bearing and will score or gouge the bearing and journal. The best prevention for this cause of bearing failure is to clean all parts thoroughly and keep everything spotlessly clean during engine assembly. Frequent and regular engine oil and filter changes are also recommended.

5   Lack of lubrication (or lubrication breakdown) has a number of interrelated causes. Excessive heat (which thins the oil), overloading (which squeezes the oil from the bearing face) and oil leakage or throw off (from excessive bearing clearances, worn oil pump or high engine speeds) all contribute to lubrication breakdown. Blocked oil passages, which usually are the result of misaligned oil holes in a bearing shell, will also oil starve a bearing and destroy it. When lack of lubrication is the cause of bearing failure, the bearing material is wiped or extruded from the steel backing of the bearing. Temperatures may increase to the point where the steel backing turns blue from overheating.

6   Driving habits can have a definite effect on bearing life. Full throttle, low speed operation (lugging the engine) puts very high loads on bearings, which tends to squeeze out the oil film. These loads cause the bearings to flex, which produces fine cracks in the bearing face (fatigue failure). Eventually the bearing material will loosen in pieces and tear away from the steel backing. Short trip driving leads to corrosion of bearings because insufficient engine heat is produced to drive off the condensed water and corrosive gases. These products collect in the engine oil, forming acid and sludge. As the oil is carried to the engine bearings, the acid attacks and corrodes the bearing material.

7   Incorrect bearing installation during engine assembly will lead to bearing failure as well. Tight fitting bearings leave insufficient bearing oil clearance and will result in oil starvation. Dirt or foreign particles trapped behind a bearing insert result in high spots on the bearing which lead to failure.

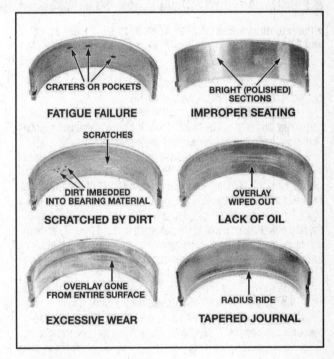

19.1 Typical bearing failures

20 Engine overhaul - reassembly sequence

1   Before beginning engine reassembly, make sure you have all the necessary new parts, gaskets and seals as well as the following items on hand:

Common hand tools
A 1/2-inch drive torque wrench
Piston ring installation tool
Piston ring compressor
Vibration damper installation tool

Short lengths of rubber or plastic hose to fit over connecting rod bolts
Plastigage
Feeler gauges
A fine-tooth file
New engine oil
Engine assembly lube or moly-base grease
Gasket sealant
Thread locking compound

2   In order to save time and avoid problems, engine reassembly must be done in the following general order:

Piston rings
Crankshaft and main bearings
Piston/connecting rod assemblies
Lower cylinder block (2.0L Zetec engines)
Oil pump
Oil pan
Cylinder head

Valve lifters
Rocker arms (1.9L engines) and camshaft(s)
Intake and exhaust manifolds
Valve cover
Timing belt
Timing belt cover(s)
Engine rear plate
Flywheel/driveplate

21 Piston rings - installation

▶ **Refer to illustrations 21.3, 21.4, 21.5, 21.9a, 21.9b, 21.12 and 21.15**

1   Before installing the new piston rings, the ring end gaps must be checked. It's assumed that the piston ring side clearance has been checked and verified correct (see Section 17).

2   Lay out the piston/connecting rod assemblies and the new ring sets so the ring sets will be matched with the same piston and cylinder during the end gap measurement and engine assembly.

3   Insert the top (number one) ring into the first cylinder and square it up with the cylinder walls by pushing it in with the top of the piston (see illustration). The ring should be near the bottom of the cylinder, at the lower limit of ring travel.

4   To measure the end gap, slip feeler gauges between the ends of the ring until a gauge equal to the gap width is found (see illustration). The feeler gauge should slide be-tween the ring ends with a slight amount of drag. Compare the measurement to this Chapter's Specifications. If the gap is larger or smaller than specified, double-check to make sure you have the correct rings before proceeding.

5   If the gap is too small, it must be enlarged or the ring ends may come in contact with each other during engine operation, which can cause serious damage to the engine. The end gap can be increased by filing the ring ends very carefully with a fine file. Mount the file in a vise

equipped with soft jaws, slip the ring over the file with the ends contacting the file face and slowly move the ring to remove material from the ends. When performing this operation, file only from the outside in (see illustration).

6   Excess end gap isn't critical unless it's greater than 0.040-inch. Again, double-check to make sure you have the correct rings for your engine.

7   Repeat the procedure for each ring installed in the first cylinder and for each ring in the remaining cylinders. Remember to keep rings, pistons and cylinders matched up.

8   Once the ring end gaps have been checked/corrected, the rings can be installed on the pistons.

9   The oil control ring (lowest one on the piston) is usually installed first. It's composed of three separate components. Slip the spacer/expander into the groove (see illustration). If an anti-rotation tang is used, make sure it's inserted into the drilled hole in the ring groove. Next, install the lower side rail. Don't use a piston ring installation tool on the oil ring side rails, as they may be damaged. Instead, place one end of the side rail into the groove between the spacer/expander and the ring land, hold it firmly in place and slide a finger around the piston while pushing the rail into the groove (see illustration). Next, install the upper side rail in the same manner.

10 After the three oil ring components have been installed, check

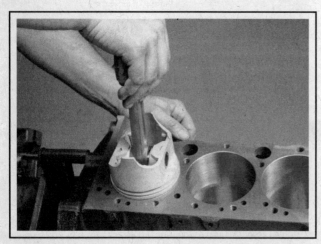

21.3 When checking piston ring end gap, the ring must be square in the cylinder bore (this is done by pushing the ring down with the top of a piston as shown)

21.4 With the ring square in the cylinder, measure the end gap with a feeler gauge

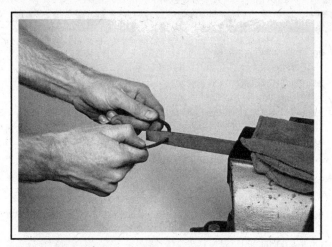

21.5 If the end gap is too small, clamp a file in a vise and file the ring ends (from the outside in only) to enlarge the gap slightly

21.9a Installing the spacer/expander in the oil control ring groove

to make sure that both the upper and lower side rails can be turned smoothly in the ring groove.

11 The number two (middle) ring is installed next. It's usually stamped with a mark which must face up, toward the top of the piston. If one side of the ring has a groove in it, install that side facing down.

➡️**Note: Always follow the instructions printed on the ring package or box - different manufacturers may require different approaches. Do not mix up the top and middle rings, as they have different cross sections.**

12 Use a piston ring installation tool and make sure the identification mark is facing the top of the piston, then slip the ring into the middle groove on the piston (see illustration). Don't expand the ring any more than necessary to slide it over the piston.

13 Install the number one (top) ring in the same manner. Make sure the mark is facing up. Be careful not to confuse the number one and number two rings.

14 Repeat the procedure for the remaining pistons and rings.

15 Position the ring gaps around the piston as shown (see illustration).

21.9b DO NOT use a piston ring installation tool when installing the oil ring side rails

21.12 Installing the compression rings with a ring expander - the mark (arrow) must face up

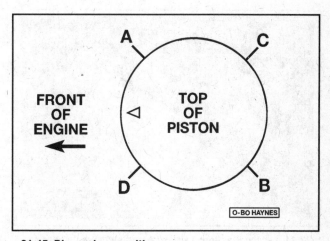

21.15 Ring end gap positions

A Oil ring rail gap - lower
B Oil ring rail gap - upper
C Top compression ring gap
D Second compression ring gap and oil ring spacer gap

22 Crankshaft - installation and main bearing oil clearance check

▶ **Refer to illustrations 22.11 and 22.15**

1   It's assumed at this point that the engine block and crankshaft have been cleaned, inspected and repaired or reconditioned.

2   Position the engine with the bottom facing up.

3   Remove the main bearing cap bolts and lift out the caps. Lay them out in the proper order to ensure correct installation.

4   If they're still in place, remove the original bearing inserts from the block and the main bearing caps. Wipe the bearing surfaces of the block and caps with a clean, lint-free cloth. They must be kept spotlessly clean.

MAIN BEARING OIL CLEARANCE CHECK

5   Clean the back sides of the new main bearing inserts and lay one in each main bearing saddle in the block. If one of the bearing inserts from each set has a large groove in it, make sure the grooved insert is installed in the block. Lay the other bearing from each set in the corresponding main bearing cap. Make sure the tab on the bearing insert fits into the recess in the block or cap.

✳✳ CAUTION:

The oil holes in the block must line up with the oil holes in the bearing insert. Do not hammer the bearing into place and don't nick or gouge the bearing faces. No lubrication should be used at this time.

6   On 1.8L engines, the thrust bearing inserts must be installed on the number four main bearing saddle with the oil grooves facing out (away from the block). On all other engines, the flanged thrust bearing must be installed in the center cap and saddle.

7   Clean the faces of the bearings in the block and the crankshaft main bearing journals with a clean, lint-free cloth.

8   Check or clean the oil holes in the crankshaft, as any dirt here can go only one way - straight through the new bearings.

9   Once you're certain the crankshaft is clean, carefully lay it in position in the main bearings.

10   Before the crankshaft can be permanently installed, the main bearing oil clearance must be checked.

11   Cut several pieces of the appropriate size Plastigage (they must be slightly shorter than the width of the main bearings) and place one piece on each crankshaft main bearing journal, parallel with the journal axis (see illustration).

12   Clean the faces of the bearings in the caps and install the caps in their respective positions (don't mix them up) with the arrows pointing toward the front of the engine. Don't disturb the Plastigage.

13   Starting with the center main and working out toward the ends, tighten the main bearing cap bolts, in three steps, to the torque listed in this Chapter's Specifications. Don't rotate the crankshaft at any time during this operation.

14   Remove the bolts and carefully lift off the main bearing caps. Keep them in order. Don't disturb the Plastigage or rotate the crankshaft. If any of the main bearing caps are difficult to remove, tap them gently from side-to-side with a soft-face hammer to loosen them.

15   Compare the width of the crushed Plastigage on each journal to the scale printed on the Plastigage envelope to obtain the main bearing oil clearance (see illustration). Check the Specifications to make sure it's correct.

16   If the clearance is not as specified, the bearing inserts may be the wrong size (which means different ones will be required). Before deciding that different inserts are needed, make sure that no dirt or oil was between the bearing inserts and the caps or block when the clearance was measured. If the Plastigage was wider at one end than the other, the journal may be tapered (refer to Section 18).

17   Carefully scrape all traces of the Plastigage material off the main bearing journals and/or the bearing faces. Use your fingernail or the edge of a credit card - don't nick or scratch the bearing faces.

FINAL CRANKSHAFT INSTALLATION

18   Carefully lift the crankshaft out of the engine.

19   Clean the bearing faces in the block, then apply a thin, uniform layer of moly-base grease or engine assembly lube to each of the bear-

22.11 Lay the Plastigage strips (arrow) on the main bearing journals, parallel to the crankshaft centerline

22.15 Compare the width of the crushed Plastigage to the scale on the envelope to determine the main bearing oil clearance (always take the measurement at the widest point of the Plastigage); be sure to use the correct scale - standard and metric ones are included

ing surfaces. Be sure to coat the thrust faces as well as the journal face of the thrust bearing.

20 Make sure the crankshaft journals are clean, then lay the crankshaft back in place in the block.

21 Clean the faces of the bearings in the caps, then apply lubricant to them.

22 Install the caps in their respective positions with the arrows pointing toward the front of the engine.

23 Install the bolts.

24 Tighten all except the thrust bearing cap bolts (number four bearing cap on 1.8L engines; center bearing cap on 1.9L and 2.0L engines) to the specified torque (work from the center out and approach the final torque in three steps).

25 Tighten the thrust bearing cap bolts to 10-to-12 ft-lbs.

26 Tap the ends of the crankshaft forward and backward with a lead

or brass hammer to line up the main bearing and crankshaft thrust surfaces.

27 Retighten all main bearing cap bolts to the specified torque, starting with the center main and working out toward the ends.

28 On manual transmission equipped models, install a new pilot bearing in the end of the crankshaft (see Chapter 8).

29 Rotate the crankshaft a number of times by hand to check for any obvious binding.

30 The final step is to check the crankshaft endplay with a feeler gauge or a dial indicator as described in Section 13. The endplay should be correct if the crankshaft thrust faces aren't worn or damaged and new bearings have been installed.

31 Refer to Part A and install a new rear main oil seal, then bolt the housing to the block.

23 Pistons/connecting rods - installation and rod bearing oil clearance check

▶ **Refer to illustrations 23.11, 23.13 and 23.17**

1 Before installing the piston/connecting rod assemblies, the cylinder walls must be perfectly clean, the top edge of each cylinder must be chamfered, and the crankshaft must be in place.

2 Remove the cap from the end of the number one connecting rod (refer to the marks made during removal). Remove the original bearing inserts and wipe the bearing surfaces of the connecting rod and cap with a clean, lint-free cloth. They must be kept spotlessly clean.

CONNECTING ROD BEARING OIL CLEARANCE CHECK

3 Clean the back side of the new upper bearing insert, then lay it in place in the connecting rod. Make sure the tab on the bearing fits into the recess in the rod. Don't hammer the bearing insert into place and be very careful not to nick or gouge the bearing face. Don't lubricate the bearing at this time.

4 Clean the back side of the other bearing insert and install it in the rod cap. Again, make sure the tab on the bearing fits into the recess in the cap, and don't apply any lubricant. It's critically important that the mating surfaces of the bearing and connecting rod are perfectly clean and oil free when they're assembled.

5 Make sure the piston ring gaps are as described in Section 21.

6 Slip a section of plastic or rubber hose over each connecting rod cap bolt.

7 Lubricate the piston and rings with clean engine oil and attach a piston ring compressor to the piston. Leave the skirt protruding about 1/4-inch to guide the piston into the cylinder. The rings must be compressed until they're flush with the piston.

8 Rotate the crankshaft until the number one connecting rod journal is at BDC (bottom dead center) and apply a coat of engine oil to the cylinder walls.

9 If you're working on a 1.8L engine, make sure the "F" mark on the connecting rod is facing the front (timing belt end) of the engine. If you're working on a 1.9L or 2.0L SPI engine, make sure the lug on the piston is toward the front (timing belt end) of the engine and the connecting rod squirt hole is on the right-hand (intake) side. If you're

working on a 2.0L Zetec engine, make sure the arrow mark on the piston is toward the front of the engine and the oil squirt groove in the connecting rod is toward the right-hand side. Gently insert the piston/connecting rod assembly into the number one cylinder bore and rest the bottom edge of the ring compressor on the engine block.

10 Tap the top edge of the ring compressor to make sure it's contacting the block around its entire circumference.

11 Gently tap on the top of the piston with the end of a wooden hammer handle (see illustration) while guiding the end of the connecting rod into place on the crankshaft journal. The piston rings may try to pop out of the ring compressor just before entering the cylinder bore, so keep some pressure on the ring compressor. Work slowly, and if any resistance is felt as the piston enters the cylinder, stop immediately. Find out what's hanging up and fix it before proceeding. Do not, for any reason, force the piston into the cylinder - you might break a ring and/or the piston.

23.11 Drive the piston gently into the cylinder bore with the end of a wooden or plastic hammer handle

23.13 Lay the Plastigage strips on each rod bearing journal, parallel to the crankshaft centerline

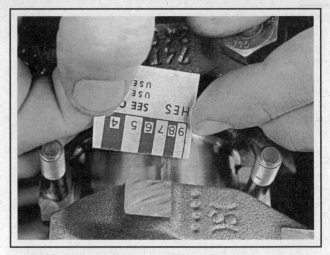

23.17 Measuring the width of the crushed Plastigage to determine the rod bearing oil clearance (be sure to use the correct scale - standard and metric ones are included)

12 Once the piston/connecting rod assembly is installed, the connecting rod bearing oil clearance must be checked before the rod cap is permanently bolted in place.

13 Cut a piece of the appropriate size Plastigage slightly shorter than the width of the connecting rod bearing and lay it in place on the number one connecting rod journal, parallel with the journal axis (see illustration).

14 Clean the connecting rod cap bearing face, remove the protective hoses from the connecting rod bolts and install the rod cap. Make sure the mating mark on the cap is on the same side as the mark on the connecting rod.

15 Install the nuts and tighten them to the torque listed in this Chapter's Specifications, working up to it in three steps.

➡**Note: Use a thin-wall socket to avoid erroneous torque readings that can result if the socket is wedged between the rod cap and nut. If the socket tends to wedge itself between the nut and the cap, lift up on it slightly until it no longer contacts the cap. Do not rotate the crankshaft at any time during this operation.**

16 Remove the nuts and detach the rod cap, being very careful not to disturb the Plastigage.

17 Compare the width of the crushed Plastigage to the scale printed on the Plastigage envelope to obtain the oil clearance (see illustration). Compare it to the Specifications to make sure the clearance is correct.

18 If the clearance is not as specified, the bearing inserts may be the wrong size (which means different ones will be required). Before deciding that different inserts are needed, make sure that no dirt or oil was between the bearing inserts and the connecting rod or cap when the clearance was measured. Also, recheck the journal diameter. If the Plastigage was wider at one end than the other, the journal may be tapered (refer to Section 18).

FINAL CONNECTING ROD INSTALLATION

19 Carefully scrape all traces of the Plastigage material off the rod journal and/or bearing face. Be very careful not to scratch the bearing - use your fingernail or the edge of a credit card.

20 Make sure the bearing faces are perfectly clean, then apply a uniform layer of clean moly-base grease or engine assembly lube to both of them. You'll have to push the piston into the cylinder to expose the face of the bearing insert in the connecting rod - be sure to slip the protective hoses over the rod bolts first.

21 Slide the connecting rod back into place on the journal, remove the protective hoses from the rod cap bolts, install the rod cap and tighten the nuts to the specified torque. Again, work up to the torque in three steps.

22 Repeat the entire procedure for the remaining pistons/connecting rods.

23 The important points to remember are:

a) *Keep the back sides of the bearing inserts and the insides of the connecting rods and caps perfectly clean when assembling them.*

b) *Make sure you have the correct piston/rod assembly for each cylinder.*

c) *If you're working on a 1.8L engine, make sure the "F" mark on the connecting rod is facing the front (timing belt end) of the engine. If you're working on a 1.9L or 2.0L SPI engine, make sure the lug on the piston is toward the front (timing belt end) of the engine and the connecting rod squirt hole is on the right-hand (exhaust) side. If you're working on a 2.0L Zetec engine, make sure the arrow mark on the piston is toward the front of the engine and the oil squirt groove in the connecting rod is toward the right-hand side.*

d) *Lubricate the cylinder walls with clean oil.*

e) *Lubricate the bearing faces when installing the rod caps after the oil clearance has been checked.*

24 After all the piston/connecting rod assemblies have been properly installed, rotate the crankshaft a number of times by hand to check for any obvious binding.

25 As a final step, the connecting rod endplay must be checked. Refer to Section 12 for this procedure.

26 Compare the measured endplay to the Specifications to make sure it's correct. If it was correct before disassembly and the original crankshaft and rods were reinstalled, it should still be right. If new rods or a new crankshaft were installed, the endplay may be inadequate. If so, the rods will have to be removed and taken to an automotive machine shop for resizing.

24 Initial start-up and break-in after overhaul

✳✳ WARNING:

Have a fire extinguisher handy when starting the engine for the first time.

1 Once the engine has been installed in the vehicle, double-check the engine oil and coolant levels.

2 With the spark plugs out of the engine and the ignition and fuel systems disabled (see Section 3), crank the engine until oil pressure registers on the gauge or the light goes out.

3 Install the spark plugs, hook up the plug wires and restore the ignition and fuel system functions (see Section 3).

4 Start the engine. It may take a few moments for the fuel system to build up pressure, but the engine should start without a great deal of effort.

➡ **Note: If backfiring occurs through the throttle body, recheck the valve timing and ignition timing.**

5 After the engine starts, it should be allowed to warm up to normal operating temperature. While the engine is warming up, make a thorough check for fuel, oil and coolant leaks.

6 Shut the engine off and recheck the engine oil and coolant levels.

7 Drive the vehicle to an area with minimum traffic, accelerate at full throttle from 30 to 50 mph, then allow the vehicle to slow to 30 mph with the throttle closed. Repeat the procedure 10 or 12 times. This will load the piston rings and cause them to seat properly against the cylinder walls. Check again for oil and coolant leaks.

8 Drive the vehicle gently for the first 500 miles (no sustained high speeds) and keep a constant check on the oil level. It is not unusual for an engine to use oil during the break-in period.

9 At approximately 500 to 600 miles, change the oil and filter.

10 For the next few hundred miles, drive the vehicle normally. Do not pamper it or abuse it.

11 After 2000 miles, change the oil and filter again and consider the engine broken in.

Specifications

1.8L engine

General

Oil pressure (at 1000 rpm)	28 to 43 psi
Compression pressure	164 to 200 psi
Maximum variation between cylinders	Lowest reading cylinder must be no less than 75-percent of highest reading cylinder

Cylinder head and valve train

Cylinder head warpage limit	0.004 inch
Valve stem-to-guide clearance	
Intake	0.0010 to 0.0024 inch
Exhaust	0.0012 to 0.0026 inch
Valve stem diameter	
Intake	0.2350 to 0.2356 inch
Exhaust	0.2348 to 0.2354 inch
Valve guide bore diameter (intake and exhaust)	0.2366 to 0.2374 inch
Valve seats	
Width (intake and exhaust)	0.031 to 0.055 inch
Angle	45 degrees
Valve springs	
Free length	1.821 inches
Out-of-square limit	0.064 inch

Specifications (continued)

Cylinder block

Head gasket surface warpage limit	0.006 inch overall
Cylinder bore	
Diameter	3.2679 to 3.2682 inches
Out-of-round limit	0.0007 inch
Taper service limit	0.0007 inch

Crankshaft

Main bearing journal diameter	1.9661 to 1.9668 inches
Connecting rod journal diameter	1.7692 to 1.7699 inches
Journal out-of-round limit	
(main or connecting rod bearing)	0.002 inch
Crankshaft runout limit	0.0016 inch
Crankshaft endplay	0.0031 to 0.0111 inch
Connecting rod bearing oil clearance	0.0011 to 0.0027 inch
Main bearing oil clearance	
Desired	0.0007 to 0.0014 inch
Maximum	0.004 inch

Connecting rods

Piston pin bore diameter	0.7875 to 0.7880 inch
Piston pin-to-bushing clearance	0.0004 to 0.0011 inch
Connecting rod-to-crankshaft side clearance (endplay)	0.014 inch maximum

Pistons and pins

Piston diameter	3.2659 to 3.2667 inches
Piston-to-bore clearance	0.0015 to 0.0020 inch
Piston pin bore diameter	0.7869 to 0.7874 inch
Piston pin diameter	0.7869 to 0.7871 inch
Piston-to-pin clearance	0.0002 to 0.0004 inch

Piston rings

Gap	
Compression (top and second)	0.006 to 0.012 inch
Oil ring (steel rail)	0.008 to 0.028 inch
Side clearance (compression rings only)	
Standard	0.0012 to 0.0028 inch
Maximum	0.006 inch

1.9L engine

General

Oil pressure (Hot 2000 rpm)	35 to 65 psi
Compression pressure	170 to 207 psi
Maximum variation between cylinders	Lowest reading cylinder must be no less than 75-percent of highest reading cylinder

1.9L engine (continued)

Cylinder head and valves

Valve guide bore diameter	
Intake	0.531 to 0.5324 inch
Exhaust	0.531 to 0.532 inch
Valve seats	
Width - intake and exhaust	0.069 to 0.091 inch
Angle	45 degrees
Runout (total indicator reading)	0.003 inch maximum
Bore diameter (insert counterbore diameter)	
Intake	
Minimum	1.572 inch
Maximum	1.573 inch
Exhaust	
Minimum	1.375 inch
Maximum	1.376 inch
Cylinder head gasket surface warpage limits	
Per inch	0.0016 inch
Per six inches	0.003 inch
Total	0.006 inch
Valve stem-to-guide clearance	
Intake	0.0008 to 0.0027 inch
Exhaust	0.0018 to 0.0037 inch
Valve head diameter	
1991	
Intake	1.65 to 1.66 inches
Exhaust	1.42 to 1.50 inches
1992 and later	
Intake	1.531 to 1.539 inch
Exhaust	1.335 to 1.343 inch
Valve face runout limit	0.002 inch
Valve face angle	45.6 degrees
Valve stem diameter	
Standard	
Intake	0.3159 to 0.3167 inch
Exhaust	0.3149 to 0.3156 inch
Oversize	
Intake	0.3474 to 0.3481 inch
Exhaust	0.347 to 0.3479 inch
Valve springs	
Compression pressure @ specified length	
Loaded	200 lbs @ 1.09 inches
Unloaded	95 lbs @ 1.461 inches
Valve springs	
Free length (approximate)	1.86 inches
Assembled height	1.48 to 1.44 inches
Out-of-square limit	0.060 inch

Specifications (continued)

Cylinder block

Head gasket surface warpage limits	
Per six inches	0.002 inch
Total	0.003 inch
Cylinder bore diameter	3.23 inches
Taper/out-of-round service limit	0.005 inch
Main bearing bore diameter	2.4523 to 2.4528 inches

Crankshaft

Main bearing journal diameter	2.2827 to 2.2835 inches
Connecting rod journal diameter	1.7279 to 1.7287 inches
Journal out-of-round limit	0.00032 inch
Journal taper limit	0.0003 inch per inch
Main journal runout limit	0.002 inch*
Thrust face runout limit	0.001 inch
Crankshaft endplay	0.004 to 0.008 inch

Connecting rod bearings

Oil clearance	
Desired	0.0008 to 0.0015 inch
Allowable	0.008 to 0.0026 inch
Bearing wall thickness (standard)	0.0581 to 0.0586 inch

Main bearings

Oil clearance	
Desired	0.0018 to 0.0026 inch
Allowable	0.018 to 0.0034 inch
Bearing wall thickness (standard)	0.0838 to 0.0833 inch

Connecting rods

Piston pin bore diameter	0.8106 to 0.8114 inch
Crankshaft bearing bore diameter	1.8460 to 1.8468 inches
Out-of-round limit, piston pin bore	0.0003 inch
Alignment (bore center-to-bore center, maximum allowable)	
Twist	0.002 inch
Bend	0.0015 inch
Side clearance (endplay)	
Standard	0.004 to 0.011 inch
Service limit	0.014 inch

Pistons, piston pins and piston rings

Piston diameter (standard)	
Coded red	3.224 to 3.225 inch
Coded blue	3.225 to 3.226 inch
0.004 inch oversize	3.226 to 3.227 inch

Pistons, piston pins and piston rings (continued)

Piston-to-bore clearance	
1991 and 1992	0.0016 to 0.0024 inch
1993 on	
Maximum allowable rebuild clearance	0.0012 to 0.0020 inch
Service limit	0.0012 to 0.0028 inch
Piston pin bore diameter	0.8123 to 0.8128 inch
Ring groove width	
Compression ring (top and second)	0.0602 to 0.061 inch
Oil ring	0.1578 to 0.1587 inch
Piston pin length	2.606 to 2.638 inches
Piston pin diameter	0.8119 to 0.8124 inch
Piston-to-pin clearance	0.0003 to 0.0005 inch
Piston pin-to-rod clearance	press fit
Piston ring width (compression rings only)	
Top	0.0578 to 0.0582 inch
Second	0.0574 to 0.0586 inch
Ring gap	
Compression (top and second)	0.010 to 0.020 inch
Oil ring (steel rail)	
1991 and 1992	0.016 to 0.055 inch
1993 on	0.016 to 0.066 inch
Piston ring side clearance (compression rings only)	
Standard	
Top ring	0.0015 to 0.0032 inch
Second ring	0.0015 to 0.0035 inch
Service limit (both rings)	0.006 inch

Runout of journals 2, 3 and 4 relative to journals 1 and 5.

2.0L SPI engine

General

Oil pressure (Hot 2000 rpm)	35 to 65 psi
Compression pressure	
Minimum	100 psi
Maximum variation between cylinders	Lowest reading cylinder must be no less than 75-percent of highest reading cylinder

Cylinder head and valve train

Cylinder head warpage limit	0.006 inch overall
Valve stem-to-guide clearance	
Intake	0.0008 to 0.0027 inch
Exhaust	0.0018 to 0.0037 inch
Valve stem diameter	
Intake	0.3159 to 0.3167 inch
Exhaust	0.3149 to 0.3156 inch
Valve guide bore diameter (intake and exhaust)	0.317 to 0.319 inch
Valve seats	
Width (intake and exhaust)	0.069 to 0.091 inch
Angle	45 degrees

Specifications (continued)

Cylinder head and valve train (continued)

Valve springs

Free length	1.86 inch
Out-of-square limit	Not specified

Cylinder block

Head gasket surface warpage limit	0.003 inch overall
Cylinder bore	
Diameter	3.34 inches
Out-of-round limit	0.0010 inch
Taper service limit	0.0005 inch

Crankshaft

Main bearing journal diameter	2.2827 to 2.2835 inches
Connecting rod journal diameter	
Through 2000, and 2002	1.8460 to 1.8500 inches
2001	1.7279 to 1.7287 inches
Journal out-of-round limit	
(main or connecting rod bearing)	0.0003 inch
Crankshaft runout limit	0.002 inch
Crankshaft endplay	0.004 to 0.012 inch
Connecting rod bearing oil clearance	0.0008 to 0.0026 inch
Main bearing oil clearance	0.0008 to 0.0026 inch

Connecting rods

Piston pin bore diameter	0.8098 to 0.8114 inch
Piston pin-to-bushing clearance	0.0006 to 0.0019 inch
Connecting rod-to-crankshaft side clearance (endplay)	
Standard	0.004 to 0.011 inch
Service limit	0.014 inch

Pistons and pins

Piston diameter	3.3374 to 3.3386 inches
Piston-to-bore clearance	
In service	0.0008 to 0.0027 inch
After rebuild	0.0008 to 0.0015 inch
Piston pin bore diameter	0.8123 to 0.8126 inch
Piston pin diameter	0.8119 to 0.8122 inch
Piston-to-pin clearance	0.0003 to 0,0005 inch

Piston rings

Gap

Compression (top and second)	0.010 to 0.030 inch
Oil ring (steel rail)	0.016 to 0.066 inch
Side clearance (compression rings)	
Top	0.0015 to 0.0032 inch
Second	0.0015 to 0.0035 inch

2.0L Zetec engine

General

Oil pressure (Hot 1500.rpm)	20 to 45 psi
Compression pressure	
Minimum	100 psi
Maximum variation between cylinders	Lowest reading cylinder must be no less than 75-percent of highest reading cylinder

Cylinder head and valve train

Cylinder head warpage limit	0.006 inch overall
Valve stem-to-guide clearance	0.0006 to 0.0025 inch
Valve stem diameter	0.2374 inch
Valve guide bore diameter (intake and exhaust)	0.2385 inch
Valve seats	
Width (intake and exhaust)	Not specified
Angle	45 degrees
Valve springs	
Free length	1.701 inch
Out-of-square limit	Not specified

Cylinder block

Head gasket surface warpage limit	0.003 inch overall
Cylinder bore	
Diameter	
Class 1	3.3385 to 3.3389 inches
Class 2	3.3389 to 3.3393 inches
Class 3	3.3393 to 3.3397 inches
Out-of-round limit	0.0010 inch
Taper service limit	0.0005 inch

Crankshaft

Main bearing journal diameter	2.2827 to 2.2835 inches
Connecting rod journal diameter	1.8460 to 1.8500 inches
Journal out-of-round limit	
(main or connecting rod bearing)	Not specified
Crankshaft runout limit	Not specified
Crankshaft endplay	0.004 to 0.012 inch
Connecting rod bearing oil clearance	0.0006 to 0.0027 inch
Main bearing oil clearance	0.0004 to 0.0028 inch

Connecting rods

Piston pin bore diameter	0.7870 to 0.7878 inch
Piston pin-to-bushing clearance	0.0006 to 0.0019 inch
Connecting rod-to-crankshaft side clearance	
(endplay)	0.0035 to 0.0125 inch

Pistons and pins

Piston diameter	
Class 1	3.3378 to 3.3385 inches
Class 2	3.3573 to 3.3358 inches

Specifications (continued)

Pistons and pins (continued)

Piston-to-bore clearance

Standard	0.0004 to 0.0012 inch
After rebuild	0.0008 to 0.0015 inch

Piston pin bore diameter .... 0.7879 to 0.7877 inch

Piston pin diameter

White	0.8118 to 0.8120 inch
Red	0.8120 to 0.8121 inch
Black or blue	0.8121 to 0.8122 inch

Piston-to-pin clearance .... 0.0004 to 0.0006 inch

Piston rings

Gap

Compression

Top	0.008 to 0.010 inch
Second	0.012 to 0.020 inch

Oil ring (steel rail) .... 0.016 to 0.035 inch

Side clearance

Compression

Top	0.0015 to 0.0028 inch
Second	0.012 to 0.019 inch

Oil ring steel rail .... 0.016 to 0.035 inch

Torque specifications   Ft-lbs (unless otherwise indicated)

➡**Note: One foot-pound (ft-lb) of torque is equivalent to 12 inch-pounds (in-lbs) of torque. Torque values below approximately 15 ft-lbs are expressed in inch-pounds, since most foot-pound torque wrenches are not accurate at these smaller values.**

Connecting rod cap nuts

1.8L engine	35 to 37
1.9L and 2.0L SPI engines	26 to 30

2.0L Zetec engine

First step	26
Second step	Tighten an additional 1/4-turn

Main bearing cap bolts

1.8L engine	40 to 43
1.9L and 2.0L SPI engines	67 to 80
2.0L Zetec engine	59 to 66

Oil jet bolt (1.8L engine only) .... 104 to 156 in-lbs

Section

Reference to other Chapters

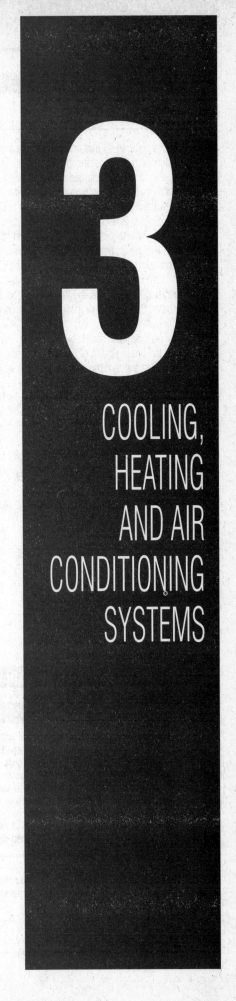

3

COOLING, HEATING AND AIR CONDITIONING SYSTEMS

1 General information

ENGINE COOLING SYSTEM

All vehicles covered by this manual employ a pressurized engine cooling system with thermostatically controlled coolant circulation. An impeller type water pump mounted on the timing belt end of the block pumps coolant through the engine. The coolant flows around each cylinder and toward the transaxle end of the engine. Cast-in coolant passages direct coolant around the intake and exhaust ports, near the spark plug areas and in close proximity to the exhaust valve guides.

A wax pellet type thermostat is located in a housing near the transaxle end of the engine. During warm up, the closed thermostat prevents coolant from circulating through the radiator. As the engine nears normal operating temperature, the thermostat opens and allows hot coolant to travel through the radiator, where it's cooled before returning to the engine.

The cooling system is sealed by a pressure type radiator cap, which raises the boiling point of the coolant and increases the cooling efficiency of the radiator. If the system pressure exceeds the cap pressure relief value, the excess pressure in the system forces the spring-loaded valve inside the cap off its seat and allows the coolant to escape through the overflow tube into a coolant reservoir. When the system cools the excess coolant is automatically drawn from the reservoir back into the radiator.

The coolant reservoir serves as both the point at which fresh coolant is added to the cooling system to maintain the proper fluid level and as a holding tank for overheated coolant.

This type of cooling system is known as a closed design because coolant that escapes past the pressure cap is saved and reused.

HEATING SYSTEM

The heating system consists of a blower fan and heater core located in the heater box, the hoses connecting the heater core to the engine cooling system and the heater/air conditioning control head on the dashboard. Hot engine coolant is circulated through the heater core. When the heater mode is activated, a flap door opens to expose the heater box to the passenger compartment. A fan switch on the control head activates the blower motor, which forces air through the core, heating the air.

AIR CONDITIONING SYSTEM

The air conditioning system consists of a condenser mounted in front of the radiator, an evaporator mounted adjacent to the heater core, a compressor mounted on the engine, a filter-drier (accumulator) which contains a high pressure relief valve and the plumbing connecting all of the above components.

A blower fan forces the warmer air of the passenger compartment through the evaporator core (sort of a radiator-in-reverse), transferring the heat from the air to the refrigerant. The liquid refrigerant boils off into low pressure vapor, taking the heat with it when it leaves the evaporator.

2 Antifreeze - general information

✺ WARNING:

Do not allow antifreeze to come in contact with your skin or painted surfaces of the vehicle. Rinse off spills immediately with plenty of water. Antifreeze is highly toxic if ingested. Never leave antifreeze lying around in an open container or in puddles on the floor; children and pets are attracted by its sweet smell and may drink it. Check with local authorities about disposing of used antifreeze. Many communities have collection centers which will see that antifreeze is disposed of safely. Never dump used antifreeze on the ground or pour it into drains.

➡Note: Non-toxic antifreeze is now manufactured and available at local auto parts stores, but even this type should be disposed of properly.

The cooling system should be filled with a 50/50 water/ethylene glycol based antifreeze solution, which will prevent freezing down to at least -20-degrees F, or lower if local climate requires it. It also provides protection against corrosion and increases the coolant boiling point. Don't use a lower concentration of antifreeze, even if the temperature never gets below freezing.

The cooling system should be drained, flushed and refilled at the specified intervals (see Chapter 1). Old or contaminated antifreeze solutions are likely to cause damage and encourage the formation of rust and scale in the system. Use distilled water with the antifreeze.

Before adding antifreeze, check all hose connections, because antifreeze tends to leak through very minute openings. Engines don't normally consume coolant, so if the level goes down, find the cause and correct it.

The exact mixture of antifreeze-to-water which you should use depends on the relative weather conditions. The mixture should contain at least 50 percent antifreeze, but should never contain more than 70 percent antifreeze. Consult the mixture ratio chart on the antifreeze container before adding coolant. Hydrometers are available at most auto parts stores to test the coolant. Use antifreeze which meets the vehicle manufacturer's specifications.

3 Thermostat - check and replacement

❋❋ WARNING:

Do not remove the radiator cap, drain the coolant or replace the thermostat until the engine has cooled completely.

CHECK

1   Before assuming the thermostat is to blame for a cooling system problem, check the coolant level (see Chapter 1), fan operation (see Section 4) and temperature gauge (or light) operation.

2   If the engine seems to be taking a long time to warm up (based on heater output or temperature gauge operation), the thermostat is probably stuck open. Replace the thermostat with a new one.

3   If the engine runs hot, use your hand to check the temperature of the upper radiator hose. If the hose isn't hot, but the engine is, the thermostat is probably stuck closed, preventing the coolant inside the engine from escaping to the radiator. Replace the thermostat.

❋❋ CAUTION:

Don't drive the vehicle without a thermostat. The computer may stay in open loop and emissions and fuel economy will suffer.

4   If the upper radiator hose is hot, it means that the coolant is flowing and the thermostat is open. Consult the *Troubleshooting* section at the front of this manual for cooling system diagnosis.

REPLACEMENT

♦ **Refer to illustrations 3.14a, 3.14b, 3.14c, 3.15a and 3.15b**

5   Disconnect the negative battery cable from the battery.

6   Disconnect the air cleaner intake tube (1.8L and 1.9L engines) or outlet tube (2.0L engines).

7   Drain the cooling system (see Chapter 1). If the coolant is relatively new or in good condition (see Chapter 1), save it and reuse it.

1.8L engine

8   Disconnect the electrical connector from the water thermoswitch, exhaust gas oxygen sensor, and the wiring harness ground strap above the thermostat housing.

1.9L and 2.0L engines

9   If you're working on a 1.9L or 2.0L SPI engine, remove the crankcase breather and the PCV hose (see Chapter 6). If you're working on a 2.0L Zetec engine, disconnect the electrical connector from the camshaft position sensor (see Chapter 6).

10   Unbolt the bracket that secures the heater hose inlet tube, then disconnect the inlet tube from the thermostat housing.

All models

11   Follow the upper radiator hose to the engine to locate the thermostat housing.

12   Loosen the hose clamp, then detach the hose from the fitting. If it's stuck, grasp it near the end with a pair of Channellock pliers and twist it to break the seal, then pull it off. If the hose is old or deteriorated, cut it off and install a new one.

13   If the outer surface of the large fitting that mates with the hose is deteriorated (corroded, pitted, etc.) it may be damaged further by hose removal. If it is, the thermostat housing cover will have to be replaced.

14   Remove the bolts and detach the housing cover (see illustrations). If the cover is stuck, tap it with a soft-face hammer to jar it loose. Be prepared for some coolant to spill as the gasket seal is broken.

15   Note how it's installed (which end is facing up), then remove the thermostat (see illustrations). If you're working on a 1.9L or 2.0L engine, remove the rubber seal as well.

16   Stuff a rag into the engine opening, then remove all traces of old gasket material and sealant from the housing and cover with a gasket scraper. Remove the rag from the opening and clean the gasket mating surfaces with lacquer thinner or acetone.

17   Install the new thermostat in the housing. Make sure the correct end faces up - the spring end is normally directed into the engine. If you're working on a 1.9L or 2.0L engine, make sure the rubber seal is fully compressed inside the housing and align the thermostat tabs with the slots in the housing.

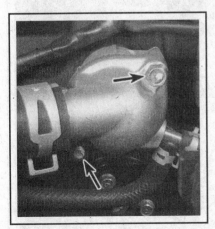

3.14a Thermostat housing fasteners (1.8L engine)

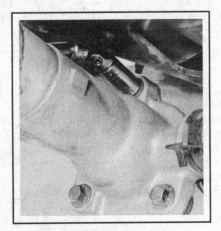

3.14b On 1.9L and 2.0L engines, disconnect the hose from the thermostat housing and remove the three bolts

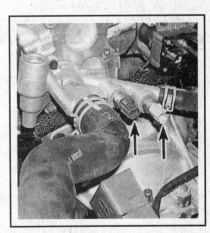

3.14c Here are the 2.0L SPI temperature senders; gauge sender (left) and engine coolant temperature (ECT) sensor (right)

3.15a On 1.8L engines, the gasket goes between the thermostat and cover; the spring end of the thermostat faces into the engine. If equipped, the "jiggle pin" must be positioned at the top

3.15b On 1.9L and 2.0L engines, be sure the tabs align with the slots; the rubber seal goes in the thermostat housing

18 Apply a thin, uniform layer of RTV sealant to both sides of the new gasket and position it on the housing.

19 Install the housing and bolts.

➡**Note: It's a good idea to use anti-seize compound on the bolt threads.**

Tighten the bolts to the torque listed in this Chapter's Specifications.

20 Reattach the hose to the fitting and tighten the hose clamp securely.

21 Refill the cooling system (see Chapter 1).

22 The remainder of installation is the reverse of the removal steps.

23 Start the engine and allow it to reach normal operating temperature, then check for leaks and proper thermostat operation (as described in Steps 2 through 4).

---

4 Engine cooling fan and motor - check, removal and installation

❋❋ **WARNING:**

To avoid possible injury or damage, DO NOT operate the engine with a damaged fan. Do not attempt to repair fan blades - replace a damaged fan with a new one.

REMOVAL AND INSTALLATION

◆ **Refer to illustrations 4.4a, 4.4b, 4.4c and 4.4d**

1 Disconnect the negative battery cable from the battery.

2 If you're working on a 1.8L engine, remove the air cleaner resonance duct from the mounts on the radiator (see Chapter 4).

3 Disconnect the fan motor electrical connector (see illustration 4.4a).

4 Unbolt the fan bracket and shroud assembly (see illustrations). Separate the harness retainer from the shroud (see illustration), then carefully lift the shroud out of the engine compartment (see illustration).

5 To detach the fan from the motor, remove the motor shaft clip.

6 To remove the bracket from the fan motor, detach the wiring harness form the retainers, then remove the mounting screws.

7 Installation is the reverse of removal.

CHECK

8 To test the motor, unplug the electrical connector at the motor and use jumper wires to connect the fan directly to the battery. If the fan still doesn't work, replace the motor.

9 If the motor tested OK, the fault lies in the coolant temperature switch or the wiring which connects the components. Carefully check all wiring and connections. If no obvious problems are found, further diagnosis should be done by a dealer service department or repair shop.

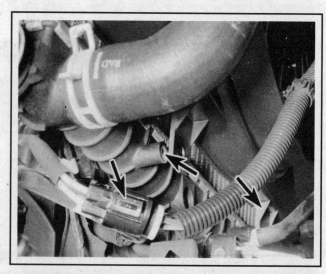

4.4a Disconnect the electrical connector (arrow) and remove the bolts that secure the side of the shroud (arrows) . . .,

4.4b . . . and remove the single bolt that secures the top of the shroud

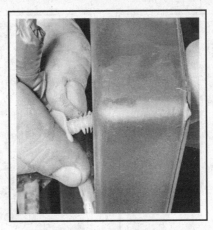

4.4c Pull and pry this harness retainer from the shroud - be careful not to damage it so it can be reused

4.4d Lift the shroud and fan assembly straight up

5 Radiator - removal and installation

♦ **Refer to illustrations 5.5, 5.6, 5.9, 5.12, 5.13 and 5.14**

✳✳ WARNING 1:

Wait until the engine is completely cool before beginning this procedure.

✳✳ WARNING 2:

1994 and later models are equipped with airbags. Before working on or near any airbag component the system must be disarmed. To do this, disconnect the cable from the negative terminal of the battery and wait one minute for the backup power supply to discharge. See Chapter 12 for more information.

1 Disconnect the negative battery cable from the battery.

2 Drain the cooling system (see Chapter 1). If the coolant is relatively new or in good condition, save it and reuse it.

3 Securely block the rear wheels so the vehicle can't roll, then raise the front end and place it on jackstands. DO NOT get under a vehicle that's supported only by a jack!

4 Remove the splash shield from the passenger side and front of the vehicle.

5 Disconnect the coolant recovery hose from the radiator filler neck (see illustration).

6 Loosen the hose clamp, then detach the lower radiator hose from the fitting (see illustration). If it's stuck, grasp each hose near the end with a pair of Channelock pliers and twist it to break the seal, then pull it off - be careful not to distort the radiator fittings! If the hose is old or deteriorated, cut it off and install a new one.

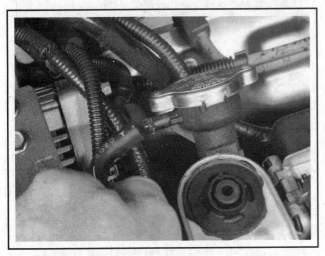

5.5 Twist the coolant recovery hose and pull it off the fitting

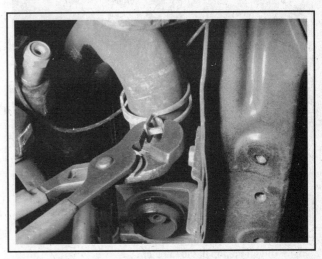

5.6 The lower radiator hose is accessible from beneath the vehicle

5.9 Hold the fitting nut with a backup wrench and remove the union bolt to disconnect the fluid cooler lines (automatic transaxle models)

5.12 Detach the top hose from the radiator fitting

7   If the vehicle is equipped with an automatic transaxle, disconnect the lower cooler line from the radiator. Use a drip pan to catch spilled fluid.

8   Remove the jackstands and lower the vehicle.

9   If you're working on a vehicle with automatic transaxle, disconnect the upper cooler line from the radiator (see illustration). If it has air conditioning as well as an automatic, remove the seal from between the radiator and fan shroud.

10   If you're working a vehicle with a 1.8L engine, remove the air cleaner resonance duct from the radiator mounts (see Chapter 4).

11   Remove the cooling fan and shroud (see Section 4).

12   Disconnect the upper hose from the radiator (see illustration).

13   Remove the radiator mounting bolts and mounts (see illustration).

14   Carefully lift out the radiator (see illustration). Don't spill coolant on the vehicle or scratch the paint.

15   With the radiator removed, it can be inspected for leaks and damage. If it needs repair, have a radiator shop or dealer service department perform the work as special techniques are required.

16   Bugs and dirt can be removed from the radiator with compressed air and a soft brush. Don't bend the cooling fins as this is done.

17   Check the radiator mounts for deterioration and make sure there's nothing in them when the radiator is installed.

18   Installation is the reverse of the removal procedure. On automatic transaxle models with gaskets at the cooler line union fittings, be sure to use new gaskets.

19   After installation, fill the cooling system with the proper mixture of antifreeze and water. Refer to Chapter 1 if necessary.

20   Start the engine and check for leaks. Allow the engine to reach normal operating temperature, indicated by the upper radiator hose becoming hot. Recheck the coolant level and add more if required.

21   If you're working on an automatic transaxle equipped vehicle, check and add fluid as needed.

5.13 Unbolt the top of the radiator . . .

5.14 . . . and lift it straight up out of the lower supports

6 Coolant reservoir and low coolant level sensor - removal and installation

※※ WARNING:

Wait until the engine is completely cool before beginning this procedure.

1 Disconnect the negative cable from the battery.

1.8L ENGINE

2 Remove the air cleaner (see Chapter 4).
3 Disconnect the electrical connector for the coolant level sensor.
4 Disconnect the overflow hose. Remove the reservoir mounting nut and lift the reservoir out.

1.9L AND 2.0L ENGINES

▶ **Refer to illustration 6.7**

5 If you're working on a 1.9L or 2.0L SPI engine model, unbolt the power steering fluid reservoir and position it out of the way without disconnecting any hoses (see Chapter 10). If you're working on a 2.0L SPI model with cruise control, disconnect the cable, unbolt the servo and move it out of the way.
6 Disconnect the electrical connector for the coolant level sensor.
7 Remove the reservoir mounting bolts. Lift the reservoir, disconnect the overflow hose and take the reservoir out (see illustration).

ALL MODELS

8 Installation is the reverse of the removal steps. Fill the reservoir to the COLD FULL mark with a 50/50 mixture of antifreeze and water.

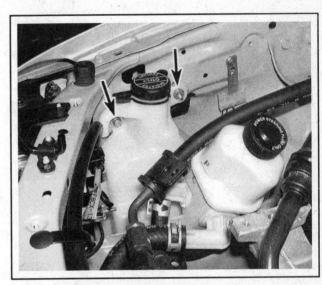

6.7 On 1.9 and 2.0L engines, remove the fasteners (arrows) and lift the reservoir, then disconnect the hose

7 Coolant temperature sending unit - check and replacement

▶ **Refer to illustration 7.1**

※※ WARNING:

Wait until the engine is completely cool before beginning this procedure.

1 The coolant temperature indicator system is composed of a temperature gauge mounted in the instrument panel and a coolant temperature sending unit mounted on the engine. The 1.8L sending unit is threaded into the cylinder head below the distributor. The 1.9L and 2.0L sending units are threaded into a coolant tube (1996 and earlier 1.9L models) or into the thermostat housing (1997 and later models) (see accompanying illustration and illustration 3.14c). The 1.9L and 2.0L SPI thermostat housings have more than one sending unit, but only one is for the temperature gauge.

※※ WARNING:

Stay clear of the electric cooling fan blades, which can come on at any time.

7.1 Coolant temperature sending unit (1996 and earlier 1.9L engine shown; on 1.8L engines, the sending unit is threaded into the cylinder head below the distributor) - the other sending units in this area are for the radiator fan and the electronic engine control system

2   If an overheating indication occurs, check the coolant level in the system and then make sure the wiring between the gauge and the sending unit is secure and all fuses are intact.

3   When the engine is first started, the gauge should be in the Cold position and gradually move to the Normal range.

4   Disconnect the wire from the temperature sender. Connect a variable resistor between the sender wire and ground (bare metal on the engine).

5   Switch on the ignition without starting the engine. With the resistance high (74 ohms on 1.8L and 1.9L engine models; 300 ohms on 2.0L engine models), the gauge pointer should be at the Cold mark. With the resistance low (9.7 ohms on 1.8L and 1.9L engine models; 45 ohms on 2.0L engine models), the gauge pointer should be at the Hot mark.

   a) If the gauge doesn't perform as described, check the wiring before replacing the gauge.
   b) If the gauge does perform as described on a 1.8L or 1.9L engine model, test the temperature sending unit as described below. No sending unit test procedure is available for 2.0L engine models; Ford recommends replacing the sending unit on these models if the gauge works during the gauge test but not during operation of the vehicle.

6   Remove the temperature sending unit from the engine (see illustration 7.1).

→Note: On 1.8L engines, the temperature sending unit for the gauge is mounted beneath the distributor. The sending unit on the other side of the thermostat housing is for the electronic engine control system.

7   Suspend the sending unit in a pan of water so it doesn't touch the sides.

❋❋ WARNING:

DO NOT use a cooking pan or it may be contaminated with poisonous antifreeze.

8   Heat the water to 176 degrees F. Measure the resistance between the sending unit terminal and case with an ohmmeter. If not approximately 9.7 ohms, replace the sending unit.

9   If the sending unit must be replaced, simply unscrew it from the engine and install the replacement. Use electrically conductive sealant on the threads. Make sure the engine is cool before removing the defective sending unit. There will be some coolant loss as the unit is removed, so be prepared to catch it. Check the coolant level after the replacement unit has been installed (see Chapter 1).

8   Water pump - check

1   A failure in the water pump can cause serious engine damage due to overheating.

2   There are three ways to check the operation of the water pump while it's installed on the engine. If the pump is defective, it should be replaced with a new or rebuilt unit.

3   With the engine running at normal operating temperature, squeeze the upper radiator hose. If the water pump is working properly, a pressure surge should be felt as the hose is released.

❋❋ WARNING:

Keep your hands away from the fan blades!

4   Water pumps are equipped with weep or vent holes. If a failure occurs in the pump seal, coolant will leak from the hole. In most cases you'll need a flashlight to find the hole on the water pump from underneath to check for leaks.

5   If the water pump shaft bearings fail there may be a howling sound at the front of the engine while it's running. Shaft wear can be felt if the water pump pulley is rocked up and down. Don't mistake drivebelt slippage, which causes a squealing sound, for water pump bearing failure.

9   Water pump - replacement

♦ **Refer to illustrations 9.8, 9.12a, 9.12b and 9.16**

❋❋ WARNING:

Wait until the engine is completely cool before beginning this procedure.

REMOVAL

1   Disconnect the negative battery cable from the battery.

2   Drain the cooling system (see Chapter 1). If the coolant is relatively new or in good condition, save it and reuse it.

3   Remove the drivebelts (see Chapter 1).

4   Remove the timing belt (see Chapter 2A).

1.8L engine

5   Securely block the rear wheels so the vehicle won't roll. Jack up the front end and place it securely on jackstands. DO NOT get under a vehicle that's supported only by a jack!

6   Unbolt the dipstick tube bracket from the water pump.

7   Unbolt the water inlet pipe from the water pump, then remove the pipe and gasket.

9.8 Water pump bolts (1.8L engine)

9.12a Disconnect the hose from the side of the water pump nearest the front of the engine . . .

9.12b . . . and the hose on the rear side

9.16 The water pump bolts on 1.9L and 2.0L engines are accessible from above (arrows)

8   Remove all of the water pump-to-engine bolts except the top one (see illustration).

9   Remove the jackstands and lower the vehicle.

10 Remove the remaining water pump-to-engine bolt and take the pump off the engine.

1.9L and 2.0L SPI engines

11 Securely block the rear wheels so the vehicle won't roll. Jack up the front end and place it securely on jackstands. DO NOT get under a vehicle that's supported only by a jack!

12 Loosen the clamps and detach the hoses from the water pump (see illustrations). If they're stuck, grasp each hose near the end with a pair of slip-joint pliers and twist it to break the seal, then pull it off. If the hoses are deteriorated, cut them off and install new ones.

13 Remove the jackstands and lower the vehicle.

14 If you're working on a 1.9L engine model, support the engine with a jack. Use a block of wood between the jack and the oil pan to protect the pan.

15 If you're working on a 1.9L engine model, unbolt the right engine

mount and roll it away from the engine (see Chapter 2A).

16 Remove the bolts (1.9L) or three bolts and one stud (2.0L SPI) and detach the water pump from the engine (see illustration).

2.0L Zetec engine

17 Securely block the rear wheels so the vehicle won't roll. Jack up the front end and place it securely on jackstands. DO NOT get under a vehicle that's supported only by a jack!

18 Remove the splash shield from under the passenger side of the engine compartment.

19 Unbolt the water pump pulley (the drivebelt will hold the pulley so it won't turn while the bolts are loosened).

20 Remove the drivebelt (see Chapter 1).

21 Unbolt the air conditioning compressor and place it out of the way (Section 18).

22 Loosen the clamps and detach the hoses from the water pump. If they're stuck, grasp each hose near the end with a pair of slip joint pliers and twist it to break the seal, then pull it off. If the hoses are deteriorated, cut them off and install new ones.

23 Remove the jackstands and lower the vehicle. Remove the bolts and detach the water pump from the center timing cover.

INSTALLATION

24 Clean the bolt threads and the threaded holes in the engine to remove corrosion and sealant.

25 Compare the new pump to the old one to make sure they're identical.

26 Remove all traces of old gasket material from the engine with a gasket scraper.

27 Clean the engine and new water pump mating surfaces with lacquer thinner or acetone.

28 Apply a thin coat of RTV sealant to the engine side of the new gasket.

29 Apply a thin layer of RTV sealant to the gasket mating surface of the new pump, then carefully mate the gasket and the pump. Slip a couple of bolts through the pump mounting holes to hold the gasket in place.

30 Carefully attach the pump and gasket to the engine and thread the bolts (and the stud on 2.0L SPI engines) into the holes finger tight.

31 Install the remaining bolts. Tighten them to the torque listed in this Chapter's Specifications in 1/4-turn increments. Don't overtighten them or the pump may be distorted.

32 Reinstall all parts removed for access to the pump.

33 Refill the cooling system and check the drivebelt tension (see Chapter 1). Run the engine and check for leaks.

10 Heater - general information

The heater circulates engine coolant through a small radiator (heater core) in the passenger compartment. Air is drawn in through an opening in the cowl, then blown (by the blower motor) through the heater core to pick up heat. The heated air is blended with varying amounts of unheated air to regulate the temperature. The heated air is then blown into the passenger compartment. Various doors in the heater control the flow of air to the floor and through the instrument panel louvers and defroster outlets.

11 Heater control assembly - removal and installation

1991 THROUGH 1996 MODELS

▶ **Refer to illustrations 11.4a, 11.4b, 11.5 and 11.6**

❄❄ **WARNING:**

1994 and later models are equipped with airbags. Before working on or near any airbag component the system must be disarmed. To do this, disconnect the cable from the negative terminal of the battery and wait one minute for the backup power supply to discharge. See Chapter 12 for more information.

Removal

1 Disconnect the negative cable from the battery.

2 Remove the screws that secure the glove compartment and slide it out (see Chapter 11).

3 Disconnect the Recirc/Fresh air cable, mode selector cable, and temperature control cable from their cams and release their retaining clips.

4 Remove the trim bezel from around the control assembly (see illustrations).

5 Remove the four screws securing the control assembly to the instrument panel (see illustration).

11.4a Carefully pry out the trim bezel that surrounds the control assembly . . .

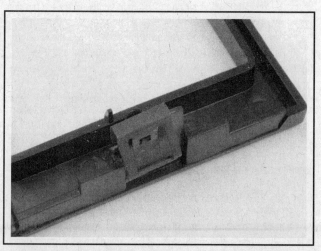

11.4b . . . if its retaining clips fall off, find them and put them back on

11.5 Remove the control assembly mounting screws (arrows) with a Torx driver

11.6 Pull the assembly partially out then detach the electrical connectors and pull it clear

6 Pull the control assembly through the opening in the instrument panel far enough to allow removal of the electrical connections (see illustration). Carefully spread the clips on the electrical connectors and disconnect the connectors for the blower switch and illumination light.

7 Remove the control assembly from the instrument panel.

8 If necessary, detach cables from the control assembly. The lever knobs are secured by screws; the blower knob pulls straight off.

Installation

9 Pull the cables through the opening in the instrument panel. Connect them to the appropriate cams and secure them with the retaining clips.

10 Connect the electrical connectors.

11 Position the control assembly on the instrument panel and install its mounting screws.

12 Check for proper operation and adjust the cables if necessary (see Section 12).

13 The remainder of installation is the reverse of the removal steps.

1997 AND LATER MODELS

14 The control assembly is removed together with the radio (see Chapter 12).

12 Heater control cables (1991 through 1996 models) - check and adjustment

CHECK

1 Move the control lever all the way from left to right.

2 If the control lever stops before the end and bounces back, the cables are out of adjustment.

ADJUSTMENT

▶ **Refer to illustrations 12.6 12.7a, 12.7b, 12.8a and 12.8b**

3 If you haven't already done so, remove the glove compartment (see Section 11).

4 Move the Recirc/Fresh air lever to the Fresh position (all the way to the right).

5 Align the cam with its alignment hole in the heater case.

6 Detach the cable from its retaining clip, then reattach it (see illustration).

7 Place the temperature lever in the Cold position, then adjust the temperature cable as described in Steps 5 and 6 (see illustrations).

8 Place the mode select lever in the Defrost position, then adjust the temperature cable as described in Steps 5 and 6 (see illustrations).

12.6 With the cam properly positioned, secure the cable in its clip (arrow)

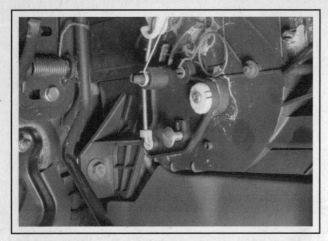

12.7a Align the temperature cable cam with the special tool
(or a 1/4-inch bolt or screw, as shown here) . . .

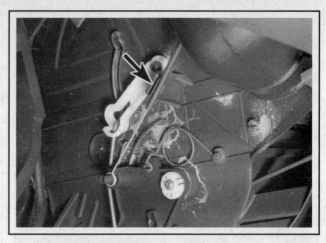

12.7b . . . then secure the cable in its clip (arrow)

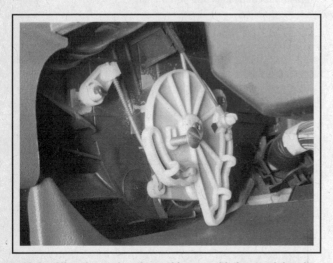

12.8a Align the mode select cable cam with the special tool
(or a 1/4-inch bolt or machine screw, as shown here) . . .

12.8b . . . then secure the cable in its clip (arrow)

13 Heater blower motor - replacement

▶ Refer to illustrations 13.4a, 13.4b, 13.5 and 13.6

1   Disconnect the negative cable from the battery.
2   Remove the trim panel from the instrument panel below the glove
compartment.
3   Unbolt the wiring bracket.
4   Disconnect the electrical connector and remove the three blower
motor attaching bolts (see illustrations).

5   Lower the blower motor assembly out of the heater assembly (see
illustration).
6   If necessary, remove the push nut on the motor shaft and remove
the blower wheel from the motor (see illustration).
7   Installation is the reverse of the removal steps. Make sure the
electrical connector is fully seated and that it "clicks" into place.

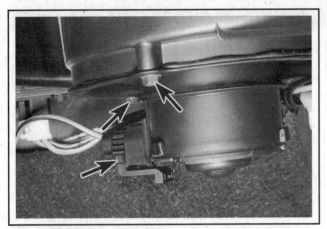

13.4a Unplug the electrical connector on the side of the blower motor, then remove the bolts behind and to the left . . .

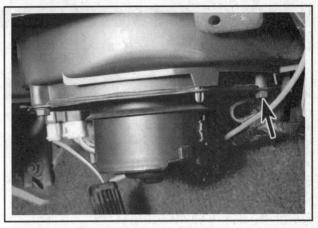

13.4b . . . and one bolt on the right . . .

13.5 . . . and carefully lower the blower motor and wheel away from the heater

13.6 The blower wheel is secured to the motorshaft by a push nut - be careful not to bend the nut if you remove it

14 Blower motor resistor - replacement

▶ **Refer to illustration 14.2**

1   Disconnect the negative cable from the battery.
2   Disconnect the resistor electrical connectors (see illustration). Remove the resistor mounting bolts and take the resistor out.
3   Installation the reverse of the removal steps.

14.2 The blower motor resistor has two electrical connectors and is secured by two bolts (arrows)

15 Heater core - replacement

Refer to illustrations 15.5, 15.15 and 15.16

✳✳ WARNING:

1994 and later models are equipped with airbags. Before working on or near any airbag component the system must be disarmed. To do this, disconnect the cable from the negative terminal of the battery and wait one minute for the backup power supply to discharge. See Chapter 12 for more information.

➡Note: This procedure requires removal of the complete instrument panel (not just the gauge cluster) and the entire heater assembly. If you decide to do it yourself, allow plenty of time.

1 Allow the cooling system to completely cool down.
2 Using a thick cloth for protection, turn the radiator filler cap to the first stop.
3 Step back and let the pressure release.
4 Once the pressure has been released, tighten the radiator cap.
5 Working within the engine compartment, loosen the clamps on the heater hoses at the engine compartment side of the firewall (see illustration). Twist the hoses and carefully separate them from the heater core tubes.
6 Plug or cap the heater core tubes to prevent coolant from spilling into the passenger compartment when the heater core is removed.
7 Place a plastic sheet on the vehicle floor to prevent stains in case the coolant spills.
8 Remove the instrument panel (see Chapter 11).
9 If you're working on a 1991 through 1996 model, disconnect the heater control cables (see Section 12). If you're working on a 1997 or later model, disconnect the vacuum harness connector.
10 Remove the defroster duct attaching screws (and retaining pins on 1997 and later models).
11 Remove one bolt that secures the heater-to-blower clamp.
12 Disconnect the radio antenna lead from the clip on the heater

unit. Remove the heater unit mounting nuts.
13 Lift the heater unit into the passenger compartment and take it out of the vehicle.
14 Remove the heater core insulator.
15 Remove four cap screws and take off the heater core cover (see illustration).
16 Lift the heater core out of the heater unit (see illustration).
17 Installation is the reverse of the removal procedure with the following additions:

   a) Fill the cooling system (see Chapter 1).
   b) Run the engine and check for coolant leaks.
   c) Adjust the heater cables (see Section 12) and test the heater. If you install a new heater unit, save the keys that are supplied with it for use in adjusting the cables.

15.5 Disconnect the heater hoses from the fittings at the firewall (arrows)

15.15 The heater core is held in by a cover - remove its four cap screws and take the cover off

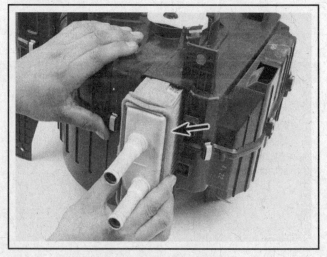

15.16 Lift the heater core out of the heater unit

16 Air conditioning system - check and maintenance

▶ Refer to illustration 16.7

❋ WARNING:

The air conditioning system is under high pressure. Do not loosen any hose fittings or remove any components until after the system has been discharged by a dealer service department or service station. Always wear eye protection when disconnecting air conditioning system fittings.

➡ **Note 1:** All 1994 and later models use "environmentally friendly" R-134a refrigerant. R-134a refrigerant, its lubricating oil and all components, including O-rings, are not compatible with the R-12 system and under no circumstances should the two different types of refrigerant and lubricating oil be intermixed. If mixed, it could result in costly compressor failure due to improper lubrication.

➡ **Note 2:** Because of recent Federal regulations proposed by the Environmental Protection Agency, 14-ounce cans of R-12 refrigerant may not be available in your area. If you choose to recharge a R-12 refrigerant system yourself, purchase a 20-pound bulk tank of R-12 refrigerant, an air conditioning manifold gauge set and refer to the Haynes Automotive Heating and Air Conditioning Manual for recharging instructions.

1   The following maintenance checks should be performed on a regular basis to ensure that the air conditioner continues to operate at peak efficiency.

    a) Check the compressor drivebelt. If it's worn or deteriorated, replace it (see Chapter 1).

    b) Check the drivebelt tension and, if necessary, adjust it (see Chapter 1).

    c) Check the system hoses. Look for cracks, bubbles, hard spots and deterioration. Inspect the hoses and all fittings for oil bubbles and seepage. If there's any evidence of wear, damage or leaks, replace the hose(s).

    d) Inspect the condenser fins for leaves, bugs and other debris. Use a "fin comb" or compressed air to clean the condenser.

    e) Make sure the system has the correct refrigerant charge.

2   It's a good idea to operate the system for about 10 minutes at least once a month, particularly during the winter. Long term non-use can cause hardening, and subsequent failure, of the seals.

3   Because of the complexity of the air conditioning system and the special equipment necessary to service it, in-depth troubleshooting and repairs are not included in this manual. However, simple checks and component replacement procedures are provided in this Chapter.

4   The most common cause of poor cooling is simply a low system refrigerant charge. If a noticeable drop in cool air output occurs, the following check will help you determine if the refrigerant level is low.

5   Warm the engine up to normal operating temperature.

6   Place the air conditioning temperature selector at the coldest setting and put the blower at the highest setting. Open the doors (to make sure the air conditioning system doesn't cycle off as soon as it cools the passenger compartment).

7   With the compressor engaged - the clutch will make an audible click and the center of the clutch will rotate - feel the evaporator inlet pipe between the orifice tube and the accumulator with one hand while placing your other hand on the surface of the accumulator housing (see illustration).

8   If both surfaces feel about the same temperature and if both feel a little cooler than the surrounding air, the refrigerant level is probably okay. Further inspection of the system is beyond the scope of the home mechanic and should be left to a professional.

9   If the inlet pipe has frost accumulation or feels cooler than the accumulator surface, the refrigerant charge is low. Add refrigerant.

16.7 The fixed orifice tube is in the engine compartment

17 Air conditioning system accumulator - removal and installation

▶ Refer to illustrations 17.4, 17.7a and 17.7b

❋ WARNING:

The air conditioning system is under high pressure. DO NOT disassemble any part of the system (hoses, compressor, line fittings, etc.) until after the system has been depressurized by a dealer service department or service station.

1   Have the air conditioning system discharged (see **Warning** above).

2   Disconnect the negative battery cable from the battery.

3   If you're working on a 1.9L or 2.0L engine model, remove the windshield washer reservoir.

4   Unplug the electrical connector from the pressure switch near the top of the accumulator (see illustration).

5   Disconnect the refrigerant line from the accumulator. The air conditioning lines use spring lock couplings, which require a special

17.4 Disconnect the electrical connector from the clutch cycling pressure switch

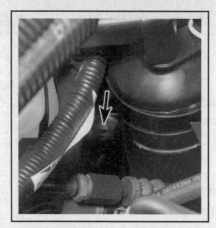

17.7a The accumulator is held in place by a strap . . .

17.7b . . . which is secured by two bolts on 1.9L and 2.0L engine models

tool to connect and disconnect (the same type used for fuel lines; see Chapter 4 for details).

➡**Note: Air conditioning spring lock couplings use O-rings made of a special material. Replace them with original equipment O-rings only.**

6 Plug the open fittings to prevent entry of dirt and moisture.

7 Loosen the mounting strap bolt (1.8L engine models) or remove the bolts and mounting strap (1.9L or 2.0L engine models) (see illustrations). Lift the accumulator out.

8 Installation is the reverse of removal. Use new O-rings on the spring lock coupling.

9 Take the vehicle back to the shop that discharged it. Have the air conditioning system evacuated, charged and leak tested.

18 Air conditioning system compressor - removal and installation

▸ **Refer to illustrations 18.5a, 18.5b and 18.6**

❄❄ **WARNING:**

The air conditioning system is under high pressure. DO NOT disassemble any part of the system (hoses, compressor, line fittings, etc.) until after the system has been depressurized by a dealer service department or service station.

➡**Note: The accumulator (see Section 17) should be replaced whenever the compressor is replaced.**

1 Have the air conditioning system discharged (see **Warning** above).

2 Disconnect the negative battery cable from the battery.

3 Disconnect the compressor clutch wiring harness.

4 Remove the drivebelt (see Chapter 1).

5 Unbolt the refrigerant line manifold from the compressor (see illustrations). Plug the open fittings to prevent entry of dirt and moisture.

6 Unbolt the compressor from the mounting brackets and lift it out of the vehicle (see illustration).

7 If a new compressor is being installed, follow the directions with the compressor regarding the draining of excess oil prior to installation.

8 The clutch may have to be transferred from the original to the new compressor.

9 Installation is the reverse of removal. Replace all O-rings with new ones specifically made for air conditioning system use and lubricate them with refrigerant oil. Position the O-rings in the manifold.

10 Have the system evacuated, recharged and leak tested by the shop that discharged it.

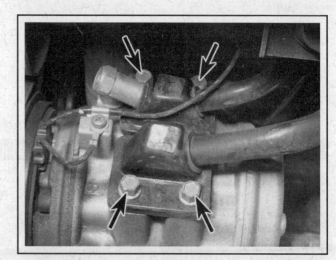

18.5a The refrigerant lines are connected to a manifold, which is secured by four bolts (arrows) on 1.8L and 1.9L engine models . . .

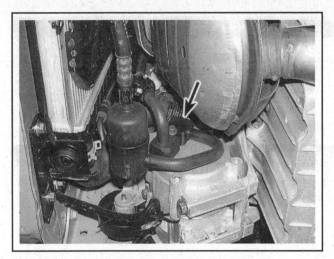

18.5b ... and one bolt on 2.0L engine models

18.6 Compressor mounting bolts (arrows) (2.0L SPI shown; others similar)

19 Air conditioning system condenser - removal and installation

▶ **Refer to illustrations 19.5 and 19.6**

※※ WARNING:

The air conditioning system is under high pressure. DO NOT disassemble any part of the system (hoses, compressor, line fittings, etc.) until after the system has been depressurized by a dealer service department or service station.

➡**Note: The accumulator (see Section 17) should be replaced whenever the condenser is replaced.**

1 Have the air conditioning system discharged (see **Warning** above).
2 Drain the cooling system (see Chapter 1).
3 Remove the radiator (see Section 5).

4 Remove the grille (see Chapter 11).
5 Use a spring lock coupling tool to disconnect the refrigerant lines from the condenser (see illustration). Plug the lines to keep dirt and moisture out.
6 Remove the mounting nuts from the condenser brackets (see illustration).
7 Lift the condenser out of the vehicle.
8 If the original condenser will be reinstalled, store it with the line fittings on top to prevent oil from draining out.
9 If a new condenser is being installed, pour one ounce of refrigerant oil into it prior to installation.
10 Reinstall the components in the reverse order of removal. Be sure the rubber pads are in place under the condenser.
11 Have the system evacuated, recharged and leak tested by the shop that discharged it.

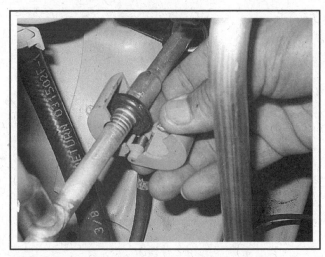

19.5 Disconnect the condenser refrigerant lines with a spring lock coupling tool

19.6 Remove the nuts that secure the condenser brackets so the condenser can be lifted out

Specifications

Radiator cap pressure	psi
Specified	13
Lower limit	12
Upper limit	15

Torque specifications — Ft-lbs (unless otherwise indicated)

➡Note: One foot-pound (ft-lb) of torque is equivalent to 12 inch-pounds (in-lbs) of torque. Torque values below approximately 15 ft-lbs are expressed in inch-pounds, since most foot-pound torque wrenches are not accurate at these smaller values.

Thermostat housing bolts	
1.8L	14 to 19
1.9L	72 to 108 in-lbs
2.0L SPI	96 to 144 in-lbs
2.0L Zetec	91 to 97 in-lbs
Water pump bolts	
1.8L	14 to 19
1.9L and 2.0L SPI	15 to 22
2.0L Zetec	17

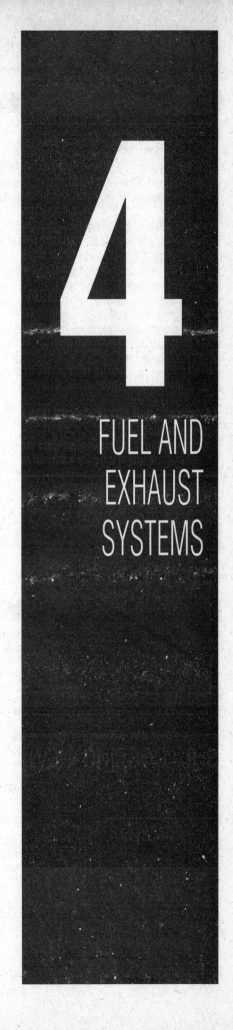

4

FUEL AND EXHAUST SYSTEMS

1 General information

FUEL SYSTEM

The fuel system consists of the fuel tank, the fuel pump, an air cleaner assembly, a fuel injection system and the various Teflon hoses, steel lines and fittings connecting the fuel delivery components together.

Vehicles covered by this manual are equipped with a Ford Electronic Fuel Injection system. The 1.8L EFI system is a multi-point simultaneous injection system. The four injectors work in pairs of two, with each pair injecting fuel every two rotations of the crankshaft (on combustion and compression strokes). The 1.9L and 2.0L EFI systems are multi-point, sequential fuel injection systems. Fuel is injected into the cylinders according to firing order sequence.

Fuel pressure on 1991 through 1997 models is controlled by a vacuum-operated fuel pressure regulator in the fuel rail. The fuel pump is capable of producing pressure above the specified operating range of the fuel injectors. When fuel pressure exceeds a specified limit, the pressure regulator routes fuel into a return line, which returns it to the fuel tank.

On 1998 and later models, the EFI system is an "electronic returnless" design. A fuel pressure sensor in the fuel rail measures the difference between fuel rail pressure and pressure in the intake manifold and sends this information to the PCM. A fuel temperature sensor is also used on vehicles equipped with the 2.0L Zetec engine. The PCM uses the input from the fuel pressure sensor (and fuel temperature sensor, if equipped) to calculate the necessary fuel pressure. The PCM controls the voltage output of the fuel pump driver module, varying the speed of the fuel pump to maintain fuel pressure within the correct range.

The fuel pump is a single, high-pressure electric pump located within the fuel tank.

EXHAUST SYSTEM

All vehicles are equipped with an exhaust manifold, a catalytic converter, an exhaust pipe and a muffler. The 1.8L exhaust system also contains a resonator. Any component of the exhaust system can be replaced. See Chapter 6 for further details regarding the catalytic converter.

2 Fuel pressure relief procedure

▶ **Refer to illustrations 2.2, 2.3 and 2.5**

✳✳ WARNING:

Gasoline is extremely flammable, so take extra precautions when you work on any part of the fuel system. Don't smoke or allow open flames or bare light bulbs near the work area, and don't work in a garage where a gas-type appliance (such as a water heater or clothes dryer) is present. Since gasoline is carcinogenic, wear latex gloves when there's a possibility of being exposed to fuel, and, if you spill any fuel on your skin, rinse it off immediately with soap and water. Mop up any spills immediately and do not store fuel-soaked rags where they could ignite. The fuel system is under constant pressure, so, if any fuel lines are to be disconnected, the fuel pressure in the system must be relieved first. When you perform any kind of work on the fuel system, wear safety glasses and have a Class B type fire extinguisher on hand.

➡Note: **After the fuel pressure has been relieved, it's a good idea to lay a shop towel over any fuel connection to be disassembled, to absorb the residual fuel that may leak out when servicing the fuel system.**

1   The "inertia switch," which shuts off fuel to the engine in the event of a collision, affords a simple and convenient means by which fuel pressure can be relieved before servicing fuel injection components.

2   The inertia switch on 1991 through 1996 models, as well as on 1998 coupes, is located in the rear of the vehicle, near the right (passenger's side) strut tower. On sedan and coupe models, open the trunk and remove the right-side trim panel. On hatchback and wagon models, there may be an access door secured by clips (see illustration), but on some models you may need to remove the lower quarter trim panel on the right side.

3   The inertia switch on 1997 and later models (except the 1998 coupe) is located to the left of the driver's footwell, behind an access door (see illustration).

4   Once you've found the switch, start the engine.

5   With the engine idling, insert a small screwdriver into the slot provided and pry the red button up (see illustration). If there's no button provided, disconnect the electrical connector from the inertia switch.

6   Let the engine run until it stalls. Crank the engine for a few seconds after it stalls (to make sure there's no residual pressure). The fuel pressure is now relieved.

✳✳ WARNING:

Although there's no pressure in the fuel system, there is still fuel in the lines, so some fuel may flow out when you disconnect fittings. Observe the fuel Warning at the beginning of this procedure and wrap shop rags around connection points before disconnecting them.

7   After repairs are completed, depress the red button on the inertia switch or re-connect the electrical connector. The fuel pump is now enabled, but it may take several seconds of cranking before the engine starts.

2.2 Here's a typical rear compartment access door for the inertia switch . . .

2.3 . . . and this type is used in the driver's footwell; pull the door off . . .

2.5 . . . insert a screwdriver into the slot (arrow) and pry up the red button to disable the fuel pump - press the red button to enable the pump

3 Inline fuel filter - replacement

▶ Refer to illustration 3.4

※ WARNING:

The fuel system pressure must be relieved before disconnecting fuel lines and fittings (see Section 2). Gasoline is extremely flammable, so take extra precautions when you work on any part of the fuel system. Don't smoke or allow open flames or bare light bulbs near the work area, and don't work in a garage where a gas-type appliance (such as a water heater or clothes dryer) is present. If you spill any fuel on your skin, rinse it off immediately with soap and water. When you perform any kind of work on the fuel system, wear safety glasses and have a Class B type fire extinguisher on hand.

1   The inline fuel filter is mounted in the engine compartment. Routine replacement of the filter is not required, although you'll want to replace it if you suspect it's clogged.

2   Relieve fuel system pressure (see Section 2).

3   Place an approved gasoline container under the fuel filter to catch any gasoline that drips.

4   Pull the plastic hairpin-type retaining clip out of the upper fuel line connector (see illustration). Push the hose off the fitting.

➡Note: See Section 4 for information on disconnecting hairpin-type connectors.

5   Loosen the filter clamp.

6   Securely block the rear wheels so the vehicle can't roll. Jack up the front end and place it on jackstands. DO NOT get under a vehicle that's supported only by a jack!

7   Pull the hairpin-type retaining clip from the hose at the bottom of the filter and disconnect the hose.

8   Lift the filter out of the engine compartment.

9   Installation is the reverse of the removal Steps.

3.4 The inline fuel filter (arrow) is mounted in the engine compartment, next to the firewall

4 Fuel lines and fittings - replacement

✳✳ WARNING:

The fuel system pressure must be relieved before disconnecting fuel lines and fittings (see Section 2). Gasoline is extremely flammable, so take extra precautions when you work on any part of the fuel system. Don't smoke or allow open flames or bare light bulbs near the work area, and don't work in a garage where a gas-type appliance (such as a water heater or clothes dryer) is present. If you spill any fuel on your skin, rinse it off immediately with soap and water. When you perform any kind of work on the fuel system, wear safety glasses and have a Class B type fire extinguisher on hand.

SPRING-LOCK COUPLINGS - DISASSEMBLY AND REASSEMBLY

▶ **Refer to illustrations 4.1, 4.2, 4.4a, 4.4b, 4.4c and 4.4d**

1 The fuel supply and return lines used on these engines may utilize spring lock couplings at some connections. The male end of the spring lock coupling, which is girded by two O-rings, is inserted into a female flared-end fitting. The coupling is secured by a garter spring which prevents disengagement by gripping the flared end of the female fitting. A clip and tether assembly provides additional security (see illustration).

2 To disconnect the spring-lock coupling supply fitting, you will need to obtain a spring-lock coupling tool, which will include (see illustration):

   a) *3/8-inch return fitting, available at most auto parts stores.*
   b) *1/2-inch supply fitting, available at most auto parts stores.*

3 Before disconnecting the line, unclip the safety clip (see illustration 4.1).

4 To disconnect and reconnect the line, refer to the accompanying illustrations and follow the information in the captions (see illustra-

tions). Always use new O-rings whenever you reassemble a spring-lock coupling.

METAL FUEL LINES

✳✳ WARNING:

Avoid using alternative tubing materials. Use of non-approved tubing could pose a hazard in service.

5 Stainless steel tubing must not be repaired using hose and hose clamps. Should the fittings or steel tubing ends become damaged, approved service parts must be used to replace the lines. Splicing such lines with seamless steel tubing or rubber hose is not recommended.

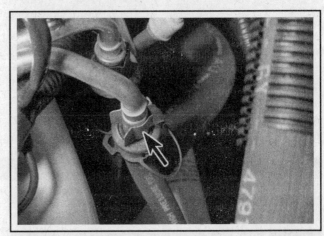

4.1 This tethered clip (arrow) must be removed before the spring lock coupling can be separated

4.2 These special tools are required to connect and disconnect spring lock couplings

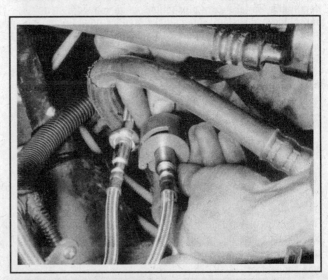

4.4a Open the tool and place it over the line . . .

HAIRPIN CLIPS

▶ **Refer to illustration 4.8**

6   Hairpin-type clips are commonly used to secure the fuel lines at the fuel filter and fuel pump. Inspect the visible portion of the fitting for dirt accumulation. Clean the fitting before disassembly.

7   Due to adhesion, the fitting may stick to the tube. Unstick it by twisting the fitting on the tube, then push and pull the fitting until it moves freely on the tube.

8   Remove the hairpin clip by first bending the shipping tab down so it will clear the body (see illustration). Spread the two clip legs about 1/8-inch each to disengage the body and push the legs into the fitting. Complete the removal by lightly pulling from the triangular end of the clip and working it clear of the tube and fitting.

➡**Note: It is recommended that the original clip not be reused.**

9   To install the new clip, insert the clip with the triangular portion pointing away from the fitting opening. Fully engage the body so the legs of the clip lock on the outside of the body.

10   Before reinstalling the fitting, wipe the tube end clean and inspect inside to ensure it is free of dirt and/or obstructions.

11   Reinstall the fitting onto the tube by aligning the fitting and tube and pushing the fitting onto the tube end until a definite click is heard.

12   Pull on the fitting to ensure it is fully engaged.

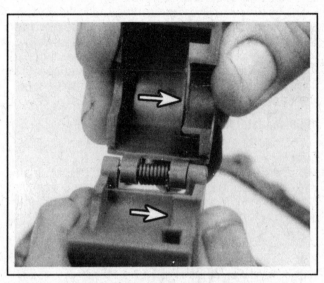

4.4b . . . then slide the tool against the fuel line fitting so the lip inside the tool (arrows) . . .

4.4c . . . pushes against the garter spring (arrow) . . .

4.4d . . . push the tool against the spring until the spring slides off the flared female end of the line (A); to reconnect the line, place the flared female end (A) over the rubber O-ring(s) on the male end and push the ends together until the flared end slips under the garter spring (B); tug on the ends to make sure they're locked, then install the safety clip

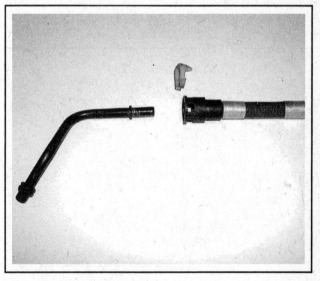

4.8 A typical hairpin clip fitting

5 Fuel pump/fuel pressure - check

✳✳ WARNING:

Gasoline is extremely flammable, so take extra precautions when you work on any part of the fuel system. See the Warning in Section 2.

➡Note 1: To perform the fuel pressure test, you will need to obtain a fuel pressure gauge and adapter set (fuel line fittings).

➡Note 2: The fuel pump will operate as long as the engine is cranking or running and the PCM is receiving ignition reference pulses from the electronic ignition system. If there are no reference pulses, the fuel pump will shut off after two or three seconds.

➡Note 3: After the fuel pressure has been relieved, it's a good idea to lay a shop towel over any fuel connection to be disassembled, to absorb the residual fuel that may leak out when servicing the fuel system.

GENERAL CHECK

1991 through 1997 models

▶ Refer to illustrations 5.2a and 5.2b

1   An electric fuel pump malfunction will usually result in a loss of fuel flow and/or pressure that is often reflected by a corresponding drop in performance (or a no-run condition).

2   Verify the pump operates. Remove the fuel filler cap and listen at the filler opening. Have an assistant turn the ignition key to ON, but don't start the engine. You should hear a brief whirring sound from the pump and pressure return noise from the fuel pressure regulator under the hood as the fuel pump comes on to pressurize the system (it normally lasts about a second). Locate the diagnostic Data Link Connector (DLC) under the hood (see illustrations). Ground the fuel pump terminal of the connector. Now the noise should be constant.

➡Note: 1996 and 1997 models may not be equipped with an underhood DLC. A SCAN tool is required to energize the fuel pump (see Chapter 6).

3   If the pump doesn't run (makes no sound), check to make sure the inertia switch is in the fuel-pump-enabled position (see Section 2). Next, check the fuel pump fuse and relay (see Chapter 12).

4   If the fuel pump operates only when the fuel pump terminal on the DLC is grounded, the control circuit of the relay is probably faulty, although the problem could also be in the wiring, fusible link or Powertrain Control Module (PCM). If you suspect the PCM, take the vehicle to a dealer service department for checking.

5   If the pump won't run and the fuse, inertia switch and relay are OK, try disconnecting the electrical connector from the fuel pump (see Section 6). Using fused jumper wires, apply battery voltage directly to the terminals at the pump and see if the pump now operates.

6   If the fuel pump still doesn't operate, replace it (see Section 6). If it runs only when jumpered to battery voltage, the problem lies somewhere in the electrical circuit to the fuel pump.

1998 and later models

7   Should the fuel system fail to deliver the proper amount of fuel, or any fuel at all, inspect it as follows.

8   Perform Step 2 above to check for the sound of the fuel pump. If you don't hear anything, check the fuel pump fuse (see Chapter 12). If the fuse is blown, replace it and see if it blows again. If it does, trace the fuel pump circuit for a short. Refer to the wiring diagrams at the end of Chapter 12 for additional wiring schematics.

9   If the fuse is good, check the fuses and the wiring circuit for the PCM, fuel pump driver module and Constant Control Relay Module (CCRM). With the key on and engine off, check for voltage at the fuel pump, then work your way back through the circuit, checking for voltage at the fuel pump driver module, inertia switch and constant control relay module. If the fuses and wiring for these components are good, have the system checked by a dealer service department or other qualified automotive repair facility.

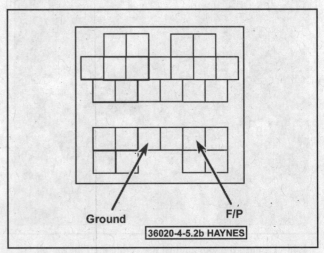

36020-4-5.2a HAYNES

5.2a To test the fuel pump, ground the fuel pump test terminal (FP lead) of the DLC connector, which is located under the hood (1.9L engine)

36020-4-5.2b HAYNES

5.2b On most 1.8L engines, the Data Link Connector is located next to the strut tower, near the battery - ground the fuel pump (F/P) terminal

OPERATING PRESSURE CHECK

1991 through 1997 models

10 Relieve the fuel pressure (see Section 2).

11 Connect a fuel pressure gauge (it must be designed for use with fuel injection systems and be capable of indicating 100 psi) to the Schrader valve on the fuel rail (1.9L engines), following the instructions included with the gauge.

➡**Note: The Schrader valve is a small valve, covered by a screw-on cap, that operates the same way as a valve core for a tire. On 1.8L engines, there may not be a Schrader valve; tee into the fuel line.**

12 Locate the diagnostic Data Link Connector (DLC) under the hood and ground the fuel pump test terminal (see illustration 5.2a or 5.2b).

➡**Note: 1996 and 1997 models may not be equipped with an underhood DLC. A SCAN tool is required to energize the fuel pump (see Chapter 6).**

13 Turn the key to ON, but do not start the engine. The fuel pump should run. If it does not, there's a problem in the fuel pump circuit (see *General check* above).

14 Observe the reading on the fuel pressure gauge and compare it to the Specifications listed in this Chapter.

    a) *If the pressure is within Specification, proceed to the next Step.*

    b) *If the pressure is higher than specified, check for a faulty fuel pressure regulator or a pinched or clogged fuel return hose or pipe.*

    c) *If the pressure is lower than specified:*

        1) *Inspect the fuel filter (see Section 3) and make sure it's not clogged.*

➡**Note: Some models have another Schrader valve in the fuel pressure line, between the fuel pump and filter. If you have this arrangement, you may want to check the fuel pressure at this Schrader valve and compare the reading to the reading you got from the Schrader valve on the fuel rail. If the fuel-rail reading is more than 5 psi lower than the reading between the pump and filter, the filter should be replaced.**

        2) *Look for a pinched or clogged fuel hose or line between the fuel tank and the fuel rail.*

        3) *With the engine running, pinch the fuel return line. If the pressure rises, the fuel pressure regulator is probably faulty.*

        4) *Look for leaks in the fuel feed lines, hoses and fuel rail.*

        5) *Check for leaking injectors.*

        6) *If all the items listed above are OK, the problem is probably in the fuel pump.*

15 Disconnect the jumper wire from the DLC connector. Start the engine and allow it to idle. Compare the fuel pressure to this Chapter's Specifications. If the fuel pressure was OK with the engine off, but is now too high or too low, the problem is probably with the pressure regulator, its vacuum hose or the source of vacuum. Also, if the pressure is now too low, the fuel pump could be faulty (delivering too little fuel to maintain sufficient pressure when the injectors are opening and closing) or the electrical circuit to the fuel pump could be faulty (causing the fuel pump to run intermittently).

16 With the engine idling, disconnect and plug the vacuum hose from the fuel pressure regulator.

❋❋ **WARNING:**

Stay away from rotating engine components!

The pressure should rise. Unplug and re-connect the hose - the pressure should drop, returning to about where it was before the hose was disconnected. If there is no change in pressure when the hose is disconnected, the pressure regulator is faulty or sufficient vacuum is not reaching the regulator (check the vacuum hose).

17 Turn the ignition key to OFF. Verify fuel pressure remains within 5 psi of specified for 1 minute after shutting off the engine. If not, inspect for a faulty fuel pressure regulator, leaks in the fuel pressure lines or leaking injectors. Also, the check valve in the fuel pump could be leaking.

18 After testing is done, relieve the fuel system pressure (see Section 2) and remove the fuel pressure gauge.

1998 and later models

▶ **Refer to illustration 5.21**

19 Relieve the fuel pressure (see Section 2).

20 Disconnect the cable from the negative terminal of the battery.

21 Remove the cap from the pressure test port and attach a fuel pressure gauge (see illustration). If you don't have the correct adapter for the test port, remove the Schrader valve and connect the gauge hose to the fitting, using a hose clamp.

22 Reconnect the negative cable to the battery.

23 Turn the key to On, but don't start the engine. Let fuel pressure reach its maximum and note the reading. Compare your readings with the values listed in this Chapter's Specifications.

24 Switch the key off and watch the pressure gauge for one minute. Fuel pressure should not drop more than 5 psi in that time.

25 If fuel pressure is below the minimum specification, check for a clogged fuel filter and check the fuel lines for kinking or restriction. One way to do this is to disconnect the fuel line at the pump and at the fuel rail, then blow low-pressure air into the pump end of the line. If the air flows freely, the lines are clear.

26 If fuel pressure drops by more than 5 psi in one minute, look for a leak in the lines. Also check the injectors to make sure they are not leaking into the engine.

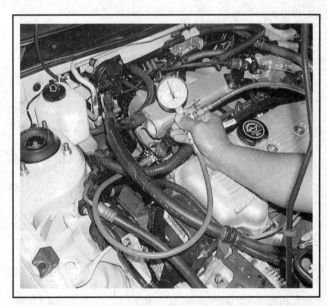

5.21 On 2.0L engines, attach a fuel pressure gauge to the pressure test port (2.0L SPI shown; 2.0L Zetec similar)

6 Fuel pump/sending unit assembly - removal, check and installation

REMOVAL

▶ **Refer to illustrations 6.4, 6.6, 6.8, 6.9a, 6.9b and 6.9c**

✳✳ WARNING:

Gasoline is extremely flammable, so take extra precautions when you work on any part of the fuel system. See the Warning in Section 2.

➡**Note: The pump/sending unit assembly is located within the fuel tank, but it can be replaced without removing the fuel tank.**

1 Relieve the fuel pressure (See Section 2). Disconnect the cable

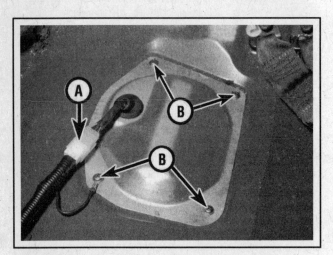

6.4 Disconnect the fuel pump/sending unit electrical connector(s) (A) (early models have a single fuel pump electrical connector while later models have two) and remove the cover screws (B)

from the negative terminal of the battery.
2 Remove the fuel tank filler cap to relieve any pressure in the fuel tank.
3 Remove the rear seat cushion (see Chapter 11).
4 Disconnect the fuel pump electrical connector(s) (see illustration).
5 Remove the fuel pump/sending unit cover screws and remove the fuel pump cover (see illustration 6.4). Note that on early models one of the covers screws secures a ground wire.
6 Disconnect the hairpin clip-type fittings from the fuel hose connections and disconnect the hoses from the pump fittings (see illustration). See Section 4 for more information on these fittings.
7 Remove any dirt that has accumulated where the fuel pump/sending unit assembly is attached to the fuel tank. Do not allow the dirt to enter the fuel tank.
8 Turn the lock ring counterclockwise until it's loose, using a hammer and a brass drift or wood dowel (see illustration).

✳✳ WARNING:

Do not use a steel drift or anything else that may cause a spark, since the fuel tank could explode!

9 Lift off the over (if equipped) and carefully pull the fuel pump/sending unit assembly from the tank (see illustrations). Don't bend the arm for the sending unit float.

✳✳ WARNING:

Place rags over the opening in the fuel tank to prevent vapors from escaping, which could lead to an explosion.

10 Remove and discard the old gasket.
11 Clean the fuel pump mounting flange, the tank mounting surface and the gasket groove.

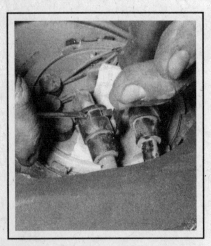

6.6 Disconnect the fuel line(s) (early models have two, later models have only one) from the pump/sending unit assembly

6.8 Use a brass punch and hammer to turn the lock ring counterclockwise

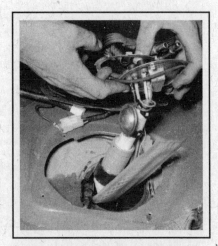

6.9a On early models, lift out the pump/sending unit and discard the gasket

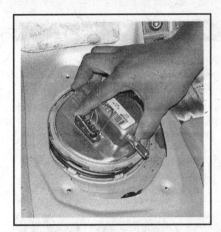

6.9b On later models, remove the cover . . .

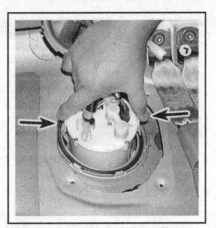

6.9c . . . then depress the two locking tabs (arrows) and lift out the pump/sending unit

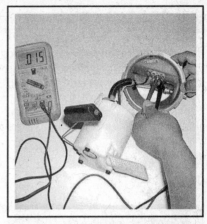

6.12 Measure resistance between the fuel level sending unit terminals with an ohmmeter (later model shown)

SENDING UNIT CHECK

▶ **Refer to illustration 6.12**

12 Position the probes of an ohmmeter on the sending unit terminals and check the resistance (see illustration). Use the 200-ohm scale on the ohmmeter.

13 With the float in the lowered position (fuel tank empty), resistance should be about 22 ohms. With the float raised (fuel tank full) the resistance should be about 145 ohms. The resistance should change smoothly as the float is moved.

14 If the readings are incorrect, replace the sending unit.

INSTALLATION

15 Installation is the reverse of the removal procedure with the following additions:

a) *Install a new gasket in the fuel tank groove.*

b) *Install the assembly into the fuel tank so that the tabs of the pump are positioned into the slots in the fuel tank. Make sure to keep the gasket in place during installation until the lock ring has been tightened properly.*

c) *Hold the fuel pump in place and tighten the lock ring clockwise until the stop is against the retainer ring tab.*

d) *Be sure the retaining clips are securely attached to the fuel lines. Before reinstalling the fuel pump cover, connect the fuel pump electrical connectors and start the engine, allowing it to run for a few minutes. Inspect the fuel line connections for leakage.*

7 Fuel tank - removal and installation

❋❋ WARNING:

Gasoline is extremely flammable, so take extra precautions when you work on any part of the fuel system. See the Warning in Section 2.

1 The following procedure is much easier to perform if the fuel tank is empty. Some tanks have a drain plug for this purpose. If the tank does not have a drain plug, siphon the gasoline once the fill pipe is disconnected.

❋❋ WARNING:

Use only siphoning equipment specifically designed for use with gasoline and follow the instructions included with the equipment. Siphon the fuel only into approved gasoline containers and cap the containers immediately after siphoning.

2 Perform Steps 1 through 6 of the previous Section.

3 Disconnect the negative cable from the battery.

4 Raise the vehicle and place it securely on jackstands.

5 Support the fuel tank with a floor jack or jackstands. Position a piece of wood between the jack head and the fuel tank to protect the tank.

6 Loosen the filler neck clamp.

7 Disconnect the hose from the filler neck. Siphon the fuel from the tank at the fill pipe opening (see the **Warning** in Step 1).

8 Compress the overflow hose clamp with pliers, then disconnect the hose from the overflow tube.

9 Disconnect the vapor hoses from the vapor tubes.

10 Remove the heat shield from the middle exhaust pipe.

11 Unbolt the fuel tank strap bolts. Unclip and remove the straps.

12 Unbolt the heat shield from the fuel tank.

13 Remove the tank from the vehicle.

14 Installation is the reverse of removal. Use new tank retaining strap bolts.

8   Fuel tank cleaning and repair general information

1   All service to the fuel tank or filler neck should be carried out by a professional who has experience in this critical and potentially dangerous work. Even after cleaning and flushing of the fuel system, explosive fumes can remain and ignite during repair of the tank.

2   If the fuel tank is removed from the vehicle, it should not be placed in an area where sparks or open flames could ignite the fumes coming out of the tank. Be especially careful inside garages where a gas-type appliance is located, because it could cause an explosion.

3   Whenever the fuel tank is steam-cleaned or otherwise serviced, the vapor valve assemblies should be replaced. All grommets and seals must be replaced to prevent possible leakage.

9   Air cleaner housing - removal and installation

1.8L ENGINE

1   Disconnect the negative cable from the battery.

2   Loosen the resonance chamber clamp at the vane air flow meter. Disconnect the chamber from the vane air flow meter.

9.8a On 1.9L engines, loosen the air intake tube clamp at the throttle body (arrow) . . .

9.8b . . . and mass airflow sensor (A); unplug the electrical connectors at the mass air flow sensor (B) . . .

3   Unplug the electrical connector at the vane air flow meter.

4   Unclamp and separate the resonance duct inlet hose from the resonance duct.

5   Remove the bolts and nut holding the air cleaner housing. Remove the housing assembly.

6   Installation is the reverse of the removal steps. Tighten all hose clamps and fittings securely.

1.9L ENGINE

▶ **Refer to illustrations 9.8a, 9.8b and 9.9**

7   Disconnect the negative cable from the battery.

8   Unclamp and disconnect the air intake tube at the throttle body and the mass air flow sensor (see illustrations). Remove the air intake duct. Cover the throttle body inlet to prevent the entry of foreign matter.

9   Disconnect the electrical connectors at the mass air flow (MAF) sensor and air charge temperature (ACT) sensor (see illustration).

10   Disconnect and remove the crankcase vent hose at the bottom of the air cleaner housing.

11   Remove the bolts and nut holding the air cleaner housing to the fender apron. Remove the housing assembly.

12   Installation is the reverse of the removal procedure. Tighten all hose clamps and fittings securely.

9.9 . . . and air charge temperature sensor (arrow)

9.13 Disconnect the IAT electrical connector (1), MAF sensor connector (2) and loosen the clamp (3) (2.0L SPI shown; 2.0L Zetec similar)

9.16 Disconnect the hose and remove the mounting bolts (arrows)

2.0L ENGINES

◆ **Refer to illustrations 9.13 and 9.16**

13 Disconnect the electrical connectors for the Intake Air Temperature (IAT) sensor and the Mass Air Flow (MAF) sensor (see illustration).

14 Disconnect the PCV and brake booster hoses form the air cleaner outlet tube. Loosen the hose clamp at each end of the tube, then detach the tube and remove it.

15 Loosen the clamp and take the cover off the air cleaner (see illustration 9.13).

16 Disconnect the PCV hose form the air cleaner housing (see illustration). Remove the housing mounting bolts and take the housing out.

17 Installation is the reverse of the removal steps.

10 Electronic fuel injection system - check

✳✳ WARNING:

Gasoline is extremely flammable, so take extra precautions when you work on any part of the fuel system. Don't smoke or allow open flames or bare light bulbs near the work area, and don't work in a garage where a gas-type appliance (such as a water heater or clothes dryer) is present. If you spill any fuel on your skin, rinse it off immediately with soap and water. When you perform any kind of work on the fuel system, wear safety glasses and have a Class B type fire extinguisher on hand.

1 Check the ground wire connections for tightness. Check all wiring and electrical connectors that are related to the system. Loose electrical connectors and poor grounds can cause many problems that resemble more serious malfunctions.

2 Check to see that the battery is fully charged, as the control unit and sensors depend on an accurate supply voltage in order to properly meter the fuel.

3 Check the air filter element - a dirty or partially blocked filter can severely impede performance and economy (see Chapter 1).

4 If a blown fuse is found, replace it and see if it blows again. If it does, search for a grounded wire in the harness related to the system.

5 Check the air intake duct from the airflow meter to the intake manifold for leaks, which will result in an excessively lean mixture. Also check the condition of the vacuum hoses connected to the intake manifold.

6 Remove the air intake duct from the throttle body and check for dirt, carbon or other residue build-up in the throttle body bore, particularly behind the throttle plate (open the plate by hand and use a flashlight to inspect thoroughly). If it's dirty, clean it with carburetor cleaner and a toothbrush (make sure the can says it's safe for use with oxygen sensors and catalytic converters).

✳✳ CAUTION:

Some models have a sludge-resistant coating inside the throttle bore, which may be damaged by carburetor cleaner. If there is a yellow ATTENTION decal on the throttle body, identifying it as having a sludge-resistant coating, do not use any solvents to clean it.

7 With the engine running, place a screwdriver or a stethoscope against each injector, one at a time, and listen through the handle for a clicking sound, indicating operation.

8 If an injector isn't operating (or sounds different than the others), turn off the engine and unplug the electrical connector from the injector. Check the resistance across the terminals of the injector and compare your reading with the resistance value listed in this Chapter's Specifications. If the resistance isn't as specified, replace the injector with a new one.

9 Check the fuel pressure (see Section 5).

10 If you're diagnosing a rough or unstable idle problem, let the engine idle and spray a little carburetor cleaner where each injector meets the cylinder head. If the idle smoothes out and stabilizes, there's probably a vacuum leak at the injector O-ring. Replace the O-rings (see Section 11, 12 or 13). This technique can also be used to find vacuum leaks at the intake manifold-to-cylinder head and throttle body-to-intake manifold gasket surfaces.

✳✳ CAUTION:

Make sure the carburetor cleaner you're using is safe for oxygen sensors and catalytic converters.

11 A rough idle, diminished performance and/or diminished fuel economy could also be caused by clogged fuel injectors. Fuel additives that can sometimes clean clogged injectors are available at auto parts stores.

12 The remainder of the system checks should be left to a dealer service department or other qualified repair shop, as there is a chance the control unit may be damaged if not performed properly.

11 Electronic fuel injection (1.8L engine) - component replacement

INTAKE PLENUM AND THROTTLE BODY

Removal

1 Disconnect the negative cable from the battery.

2 Remove the inlet air duct from between the throttle body and resonance chamber.

3 Label and disconnect the electrical connectors and vacuum lines that secure the intake plenum and air intake throttle body to the engine and body.

4 Disconnect the idle speed control and bypass air hoses from the intake plenum.

5 Disconnect the accelerator cable from the throttle cam. If equipped with an automatic transaxle, disconnect the kickdown cable from the throttle cam. Remove the cable bracket from the plenum.

6 Remove the upper mounting bolts and nuts holding the intake plenum to the intake manifold.

7 Raise the vehicle and place it securely on jackstands.

8 Remove the lower mounting bolts holding the intake plenum to the intake manifold.

9 Remove the jackstands and lower the vehicle to the ground.

10 Lift the plenum and throttle body together off the lower intake manifold.

Installation

11 Thoroughly clean all old gasket material from the mating surfaces of plenum and lower intake manifold.

12 Install a new gasket on the lower manifold, then install the plenum and tighten the upper bolts and nuts evenly to the torque listed in this Chapter's Specifications.

13 The remainder of installation is the reverse of the removal steps.

AIR INTAKE THROTTLE BODY

14 Remove the inlet air duct between the throttle body and resonance chamber.

15 Label and disconnect the electrical connectors and vacuum lines that connect the intake plenum and air intake throttle body.

16 Disconnect the idle speed control and bypass air hoses from the ISC valve.

17 Disconnect the accelerator cable from the throttle cam. If equipped with an automatic transaxle, disconnect the kickdown cable from the throttle cam. Remove the cable bracket from the plenum.

18 Remove the four throttle body mounting screws. Remove the throttle body and gasket from the intake plenum.

19 Carefully clean all old gasket material from the mating surface of throttle body and intake plenum.

✳✳ CAUTION:

Don't let gasket material fall into the plenum.

20 Place a new gasket on the plenum, then install the throttle body and tighten its screws to the torque listed in this Chapter's Specifications.

21 The remainder of installation is the reverse of the removal steps.

FUEL RAIL AND INJECTORS

Removal

22 Before starting, steam clean the engine to prevent dirt from contaminating exposed fittings and fuel metering orifices.

23 Relieve fuel system pressure (see Section 2).

24 Disconnect the negative cable from the battery. Tie the cable back out of the way so it can't accidentally contact the battery and restore power to the fuel injection system.

25 Disconnect the fuel supply and return lines (see Section 3).

26 Disconnect the PCV hose between the intake plenum and cylinder head cover.

27 Disconnect the vacuum line at the fuel pressure regulator.

28 Disconnect the fuel injector wiring harness electrical connectors.

29 Remove the fuel rail mounting bolts. Carefully remove the fuel rail and injectors with a rocking, pulling motion.

30 Detach the injectors from the fuel rail as follows:

a) *Disconnect the injector electrical connector from the individual injector(s).*

b) *Remove the injector retaining clip(s).*

c) *Carefully pull the injector out of the fuel rail with a rocking motion.*

Installation

▶ **Refer to illustration 11.31**

31 Check the injector O-rings for damage or deterioration and replace as needed (see illustration).

➡**Note: We recommend replacing the O-rings whenever the injectors are removed.**

32 Inspect the plastic "hat" that covers the end of each injector If it's not on the injector, it may be in the intake manifold. Replace the hat if it's damaged or deteriorated.

33 Lubricate the injector O-rings with light engine oil. Each injector uses two O-rings.

✳✳ CAUTION:

Don't lubricate the O-rings with silicone grease. It will clog the injectors.

34 Install the injectors in the fuel rail with a light rocking motion.

35 The remainder of installation is the reverse of the removal steps.

36 Turn the ignition key On and Off several times (without starting the engine) to pressurize the fuel system. Check all fuel system connections for leaks.

FUEL PRESSURE REGULATOR

▶ **Refer to illustration 11.41**

37 Disconnect the negative cable from the battery.

38 Relieve fuel system pressure (see Section 2).

39 Disconnect the vacuum line from the pressure regulator.

40 Disconnect the fuel return line from the pressure regulator.

41 Remove the regulator mounting bolts. Remove the regulator and O-ring. Discard the O-ring (see illustration).

42 Check the fuel return line for kinks or worn spots and replace as needed.

43 Lubricate the O-ring with light engine oil

➡**Note: Don't lubricate the O-ring with silicone grease. It will clog the injectors.**

44 The remainder of installation is the reverse of the removal steps. Tighten the pressure regulator bolts to the torque listed in this Chapter's Specifications.

BYPASS AIR VALVE

➡**Note: The bypass air valve allows additional air into the intake manifold during warm-up. This allows a higher, more stable idle speed when the engine is cold. The valve is controlled by a thermo-valve (threaded into a coolant jacket on the engine). When the engine is cold, the valve is fully open, allowing additional air to the intake manifold. As the engine warms up, the valve progressively closes until, when the engine is fully warmed up, the valve is completely closed. The PCM (computer) does not control this valve in any way.**

45 Remove the intake plenum as described in this section.

46 Remove the mounting screws, then take off the valve and gasket.

47 Thoroughly clean all old gasket material from the valve and its mounting surface.

48 Install the valve with a new gasket and tighten its bolts to the torque listed in this Chapter's Specifications.

49 Reinstall the intake plenum as described in this section.

THROTTLE POSITION (TP) SENSOR

▶ **Refer to illustrations 11.53a and 11.53b**

50 Locate the throttle position sensor on the intake air throttle body.

51 Disconnect the electrical connector from the throttle position sensor.

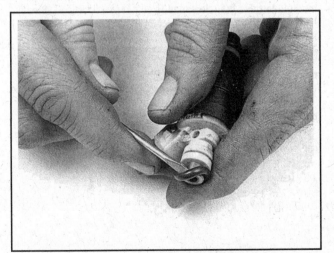

11.31 Each injector uses two O-rings; the injector pintle is protected by a plastic "hat" (1.8L engine)

11.41 Install a new O-ring on the fuel pressure regulator whenever the regulator is removed

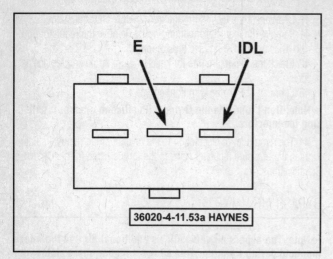

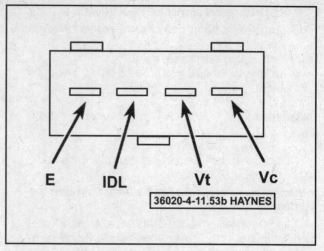

11.53a Throttle position sensor terminal identification (1.8L manual transaxle models)

11.53b Throttle position sensor terminal identification (1.8L automatic transaxle models)

52 Remove the two screws and take the throttle position sensor off the air intake throttle body.

53 Installation is the reverse of the removal steps, with the following adjustment steps required:

a) Connect an ohmmeter between the E and IDL terminals on the throttle position sensor (see illustrations).

b) Insert a 0.016 inch feeler gauge (manual transaxle models) or 0.010 inch feeler gauge (automatic transaxle models) between the throttle stop screw and the stop lever.

c) Loosen the throttle position sensor screws just enough to allow sensor movement.

d) Rotate the sensor clockwise about 30 degrees, then rotate it counterclockwise until the ohmmeter shows continuity.

e) Remove the feeler gauge installed between the stop screw and stop lever. Replace it with a 0.027 inch feeler gauge (manual transaxle models) or 0.016 inch feeler gauge (automatic transaxle models). With the larger feeler gauge in place, the ohmmeter should not show continuity. If it does, repeat this procedure.

f) Hold the sensor to prevent it from moving and tighten the mounting screws to the torque listed in this Chapter's Specifications.

g) Operate the throttle plate manually between its wide open and closed positions, then recheck adjustment by installing the thin feeler gauge between the stop screw and stop lever. The ohmmeter should show continuity until the thin feeler gauge is replaced by the thicker one.

h) If you're working on a vehicle with an automatic transaxle, check the resistance between sensor terminals E and Vt (see illustration 11.53b). If it isn't approximately 5,000 ohms, repeat the adjustment.

VANE AIR FLOW (VAF) METER

➡**Note: The Vane Air Temperature (VAT) sensor is an integral part of the VAF.**

54 Disconnect and remove the hose between the resonance chamber and vane air flow meter. Reposition the resonance chamber and air duct to provide working access.

55 Disconnect the vane air flow meter electrical connector.

56 Remove the ignition coil wire routing bracket.

57 Remove the vane air flow meter mounting nuts. Remove the air flow meter assembly and gasket.

58 Thoroughly clean all old gasket material from the vane air flow meter and its mounting surface.

59 Install the vane air flow meter with a new gasket and tighten its bolts to the torque listed in this Chapter's Specifications.

60 Reinstall the coil wire routing bracket and connect the electrical connector.

IDLE SPEED CONTROL (ISC) VALVE

➡**Note: The ISC valve maintains a steady idle speed when heavy mechanical or electrical loads are placed on the engine. It is a solenoid valve that allows additional air into the intake manifold to raise the idle speed to compensate for load. Since the ISC is controlled by the PCM (computer), the only check the home mechanic should perform is ISC valve resistance. To do this, remove the electrical connector from the valve and check the resistance across its electrical terminals with a digital ohmmeter. Compare the reading to this Chapter's Specifications. Replace the valve if it is not within specifications. Any further diagnosis should be left to a dealer service department or other qualified shop.**

61 Remove the air intake throttle body (see the procedure starting at Step 14 above).

62 Remove the ISC valve mounting screws and lift off the ISC valve.

63 Remove all traces of old gasket material, then install the valve, using a new gasket.

64 Install the air intake throttle body.

12 Electronic fuel injection (1.9L engine) - component replacement

AIR INTAKE THROTTLE BODY

▶ **Refer to illustrations 12.1, 12.3 and 12.5**

1 Disconnect the air intake tube at the air intake throttle body and disconnect the electrical connector for the idle air control valve (see illustration).

2 Disconnect the throttle position sensor electrical connector (see illustration 12.40).

3 Disconnect the vacuum line at the bottom of the air intake throttle body (see illustration).

4 Disconnect the accelerator cable from the throttle lever. If equipped with an automatic transaxle, disconnect the kickdown cable from the throttle lever.

5 Remove the four throttle body mounting bolts (see illustration). Remove the throttle body and gasket from the air intake manifold.

6 Carefully clean all traces of old gasket material from the mating surface of the air intake throttle body and air intake manifold.

✳ CAUTION:

Don't let gasket material fall into the air intake manifold; stuff a rag into the opening. If you scrape off the old gasket material, be very careful not to scratch or gouge the delicate aluminum.

7 Place a new gasket on the air intake manifold, then install the air intake throttle body and tighten its bolts to the torque listed in this Chapter's Specifications.

8 The remainder of installation is the reverse of the removal steps.

IDLE AIR CONTROL (IAC) VALVE

▶ **Refer to illustration 12.9**

➡ **Note: The IAC valve maintains a steady idle speed when heavy mechanical or electrical loads are placed on the engine. It also**

increases idle speed during warm-up. It is a solenoid valve that allows additional air into the intake manifold to raise the idle speed to compensate for load or a cold engine. Idle speed should not require adjustment on these models. Since the ISC is controlled by the PCM (computer), any diagnosis (other than checking for trouble codes - see Chapter 6) should be left to a dealer service department or other qualified shop.

9 Disconnect the idle air control valve electrical connector and remove the two mounting bolts (see illustration).

10 Take off the valve and gasket.

11 Thoroughly clean all old gasket material from the valve and its mounting surface.

✳ CAUTION:

Don't let gasket material fall into the upper manifold and, if you're using a scraper to remove the gasket, be careful not to gouge or scratch the delicate aluminum surfaces.

12.1 The air intake tube is secured by a clamp and the electrical connector by a single tab (1.9L engine)

12.3 This vacuum line is connected to a fitting on the underside of the throttle body (1.9L engine)

12.5 The throttle body is secured by four bolts (arrows) (1.9L engine)

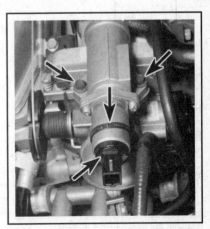

12.9 The idle air control valve has a single electrical connector and two mounting bolts; the harness tie wrap must also be detached (arrows) (1.9L engine)

12.20 The fuel rail is secured by two bolts (arrows) (1.9L engine)

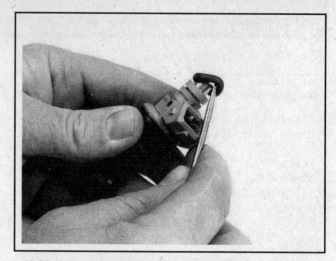

12.22 Remove the old O-rings from the injectors and install new ones

21 Detach the injectors from the fuel rail as follows:
   a) *Remove the injector retaining clip(s).*
   b) *Carefully pull the injector out of the fuel rail with a rocking motion.*

Installation

▶ **Refer to illustration 12.22**

22 Check the injector O-rings for damage or deterioration and replace as needed (see illustration).

23 Inspect the plastic "hat" that covers the end of each injector (see illustration 11.31). If it's not on the injector, it may be in the intake manifold. Replace the hat if damaged or deteriorated.

24 Lubricate the injector O-rings with light engine oil. Each injector uses two O-rings.

> ⁑ **CAUTION:**
>
> **Don't lubricate the O-rings with silicone grease. It will clog the injectors.**

25 Install the injectors in the fuel rail with a light rocking motion.

26 The remainder of installation is the reverse of the removal steps.

27 Turn the ignition key On and Off several times (without starting the engine) to pressurize the fuel system. Check all fuel system connections for leaks.

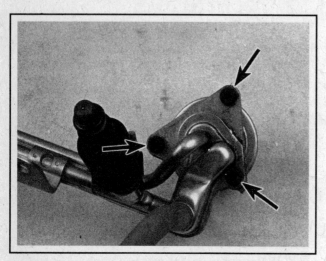

12.30 The fuel pressure regulator is retained by three screws (1.9L engine)

12 Install the valve with a new gasket and tighten its bolts securely.

13 Connect the electrical connector.

FUEL RAIL AND INJECTORS

▶ **Refer to illustration 12.20**

Removal

14 Before starting, steam clean the engine to prevent dirt from contaminating exposed fittings and fuel metering orifices.

15 Relieve fuel system pressure (see Section 2).

16 Disconnect the negative cable from the battery. Tie the cable back out of the way so it can't accidentally contact the battery and restore power to the fuel injection system.

17 Disconnect the vacuum line at the fuel pressure regulator.

18 Disconnect the fuel supply and return lines (see Section 4).

19 Disconnect the electrical connector at each fuel injector.

20 Remove two bolts that secure the fuel rail (see illustration). Carefully lift the fuel rail and injectors out with a rocking, pulling motion.

FUEL PRESSURE REGULATOR

▶ **Refer to illustration 12.30**

28 Relieve fuel system pressure (see Section 2).

29 Remove the fuel rail as described in this Section.

30 Remove the three mounting screws from the regulator (see illustration).

31 Remove the pressure regulator, gasket and O-ring from the fuel rail. Discard the gasket and O-ring.

32 Check the fuel return line for kinks or worn spots and replace as needed.

33 Lubricate the new O-ring (if equipped) with light engine oil.

➡**Note: Don't lubricate the O-ring with silicone grease. It will clog the injectors.**

34 The remainder of installation is the reverse of the removal Steps. Be sure to use a new gasket and/or O-ring.

AIR CHARGE TEMPERATURE (ACT) SENSOR

35 Disconnect the electrical connector from the air charge temperature sensor (see illustration 9.9).

36 Unscrew the sensor from the air cleaner housing.

37 Installation is the reverse of the removal steps.

THROTTLE POSITION (TP) SENSOR

◆ **Refer to illustration 12.40**

38 Disconnect and remove the air intake tube.

39 Look for scribed alignment marks on the throttle position sensor and throttle body. If they aren't visible, make your own.

40 Disconnect the electrical connector from the throttle position sensor and remove the two mounting screws (see illustration).

41 Carefully take the sensor off, noting the position of the tangs which engage with the throttle body.

42 Installation is the reverse of the removal steps, with the following additions:

a) *Be sure the rotary tangs on the sensor are aligned properly. Slide them into position over the throttle shaft blade, then rotate the throttle position sensor clockwise only to align the scribe marks. Rotating the sensor counterclockwise may cause excessive idle speeds.*

b) *Be sure the electrical leads are pointing down.*

c) *Tighten the screws to the torque listed in this Chapter's Specifications.*

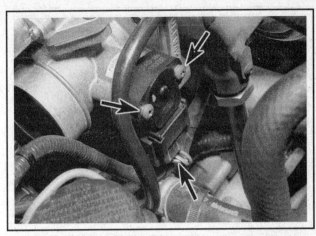

12.40 The throttle position sensor is secured by two screws and has a single electrical connector (arrows) (1.9L engine)

MASS AIR FLOW (MAF) SENSOR

43 Disconnect the negative cable from the battery.

44 Disconnect and remove the air intake tube between the MAF sensor and air intake throttle body (see illustration 9.8b).

45 Disconnect the MAF sensor electrical connector.

46 Remove the four screws and take the mass air flow sensor off the air cleaner lid. Remove the sensor gasket.

✳✳ CAUTION:

If the sensor gasket has deteriorated and requires scraping to remove it, work carefully to prevent damage to the air cleaner lid or the sensor gasket surfaces.

47 Installation is the reverse of removal.

13 Electronic fuel injection (2.0L engines) - component replacement

AIR INTAKE THROTTLE BODY

◆ **Refer to illustrations 13.1 and 13.5**

1 Disconnect the air intake tube at the air intake throttle body (see illustration).

2 Disconnect the idle air control valve and throttle position sensor electrical connectors.

3 Disconnect the vacuum line at the bottom of the air intake throttle body.

4 Disconnect the accelerator cable from the throttle lever. If equipped with an automatic transaxle, disconnect the kickdown cable from the throttle lever. If equipped with cruise control, detach the activator from the throttle pulley.

5 Remove the four throttle body mounting bolts (see illustration). Remove the throttle body and gasket from the air intake manifold.

6 Carefully clean all traces of old gasket material from the mating

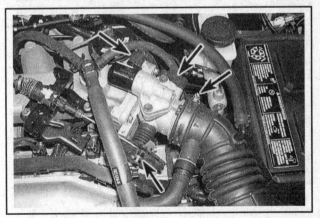

13.1 Disconnect the electrical connectors from the IAC valve and TPS and remove the air cleaner outlet tube and throttle cable from the throttle body

13.5 Remove the throttle body mounting bolts (arrows)

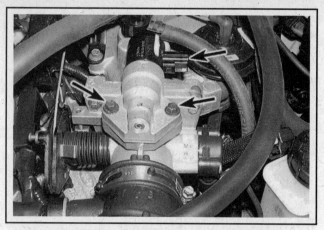

13.9 Idle air control valve mounting screws and electrical connector (arrows) (2.0L SPI shown; 2.0L Zetec similar)

13.20 Fuel pressure sensor and fuel injector electrical connectors (arrows) (2.0L SPI shown; 2.0L Zetec similar)

surface of the air intake throttle body and air intake manifold.

✳✳ CAUTION:

Don't let gasket material fall into the air intake manifold; stuff a rag into the opening. If you scrape off the old gasket material, be very careful not to scratch or gouge the delicate aluminum.

7   Place a new gasket on the air intake manifold, then install the air intake throttle body and tighten its bolts to the torque listed in this Chapter's Specifications.

8   The remainder of installation is the reverse of the removal steps.

IDLE AIR CONTROL VALVE

▶ Refer to illustration 13.9

➡ **Note:** The idle air control valve maintains a steady idle speed when heavy mechanical or electrical loads are placed on the engine. It also increases idle speed during warm-up. It is a solenoid valve that allows additional air into the intake manifold to raise the idle speed to compensate for load or a cold engine. Idle speed should not require adjustment on these models.

Since the idle air control valve is controlled by the PCM, any diagnosis (other than checking for trouble codes - see Chapter 6) should be left to a dealer service department or other qualified shop.

9   Disconnect the idle air control valve electrical connector and remove the two mounting bolts (see illustration). The 2.0L SPI valve is on top of the throttle body. The 2.0L Zetec is underneath.

10   Carefully remove the valve and gasket.

11   Thoroughly clean all old gasket material from the valve and its mounting surface.

✳✳ CAUTION:

Don't let gasket material fall into the upper manifold and, if you're using a scraper to remove the gasket, be careful not to gouge or scratch the delicate aluminum surfaces.

12   Install the valve with a new gasket and tighten its bolts securely.

13   Connect the electrical connector.

FUEL RAIL AND INJECTORS

▶ Refer to illustrations 13.20 and 13.21

Removal

14   Before starting, clean the area around the injectors to prevent dirt from contaminating exposed fittings and fuel metering orifices.

15   Relieve fuel system pressure (see Section 2).

16   Disconnect the negative cable from the battery.

17   If you're working on a 2.0L SPI engine, disconnect the electrical connector at the crankshaft position sensor and the two main harness connectors above the passenger's side wheel well in the engine compartment.

18   If you're working on a 2.0L Zetec engine, remove the air cleaner outlet tube and the throttle body as described above.

19   Disconnect the fuel supply line (see Section 4).

20   Move the protective rail for the fuel injection wiring harness out of the way. Disconnect the vacuum line and electrical connector at the fuel pressure regulator or fuel pressure sensor and the electrical connectors at each fuel injector (see illustration). If you're working on a 2.0L SPI engine model, disconnect the electrical connector from the

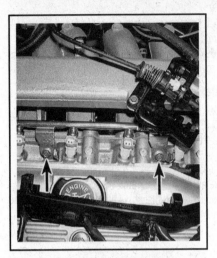

13.21 Fuel rail mounting bolts (arrows) (2.0L SPI shown; 2.0L Zetec similar)

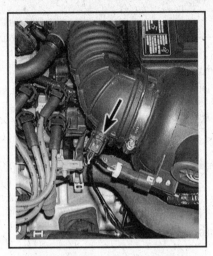

13.34 Intake Air Temperature (IAT) sensor electrical connector (2.0L SPI shown; 2.0L Zetec similar)

13.39 Throttle position sensor mounting screws (arrows) (2.0L SPI shown; 2.0L Zetec similar)

camshaft position sensor (see Chapter 6).

21 Remove two bolts that secure the fuel rail (see illustration). Carefully lift the fuel rail and injectors out with a rocking, pulling motion.

22 Detach the injectors from the fuel rail as follows:

   a) *Remove the injector retaining clip(s) (2.0L Zetec only).*

   b) *Carefully pull the injector out of the fuel rail with a rocking motion.*

Installation

23 Check the injector O-rings for damage or deterioration and replace as needed.

24 Inspect the cap and body of each injector. Replace the injector if damaged or deteriorated.

25 Lubricate the injector O-rings with light engine oil. Each injector uses two O-rings.

✷✷ CAUTION:

Don't lubricate the O-rings with silicone grease. It will clog the injectors.

26 Install the injectors in the fuel rail with a light rocking motion.

27 The remainder of installation is the reverse of the removal steps.

28 Turn the ignition key On and Off several times (without starting the engine) to pressurize the fuel system. Check all fuel system connections for leaks.

FUEL PRESSURE SENSOR

➡**Note: Refer to Section 12 for fuel pressure regulator replacement on 1997 models.**

29 Relieve fuel system pressure (see Section 2).

30 Disconnect the electrical connector and vacuum line from the sensor. Remove the mounting screws from the sensor (see illustration 13.20).

31 Remove the sensor and O-rings from the fuel rail. Discard the O-rings.

32 Lubricate the new O-rings with light engine oil.

➡**Note: Don't lubricate the O-ring with silicone grease. It will clog the injectors.**

33 The remainder of installation is the reverse of the removal steps. Be sure to use new O-rings.

INTAKE AIR TEMPERATURE (IAT) SENSOR

♦ **Refer to illustration 13.34**

34 Disconnect the electrical connector from the intake air temperature sensor (see illustration).

35 Twist the sensor counterclockwise and pull it from the air cleaner housing.

36 Installation is the reverse of the removal steps.

THROTTLE POSITION (TP) SENSOR

♦ **Refer to illustration 13.39**

37 Disconnect and remove the air cleaner outlet tube.

38 Look for scribed alignment marks on the throttle position sensor and throttle body. If they aren't visible, make your own.

39 Disconnect the electrical connector from the throttle position sensor and remove the two mounting screws (see illustration).

40 Carefully take the sensor off, noting the position of the tangs which engage with the throttle body.

41 Installation is the reverse of the removal steps, with the following additions:

   a) *Be sure the rotary tangs on the sensor are aligned properly. Turn the throttle position sensor 1/4-turn clockwise from its installed position, then slide it into position over the throttle shaft blade and rotate the throttle position sensor counterclockwise only to align the scribe marks. Rotating the sensor clockwise may cause excessive idle speeds.*

   b) *Be sure the electrical leads are pointing down.*

   c) *Tighten the screws to the torque listed in this Chapter's Specifications.*

MASS AIR FLOW (MAF) SENSOR

42 Disconnect the negative cable from the battery.

43 Disconnect the air cleaner outlet tube and remove the air cleaner.

44 Pry the MAF sensor electrical connector's grommet out of the MAF sensor, then disconnect the electrical connector (see illustration 9.13).

45 Pry out the MAF sensor cover with a screwdriver, then remove the two mounting nuts and the MAF sensor.

46 Installation is the reverse of removal.

FUEL PUMP DRIVER MODULE

Coupe and sedan models

47 Working inside the luggage compartment, remove the rear panel trim cover. Remove the left (driver's-side) quarter panel trim cover.

48 Remove the nuts retaining the fuel pump driver module to the body brace, pull the module out and disconnect the electrical connector.

49 Installation is the reverse of removal.

Station wagon models

50 Working inside the luggage compartment, remove the rear panel trim cover.

51 Lay the left rear seat back down and remove the left rear radio speaker and grille.

52 Pull the carpet back and remove the left quarter panel trim cover.

53 Remove the nuts retaining the fuel pump driver module to the body brace, pull the module out and disconnect the electrical connector.

54 Installation is the reverse of removal.

14 Variable Inertia Charging System (VICS) - general information

The 1.8L air intake system incorporates a variable inertia charging system in the air intake plenum. This system is designed to increase the length of the air intake path in the intake manifold at engine speeds above 5,000 RPM to produce greater engine torque with a wider torque band at high engine speeds.

The system consists of four normally-closed shutter valves mounted on a single rod inside a dual-port intake plenum. The rod is externally connected to a vacuum-operated shutter valve actuator mounted on the passenger's side of the plenum. A manifold port below the shutter valve actuator routes vacuum to a vacuum storage canister. The canister contains a check valve to prevent vacuum back flow, and is connected to a 3-way solenoid valve controlled by the PCM.

The system applies vacuum to the shutter valve actuator to hold the shutters closed at engine speeds below 5,000 RPM. When this engine speed is reached, the PCM signals the actuator to vent vacuum to the atmosphere. This opens the shutter valves, increasing the air intake path and altering the resonance-induced inertia charging effect. When engine speed drops below 5,000 RPM, the PCM reapplies vacuum to the actuator to close the shutter valves.

The vacuum storage canister also provides vacuum to hold the shutter valves closed during momentary periods of low vacuum, as during high engine load or wide open throttle conditions.

The only serviceable parts of the VICS system are the shutter valve actuator, vacuum storage canister and the 3-way solenoid valve.

Beyond checking for the presence or absence of vacuum, diagnosis of the VICS system is well beyond the ability of the home mechanic. If engine performance deteriorates, take the vehicle to a dealer service department to have the VICS system checked.

15 Intake Manifold Runner Control (IMRC) system - general information

♦ **Refer to illustration 15.1**

1997 and later 2.0L SPI models are equipped with an Intake Manifold Runner Control (IMRC) system. The IMRC system consists of the IMRC valves (located inside the IMRC housing between the intake manifold and cylinder head), IMRC valve actuator and the PCM (see Illustration).

The IMRC valves divert the path of the incoming air through the intake manifold. The intake manifold is constructed with two separate air passages for each cylinder. One passage is open at all times and the other passage is opened and closed by the butterfly valves inside the IMRC housing. At low engine speeds (below 3000 rpm) the valves are closed and air is diverted through one path to enhance maximum torque at low speed. At a preset engine speed (3000 rpm) the PCM energizes the IMRC valve actuator and the IMRC valves open. Air is then drawn through both passages enhancing high speed power.

15.1 The Intake Manifold Runner Control actuator (arrow) is located at the end of the IMRC valve housing

16 Fuel pump inertia switch - removal and installation

1   The fuel pump switch - sometimes called the "inertia switch" - shuts off fuel to the engine in the event of a collision (any sudden jolt will trip it). See Section 2 for switch locations.

2   Relieve fuel system pressure (see Section 2).

3   Remove trim panel(s) as necessary for access to the switch.

4   Unplug the inertia switch electrical connector.

5   Remove the inertia switch mounting screws.

6   Reconnect the electrical connector to the switch and push the reset button on the top of the switch. Reinstall the trim panel.

17 Exhaust system servicing - general information

❊❊ WARNING:

Inspection and repair of exhaust system components should be done only after enough time has elapsed after driving the vehicle to allow the system components to cool completely. Also, when working under the vehicle, make sure it is securely supported on jackstands.

1   The 1.8L exhaust system is a five-piece assembly consisting of an exhaust manifold, the inlet pipe, the catalytic converter, the outlet pipe/resonator/middle pipe assembly, the muffler and tailpipe assembly, and all attaching brackets, heat shields, hangers and clamps.

2   The 1.9L and 2.0L exhaust system is a four-piece assembly consisting of an exhaust manifold, the catalytic converter and outlet pipe, middle pipe assembly, the muffler and tailpipe assembly, and all attaching brackets, heat shields, hangers and clamps.

3   The exhaust system is attached to the body with mounting brackets and rubber hangers (it's also bolted to the engine oil pan on 1.9L engine models). If any of these components are improperly installed, excessive noise and vibration will be transmitted to the body.

4   Conduct regular inspections of the exhaust system to keep it safe and quiet. Look for any damaged or bent parts, open seams, holes, loose connections, excessive corrosion or other defects which could allow exhaust fumes to enter the vehicle. Deteriorated exhaust system components should not be repaired; they should be replaced with new parts.

5   If the exhaust system components are extremely corroded or rusted together, welding equipment will probably be required to remove them. The convenient way to accomplish this is to have a muffler repair shop remove the corroded sections with a cutting torch. If, however, you want to save money by doing it yourself (and you don't have a welding outfit with a cutting torch), simply cut off the old components with a hacksaw. If you have compressed air, special pneumatic cutting chisels can also be used. If you do decide to tackle the job at home, be sure to wear safety goggles to protect your eyes from metal chips and work gloves to protect your hands.

6   Here are some simple guidelines to follow when repairing the exhaust system:

a) *Work from the back to the front when removing exhaust system components.*

b) *Apply penetrating oil to the exhaust system component fasteners to make them easier to remove.*

c) *Use new gaskets, hangers and clamps when installing exhaust systems components.*

d) *Apply anti-seize compound to the threads of all exhaust system fasteners during reassembly.*

e) *Be sure to allow sufficient clearance between newly installed parts and all points on the underbody to avoid overheating the floor pan and possibly damaging the interior carpet and insulation. Pay particularly close attention to the catalytic converter and heat shields.*

Specifications

General

Fuel injector resistance	11 to 18 ohms
ISC valve resistance	6 to 14 ohms
Fuel pressure	
1.8L and 1.9L engines	
Engine not running	35 to 45 psi
Engine running	30 to 40 psi
2.0L engines	
1997	
Engine not running	35 to 45 psi
Engine running	30 to 40 psi
1998 and later	
Engine not running	50 to 85 psi
Engine running	25 to 35 psi

Torque specifications — Ft-lbs (unless otherwise indicated)

➡ Note: One foot-pound (ft-lb) of torque is equivalent to 12 inch-pounds (in-lbs) of torque. Torque values below approximately 15 ft-lbs are expressed in inch-pounds, since most foot-pound torque wrenches are not accurate at these smaller values.

1.8L engine

Fuel pressure regulator bolt	69 to 95 in-lbs
Fuel rail mounting bolts	14 to 19
Intake plenum bolts and nuts	14 to 19
Throttle body mounting bolts	14 to 19

1.9L engine

Fuel pressure regulator mounting screws	27 to 40 in-lbs
Fuel rail mounting bolts	15 to 22
Mass air flow sensor screws	72 to 108 in-lbs
Throttle body mounting bolts	15 to 22
Throttle position sensor screws	25 to 30 in-lbs

2.0L engines

Idle Air Control (IAC) valve bolts	62 to 88 in-lbs
Throttle position sensor screws	26 in-lbs
Mass Air Flow (MAF) sensor nuts	71 to 106 in-lbs
Fuel pressure sensor bolts	27 to 40 in-lbs
Throttle body bolts	
2.0L SPI	15 to 22
2.0L Zetec	71 to 106 in-lbs
Fuel pressure relief valve	70 in-lbs
Fuel rail bolts	
2.0L SPI	15 to 22
2.0L Zetec	71 to 106 in-lbs

Section

Reference to other Chapters

CHECK ENGINE light on - See Chapter 6

5

ENGINE ELECTRICAL SYSTEMS

1 General information

The engine electrical systems include all ignition, charging and starting components. Because of their engine-related functions, these components are considered separately from chassis electrical devices like the lights, instruments, etc.

Be very careful when working on the engine electrical components. They are easily damaged if checked, connected or handled improperly. The alternator is driven by an engine drivebelt which could cause serious injury if your hands, hair or clothes become entangled in it with the engine running. Both the starter and alternator are connected directly to the battery and could arc or even cause a fire if mishandled, overloaded or shorted out.

Never leave the ignition switch on for long periods of time with the engine off. Don't disconnect the battery cables while the engine is running. Correct polarity must be maintained when connecting battery cables from another source, such as another vehicle, during jump starting. Always disconnect the negative cable first and hook it up last or the battery may be shorted by the tool being used to loosen the cable clamps.

Additional safety related information on the engine electrical systems can be found in *Safety first* near the front of this manual. It should be referred to before beginning any operation included in this Chapter.

2 Battery - removal and installation

♦ **Refer to illustrations 2.1a, 2.1b and 2.5**

1   Disconnect both cables from the battery terminals (see illustrations).

✳✳ CAUTION:

Always disconnect the negative cable first and hook it up last or the battery may be shorted by the tool being used to loosen the cable clamps.

2   Loosen the two battery hold-down clamp nuts enough to disengage the hold-down legs from the battery tray. Remove the hold-down clamp as an assembly.

3   On models so equipped, disengage the battery shroud from the battery duct. Remove the battery shroud.

4   Lift out the battery. Special straps or clamps that attach to the battery are available - lifting and moving the battery is much easier if you use one.

5   If necessary, unbolt the battery tray and lift it out (see illustration).

6   Installation is the reverse of the removal steps. Make sure the battery cables and battery posts are free of corrosion. Clean them if necessary (see Section 4).

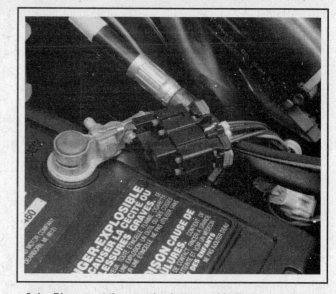

2.1a Disconnect the negative battery cable first . . .

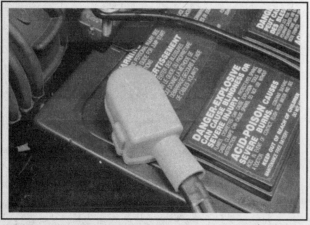

2.1b . . . then disconnect the positive cable (its clamp is located beneath a plastic cover)

2.5 Unbolt the battery tray and lift it out

3   Battery - emergency jump starting

Refer to the *Booster battery (jump) starting* procedure at the front of this manual.

4   Battery cables - check and replacement

1   Periodically inspect the entire length of each battery cable for damage, cracked or burned insulation and corrosion. Poor battery cable connections can cause starting problems and decreased engine performance.

2   Check the cable-to-terminal connections at the ends of the cables for cracks, loose wire strands and corrosion. The presence of white, fluffy deposits under the insulation at the cable terminal connection is a sign that the cable is corroded and should be replaced. Check the terminals for distortion, missing mounting bolts and corrosion.

3   When replacing the cables, always disconnect the negative cable first and hook it up last or the battery may be shorted by the tool used to loosen the cable clamps. Even if only the positive cable is being replaced, be sure to disconnect the negative cable from the battery first.

4   Disconnect and remove the cable. Make sure the replacement cable is the same length and wire size (diameter).

5   Clean the threads of the starter relay or ground connection with a wire brush to remove rust and corrosion. Apply a light coat of petroleum jelly to the threads to prevent future corrosion.

6   Attach the cable to the starter relay or ground connection and tighten the mounting nut/bolt to the torque listed in this Chapter's Specifications.

7   Before connecting the new cable to the battery, make sure that it reaches the battery post without having to be stretched. Clean the battery posts and cable ends thoroughly and apply a light coat of petroleum jelly to prevent corrosion (see Chapter 1).

8   Connect the positive cable first, followed by the negative cable.

5   Ignition system - general information

➡**Note: Many ignition system components are covered by a Federally mandated extended warranty (5 years or 50,000 miles at the time this manual was written). Check with a dealer service department before replacing components yourself.**

ELECTRONIC SPARK ADVANCE (ESA) SYSTEM (1.8L ENGINE MODELS)

The 1.8L engine ignition system is a solid state electronic design consisting of an ignition module, coil, distributor, the spark plug wires and the spark plugs. The distributor is mounted on the flywheel end of the engine and driven directly by the camshaft at one-half crankshaft speed. Two drive tangs on the distributor shaft engage with corresponding slots in the camshaft. The distributor contains a crankshaft position (CP) sensor, a cylinder identification sensor and the rotor. It rotates counterclockwise as seen from the driver's side of the vehicle.

Mechanically, the system is similar to a breaker point system, except that the distributor cam and ignition points are replaced by two photo diodes and a revolving disc containing slots that provide the crankshaft position and cylinder identification signals. The coil primary circuit is controlled by the ignition module.

When the ignition is switched on, the ignition primary circuit is energized. As the four slots in the outer edge of the disc pass through one of the photo diodes, four evenly spaced signals are created with every revolution of the disc. These signals control the transistors in the ignition module to make and break the ignition coil primary circuit. The signals also are sent to the ECA where they are used for control of ignition timing and determination of engine speed. A timing circuit in the module turns the coil current back on after the coil field has collapsed.

➡**Note: The second photo diode produces one signal per distributor revolution as the single slot on the inside of the disc passes by it. This cylinder identification signal is used by the ECA for calculation of fuel injection timing.**

When the coil is on, current flows from the battery through the ignition switch, the coil primary winding, the ignition module and then to ground. When the current is interrupted, the magnetic field in the ignition coil collapses, inducing a high voltage in the coil secondary windings. The voltage is conducted to the distributor where the rotor directs it to the appropriate spark plug. This process is repeated continuously.

Ignition timing is controlled by the powertrain control module (PCM). The distributor transmits crankshaft position, engine rpm, and piston travel data to the PCM, which signals the ignition module when to fire the coil.

ELECTRONIC DISTRIBUTORLESS (EDIS) TYPE (1.9L AND 2.0L ENGINE MODELS)

The 1.9L and 2.0L engines are equipped with the Electronic Distributorless Ignition System (EDIS) that is a solid state electronic design. It consists of a crankshaft position sensor (or VRS), EDIS module (1.9L engine only), EDIS coil pack, the spark angle portion of the EEC, the spark plug wires and the spark plugs.

This ignition system does not have any moving parts (no distributor) and all engine timing and spark distribution is handled electronically. This system has fewer parts that require replacement and provides more accurate spark timing. During engine operation, the EDIS ignition module and the EEC module calculate spark angle and determine the turn on and firing time of the ignition coil. The EDIS module consists of a microprocessor and coil drivers.

The crankshaft position sensor is a variable reluctance-type consisting of a 36-tooth trigger wheel with one missing tooth that is pressed onto the rear of the crankshaft front damper. The signal generated by this sensor is called a Variable Reluctance Sensor signal (VRS) and it provides the base timing and engine rpm information to the EDIS ignition module. The main function of the EDIS module is to synchronize the ignition coils so they are turned on and off in the proper sequence for accurate spark control. 2.0L engines are not equipped with an EDIS module. The PCM controls ignition timing and spark distribution.

6   Ignition system - check

▶ **Refer to illustration 6.2**

> ✳✳ **WARNING:**
>
> **Because of the very high secondary (spark plug) voltage generated by the ignition system, extreme care should be taken when this check is done.**

1   Disconnect the spark plug lead from any spark plug and attach it to a calibrated ignition tester (available at most auto parts stores).

2   Connect the clip on the tester to a bolt or metal bracket on the engine (see illustration), crank the engine and watch the end of the tester to see if bright blue, well-defined sparks occur.

3   If sparks occur, sufficient voltage is reaching the plug to fire it. Repeat the check at the remaining plug wires to verify that the wires and distributor cap and rotor (1.8L) or ignition coil pack (1.9L) are OK. However, the plugs themselves may be fouled, so remove and check them as described in Chapter 1 or install new ones.

4   If no sparks or intermittent sparks occur, remove the wires and distributor cap (1.8L engine models only) and check the cap and rotor as described in Chapter 1. If moisture is present, dry out the cap and rotor, then reinstall the cap and repeat the spark test. On all models, check the spark plug wires (see Chapter 1).

5   On all models, make sure there are no stored trouble codes (see Chapter 6). Further testing should be left to a dealer service department.

6.2 To use a calibrated ignition tester (available at most auto parts stores), simply disconnect a spark plug wire, attach the wire to the tester, clip the tester to a convenient ground (like a valve cover bolt) and operate the starter - if there's enough power to fire the plug, sparks will be visible between the electrode tip and the tester body

7   Ignition coil pack (1.9L and 2.0L engine models) – removal and installation

▶ **Refer to illustrations 7.2 and 7.4**

➡ **Note: Checking the coil pack is beyond the scope of the home mechanic, since special test equipment is required. If there are no stored trouble codes (see Chapter 6), take the vehicle to a dealer service department for further diagnosis.**

1   Disconnect the negative cable from the battery.

2   Disconnect the electrical connector at the coil pack and capacitor assembly (see illustration).

3   Using pieces of numbered tape, mark the spark plug wires to the coil terminals (if no numbers are present on the spark plug wires and the coil terminals). Squeeze the locking tabs of the spark plug wire connectors by hand and remove each spark plug wire from the ignition coil assembly with a twisting and pulling motion (see illustration 7.2). DO NOT just pull on the wires to disconnect them. Disconnect all spark plug wires.

4   Remove the four bolts securing the ignition coil pack and capacitor assembly (see illustration). Save the capacitor for reuse and remove the coil pack.

5   If bracket removal is required, remove the three mounting bolts and detach the coil bracket.

6   Installation is the reverse of the removal procedure with the following additions:

a) *Whenever a spark plug wire is removed from either the spark plug or the ignition coil pack, the boot should be coated with silicone dielectric compound*

b) *Insert each spark plug wire into the proper terminal of the ignition coil pack (see illustration 7.2). Push the wire into the terminal and make sure the boots are fully seated and both locking tabs are engaged properly.*

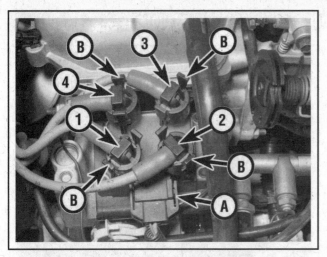

7.2 Disconnect the connector (A), then squeeze the locking tabs (B) to disconnect the wires - refer to the cylinder numbers to make sure the wires are reconnected to the proper terminals

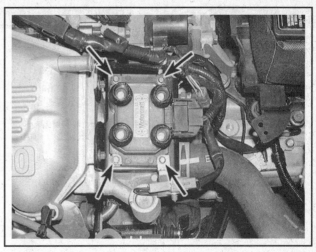

7.4 Remove the ignition coil pack mounting bolts (arrows) (one of the bolts also secures the condenser)

8   Crankshaft position sensor - removal and installation

1.8L ENGINE

The crankshaft position sensor is an integral part of the distributor and cannot be removed or serviced. If the sensor is defective, the entire distributor assembly must be replaced.

1.9L AND 2.0L ENGINES

♦ **Refer to illustration 8.5**

1   Disconnect the negative cable from the battery.

2   Raise the vehicle with a jack and support it securely on jackstands.

3   If you're working on a 1.9L model or a 2.0L SPI model, remove the splash shield from under the front of the vehicle.

4   If you're working on a 2.0L Zetec model (coupe), remove the exhaust manifold (see Chapter 4).

5   Locate the crankshaft position sensor at the front of the engine and disconnect its electrical connector (see illustration).

6   Remove the two mounting bolts (1.9L and 2.0L SPI) or one mounting bolt (2.0L Zetec) and take the sensor off the engine.

7   Installation is the reverse of the removal steps. Tighten the mounting screws to the torque listed in this Chapter's Specifications.

8.5 Crankshaft position sensor location (arrow)

9   Ignition module (1995 and earlier 1.9L engine models) - removal and installation

‣ Refer to illustration 9.2

➡ Note 1: 1996 and later models are equipped with ignition modules built into the PCM. Have vehicle tested by dealership service department or other automotive repair facility.

➡ Note 2: On 1995 and earlier models the EDIS module is mounted on the driver's side fender apron in front of the strut tower.

1   Disconnect the negative cable from the battery.
2   Remove the three module sub-bracket nuts (see illustration).
3   Carefully pull the module and sub-bracket assembly straight up and disconnect the electrical connector from the EDIS ignition module.
4   Remove the two screws holding the module to the sub-bracket, then separate the module and sub-bracket.
5   Installation is the reverse of the removal procedure. Tighten the fasteners to the torque listed in this Chapter's Specifications.

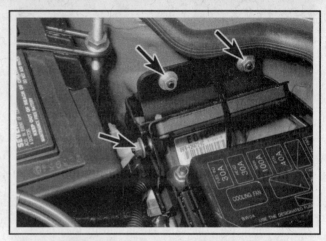

9.2 The EDIS ignition module sub-bracket is secured by three nuts (arrows) - 1995 and earlier models

10   Distributor (1.8L engine models) - removal and installation

REMOVAL

1   Disconnect the negative cable from the battery.
2   Disconnect the coil wire at the distributor cap.
3   Remove the distributor cap (see Chapter 1). Move the cap and spark plug wires out of the way. Mark the rotor position on the distributor body to permit correct timing on installation.
4   Disconnect the distributor electrical connector.
5   Make a mark across the distributor base flange and the cylinder head. This mark will permit correct installation without changing the timing.
6   Remove the two distributor mounting bolts and remove the distributor by pulling it straight out from the cylinder head.

✻✻ CAUTION:

DO NOT turn the engine while the distributor is removed, or the alignment marks will be useless.

INSTALLATION

7   Insert the distributor into the engine in exactly the same relationship to the cylinder head that it was in when removed. Make sure the drive tangs engage the camshaft slots.
8   If the same distributor is being installed, align the reference marks made before removal and tighten the mounting bolts to the torque value listed in this Chapter's Specifications.

➡ Note: If the crankshaft has been moved while the distributor is out, locate Top Dead Center (TDC) for the number one piston (see Chapter 2) and position the distributor and rotor accordingly.

9   If a new distributor is being installed, install and tighten the mounting bolts finger-tight.
10 Reconnect the distributor electrical connector.
11 Install the distributor cap (see Chapter 1).
12 Reconnect the coil wire to the distributor cap.
13 Connect the negative cable to the battery.
14 If a new distributor was installed, check the ignition timing (refer to Section 14) and tighten the distributor mounting bolts to the torque listed in this Chapter's Specifications.

11   Ignition coil (1.8L engine models) - removal and installation

1   Disconnect the negative cable from the battery.
2   Unplug the coil secondary wire.
3   Disconnect the coil primary electrical connector.
4   Remove both bracket mounting nuts and detach the coil and bracket as an assembly.

5   Installation is the reverse of the removal procedure with the following addition.
6   Whenever a spark plug wire is removed from either the spark plug or the ignition coil, the boot should be coated with silicone dielectric compound.

12 Ignition module (1.8L engine models) - removal and installation

✳✳ CAUTION:

The ignition module is a delicate and relatively expensive electronic component. Failure to follow the step-by-step procedures could damage the module or other electronic devices, including the PCM microprocessor itself. Additionally, all devices under computer control are protected by a Federally mandated extended warranty. Check with your dealer before attempting to replace them yourself.

1   Disconnect the negative cable from the battery.
2   Disconnect the electrical connector at the ignition module.
3   Remove the mounting screws and nuts from the module. Remove the module.
4   Installation is the reverse of the removal procedure.

13 Suppression capacitor (1.8L engine models) - removal and installation

1   Disconnect the negative cable from the battery.
2   Disconnect the capacitor electrical connector and remove the mounting nut.
3   Installation is the reverse of the removal procedure.

14 Ignition timing procedure (1.8L engine models)

▶ **Refer to illustrations 14.4, 14.5 and 14.6**

➡**Note:** This procedure applies to all models equipped with the 1.8L engine and ESA ignition system. However, check the Vehicle Emission Control Information (VECI) label on your vehicle to see if it specifies additional steps or a different procedure. If it does, follow the label instructions. No timing adjustments are possible on vehicles equipped with electronic distributorless (EDIS) ignition systems.

1   Apply the parking brake and block the wheels. Place the transmission in Park (automatic) or Neutral (manual). Turn off all accessories (heater, air conditioner, etc.).
2   Start the engine and warm it up. Once it has reached operating temperature, turn it off.

3   Connect an inductive timing light and tune-up tachometer in accordance with the manufacturer's instructions.

✳✳ CAUTION:

Make sure that the timing light and tachometer wires don't hang anywhere near the fan or they may become entangled in the fan blades when the engine runs.

4   Install a jumper wire between the Ground and TEN terminals in the diagnosis connector (see illustration).
5   Connect a tachometer between the negative battery post and the IG terminal in the diagnosis connector (see illustration).

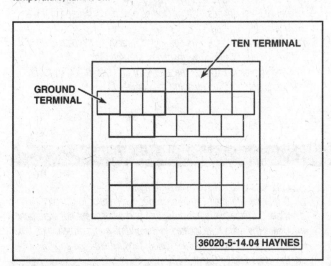

14.4 **Diagnosis connector terminals**

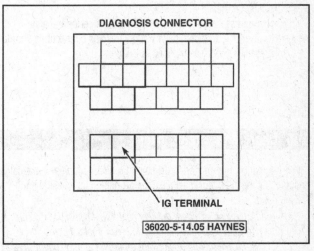

14.5 **Tachometer connection to diagnosis terminal**

14.6 Timing mark locations - typical

6   Locate the yellow timing mark on the crankshaft pulley and the corresponding timing mark on the timing belt cover (see illustration).
7   Start the engine again.
8   Point the timing light at the timing marks and note whether the timing marks are correctly aligned. Unless the VECI label specifies dif-

ferently, the correct ignition timing should be 9 to 11 degrees BTDC at 700 to 800 rpm.

✳✳ WARNING:

The crankshaft pulley may appear to be standing still under the timing light. It's actually rotating at high speed and can cause serious injury. Keep your hands, hair and clothes away from the pulley and drivebelts.

9   If the marks are not correctly aligned, loosen the distributor mounting bolts. Turn the distributor to change timing until the marks are correctly aligned. Tighten the distributor mounting bolts securely when the timing is correct and recheck it to make sure it didn't change when the bolts were tightened.
10   Turn off the engine.
11   Remove the jumper wire from the diagnosis connector.
12   Restart the engine and check the idle speed. Because fuel injected models are equipped with automatic idle speed control, idle rpm is not adjustable. If the idle rpm is not within the specified range, take the vehicle to a dealer service department or repair shop.
13   Turn off the engine.
14   Remove the timing light and tachometer.

15 Charging system - general information and precautions

The 1.8L engine uses a 65 amp alternator with an integral IC regulator. The 1.9L engine uses a 75 amp alternator with an integral solid-state voltage regulator (IAR). The 2.0L SPI engine (1997 and later sedan and wagon) uses a 75 amp alternator. The 2.0L Zetec engine (1997 and later coupe) uses a 95 amp alternator. All charging systems include a charge indicator light, the battery, a fusible link and the wiring between all the components. The charging system supplies electrical power for the ignition system, the lights, the radio, etc. The alternator is driven by a drivebelt at the front of the engine.

The purpose of the voltage regulator is to limit the alternator's voltage to a preset value. This prevents power surges, circuit overloads, etc., during peak voltage output. The solid state regulator is housed inside the alternator itself.

The charging system doesn't ordinarily require periodic maintenance. However, the drivebelt, battery and wires and connections should be inspected at the intervals outlined in Chapter 1.

Be very careful when making electrical circuit connections to the vehicle and note the following:

a)   *When reconnecting wires to the alternator from the battery, be sure to note the polarity.*
b)   *Before using arc welding equipment to repair any part of the vehicle, disconnect the wires from the alternator and the battery terminals.*
c)   *Never start the engine with a battery charger connected.*
d)   *Always disconnect both battery leads before using a battery charger.*
e)   *The alternator is turned by a drivebelt which could cause serious injury if your hands, hair or clothes become entangled in it with the engine running.*
f)   *Because the alternator is connected directly to the battery, it could arc or cause a fire if overloaded or shorted out.*
g)   *Wrap a plastic bag over the alternator and secure it with rubber bands before steam cleaning the engine.*

16 Charging system - check

1   If a malfunction occurs in the charging circuit, don't automatically assume that the alternator is causing the problem. First check the following items:

a)   *The battery cables where they connect to the battery. Make sure the connections are clean and tight (see Chapter 1).*
b)   *Check the external alternator wiring harness and the connectors at the alternator and voltage regulator. They must be in good condi-*

tion, clean, free of corrosion and tight.
c)   *Check the drivebelt condition and tension (refer to Chapter 1).*
d)   *Make sure the alternator mounting and adjustment bolts are tight.*
e)   *Check the main fuse located in the engine compartment fuse box. If it's burned, determine the cause, repair the circuit and replace the fuse (refer to Chapter 12).*
f)   *Run the engine and check the alternator for abnormal noise.*

1.8L CHARGING SYSTEM

2   Start the engine and make sure the charging indicator lamp goes out. If it does, continue with Step 6. If it does not, continue with Step 3.

3   With the ignition switch on and the engine off, check the voltage at the B, L and S terminals. The meter should read 12 volts at terminals B and S, and one volt at terminal L.

4   Start the engine and run at idle. Recheck the voltage at the B, L and S terminals. The meter should read between 14.1 and 14.7 volts at each terminal. Shut the engine off.

5   If the voltage readings in Step 3 and Step 4 are not as specified, check the wiring harness between terminal B and the battery. If nothing is wrong with the harness, replace the alternator.

6   Disconnect the B terminal connector at the alternator. Using a suitable ammeter, connect the positive test lead to the B terminal connector and the negative test lead to the B terminal on the alternator.

7   Connect a tachometer according to manufacturer's instructions.

8   Start the engine and run at idle. Make sure all lights and accessories are off, then depress and hold the brake pedal.

9   Increase engine speed to 2,500-3,000 rpm and note the tester reading of the alternator output current. If the reading is 65 amps or more, the charging system is operating properly. If the reading is below 65 amps, replace the alternator.

10 Shut the engine off. Disconnect the tester and reconnect the B terminal connector to the alternator.

1.9L AND 2.0L CHARGING SYSTEMS

11 Turn the headlights on for 10 to 15 seconds to remove any surface charge from the battery. Wait 3 to 5 minutes for the battery voltage to stabilize before continuing with Step 12.

12 Connect a voltmeter between the battery terminals and check the battery voltage with the engine off. It should be approximately 12- volts.

13 Turn off all electrical loads (be sure your foot is off the brake and the doors are closed so the dome light doesn't come on). Run the engine at a fast idle (approximately 1500 rpm) and check the battery voltage again after the voltage stops rising. This may take a few minutes. It should now be higher than battery voltage, but not more than 3-volts higher.

14 If the voltage reading is less than the specified charging voltage, perform the Under-voltage test in this section. If it is higher, perform the Over-voltage test.

15 Turn on the high beam headlights and turn the heater or air conditioner blower to its highest setting. Run the engine at 2,000 rpm and check the voltage reading. It should now be at least 0.5 volt higher than battery voltage. If not, perform the Under-voltage test.

16 If the voltage readings are correct in the preceding Steps, the charging system is working properly. Use a 12-volt test light and the wiring diagrams (see Chapter 12) to check for a battery drain.

Under-voltage test

◆ **Refer to illustrations 16.17, 16.18 and 16.20**

17 Unplug the electrical connector from the regulator. Connect an ohmmeter between the A and F terminal screws (see illustration). The ohmmeter should indicate at least 2.4 ohms.

a) If the ohmmeter reading is too low, the regulator is defective.

➡**Note: The regulator failure may have been caused by a shorted rotor or field circuit. These must be checked before replacing the regulator or the new regulator may fail as well. Checking the rotor and field circuit should be done by a dealer or electrical shop.**

b) If the ohmmeter reading is within specifications, reconnect the electrical connector to the regulator and perform Step 18.

18 Connect the voltmeter negative lead to the alternator rear housing and the positive lead to the regulator A terminal screw (see illustration). The voltmeter should indicate battery voltage. If not, check the A circuit for breaks or bad connections (refer to wiring diagrams in Chapter 12).

19 Repeat the load test (Step 15).

16.17 Connect an ohmmeter between the A and F terminal screws

16.18 Connect the voltmeter negative lead to the alternator rear housing, and the positive lead to the regulator A terminal screw

16.20 Connect the voltmeter negative lead to the alternator frame, and the positive lead to the F terminal screw

20 If the voltmeter indicates battery voltage in Step 18, place the ignition key in the Off position. Connect the voltmeter negative lead to the alternator frame and the positive lead to the F terminal screw (see illustration).

a) *If the voltmeter indicates no voltage, replace the alternator.*
b) *If the voltmeter indicates battery voltage, proceed to Step 21.*

21 Turn the ignition key to the Run position, but don't start the engine. Touch the voltmeter negative lead to the rear of the alternator and the positive lead to the F terminal screw on the regulator.

a) *If the voltmeter indicates more than 2 volts, perform the I circuit test in this Section.*
b) *If the voltmeter indicates 2 volts or less, proceed to Step 22.*

22 Disconnect the alternator electrical connector. Connect 12-gauge jumper wires between the alternator B+ terminals and their corresponding terminals in the electrical connector. Perform the load test (Step 5) with the voltmeter positive terminal connected to one of the B+ jumper wire terminals.

a) *If voltage increases to more than 0.5-volt above battery voltage, check the wiring from alternator to starter relay for breaks or bad connections.*
b) *If the voltage does not increase to more than 0.5 volt above battery voltage, perform Step 23.*

23 Connect a jumper wire between the alternator rear housing and the regulator F terminal screw. Repeat the load test (Step 5) with the voltmeter positive lead connected to one of the B+ jumper wire terminals.

a) *If voltage increases by more than 0.5 volt, replace the regulator.*
b) *If voltage doesn't increase by more than 0.5 volt, replace the alternator.*

Over-voltage test

24 Turn the key to the On position but leave the engine off.
25 Connect the voltmeter negative lead to the alternator rear housing, then connect the positive lead to the A terminal screw and the regulator grounding screw in turn. If the voltage readings differ by more than 0.5 volt, check the A circuit for breaks or bad connections (refer to wiring diagrams in Chapter 12).
26 Check for loose regulator grounding screws and tighten as needed to the torque listed in this Chapter's Specifications.
27 If the voltage reading is still too high, place the ignition key in the Off position. Connect the voltmeter negative lead to the alternator frame. Connect the voltmeter positive lead to the A terminal screw, then to the F terminal screw (see illustration 16.18).

a) *If the voltage readings at the two screw heads are different, replace*

the alternator.
b) *If the voltage readings at the two screw heads are the same, replace the regulator.*

S and/or I circuit test

28 Start the engine and let it idle. With the engine running, disconnect the electrical connector at the voltage regulator.

a) *If the charge indicator lamp comes on, check the I circuit for a short to ground (see the wiring diagrams in Chapter 12).*
b) *If the lamp stays off, go to Step 29.*

29 Reconnect the voltage regulator connector. With the engine running, check S circuit voltage at the alternator and regulator (see the wiring diagrams in Chapter 12).

a) *If there's no voltage at either point, replace the alternator.*
b) *If the voltmeter indicates approximately half of the battery voltage reading at the alternator, but not at the regulator, check the S circuit wiring for a break or bad connection.*
c) *If the voltmeter indicates approximately half of battery voltage at both points, go to Step 30.*

30 With the engine running at 2,000 rpm, check battery voltage.

a) *If it's below 14 volts, replace the regulator.*
b) *If it's above 14 volts, the alternator brushes or rotor may be shorted to ground. Perform Steps 25 through 27. If the test results are correct, check the A circuit for a break or bad connection. If the circuit is good, replace the regulator.*

BATTERY DRAIN TEST

31 Perform this test with all electrical loads switched off. Make sure the doors are closed. If they've been opened, close them and wait for about 50 minutes before doing the test.
32 Disconnect the cable from the negative terminal of the battery. Set an ammeter to the milliamps setting and connect it between the terminal and the disconnected end of the cable.

✳✳ CAUTION:

Don't connect the ammeter between the battery positive and negative terminals. This will blow the ammeter's internal fuse or ruin the ammeter.

33 Check the reading on the ammeter. A reading of 10 milliamps or somewhat more may be caused by a vehicle computer and is acceptable. A reading of 50 milliamps or more indicates a problem. To isolate it, remove and reinstall the vehicle's fuses one at a time while watching the ammeter. If the current reading suddenly drops when you remove a fuse, check the circuit related to that fuse for a short.

➡**Note: An ammeter reading of about one amp may be caused by a dome light, trunk light or engine compartment light staying on.**

34 Some current drains may stop when the battery is disconnected, then start up again after you disconnect the ammeter and reconnect the battery. To check for this type of current drain, leave the ammeter connected and turn the ignition key to On, then to Off, then repeat Step 33.

✳✳ CAUTION:

Don't turn the key to Start.

➡**Note: If the vehicle is equipped with illuminated entry, wait for the illuminated entry lights to go out.**

17 Alternator - removal and installation

1.8L ENGINE MODELS

1 Disconnect the negative cable from the battery.
2 Remove the nut holding the electrical connector to the alternator.
3 Disconnect the field terminal electrical connector.
4 Remove the upper mounting bolt from the alternator bracket.
5 Loosen the lower mounting bolt, then pivot the alternator forward.
6 Remove the drivebelt from the alternator pulley.
7 Raise the vehicle with a jack and place on jackstands.
8 Unbolt and remove the lower splash shield protecting the drivebelts.
9 Remove the lower mounting bolt.
10 Work the alternator free of the bracket and over the driveaxle, then remove it from the vehicle.
11 Installation is the reverse of removal.

1.9L ENGINE MODELS

▶ **Refer to illustrations 17.14, 17.15a, 17.15b, 17.15c, 17.15d, 17.16, 17.17, 17.19a and 17.19b**

12 Disconnect the negative cable from the battery.
13 Remove the drivebelt (see Chapter 1).
14 Unbolt the air conditioning hose bracket from the alternator bracket (see illustration). Move the bracket out of the way.
15 Disconnect the alternator electrical connectors (see illustrations).
16 Remove the lower mounting bolt (see illustration).

17.14 Unbolt and reposition the air conditioning hose bracket (1.9L engine models)

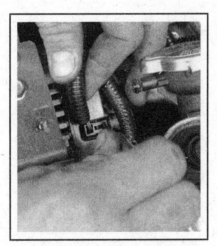

17.15a Lift the retaining tab of the small connector with a pointed tool, then pull the connector off

17.15b Use the same technique on the larger connector

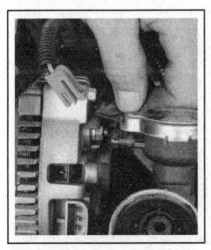

17.15c Pull back the rubber boot from the B terminal . . .

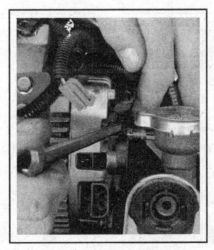

17.15d . . . and remove the nut to free the wire

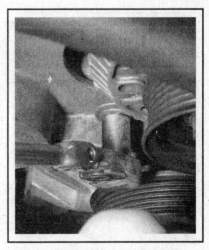

17.16 Remove the alternator lower mounting bolt

17 Remove the upper mounting bolt (see illustration).

18 Unbolt the power steering reservoir and move it to one side.

19 Pry the alternator loose from the bracket, then lift it out (see illustrations).

20 Installation is the reverse of the removal steps.

2.0L ENGINE MODELS

Coupe

21 Disconnect the cable from the negative terminal of the battery.

22 Remove the drivebelt (see Chapter 1).

23 Remove the coolant reservoir (see Chapter 3).

24 Disconnect both of the small electrical connectors from the alternator.

25 Remove the alternator mounting bolts (two underneath and one above). Lift the alternator out, pull back the rubber cover from the B+

terminal nut and disconnect the B+ terminal cable.

26 Installation is the reverse of the removal steps.

Sedan and Wagon

▶ **Refer to illustrations 17.30 and 17.31**

27 Disconnect the cable from the negative terminal of the battery.

28 Remove the drivebelt (see Chapter 1).

29 Free the oxygen sensor wiring harness from its retainer on the alternator bracket.

30 Unbolt the air conditioning and power steering hose bracket from the top of the alternator (see illustration). Remove the alternator mounting bolts.

31 Lift the alternator out and disconnect the electrical connectors (see illustration). Pull back the rubber cover from the B+ terminal nut and disconnect the B+ terminal cable.

32 Installation is the reverse of the removal steps.

17.17 Remove the upper alternator mounting bolt

17.19a Hold the alternator pulley with one hand and GENTLY pry the alternator from the bracket . . .

17.19b . . . then lift it away from the engine

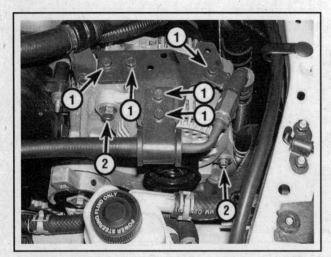

17.30 Remove the bracket bolts (1) and alternator mounting bolts (2)

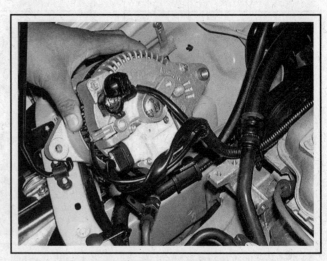

17.31 Lift the alternator out for access to the electrical connectors

18 Starting system - general information and precautions

The starting system is composed of a permanent magnet gear-reduction starter motor, solenoid, battery, ignition switch, manual lever position or clutch engage switch and connecting wires.

Turning the ignition key to the Start position actuates the starter solenoid through the starter control circuit. The starter solenoid then connects the battery to the starter. The battery supplies the electrical energy to the starter motor, which does the actual work of cranking the engine.

Vehicles equipped with an automatic transaxle have a manual lever position switch in the starter control circuit, which prevents operation of the starter unless the shift lever is in Neutral or Park. The circuit on vehicles with a manual transaxle prevents operation of the starter motor unless the clutch pedal is depressed.

Never operate the starter motor for more than 15 seconds at a time without pausing to allow it to cool for at least two minutes. Excessive cranking can cause overheating, which can seriously damage the starter.

19 Starter motor - testing in vehicle

➡Note: **Before diagnosing starter problems, make sure the battery is fully charged.**

1   If the starter motor does not turn at all when the switch is operated, make sure that the shift lever is in Neutral or Park (automatic transaxle) or that the clutch pedal is depressed (manual transaxle).

2   Make sure that the battery is charged and that all cables, both at the battery and starter solenoid terminals, are clean and secure.

3   If the starter motor spins, but the engine is not cranking, the overrunning clutch in the starter motor is slipping and the starter motor must be replaced. Also, the flywheel or driveplate ring gear could be damaged.

4   If, when the switch is actuated, the starter motor does not operate at all but the solenoid clicks, the problem lies with either the battery, the main solenoid contacts or the starter motor itself (or the engine is seized).

5   If the solenoid plunger cannot be heard when the switch is actuated, the battery is bad, the fuse or fusible link is burned (the circuit is open) or the solenoid itself is defective.

6   To check the solenoid, connect a jumper lead between the battery (+) and the ignition switch wire terminal (the small terminal, sometimes marked "S") on the solenoid. If the starter motor now operates, the solenoid is OK and the problem is in the ignition switch, neutral (or clutch) start switch or the wiring.

7   If the starter motor still does not operate, remove the starter/solenoid assembly for disassembly, testing and repair.

8   If the starter motor cranks the engine at an abnormally slow speed, first make sure the battery is fully charged and that all terminal connections are tight. If the engine is partially seized or has the wrong viscosity oil in it (in cold weather), it will crank slowly. Also, verify the battery's Cold Cranking Amp (CCA) rating is sufficient for the engine (an auto parts store can usually tell you what the minimum should be).

9   Run the engine until normal operating temperature is reached, then disconnect the coil wire from the distributor cap and ground it on the engine.

10   Connect a voltmeter positive lead to the positive battery post and connect the negative lead to the negative post. A fully charged battery should read about 12.6 volts. If the reading is lower, charge the battery before proceeding.

11   Crank the engine and take the voltmeter readings as soon as a steady figure is indicated. Do not allow the starter motor to turn for more than 15 seconds at a time. A reading of 9 volts or more, with the starter motor turning at normal cranking speed, is normal. If the reading is 9 volts or more, but the cranking speed is slow, the solenoid contacts are burned, there is a bad connection or the starter motor is faulty. If the reading is less than 9 volts and the cranking speed is slow, the starter motor is bad or the battery is discharged.

20 Starter motor - removal and installation

➡Note: **To remove the starter solenoid, first remove the starter motor, then disconnect the brush lead from the bottom of the solenoid and remove the two screws near the drive end of the starter motor. The solenoid should pull off the motor.**

1.8L ENGINE MODELS

1   Disconnect the negative cable from the battery.

2   Remove the air duct between the throttle body and resonance chamber.

3   Remove the upper mounting bolts from the starter motor.

4   Raise the vehicle and support it securely on jackstands.

5   Unbolt and remove the intake plenum support bracket.

6   Disconnect the starter cable and push-on connector from the starter solenoid B and S terminals.

❋❋ CAUTION:

Disconnect the connector at the solenoid S terminal by grasping it, depressing the plastic tab, and pulling the connector straight off to prevent damage to the connector and terminal.

7   Remove the lower bolt and remove the starter from the engine.

8   Installation is the reverse of the removal procedure. Tighten the mounting bolts securely.

20.12a The starter motor lower bolt (arrow) is accessible from beneath the vehicle (1.9L and 2.0L engine models)

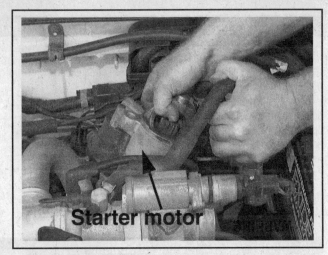

20.12b Lift the starter out from above (1.9L and 2.0L engine models)

1.9L AND 2.0L SPI ENGINE MODELS

▶ **Refer to illustrations 20.12a and 20.12b**

9   Disconnect the negative cable from the battery.

10 If equipped with an automatic transmission, remove the kickdown cable routing bracket from the engine block.

11 Disconnect the starter cable and push-on connector from the starter solenoid B and S terminals.

✳✳ CAUTION:

Disconnect the connector at the solenoid S terminal by grasping it, depressing the plastic tab, and pulling the connector straight off to prevent damage to the connector and terminal.

12 Remove the upper and lower starter motor mounting bolts (see illustration). Lift the starter motor up and remove it from the engine (see illustration).

13 Installation is the reverse of the removal steps. Tighten the mounting bolts securely.

2.0L ZETEC ENGINE MODELS

14 Disconnect the negative cable from the battery.

15 Remove the outlet tube from the air cleaner housing (see Chapter 4).

16 Jack up the front end of the vehicle and support it securely on jackstands.

17 Remove the starter motor's lower mounting bolt, then remove the jackstands and lower the vehicle.

18 Remove the starter motor's upper mounting bolts. Lift the starter away from the engine for access to the wiring.

19 Remove the nuts that secure the integral connector, then detach the starter wires and remove the starter.

20 Installation is the reverse of the removal steps.

Torque specifications   **Ft-lbs (unless otherwise indicated)**

➡**Note: One foot-pound (ft-lb) of torque is equivalent to 12 inch-pounds (in-lbs) of torque. Torque values below approximately 15 ft-lbs are expressed in inch-pounds, since most foot-pound torque wrenches are not accurate at these smaller values.**

Alternator
    Electrical connector nuts

1.8L and 1.9L engines	25 to 35 in-lbs
2.0L engines (B+ terminal)	60 to 84 in-lbs

    Mounting bracket bolts
        All except 2.0L Zetec

Upper bolt	14 to 22
Lower bolt	29 to 40
2.0L Zetec	29 to 40

    Pulley nut

1.8L and 1.9L engines	43 to 72
2.0L engines	60 to 99
Regulator grounding screw (1.8L and 1.9L)	16 to 24 in-lbs
Regulator mounting screws (2.0L)	26 to 41 in-lbs
Through bolts (1.8L)	36 to 48 in-lbs

Crankshaft position sensor

Screws (1.9L)	40 to 61 in-lbs
Bolts (2.0L SPI)	45 to 61 in-lbs
Bolt (2.0L Zetec)	53 to 80 in-lbs
Distributor mounting bolts (1.8L)	14 to 19

EDIS coil pack mounting bolts

1.9L engine	40 to 61 in-lbs
2.0L engines	44 to 62 in-lbs
EDIS ignition module mounting screws (1.9L)	24 to 35 in-lbs
EDIS ignition module sub-bracket nuts (1.9L)	62 to 88 in-lbs

Starter

Brush end plate screws	20 to 30 in-lbs

    Mounting bolts

All except 2.0L SPI engine	15 to 20
2.0L SPI engine	18 to 20
Cable nut (1.8L and 1.9L)	80 to 120 in-lbs
Cable nut (2.0L SPI)	80 to 115 in-lbs
Integral solenoid connector nuts (2.0L Zetec)	61 in-lbs

Notes

Section

6

EMISSIONS
AND ENGINE
CONTROL
SYSTEMS

1 General information

▶ **Refer to illustration 1.7**

To prevent pollution of the atmosphere from incompletely burned and evaporating gases, and to maintain good driveability and fuel economy, a number of emission control systems are incorporated. They include the:

Electronic Engine Control system
Exhaust Gas Recirculation (EGR) system
Fuel evaporative emission control system
Positive Crankcase Ventilation (PCV) system
Catalytic converter

All of these systems are linked, directly or indirectly, to the emission control system.

The Sections in this Chapter include general descriptions, checking procedures within the scope of the home mechanic and component replacement procedures (when possible) for each of the systems listed above.

Before assuming that an emissions control system is malfunctioning, check the fuel and ignition systems carefully. The diagnosis of some emission control devices requires specialized tools, equipment and training. If checking and servicing become too difficult or if a procedure is beyond your ability, consult a dealer service department or other qualified repair shop. Remember, the most frequent cause of emissions problems is simply a loose or broken vacuum hose or wire, so always check the hose and wiring connections first.

This doesn't mean, however, that emission control systems are particularly difficult to maintain and repair. You can quickly and easily perform many checks and do most of the regular maintenance at home with common tune-up and hand tools.

➡**Note: Because of a Federally mandated extended warranty which covers the emission control system components, check with your dealer about warranty coverage before working on any emissions-related systems. Once the warranty has expired, you may wish to perform some of the component checks and/or replacement procedures in this Chapter to save money.**

Pay close attention to any special precautions outlined in this Chapter. It should be noted that the illustrations of the various systems may not exactly match the system installed on the vehicle you're working on because of changes made by the manufacturer during production or from year-to-year.

A Vehicle Emissions Control Information label is located in the engine compartment (see illustration). This label contains important emissions specifications and adjustment information, as well as a vacuum hose schematic with emissions components identified. When servicing the engine or emissions systems, the VECI label in your particular vehicle should always be checked for up-to-date information. A calibration revision decal may also be used. The calibration revision number indicates running changes in designs or specifications.

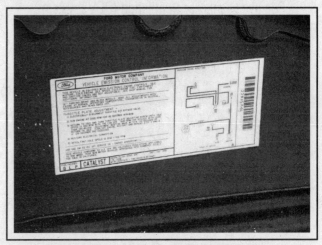

1.7 The Vehicle Emissions Control Information (VECI) label is located in the engine compartment and it contains important emissions specifications and adjustment information, as well as a vacuum hose schematic

2 Electronic Engine Control (EEC) system and trouble codes

GENERAL DESCRIPTION

1   All vehicles with 1.9L or 2.0L engines use the EDIS or Electronic Distributorless Ignition System (see Chapter 5) and the Electronic Engine Control (EEC) system. All vehicles with 1.8L engines use the ESA or electronic spark advance ignition system (see Chapter 5) and an Electronic Engine control (EEC) system. The EEC system consists of an onboard computer, known as the Electronic Control Assembly (ECA) or Powertrain Control Module (PCM), and the information sensors, which monitor various functions of the engine and send data to the computer. Based on the data and the information programmed into the computer's memory, the computer generates output signals to control various engine functions via control relays, solenoids and other actuators.

2   The computer located under the instrument panel on the floor tunnel ahead of the floor console is the "brain" of the EEC system. It

receives data from a number of sensors and other electronic components (switches, relays, etc.). Based on the information it receives, the computer generates output signals to control various relays, solenoids and other actuators (see the following Sections). The computer is specifically calibrated to optimize the emissions, fuel economy and driveability of the vehicle.

3   Because of a Federally mandated extended warranty which covers the computer, the information sensors and all components under its control, and because any owner-induced damage to the computer, the sensors and/or the control devices may void the warranty, it isn't a good idea to attempt diagnosis or replacement of the computer at home while the extended warranty is in effect. Take your vehicle to a dealer service department if the computer or a system component malfunctions during this time.

INFORMATION INPUT SENSORS

➡Note: Not all of the following devices will be on every vehicle. The VECI label is the most specific and accurate source of information for determining what sensors are on the vehicle.

4   When battery voltage is applied to the air conditioning compressor clutch, a signal is sent to the computer, which interprets the signal as an added load created by the compressor and increases engine idle speed accordingly to compensate.

5   The Intake Air Temperature (IAT) sensor is mounted in the Vane Air Flow (VAF) meter on 1.8L engine models, and in the air intake resonator on 2.0L engine models. The Air Charge Temperature sensor (ACT) is threaded into the air cleaner lid on 1.9L engine models. These devices provide the computer with fuel/air mixture temperature information.

6   The Engine Coolant Temperature (ECT) sensor, which is threaded into a coolant passage in the cylinder head (1.8L and 2.0L Zetec engines) or the heater hose inlet pipe (1.9L and 2.0L SPI engines) monitors engine coolant temperature. The ECT sends the computer a constantly varying voltage signal which influences computer control of the fuel mixture, ignition timing and EGR operation.

7   The (Heated) Exhaust Gas Oxygen (O2S or HO2S) sensor constantly monitors the oxygen content of the exhaust gas. Both heated and unheated types perform the same function, but the HO2S is heated by electrical current so it can start functioning faster. A voltage signal which varies in accordance with the difference between the oxygen content of the exhaust gases and the surrounding atmosphere is sent to the computer. The computer converts this exhaust gas oxygen content signal to the fuel/air ratio, compares it to the ideal ratio for current engine operating conditions and alters the signal to the injectors accordingly. Later models use two HO2S sensors, one upstream of the catalytic converter and one downstream. The PCM compares the readings of the upstream and downstream sensors to determine the effectiveness of the catalytic converter.

8   The Throttle Position Sensor (TPS), which is mounted on the side of the throttle body (see Chapter 4) and connected directly to the throttle shaft, senses throttle movement and position, then transmits an electrical signal proportional to the throttle plate angle to the computer. This signal enables the computer to determine when the throttle is closed, in its normal cruise condition or wide open.

9   The Mass Air Flow (MAF) sensor, which is mounted in the air cleaner intake passage on 1.9L and 2.0L engines, measures the mass of the air entering the engine (see Chapter 4). Because air mass varies with air temperature (cold air is denser than warm air), measuring air mass provides the computer with a very accurate way of determining the

correct amount of fuel to obtain the ideal fuel/air mixture.

10   The Vane Air Flow (VAF) meter, which is mounted in the air resonance chamber near the front of the air intake system on 1.8L engines, serves a similar function to the MAF sensor on 1.9L engines in providing the computer with the necessary data to determine the correct amount of fuel. However, the VAF signal is also used by the computer in determining timing advance.

11   The knock sensor, which is located on the right side of the cylinder head on 2.0L SPI models, detects the sound of spark knock (detonation) occurring in the combustion chambers. The knock sensor sends a voltage signal to the PCM, which then retards ignition timing.

12   The Camshaft Position (CMP) sensor, which is located at the front of the engine on 1.9L and 2.0L models, tells the PCM when no. 1 piston is at TDC on its compression stroke.

13   The Crankshaft Position (CKP) sensor, used on 2.0L engine models, determines engine rpm and the position of the crankshaft and signals this information to the PCM.

OUTPUT DEVICES

➡Note: Not all of the following devices will be on every vehicle. Also, the location and appearance of the following devices may differ somewhat on the vehicle from those described below. The VECI label is the most specific and accurate source of information for determining what devices are on he vehicle.

14   The air conditioning and cooling fan controller module is operated by the computer, the coolant temperature switch and the brake light switch. The controller module provides an output signal which controls operation of the air conditioning compressor clutch and the engine cooling fan.

15   The EEC power relay, which is activated by the ignition switch, supplies battery voltage to the computer when the switch is on.

16   The canister purge solenoid (CANP) switches manifold vacuum to operate the canister purge valve when a signal is received from the computer. Vacuum opens the purge valve when the solenoid is energized allowing fuel vapor to flow from the canister to the intake manifold.

17   The solenoid operated fuel injectors are located in the intake ports of vehicles equipped with EFI. The computer controls the length of time the injector is open. The "open" time of the injector determines the amount of fuel delivered. For information regarding injector replacement, refer to Chapter 4.

18   The fuel pump relay is activated by the computer with the ignition switch in the On position. When the ignition switch is turned to the On position, the relay is activated to supply initial line pressure to the system. For information regarding fuel pump checking and replacement, refer to Chapter 4.

19   The EDIS ignition module used on 1.9L engine models triggers the ignition coil and determines dwell. The computer uses a signal from the Profile Ignition Pick-Up to determine crankshaft position. Ignition timing is determined by the computer, which then signals the module to fire the EDIS coil pack. For further information regarding the EDIS module, refer to Chapter 5.

20   The ESA ignition module used on 1.8L engine models triggers the ignition coil and determines dwell. The computer uses a signal from sensors in the distributor to determine crankshaft position, cylinder identification and engine speed. The computer uses this information to signal the module to fire the coil at the correct time. For further information regarding the ESA module, refer to Chapter 5.

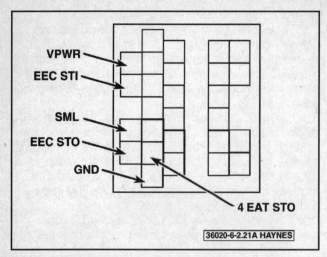

2.21a Diagnostic test connector terminals (1.8L engine)

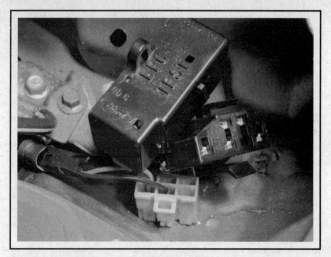

2.21b Diagnostic test connector location (1.9L engine)

OBTAINING DIAGNOSTIC TROUBLE CODES (1995 AND EARLIER MODELS)

▶ **Refer to illustrations 2.21a, 2.21b and 2.21c**

21 Trouble codes on 1995 and earlier 1.8L and 1.9L engine models can be read with an analog voltmeter or by using the Check Engine light. Locate the EEC diagnostic or self-test connector located behind the battery in the engine compartment.

 a) *1.8L engine, testing with an analog voltmeter: With the ignition key in the Off position, connect the voltmeter positive lead to the EEC STO line and the negative lead to ground (see illustration). Connect the EEC STI terminal to ground with a jumper wire. Set the voltmeter on a 20-volt scale.*

 b) *1.8L engine, testing with the Check Engine light: Connect the EEC STI terminal to ground with a jumper wire (see illustration 2.21a).*

 c) *1.9L engine, testing with an analog voltmeter: With the ignition key in the Off position, connect the voltmeter positive lead to the battery positive terminal and the negative lead to the STO terminal in the diagnostic connector (see illustrations). Jumper the STI connector, then set the voltmeter to the 20-volt scale.*

 d) *1.9L engine, testing with the Check Engine light: With the ignition off, jumper the STI terminal (see illustration 2.21c).*

22 The three types of codes this test will provide are:

 O - Key On Engine Off (KOEO) (on demand codes with the engine off)

 C - Continuous Memory (codes stored when the engine was running)

 R - Engine Running (ER) (codes produced as the engine is running)

O (KOEO)

23 Turn the ignition on. Disconnect and reconnect the STI terminal jumper wire. Watch the Check Engine lamp or voltmeter needle. Codes will be retrieved through flashing of the light or counting the sweeps of the voltmeter needle. For example, two flashes of the light or sweeps of the needle followed by three flashes or sweeps is code 23, with a four second delay between codes. Write the codes down for reference. The codes will appear in numerical order, repeating once.

C (Continuous Memory)

24 After the KOEO codes are reported, turn the ignition key to the Off position. Start and run the engine at 2,000 rpm for five minutes to warm up the EGO or HEGO sensor, then turn the engine off. Wait 10 seconds and restart the engine.

➡**Note: With the 1.9L engine, the first code will be an identification code. As soon as it appears, depress and release the brake pedal, then turn the steering wheel one-half turn and release. There will be a short pause and any stored Continuous Memory codes will appear in order. Remember that the "Pass" code is 11, or flash/sweep, two second pause, flash/sweep.**

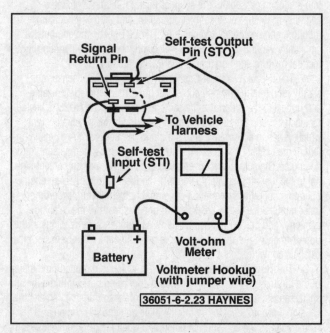

2.21c To read any stored trouble codes on the 1.9L engine, connect a voltmeter to the self-test connector as shown, then connect a jumper wire between the self-test input and the signal return pin - turn the ignition On and watch the voltmeter needle (you can also watch the Check Engine light on the dash if you don't have a voltmeter)

R (Engine Running)

25 Start the engine. The first part of this test makes sure the system can advance the timing. Check the ignition timing. It should be advanced about 20-degrees above base timing (check the VECI label for the base timing specification). Shut off the engine, restart it and run it for two minutes, then turn it off for ten seconds before restarting it.

1.8L TROUBLE CODES

Code	Condition
02	No crankshaft position sensor signal
03	No cylinder ID sensor signal
08	Vane air flow meter signal
09	Electronic coolant temperature sensor
10	Vane air temperature sensor
12	Throttle position sensor
14	Barometric pressure sensor
15	Exhaust gas oxygen sensor - voltage stays below 0.55 volts (lean)
17	Exhaust gas oxygen sensor - voltage does not change (rich)
25	Fuel pressure regulator control solenoid
26	Canister purge control solenoid
34	Idle speed control solenoid
41	High speed inlet air control solenoid

1.9L TROUBLE CODES (1991)

Code	Test condition	Probable cause
11	O,R,C	System OK, testing complete
12	R	RPM out of specified range during self test high rpm check
13	R	RPM out of specified range during self test low rpm check
14	C	Profile ignition pickup circuit failure
15	O	Read Only Memory (computer) test failure
15	C	Keep Alive Memory (computer) test failure
18	R	Spark Angle Word (SAW) circuit failure
18	C	Ignition Diagnostic Monitor (IDM) circuit failure or SPOUT circuit grounded

The Check Engine lamp should flash three times (1.8L) or the voltmeter needle should make three quick sweeps (1.9L), then show an engine code. After another pause will be one flash/sweep, the signal to blip the throttle so the system can check throttle component operation. After this there will be a pause, followed by the Engine Running codes which will appear in the same manner as before, repeating twice.

Code	Test condition	Probable cause
19	O	Computer internal voltage failure
19	C	Cylinder ID circuit failure
21	O,R	Engine coolant Temperature (ECT) sensor out of specified range
23	O,R	Throttle Position (TP) sensor out of specified range
24	O,R	Air Charge Temperature (ACT) sensor out of specified range
26	O,R	Mass Air Flow (MAF) sensor out of self-test range
29	C	Insufficient input from Vehicle Speed Sensor
31	O,R,C	Pressure Feedback EGR (PFE) circuit voltage below minimum
32	R,C	Low PFE circuit voltage
33	R,C	EGR valve opening not detected
34	O	PFE sensor voltage out of range
34	R,C	PFE circuit voltage and/or exhaust pressure high
35	O,R,C	PFE circuit voltage above maximum
41	R	Heated exhaust gas oxygen sensor (HEGO) circuit indicates system lean
41	C	No HEGO switch detected
42	R	HEGO sensor circuit indicates system rich
45	C	Coil 1 primary circuit failure
46	C	Coil 2 primary circuit failure
51	O,C	ECT (engine coolant temperature) sensor indicates -40 degree F/circuit open
53	O,C	TP circuit voltage above maximum
54	O,C	ACT sensor -40 degree F/circuit open
56	O,R,C	MAF sensor circuit voltage above maximum
61	O,C	ECT indicates 254 degree F/circuit grounded
63	O,C	TP circuit voltage below minimum

Code	Test condition	Probable cause
64	O,C	ACT sensor 254 degree F/circuit grounded
66	R,C	MAF sensor circuit voltage below minimum
67	O,R	Neutral Drive Switch (NDS) circuit open
67	C	Clutch Engage Switch (CES) circuit failure
67	C	Clutch Engage Switch (CES) circuit failure
72	R	Insufficient MAF change during dynamic response test
73	R	Insufficient throttle position change during dynamic response test
74	R	Brake On/Off (BOO) switch circuit failure or not actuated during self-test
77	R	Brief wide open throttle not sensed during self-test or operator error
79	O	Air conditioning on or defrost on during self-test
83	O	High Speed Electro Drive Fan (HEDF) circuit failure
84	O	EGR Vacuum Regulator (EVR) circuit failure
87	O,C	Fuel pump primary circuit failure
88	O	Electro Drive Fan (EDF) circuit failure
95	O,C	Fuel pump secondary circuit failure
96	O,C	Fuel pump secondary circuit failure
98	R	Hard fault is present - Failure Mode Effects Management (FMEM)
No Codes		Unable to initiate self-test or unable to output codes

1.9L TROUBLE CODES (1992 THROUGH 1995)

Code	Test condition	Probable cause
111	O,R,C	System OK, testing complete
112	O,C	Air Charge Temperature sensor indicates 254 degree F/circuit grounded
113	O,C	ACT indicates -40 degree F/circuit grounded
114	O,R	ACT out of self-test range
116	O,	Engine Coolant Temperature out of self-test range

Code	Test condition	Probable cause
117	O,C	ECT indicates 254 degree F/circuit grounded
118	O,C	ECT indicates -40 degree F/circuit grounded
121	O,R,C	Throttle Position (TP) circuit voltage higher or lower than expected
122	O,C	Throttle Position (TP) circuit voltage below minimum
123	O,C	Throttle Position (TP) circuit voltage above maximum
124	C	Throttle Position (TP) sensor voltage higher than expected
125	C	Throttle Position (TP) sensor voltage lower than expected
129	R	Insufficient Mass Air Flow (MAF) change during Dynamic Response test
157	C	Mass Air Flow (MAF) sensor voltage below minimum
158	O,C	Mass Air Flow (MAF) sensor voltage above maximum
159	O,R	Mass Air Flow (MAF) sensor higher or lower than expected during KOEO, KOER
167	R	Insufficient Throttle Position (TP) change during Dynamic Response test
171	C	Fuel system at adaptive limits, oxygen sensor (HEGO) unable to switch
172	R,C	Lack of HEGO switches, indicates lean
173	R,C	Lack of HEGO switches, indicates rich
179	C	Fuel system at lean adaptive limit at part throttle, system rich
181	C	Fuel system at rich adaptive limit at part throttle, system lean
182	C	Fuel system at lean adaptive limit at idle, system rich
183	C	Fuel system at rich adaptive limit at idle, system lean
184	C	Mass Air Flow (MAF) higher than expected
185	C	Mass Air Flow (MAF) lower than expected
186	C	Injector pulse width higher than expected
187	C	Injector pulse width lower than expected

Code	Test condition	Probable cause
211	C	Profile Ignition Pickup (PIP) circuit fault
212	C	Loss of Ignition Diagnostic Monitor (IDM) input to computer/SPOUT circuit grounded
213	R	SPOUT circuit open
214	C	Cylinder ID circuit failure
215	C	Coil 1 primary circuit failure
216	C	Coil 2 primary circuit failure
226	O	Identification Diagnostic Monitor (IDM) signal not received
326	R,C	Pressure Feedback EGR (PFE) circuit voltage low
327	O,R,C	Pressure Feedback EGR (PFE) circuit below minimum voltage
332	R,C	EGR valve opening not detected
335	O	Pressure Feedback EGR (PFE) sensor voltage out of range
336	R,C	Exhaust pressure high/PFE circuit voltage high
337	O,R,C	PFE circuit above maximum voltage
338	C	Engine coolant temperature lower than normal
339	C	Engine coolant temperature higher than normal
341	O	Octane Adjust (OCT ADJ) circuit open
411	R	RPM out of specified range during self test low rpm check
412	R	RPM out of specified range during self test high rpm check
452	R	Insufficient input from Vehicle Speed Sensor (VSS)
511	O	Read Only Memory (ROM) (computer) test failure
512	C	Keep Alive Memory (KAM) (computer) test failure
513	O	Computer internal voltage failure
522	O	Vehicle not in Park or Neutral during KOEO/Neutral Drive Switch (NDS) circuit open
528	C	Clutch Engage Switch (CES) circuit failure
536	R,C	Brake On/Off (BOO) circuit failure or not actuated during self-test
538	R	Brief wide open throttle not sensed during self-test or operator error

Code	Test condition	Probable cause
539	O	Air conditioning on or defrost on during self-test
542	O,C	Fuel pump secondary circuit failure
543	O,C	Fuel pump secondary circuit failure
556	O,C	Fuel pump relay primary circuit failure
558	O	EGR Vacuum Regulator (EVR) circuit failure
563	O	High Electro Drive Fan (HEDF) circuit failure
564	O	Electro Drive Fan (EDF) circuit failure
565	O	Canister Purge (CANP) circuit failure
621	O,C	Shift solenoid 1 circuit failure
622	O,C	Shift solenoid 2 circuit failure
634	C	Error in Transmission Select Switch (TSS) circuits
636	O,R	Transmission Oil Temperature (TOT) sensor out of self-test range
637	O,C	TOT sensor voltage above maximum
638	O,C	TOT sensor voltage below minimum
639	R,C	Insufficient input from Transmission Speed Sensor (TSS)
641	O,C	Shift solenoid 3 circuit failure
643	O,C	Converter clutch control circuit failure
998	R	Hard fault is present - Failure Mode Effects Management (FMEM)
No Codes		Unable to initiate self-test or unable to output codes

OBD-II GENERIC TROUBLE CODES (1996 AND LATER)

Code	Probable cause
P0100	Mass air flow or volume air flow circuit malfunction
P0102	Mass air flow or volume air flow circuit, low input
P0103	Mass air flow or volume air flow circuit, high input
P0110	Intake air temperature circuit malfunction
P0112	Intake air temperature circuit, low input
P0113	Intake air temperature circuit, high input
P0117	Engine coolant temperature circuit, low input

Code	Probable cause
P0118	Engine coolant temperature circuit, high input
P0120	Throttle position sensor circuit malfunction
P0121	Throttle position sensor circuit, range or performance problem
P0122	Throttle position sensor circuit, low input
P0123	Throttle position sensor circuit, high input
P0125	Insufficient coolant temperature for closed loop fuel control
P0130	O2 sensor circuit malfunction
P0131	O2 sensor circuit, low voltage
P0133	O2 sensor circuit, slow response
P0134	O2 sensor circuit – no activity detected
P0135	O2 sensor heater circuit malfunction
P0136	O2 sensor circuit malfunction
P0140	O2 sensor circuit – no activity detected
P0141	O2 sensor heater circuit malfunction
P0150	O2 sensor circuit malfunction
P0151	O2 sensor circuit, low voltage
P0153	O2 sensor circuit, slow response
P0154	O2 sensor circuit – no activity detected
P0155	O2 sensor heater circuit malfunction
P0156	O2 sensor circuit malfunction
P0160	O2 sensor circuit – no activity detected
P0161	O2 sensor heater circuit malfunction
P0170	Fuel trim malfunction
P0171	System too lean
P0172	System too rich
P0173	Fuel trim malfunction
P0174	System too lean
P0175	System too rich
P0176	Fuel composition sensor circuit malfunction
P0180	Fuel temperature sensor circuit malfunction
P0181	Fuel temperature sensor circuit, range or performance problem

Code	Probable cause
P0182	Fuel temperature sensor circuit, low input
P0183	Fuel temperature sensor circuit, high input
P0190	Fuel rail pressure sensor circuit malfunction
P0191	Fuel rail pressure sensor circuit, range or performance problem
P0192	Fuel rail pressure sensor circuit, low input
P0193	Fuel rail pressure sensor circuit, high input
P0230	Fuel pump primary circuit malfunction
P0231	Fuel pump secondary circuit, low
P0232	Fuel pump secondary circuit, high
P0300	Random/multiple cylinder misfire detected
P0301	Cylinder no. 1 misfire detected
P0302	Cylinder no. 2 misfire detected
P0303	Cylinder no. 3 misfire detected
P0304	Cylinder no. 4 misfire detected
P0320	Ignition/distributor engine speed input circuit malfunction
P0325	Knock sensor circuit malfunction
P0326	Knock sensor circuit, range or performance problem
P0330	Knock sensor circuit malfunction
P0331	Knock sensor circuit, range or performance problem
P0335	Crankshaft position sensor circuit malfunction
P0340	Camshaft position sensor circuit malfunction
P0350	Ignition coil primary or secondary circuit malfunction
P0351	Ignition coil primary or secondary circuit malfunction
P0352	Ignition coil primary or secondary circuit malfunction
P0353	Ignition coil primary or secondary circuit malfunction
P0354	Ignition coil primary or secondary circuit malfunction
P0355	Ignition coil primary or secondary circuit malfunction
P0356	Ignition coil primary or secondary circuit malfunction
P0357	Ignition coil primary or secondary circuit malfunction
P0358	Ignition coil primary or secondary circuit malfunction
P0359	Ignition coil primary or secondary circuit malfunction

Code	Probable cause
P0360	Ignition coil primary or secondary circuit malfunction
P0385	Crankshaft position sensor circuit malfunction
P0400	Exhaust gas recirculation flow malfunction
P0401	Exhaust gas recirculation, insufficient flow detected
P0402	Exhaust gas recirculation, excessive flow detected
P0411	Secondary air injection system, incorrect flow detected
P0412	Secondary air injection system switching valve, circuit malfunction
P0413	Secondary air injection system switching valve, open circuit
P0414	Secondary air injection system switching valve, shorted circuit
P0416	Secondary air injection system switching valve, open circuit
P0417	Secondary air injection system switching valve, shorted circuit
P0420	Catalyst system efficiency below threshold
P0430	Catalyst system efficiency below threshold
P0440	Evaporative emission control system malfunction
P0442	Evaporative emission control system, small leak detected
P0443	Evaporative emission control system, purge control valve circuit malfunction
P0452	Evaporative emission control system, pressure sensor low input
P0453	Evaporative emission control system, pressure sensor high input
P0455	Evaporative emission control system, pressure sensor intermittent
P0460	Fuel level sensor circuit malfunction
P0500	Vehicle speed sensor malfunction
P0501	Vehicle speed sensor, range or performance problem
P0503	Vehicle speed sensor circuit, intermittent, erratic or high input
P0505	Idle control system malfunction
P0510	Closed throttle position switch malfunction
P0552	Power steering pressure sensor circuit, low input
P0553	Power steering pressure sensor circuit, high input

Code	Probable cause
P0602	Control module, programming error
P0603	Internal control module, Keep Alive Memory (KAM) error
P0605	Internal control module, Read Only Memory (ROM) error
P0703	Torque converter/brake switch, circuit malfunction
P0704	Clutch switch input circuit malfunction
P0705	Transmission range sensor, circuit malfunction (PRNDL input)
P0707	Transmission range sensor circuit, low input
P0708	Transmission range sensor circuit, high input
P0710	Transmission fluid temperature sensor, circuit malfunction
P0712	Transmission fluid temperature sensor circuit, low input
P0713	Transmission fluid temperature sensor circuit, high input
P0715	Input/turbine speed sensor circuit malfunction
P0717	Input/turbine speed sensor circuit, no signal
P0720	Output speed sensor malfunction
P0721	Output speed sensor circuit, range or performance problem
P0722	Output speed sensor circuit, no signal
P0723	Output speed sensor circuit, intermittent signal
P0731	Incorrect gear ratio, first gear
P0732	Incorrect gear ratio, second gear
P0733	Incorrect gear ratio, third gear
P0734	Incorrect gear ratio, fourth gear
P0735	Incorrect gear ratio, fifth gear
P0736	Incorrect gear ratio, reverse gear
P0740	Torque converter clutch, circuit malfunction
P0741	Torque converter clutch, circuit performance or stuck in off position
P0743	Torque converter clutch circuit, electrical problem
P0745	Pressure control solenoid malfunction
P0746	Pressure control solenoid, performance problem or stuck in off position
P0750	Shift solenoid malfunction
P0751	Shift solenoid, performance problem or stuck in off position

Code	Probable cause
P0755	Shift solenoid malfunction
P0756	Shift solenoid, performance problem or stuck in off position
P0760	Shift solenoid malfunction
P0761	Shift solenoid, performance problem or stuck in off position
P0765	Shift solenoid malfunction

Code	Probable cause
P0779	Shift malfunction
P0781	First-to-second shift malfunction
P0782	Second-to-third shift malfunction
P0783	Third-to-fourth shift malfunction
P0784	Fourth-to-fifth shift malfunction

CLEARING CODES (1995 AND EARLIER MODELS)

26 To clear the trouble codes on a 1.8L model, disconnect the jumper wire from the STI terminal at the diagnostic test connector, then disconnect the negative battery cable from the battery and depress the brake pedal for five to ten seconds.

27 To clear the trouble codes on a 1.9L model, start the KOEO test. When the trouble codes begin to appear, remove the jumper wire from the STI terminal. DO NOT disconnect the battery to clear codes on a 1.9L model.

OBTAINING AND CLEARING DIAGNOSTIC TROUBLE CODES (1996 AND LATER MODELS)

▶ Refer to illustrations 2.28a and 2.28b

28 As specified by CARB and EPA regulations, the manufacturer has incorporated the second generation self diagnosis system, referred to as On Board Diagnosis II (OBD-II), into the engine control system on 1996 and later models. This system incorporates a series of diagnostic moni-tors that detect and identify emissions and engine control systems faults and stores the information in the computer memory. This updated system also tests sensors and output actuators, diagnoses drive cycles and freezes data during a malfunction for later retrieval. An OBD-II compliant scan tool is required to obtain and clear the diagnostic trouble codes on 1996 and later models. The system is accessed at the 16 pin Data Link Connector (DLC) located under the driver's dash area (see illustrations). Several generic OBD-II scan tools are available for the home mechanic. Inquire at your local auto parts store for additional information and availability. Follow the scan tool manufactures specific instructions for obtaining and clearing diagnostic trouble codes.

COMPONENT REPLACEMENT

➡Note: Because of the Federally mandated warranty which covers the computer, input sensors and output devices, it isn't a good idea to attempt diagnosis or replacement of the PCM at home while the vehicle is under warranty. Take the vehicle to a dealer service department if the PCM or a system component malfunctions.

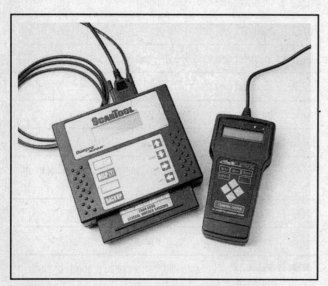

2.28a Generic scanners are powerful diagnostic aids - programmed with comprehensive diagnostic information, they can tell you just about anything you want to know about your engine management system

2.28b Typical Data Link Connector (DLC) location (1996 and later OBD-II models)

Air Charge Temperature (ACT) sensor (1.8L and 1.9L engines)

29 Refer to Chapter 4 for the removal and installation procedure.

Engine Coolant Temperature (ECT) Sensor (1.8L engine)

※※ WARNING:

Wait until the engine is completely cool before beginning this procedure.

30 Disconnect the negative cable from the battery.
31 Locate the ECT sensor on the cylinder head near the coil.
32 Unplug the electrical connector from the sensor.
33 Wrap the threads of the new sensor with thread-sealing tape to prevent coolant leakage.
34 Remove the sensor with a wrench. Be prepared for coolant leakage.
35 Installation is the reverse of removal. Add coolant as needed (see Chapter 1).

Engine Coolant Temperature (ECT) sensor (1.9L engine)

♦ Refer to illustration 2.40

※※ WARNING:

Wait until the engine is completely cool before beginning this procedure.

36 Disconnect the cable from the negative terminal of the battery.
37 Remove the air intake duct (see Chapter 4).
38 Unplug the electrical connector from the sensor.
39 Wrap the threads of the new sensor with thread-sealing tape to prevent coolant leakage.

40 Brace the heater hose inlet pipe with one hand and unscrew the sensor (see illustration).
41 Installation is the reverse of removal. Add coolant as needed (see Chapter 1).

Engine Coolant Temperature (ECT) sensor (2.0L engines)

♦ Refer to illustration 2.45

※※ WARNING:

Wait until the engine is completely cool before beginning this procedure.

42 Disconnect the cable from the negative terminal of the battery.
43 Disconnect the electrical connector from the sensor.
44 Wrap the threads of the new sensor with thread-sealing tape to prevent coolant leakage.
45 If you're working on a 2.0L SPI engine, brace the heater hose inlet pipe with one hand and unscrew the sensor (see illustration). If you're working on a 2.0L Zetec engine, unscrew the sensor form the cylinder head.
46 Installation is the reverse of removal. Add coolant as needed (see Chapter 1).

Exhaust Gas Oxygen (EGO) sensor (1.8L engine)

47 Disconnect the negative cable from the battery.
48 Locate the EGO sensor on the lower side of the exhaust manifold.
49 Unplug the electrical connector from the EGO sensor.
50 Unbolt and remove the exhaust manifold heat shield.
51 Raise the vehicle and place it securely on jackstands.
52 Remove the sensor from the exhaust manifold with a suitable socket or box wrench.
53 Coat the threads of the new sensor with anti-seize compound to prevent the threads from welding themselves to the manifold.
54 Installation is the reverse of removal.

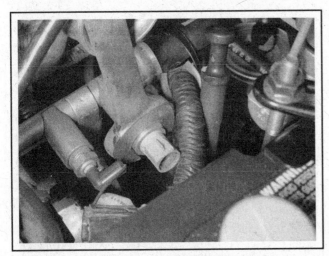

2.40 The 1.9L ECT sensor is installed in the heater hose inlet pipe

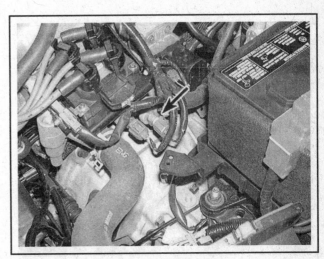

2.45 ECT sensor location (2.0L SPI models; 2.0L Zetec similar)

Heated Exhaust Gas Oxygen (HEGO) sensor (1.9L and 2.0L engines)

▶ **Refer to illustration 2.55**

55 Disconnect the electrical connector from the HEGO sensor. Unscrew the sensor from the catalytic converter inlet pipe (or outlet pipe if you're replacing a downstream sensor) (see illustration).

56 Coat the threads of the new sensor with anti-seize compound to prevent the threads from welding themselves to the manifold.

57 Installation is the reverse of the removal steps.

Throttle Position (TP) sensor

58 Refer to Chapter 4 for the replacement procedure.

Camshaft Position (CP) sensor (1.9L engine)

▶ **Refer to illustration 2.60**

➡ **Note: The CP sensor on the 1.8L engine is an integral part of the distributor and is serviced by distributor replacement. The**

CP sensor on 1.9L engines is mounted on the intake side of the cylinder head under the intake manifold.

59 Remove the intake manifold (see Chapter 2A).

60 Remove the bolt and take the camshaft position sensor off the cylinder head (see illustration).

61 Check the sensor O-rings for damage. Replace them if they are cracked or hardened. Lubricate the O-rings with a light coat of engine oil.

62 Installation is the reverse of removal.

Camshaft Position (CMP) sensor (2.0L engines)

▶ **Refer to illustrations 2.63 and 2.64**

63 Locate the camshaft position sensor at the front of the cylinder head and disconnect its electrical connector (see illustration).

64 Remove the bolt and take the camshaft position sensor off the cylinder head (see illustration).

65 Check the sensor O-ring for damage. Replace it if it's cracked or hardened. Lubricate the O-ring with a light coat of engine oil.

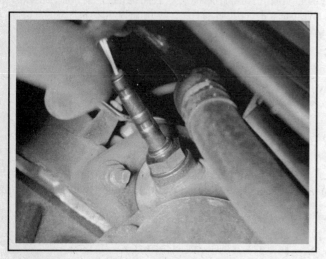

2.55 HEGO sensor location - 1.9L engine (2.0L engines similar)

2.60 The 1.9L camshaft position sensor is located on the cylinder head above the intake manifold

2.63 Camshaft Position Sensor (CMP) - 2.0L SPI models (2.0L Zetec similar)

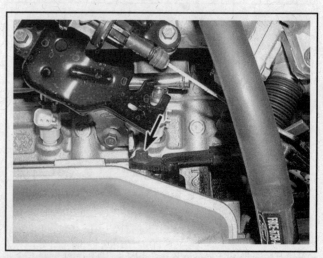

2.64 Disconnect the electrical connector and remove the mounting bolt (arrow)

66 Installation is the reverse of removal.

Crankshaft Position (CKP) sensor (1.9L and 2.0L engines)

67 Refer to Chapter 5 for the removal and installation procedure.

Mass Air Flow (MAF) sensor (1.9L and 2.0L engines)

68 Refer to Chapter 4 for the removal and installation procedure.

Vane Air Flow (VAF) meter (1.8L engine)

69 Refer to Chapter 4 for the removal and installation procedure.

Knock sensor (2.0L SPI engine)

♦ Refer to illustration 2.72

☀☀ WARNING:

Wait until the engine is completely cool before starting this procedure.

70 Disconnect the cable from the negative terminal of the battery.
71 Jack up the front end of the vehicle and support it securely on jackstands.
72 Locate the knock sensor on the right side of the engine block (see illustration).
73 Disconnect the electrical connector and remove the knock sensor

mounting bolt.

☀☀ WARNING:

Some knock sensors thread into the water jacket - be prepared for coolant spillage.

74 Installation is the reverse of the removal steps.

2.72 The knock sensor is mounted on the right side of the engine block (arrow)

---

3 | Fuel Evaporative Emission Control (EVAP) system

♦ Refer to illustration 3.2

1 This system is designed to prevent hydrocarbons from being released into the atmosphere by trapping and storing fuel vapor from the fuel tank or fuel injection system.

2 The serviceable parts of the system include a charcoal filled canister (see illustration), purge solenoid (1.8L or 1.9L), purge valve (2.0L) and the connecting lines between the fuel tank, fuel tank filler cap and the fuel injection system.

3 Vapor trapped in the gas tank is vented through two valves in the top of the tank. From the valves, the vapor is routed through vapor tubes to a carbon canister, where it's stored until the next time the engine is started. Purging of the canister occurs with the engine at operating temperature and off-idle. The canister on 1.8L and 1.9L engines is located in the engine compartment near the radiator. On 2.0L engines, it's mounted at the rear of the vehicle near the fuel tank.

SYSTEM CHECKING

4 There are no moving parts and nothing to wear in the canister. Check for loose, missing, cracked or broken fittings and inspect the canister for cracks and other damage. If the canister is damaged, replace it (see following).

5 Check for fuel smells around the vehicle. Make sure the gas cap is in good condition and properly installed.

COMPONENT REPLACEMENT

Charcoal canister

1.8L and 1.9L engine models

6 Locate the canister in the driver's side wheel well (see illustration 3.2).

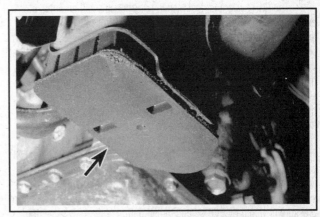

3.2 The charcoal canister on 1996 and earlier models is located in the driver's side wheel well (arrow)

7 From inside the engine compartment, remove the single mounting bolt and lower the canister.

8 Clearly label the hoses and detach them from the canister.

9 Installation is the reverse of the removal steps.

2.0L engine models

10 Block the front wheels so the vehicle won't roll. Jack up the rear end of the vehicle and support it securely on jackstands.

11 Disconnect the canister vent solenoid electrical connector, the canister tube and the canister purge outlet tube.

12 Unbolt the canister bracket and remove it together with the canister, then detach the canister from the bracket.

13 Installation is the reverse of the removal steps.

Canister Purge Solenoid (1.8L and 1.9L engine models)

14 Disconnect the negative cable from the battery.

15 Locate the canister purge solenoid in the engine compartment (in the vacuum hose running from the evaporative emissions control canister behind the driver's side headlight).

16 Disconnect the electrical connector from the solenoid.

17 Label the vacuum hoses and ports, then detach the hoses.

18 Remove the solenoid.

19 Installation is the reverse of removal.

Canister Purge Valve (2.0L engine models)

20 Disconnect the negative cable from the battery.

21 Locate the canister purge solenoid in right rear corner of the engine compartment.

22 Disconnect the electrical connector from the solenoid.

23 Label the vacuum hoses and ports, then detach the hoses.

24 Remove the solenoid mounting bolts and remove the solenoid.

25 Installation is the reverse of removal.

All other components

26 Referring to the VECI label of the vehicle, locate the component you intend to replace.

27 Label the hoses, then detach them and remove the component.

28 Installation is the reverse of removal.

4 Exhaust Gas Recirculation (EGR) system (1.9L and 2.0L SPI engines)

➡**Note: 1.8L engines and 2.0L Zetec engines are not equipped with an EGR system.**

GENERAL DESCRIPTION

1 The EGR system is designed to reintroduce small amounts of exhaust gas into the combustion chambers to reduce the combustion temperature, thus reducing the generation of oxides of nitrogen (NOx) emissions. The amount of exhaust gas introduced and the timing of the cycle is controlled by various factors such as engine speed, altitude, manifold vacuum, exhaust system back pressure, coolant temperature and throttle angle. All EGR valves are vacuum actuated (the vacuum diagram for each vehicle is shown on the Vehicle Emissions Control Information [VECI] label in the engine compartment).

2 A Pressure Feedback Electronic (PFE) EGR system with ported EGR valve is used. The PFE EGR system consists of the EGR valve, EGR backpressure transducer, EGR vacuum regulator (EVR) valve and the computer. PFE is a subsonic closed loop system that monitors the pressure drop across a remote orifice to control EGR flow rate. Since control pressure is varied by EVR solenoid modulation of the EGR valve, the back pressure transducer acts as the feedback device. The EGR valve in this type of system acts as a pressure regulator instead of a flow metering device.

3 The computer determines EGR flow according to input from the Engine Coolant Temperature (ECT) sensor, Throttle Position (TP) sensor, and on 1.9L models, the ignition coil, neutral safety switch and the 4EAT transaxle control unit.

4 The ported EGR valve is operated by a vacuum signal from the EVR valve, which actuates the valve diaphragm. As the vacuum increases sufficiently to overcome the spring, the valve is modulated, allowing EGR flow. The amount of flow is contingent upon the tapered pintle or the poppet position, which is affected by the vacuum signal and exhaust gas pressure.

CHECKING

5 Make sure that all vacuum lines are properly routed (see the VECI label in the engine compartment), secure and in good condition (not cracked, kinked or broken off).

6 When the engine is cold, there should be no vacuum to operate the EGR valve. If there is vacuum, check the EGR vacuum regulator (EVR) solenoid and replace it as required.

7 There should be no vacuum to the valve at curb idle (engine warm).

8 There should be vacuum to the valve above 1500 rpm. If there is no vacuum, check the EGR vacuum regulator (EGR) solenoid and

4.14 Hold the lower nut (arrow) with a wrench and loosen the upper nut to detach the EGR tube from the exhaust pipe

4.15a Here's the EGR valve used on 1.9L engine models

replace it as required.

9   With the engine at idle, apply 8-inch Hg vacuum to the valve. The valve stem should move, opening the valve, and the engine should stall or run roughly. If the valve stem moves but the engine doesn't respond, remove and clean the inlet and outlet ports with a wire brush.

✳✳ CAUTION:

Do not sandblast or clean the valve with gasoline or damage will result!

10 With the engine at idle, trap 4 in-Hg vacuum in the valve. Vacuum shouldn't drop more than 1 in-Hg in 30 seconds. If it does, replace the valve.

11 When the valve is suspected of leaking (indicated by a rough idle or stalling) perform the following simple check:

a) Insert a blocking gasket (no flow holes) between the valve and base and reinstall the valve.

b) If the engine idle improves, replace the valve and remove the blocking gasket. If the idle doesn't improve, take the vehicle to a dealer service department.

COMPONENT REPLACEMENT

♦ **Refer to illustrations 4.14, 4.15a, 4.15b and 4.16**

12 Disconnect the negative cable from the battery.

13 When replacing any vacuum hoses, remove only one hose at a time and make sure that the replacement hose is of the same quality and size as the hose being replaced.

14 Working beneath the vehicle, unscrew the threaded fitting that attaches the EGR pipe to the exhaust pipe (see illustration).

15 Remove the EGR valve mounting bolts (see illustration).

16 Lift the valve out together with the EGR tube (see illustration). Separate the tube from the valve.

17 Remove the old gasket. Be sure to thoroughly clean the gasket surfaces of the valve and the intake manifold. Use a new gasket when installing the valve and check for leaks when the job is completed.

18 Installation is the reverse of the removal steps.

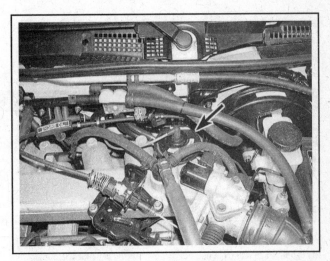

4.15b EGR valve location (arrow) - 2.0L SPI models

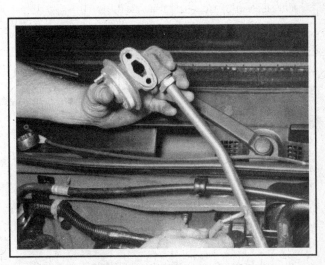

4.16 Lift out the EGR valve together with the EGR tube

5 Positive Crankcase Ventilation (PCV) system

GENERAL DESCRIPTION

1   The Positive Crankcase Ventilation (PCV) system cycles crankcase vapors back through the engine where they are burned. The valve regulates the amount of ventilating air and blow-by gas to the intake manifold and prevents backfire from traveling into the crankcase.

2   The PCV system consists of a replaceable PCV valve, a crankcase ventilation filter and the connecting hoses.

3   The air source for the crankcase ventilation system is in the air cleaner. Air passes through the PCV filter and through a hose connected to the air cleaner housing. From the PCV filter, the air flows into the valve cover and the crankcase, from which it circulates up into another section of the valve cover and finally enters a spring loaded regulator valve (PCV valve) that controls the amount of flow as operating conditions vary. The vapors are routed to the intake manifold through the crankcase vent hose tube and fittings. This process goes on continuously while the engine is running.

CHECKING

4   Checking procedures for the PCV system components are included in Chapter 1.

COMPONENT REPLACEMENT

5   Component replacement involves simply installing a new valve, filter or hose in place of the one removed during the checking procedure.

6 Catalytic converter

➡Note: Because of a Federally mandated extended warranty which covers emissions-related components such as the catalytic converter, check with a dealer service department before replacing the converter at your own expense.

GENERAL DESCRIPTION

1   The catalytic converter is an emission control device added to the exhaust system to reduce pollutants from the exhaust gas stream. There are two types of converters. The conventional oxidation catalyst reduces the levels of hydrocarbon (HC) and carbon monoxide (CO). The three-way catalyst lowers the levels of oxides of nitrogen (NOx) as well as hydrocarbons (HC) and carbon monoxide (CO).

CHECK

2   The test equipment for a catalytic converter is expensive and highly sophisticated. If you suspect that the converter on your vehicle is malfunctioning, take it to a dealer or authorized emissions inspection facility for diagnosis and repair.

3   Whenever the vehicle is raised for servicing of underbody components, check the converter for leaks, corrosion, dents and other damage. Check the welds/flange bolts that attach the front and rear ends of the converter to the exhaust system. If damage is discovered, the converter should be replaced.

4   Although catalytic converters don't break too often, they do become plugged. The easiest way to check for a restricted converter is to use a vacuum gauge to diagnose the effect of a blocked exhaust on intake vacuum.

a) Open the throttle until the engine speed is about 2000 RPM.

b) Release the throttle quickly.

c) If there is no restriction, the gauge will quickly drop to not more than 2 in Hg or more above its normal reading.

d) If the gauge does not show 5 in Hg or more above its normal reading, or seems to momentarily hover around its highest reading for a moment before it returns, the exhaust system, or the converter, is plugged (or an exhaust pipe is bent or dented, or the core inside the muffler has shifted).

COMPONENT REPLACEMENT

5   The converter is bolted to the exhaust system. Refer to the exhaust system removal and installation in Chapter 4.

Section

Reference to other Chapters

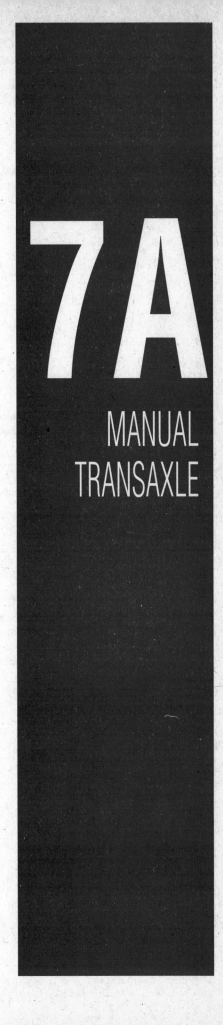

7A

MANUAL
TRANSAXLE

1 General information

The vehicles covered by this manual are equipped with either a four or five-speed manual transaxle or a four speed automatic transaxle. Information on the manual transaxle is included in this Part of Chapter 7. Service procedures for the automatic transaxle are contained in Chapter 7B.

The manual transaxle is a compact, two piece, lightweight aluminum alloy housing containing both the transmission and differential assemblies.

Because of the complexity, unavailability of replacement parts and special tools required, internal repair of the manual transaxle by the home mechanic is not recommended. For readers who wish to tackle a transaxle rebuild, a brief *Transaxle overhaul - general information* Section is provided. The bulk of information in this Chapter is devoted to removal and installation procedures.

2 Shift lever and linkage - removal and installation

REMOVAL

▶ **Refer to illustrations 2.2, 2.3, 2.6, 2.7 and 2.8**

1 Securely block both rear wheels so the vehicle can't roll, then jack up the front end and place it securely on jackstands. DO NOT get under a vehicle that's supported only by a jack!

2 Remove the shift control rod nut and bolt (see illustration).

3 Working inside the vehicle, unscrew the shift knob (see illustration).

4 Remove the shift console (see Chapter 11).

5 If necessary, remove four screws that secure the shift boot (see illustration). Remove the shift boot and its gasket.

6 Pry out the shifter spring with a screwdriver (see illustration).

7 Lift the shift lever and its ball seats out of the shift housing (see illustration).

8 If it's necessary to remove the linkage as well as the lever, remove the nuts and washers that secure the shift housing on the end of the extension bar to the vehicle (see illustration). Detach the extension bar from the transaxle, lower the shift housing and detach the shift control rod from the transaxle.

INSTALLATION

9 Installation is the reverse of the removal Steps, with the following additions:

a) Lubricate all joints and friction points with multipurpose grease.

b) Tighten all fasteners to the torques listed in this Chapter's Specifications.

c) Make sure the shift lever spring is securely seated in its groove (see illustration).

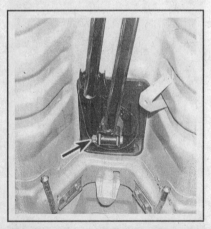

2.2 The shift control rod is attached to the bottom of the shift lever by a nut and bolt

2.3 The shift knob unscrews from the lever

2.6 Pry out the shifter spring to release the shift lever from the shift housing . . .

2.7 . . . and lift the lever out, together with its ball seats

2.8 The shift housing, located on the end of the extension bar, is secured to the vehicle by four nuts and washers

3 Manual transaxle - removal and installation

1991 THROUGH 1996 MODELS

Removal

1 Disconnect the negative cable from the battery.

2 Remove the battery and the battery tray (see Chapter 5).

3 Remove the air cleaner air hose and resonance chamber (see Chapter 4).

4 Disconnect the speedometer cable from the vehicle speed sensor at the transaxle.

5 Remove the clutch line clip. Disconnect the clutch line from the clutch hose and plug the disconnected ends (see Chapter 8).

6 Disconnect the transaxle ground strap and the three electrical connectors above the transaxle. Remove the connector bracket.

7 Support the engine with a three-bar type engine support, or equivalent, attached to the engine lifting brackets.

8 Remove three nuts that secure the transaxle upper mount (see Chapter 2A). Loosen the mount pivot nut, rotate the mount out of the way and remove the mount bracket.

9 Remove the two upper bolts that secure the transaxle to the engine.

10 Loosen the front wheel lug nuts. Securely block both rear wheels so the vehicle can't roll, then jack up the front end and place it securely on jackstands. DO NOT get under a vehicle that's supported only by a jack!

11 Remove the front wheels.

12 Remove the splash shields for the inner fenders.

13 Drain the transaxle lubricant (see Chapter 1), then reinstall the drain plug. Tighten now, so you don't forget to do it later.

14 Remove the driveaxles (see Chapter 8). Install transaxle plugs in the driveaxle holes so the differential gears don't fall out of position.

15 Unbolt the plenum support bracket and remove it (see Chapter 2A).

16 Remove the starter (see Chapter 5).

17 Detach the extension bar and shift control rod from the transaxle (see Section 2).

18 Remove both splash shields from under the front of the vehicle.

19 Remove two nuts that secure the transaxle mount to the crossmember, then remove the crossmember.

20 Remove the front transaxle mount and tubing bracket.

21 Support the transaxle with a transmission jack. These are available from rental outlets and include cradles which will prevent the transaxle from falling.

22 Remove the five lower bolts that secure the transaxle to the engine.

23 Make a final check that all wires and hoses have been disconnected from the transaxle, then carefully pull the transaxle and jack away from the engine.

24 Once the input shaft is clear, lower the transaxle and remove it from under the vehicle.

❋❋ CAUTION:

Do not depress the clutch pedal while the transaxle is out of the vehicle.

25 With the transaxle removed, the clutch components are now accessible and can be inspected. In most cases, new clutch components should be routinely installed when the transaxle is removed.

Installation

26 If removed, install the clutch components (see Chapter 8).

27 With the transaxle secured to the jack with a chain, raise it into position behind the engine, then carefully slide it forward, engaging the input shaft with the clutch plate hub splines. Do not use excessive force to install the transaxle - if the input shaft does not slide into place, readjust the angle of the transaxle so it is level and/or turn the input

shaft so the splines engage properly with the clutch plate hub.

28 Install the transaxle-to-engine bolts. Tighten the bolts securely.

29 Install the transaxle mount nuts or bolts and the crossmember.

30 Remove the jacks supporting the transaxle and engine.

31 Install the various items removed previously, referring to Chapter 8 for installation of the driveaxles.

32 Make a final check that all wires, hoses, linkages and the speedometer cable have been connected and that the transaxle has been filled with lubricant to the proper level (see Chapter 1).

33 Connect the negative battery cable. Road test the vehicle for proper operation and check for leaks.

1997 AND LATER MODELS

Removal

34 Perform Steps 1, 2 and 5 above.

35 Disconnect the electrical connectors for the oxygen sensor and backup lights, unbolt the connector suppprt bracket, then disconnect the electrical connectors for the vehicle speed sensor and Park/Neutral switch.

36 Support the engine with an approved support bar, or equivalent, attached to the engine lifting brackets.

37 Remove three nuts and washers that secure the left-hand support insulator.

38 Remove the upper front and upper rear bolts that secure the transaxle to the engine block.

39 Remove the starter motor (see Chapter 5).

40 Remove the driveaxles (see Chapter 8).

41 Drain the transaxle oil (see Chapter 1).

42 Follow the air conditioning refrigerant line to its retainer on the engine crossmember, then free the line from the retainer. With the engine securely supported, unbolt the front and rear ends of the crossmember from the vehicle (two bolts at the front end of the crossmember and two bolts at the rear, accessible from beneath). Then, working from beneath, remove the two nuts that secure the crossmember to the front engine mount insulator and two more that secure the crossmember to the rear engine mount insulator.

43 Lower the crossmember away from the vehicle.

44 Unbolt the gearshift rod from the input shift shaft on the transaxle (see illustration 2.2). Remove the nut that secures the gearshift stabilizer bar to the transaxle, then slide the bar off the stud.

45 Remove the clutch slave cylinder (see Chapter 8).

46 Remove the two lower bolts that secure the transaxle to the engine.

47 Support the transaxle with a transmission jack. These are available from rental outlets and include cradles that will keep the transaxle from falling.

48 Remove the catalytic converter (see Chapter 4). If parts are corroded, you may find it easier to remove the entire exhaust system.

49 With the transaxle securely supported, remove the last three bolts that secure the transaxle to the engine. Carefully lower the transaxle and pull it away from the engine.

Installation

50 Perform Steps 26 through 33 to install the transaxle.

4   Transaxle overhaul - general information

Overhauling a manual transaxle is a difficult job for the do-it-yourselfer. It involves the disassembly and reassembly of many small parts. Numerous clearances must be precisely measured and, if necessary, changed with select fit spacers and snap-rings. As a result, if transaxle problems arise, it can be removed and installed by a competent do-it-yourselfer, but overhaul should be left to a transmission repair shop. Rebuilt transaxles may be available - check with your dealer parts department and auto parts stores. At any rate, the time and money involved in an overhaul is almost sure to exceed the cost of a rebuilt unit.

Nevertheless, it's not impossible for an inexperienced mechanic to rebuild a transaxle if the special tools are available and the job is done in a deliberate step-by-step manner so nothing is overlooked.

The tools necessary for an overhaul include internal and external snap-ring pliers, a bearing puller, a slide hammer, a set of pin punches, a dial indicator and possibly a hydraulic press. In addition, a large, sturdy workbench and a vise or transaxle stand will be required.

During disassembly of the transaxle, make careful notes of how each piece comes off, where it fits in relation to other pieces and what holds it in place. Actually noting how they are installed when you remove the parts will make it much easier to get the transaxle back together.

Before taking the transaxle apart for repair, it will help if you have some idea what area of the transaxle is malfunctioning. Certain problems can be closely tied to specific areas in the transaxle, which can make component examination and replacement easier. Refer to the *Troubleshooting* section at the front of this manual for information regarding possible sources of trouble.

Torque specifications — Ft-lbs (unless otherwise indicated)

➡Note: One foot-pound (ft-lb) of torque is equivalent to 12 inch-pounds (in-lbs) of torque. Torque values below approximately 15 ft-lbs are expressed in inch-pounds, since most foot-pound torque wrenches are not accurate at these smaller values.

1991 through 1996 models

Lower transaxle-to-engine bolts	27 to 38
Front transaxle mount bolts	12 to 17
Lower crossmember nuts and bolts	47 to 66
Transaxle mount-to-crossmember nuts	27 to 38
Shift control rod bolt and nut	23 to 34
Extension bar nut	12 to 17
Upper engine to transaxle bolts	47 to 66
Upper transaxle mount nuts	
1.8L engine models	47 to 66
1.9L engine models	49 to 69
Shift housing nuts	96 to 132 in-lbs
Control rod-to-shift lever nut	12 to 17

1997 and later models

Lower transaxle-to-engine bolts	28 to 38
Center transaxle-to-engine bolts	28 to 38
Upper transaxle-to-engine bolts	28 to 38
Insulator through-bolts	50 to 68
Left insulator nuts and washers	50 to 68
Shift control rod bolt and nut	12 to 17
Extension bar nut	23 to 34
Shift housing nuts	96 to 132 in-lbs
Control rod-to-shift lever nut	104 to 122 in-lbs
Crossmember insulator nuts	28 to 37
Crossmember mounting nuts	47 to 65
Vehicle speed sensor bolt	70 to 99 in-lbs

Notes

Section

7B

AUTOMATIC
TRANSAXLE

1 General information

All vehicles covered in this manual come equipped with either a five-speed manual transaxle or an automatic transaxle. All information on the automatic transaxle is included in this Part of Chapter 7. Information for the manual transaxle can be found in Chapter 7A.

Due to the complexity of the automatic transaxles covered in this manual and the need for specialized equipment to perform most service operations, this Chapter contains only general diagnosis and removal and installation procedures.

If the transaxle requires major repair work, it should be left to a dealer service department or an automotive or transmission repair shop. You can, however, remove and install the transaxle yourself and save the expense, even if the repair work is done by a transmission shop.

2 Diagnosis - general

➡**Note: Automatic transaxle malfunctions may be caused by five general conditions: poor engine performance, improper adjustments, hydraulic malfunctions, mechanical malfunctions or malfunctions in the computer or its signal network. Diagnosis of these problems should always begin with a check of the easily repaired items: fluid level and condition (see Chapter 1), shift linkage adjustment and throttle linkage adjustment. Next, perform a road test to determine if the problem has been corrected or if more diagnosis is necessary. If the problem persists after the preliminary tests and corrections are completed, additional diagnosis should be done by a dealer service department or transmission repair shop. Refer to the Troubleshooting section at the front of this manual for transaxle problem diagnosis.**

PRELIMINARY CHECKS

1   Drive the vehicle to warm the transaxle to normal operating temperature.

2   Check the fluid level as described in Chapter 1:

a) *If the fluid level is unusually low, add enough fluid to bring the level within the designated area of the dipstick, then check for external leaks.*

b) *If the fluid level is abnormally high, drain off the excess, then check the drained fluid for contamination by coolant. The presence of engine coolant in the automatic transmission fluid indicates that a failure has occurred in the internal radiator walls that separate the coolant from the transmission fluid (see Chapter 3).*

c) *If the fluid is foaming, drain it and refill the transaxle, then check for coolant in the fluid or a high fluid level.*

3   Check the engine idle speed.

➡**Note: If the engine is malfunctioning, do not proceed with the preliminary checks until it has been repaired and runs normally.**

4 . Check the electrical connectors - make sure they're securely connected and not corroded or damaged (see illustrations 4.5a and 4.5b).

5   Inspect the shift control cable (see illustration 4.3a). Make sure that it's properly adjusted and that the linkage operates smoothly.

FLUID LEAK DIAGNOSIS

6   Most fluid leaks are easy to locate visually. Repair usually consists of replacing a seal or gasket. If a leak is difficult to find, the following procedure may help.

7   Identify the fluid. Make sure it's transmission fluid and not engine oil or brake fluid (automatic transmission fluid is a deep red color).

8   Try to pinpoint the source of the leak. Drive the vehicle several miles, then park it over a large sheet of cardboard. After a minute or two, you should be able to locate the leak by determining the source of the fluid dripping onto the cardboard.

9   Make a careful visual inspection of the suspected component and the area immediately around it. Pay particular attention to gasket mating surfaces. A mirror is often helpful for finding leaks in areas that are hard to see.

10 If the leak still cannot be found, clean the suspected area thoroughly with a degreaser or solvent, then dry it.

11 Drive the vehicle for several miles at normal operating temperature and varying speeds. After driving the vehicle, visually inspect the suspected component again.

12 Once the leak has been located, the cause must be determined before it can be properly repaired. If a gasket is replaced but the sealing flange is bent, the new gasket will not stop the leak. The bent flange must be straightened.

13 Before attempting to repair a leak, check to make sure that the following conditions are corrected or they may cause another leak.

➡**Note: Some of the following conditions cannot be fixed without highly specialized tools and expertise. Such problems must be referred to a transmission shop or a dealer service department.**

Gasket leaks

14 Check the pan periodically. Make sure the bolts are tight, no bolts are missing, the gasket is in good condition and the pan is flat (dents in the pan may indicate damage to the valve body inside).

15 If the pan gasket is leaking, the fluid level or the fluid pressure may be too high, the vent may be plugged, the pan bolts may be too tight, the pan sealing flange may be warped, the sealing surface of the transaxle housing may be damaged, the gasket may be damaged or the transaxle casting may be cracked or porous. If sealant instead of gasket material has been used to form a seal between the pan and the transaxle housing, it may be the wrong sealant.

Seal leaks

16 If a transaxle seal is leaking, the fluid level or pressure may be too high, the vent may be plugged, the seal bore may be damaged, the seal itself may be damaged or improperly installed, the surface of the shaft protruding through the seal may be damaged or a loose bearing may be causing excessive shaft movement.

17 Make sure the dipstick tube seal is in good condition and the tube is properly seated. Periodically check the area around the speedometer gear or sensor for leakage. If transmission fluid is evident, check the O-ring for damage. Also inspect the side gear shaft oil seals for leakage.

Case leaks

18 If the case itself appears to be leaking, the casting is porous and will have to be repaired or replaced.

19 Make sure the oil cooler hose fittings are tight and in good condition.

Fluid comes out vent pipe or fill tube

20 If this condition occurs, the transaxle is overfilled, there is coolant in the fluid, the case is porous, the dipstick is incorrect, the vent is plugged or the drain back holes are plugged.

3   Oil seal replacement

▶ **Refer to illustrations 3.7 and 3.10**

1   Oil leaks frequently occur due to wear of the driveaxle oil seals. Replacement of these seals is relatively easy, since the repairs can usually be performed without removing the transaxle from the vehicle.

2   The driveaxle oil seals are located at the sides of the transaxle, where the driveaxles are attached. If leakage at the seal is suspected, raise the vehicle and support it securely on jackstands. If the seal is leaking, lubricant will be found on the sides of the transaxle.

3   Disconnect the tie rod ends and balljoints from the steering knuckles (see Chapter 10).

4   Support the engine with a hoist.

5   Remove the crossmember from beneath the transaxle.

6   If you're working on a vehicle with a 1.8L engine, remove the bracket that supports the passenger side driveaxle.

7   Pry the inner ends of the driveaxles out of the transaxle with a flat pry bar (see illustration). Support the driveaxles with rope or wire.

❈❈ CAUTION:

Don't let the driveaxles hang free or the CV joints may be damaged.

8   Using a screwdriver or pry bar, carefully pry the oil seal out of the transaxle bore.

9   If the oil seal cannot be removed with a screwdriver or pry bar, a special oil seal removal tool (available at auto parts stores) will be required.

10   Using a large section of pipe or a large deep socket as a drift, install the new oil seal (see illustration). Drive it into the bore squarely and make sure it's completely seated.

11   Install the driveaxle(s). Be careful not to damage the lip of the new seal.

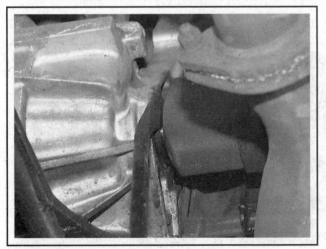

3.7 Insert a prybar between the halfshaft and transaxle case. Gently pry outward to release the halfshaft from the differential side gear

3.10 Drive in the oil seal using a socket

4 Automatic transaxle - removal and installation

1991 THROUGH 1996 MODELS

Refer to illustrations 4.3a, 4.3b, 4.5a, 4.5b, 4.5c, 4.6, 4.10, 4.11, 4.12, 4.20, 4.21a, 4.21b, 4.21c, 4.26a and 4.26b

Removal

1 Remove the battery and the battery tray (see Chapter 5).

2 Remove the air cleaner (see Chapter 4).

3 Disconnect the shift control cable from the manual lever on the transaxle (see illustration). Remove the cable clip (see illustration).

4 Remove the speedometer cable clip and pull the cable out.

5 Disconnect the transaxle electrical connectors and detach the harnesses from the clips (see illustrations).

6 At the top of the transaxle, disconnect the ground cables and remove the manual lever position switch wiring brackets (see illustration).

7 Remove the starter (see Chapter 5).

8 Support the engine with a hoist or support bar.

4.3a The shift control cable is secured to the manual lever on top of the transaxle by a clip

4.3b Pull out the clip with pliers and separate the cable from its bracket

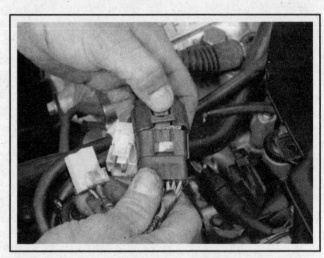

4.5a Disconnect the large electrical connectors . . .

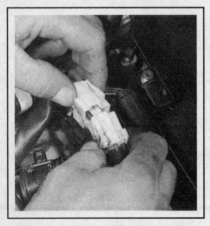

4.5b . . . and the small one . . .

4.5c . . . and squeeze the retainers with pliers to separate them from the clips

4.6 Disconnect the ground wires and wiring brackets on the top of the transaxle

9 Disconnect the kickdown cable from the throttle cam (see Chapter 2 Part A).

10 Place a drain pan under the transaxle to catch the fluid. Disconnect the transaxle cooler lines from the transaxle, then plug the disconnected ends and fittings (see illustration).

11 Remove the upper transaxle mount (see illustration).

12 Remove the upper transaxle mounting bolts (see illustration).

13 Disconnect the electrical connectors for the exhaust gas oxygen sensor and the speed sensor.

14 Disconnect the vent hose from the transaxle.

15 Loosen the wheel lug nuts. Securely block the rear wheels so the vehicle can't roll. Jack up the front end and place it securely on jackstands. DO NOT get under a vehicle that's supported only by a jack!

16 Remove the front wheels.

17 Remove the driveaxles (see Chapter 8).

18 Remove three lower splash shields from beneath the engine and transaxle.

19 Remove the front part of the exhaust system (see Chapter 4).

20 Remove the torque converter inspection plate (see illustration).

21 Mark one of the torque converter-to-driveplate studs and its location on the driveplate with white paint, then remove the nut (see illustrations). Rotate the crankshaft to provide access to the remaining torque converter-to-driveplate nuts and remove the nuts (see illustration).

22 Unbolt the transaxle oil pan from the engine.

23 Remove the lower crossmember.

24 Drain the fluid from the transaxle pan and differential (see Chapter 1).

4.10 The fluid cooler lines are secured to the transaxle by spring clips

4.11 Remove three nuts to detach the upper transaxle mount

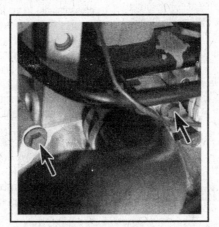

4.12 Remove the upper transaxle mounting bolts (arrows)

4.20 Remove the torque converter inspection plate

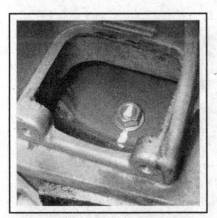

4.21a Paint an alignment mark on one of the converter studs and the driveplate so they can be reassembled in their same relative positions

4.21b Then remove the converter-to-driveplate nuts

4.21c Reach through the access hole with a large screwdriver or small pry bar and turn the engine crankshaft to bring each of the torque converter-to-driveplate nuts within reach

25 Place a transmission jack under the transaxle. For safety, secure the transaxle to the jack with a chain so it can't fall and cause injury.

26 Remove the lower bolts that secure the transaxle to the engine (see illustrations).

27 Slide the transaxle away from the engine and lower it clear of the vehicle.

Installation

28 Prior to installation, make sure that the torque converter hub is securely engaged in the pump.

29 With the transaxle secured to the jack, raise it into position. Be sure to keep it level so the torque converter does not slide out. Connect the fluid cooler lines.

30 Turn the torque converter to line up the drive studs with the holes in the driveplate. The white paint mark on the torque converter and the stud made in Step 21 must line up.

31 Move the transaxle forward carefully until the dowel pins and the torque converter are engaged.

32 Install the transaxle housing-to-engine bolts. Tighten them securely.

33 Install the torque converter-to-driveplate nuts. Tighten the nuts to the torque listed in this Chapter's Specifications.

34 Install the transaxle and any suspension and chassis components which were removed. Tighten the bolts and nuts to the specified torque.

35 If you're installing a new or rebuilt transaxle, remove the throttle cam securing pin. Coat the threads of the bolt from the old transaxle with sealant, then use it to replace the pin.

36 The remainder of installation is the reverse of the removal steps.

37 Fill the transaxle (see Chapter 1), run the vehicle and check for fluid leaks.

1997 AND LATER MODELS

Removal

38 Perform Steps 1 through 3.

39 Remove the computer control relay module and bracket (see Chapter 6).

40 Disconnect the following electrical connectors:

a) *Transmission range sensor*
b) *Transmission solenoid*
c) *Turbine shaft speed sensor*
d) *Vehicle speed sensor*
e) *Downstream catalyst monitor*

41 Remove the starter motor (see Chapter 5).

42 Support the engine with a support fixture or an engine hoist, attached to the engine lifting brackets.

43 Drain the transaxle fluid (see Chapter 1). Disconnect both fluid cooler hoses where they meet the metal lines.

44 Remove three nuts and washers that secure the left-hand support insulator.

45 Remove the upper bolts that secure the transaxle to the engine block.

46 Remove the driveaxles (see Chapter 8).

47 Detach the clip that secures the oxygen sensor wire, then remove four bolts and the small crossmember, working from beneath.

48 Remove the catalytic converter (see Chapter 4). If parts are corroded, you may find it easier to remove the entire exhaust system.

49 Follow the air conditioning refrigerant line to its retainer on the front engine crossmember, then free the line from the retainer. With the engine securely supported, unbolt the front and rear ends of the crossmember from the vehicle (two bolts at the front end of the crossmember and two bolts at the rear, accessible from beneath). Then, working from beneath, remove the two nuts that secure the crossmember to the front engine mount insulator and two more that secure the crossmember to the transmission mount insulator.

50 Lower the crossmember away from the vehicle.

51 Unbolt the transmission housing cover for access to the torque converter-to-drive plate nuts and studs. Mark one of the studs and its location on the driveplate with white paint, then remove the nut (see illustrations 4.21a and 4.21b). Rotate the crankshaft to provide access to the remaining torque converter-to-driveplate nuts and remove the nuts.

52 Support the transaxle with a transmission jack. These are available from rental outlets and include cradles that will keep the transaxle from falling.

53 With the transaxle securely supported, remove the last five bolts that secure the transaxle to the engine. Carefully lower the transaxle and pull it away from the engine.

Installation

54 Perform Steps 28 through 37 to install the transaxle.

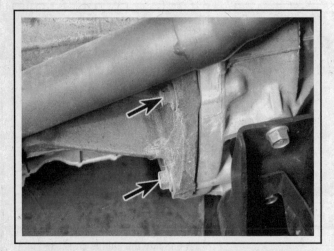

4.26a There are lower mounting bolts on the forward side of the transaxle . . .

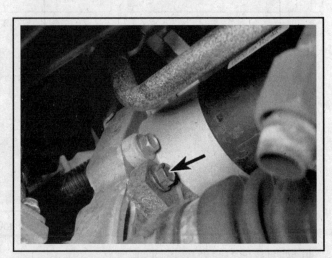

4.26b . . . and on the rear side (arrow); the upper bolt in this photo is a starter lower mounting bolt

Torque specifications   **Ft-lbs (unless otherwise indicated)**

➡**Note: One foot-pound (ft-lb) of torque is equivalent to 12 inch-pounds (in-lbs) of torque. Torque values below approximately 15 ft-lbs are expressed in inch-pounds, since most foot-pound torque wrenches are not accurate at these smaller values.**

Lower transaxle-to-engine bolts (not to oil pan)	41 to 59
Torque converter-to-drive plate nuts	25 to 36
Lower crossmember-to-transaxle mount nuts	27 to 38
Crossmember-to-vehicle nuts and bolts	47 to 66
Lower transaxle-to-oil pan bolts	27 to 38
Upper transaxle-to-engine bolts	41 to 59
Upper transaxle mount nuts	49 to 69
Throttle cam bolt	69 to 95 in-lbs

Notes

Section

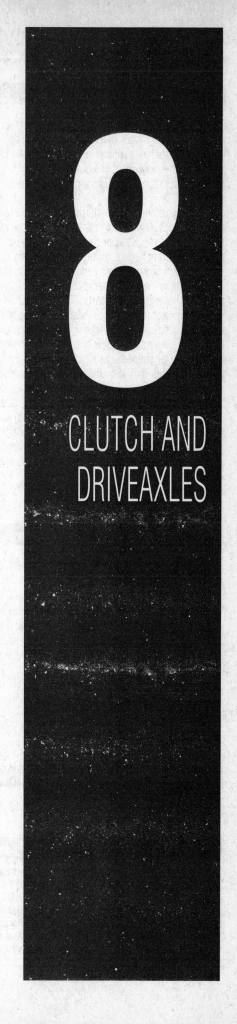

8

CLUTCH AND
DRIVEAXLES

1 General information

All of the models covered by this manual that are equipped with a manual transaxle have a single dry plate, diaphragm spring type clutch. The clutch plate has a splined hub which allows it to slide along the splines on the input shaft. The clutch and pressure plate are held in contact by spring pressure exerted by the diaphragm spring in the pressure plate.

During gear shifting, the clutch pedal is depressed, which transmits hydraulic pressure from the master cylinder to the release cylinder, pushing on the release lever so the throwout bearing pushes on the diaphragm spring fingers, disengaging the clutch.

The clutch pedal requires periodic adjustment (see Chapter 1).

Power from the engine passes through the clutch and transaxle to the front wheels by two driveaxles. The driveaxles are of unequal length.

On all except the passenger side of 1.8L engine models, the driveaxles consist of three sections: the inner splined ends which are held in the differential by clips or springs, two constant velocity (CV) joints and outer splined ends which are held in the hub by a nut. A dynamic damper is used on the passenger-side driveaxle of 1.9L engine models.

On the passenger side of 1996 and earlier 1.8L engine models and 1998 and later coupe models (2.0L Zetec engine) with manual transaxle, the driveaxle shaft consists of two sections which are splined together. CV joints are used at both ends of the outer driveaxle section. A dynamic damper bearing assembly, bolted to the engine block, supports the center of the driveaxle.

The CV joints contain ball bearings which allow them to operate at various lengths and angles as the suspension is compressed and extended and the steering wheel turned. The CV joints are lubricated with special grease and are protected by rubber boots which must be inspected periodically for cracks, holes, tears and signs of leakage, which could lead to damage of the joints and failure of the driveaxle.

It should be noted that the terms used in this manual to describe various clutch components may vary somewhat from those used by parts vendors. For example, such terms as slave cylinder, clutch plate, pressure plate and release bearing are used throughout this Chapter. An auto parts store or dealer parts department, however, might use the terms release cylinder, clutch disc, clutch cover and throwout bearing, respectively, for the above parts. The important thing is to keep in mind that the terms are interchangeable - they mean the same thing.

✳✳ WARNING:

Dust produced by clutch wear and deposited on clutch components is hazardous to your health. DO NOT blow it out with compressed air and DO NOT inhale it. DO NOT use gasoline or petroleum-based solvents to remove the dust. Brake system cleaner should be used to flush the dust into a drain pan. After the clutch components are wiped clean with a rag. dispose of the contaminated rags and cleaner in a covered container.

2 Clutch operation - check

Other than to replace components with obvious damage, some preliminary checks should be done to diagnose clutch problems.

a) *The first check should be of the fluid level in the clutch master cylinder. If the fluid level is low, add fluid as necessary and retest. If the master cylinder runs dry, or if any of the hydraulic components are serviced, bleed the hydraulic system (see Section 7).*

b) *To check clutch "spin down" time, run the engine at normal idle speed with the transaxle in Neutral (clutch pedal up - engaged). Disengage the clutch (pedal down), wait several seconds and shift the transaxle into Reverse. No grinding noise should be heard. A grinding noise would indicate component failure in the clutch plate or pressure plate.*

c) *To check for complete clutch release, run the engine (with the parking brake on to prevent movement) and hold the clutch pedal approximately 1/2-inch from the floor mat. Shift the transmission between First gear and Reverse several times. If the shifts are smooth, the clutch is releasing properly. If they aren't, the clutch is not releasing completely. Check the pedal, lever and clutch fluid level.*

d) *Check that the clutch release lever is properly mounted on its ballstud.*

3 Clutch components - removal, inspection and installation

▶ **Refer to illustrations 3.3, 3.4, 3.9 and 3.12**

✳✳ WARNING:

Dust produced by clutch wear and deposited on clutch components is hazardous to your health. DO NOT blow it out with compressed air and DO NOT inhale it. DO NOT use gasoline or petroleum-based solvents to remove the dust. Brake system cleaner should be used to flush the dust into a drain pan. After the clutch components are wiped clean with a rag, dispose of the contaminated rags and cleaner in a covered container.

REMOVAL

1 Remove the transaxle from the vehicle (see Chapter 7A).

2 Use a center-punch to mark the position of the pressure plate assembly on the flywheel so it can be installed in the same position.

3 Loosen the pressure plate bolts a little at a time, in a criss-cross pattern, to prevent warping the pressure plate (see illustration).

4 Remove the bolts and detach the pressure plate and clutch plate from the flywheel.

5 Handle the clutch carefully, trying not to touch the lining surface, and set it aside.

3.3 Prevent the flywheel from turning with a locking tool - if you don't have one, use a large screwdriver or prybar braced against a transaxle-to engine block bolt

3.4 Remove the clutch cover, and take out the friction disc

EXCESSIVE WEAR

NORMAL FINGER WEAR   **EXCESSIVE FINGER WEAR**   **BROKEN OR BENT FINGERS**

3.9 Replace the pressure plate if any of these conditions are noted

INSPECTION

6   Inspect the friction surfaces of the clutch plate, pressure plate and flywheel for signs of uneven contact, indicating improper installation or damaged clutch springs. Also look for score marks, burned areas, deep grooves, cracks and other types of wear and damage. If the flywheel is worn or damaged, remove it and take it to an automotive machine shop to see if it can be resurfaced (if it can't, a new one will be required). If the flywheel is glazed, rough it up with fine emery cloth.

7   To see how worn the clutch plate is, measure the distance from the rivet heads to the lining surface. There should be at least 1/16-inch of lining above the rivet heads. However, the clutch plate is ordinarily replaced with a new one whenever it's removed for any reason (due to the relatively low cost of the part and the work involved to get to it). Check the lining for contamination by oil or grease and replace the clutch plate with a new one if any is present. Check the hub for cracks, blue discolored areas, broken springs and contamination by grease or oil. Slide the clutch plate onto the input shaft to make sure the fit is snug and the splines are not burred or worn.

8   Remove and inspect the release bearing and release lever as described in Section 4.

9   Check the flatness of the pressure plate with a straightedge. Look for signs of overheating, cracks, deep grooves and ridges. The inner end of the diaphragm spring fingers should not show any signs of uneven wear. Replace the pressure plate with a new one if its condition is in doubt (see illustration).

10   Make sure the pressure plate fits snugly on the flywheel dowels. Replace it with a new one if it fits loosely on the dowels.

11   Check the pilot bearing in the end of the flywheel for smooth operation. If it's noisy or feels rough when turned, remove it with a slide hammer and puller attachment. Install the new pilot bearing using a bushing driver or a socket with an outside diameter slightly smaller than that of the pilot bearing.

➡**Note: If you're replacing the clutch components, it's a good idea to go ahead and replace the pilot bearing also, regardless of its condition.**

INSTALLATION

12 Position the clutch plate on the flywheel, centering it with an alignment tool (see illustration).

13 With the clutch plate held in place by the alignment tool, place the pressure plate in position on the flywheel dowels, aligning it with the marks made at the time of removal.

14 Install the bolts and tighten them in a criss-cross pattern, one or two turns at a time, until they're at the torque listed in this Chapter's Specifications.

15 Install the release lever and release bearing, if removed (refer to Section 4).

16 Install the transaxle (refer to Chapter 7A).

3.12 Use a clutch alignment tool to center the friction disc

---

4 Clutch release bearing and lever - removal, inspection and installation

▶ **Refer to illustration 4.5**

☀ WARNING:

Dust produced by clutch wear and deposited on clutch components is hazardous to your health. DO NOT blow it out with compressed air and DO NOT inhale it. DO NOT use gasoline or petroleum-based solvents to remove the dust. Brake system cleaner should be used to flush the dust into a drain pan. After the clutch components are wiped clean with a rag. dispose of the contaminated rags and cleaner in a covered container.

REMOVAL

1 Remove the transaxle from the vehicle and clean the clutch housing as described in the **Warning** above.

2 Detach the release bearing from the release lever and slide the bearing off the input shaft sleeve.

3 Pull the release lever off its ballstud, detach it from the boot and take it out of the clutch housing.

INSPECTION

4 Check the lever for excessive wear and galling.

5 Inspect the bearing for damage, wear and cracks. Hold the center of the bearing and spin the outer race (see illustration). If the bearing doesn't turn smoothly or if it's noisy, replace it with a new one. It's common practice to replace the bearing with a new one whenever a clutch job is performed, to decrease the possibility of a bearing failure in the future.

INSTALLATION

6 Wipe the old grease from the release bearing if the bearing is to be reused. Do not clean it by immersing it in solvent; it's sealed at the factory and would be ruined if solvent got into it. Fill the cavities and coat the inner surface, as well as the input shaft sleeve with high temperature multi-purpose grease.

7 Lubricate the pocket in the release lever with multi-purpose grease. Pass the end of the lever through the boot and snap it down onto the ballstud. Lubricate the release lever arms where they contact the bearing with high temperature multi-purpose grease.

8 Slide the release bearing over the input shaft sleeve and position it in the release lever arms with the ears on the bearing straddling the lever arms.

9 Operate the clutch release lever by hand to verify smooth operation of the release bearing.

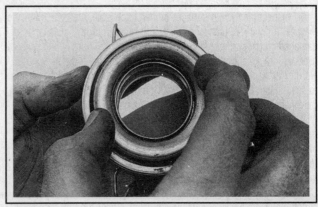

4.5 Hold the release bearing with one hand and spin it with the other; replace it if there's any roughness or abnormal noise

5 Clutch slave cylinder - removal, overhaul and installation

REMOVAL

1   Disconnect the hydraulic line nut from the cylinder with a flare nut wrench, if available. Plug the line to keep the fluid in and dirt out.

2   Remove the slave cylinder mounting bolts and take it off the clutch housing.

OVERHAUL

➡**Note: The piston and cup should be replaced as an assembly whenever the release cylinder is disassembled.**

3   Work the boot off the cylinder body and pull out the pushrod.

4   Tap the cylinder against a block of wood to eject the piston. If it sticks, it may be necessary to force it out with compressed air.

✳✳ WARNING:

If this method is used, the piston may shoot out forcefully enough to cause injury. Keep your fingers out of the way and don't point the cylinder anywhere but at a block of wood or a bundle of rags. Apply air pressure gradually and use just enough to ease the piston out.

5   Remove the spring from the bore.

6   Remove the bleed valve cap, unscrew the bleed valve and remove the bleed valve ball.

7   Clean all parts with clean brake fluid or brake system cleaner.

8   Check all parts for wear or damage. Replace the release cylinder as an assembly if any parts except the piston and cup are worn or damaged. The piston and cup can be replaced separately.

9   Coat the cylinder bore with clean brake fluid.

10 Install the spring in the bore, wide end first. Install a new piston and cup, taking care not to bend back the lip of the cup.

11 Install the pushrod, then install the boot and engage it with the grooves in the pushrod and cylinder body.

INSTALLATION

12 Installation is the reverse of the removal steps.

13 Bleed the clutch hydraulic system (see Section 7).

6 Clutch master cylinder - removal, overhaul and installation

REMOVAL

1   Remove the battery and battery tray (see Chapter 5).

2   Disconnect the clutch line from the master cylinder with a flare nut wrench, if available.

3   Remove the clamp and disconnect the hose from the master cylinder body. Plug the hose to prevent excessive fluid loss.

4   Remove the cylinder mounting nuts, one in the engine compartment and the other in the passenger compartment.

5   Remove the clutch master cylinder.

OVERHAUL

6   Remove the inlet tube and bushing.

7   Push the piston into the bore with a Phillips screwdriver or blunt punch. While you hold the piston in, remove the snap-ring with snap-ring pliers.

8   Tap the cylinder against a block of wood to eject the piston. If it won't come out, blow air into the fluid line fitting to force the piston out.

✳✳ WARNING:

The piston may shoot out forcefully enough to cause injury. Keep your fingers out of the way and don't point the cylinder anywhere but at a block of wood or a bundle of rags. Apply air pressure gradually and use just enough to ease the piston out.

9   Remove the spacer, primary cup and spring from the bore. Carefully note which way they face so they can be reinstalled correctly.

10 Clean all parts with clean brake fluid.

11 Check all parts for wear or damage. Replace the release cylinder as an assembly if any parts except the piston and cup are worn or damaged. The piston and cup can be replaced separately.

12 Coat the cylinder bore with clean brake fluid.

13 Install the return spring, a new primary cup and the spacer. Be sure the lip of the cup faces into the bore.

14 Install the piston and secondary cup. Push the piston into the bore and install the snap-ring.

15 Install the bushing and hose fitting tube.

INSTALLATION

16 Installation is the reverse of the removal steps.

17 Bleed the system (see Section 7).

18 Operate the clutch to make sure it works correctly.

7 Clutch hydraulic system - bleeding

1   Remove the rubber cap from the bleed valve on the slave cylinder. Fit a clear vinyl tube over the bleeder screw and immerse the other end in a container of clean brake fluid.

2   Have an assistant pump the clutch pedal slowly several times, then hold it down.

3   Loosen the bleed valve to let air escape. When air bubbles stop flowing from the tube, tighten the bleed valve.

➡ **Note: The fluid level in the master cylinder reservoir will drop during this step. Don't let it fall below 1/2 full or air may be sucked into the system and the whole bleeding process will have to be repeated.**

4   Repeat Steps 2 and 3 until no more bubbles can be seen flowing from the tube.

5   Close the bleed valve and install the rubber cap.

6   Operate the clutch to make sure it works properly.

8 Clutch pedal - removal and installation

1   Working beneath the instrument panel, remove the clip from the pushrod clevis pin. Pull out the pin and remove the spacers.

2   Remove the nut and washer from the pedal pivot bolt. Remove the pivot bolt and return spring and take the pedal out.

3   Installation is the reverse of the removal steps with the following additions:

  a) *Apply multi-purpose grease to all friction points.*
  b) *Check pedal height and freeplay and adjust if necessary (see Chapter 1).*

9 Clutch switch - removal and installation

1   Disconnect the electrical connector from the switch.

2   Remove the lock nut and unscrew the switch.

3   Installation is the reverse of the removal steps. Adjust pedal height (see Chapter 1).

10 Clutch engage switch - removal and installation

1   Disconnect the electrical connector from the switch.

2   Remove the two mounting nuts and take the switch out.

3   Installation is the reverse of the removal steps.

11 Driveaxles, constant velocity (CV) joints and boots - check

1   The driveaxles, CV joints and boots should be inspected periodically and whenever the vehicle is raised for any reason. The most common symptom of driveaxle or CV joint failure is knocking or clicking noises when turning.

2   Raise the vehicle and support it securely on jackstands.

3   Inspect the CV joint boot for cracks, leaks and broken retaining bands. If lubricant leaks out through a hole or crack in the boot, the CV joint will wear prematurely and require replacement. Replace any damaged boots immediately (see Section 14). It's a good idea to disassemble, clean, inspect and repack the CV joint whenever replacing a CV joint boot, to ensure that the joint is not contaminated with moisture or dirt, which could cause premature CV joint failure.

4   Check the entire length of each axle to make sure they aren't cracked, dented, twisted or bent.

5   Grasp each axle and rotate it in both directions while holding the CV joint housings to check for excessive movement, indicating worn splines or loose CV joints.

6   If a boot is damaged or loose, remove the driveaxle as described in Section 12. Disassemble and inspect the CV joint as outlined in Section 14.

➡ **Note: Some auto parts stores carry "split" type replacement boots, which can be installed without removing the driveaxle from the vehicle. This is a convenient alternative; however, it's recommended that the driveaxle be removed and the CV joint disassembled and cleaned to ensure that the joint is free from contaminants such as moisture and dirt, which will accelerate CV joint wear.**

12 Left driveaxle (all models) and right driveaxle (1.9L engine models) - removal and installation

❋❋ CAUTION:

Whenever both driveaxles are removed at the same time, the differential side gears must be supported so they don't fall into the transaxle case. A wooden dowel, approximately 15/16-inch in diameter, inserted into each side gear will work. If this precaution is not heeded and the side gears do drop, the differential will have to be removed from the transaxle to realign the gears (which will necessitate towing the vehicle to a Ford dealer service department or other repair shop).

REMOVAL

▶ **Refer to illustrations 12.2, 12.3, 12.8, 12.10, 12.11a, 12.11b, 12.11c and 12.13**

1 Remove the hubcap from the wheel.
2 Use a hammer and a chisel or punch to raise the staked part of the driveaxle retaining nut out of the groove (see illustration).
3 Remove the retaining nut from the driveaxle (see illustration).

❋❋ CAUTION:

Don't roll the vehicle with the driveaxle/hub nut removed - damage to the front hub bearings may result.

4 Raise the vehicle and support it securely on jackstands. Remove the splash shield from the side of the vehicle you're working on.
5 Tap the end of the driveaxle with a hammer and punch to free it from the hub. Don't try to drive it all the way out at this time.
6 Remove the pinch bolt and detach the balljoint stud from the steering knuckle (see Chapter 10).
7 Turn the steering wheel all the way toward the side from which you're removing the driveaxle (to the left if you're removing the driver's side driveaxle; to the right if you're removing the passenger side driveaxle).
8 Pull the hub and knuckle out while you push the driveaxle out of the hub (see illustration).
9 Swivel the end of the driveaxle forward and support it with a piece of wire so the inner CV joint isn't damaged.

12.2 Raise the staked portion of the retaining nut with a hammer and chisel or punch . . .

12.3 . . . then loosen the driveaxle nut with a socket and breaker bar

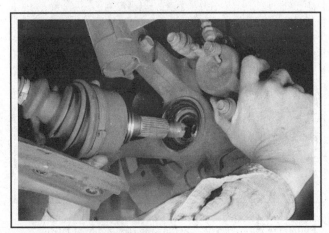

12.8 Push the hub off the driveaxle end

12.10 Support the engine with a jack and block of wood

Left driveaxle

10 Support the engine with a jack and block of wood positioned beneath the oil pan (see illustration).

11 Remove the transaxle crossmember (see illustrations).

Both driveaxles

12 Place a drain pan under the transaxle to catch the fluid.

13 Insert a prybar between the inner CV joint and the transaxle case (see illustration). Pry the driveaxle out of the transaxle. Be careful not to damage the CV joint, its boot, the transaxle case or the oil seal with the prybar.

14 If both driveaxles are being removed insert a snug-fitting wooden dowel into each of the differential side gears.

INSTALLATION

▶ **Refer to illustration 12.15**

15 Position the circlip on the inner stub shaft splines so its gap is at the top (see illustration). Lubricate the splines with multi-purpose grease.

16 Coat the differential seal lips with multi-purpose grease and insert the stub shaft into the differential side gear until the shaft is seated and the circlip snaps into place.

17 Pull out on the strut/knuckle assembly and insert the outer CV joint stub shaft in the hub (make sure the splines are aligned). Push the shaft as far into the hub as possible.

18 Reattach the balljoint to the steering knuckle and tighten the pinch bolt to the torque listed in the Chapter 10 Specifications.

19 Install the transaxle crossmember. Tighten its nuts and bolts to the torque values listed in Chapter 7 Part A or B.

20 Install a new driveaxle/hub nut. Tighten the nut to the torque listed in this Chapter's Specifications while preventing the hub from turning by placing a screwdriver between two wheel studs. If you can't reach the full torque using this method, tighten the nut as tight as possible and wait until the wheel is installed and the vehicle is resting on the ground, then tighten the nut to the specified torque.

21 Stake the nut with a rounded chisel or a center-punch. Don't use a sharp-edged tool. If the collar on the nut cracks or splits while you're staking it, discard it and install another new nut.

22 The remainder of installation is the reverse of the removal steps.

23 Check transaxle fluid level and top it off as needed (see Chapter 1).

12.11a Detach the crossmember from the vehicle at the front end . . .

12.11b . . . at the rear end . . .

12.11c . . . and at the center

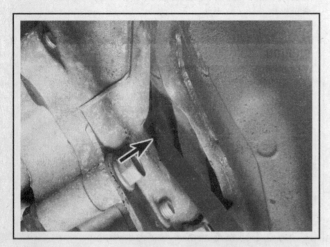

12.13 Use a large screwdriver or prybar (arrow) to carefully pry the CV joint out of the transaxle

12.15 Always replace the circlip before installing the inner CV joint in the transaxle, position the circlip gap at the top and lubricate the splines with multi-purpose grease

13 Right driveaxle and intermediate shaft (1.8L engine and 1998 and later manual transaxle coupe models) - removal and installation

➡**Note: It's possible to remove the drive-axle/intermediate shaft in two sections or as a single assembly. If you're going to remove both sections as a single assembly and don't have the need to separate them, begin this procedure with Step 20.**

DRIVEAXLE

1 Perform Steps 1 through 9 of Section 12.

2 Insert a flat prybar between the driveaxle and the bearing support bracket. Pry the driveaxle away from the intermediate shaft and take it out.

3 Installation is the reverse of the removal steps, with the following additions:

a) *Tighten all fasteners to the torque values listed in this Chapter's Specifications and in the Chapter 10 Specifications.*

b) *Use a new driveaxle/hub nut. Tighten and stake it as described in Steps 20 and 21 of Section 12.*

INTERMEDIATE SHAFT AND BEARING SUPPORT BRACKET

➡**Note 1: Steps 9 through 15 following, which describe replacement of the intermediate shaft bearing and seals, apply only to 1.8L engine models. If inspection shows a problem with the bearing or seals on a 1998 or later coupe (2.0L Zetec engine), replace the intermediate shaft and bearing as a unit.**

➡**Note 2: Steps 9 through 15 require a hydraulic press. If you don't have one, remove the intermediate shaft and take it to an automotive machine shop for bearing replacement.**

4 Remove the driveaxle (see Steps 1 through 3).

5 Remove the three bolts that secure the bearing support bracket to the engine block.

6 Place a drain pan beneath the transaxle to catch the fluid.

7 Insert a prybar between the bearing support bracket and the starter brace and pry the intermediate shaft out of the transaxle.

8 Install a plug in the differential side gear so it can't fall out of position (read the Caution at the beginning of Section 12).

9 Press the intermediate shaft out of the bearing.

10 Press the bearing and inner seal out of the support bracket, then discard them.

11 Remove the outer seal from the bracket with a seal puller.

12 Drive in a new outer seal.

13 Press in a new bearing.

14 Press in a new inner seal.

15 Press the intermediate shaft into the bracket, then install a new circlip.

16 Remove the plug from the differential side gear.

17 Align the splines of the shaft with those in the differential, then push the shaft into the transaxle.

18 Install the bearing support bracket bolts, tightening the bolts to the torque listed in this Chapter's Specifications.

19 Install the driveaxle as described earlier in this Section.

COMPLETE DRIVEAXLE ASSEMBLY

20 Perform Steps 1 through 9 of Section 12.

21 Perform Steps 5 through 8 above.

22 Remove the driveaxle/intermediate shaft assembly.

23 Installation is the reverse of the removal steps with the following additions:

a) *Install a new driveaxle/hub nut. Tighten the nut to the torque listed in this Chapter's Specifications while preventing the hub from turning by placing a screwdriver between two wheel studs. If you can't reach the full torque using this method, tighten the nut as tight as possible and wait until the wheel is installed and the vehicle is resting on the ground, then tighten the nut to the specified torque.*

b) *Stake the nut with a rounded chisel or a center-punch. Don't use a sharp-edged tool. If the collar on the nut cracks or splits while you're staking it, discard it and install another new nut.*

c) *Check the transaxle fluid level and top it off as needed (see Chapter 1).*

14 Constant velocity (CV) joints and boots - boot replacement and CV joint overhaul

➡**Note: If the outer boot is damaged and must be replaced, the inner boot must also be removed, since the outer CV joint can't be removed from the driveaxle shaft.**

DISASSEMBLY

1 Remove the driveaxle (see Section 12 or 13).

Inner CV joint and boot

▶ **Refer to illustrations 14.2a, 14.2b, 14.3, 14.5 14.6 and 14.7**

2 Pry open and remove the boot bands (see illustrations). Pull the boot out of the way and wipe off any excess grease.

3 Make alignment marks on the shaft and the CV joint housing so they can be reassembled in their same relative positions (see illustration).

14.2a Bend up the locking tabs, then remove the bands with pliers

14.2b Remove both boot clamps, then slide the boot down the axleshaft so it's out of the way

14.3 Be sure to make alignment marks on the tripod housing and shaft

14.5 Use snap-ring pliers to remove the snap-ring

14.6 Use a center-punch to make match marks (arrows) on the tripod and driveaxle to ensure they're reassembled properly

14.7 Drive the tripod joint off the driveaxle with a brass drift and hammer - be careful not to damage the bearing surfaces or the splines on the shaft

4   Remove the retainer ring from the housing, then take the joint housing off the shaft.

5   Remove the tripod snap-ring with snap-ring pliers (see illustration).

6   Make match marks on the tripod and driveaxle (see illustration).

7   Carefully tap the tripod off the shaft with a hammer and a brass drift (see illustration).

8   Remove the boot.

Outer CV joint and boot

▶ **Refer to illustration 14.9**

9   If you're working on the passenger side driveaxle of a model with a 1.9L engine and you plan to replace the outer CV joint boot, remove the dynamic damper (see illustration). Pry up the locking clips on the retaining band, take the band off with pliers and slide the damper off the shaft.

10   Remove the boot bands from the outer joint boot in the same way

you removed them from the inner joint boot (see Step 2).

INSPECTION

▶ **Refer to illustration 14.12**

11   Clean the components with solvent to remove all traces of grease. Inspect the tripod and housing for pitting, score marks, cracks and other signs of wear and damage. Shiny, polished spots are normal and will not adversely affect CV joint performance.

➡ **Note: Since the outer CV joint can't be disassembled, it is difficult to wash away all the old grease and to rid the joint of solvent once it's clean. But it is imperative that the job be done thoroughly, so take your time and do it right.**

12   Bend the outer CV joint housing at an angle to the driveaxle to expose the bearings, inner race and cage (see illustration). Inspect the bearing surfaces for signs of wear. If the bearings are damaged or worn, replace the driveaxle.

14.9 The passenger side driveaxle on 1.9L engine models uses a dynamic damper, secured by a clamp

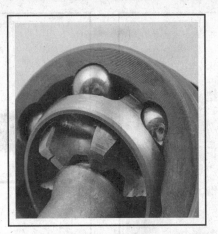

14.12 After the outer joint has been cleaned, rotate it through its full range of motion and inspect the bearing surfaces

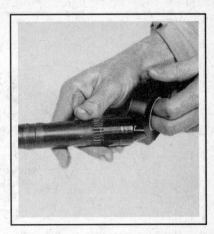

14.13 Before sliding the boot onto the shaft, tape the end of the shaft to protect the boot as it passes over the splines

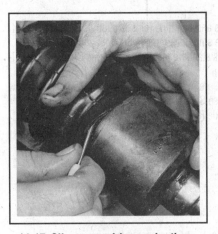

14.17 Slip a screwdriver under the edge of the boot to equalize the pressure inside the boot

14.18a Install the boot bands with the ends facing away from the forward rotating direction of the driveaxle - pull the bands tight with pliers and bend the tang down . . .

14.18b . . . then bend over the locking tabs to secure the end

ASSEMBLY

◆ **Refer to illustrations 14.13, 14.17, 14.18a, 14.18b, 14.23 and 14.28**

13 Wrap the shaft splines with tape to protect the boots during installation (see illustration).

14 If the boot was removed from the outer end, slip it part way onto the shaft. The inner and outer boots are different sizes; measure the large diameter opening of each boot and compare with the Specifications at the end of this Chapter to make sure you're installing them in the correct locations.

15 Thoroughly pack the outer joint housing with CV joint grease. Also apply a liberal amount of grease to the inside of the boot.

16 Position the outer boot on the housing and make sure it's seated securely in the housing and the shaft groove.

17 Lift the boot with a screwdriver to release excess trapped air (see illustration).

18 Install new bands on the boot so their ends face away from the forward rotating direction of the shaft. Wrap the bands around the boot, bend the tangs down and secure the ends with the locking tabs (see illustrations).

19 Flex the joint through its normal range of travel. If it doesn't move smoothly, remove the boot and find out why.

20 If you're working on the passenger side driveaxle of a 1.9L or 2.0L engine model, install the rubber damper. On 2.0L engine models, position the damper 16-11/16 to 16-15/16 inches from the outer end of the outer joint. Secure the damper with a new band, installed in the same way as the boot bands.

21 Slip the small boot band and the inner boot onto the driveaxle.

22 Line up the marks made during disassembly on the tripod and the shaft, then install the tripod. Tap it gently with a soft-faced mallet if

14.23 Pack the tripod housing with CV joint grease and coat the tripod with the same grease (be sure to force the grease into the rollers)

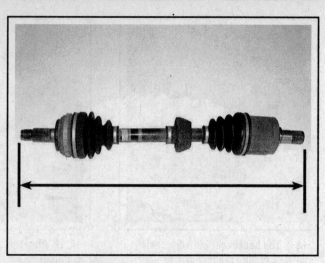

14.28 Set the driveaxle to its standard length before tightening the boot band

necessary. Once it's fully installed, secure it with the snap-ring.

23 Pack the inner CV joint housing with CV joint grease (see illustration). Coat the tripod with the same lubricant, forcing it into the rollers.

24 Line up the marks made during removal and install the housing over the tripod.

25 Secure the housing with the retainer ring.

26 Position the boot on the housing and make sure it's securely seated in the housing and the shaft grooves. Tighten the small band (see Step 18).

27 Extend, compress and bend the joint through its normal range of travel. If it doesn't move smoothly, remove the boot and find out why.

28 Set the shaft to its standard length listed in this Chapter's Specifications (see illustration).

29 Equalize the pressure in the boot (see Step 17), then install a new band on the housing (see Step 18).

30 Install the driveaxle (see Section 12 or 13).

Specifications

CV joint boot diameter

1.8L engine
Inner	3-35/64 inches
Outer	3-11/32 inches

1.9L engine
Right side inner	3-35/64 inches
Left side inner	3-5/16 inches
Outer	3-1/2 inches

2.0L engine	Not specified

Driveaxle standard length

1.8L engine
Right side	24-55/64 inches
Left side	24-31/64 inches

1.9L engine
Right side	36-5/32 inches
Left side	25-7/32 inches

2.0L engine (coupe)
Manual transaxle	24-1/2 inches
Automatic transaxle left side	24-1/2 inches
Automatic transaxle right side	36-19/32 inches

2.0L engine (sedan and wagon)
Manual transaxle left side	24-7/8 inches
Manual transaxle right side	36-19/32 inches

Automatic transaxle left side
Through 1998	35-31/32 inches
1999 and 2000	24-31/32 inches

Automatic transaxle right side
Through 1998	36-19/32 inches
1999 and 2000	35-15/16 inches

Clutch disc minimum thickness
(depth to rivet head)

	1/32 inch

Torque specifications	Ft-lbs
Clutch pressure plate bolts	13 to 20
Master cylinder mounting nuts	14 to 19
Slave cylinder mounting bolts/nuts	12 to 17
Driveaxle retaining nut	174 to 235
Intermediate shaft bearing support bracket bolts (1.8L engine and 1998 and later coupe with manual transaxle)	32 to 46

Notes

Section

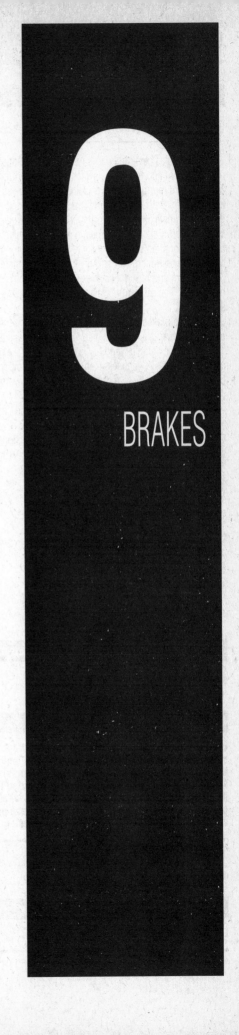

9

BRAKES

1 General information

DESCRIPTION

The vehicles covered by this manual are equipped with hydraulically operated front and rear brake systems. The front brakes are disc type. The standard rear brakes are drum type with rear disc brakes available as an option. Both the front and rear brakes are self adjusting. The disc brakes automatically compensate for pad wear, while the rear drum brakes incorporate an adjustment mechanism which is activated as the brakes are applied when the vehicle is driven in reverse. Some later models are equipped with an Anti-lock Brake System (ABS).

The front and rear disc brakes feature a single piston, floating caliper design. The rear drum brakes are leading/trailing shoe types with a single pivot.

The disc brakes automatically compensate for pad wear during usage. The rear drum brakes also feature automatic adjustment.

Front drive vehicles tend to wear the front brake pads at a faster rate than rear drive vehicles. Consequently, it's important to inspect the brake pads frequently to make sure they haven't worn to the point where the disc itself is scored or damaged.

All models are equipped with a cable actuated parking brake which operates the rear brakes.

The hydraulic system is a diagonally split design, meaning there are separate circuits for the left front/right rear and the right front/left rear brakes. If one circuit fails, the other circuit will remain functional and a warning indicator will light up on the dash when a substantial amount of brake fluid is lost, showing that a failure has occurred. The hydraulic system also incorporates a proportioning valve that reduces the pressure to the rear brakes in order to limit rear wheel lockup during hard braking.

PRECAUTIONS

Use only DOT 3 brake fluid.

The brake pads and linings may contain asbestos fibers, which are hazardous to your health if inhaled. When working on brake system components, carefully clean all parts with brake system cleaner. Don't allow the fine dust to become airborne.

Safety should be paramount when working on brake system components. Don't use parts or fasteners that aren't in perfect condition and be sure that all clearances and torque specifications are adhered to. If you're at all unsure about a certain procedure, seek professional advice. When finished working on the brakes, test them carefully under controlled conditions before driving the vehicle in traffic. If a problem is suspected in the brake system, don't drive the vehicle until the fault is corrected.

2 Front disc brake pads - replacement

▶ **Refer to illustrations 2.4a through 2.4f**

✳✳ WARNING:

Disc brake pads must be replaced on both front wheels at the same time - never replace the pads on only one wheel. Also, the dust created by the brake system is harmful to your health. Never blow it out with compressed air and don't inhale any of it. An approved filtering mask should be worn when working on the brakes. Do not, under any circumstances, use petroleum-based solvents to clean brake parts. Use brake system cleaner only!

1 Remove about two-thirds of the fluid from the master cylinder reservoir.

✳✳ CAUTION:

Don't spill brake fluid on the vehicle's paint.

2 Loosen the wheel lug nuts, raise the vehicle and support it securely on jackstands. Remove the front wheels.

3 Check the disc carefully as outlined in Section 4. If machining is necessary, follow the procedure in Section 4 to remove the disc.

4 Follow the accompanying photos, beginning with illustration 2.4a, for the actual pad replacement procedure. Be sure to stay in order and read the information in the caption under each illustration.

5 Once the new pads are in place and the caliper pins have been installed and properly tightened, install the wheels and lower the vehicle to the ground.

➡**Note: If the brake hose was disconnected from the caliper for any reason, the brake system must be bled as described in Section 13.**

6 Fill the master cylinder reservoir(s) with new brake fluid and slowly pump the brakes a few times to seat the pads against the disc.

7 Check the fluid level in the master cylinder reservoir(s) one more time and then road test the vehicle carefully before driving it in traffic.

2.4a Remove the pad pin retaining spring (W-shaped) . . .

2.4b . . . the pad retaining pins and M-shaped spring . . .

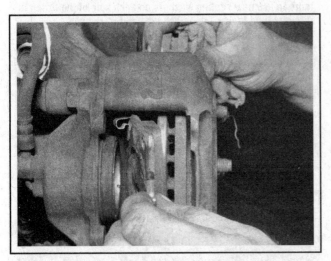

2.4c . . . then pull the pads and shims out of the caliper

2.4d Use a C-clamp and one of the old pads to press the piston into the caliper to make room for the new pads

2.4e Install the pads and shims in the caliper . . .

2.4f . . . then install the lower retaining pin, M-shaped spring, upper retaining pin and W-shaped spring

3 Disc brake caliper - removal, overhaul and installation

✳ WARNING:

Disc brake pads must be replaced on both front wheels at the same time - never replace the pads on only one wheel. Also, the dust created by the brake system is harmful to your health. Never blow it out with compressed air and don't inhale any of it. An approved filtering mask should be worn when working on the brakes. Do not, under any circumstances, use petroleum-based solvents to clean brake parts. Use brake system cleaner only!

➡Note: If an overhaul is indicated (usually because of fluid leakage), explore all options before beginning the job. New and factory-rebuilt calipers are available on an exchange basis, which makes this job quite easy. If you decide to rebuild the calipers, make sure that a rebuild kit is available before proceeding. Always rebuild the calipers in pairs - never rebuild just one of them.

REMOVAL

◆ Refer to illustrations 3.3, 3.4, 3.5a and 3.5b

1 Loosen the wheel lug nuts, raise the vehicle and support it securely on jackstands.
2 Remove the wheel.
3 Remove the brake hose bolt and disconnect the brake hose from the back of the caliper (see illustration). Have a rag handy for fluid spills and wrap a plastic bag around the end of the hose to prevent fluid loss and contamination. Discard the fitting washers - new ones should be used during installation. If the caliper is only being removed to get at the disc, don't detach the hose. This will save the trouble of bleeding the brake system.
4 Remove the caliper mounting bolts (sometimes referred to as caliper pins) and lift the caliper off (see illustration 3.3). If you're leaving the hose connected, suspend the caliper with a piece of wire from the suspension (see illustration).
5 If you're removing the caliper to remove a suspension strut, pull the brake line clip out with pliers (see illustration). Move the brake line forward out of the clip (see illustration).

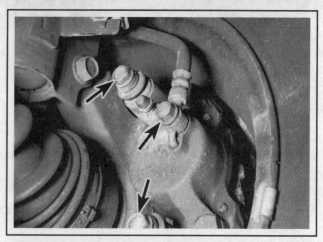

3.3 Removing the brake hose fitting bolt (center arrow) (be sure to use new sealing washers on each side of the fitting to prevent fluid leaks) - to detach the caliper, remove the two mounting bolts (upper and lower arrows)

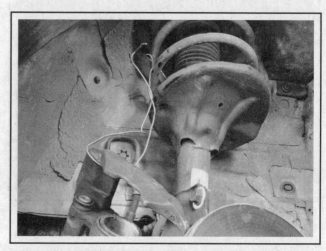

3.4 To avoid damage to the brake hose, suspend the caliper with a piece of wire

3.5a To detach the brake hose from the strut, pull out the clip . . .

3.5b . . . and pass the hose through the opening in the bracket

OVERHAUL

▶ **Refer to illustrations 3.7, 3.8, 3.9 and 3.10**

6   Clean the exterior of the caliper with brake system cleaner. Never use petroleum-based cleaning solvents. Place the caliper on a clean workbench.

7   Position a wood block or several shop rags in the caliper as a cushion, then use compressed air to remove the piston from the caliper (see illustration). Use only enough air pressure to ease the piston out of the bore. If the piston is blown out, even with the cushion in place, it may be damaged.

✳✳ WARNING:

Never place your fingers in front of the piston in an attempt to catch or protect it when applying compressed air, as serious injury could occur.

8   Pry the retaining ring from the dust boot, then remove the boot from the caliper bore (see illustration).

9   Using a wood or plastic tool, remove the piston seal from the groove in the caliper bore (see illustration). Metal tools may cause bore damage.

10   Remove the pin sleeves and boots (see illustration).

11   Remove the caliper bleeder screw and discard all rubber parts.

12   Clean the remaining parts with brake system cleaner, then blow them dry with compressed air, if available.

13   Carefully examine the piston for nicks and burrs and loss of plating. If surface defects are present, the caliper must be replaced. Check the caliper bore in a similar way.

14   Discard the pin sleeves if they're corroded or damaged.

15   When assembling, lubricate the piston bore and seal with clean brake fluid. Install the seal in the caliper bore groove. Make sure the seal does not become twisted and that it is firmly seated in the groove.

16   Lubricate the piston with clean brake fluid, insert the piston squarely into the caliper bore, then use a C-clamp and brake pad to press the piston in until it bottoms out (see illustration 2.4d).

3.7 Force the piston out of the caliper with compressed air - use only enough pressure to ease the piston out, and keep your fingers out of the way to avoid injury

3.8 Pry off the dust boot retaining ring, then remove the boot

3.9 The piston seal should be removed with a wooden or plastic tool to avoid damage to the bore and seal groove - a pencil will do the job

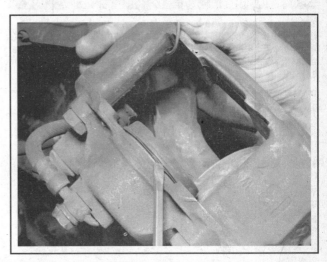

3.10 Push the pin sleeve on each side of the caliper through the boot and pull it free, then remove the boot

17 Seat the lip of the dust boot in the groove on the piston. Install the dust boot retaining ring.

18 Install the pin sleeves and boots.

19 Install the bleeder screw.

INSTALLATION

20 Installation is the reverse of the removal steps with the following additions.

a) Tighten the caliper mounting bolts to the torque listed in this Chapter's Specifications.

b) After the caliper is reinstalled, reconnect the brake hose using new washers on each side of the brake hose fitting bolt. Tighten the bolt to the torque listed in this Chapter's Specifications.

c) Pump the brake pedal several times to bring the pads into contact with the disc.

d) Bleed the brakes as described in Section 13. This isn't necessary if the brake hose was left connected to the caliper.

e) Install the wheel and lower the vehicle. Check brake operation carefully before driving the vehicle in traffic.

4 Front brake disc - inspection, removal and installation

❄❄ WARNING:

The dust created by the brake system is harmful to your health. Never blow it out with compressed air and don't inhale any of it. An approved filtering mask should be worn when working on the brakes. Do not, under any circumstances, use petroleum-based solvents to clean brake parts. Use brake system cleaner only!

INSPECTION

▶ **Refer to illustrations 4.2, 4.3a, 4.3b, 4.4a and 4.4b**

1 Securely block the rear wheels so the vehicle can't roll. Loosen the wheel lug nuts, raise the vehicle and support it securely on jackstands. Remove the wheel and install two lug nuts to hold the disc in place.

2 Visually inspect the disc surface for score marks and other damage. Light scratches and shallow grooves are normal after use and may not be detrimental to brake operation. Deep score marks - deep enough to catch a fingernail - require disc removal and refinishing by an automotive machine shop. Be sure to check both sides of the disc (see illustration).

3 To check disc runout, attach a dial indicator to the brake caliper and locate the stem about 1/2-inch from the outer edge of the disc (see illustration). Set the indicator to zero and turn the disc. The indicator reading should not exceed that listed in this Chapter's Specifications. If it does, the disc should be resurfaced by an automotive machine shop.

➡Note: **Professionals recommend resurfacing of brake discs regardless of the dial indicator reading (to produce a smooth, flat surface that will eliminate brake pedal pulsations and other undesirable symptoms related to questionable discs). At the very least, if you elect not to have the discs resurfaced, deglaze the brake pad surface with sandpaper or emery cloth (use a swirling motion to ensure a non-directional finish) (see illustration).**

4.2 The brake pads on this vehicle were obviously neglected, as they wore down to the rivets and cut deep grooves into the disc - wear this severe will require replacement of the disc

4.3a With two lug nuts installed to hold the disc in place, check disc runout with a dial indicator - if the reading exceeds the maximum allowable runout limit, the disc will have to be machined or replaced

4.3b Using a swirling motion, remove the glaze from the disc with sandpaper or emery cloth

4.4a The minimum allowable disc thickness is cast into the inside of the disc (typical disc shown)

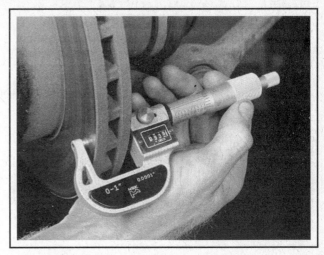

4.4b A micrometer is used to measure disc thickness

4   The disc should never be machined to a thickness under the specified minimum allowable thickness, which is cast into the inside of the disc itself (see illustration). The disc thickness can be checked with a micrometer (see illustration).

REMOVAL AND INSTALLATION

5   Refer to Section 3 and remove the brake caliper.

✲✲ WARNING:

Don't allow the caliper to hang by the brake hose and don't disconnect the hose from the caliper.

6   Remove the two lug nuts that were put on to hold the disc in place and slide the disc off the hub.
7   Installation is the reverse of removal.

---

5   Rear brake drum - removal, inspection and installation

✲✲ WARNING:

The dust created by the brake system is harmful to your health. Never blow it out with compressed air and don't inhale any of it. An approved filtering mask should be worn when working on the brakes. Do not, under any circumstances, use petroleum-based solvents to clean brake parts. Use brake system cleaner only!

REMOVAL

▶ **Refer to illustration 5.2**

1   Loosen the wheel lug nuts, raise the rear of the vehicle and support it securely on jackstands. Block the front wheels, then remove the rear wheel.
2   Remove the two screws that secure the brake drum (see illustration).
3   Grasp the brake drum and pull it off. If it won't come off, thread

5.2 The drum securing screws may be difficult to remove - it's a good idea to use an impact driver to prevent the heads from being rounded out

5.4a Remove glaze from the drum surface with sandpaper or emery cloth

5.4b The maximum allowable diameter is cast into the drum (typical drum shown - see this Chapter's Specifications for the actual maximum allowable diameter)

two bolts of the correct size and thread pitch into the two threaded holes near the hub of the drum. Tighten the bolts and the drum will be forced off the hub.

INSPECTION

▶ **Refer to illustrations 5.4a and 5.4b**

4   Check the drum for cracks, score marks, deep grooves and signs of overheating of the shoe contact surface. If the drums have blue spots, indicating overheated areas, they should be replaced. Also, look for grease or brake fluid on the shoe contact surface. Grease and brake fluid can be removed from the drum with brake system cleaner, but the brake shoes must be replaced if they are contaminated. Surface glazing, which is a glossy, highly polished finish, can be removed with sandpaper or emery cloth (see illustration).

➡ **Note: Professionals recommend resurfacing the drums whenever a brake job is done. Resurfacing will eliminate the possibility of out-of-round drums. If the drums are worn so much that they can't be resurfaced without exceeding the maximum allowable diameter stamped into the drum (see illustration), then new ones will be required.**

INSTALLATION

5   Place the drum on the hub and install the securing screws.
6   Install the wheel, lower the vehicle and tighten the lug nuts to the torque listed in the Chapter 1 Specifications.

6   Rear brake shoes - replacement

▶ **Refer to illustrations 6.6a through 6.6i and 6.7a, 6.7b, 6.7c, 6.8, 6.9 and 6.10**

✳✳ WARNING:

The brake shoes must be replaced on both rear wheels at the same time - never replace the shoes on only one wheel. Also, brake system dust is harmful to your health. Never blow it out with compressed air and don't inhale any of it. Do not, under any circumstances, use petroleum-based solvents to clean brake parts. Use brake system cleaner only.

➡ **Note: Whenever the brake shoes are replaced, the return and hold-down springs should also be replaced. Due to the continuous heating/cooling cycle that the springs are subjected to, they** lose their tension over a period of time and may allow the shoes to drag on the drum and wear at a much faster rate than normal.

1   Remove about one-third of the brake fluid from the master cylinder reservoir.
2   Loosen the wheel lug nuts, raise the rear of the vehicle and support it on jackstands. Block the front wheels and remove the rear wheels from the vehicle.
3   Refer to Section 5 in this Chapter and remove the brake drums.
4   Carefully inspect the brake drums as outlined in Section 5 of this Chapter. Also inspect the wheel cylinder for fluid leakage as described in Chapter 1.
5   Clean the brake assembly with brake cleaner and allow the components to dry (be sure to place a drain pan under the brake).
6   Follow the accompanying photographs (see illustrations 6.6a through 6.6i) to remove the shoes. Be sure to stay in order and read the information in the caption under each illustration.

6.6a Twist the pins and remove the shoe retaining springs . . .

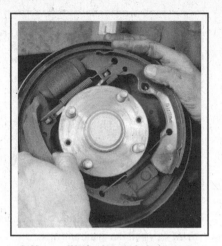

6.6b . . . lift the forward shoe away from the backing plate to create slack in the springs . . .

6.6c . . . unhook the lower spring . . .

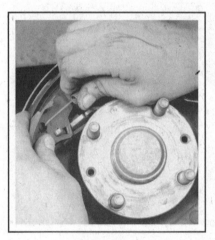

6.6d . . . and the upper spring

6.6e Remove the forward shoe

6.6f Unhook the adjusting quadrant retaining spring . . .

6.6g . . . and remove the rear shoe

6.6h Unhook the parking brake cable spring . . .

6.6i . . . and the cable, then remove the adjusting quadrant

6.7a The adjusting quadrant may be positioned like this after it is removed . . .

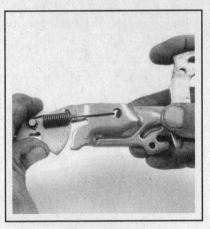

6.7b . . . pull the quadrant apart against the spring tension . . .

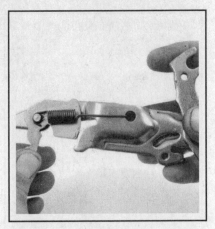

6.7c . . . and reposition it as shown here - the drum should just fit over the shoes if the adjuster is set correctly

6.8 After the quadrant is installed, apply a thin coat of high-temperature grease to the points where the brake shoes ride against the backing plate

6.9 After installation, the brake assembly should look like this

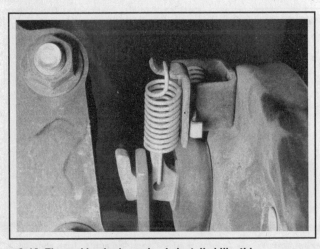

6.10 The parking brake spring is installed like this

7   Position the adjusting quadrant (see illustrations) in a notch that will allow the shoes to just clear the drum when it's installed.

8   Install the adjusting quadrant in the backing plate (see illustration).

9   Reverse the removal procedure to install the shoes (see illustration).

10 Connect the parking brake cable and spring (see illustration).

11 Once the new shoes are in place and adjusted, install the drum as outlined in Section 5.

12 Repeat the procedure on the opposite wheel.

13 Install the wheels and lower the vehicle. Tighten the lug nuts to the torque listed in the Chapter 1 Specifications.

14 Adjust the parking brake as described in Section 14 of this Chapter.

15 Top up the master cylinder with brake fluid and pump the pedal several times. Lower the vehicle and check brake operation before driving the vehicle in traffic.

7. Wheel cylinder - removal and installation

♦ Refer to illustrations 7.3 and 7.4

❋ WARNING:

The dust created by the brake system is harmful to your health. Never blow it out with compressed air and don't inhale any of it. An approved filtering mask should be worn when working on the brakes. Do not, under any circumstances, use petroleum-based solvents to clean brake parts. Use brake system cleaner only!

➡Note: If the wheel cylinder is leaking or malfunctioning, replace it with a new or factory rebuilt unit.

REMOVAL

1 Loosen the wheel lug nuts, raise the rear of the vehicle and support it on jackstands, then block the front wheels. Remove the rear wheel(s).

2 Remove the rear brake drum (see Section 5). If you're going to replace the brake shoes, remove them (see Section 6). If you don't plan to replace the brake shoes, just remove the upper return spring.

3 Loosen the fitting at the wheel cylinder with a flare nut wrench (see illustration). Don't try to pull the line away from the wheel cylinder yet.

4 Pull the brake hose clip out of its bracket (see illustration). Separate the hose from the bracket, then separate the line from the wheel cylinder. Plug the end of the line to prevent excessive fluid loss and contamination.

5 Unbolt the wheel cylinder and remove it from the backing plate. Remove and discard the gasket. Clean the backing plate and wheel cylinder mating surfaces.

INSTALLATION

6 Place the wheel cylinder and a new gasket into position on the backing plate. Make sure the brake shoes seat properly on the wheel cylinder pistons.

7 Install the two wheel cylinder mounting bolts and tighten them to the torque listed in this Chapter's Specifications.

8 Carefully insert the brake line fitting into the cylinder and tighten it by hand to be sure it isn't cross threaded.

9 Install the brake hose in the bracket and secure it with the clip. Tighten the brake line fitting securely.

10 Install the upper return spring (or brake shoes, if they were removed).

11 Install the brake drum (see Section 5).

12 Bleed the brakes (see Section 13).

13 Pump the brake pedal several times to operate the adjuster.

14 Install the wheels and lower the vehicle. Tighten the lug nuts to the torque listed in the Chapter 1 Specifications.

15 Check brake operation before driving the vehicle on the road.

7.3 Loosen the wheel cylinder line nut completely with a flare nut wrench, but don't separate the line from the cylinder . . .

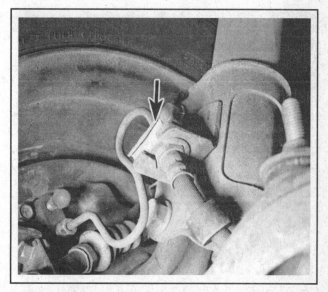

7.4 . . . until you've removed the brake hose clip (arrow) and separated the hose from the bracket

8 Rear disc brake pads - removal and installation

1 Loosen the rear wheel lug nuts. Securely block both front wheels so the vehicle won't roll. Jack up the rear end and place it securely on jackstands.

2 Remove the rear wheels.

3 If the pads are tight against the disc, remove the screw plug that covers the adjustment gear on the back of the caliper. Turn the gear counterclockwise with an Allen wrench to retract the piston.

4 Remove the caliper lower lock-bolt.

5 Pivot the caliper off the pads with a screwdriver.

6 Remove the brake pads, the M-spring, the shims and the guides.

7 Apply a thin film of high-temperature disc brake grease between the caliper and pads. Install the pads, M-spring, shims and guides on the caliper bracket.

8 Pivot the caliper down over the pads. Lubricate the lower lock-bolt with a bit of high-temperature disc brake grease, then install it and tighten to the torque listed in this Chapter's Specifications.

9 Turn the adjustment gear clockwise with an Allen wrench until the pads just touch the disc (to check, look through the caliper inspection hole and spin the disc to check for tightness). Back off the gear 1/3 turn, then install the screw plug and tighten it securely.

10 Install the wheels, lower the vehicle and tighten the wheel lug nuts to the torque listed in the Chapter 1 Specifications

11 Check the operation of the brakes before driving the vehicle in traffic.

9 Rear disc brake caliper - removal, overhaul and installation

REMOVAL

1 Remove the rear brake pads (see Section 8).

2 Unbolt the parking brake cable bracket and move the bracket out of the way.

3 Disconnect the parking brake cable from the operating lever (see Section 15).

4 Clamp off the brake hose with locking pliers. Be sure to wrap a rag around the hose first and don't tighten the pliers excessively, or the hose will be damaged. Remove the brake line bolt. Remove and discard the brake line washers.

5 Slide the caliper off the upper pivot.

OVERHAUL

6 Remove the screw plug that covers the adjustment gear.

7 Turn the adjustment gear clockwise until it is loose, then remove it from the caliper.

8 Place a block of wood or some rags between the piston and cali-per and force the piston out with compressed air (see illustration 3.7). DO NOT place your fingers in front of the piston; it may come out with enough force to cause injury. Use only enough air pressure to ease the piston out.

9 Take the dust seal off the piston and discard it.

10 Remove the snap ring, adjusting bolt, O-ring and connecting link. Discard the O-ring.

11 Carefully remove the piston seal from the bore with a plastic or wooden tool (such as a pencil) (see illustration 3.9). Don't use a metal tool or the bore may be scratched. Discard the seal.

12 Remove the operating lever spring, then remove the lever.

13 Unscrew the bleed valve.

14 Check all parts for wear, damage and corrosion. Refer to Section 3 for piston and bore inspection procedures.

15 Assembly is the reverse of disassembly, with the following additions:

a) Be sure the piston seal isn't twisted and is seated securely in its groove.

b) Lubricate the piston seal, connecting link, O-ring, adjusting bolt and dust seal with clean brake fluid during assembly.

INSTALLATION

16 Installation is the reverse of the removal steps with the following additions.

a) Use new washers on the brake line fitting.

b) Bleed the brakes (see Section 13).

c) Adjust the caliper as described in Section 8, Step 9.

d) Check operation of the brakes before driving the vehicle in traffic.

10 Rear brake disc - inspection, removal and installation

✳✳ WARNING:

The dust created by the brake system is harmful to your health. Never blow it out with compressed air and don't inhale any of it. An approved filtering mask should be worn when working on the brakes. Do not, under any circumstances, use petroleum-based solvents to clean brake parts. Use brake system cleaner only!

1 The rear brake discs are inspected in the same way as the front brake discs (see Section 4).
2 Remove the brake pads (see Section 8).
3 Remove the brake disc retaining screws. An impact screwdriver may be necessary to loosen the screws (see illustration 5.2).
4 Installation is the reverse of the removal steps.

11 Master cylinder - removal and installation

▶ Refer to illustrations 11.3 and 11.6

➡Note: If service is indicated (usually because of insufficient pedal resistance or no resistance at all, or external fluid leakage) it's recommended that the master cylinder be replaced rather than attempting to rebuild it. New and factory rebuilt units are available on an exchange basis, which makes this job quite easy and will ensure that the master cylinder is in top condition.

REMOVAL

1 Remove the battery (see Chapter 5).
2 Place rags under the fittings and prepare caps or plastic bags to cover the ends of the lines once they are disconnected. Remove as much fluid as possible with a suction gun before starting this procedure.

✳✳ CAUTION:

Brake fluid will damage paint. Cover all body parts and be careful not to spill fluid during this procedure.

3 Loosen the fittings at the ends of the brake lines where they enter the master cylinder (see illustration). To prevent rounding off the flats, use a flare-nut wrench, which wraps around the nut.
4 Pull the brake lines away from the master cylinder slightly and plug the ends to prevent contamination.
5 If you're working on a vehicle with a manual transaxle, remove the clamp and disconnect the clutch fluid line from the side of the master cylinder reservoir. Cap the line and the master cylinder fitting to prevent fluid leaks.
6 Unplug the electrical connector at the master cylinder, then remove the two nuts attaching the master cylinder to the power booster (see illustration). Pull the master cylinder off the studs and lift it out of the engine compartment. Again, be careful not to spill any fluid as this is done.

INSTALLATION

7 Install the master cylinder over the studs on the power brake booster and tighten the nuts only finger tight at this time.
8 Using your fingers, thread the brake line fittings into the master cylinder. Since the master cylinder is still a bit loose, it can be moved

11.3 Loosen the master cylinder brake line fittings with a flare nut wrench

11.6 The master cylinder is retained by two nuts

slightly in order for the fittings to thread in easily. Don't strip the threads as the fittings are tightened.

9 Tighten the brake line fittings and the two mounting nuts.

10 Fill the master cylinder reservoir with brake fluid. It will be necessary to bleed the master cylinder to remove any air that may be present.

11 Place plenty of rags or newspapers under and around the master cylinder to absorb the brake fluid that will escape during the bleeding process. It is also recommended that eye protection be worn while performing the bleeding procedure.

12 With an assistant seated in the driver's seat, loosen the upper secondary brake line fitting (the one closest to the front of the vehicle) approximately 3/4-turn. Have your assistant push the brake pedal slowly to the floor and hold it there. Tighten the fitting and have the assistant slowly return the pedal to the released position. Wait five seconds, then repeat this operation until the stream of fluid from the loosened fitting is free of air bubbles.

13 Repeat the procedure at the upper primary brake line fitting (the one closest to the power booster). Be sure to keep an eye on the fluid level.

14 Fill the reservoir to the MAX indicator and install the filler cap.

15 Remove the newspapers or rags. Be careful not to let any brake fluid drip on the vehicle's paint. Rinse the area around the master cylinder with water immediately to wash away residual fluid that will damage the engine compartment paint.

16 Refer to Section 13 for further brake hydraulic system bleeding.

12 Brake hoses and lines - inspection and replacement

INSPECTION

1 About every six months, with the vehicle raised and supported securely on jackstands, the rubber hoses which connect the steel brake lines with the front and rear brake assemblies should be inspected for cracks, chafing of the outer cover, leaks, blisters and other damage). These are important and vulnerable parts of the brake system and inspection should be complete. A light and mirror will be helpful for a thorough check. If a hose exhibits any of the above conditions, replace it with a new one.

FLEXIBLE HOSE REPLACEMENT

2 Clean all dirt away from the ends of the hose.

3 Disconnect the metal brake line(s) from the hose fitting(s) using a back-up wrench on the fitting. Be careful not to bend the frame bracket or line. If necessary, soak the connections with penetrating oil.

4 Remove the clip from the fitting at the bracket and remove the hose from the bracket.

5 Disconnect the hose from the caliper, discarding the copper washers on either side of the fitting block.

6 When attaching a new brake hose to the caliper, use new copper washers.

7 Install the clip in the female fitting at the frame bracket.

8 Attach the metal brake line to the hose fitting using a back-up wrench on the fitting.

9 Carefully check to make sure the suspension or steering components don't make contact with the hose. Have an assistant push on the vehicle and - for front brake hoses - also turn the steering wheel from lock-to-lock during inspection.

10 Bleed the brake system as described in Section 13.

METAL LINE REPLACEMENT

11 When replacing brake lines, be sure to use the correct parts. Don't use copper tubing for any brake system components. Purchase genuine steel brake lines from a dealer or auto parts store.

12 Prefabricated brake line, with the tube ends already flared and fittings installed, is available at auto parts stores and dealers. These lines are also bent to the proper shapes.

13 When installing the new line make sure it's securely supported in the brackets and has plenty of clearance from moving or hot components.

14 After installation, check the master cylinder fluid level and add fluid as necessary. Bleed the brake system (see Section 13) and test the brakes carefully before driving the vehicle in traffic.

13 Brake hydraulic system - bleeding

▶ **Refer to illustrations 13.10 and 13.11**

✻✻ WARNING:

Wear eye protection when bleeding the brake system. If the fluid comes in contact with your eyes, immediately rinse them with water and seek medical attention.

1 Bleeding the hydraulic system is necessary to remove any air that manages to find its way into the system as a result of removal and installation of a hose, line, caliper or master cylinder. Use only the specified fluid in this system or extensive damage could result. It will probably be necessary to bleed the system at the master cylinder and all four brakes if air has entered the system due to low fluid level, or if the brake lines have been disconnected at the master cylinder.

2 If a brake line was disconnected only at one wheel, then only that

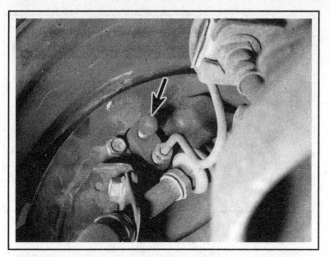

13.10 The bleed valve at each rear wheel cylinder is under a rubber cap (arrow)

13.11 When bleeding the brakes, a hose is connected to the bleeder screw and then submerged in brake fluid - air will be seen as bubbles in the container and the hose (all air must be removed before continuing to the next wheel)

caliper (or wheel cylinder) must be bled.

3   If a brake line is disconnected at a fitting located between the master cylinder and any of the brakes, that part of the system served by the disconnected line must be bled. Always work from the bleed valve farthest from the disconnection point to the bleed valve nearest to it.

4   Remove any residual vacuum from the power brake booster by applying the brake several times with the engine off.

5   Remove the master cylinder reservoir cap and fill the reservoir with brake fluid. Reinstall the cap.

➠Note: Check the fluid level often during the bleeding operation and add fluid as necessary to prevent the level from falling low enough to allow air bubbles into the master cylinder.

6   Have an assistant on hand, as well as a supply of new brake fluid, an empty clear plastic container, a length of clear tubing to fit over the bleeder screw and a wrench to open and close the bleeder screw.

7   Loosen, but don't disconnect, one of the master cylinder hydraulic line fittings. Wrap the fitting with a rag to catch dripping brake fluid.

8   Have an assistant slowly push the brake pedal to the floor to force trapped air out of the master cylinder. While the assistant holds the pedal down, tighten the fitting.

9   Let the pedal up. Repeat Step 8 until no more air escapes from the hydraulic line fittings.

10   Move to the right rear wheel. Loosen the bleeder screw slightly, then tighten it to a point where it's snug but can still be loosened

quickly and easily (see illustration).

11   Place one end of the tubing over the bleeder screw and submerge the other end in brake fluid in the container (see illustration).

12   Loosen the bleed valve approximately 3/4 turn. Have the assistant slowly push the pedal to the floor.

13   While the pedal is held down, watch for air bubbles to exit the submerged end of the tube. When the fluid flow slows after a couple of seconds, tighten the screw and have your assistant release the pedal.

14   Repeat Steps 10 through 13 until no more air is seen leaving the tube, then tighten the bleeder screw and proceed to the left front wheel, the left rear wheel and the right front wheel, in that order, and perform the same procedure. Be sure to check the fluid in the master cylinder reservoir frequently.

15   Never use old brake fluid. It contains moisture which can boil, rendering the brake system useless.

16   Refill the master cylinder with fluid at the end of the operation.

17   Check the operation of the brakes. The pedal should feel solid when depressed, with no sponginess. If necessary, repeat the entire process.

❋❋ **WARNING:**

DO NOT operate the vehicle if you are in doubt about the effectiveness of the brake system.

14 Parking brake - adjustment

▶ Refer to illustration 14.4

1   Start the engine and shift to Reverse. With the vehicle moving backwards, firmly depress the brake pedal several times to seat the shoes in the brake drum. Turn off the engine.

2   Remove the console trim surrounding the parking brake lever.

➠Note: This isn't necessary if you have a deep socket and a long extension.

3   Pull up on the parking brake lever until the seventh notch is engaged (listen for the clicks). It should take approximately 22 pounds of force to raise the lever five to seven notches.

4   If the lever is out of adjustment, correct it by turning the parking brake adjusting nut (see illustration).

5   Release the lever. Securely block the front wheels so the vehicle can't roll, jack up the rear end and place it securely on jackstands. DO NOT get under a vehicle that's supported only by a jack!

6   With the transaxle in Neutral and the parking brake released, rotate the rear wheels. The wheels should turn freely, but a slight drag is acceptable.

7   If the brake lever travels too far or the parking brake fails to hold the vehicle on a hill, tighten the adjusting nut a little more and recheck the operation of the parking brake.

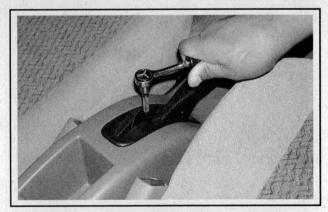

14.4 Turn the adjusting nut until the parking brake lever stroke is within five to seven notches

15 Parking brake cables - removal and installation

▶ **Refer to illustrations 15.3, 15.5, 15.6a, 15.6b, and 15.7**

1   Remove the console trim that surrounds the parking brake lever. Remove the cable adjusting nut (see Section 14).

2   Remove the heat shields for the rear exhaust pipe and resonator.

3   Unhook the return spring from the equalizer (see illustration).

4   Move the equalizer to create slack in the cables, then turn it so its slots allow the cable ends to be slipped out.

5   Unclip the cable from the retaining bracket (see illustration).

6   Detach the cable routing brackets from the floorpan and trailing link (see illustrations).

7   Unbolt the cable retaining bracket from the backing plate (see illustration).

8   Unhook the cable from the parking brake activating lever (see illustrations 6.6h and 6.6i). Take the cable out from under the vehicle.

9   Installation is the reverse of the removal steps.

10   Adjust the parking brake cable (see Section 14).

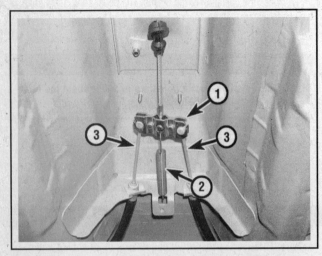

15.3 Unhook the return spring, then pivot the equalizer so the cable can be slipped out of the slot

1   Equalizer   3   Cables
2   Return spring

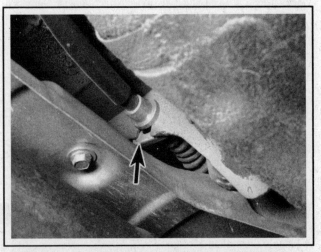

15.5 Pull out the retaining clip (arrow) and separate the cable from the bracket

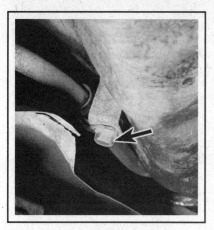

15.6a Unbolt the cable bracket (arrow) from the floorpan

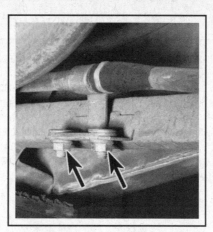

15.6b Remove two nuts (arrows) that attach the cable bracket to the trailing link

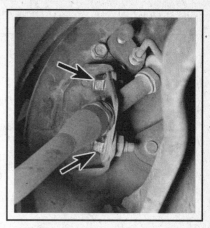

15.7 Two bolts (arrows) secure the cable retaining bracket to the brake backing plate

16 Power brake booster - check valve test, removal, installation and adjustment

♦ **Refer to illustrations 16.2 and 16.7**

1 The power brake booster unit requires no special maintenance apart from periodic inspection of the vacuum hose and the case. Dismantling of the brake booster requires special tools and is not ordinarily done by the home mechanic. If a problem develops, install a new or factory rebuilt unit.

CHECK VALVE TEST

2 The check valve is mounted inside the brake booster vacuum hose (see illustration).
3 Disconnect the hose from the engine and brake booster.
4 Try to blow air through it in both directions. Air should only flow only toward the engine side of the hose. If it flows both ways or neither way, replace the hose and check valve.

REMOVAL

5 Remove the master cylinder (see Section 11).
6 Disconnect the vacuum hose where it attaches to the power brake booster (see illustration 16.2).
7 Working in the passenger compartment under the steering column, remove the pin that secures the brake pedal clevis pin (see illustration). Pull the clevis pin out.
8 Remove the nuts attaching the brake booster to the firewall.
9 Carefully detach the booster from the firewall and lift it out of the engine compartment.

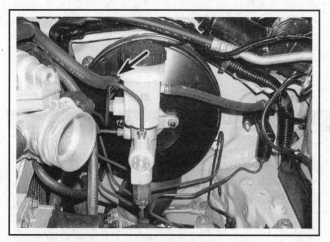

16.2 The brake booster check valve is located inside the vacuum hose

16.7 Remove the clip and clevis pin (top arrow), then remove the booster mounting nuts (arrows) - one nut is hidden behind the pedal bracket

INSTALLATION

10 Place the booster into position on the firewall and tighten the mounting nuts. Connect the booster clevis to the brake pedal. Install the retaining clip in the clevis pin.

11 Install the master cylinder and vacuum hose. Refer to Section 11 for the master cylinder bleeding procedure.

12 Carefully check the operation of the brakes before driving the vehicle in traffic.

ADJUSTMENT

13 Some boosters feature an adjustable pushrod. They are matched to the booster at the factory and most likely will not require adjustment. If a misadjusted pushrod is suspected, a special gauge is required. Have adjustment done by a local dealer or brake shop.

14 Some common symptoms caused by a misadjusted pushrod include dragging brakes (if the pushrod is too long) or excessive brake pedal travel accompanied by a groaning sound from the brake booster (if the pushrod is too short).

17 Brake light switch - removal, installation and adjustment

▸ **Refer to illustration 17.2**

1 Remove the under dash panel.

2 Locate the switch near the top of the brake pedal and disconnect the electrical connector (see illustration).

3 Loosen the switch lock nut and unscrew the switch from the bracket.

4 Installation is the reverse of the removal steps, with the following additions:

a) *Measure pedal height from the floor. If it's within the range listed in this Chapter's Specifications, no further steps are necessary.*

b) *If pedal height isn't as specified, continue with the procedure.*

c) *Disconnect the electrical connector from the brake light switch. Loosen the switch lock nut and turn the switch until its plunger is clear of the brake pedal.*

d) *Loosen the lock nut on the pedal pushrod. Turn the pushrod to bring pedal height within the range listed in this Chapter's Specifications, then tighten the lock nut.*

e) *Turn the brake light switch clockwise until its plunger touches the brake pedal, then turn it one-half turn more and tighten its lock nut.*

17.2 The brake light switch is threaded into a bracket - to remove the switch, loosen the locknut and unscrew the switch

18 Brake pedal - removal and installation

1 Disconnect the negative cable from the battery.

2 Unplug the electrical connector at the brake light switch.

3 Remove the clip the secures the brake pedal clevis pin (see illustration 16.7). Pull the pin out to detach the brake pedal from the booster pushrod.

4 Remove the nut, washer and pivot bolt from the top of the pedal.

5 Unhook the pedal return spring and take the pedal out.

6 Remove the pedal bushings.

7 Lubricate the pedal bushings with multi-purpose grease and install them in the bracket.

8 The remainder of installation is the reverse of the removal steps.

9 Adjust the brake light switch and pedal height as described in Section 17.

19 Anti-lock Brake System (ABS) - general information and trouble codes

1   The Anti-lock Brake System, which was introduced in 1994, is designed to maintain vehicle steerability, directional stability and optimum deceleration under severe braking conditions and on most road surfaces. It does so by monitoring the rotational speed of each wheel and, when necessary, controlling the brake line pressure to each wheel during braking. This prevents the wheel from locking up.

COMPONENTS

2   In addition to the master cylinder, power booster and the brakes at the wheels, the ABS system consists of an ABS control module, an ABS relay, a hydraulic actuator assembly, a speed sensor and rotor on each wheel and a brake pressure control valve.

ABS control module

3   The ABS control module, located under the passenger seat, is the "brain" of the system. The function of the control module is to accept and process information received from the wheel speed sensors to control the hydraulic line pressure, avoiding wheel lock-up. The module also constantly monitors the system, even under normal driving conditions, to find faults within the system. If a fault is found, a trouble code will be stored in the computer's memory and an ABS warning indicator on the dash will light up.

ABS relay

4   The ABS relay is located under the hood on the left inner fender panel, near the coolant reservoir. It performs two functions: It supplies power to the solenoids in the hydraulic actuator (when energized) and also serves as the ground for the ABS warning indicator (when deenergized).

Hydraulic actuator assembly

5   The hydraulic actuator assembly is located below the brake master cylinder. It contains an electric hydraulic pump motor, flow control valves, solenoid valves and buffer chambers.

6   The actuator is controlled by the ABS control module. During normal braking the solenoid valves are at rest, held closed by spring pressure. When the control module senses a wheel is about to lock up, it sends a signal to the modulator which opens the solenoid valve of the affected brake. This causes the flow control valve to seal off the passage from the master cylinder to the brake that is locking up. In addition, fluid from the caliper flows past the spool orifice in the flow control valve into the reservoir, relieving pressure in the affected brake and preventing wheel lock-up.

Speed sensors and signal rotors

7   The speed sensors, which are located at each wheel, generate small electrical pulsations when the toothed signal rotors are turning, sending a variable voltage signal to the ABS control module indicating wheel rotational speed.

8   The front speed sensors are mounted on the steering knuckles in close relationship to the toothed signal rotors, which are integral with the outer constant velocity (CV) joints. The rear wheel speed sensors are mounted on the rear spindles, with the signal rotors being a part of the rear hubs.

DIAGNOSTIC CODES

9   The ABS control module has a built-in self-diagnosis system which detects malfunctions in the system and alerts the driver by illuminating an ABS warning light on the instrument panel. The computer stores the failure code until the diagnostic system is cleared or the malfunction is repaired.

10   The ABS warning light should come on when the ignition switch is placed in the On position. When the engine is started, the warning light should go out. If the light remains on, the diagnostic system has detected a malfunction or abnormality in the system. If the light doesn't remain on but a symptom of an anti-lock braking problem exists, a past or intermittent problem may have occurred.

1994 through 1996 models

▶ **Refer to illustration 19.11**

11   The codes for the ABS system can be accessed by using an analog volt-ohmmeter and a jumper wire. Locate the data link connector in the engine compartment, next to the battery. With the ignition key off, connect the jumper wire between terminals TBS (Test Brake System) and GND (ground) (see illustration). Now, connect the leads of the voltmeter between terminals FBS (Failure Brake System) and an engine ground. Set the voltmeter to the 20-volt DC scale.

12   Turn the ignition key to the On position. The voltmeter needle will deflect, indicating any stored trouble codes. One sweep of the needle followed by another relatively shorter sweep indicates a code 11. One sweep of the needle, followed by two relatively shorter sweeps indicates

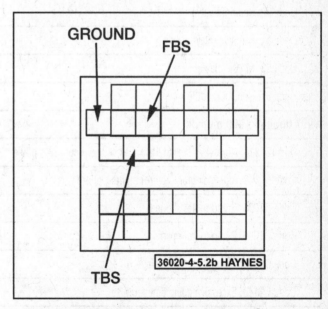

19.11 To output trouble codes with an analog voltmeter, connect a jumper wire between TBS and GND of the data link connector (ignition key Off). Then, connect the voltmeter positive lead to terminal FBS and the negative lead to a good ground - turn on the key and codes will be displayed as sweeps of the meter needle

a code 12. Two sweeps of the needle followed by two relatively shorter sweeps indicates a code 22, and so on. After all stored trouble codes have been shown once, the sequence will repeat. Refer to the accompanying table for a list of the trouble codes and the possible causes of failure.

❋❋ WARNING:

This diagnostic procedure is intended to help the home mechanic find the general area or circuit in which the failure lies. Checks to the system should be limited to:

a) Brake fluid level
b) Fuses
c) Electrical connectors at the control module, hydraulic actuator, and wheel speed sensors
d) Wiring harnesses

Clearing codes

➥Note: ABS trouble codes can't be erased by disconnecting the cables from the battery.

13 To clear any stored ABS trouble code, enter the code access mode by following the procedure described in Steps 11 and 12. After all of the trouble codes have been displayed and the first code repeats, depress the brake pedal ten times in less than ten seconds, then turn the key off. Remove the jumper wire and the voltmeter.

1997 and later models

14 Code retrieval on 1997 and later models requires a scan tool of the type described in Chapter 6. If the amber ABS warning light on the dash comes on and stays on, it indicates a problem with the ABS system rather than the main brake system. Take the vehicle to a dealer service department or other qualified repair facility for diagnosis.

1994 through 1996 models

Code 11: Right-hand front anti-lock sensor (wheel speed sensor) or sensor indicator

Code 12: Left-hand front anti-lock sensor (wheel speed sensor) or sensor indicator

Code 13: Right-hand rear anti-lock sensor (wheel speed sensor) or sensor indicator

Code 14: Left-hand rear anti-lock sensor (wheel speed sensor) or sensor indicator

Code 15: Front and rear anti-lock sensor (wheel speed sensor)

Code 22: Solenoid valve

Code 51: Fail safe relay

Code 53: Motor relay

Code 61: Control module

1997 through 1999 models:

Code B1318: No/low voltage to the anti-lock brake control module

Code B1342: Anti-lock brake control module failure

Code C1095: Pump motor shorted

Code C1096: Pump motor open

Code C1115: Shorted anti-lock relay

Code C1140: Excessive dump time fault

Code C1145: Right front anti-lock brake sensor (static)

Code C1148/C1234: Right front anti-lock brake sensor (dynamic)

Code C1155: Left front anti-lock brake sensor (static)

Code C1158/C1233: Left front anti-lock brake sensor (dynamic)

Code C1165: Right rear anti-lock brake sensor (static)

1997 through 1999 models (continued):

Code C1168/1235: Right rear anti-lock brake sensor (dynamic)

Code C1175: Left rear anti-lock brake sensor (static)

Code C1178/C1236: Left rear anti-lock brake sensor (dynamic)

Code C1184: Excessive ABS isolation

Code C1185: Open anti-lock relay

Code C1194/C1196: Open or shorted left front dump valve solenoid

Code C1198/C1200: Open or shorted left front isolation valve solenoid

Code C1220: Anti-lock brake warning indicator shorted

Specifications

General

Brake fluid type	See Chapter 1
Brake pedal height	7.60 to 7.72 inches

Front disc brakes

Disc thickness	
Standard	0.79 to 0.87 inch
Minimum	Refer to numbers cast into the disc
Disc runout limit	
1996 and earlier	0.004 inch
1997 on	0.002 inch
Minimum brake pad thickness	See Chapter 1

Rear drum brakes

Standard drum diameter	
1991 and 1992	9.0 inches
1993 through 1996	7.87 inches
1997 on	9.06 inches
Maximum drum diameter	Refer to numbers cast into the drum
Minimum brake lining thickness	See Chapter 1

Rear disc brakes

Disc thickness	
Standard	0.28 to 0.35 inch
Minimum	Refer to numbers cast into the disc
Disc runout limit	
1996 and earlier	0.004 inch
1997 on	0.002 inch

Torque specifications   **Ft-lbs (unless otherwise indicated)**

➡**Note: One foot-pound (ft-lb) of torque is equivalent to 12 inch-pounds (in-lbs) of torque. Torque values below approximately 15 ft-lbs are expressed in inch-pounds, since most foot-pound torque wrenches are not accurate at these smaller values.**

Front disc brake caliper mounting bolts	29 to 36
Brake hose-to-caliper bolt	16 to 20
Rear disc brake caliper lock-bolt	33 to 43
Master cylinder mounting nuts	96 to 144 in-lbs
Brake booster mounting nuts	14 to 19
Wheel cylinder bolts	89 to 115 in-lbs
Wheel lug nuts	See Chapter 1

Section

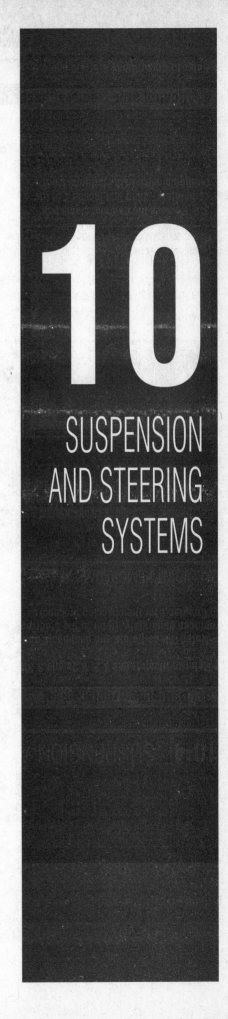

10

SUSPENSION AND STEERING SYSTEMS

1 General information

▶ **Refer to illustrations 1.1 and 1.2**

The front suspension is a MacPherson strut design. The steering knuckle is located by a control arm and both front control arms are connected by a stabilizer bar, to reduce body lean during cornering (see illustration).

The rear suspension also utilizes MacPherson struts. Longitudinal movement is controlled by trailing links mounted between the body and the rear spindles (see illustration). Side-to-side movement is controlled by front and rear lateral links. A stabilizer bar minimizes body lean during cornering.

The rack-and-pinion steering gear is located behind the engine/transaxle assembly and actuates the steering arms which are integral with the steering knuckles. Some vehicles are equipped with power steering. The steering column is connected to the steering gear through an articulated intermediate shaft. The steering column is designed to collapse in the event of an accident.

✴✴ WARNING:

Whenever steering and suspension fasteners are replaced, use new ones of the same part number or of original equipment quality and design. Torque specifications must be followed for proper reassembly and component retention. Never attempt to heat, straighten or weld any suspension or steering component. Instead, replace any bent or damaged part with a new one.

1.1 Front suspension and related components

1	Front stabilizer bar link bolt	2	Support crossmember
	Note: *Stabilizer bar and clamps not*	3	Control arm
	shown	4	Balljoint

5	Strut/coil spring assembly
6	Right driveaxle assembly
7	Left driveaxle assembly
8	Rack-and-pinion steering gear

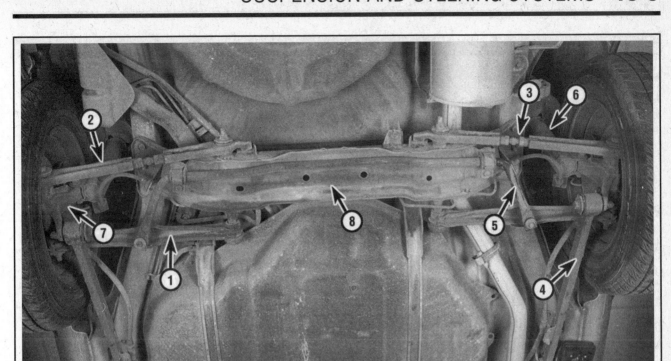

1.2 Rear suspension components

1	Rear lateral suspension arm - No. 1	4	Strut rod (trailing link)	7	Rear spindle
2	Rear lateral suspension arm - No. 2	5	Rear stabilizer bar	8	Rear suspension crossmember
3	Rear arm toe adjuster	6	Strut/coil spring assembly		

2   Front stabilizer bar - removal and installation

▶ **Refer to illustration 2.12**

REMOVAL

1   Loosen the front wheel lug nuts. Block the rear wheels so the vehicle can't roll. Raise the vehicle and support it securely on jackstands.

2   Attach a hoist or support fixture to the engine. The device must be capable of supporting the engine's weight throughout the procedure.

3   Remove the front wheels.

4   Remove the steering gear mounting bracket nuts (see Section 18). Move the steering gear slightly away from the firewall to provide removal access for the stabilizer bar.

5   Remove the connecting hardware that attaches the stabilizer bar to the control arms.

6   Be sure the hoist or support bracket is supporting the engine's weight.

7   Remove the crossmember rear mounting nuts.

8   Loosen, but don't remove, the crossmember front mounting nuts. Lower the rear end of the crossmember.

9   Unbolt the chassis frame from the vehicle frame. Lower the chassis frame (it will be supported by the engine and transaxle mounts).

10   Unbolt the stabilizer bar brackets from the chassis frame and take it out.

11   Inspect the bushings for cracks, wear and deterioration. Install new ones if there's any doubt about their condition.

INSTALLATION

12   Installation is the reverse of the removal steps. Tighten all fasteners to the torque values listed in this Chapter's Specifications. Tighten the stabilizer bar-to-control arm nuts until 5/8 to 3/4-inch of threads is exposed (see illustration).

2.12 Tighten the nuts on the stabilizer bar-to-control arm bolts until the exposed threads measure approximately 5/8 to 3/4-inch

3 Balljoints - replacement

♦ Refer to illustrations 3.2, 3.3a and 3.3b

➡Note: The balljoints and dust boots on this vehicle can be replaced separately. Refer to the Steering and suspension check in Chapter 1 for the checking procedure.

BALLJOINT REMOVAL

1 Block the rear wheels so the vehicle can't roll. Jack up the front end and place it securely on jackstands.
2 Remove the balljoint clamp bolt and nut (see illustration). Remove the bolt completely, don't just loosen it.
3 Remove the two bolts holding the balljoint to the control arm and take it off (see illustrations).

BOOT REPLACEMENT

4 Place the balljoint in a vise. Gently tap the boot off with a hammer and chisel.
5 Place the new boot over the balljoint stud. Press it into position with a suitable size driver, such as a deep socket or piece of pipe.

BALLJOINT INSTALLATION

6 Attach the balljoint to the control arm, then install the clamp bolt and nut. Tighten all fasteners to the torque values listed in this Chapter's Specifications.
7 The remainder of installation is the reverse of the removal steps.

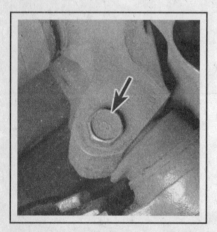

3.2 Remove the balljoint clamp bolt completely - don't just loosen it (it fits through a notch in the balljoint stud)

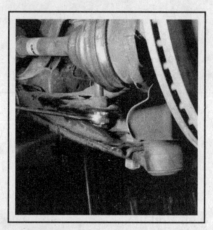

3.3a Remove the nut on the upper side of the control arm . . .

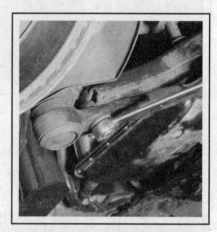

3.3b . . . and one on the lower side of the control arm, then remove the balljoint

4 Control arm - removal, inspection and installation

♦ Refer to illustrations 4.5, 4.6 and 4.9

REMOVAL

1 Block the rear wheels so the vehicle won't roll. Loosen the wheel lug nuts on the side to be disassembled, raise the front of the vehicle and support it securely on jackstands. Remove the wheel.
2 Remove the stabilizer bar-to-control arm nut and bolt (see Section 2).
3 Remove the balljoint clamp bolt and nut from the steering knuckle (see illustration 3.2).
4 Pry the control arm down to separate it from the steering knuckle.
5 Remove the bolt and washer from the control arm front pivot (see illustration).
6 Unbolt the control arm rear bushing retaining strap (see illustration).
7 Remove the control arm from the vehicle.

4.5 Remove the front pivot bolt

4.6 Remove the bolts and detach the rear of the control arm from the vehicle

4.9 To separate the rear bushing from the control arm, remove the nut and lockwasher, then slide the bushing and washers off the shaft

INSPECTION

8   Check the control arm for distortion and the bushings for wear, damage and deterioration. Replace a damaged or bent control arm with a new one. Replace defective bushings.

9   If the rear bushing is worn, remove the nut and take the rear bushing off the control arm (see illustration).

INSTALLATION

10 If removed, install the washer, rear bushing, second washer, lock- washer and nut on the control arm. Tighten the nut to the torque listed in this Chapter's Specifications.

11 Insert the balljoint stud into the steering knuckle. Install the clamp bolt and nut and tighten the nut to the torque listed in this Chapter's Specifications.

12 Raise the control arm into position and attach the rear bushing strap to the vehicle frame. Tighten the bolts to the torque listed in this Chapter's Specifications.

13 Align the front bushing with its holes in the frame and install the pivot bolt. Install the lockwasher and tighten the nut to the torque listed in this Chapter's Specifications.

14 The remainder of installation is the reverse of the removal steps.

5   Strut assembly (front) - removal, inspection and installation

▶ **Refer to illustration 5.3 and 5.4**

REMOVAL

1   Block the rear wheels so the vehicle can't roll. Loosen the wheel lug nuts on the side to be dismantled, raise the front of the vehicle and support it securely on jackstands. Remove the wheel.

2   Pull out the clip that secures the brake hose to the strut (don't disconnect the hose from the line or caliper).

3   Remove the nuts and bolts that secure the bottom of the strut to the steering knuckle (see illustration).

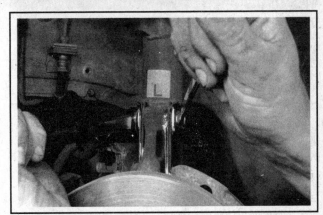

5.3 Remove the strut-to-steering knuckle bolts

5.4 Note the direction indicator on the mounting block (arrow) (it must be toward the center of the vehicle when installed), then remove the four mounting block nuts

4 Remove the strut mounting block nuts while supporting the strut assembly so it doesn't fall (see illustration).

5 Carefully guide the strut and spring assembly out of the wheel well.

INSPECTION

6 Check the strut body for leaking fluid, dents, cracks and other obvious damage which would warrant repair or replacement. Check the coil spring for cracks or chips in the spring coating (this may cause spring failure due to corrosion). Inspect the spring seat for cuts, hardness and general deterioration. If any undesirable conditions exist, proceed to Section 6 for the strut disassembly procedure.

INSTALLATION

7 To install the strut, place it in position with the studs extending up through the upper mounting holes. Be sure the direction indicator on the mounting block points toward the center of the vehicle. Install the nuts and tighten them to the torque listed in this Chapter's Specifications.

8 Install the nuts and bolts that secure the lower end of the strut to the steering knuckle. Tighten them to the torque listed in this Chapter's Specifications.

9 Attach the brake hose to the strut with the clip. Make sure the hose isn't twisted.

10 Install the wheel and lug nuts, lower the vehicle and tighten the lug nuts to the torque listed in the Chapter 1 Specifications.

---

6 Strut/coil spring (front) - replacement

▶ **Refer to illustration 6.4**

1 If the struts exhibit the telltale signs of wear (leaking fluid, loss of damping capability) explore all options before beginning any work. The strut assemblies are not serviceable and must be replaced if a problem develops. However, strut assemblies complete with springs may be available on an exchange basis, which eliminates much time and work. Whichever route you choose to take, check on the cost and availability of parts before disassembling the vehicle.

✳✳ WARNING:

Disassembling a strut is dangerous - be very careful and follow all instructions or serious injury could result. Use only a high quality spring compressor and carefully follow the manufacturer's instructions furnished with the tool. After removing the coil spring from the strut assembly, set it aside in a safe, isolated area.

2 Remove the strut and spring assembly following the procedure described in Section 5. Mount the strut assembly in a vise, with the jaws of the vise clamping onto the mounting block.

3 Remove the cap from the piston rod nut. Loosen the nut one turn. DO NOT loosen it further than this yet or the coil spring may fly out and cause injury.

4 Following the tool manufacturer's instructions, install the spring compressor (which can be obtained at most auto parts stores or equipment yards on a daily rental basis) on the spring and compress it sufficiently to relieve all pressure from the spring seat (see illustration).

5 Remove the piston rod nut. Take off the mounting block, thrust bearing, upper spring seat, rubber spring seat and bound stopper. Inspect the bearing for smooth operation and replace it if necessary.

6 Carefully remove the compressed spring and set it in a safe place.

✳✳ WARNING:

Never place your head near the end of the spring!

6.4 Install a spring compressor and compress the spring until there is no pressure being exerted on the bearing and seat assembly

7 Assemble the strut beginning with the bound stopper, then the spring, then the rubber spring seat, upper spring seat, thrust bearing and mounting block. Position the direction indicator on the mounting block so it will face in when the strut is installed (opposite the mounting flange on the bottom of the strut).

8 Install the piston rod nut and tighten it to the torque listed in this Chapter's Specifications.

9 Carefully remove the spring compressor. As you release the tension, make sure the spring seats correctly in the upper and lower seats.

10 Install the cap on the piston rod nut.

7 Steering knuckle and hub - removal, wheel bearing and seal replacement and installation

REMOVAL

1 Remove the hubcap and loosen the driveaxle retaining nut (see Chapter 8).

2 Securely block the rear wheels so the vehicle can't roll. Loosen the wheel lug nuts on the side to be disassembled, raise the front of the vehicle and support it securely on jackstands. Remove the wheel and the driveaxle nut. Tap the end of the driveaxle with a hammer and a brass drift to loosen the splines in the hub.

3 Remove the brake caliper and support it with a piece of wire as described in Chapter 9. Separate the brake disc from the hub.

4 Separate the tie-rod from the steering knuckle arm (see Section 16). If the vehicle is equipped with ABS, unbolt the wheel speed sensor from the knuckle.

5 Unbolt the strut from the steering knuckle (see illustration 5.3).

6 Remove the clamp bolt and nut and detach the balljoint from the steering knuckle (see illustration 3.2).

7 Pull the hub and steering knuckle off the driveaxle.

WHEEL BEARING AND SEAL REPLACEMENT

▸ **Refer to illustrations 7.9 and 7.13**

8 This procedure requires a hydraulic press. If you don't have one, take the knuckle and hub to a machine shop and have the bearing and seal replaced.

9 Take the oil seal out of the hub (see illustration).

10 Press the hub out of the bearing with an appropriate size drift.

11 If the bearing inner race stays on the hub, grind a portion of the inner race until it is 0.020-inch thick, then cut it off with a chisel.

12 Take the snap-ring out of the steering knuckle.

13 Press the bearing out of the steering knuckle with an appropriate size drift (see illustration).

14 The dust cover can't be removed without damaging it, so don't remove it unless you plan to install a new one.

➡**Note: Don't do this unless you plan to replace the dust cover.**

15 Scribe alignment marks on the dust cover and steering knuckle. Drive the dust cover off with a hammer and chisel.

➡**Note: Don't do this unless you plan to replace the dust cover.**

16 If the wheel studs are damaged, press them out and press new ones in. They must be replaced with new ones once they are removed, so don't remove them unless it's necessary.

17 If the dust cover was removed, scribe an alignment mark on it in the same position as the mark you made on the old one. Press the new dust cover onto the knuckle.

18 Press the bearing into the knuckle and install the snap-ring.

19 Press the hub into the bearing and steering knuckle.

20 Tap a new oil seal into place with an appropriate seal driver. The seal must be flush with the steering knuckle.

INSTALLATION

21 Position the steering knuckle on the balljoint stud. Install the clamp bolt and nut and tighten them to the torque listed in this Chapter's Specifications.

22 Attach the tie-rod end to the steering knuckle arm (see Section 16).

23 Bolt the steering knuckle to the strut. Tighten the nuts and bolts to the torque listed in this Chapter's Specifications.

24 Install a new driveaxle retaining nut.

25 Install the brake disc and caliper (see Chapter 9).

26 Tighten the driveaxle retaining nut to the torque listed in the Chapter 8 Specifications.

27 The remainder of installation is the reverse of the removal steps.

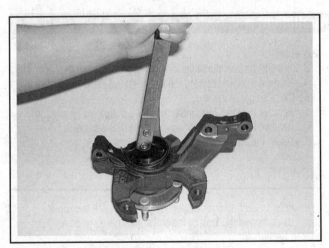

7.9 Remove the seal from the steering knuckle

7.13 Press the bearing out of the steering knuckle

8 Rear stabilizer bar - removal and installation

◆ **Refer to illustration 8.2, 8.3 and 8.6**

1   Securely block both front wheels so the vehicle won't roll. Jack up the rear end and place it securely on jackstands.

2   Remove the bolts and mounting hardware from the ends of the stabilizer bar (see illustration).

3   Look for paint marks that indicate the position of the stabilizer bar in the bushings (see illustration). Unbolt the stabilizer bar brackets from the crossmember and take the stabilizer bar out.

4   Check the bushings and mounting hardware for deterioration, wear or damage. Replace parts as necessary.

5   Make sure the bushings are aligned with the paint marks on the bar.

6   Install the stabilizer bar on the vehicle. Tighten the bracket bolts securely. Tighten the end nuts and bolts so 5/8 to 3/4-inch of threads is exposed (see illustration).

7   The remainder of installation is the reverse of the removal steps.

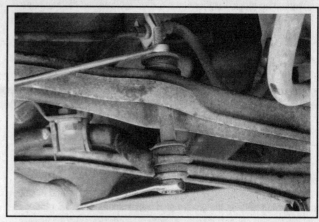

8.2 Remove the stabilizer bar-to-lateral link bolts and nuts (note how the bushings, spacers and washers are arranged)

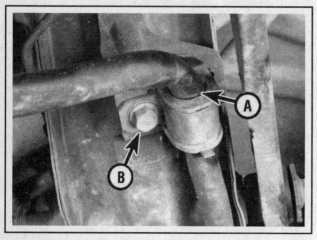

8.3 If there aren't paint marks on the bar to indicate the bushing positions (A), make your own, then remove the bolts that secure the bushing brackets (B)

8.6 Tighten the stabilizer nuts and bolts until 5/8 to 3/4-inch of the threaded bolt is exposed

9 Strut assembly (rear) - removal, inspection and installation

◆ **Refer to illustrations 9.1a, 9.1b, 9.1c, 9.5, 9.6a, 9.6b and 9.6c**

REMOVAL

1   If you're working on a station wagon or a hatchback model, remove the speaker grille and the seat back outer extension from the side of the vehicle being worked on (see illustrations). On 1996 and earlier models with a trunk, simply open the trunk lid for access to the strut upper mounting nuts. On 1997 and later models with a trunk, remove the package tray and rear seat trim for access to the upper mounting nuts.

2   Loosen the rear wheel lug nuts, raise the rear of the vehicle and support it securely on jackstands. Block the front wheels. Remove the

rear wheel.

3   Support the spindle of the side being worked on with a floor jack.

4   Remove the clip securing the flexible brake hose to the strut and move the hose out of the way.

5   Remove the strut-to-spindle mounting bolts (see illustration).

6   Remove the upper mounting nuts (see illustrations).

7   Lower the strut and remove it from the vehicle.

INSPECTION

8   Refer to Section 5 for inspection procedures. If the shock absorber portion of the strut or the coil spring needs to be replaced, refer to Section 10.

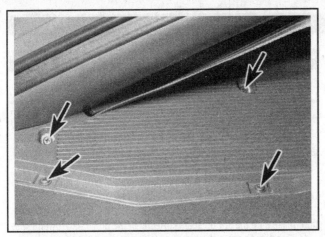

9.1a On station wagon and hatchback models, remove the screws that secure the speaker grille . . .

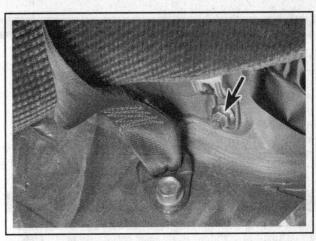

9.1b . . . remove the rear seat cushion and unscrew the nut that secures the seat outer extension . . .

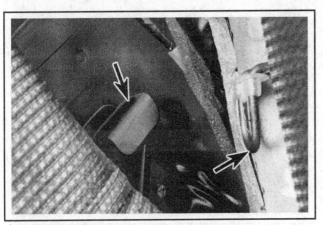

9.1c . . . and lift the extension retainer out of its slot (arrows)

9.5 Remove the bolts and nuts to separate the lower end of the strut from the spindle

9.6a One of the upper mounting nuts is accessible through the speaker grille opening . . .

9.6b . . . and the other through the seat extension opening (station wagon and hatchback models)

9.6c On 1997 and later models with a trunk, the strut upper mounting nuts are accessible after the rear seat trim and package tray have been removed

INSTALLATION

9   Position the strut assembly on the vehicle. Slide the mounting block studs into their holes, install the nuts and tighten them to the torque listed in this Chapter's Specifications.

10 Position the spindle in the strut flange, install the bolts and tighten them to the torque listed in this Chapter's Specifications.

11 Install the wheel and lug nuts, lower the vehicle and tighten the lug nuts to the torque listed in the Chapter 1 Specifications.

10 Strut/coil spring (rear) - replacement

▶ **Refer to illustration 10.5**

1   If the struts exhibit the telltale signs of wear (leaking fluid, loss of damping capability) explore all options before beginning any work. The strut/shock absorber assemblies are not serviceable and must be replaced if a problem develops. However, strut assemblies complete with springs may be available on an exchange basis, which eliminates much time and work. Whichever route you choose to take, check on the cost and availability of parts before disassembling the vehicle.

❊❊ **WARNING:**

Disassembling a strut is dangerous - be very careful and follow all instructions or serious injury could result. Use only a high quality spring compressor and carefully follow the manufacturer's instructions furnished with the tool. After removing the coil spring from the strut assembly, set it aside in a safe, isolated area.

2   Remove the strut and spring assembly following the procedure described in Section 9. Mount the strut assembly in a vise, with the jaws of the vise clamping onto the mounting block.

3   Remove the cap from the piston rod nut. Loosen the nut one turn only. DO NOT loosen it further than this yet or the coil spring may fly out and cause injury.

4   Remove the strut from the vise and reinstall it with the vise griping the lower mounting bracket. Following the tool manufacturer's instructions, install the spring compressor (which can be obtained at most auto parts stores or equipment yards on a daily rental basis) on the spring and compress it sufficiently to relieve all pressure from the spring seat (see illustration 6.4).

5   Hold the retainer with pliers and unscrew the piston rod nut (see illustration). Remove the washer, retainer and mounting block.

6   Carefully remove the compressed spring and set it in a safe place.

❊❊ **WARNING:**

Never place your head near the end of the spring!

7   Remove the bound stopper seat and bound stopper.

8   Assemble the strut beginning with the bound stopper, then the seat, coil spring and mounting block. Align the mounting block studs with the lower mounting bracket on the strut.

9   Install the retainer, washer and piston rod nut. Tighten the nut to the torque listed in this Chapter's Specifications.

10 Carefully remove the spring compressor. As you release the tension, make sure the spring seats correctly in the upper and lower seats.

11 Install the cap on the piston rod nut.

10.5 Hold the retainer from turning with pliers and remove the piston rod nut

11 Rear suspension links - removal and installation

1   Loosen the rear wheel lug nuts on the side of the vehicle being disassembled. Securely block both front wheels so the vehicle won't roll. Jack up the rear end and place it securely on jackstands.

2   Remove the rear wheel(s).

LATERAL LINKS

▶ **Refer to illustrations 11.4, 11.5, 11.6, 11.7a, 11.7b and 11.8**

3   Remove the rear stabilizer bar (see Section 8).

4   Remove the cap from the lateral link pivot bolt (see illustration).

5   Support the rear suspension crossmember with a floor jack (see illustration).

6   Unbolt the crossmember from the vehicle frame and lower it with the floor jack (see illustration). Be sure to detach the brake lines from the clips on the floorpan. Lower the crossmember just enough to allow the lateral link pivot bolts to be removed.

7   Remove the pivot bolt and separate the lateral links from the crossmember (see illustrations).

8   Unbolt the lateral links from the spindle and take them out (see illustration).

9   Installation is the reverse of removal. Tighten all fasteners to the torque values listed in this Chapter's Specifications.

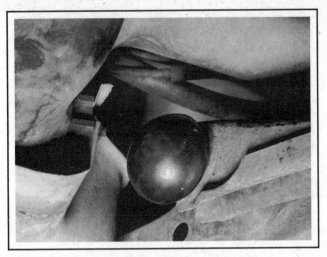

11.4 The lateral link pivot bolt head is covered by a plastic cap

11.5 Support the crossmember with a floor jack (a transmission jack is shown here and is preferable because of its width)

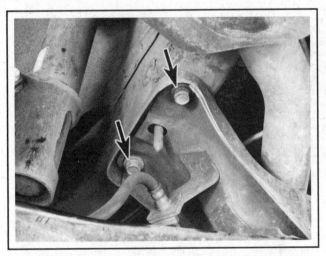

11.6 Remove the crossmember mounting bolts on each side (arrows) and lower the crossmember enough for removal access, but don't kink the brake lines

11.7a Remove the nut and bolt to free the inner end of the lateral link; here's the 1991 through 1996 design . . .

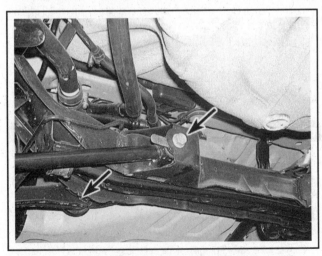

11.7b . . . and here's the 1997 and later version; note the L or R mark on the alignment tab

11.8 A long bolt secures each of the lateral links to the spindle

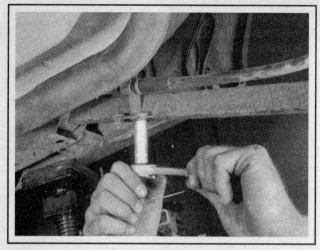

11.10 The parking brake cable bracket is secured to the trailing link by one or two nuts, depending on model

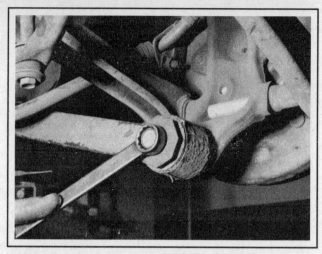

11.11a Remove the pivot bolt at the rear end of the trailing link . .

11.11b . . . and at the front end . . .

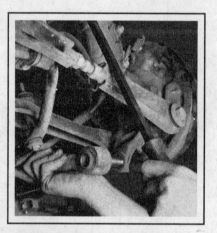

11.11c . . . pull or pry the hub forward to detach the rear end of the trailing arm . . .

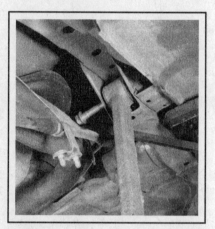

11.11d . . . and pry the front end out of the bracket

TRAILING LINK

▶ **Refer to illustrations 11.10, 11.11a, 11.11b, 11.11c and 11.11d**

10 Detach the parking brake cable bracket from the trailing link (see illustration).

11 Remove the pivot bolts at the front and rear ends of the trailing link and detach the link from the frame and spindle (see illustrations).

12 Installation is the reverse of the removal steps. Tighten all fasteners to the torque values listed in this Chapter's Specifications.

12 Rear wheel hub and spindle - removal, inspection and installation

▶ **Refer to illustrations 12.2a, 12.2b and 12.4**

HUB REMOVAL

1   Loosen the rear wheel lug nuts on the side of the vehicle being disassembled. Securely block both front wheels so the vehicle won't roll. Raise the rear end and place it securely on jackstands.

2   Remove the cap from the hub with a hammer, chisel and pliers (see illustrations).

Drum brake models

3   Remove the brake drum and shoes (see Chapter 9).

4   Raise the staked portion of the spindle nut with a hammer and

12.2a Tap gently under one side of the dust cap with a chisel to loosen it, then turn the hub 180-degrees and tap under the other side

12.2b Work the cap back and forth with pliers to remove it

punch, then remove the nut and discard it (see illustration).

5 Remove the rear brake backing plate.

Disc brake models

6 Remove the caliper and brake disc (see Chapter 9). If the vehicle is equipped with ABS, unbolt the wheel speed sensor from the spindle.

7 Perform Step 4 above.

8 Remove the brake dust shield.

SPINDLE REMOVAL

9 Unbolt the strut from the spindle (see illustration 9.5).

10 Unbolt the trailing link from the spindle (see illustration 11.11a).

11 Unbolt the lateral links from the spindle (see illustration 11.8).

12 Remove the spindle.

INSPECTION

13 If there's any sign of wear or damage to the hub bearing, have it replaced by a dealer service department or machine shop.

INSTALLATION

14 Bolt the spindle to the strut. Tighten the nuts and bolts to the torque listed in this Chapter's Specifications.

15 Bolt the trailing link to the spindle, then connect the lateral links to the spindle. Tighten the fasteners to the torque values listed in this Chapter's Specifications.

16 Install the stabilizer bar (see Section 8).

17 Install the brake backing plate.

18 Install the hub on the spindle. Install a new retaining nut, tighten it to the torque listed in this Chapter's Specifications and stake the nut

12.4 Use a punch and hammer to raise the staked portion of the spindle nut out of the groove, then unscrew the nut

with a rounded chisel.

✳✳ WARNING:

Don't stake the nut with a sharp chisel or it may work loose and allow the hub to fall off while the vehicle is being driven.

19 The remainder of installation is the reverse of the removal steps. Tighten the wheel lug nuts to the torque listed in the Chapter 1 Specifications.

13 Rear hub bearing endplay - check and adjustment

1   Securely block the front wheels so the vehicle won't roll. Raise the rear end and place it on jackstands.

2   Remove the rear brake drum or caliper (see Chapter 9).

3   Check the bearings for proper lubrication and excessive wear by spinning the hub. If movement is rough or noisy, remove the spindle (see Section 12) and have it replaced.

4   Set up a dial indicator to measure endplay. Pull the hub out and push it in and note the reading on the gauge. If it exceeds the endplay listed in this Chapter's Specifications, try tightening the bearing nut to the torque listed in this Chapter's Specifications. If the endplay then falls within the allowable range, remove the nut and install a new one. If tightening the nut doesn't work, remove the hub and have the bearing replaced.

14 Steering system - general information

All models are equipped with rack-and-pinion steering. Some are power assisted. The steering gear is bolted to the crossmember and operates the steering arms via tie-rods. The inner ends of the tie-rods are protected by rubber boots which should be inspected periodically for secure attachment, tears and leaking lubricant.

The power assist system consists of a belt-driven pump and associated lines and hoses. The fluid level should be checked periodically (see Chapter 1).

The steering wheel operates the steering shaft, which actuates the steering gear through universal joints and the intermediate shaft. Looseness in the steering can be caused by wear in the steering shaft universal joints, the steering gear, the tie-rod ends and loose retaining bolts.

15 Steering wheel - removal and installation

▶ Refer to illustrations 15.2a, 15.2b, 15.3, 15.4 and 15.6

✳✳ WARNING:

1994 and later models are equipped with airbags. Before working on or near any airbag component the system must be disarmed. To do this, disconnect the cable from the negative terminal of the battery and wait one minute for the backup power supply to discharge. See Chapter 12 for more information.

REMOVAL

1   Disconnect the negative cable from the battery.

2   Remove the screws securing the horn pad to the steering wheel (see illustration). If the vehicle is equipped with an airbag, remove the bolt from each side of the back of the steering wheel (see illustration). Pull the airbag module out, disconnect the electrical connector and remove the module from the steering wheel.

✳✳ WARNING:

Carry the airbag module with the soft face away from your body. When you set it down, make sure the soft face is pointing up.

3   Remove the horn pad and disconnect the horn wire electrical connector (see illustration).

4   Mark the relationship of the steering wheel to the steering shaft (see illustration). These marks will be used during installation.

5   Remove the steering wheel nut or bolt. Discard the bolt or nut.

6   Use a puller to remove the steering wheel (see illustration).

✳✳ CAUTION:

Don't hammer on the shaft to remove the steering wheel.

INSTALLATION

7   Align the index mark on the steering wheel hub with the mark on the shaft and slip the wheel onto the shaft.

8   Install a new nut or bolt and tighten it to the torque listed in this Chapter's Specifications.

9   Reconnect the horn wire electrical connector and install the horn pad; or, if equipped with an airbag, connect the airbag electrical connector and install the airbag module.

10 Reconnect the negative battery cable.

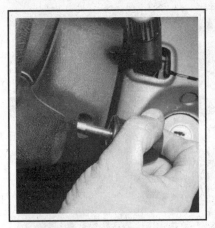

15.2a Two-spoke steering wheels have two screws securing the horn pad; four-spoke steering wheels have four screws

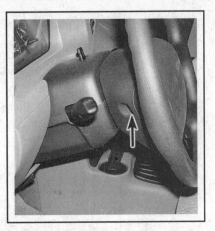

15.2b The airbag module is secured to the steering wheel with two bolts (one on each side of the back of the steering wheel)

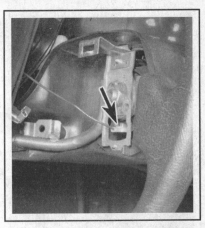

15.3 Lift the horn pad and disconnect the electrical connector (arrow)

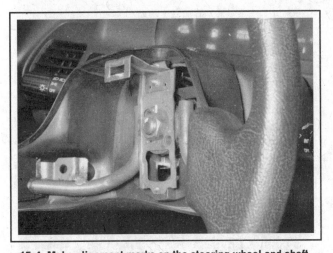

15.4 Make alignment marks on the steering wheel and shaft

15.6 Remove the steering wheel with a puller

16 Tie-rod ends - removal and installation

♦ Refer to illustrations 16.2a, 16.2b, 16.3 and 16.5

➡ Note: If that doesn't work, use a two-jaw puller to force the stud out of the steering knuckle arm. Remove the tie-rod end.

REMOVAL

1   Loosen the front wheel lug nuts. Block the rear wheels so the vehicle won't roll. Raise the front of the vehicle and support it securely on jackstands. Remove the front wheel.

2   Hold the tie-rod with a wrench and loosen the jam nut enough to mark the position of the tie-rod end in relation to the threads (see illustrations).

3   Remove the cotter pin from the tie-rod end stud (see illustration). Discard the cotter pin.

4   Remove the nut from the tie-rod end stud.

5   Strike the knuckle arm a sharp blow with a hammer to free the stud (see illustration). Separate the stud from the knuckle arm.

INSTALLATION

6   Thread the tie-rod end on to the marked position and insert the tie-rod end stud into the steering knuckle arm. Tighten the jam nut securely.

7   Install the nut on the stud and tighten it to the torque listed in this Chapter's Specifications. Install a new cotter pin and bend the ends over completely.

8   Install the wheel and lug nuts. Lower the vehicle and tighten the lug nuts to the torque listed in the Chapter 1 Specifications.

9   Have the alignment checked by a dealer service department or an alignment shop.

16.2a Loosen the jam nut while holding the tie-rod with a wrench (or pair of locking pliers) on the flat portion of the rod to prevent it from turning

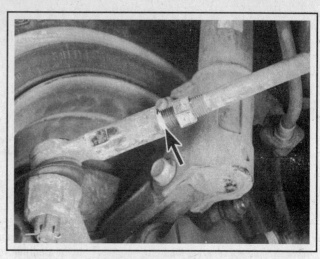

16.2b Mark the position of the jam nut on the threads so you can reset the tie-rod to the same length

16.3 Bend back the ends of the cotter pin and pull it out of the tie-rod stud

16.5 Rap the steering knuckle with a hammer to free the tie-rod end

17 Steering gear boots - replacement

1 Loosen the front wheel lug nuts. Raise the front of the vehicle, support it securely, block the rear wheels and set the parking brake. Remove the front wheel.

2 Refer to Section 16 and remove the tie-rod end and jam nut.

3 Remove the wire retainer or clamp from the inner end of the boot and remove the clip from the outer end, then slip the boot off.

4 Before installing the new boot, wrap the threads and serrations on the end of the steering rod with a layer of tape so the small end of the new boot isn't damaged.

5 Slide the new boot into position on the steering gear. If it's hard to install, lubricate the boot with silicone spray.

6 Install a new wire retainer on the large end of the boot. Make sure the boot isn't twisted, then secure the small end with the clip.

7 Remove the tape and install the tie-rod end (see Section 16).

8 Install the wheel and lug nuts. Lower the vehicle and tighten the lug nuts to torque listed in the Chapter 1 Specifications.

18 Steering gear - removal and installation

♦ Refer to illustration 18.4, 18.8, 18.13a and 18.13b

❊❊ WARNING:

On airbag-equipped models, make sure the steering shaft is not turned while the steering gear is removed or you could damage the airbag system. To prevent the shaft from turning, turn the ignition key to the lock position before beginning work or run the seat belt through the steering wheel and clip the seat belt into place. Due to the possible damage to the airbag system, we recommend only experienced mechanics attempt this procedure.

REMOVAL

1 Set the front wheels to the straight-ahead position.

2 Disconnect the negative cable from the battery.

3 Follow the steering column down to the floor and remove the set plate surrounding the bottom of the steering column.

4 Reach through the set plate opening and remove the pinch bolt that secures the pinion shaft to the intermediate shaft (see illustration).

5 Loosen the front wheel lug nuts. Block the rear wheels so the vehicle can't roll. Raise the front of the vehicle and support it on jackstands.

6 Remove both front wheels.

Power steering models

7 Remove the splash shield from the driver's side wheel well.

8 Place a pan under the steering gear. Disconnect the lines and cap the ends to prevent excessive fluid loss and contamination (see illustration). Cap the fittings on the gear as well.

9 Remove and discard the strap that secures the power steering lines to the gear.

10 If you're working on a vehicle with a manual transaxle, disconnect the shift control rod from the transaxle (see Chapter 7 Part A).

All models

11 If you're working on a vehicle with a manual transaxle, detach the extension bar from the transaxle (see Chapter 7 Part A).

12 Separate the tie-rod ends from the steering knuckle arms (see Section 16).

13 Remove the nuts from the steering gear brackets (see illustrations).

14 Gently pull the steering gear assembly forward and down, away from the firewall. Have an assistant pull up on the lower shaft from inside the vehicle to dislocate it from the steering gear input shaft.

15 Carefully remove the entire assembly through the left wheel well.

18.4 Remove the pinch bolt

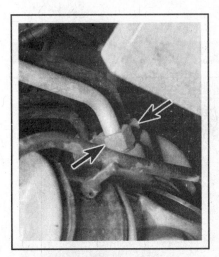

18.8 Disconnect the power steering line fittings (arrows)

18.13a Remove the upper and lower nuts that secure the mounting bracket on the passenger side . . .

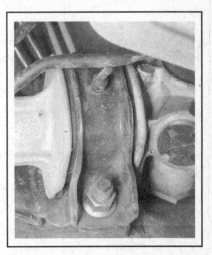

18.13b . . . and detach the bracket on the driver's side to separate the gear from the crossmember

INSTALLATION

16 If a new rack-and-pinion assembly is being installed, the tie-rod ends must be removed from the original assembly and installed on the new unit at the approximate same setting. The most important thing is that the tie-rod ends are screwed on an equal amount at this stage.

17 Make sure the steering gear is centered. Turn the pinion shaft to full lock in one direction, then count and record the number of turns required to rotate it to the opposite full lock position. Turn the pinion shaft back through one-half the number of turns just counted to center the assembly.

18 Check that the front wheels are in the straight-ahead position.

19 The remainder of installation is the reverse of the removal steps with the following additions:

a) *If you're working on a vehicle with power steering, fill the fluid reservoir with the specified fluid and refer to Section 21 for the power steering bleeding procedure.*

b) *Have the front end alignment checked by a dealer service department or alignment shop.*

19 Power steering fluid reservoir - removal and installation

▶ **Refer to illustration 19.1**

1 Remove the reservoir mounting bolts (see illustration).

2 Squeeze the spring clamps on the supply and return hoses and slide them down the hoses, away from the reservoir fittings.

3 Work the hoses off the fittings (twist them back and forth if they're tight).

4 Tilt the fittings up to prevent fluid loss and lift the reservoir out.

5 Installation is the reverse of the removal steps. Fill the reservoir with the fluid recommended in the Chapter 1 Specifications.

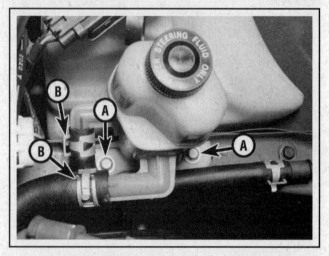

19.1 The power steering fluid reservoir is secured by two mounting bolts (A); the supply and return hoses are secured by spring clamps (B)

20 Power steering pump - removal and installation

1.8L ENGINE MODELS

▶ **Refer to illustration 20.2**

1 Remove the fluid reservoir (see Section 19).

2 Disconnect the electrical connector from the pressure switch on the pump (see illustration).

3 Remove the nut from the high pressure line. Disconnect the line from the pump and cap the line and fittings to prevent leakage and contamination.

4 Securely block the rear wheels so the vehicle won't roll. Jack up the front end and place it on jackstands.

5 Remove the passenger side under cover.

6 Remove the pump drivebelt (see Chapter 1).

7 Remove the jackstands and lower the vehicle.

8 Remove the pump mounting bracket bolts, then take out the pump together with the bracket.

9 Remove the nuts and bolts that secure the pump, tensioner and bracket together.

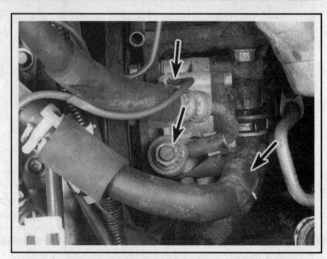

20.2 Unplug the electrical connector and detach the fluid hoses (1.8L engine models)

10 Installation is the reverse of the removal steps. Be sure to fill the fluid reservoir with the recommended fluid (see Chapter 1) and bleed the system (see Section 21).

1.9L ENGINE MODELS

▶ **Refer to illustration 20.19**

11 Drain the cooling system (see Chapter 1).

12 Remove the drivebelt (see Chapter 1). Unbolt the drivebelt tensioner from the engine and take it off.

13 Place a floor jack beneath the oil pan to support the engine. Use a block of wood between the jack and oil pan so the pan won't be damaged.

14 Remove the vibration damper from the engine mount (see Chapter 2 Part A). Remove the engine mount nuts, loosen the through-bolt and pivot the engine mount away from the engine.

15 Raise the engine with a jack just enough to provide access to the power steering pump pulley. Take care not to strain any lines or hoses.

16 Hold the pulley from turning (a strap wrench or chain wrench will work) and remove the three pulley mounting bolts. Take the pulley off.

17 Lower the engine to its installed height.

18 Swivel the engine mount back into position and install the two nuts.

19 Disconnect the pressure and return lines from the pump (see illustration).

20 Securely block the rear wheels so the vehicle won't roll. Jack up the front end and place it on jackstands. DO NOT get under a vehicle that's supported only by a jack!

21 Remove both splash shields from the passenger side of the vehicle.

22 Unbolt the air conditioning compressor and set it aside without disconnecting any lines (see Chapter 3).

23 Remove the lower radiator hose (see Chapter 3).

24 Unbolt the pump and take it out.

25 Installation is the reverse of the removal steps.

26 Fill and bleed the power steering system (see Section 21).

27 Run the engine and make sure there aren't any fluid leaks.

1997 AND LATER 2.0L ENGINE MODELS (EXCEPT ZETEC)

28 Remove the power steering fluid reservoir (Section 19).

29 Disconnect the negative cable from the battery.

30 Unbolt the retainers and support bracket that secure the power steering pressure hose.

31 Remove the accessory drivebelt (see Chapter 1).

32 Unbolt the alternator and set it aside out of the way (see Chapter 5).

33 Hold the power steering pump pulley with a strap wrench or similar tool and remove the three pulley mounting bolts. Take the pulley off the pump.

34 Securely block the rear wheels so the vehicle won't roll. Jack up the front end and place it on jackstands.

35 Remove the passenger side under cover.

36 Disconnect the pressure and return hoses from the power steering pump.

20.19 Power steering pump lines (1.9L engine models)

37 Remove the jackstands and lower the vehicle.

38 Unbolt the power steering pump and take it off.

39 Perform Steps 25 through 27 to install the pump. Tighten the pump mounting bolts to the torque listed in this Chapter's Specifications.

2.0L ZETEC ENGINE MODELS

40 Disconnect the negative cable from the battery.

41 Disconnect the coolant overflow hose form the radiator filler neck and position it out of the way.

42 Unbolt the clamp that secures the air conditioning refrigerant hose, unclip the cruise control cable from the air conditioner hose bracket and unbolt the bracket.

43 Securely block the rear wheels so the vehicle won't roll. Jack up the front end and place it on jackstands.

44 Remove the passenger side under cover.

45 Remove the accessory drivebelt (see Chapter 1).

46 Disconnect the pressure hose from the power steering pump.

47 Remove the jackstands and lower the vehicle. Leave the rear wheels blocked; you'll need to jack up the vehicle again later.

48 Disconnect the power steering pressure hoses from each other at their junction. Unbolt the pressure hose brackets and move them out of the way.

49 Disconnect the electrical connector from the oxygen sensor (see Chapter 6).

50 Unbolt the ground bracket from the cylinder block.

51 Squeeze the clamp on the power steering return hose and slide it up the hose, then disconnect the hose from the fitting.

52 Once again, securely block the rear wheels so the vehicle won't roll. Jack up the front end and place it on jackstands.

53 Take the pressure hose out of the engine compartment.

54 Unbolt the power steering pump from the engine and remove it. Discard the heat shield; you'll need to install a new one.

55 Perform Steps 25 through 27 to install the pump. Use new Teflon seals on the pressure hose fittings. Install a new heat shield and tighten the pump mounting bolts to the torque listed in this Chapter's Specifications.

21 Power steering system - bleeding

1   The power steering system must be bled whenever a line is disconnected. Bubbles can be seen in power steering fluid which has air in it and the fluid will often have a tan or milky appearance. A low fluid level can cause air to mix with the fluid, resulting in a noisy pump as well as foaming of the fluid.

2   Open the hood and check the fluid level in the reservoir, adding the specified fluid necessary to bring it up to the proper level (see Chapter 1).

3   Securely block the rear wheels so the vehicle won't roll. Jack up the front end and place it on jackstands.

4   If you're working on a vehicle with a 1.8L engine, disconnect the coil wire from the distributor cap and ground it on the engine.

5   If you're working on a vehicle with a 1.9L engine, or a 1997 model, disconnect the electrical connector from the ignition coil pack.

6   If you're working on a 1998 or later model, remove the ENGINE fuse from the fuse block (see Chapter 12).

7   Crank the engine with the starter (but not for more than 15 seconds at a time) and slowly turn the steering wheel several times from left-to-right and back again.

✳✳ CAUTION:

Don't turn the steering wheel unless the front wheels are off the ground.

8   Check the fluid level, topping it up as necessary until it remains steady and no more bubbles are visible.

22 Wheel alignment - general information

▶ **Refer to illustration 22.1**

A wheel alignment refers to the adjustments made to the wheels so they are in proper angular relationship to the suspension and the ground (see illustration). Wheels that are out of proper alignment not only affect vehicle control, but also increase tire wear. The only front end adjustment normally required on these vehicles is toe-in, but camber and caster can also be adjusted. Toe-in is adjustable on the rear wheels also.

Getting the proper wheel alignment is a very exacting process, one in which complicated and expensive machines are necessary to perform the job properly. Because of this, you should have a technician with the proper equipment perform these tasks. We will, however, use this space to give you a basic idea of what is involved with a wheel alignment so you can better understand the process and deal intelligently with the shop that does the work.

Toe-in is the turning in of the wheels. The purpose of a toe specification is to ensure parallel rolling of the wheels. In a vehicle with zero toe-in, the distance between the front edges of the wheels will be the same as the distance between the rear edges of the wheels. On the front end, the amount of toe-in is controlled by the tie-rod end position on the tie-rod. On the rear wheels it's controlled by an adjustable lateral link. Incorrect toe-in will cause the tires to wear improperly by making them scrub against the road surface.

Camber is the tilting of the wheels from vertical when viewed from one end of the vehicle. When the wheels tilt in at the top, the camber is negative (-). When the wheels tilt out at the top, the camber is positive (+). The amount of tilt is measured in degrees from vertical and this measurement is called the camber angle. This angle affects the amount of tire tread which contacts the road and compensates for changes in suspension geometry when the vehicle is cornering or travelling over and undulating surface. Camber is adjusted by changing the position of the strut mounting block in the strut tower.

Caster is the tilting of the steering axis from vertical. A tilt toward the rear is positive caster and a tilt toward the front is negative caster. Caster is also adjusted by changing the position of the strut mounting block in the strut tower.

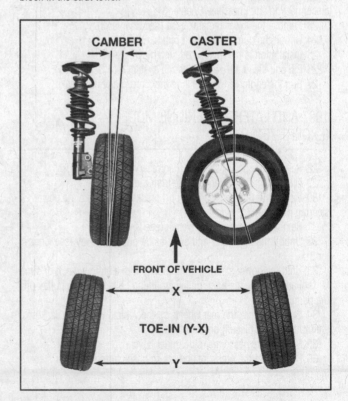

22.1 Camber, caster and toe-in angles

23 Wheels and tires - general information

▶ **Refer to illustration 23.1**

All vehicles covered by this manual are equipped with metric-size fiberglass or steel belted radial tires (see illustration). The use of other size or type tires may affect the ride and handling of the vehicle. Don't mix different types of tires, such as radials and bias belted, on the same vehicle, since handling may be seriously affected. Tires should be replaced in pairs on the same axle, but if only one tire is being replaced, be sure it's the same size, structure and tread design as the other.

Because tire pressure affects handling and wear, the tire pressures should be checked at least once a month or before any extended trips (see Chapter 1).

Wheels must be replaced if they're bent, dented, leak air, have elongated bolt holes, are heavily rusted, out of vertical symmetry or if the lug nuts won't stay tight. Wheel repairs by welding or peening aren't recommended.

Tire and wheel balance is important to the overall handling, braking and performance of the vehicle. Unbalanced wheels can adversely affect handling and ride characteristics as well as tire life. Whenever a tire is installed on a wheel, the tire and wheel should be balanced by a shop with the proper equipment.

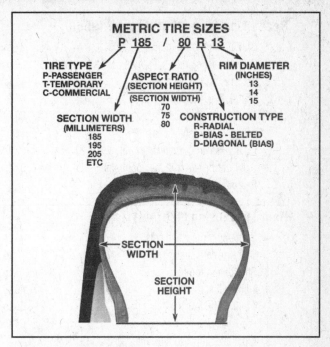

23.1 Metric tire size code

Specifications

General

Power steering fluid type	See Chapter 1
Steering gear type	Rack and pinion with optional power assist
Rear wheel hub bearing endplay	0.002 inch

Torque specifications

	Ft-lbs

Front suspension

Strut upper mounting nuts	22 to 30
Strut-to-steering knuckle bolts/nuts	69 to 93
Strut piston rod nut	58 to 81
Control arm retaining strap bolts	69 to 86
Control arm rear bushing nut	69 to 86
Control arm front pivot nut	69 to 93
Balljoint clamp bolt and nut	32 to 43
Balljoint-to-control arm nuts	69 to 86
Stabilizer bar bracket bolts	32 to 43
Chassis frame-to-vehicle frame bolts and nuts	69 to 93

Torque specifications (continued)	Ft-lbs

Rear suspension (1991 through 1996)

Strut upper mounting nuts	22 to 27
Strut-to-rear spindle bolts/nuts	69 to 93
Strut piston rod nut	41 to 50
Trailing link front bolt	46 to 69
Trailing link rear bolt	69 to 93
Lateral link-to-spindle nut	63 to 86
Lateral link-to-crossmember nut	50 to 70
Stabilizer bar-to-crossmember bolts	32 to 43
Rear hub retaining nut	130 to 174

Rear suspension (1997 on)

Strut upper mounting nuts	34 to 46
Strut-to-rear spindle bolts/nuts	76 to 100
Strut piston rod nut	41 to 49
Trailing link front bolt	46 to 69
Trailing link rear bolt	69 to 94
Front lateral link-to-spindle nut	64 to 86
Front lateral link-to-crossmember nut	
All 1997, 1998 coupe	50 to 70
1998 except coupe, all 1999	63 to 86
Stabilizer bar-to-crossmember bolts	32 to 43
Rear hub retaining nut	130 to 174

Steering (1991 through 1996)

Steering gear mounting nuts	28 to 38
Power steering pump bolts	30 to 45
Power steering pump pulley bolts	15 to 22
Steering column shaft-to-universal joint bolt	29 to 36
Tie-rod end-to-steering knuckle nut	31 to 42
Steering wheel lock bolt	36 to 46

Steering (1997 on)

Steering gear mounting nuts	28 to 38
Power steering pump bolts	
1997	30 to 35
1998 on	15 to 22
Power steering pump pulley bolts	15 to 22
Steering column shaft-to-universal joint bolt	30 to 36
Tie-rod end-to-steering knuckle nut	33

Section

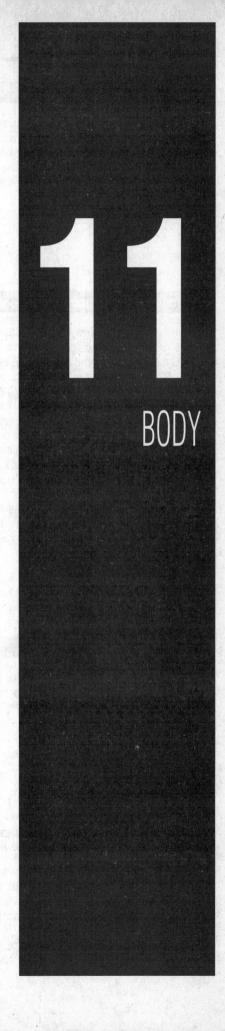

11

BODY

1 General information

These models feature a "unibody" layout, using a floor pan with front and rear frame side rails which support the body components, front and rear suspension systems and other mechanical components.

Certain components are particularly vulnerable to accident damage and can be unbolted and repaired or replaced. Among these parts are the body moldings, bumpers, the hood and trunk lids and all glass.

Only general body maintenance practices and body panel repair procedures within the scope of the do-it-yourselfer are included in this Chapter.

2 Body - maintenance

1 The condition of your vehicle's body is very important, because the resale value depends a great deal on it. It's much more difficult to repair a neglected or damaged body than it is to repair mechanical components. The hidden areas of the body, such as the wheel wells, the frame and the engine compartment, are equally important, although they don't require as frequent attention as the rest of the body.

2 Once a year, or every 12,000 miles, it's a good idea to have the underside of the body steam-cleaned. All traces of dirt and oil will be removed and the area can then be inspected carefully for rust, damaged brake lines, frayed electrical wires, damaged cables and other problems.

3 At the same time, clean the engine and the engine compartment with a steam cleaner or water-soluble degreaser.

4 The wheel wells should be given close attention, since undercoating can peel away and stones and dirt thrown up by the tires can cause the paint to chip and flake, allowing rust to set in. If rust is found, clean down to the bare metal and apply an anti-rust paint.

5 The body should be washed about once a week. Wet the vehicle thoroughly to soften the dirt, and then wash it down with a soft sponge and plenty of clean soapy water. If the surplus dirt is not washed off very carefully, it can wear down the paint.

6 Spots of tar or asphalt thrown up from the road should be removed with a cloth soaked in kerosene. Scented lamp oil is available in most hardware stores and the smell is easier to work with than straight kerosene.

7 Once every six months, wax the body and chrome trim. If chrome cleaner is used to remove rust from any of the vehicle's plated parts, remember that the cleaner also removes part of the chrome, so use it sparingly. On any plated parts where chrome cleaner is used, use a good paste wax over the plating for extra protection.

3 Vinyl trim - maintenance

Don't clean vinyl trim with detergents, caustic soap or petroleum-based cleaners. Plain soap and water works just fine, with a soft brush to clean dirt that may be ingrained. Wash the vinyl as frequently as the rest of the vehicle.

After cleaning, application of a high quality rubber and vinyl protectant will help prevent oxidation and cracks. The protectant can also be applied to weather stripping, vacuum lines and rubber hoses, which often fail as a result of chemical degradation, and to the tires.

4 Upholstery and carpets - maintenance

1 Every three months, remove the floormats and clean the interior of the vehicle (more frequently if necessary). Use a stiff whisk broom to brush the carpeting and loosen dirt and dust, and then vacuum the upholstery and carpets thoroughly, especially along seams and crevices.

2 Dirt and stains can be removed from carpeting with basic household or automotive carpet shampoos available in spray cans. Follow the directions and vacuum again, then use a stiff brush to bring back the nap of the carpet.

3 Most interiors have cloth or vinyl upholstery, either of which can be cleaned and maintained with a number of material-specific cleaners or shampoos available in auto supply stores. Follow the directions on the product for usage, and always spot-test any upholstery cleaner on an inconspicuous area (bottom edge of a backseat cushion) to ensure

that it doesn't cause a color shift in the material.

4   After cleaning, vinyl upholstery should be treated with a protectant.

➡**Note: Make sure the protectant container indicates the product can be used on seats - some products may make a seat too slippery.**

❊❊ **CAUTION:**

Do not use protectant on steering wheels.

5   Leather upholstery requires special care. It should be cleaned regularly with saddlesoap or leather cleaner. Never use alcohol, gasoline, nail polish remover or thinner to clean leather upholstery.

6   After cleaning, regularly treat leather upholstery with a leather conditioner, rubbed in with a soft cotton cloth. Never use car wax on leather upholstery.

7   In areas where the interior of the vehicle is subject to bright sunlight, cover leather seating areas of the seats with a sheet if the vehicle is to be left out for any length of time.

5   Body repair - minor damage

FLEXIBLE PLASTIC BODY PANELS (FRONT AND REAR BUMPER FASCIA)

The following repair procedures are for minor scratches and gouges. Repair of more serious damage should be left to a dealer service department or qualified auto body shop. Below is a list of the equipment and materials necessary to perform the following repair procedures on plastic body panels. Although a specific brand of material may be mentioned, it should be noted that equivalent products from other manufacturers may be used instead.

   Wax, grease and silicone removing solvent
   Cloth-backed body tape
   Sanding discs
   Drill motor with three-inch disc holder
   Hand sanding block
   Rubber squeegees
   Sandpaper
   Non-porous mixing palette
   Wood paddle or putty knife
   Curved-tooth body file
   Flexible parts repair material

1   Remove the damaged panel, if necessary or desirable. In most cases, repairs can be carried out with the panel installed.

2   Clean the area(s) to be repaired with a wax, grease and silicone removing solvent applied with a water-dampened cloth.

3   If the damage is structural, that is, if it extends through the panel, clean the backside of the panel area to be repaired as well. Wipe dry.

4   Sand the rear surface about 1-1/2 inches beyond the break.

5   Cut two pieces of fiberglass cloth large enough to overlap the break by about 1-1/2 inches. Cut only to the required length.

6   Mix the adhesive from the repair kit according to the instructions included with the kit, and apply a layer of the mixture approximately 1/8-inch thick on the backside of the panel. Overlap the break by at least 1-1/2 inches.

7   Apply one piece of fiberglass cloth to the adhesive and cover the cloth with additional adhesive. Apply a second piece of fiberglass cloth to the adhesive and immediately cover the cloth with additional adhesive in sufficient quantity to fill the weave.

8   Allow the repair to cure for 20 to 30 minutes at 60-degrees to 80-degrees F.

9   If necessary, trim the excess repair material at the edge.

10   Remove all of the paint film over and around the area(s) to be repaired. The repair material should not overlap the painted surface.

11   With a drill motor and a sanding disc (or a rotary file), cut a V along the break line approximately 1/2-inch wide. Remove all dust and loose particles from the repair area.

12   Mix and apply the repair material. Apply a light coat first over the damaged area; then continue applying material until it reaches a level slightly higher than the surrounding finish.

13   Cure the mixture for 20 to 30 minutes at 60-degrees to 80-degrees F.

14   Roughly establish the contour of the area being repaired with a body file. If low areas or pits remain, mix and apply additional adhesive.

15   Block sand the damaged area with sandpaper to establish the actual contour of the surrounding surface.

16   If desired, the repaired area can be temporarily protected with several light coats of primer. Because of the special paints and techniques required for flexible body panels, it is recommended that the vehicle be taken to a paint shop for completion of the body repair.

STEEL BODY PANELS

◆ **See photo sequence**

Repair of minor scratches

17   If the scratch is superficial and does not penetrate to the metal of the body, repair is very simple. Lightly rub the scratched area with a fine rubbing compound to remove loose paint and built up wax. Rinse the area with clean water.

18   Apply touch-up paint to the scratch, using a small brush. Continue to apply thin layers of paint until the surface of the paint in the scratch is level with the surrounding paint. Allow the new paint at least two weeks to harden, and then blend it into the surrounding paint by rubbing with a very fine rubbing compound. Finally, apply a coat of wax to the scratch area.

19   If the scratch has penetrated the paint and exposed the metal of the body, causing the metal to rust, a different repair technique is required. Remove all loose rust from the bottom of the scratch with a pocket knife, and then apply rust inhibiting paint to prevent the formation of rust in the future. Using a rubber or nylon applicator, coat the scratched area with glaze-type filler. If required, the filler can be mixed with thinner to provide a very thin paste, which is ideal for filling narrow scratches. Before the glaze filler in the scratch hardens, wrap a piece of smooth cotton cloth around the tip of a finger. Dip the cloth in thinner and then quickly wipe it along the surface of the scratch. This will ensure that the surface of the filler is slightly hollow. The scratch can now be painted over as described earlier in this Section.

These photos illustrate a method of repairing simple dents. They are intended to supplement Body repair - minor damage in this Chapter and should not be used as the sole instructions for body repair on these vehicles.

1 If you can't access the backside of the body panel to hammer out the dent, pull it out with a slide-hammer-type dent puller. In the deepest portion of the dent or along the crease line, drill or punch hole(s) at least one inch apart . . .

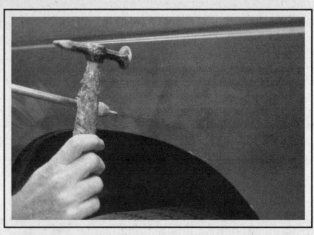

2 . . . then screw the slide-hammer into the hole and operate it. Tap with a hammer near the edge of the dent to help 'pop' the metal back to its original shape. When you're finished, the dent area should be close to its original contour and about 1/8-inch below the surface of the surrounding metal

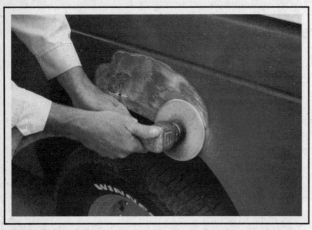

3 Using coarse-grit sandpaper, remove the paint down to the bare metal. Hand sanding works fine, but the disc sander shown here makes the job faster. Use finer (about 320-grit) sandpaper to feather-edge the paint at least one inch around the dent area

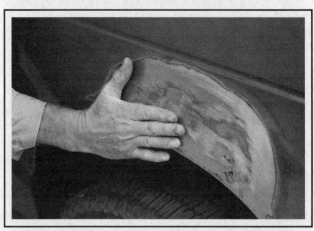

4 When the paint is removed, touch will probably be more helpful than sight for telling if the metal is straight. Hammer down the high spots or raise the low spots as necessary. Clean the repair area with wax/silicone remover

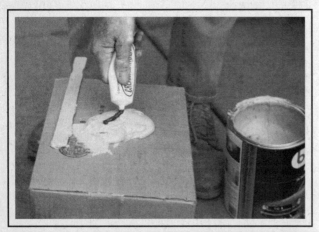

5 Following label instructions, mix up a batch of plastic filler and hardener. The ratio of filler to hardener is critical, and, if you mix it incorrectly, it will either not cure properly or cure too quickly (you won't have time to file and sand it into shape)

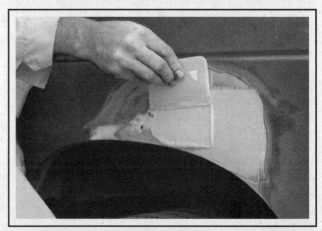

6 Working quickly so the filler doesn't harden, use a plastic applicator to press the body filler firmly into the metal, assuring it bonds completely. Work the filler until it matches the original contour and is slightly above the surrounding metal

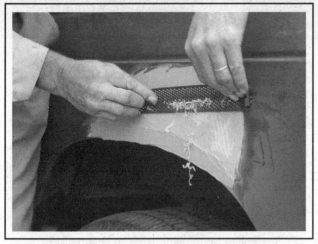

7 Let the filler harden until you can just dent it with your fingernail. Use a body file or Surform tool (shown here) to rough-shape the filler

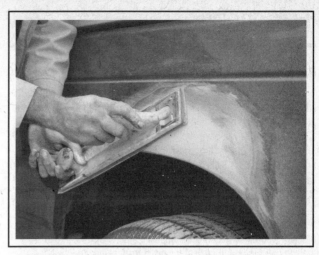

8 Use coarse-grit sandpaper and a sanding board or block to work the filler down until it's smooth and even. Work down to finer grits of sandpaper - always using a board or block - ending up with 360 or 400 grit

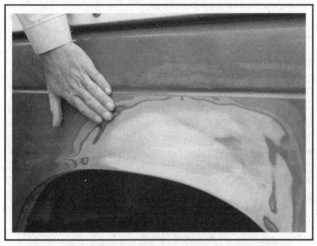

9 You shouldn't be able to feel any ridge at the transition from the filler to the bare metal or from the bare metal to the old paint. As soon as the repair is flat and uniform, remove the dust and mask off the adjacent panels or trim pieces

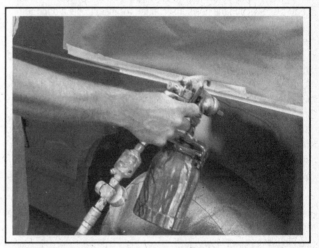

10 Apply several layers of primer to the area. Don't spray the primer on too heavy, so it sags or runs, and make sure each coat is dry before you spray on the next one. A professional-type spray gun is being used here, but aerosol spray primer is available inexpensively from auto parts stores

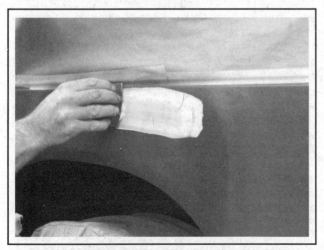

11 The primer will help reveal imperfections or scratches. Fill these with glazing compound. Follow the label instructions and sand it with 360 or 400-grit sandpaper until it's smooth. Repeat the glazing, sanding and respraying until the primer reveals a perfectly smooth surface

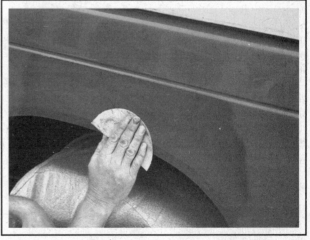

12 Finish sand the primer with very fine sandpaper (400 or 600-grit) to remove the primer overspray. Clean the area with water and allow it to dry. Use a tack rag to remove any dust, then apply the finish coat. Don't attempt to rub out or wax the repair area until the paint has dried completely (at least two weeks)

Repair of dents

20 When repairing dents, the first job is to pull the dent out until the affected area is as close as possible to its original shape. There is no point in trying to restore the original shape completely as the metal in the damaged area will have stretched on impact and cannot be restored to its original contours. It is better to bring the level of the dent up to a point that is about 1/8-inch below the level of the surrounding metal. In cases where the dent is very shallow, it is not worth trying to pull it out at all.

21 If the back side of the dent is accessible, it can be hammered out gently from behind using a soft-face hammer. While doing this, hold a block of wood firmly against the opposite side of the metal to absorb the hammer blows and prevent the metal from being stretched.

22 If the dent is in a section of the body that has double layers, or some other factor makes it inaccessible from behind, a different technique is required. Drill several small holes through the metal inside the damaged area, particularly in the deeper sections. Screw long, self-tapping screws into the holes just enough for them to get a good grip in the metal. Now the dent can be pulled out by pulling on the protruding heads of the screws with locking pliers.

23 The next stage of repair is the removal of paint from the damaged area and from an inch or so of the surrounding metal. This is easily done with a wire brush or sanding disk in a drill motor, although it can be done just as effectively by hand with sandpaper. To complete the preparation for filling, score the surface of the bare metal with a screwdriver or the tang of a file or drill small holes in the affected area. This will provide a good grip for the filler material. To complete the repair, see the Section on filling and painting.

Repair of rust holes or gashes

24 Remove all paint from the affected area and from an inch or so of the surrounding metal using a sanding disk or wire brush mounted in a drill motor. If these are not available, a few sheets of sandpaper will do the job just as effectively.

25 With the paint removed, you will be able to determine the severity of the corrosion and decide whether to replace the whole panel, if possible, or repair the affected area. New body panels are not as expensive as most people think and it is often quicker to install a new panel than to repair large areas of rust.

26 Remove all trim pieces from the affected area except those which will act as a guide to the original shape of the damaged body, such as headlight shells, etc. Using metal snips or a hacksaw blade, remove all loose metal and any other metal that is badly affected by rust. Hammer the edges of the hole in to create a slight depression for the filler material.

27 Wire brush the affected area to remove the powdery rust from the surface of the metal. If the back of the rusted area is accessible, treat it with rust inhibiting paint.

28 Before filling is done, block the hole in some way. This can be done with sheet metal riveted or screwed into place, or by stuffing the hole with wire mesh.

29 Once the hole is blocked off, the affected area can be filled and painted. See the following subsection on filling and painting.

Filling and painting

30 Many types of body fillers are available, but generally speaking, body repair kits which contain filler paste and a tube of resin hardener are best for this type of repair work. A wide, flexible plastic or nylon applicator will be necessary for imparting a smooth and contoured finish to the surface of the filler material. Mix up a small amount of filler on a clean piece of wood or cardboard (use the hardener sparingly). Follow the manufacturer's instructions on the package, otherwise the filler will set incorrectly.

31 Using the applicator, apply the filler paste to the prepared area. Draw the applicator across the surface of the filler to achieve the desired contour and to level the filler surface. As soon as a contour that approximates the original one is achieved, stop working the paste. If you continue, the paste will begin to stick to the applicator. Continue to add thin layers of paste at 20-minute intervals until the level of the filler is just above the surrounding metal.

32 Once the filler has hardened, the excess can be removed with a body file. From then on, progressively finer grades of sandpaper should be used, starting with a 180-grit paper and finishing with 600-grit wet-or-dry paper. Always wrap the sandpaper around a flat rubber or wooden block, otherwise the surface of the filler will not be completely flat. During the sanding of the filler surface, the wet-or-dry paper should be periodically rinsed in water. This will ensure that a very smooth finish is produced in the final stage.

33 At this point, the repair area should be surrounded by a ring of bare metal, which in turn should be encircled by the finely feathered edge of good paint. Rinse the repair area with clean water until all of the dust produced by the sanding operation is gone.

34 Spray the entire area with a light coat of primer. This will reveal any imperfections in the surface of the filler. Repair the imperfections with fresh filler paste or glaze filler and once more smooth the surface with sandpaper. Repeat this spray-and-repair procedure until you are satisfied that the surface of the filler and the feathered edge of the paint are perfect. Rinse the area with clean water and allow it to dry completely.

35 The repair area is now ready for painting. Spray painting must be carried out in a warm, dry, windless and dust free atmosphere. These conditions can be created if you have access to a large indoor work area, but if you are forced to work in the open, you will have to pick the day very carefully. If you are working indoors, dousing the floor in the work area with water will help settle the dust that would otherwise be in the air. If the repair area is confined to one body panel, mask off the surrounding panels. This will help minimize the effects of a slight mismatch in paint color. Trim pieces such as chrome strips, door handles, etc., will also need to be masked off or removed. Use masking tape and several thickness of newspaper for the masking operations.

36 Before spraying, shake the paint can thoroughly, and then spray a test area until the spray-painting technique is mastered. Cover the repair area with a thick coat of primer. The thickness should be built up using several thin layers of primer rather than one thick one. Using 600-grit wet-or-dry sandpaper, rub down the surface of the primer until it is very smooth. While doing this, the work area should be thoroughly rinsed with water and the wet-or-dry sandpaper periodically rinsed as well. Allow the primer to dry before spraying additional coats.

37 Spray on the top coat, again building up the thickness by using several thin layers of paint. Begin spraying in the center of the repair area and then, using a circular motion, work out until the whole repair area and about two inches of the surrounding original paint is covered. Remove all masking material 10 to 15 minutes after spraying on the final coat of paint. Allow the new paint at least two weeks to harden, then use a very fine rubbing compound to blend the edges of the new paint into the existing paint. Finally, apply a coat of wax.

6 Body repair - major damage

1   Major damage must be repaired by an auto body shop specifically equipped to perform unibody repairs. These shops have the specialized equipment required to do the job properly.

2   If the damage is extensive, the body must be checked for proper alignment or the vehicle's handling characteristics may be adversely affected and other components may wear at an accelerated rate.

3   Due to the fact that some of the major body components (hood, fenders, doors, etc.) are separate and replaceable units, any seriously damaged components should be replaced rather than repaired. Sometimes the components can be found in a wrecking yard that specializes in used vehicle components, often at considerable savings over the cost of new parts.

7 Hinges and locks - maintenance

Once every 3000 miles, or every three months, the hinges and latch assemblies on the doors, hood and trunk should be given a few drops of light oil or lock lubricant. The door latch strikers should also be lubricated with a thin coat of grease to reduce wear and ensure free movement. Lubricate the door and trunk locks with spray-on graphite lubricant.

8 Hood - removal, installation and adjustment

➡**Note: The hood is heavy and somewhat awkward to remove and install. At least two people should perform this procedure.**

REMOVAL AND INSTALLATION

♦ **Refer to illustration 8.2**

1   Use blankets or pads to cover the cowl area of the body and the fenders. This will protect the body and paint as the hood is lifted off.

2   Scribe or paint alignment marks around the bolt heads to insure proper alignment during installation (see illustration).

3   Disconnect any cables or wire harnesses which will interfere with removal.

4   Have an assistant support the weight of the hood. Remove the hinge-to-hood nuts or bolts.

5   Lift off the hood.

6   Installation is the reverse of removal.

ADJUSTMENT

♦ **Refer to illustration 8.10**

7   Fore-and-aft and side-to-side adjustment of the hood is done by moving the hood in relation to the hinge plate after loosening the bolts or nuts.

8   Scribe a line around the entire hinge plate so you can judge the amount of movement (see illustration 8.2).

9   Loosen the bolts or nuts and move the hood into correct alignment. Move it only a little at a time. Tighten the hinge bolts or nuts and carefully lower the hood to check the alignment.

10 If necessary after installation, the entire hood latch assembly can be adjusted up-and-down as well as from side-to-side on the radiator support so the hood closes securely and is flush with the fenders. To do this, scribe a line around the hood latch mounting bolts to provide a reference point. Then loosen the bolts and nut and reposition the latch assembly as necessary. Following adjustment, retighten the mounting bolts and nut (see illustration).

11 The hood latch assembly, as well as the hinges, should be periodically lubricated with white lithium-base grease to prevent sticking and wear.

8.2 Mark around the hood hinges so the hood can be aligned easily during installation

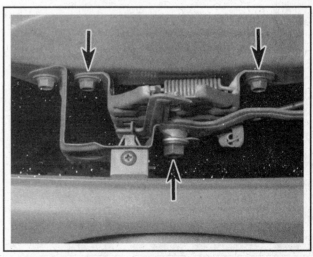

8.10 The hood latch is secured by two bolts and a nut (arrows)

9 Hood latch and cable - removal and installation

▶ **Refer to illustration 9.5**

1   Remove the hood latch bolts and nut (see illustration 8.10).
2   Remove the cable retaining clip to detach the cable from the latch. Take the latch out.
3   Follow the cable through the engine compartment and wheel well, disconnecting the cable retainers as you go.
4   Securely attach a length of mechanic's wire to the end of the cable.

➡ **Note: Be sure the wire is securely attached. If it falls off, it will be difficult or impossible to route the new cable.**

5   Loosen the nut and detach the cable housing from the dash (see illustration). Pull the cable into the passenger compartment.
6   Attach the mechanic's wire to the latch end of the new cable.
7   Pull on the wire to guide the new cable into position.
8   The remainder of installation is the reverse of the removal steps.

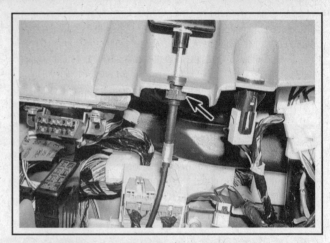

9.5 Loosen the nut and slip the cable off the dash

10 Doors - removal, installation and adjustment

REMOVAL AND INSTALLATION

▶ **Refer to illustrations 10.1 and 10.2**

➡ **Note: This procedure requires two people.**

1   Open the door. Tap the door checker pin out of its fitting (see illustration).

2   Carefully pull the rubber conduit away from the body. Pry the electrical connector out of the body, then disconnect it (see illustration).
3   Support the door with a jack padded with rags.
4   Have an assistant balance the door on the jack and remove the hinge-to-door bolts.
5   Lift the door off.
6   Installation is the reverse of the removal steps. If necessary, adjust the door.

10.1 The door checker pin prevents the door from opening too far - tap it out of its fitting to remove the door

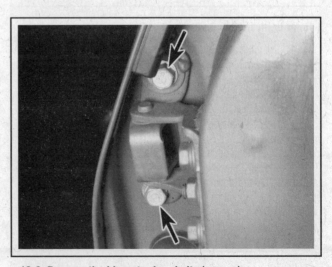

10.2 Remove the hinge-to-door bolts (arrows)

ADJUSTMENT

◆ **Refer to illustration 10.7**

7 Open the door. Loosen the hinge-to-body bolts (and nut on upper hinges) just enough to allow movement (see illustration).

8 Align the door with the body, then tighten the hinge-to-body bolts.

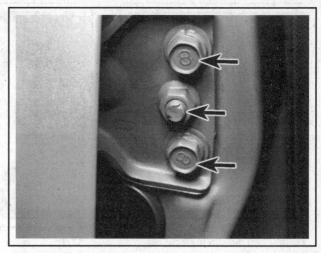

10.7 To adjust the door, loosen the hinge-to-body bolts (upper hinges also have a nut)

11 Door trim panel - removal and installation

◆ **Refer to illustrations 11.1a, 11.1b, 11.3a, 11.3b, 11.3c, 11.3d, 11.4a, 11.4b, 11.6, 11.7 and 11.9**

1 If you're working on a vehicle with manual windows, slip a clean rag behind the window crank and hook the clip (see illustration). Pull the clip off the crank and slide the crank off the shaft. Find the clip and put it back on the crank (see illustration).

2 If you're working on a vehicle with power windows, remove the window switch and disconnect the electrical connector.

3 Remove the screw that secures the inside door handle (see illustration). Carefully pry the handle trim away from the door, disengage the handle rod and take the handle out (see illustrations).

4 Remove the arm rest screws (see illustrations). Don't try to take the arm rest off separately; it's part of the door panel.

5 If you're working on a 1997 or later coupe, pry out the trim covers from the panel screws (two at the leading edge of the door and one at the trailing edge) and remove the screws.

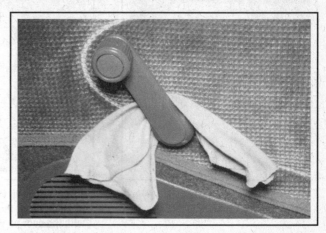

11.1a Slip a cloth behind the window crank and hook the clip

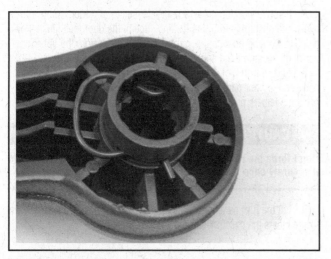

11.1b Locate the clip (it may fall on the floor) and put it back on the window crank

11.3a Remove the screw and pull out the door handle . . .

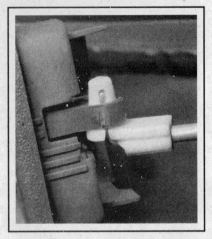

11.3b . . . if the clip is plastic like this one . . .

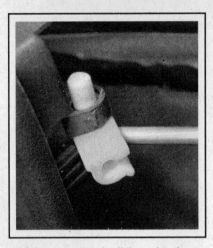

11.3c . . . rotate it off the rod and detach the rod

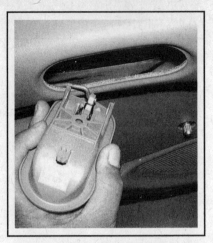

11.3d Later models don't use a clip; simply twist the handle off the "Z" portion of the bar

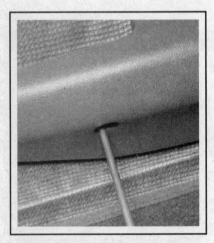

11.4a The arm rest screws may be in the side of the arm rest like this . . .

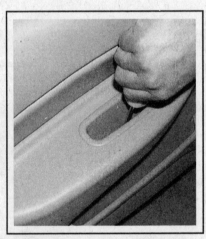

11.4b . . . or in the bottom like this; in either case, the arm rest comes off with the door panel

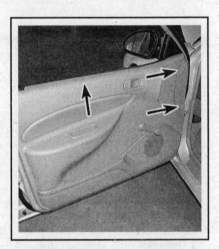

11.6 Door trim master locator (at top center) and push-pin locations

11.7 The retainers will pop out of the door if pried carefully; don't pry too hard or they'll tear out of the panel

6   If you're working on a 1997 or later sedan or wagon, remove the two-piece push pins from the leading edge of the door (see illustration). If you're working on a coupe, remove one push pin from the upper corner of the leading edge and two from the trailing edge.

7   Slide a trim tool, a wide-bladed screwdriver or a putty knife between the door panel and door, next to each retainer in turn. Carefully pry the retainers out of the door (see illustration).

✳✳ CAUTION:

Don't force the retainers out of the trim panel, or they won't hold it securely once it's installed.

8   Lift the trim panel and slide it rearward so the upper bolster down flange clears the sheet metal on the door.

9   If you need access to the door mechanism, carefully peel back the weather sheet (see illustration). If necessary, remove the radio speaker so the sheet can be peeled off completely (see Chapter 12).

10 Installation is the reverse of the removal steps, with the following additions:

a) *If the weather sheet won't fasten securely with the original sealer, reinforce it with duct tape.*

b) *Be sure the master locator is in its hole at the top center of the door (see illustration 11.6).*

c) *When installing a manual window crank, put the clip on the crank first, then push the crank onto the shaft until the clip locks into position.*

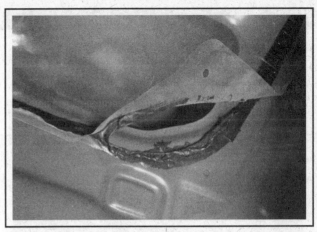

11.9 To avoid tearing the weather sheet, slip a putty knife along the sealer as you pull the sheet away (note that there's a strand of wire embedded in the sealer)

12 Door lock - removal and installation

▶ **Refer to illustrations 12.2a and 12.2b**

1   Remove the door trim panel and weather sheet (see Section 11).
2   Remove the lock cylinder retaining clip and detach the linkage

rod from the lock cylinder (see illustrations).
3   Pull the lock cylinder out of the door from the outside.
4   Installation is the reverse of the removal steps.

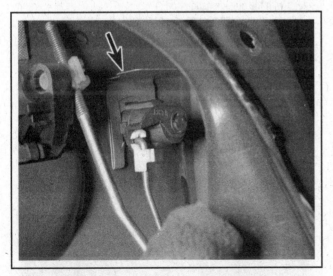

12.2a On 1996 and earlier models, pull out the retaining clip (arrow), rotate the plastic clip off the linkage rod, detach the rod from the cylinder and remove the cylinder from the door

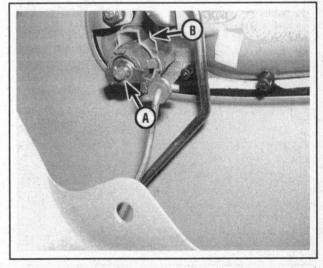

12.2b On 1997 and later models, remove the E-clip (A) from the lock cylinder, then remove the retaining clip (B) and remove the lock cylinder from the door handle

13 Outside handle - removal and installation

▶ **Refer to illustrations 13.2a and 13.2b**

1   Remove the door trim panel and weather sheet (see Section 11).

2   Remove the retaining clip and detach the lock rod from the handle (see illustrations). On 1997 and later models, also detach the lever from the lock cylinder.

3   Remove the handle mounting nuts and take the handle out of the door.

4   Installation is the reverse of he removal steps.

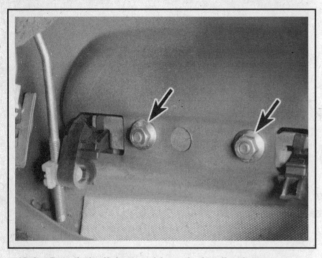

13.2a Detach the linkage rod from the handle, then remove the mounting nuts (arrows) - 1996 and earlier models

13.2b Door handle mounting nuts - 1997 and later models

14 Door latch assembly - removal and installation

FRONT DOORS

▶ **Refer to illustration 14.6**

1   Remove the door trim panel and weather sheet (see Section 11). If you're working on a 1997 or later model, remove the access cover screws and take the cover off the door latch access hole.

2   Detach the outside handle rod from the handle.

3   Disconnect the lock rod from the latch and remove the rod through the top of the door.

4   Disconnect the lock cylinder rod from the lock cylinder (see illustration 12.2a or 12.2b).

5   If you're working on a vehicle with power door locks, disconnect the actuator rod from the latch and disconnect the power lock electrical connector.

6   Remove the latch mounting screws (see illustration). Take the latch out of the door together with the inside and outside handle rods and lock cylinder rod.

7   Installation is the reverse of the removal steps.

REAR DOORS

8   Remove the door trim panel and weather sheet (see Section 11).

9   Disconnect the bellcrank rod from the latch and lower the rod to the bottom of the door (see illustration).

10 If you're working on vehicle with power door locks, disconnect the lock actuator rod from the latch.

11 Remove the latch mounting screws. Take the latch out of the door together with the outside handle rod.

12 Installation is the reverse of the removal steps.

14.6 These three screws secure the latch to the door (1996 and earlier models)

15 Power door lock actuator - removal and installation

1   Remove the door trim panel and weather sheet (see Section 11).
2   Disconnect the power lock actuator rod from the latch and disconnect the electrical connector.

3   Unbolt the actuator from the door and take it out.
4   Installation is the reverse of the removal steps.

16 Door latch striker - removal, installation and adjustment

▶ **Refer to illustration 16.1**

1   Remove the striker screws with a Torx bit and take the striker off (see illustration).
2   Installation is the reverse of the removal procedure with the following additions:
3   The striker can be adjusted vertically and side to side.
4   Don't use the door latch striker to compensate for door misalignment.
5   Before adjusting the striker, make sure the door opens and closes easily and isn't loose.
6   Check door alignment along the rear edge. Adjust the striker side to side if the door closes too far or not far enough.

16.1 The door latch striker is secured by Torx screws

17 Front door window glass - removal and installation

▶ **Refer to illustration 17.4**

1   If you're working on a 1991 through 1996 model, raise the window 4-5/16 inch from the fully open position. If you're working on a 1997 or later model, open the window all the way.
2   Disconnect the negative cable from the battery.
3   Remove the door trim panel and weather sheet (see Section 11).
4   Remove the glass retaining screws (see illustration).
5   Tilt the front end of the glass down, separate it from the channel and lift it out of the door.
6   Installation is the reverse of the removal steps.

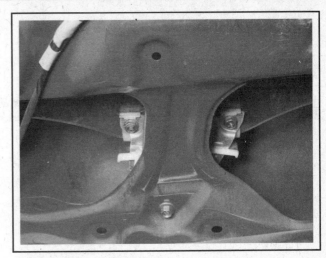

17.4 Remove the glass retaining screws (the glass will remain resting on the support clips)

18 Front door window regulator - removal and installation

MANUAL WINDOWS

Removal

▶ **Refer to illustrations 18.2 and 18.3**

1   Remove the front door glass (see Section 17).
2   Remove two nuts and one screw that secure the regulator (see illustration).
3   Remove the regulator drive nuts (see illustration).
4   Remove the regulator through the access hole in the bottom of the door.

Installation

5   Rotate the regulator drive unit so the gray cable is toward the glass and the black cable is toward the inner door panel.
6   Insert the regulator into the access hole in the bottom of the door. Install the regulator drive nuts, then the regulator nuts and screw.
7   The remainder of installation is the reverse of the removal steps.

POWER WINDOWS

8   Remove the front door glass (see Section 17).
9   Detach the retainers that secure the electrical harness conduit to the door. Disconnect the electrical connector.
10 Remove the upper nuts and lower bolts that secure the regulator to the door, then remove the regulator through the access hole.
11 Installation is the reverse of the removal steps.

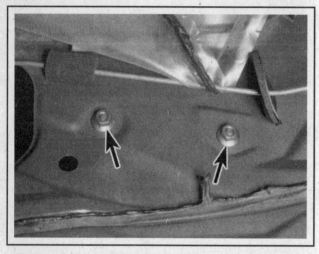

18.2 The manual window regulator is secured by two nuts (arrows) and a screw

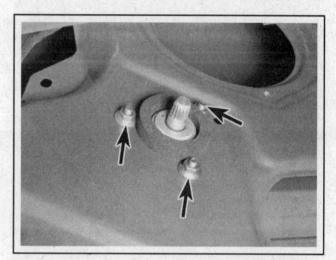

18.3 The regulator drive is secured by three nuts (arrows)

19 Rear door window glass - removal and installation

1   Open the rear window all the way.
2   Disconnect the negative cable from the battery.
3   Remove the door trim panel and weather sheet (see Section 11).
4   Detach the weatherstrip from the top of the door.
5   Unscrew both retainers. Remove the center channel and division bar.
6   Remove the regulator roller through the large hole in the lift bracket. Tilt the window and remove it from the door.
7   If necessary, pull the fixed window out of its channel and remove it.
8   Installation is the reverse of the removal steps.

20 Rear window regulator - removal and installation

◆ **Refer to illustration 20.3**

1   Remove the rear door window (see Section 19).
2   If you're working on a vehicle with power windows, disconnect the electrical connector.
3   Remove the regulator mounting bolts (see illustration). Lower the regulator and remove it through the access hole.
4   Installation is the reverse of the removal steps.

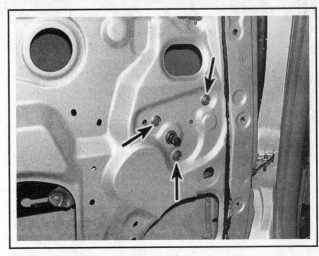

20.3a Rear door regulator mounting details (manual windows)

21 Fixed glass - replacement

Replacement of the windshield and fixed glass requires the use of special fast-setting adhesive/caulk materials and some specialized tools and techniques. These operations should be left to a dealer service department or a shop specializing in glass work.

22 Deck lid - removal, installation and adjustment

REMOVAL AND INSTALLATION

◆ **Refer to illustration 22.3**

➡**Note: This procedure requires two people.**

1   Open the deck lid. Place a thick layer of rags between the deck lid and the body.
2   Separate the deck lid release cable from the deck lid and hinge. Disconnect the electrical connectors and separate the wiring harness from the hinge.
3   Mark the locations of the hinges on the deck lid (see illustration).
4   While an assistant helps support the deck lid, remove the hinge bolts. Take the deck lid off.
5   Installation is the reverse of the removal steps.

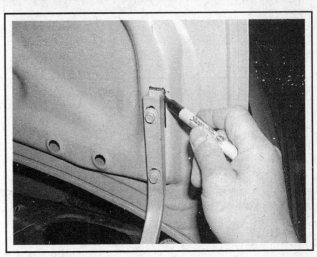

22.3 Mark the hinge locations, then unbolt the hinges while an assistant supports the deck lid

ADJUSTMENT

▶ **Refer to illustration 22.9**

6 Loosen the deck lid hinges just enough so the lid can be moved.
7 Close the deck lid and check its alignment with the body.
8 Reposition the deck until it's correctly aligned, then tighten the hinge bolts.
9 To align the deck lid vertically with the fenders, loosen the latch striker bolts (see illustration). Move the striker as needed and tighten the bolts.

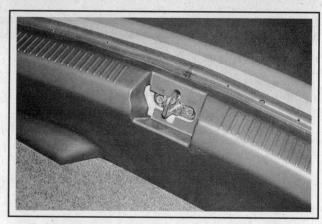

22.9 The deck lid latch striker is used to make vertical adjustments

23 Deck lid latch - removal and installation

▶ **Refer to illustrations 23.1 and 23.2**

1 Remove the deck lid latch cover (see illustration).
2 Detach the control link rod from the latch (see illustration). Remove the latch mounting bolts.

3 If you're working on a 1996 or earlier model, detach the release cable from the latch. If you're working on a 1997 or later model, unplug the electrical connector. Take the latch out.
4 Installation is the reverse of the removal steps.

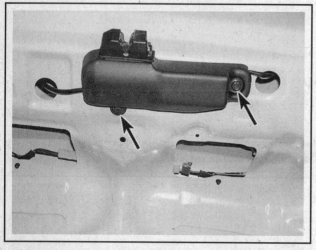

23.1 Remove the deck lid latch cover (1997 and later models shown)

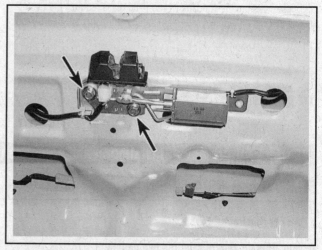

23.2 Disconnect the control link rod and remove the mounting bolts

24 Deck lid release cable (1996 and earlier models only) - removal and installation

1 Remove trim panels as needed to gain access to the cable.
2 Remove the latch (see Section 23).
3 Separate the cable from the clips, detach it from the release lever

and take it out.
4 Installation is the reverse of the removal steps.

25 Deck lid lock cylinder - removal and installation

▶ **Refer to illustration 25.2**

1   Open the deck lid.
2   Disconnect the control link rod from the lock cylinder (see illustration). Slide the retainer out and remove the lock cylinder from the outside.
3   Installation is the reverse of the removal steps.

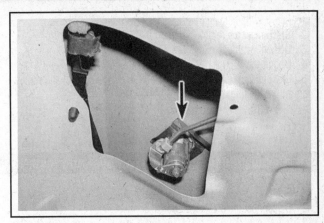

25.2 Detach the rod clip and pull out the retainer (arrow), then remove the lock cylinder

26 Liftgate trim panel - removal and installation

▶ **Refer to illustration 26.1**

1   Open the liftgate. Remove three push-in retainers that secure the high-mount brake light (if equipped) (see illustration).
2   Remove the seaming welt from the edge of the trim panel.
3   Detach the trim panel retainers if equipped, then lift the panel off the liftgate.
4   If necessary, remove the luggage compartment lamp.
5   Installation is the reverse of the removal steps. Be sure the seaming welt covers the flange on the upper edge of the trim panel.

26.1 To remove the push-in retainers, catch the edges of the center pin with fingernails and pull it out; the retainer can then be lifted out of the panel - to reinstall, place the retainer in the hole, then push in the center pin

27 Liftgate - removal, installation and adjustment

REMOVAL AND INSTALLATION

➡ **Note: This procedure requires two people.**

1   Remove the upper and lower quarter trim panels and the rear header trim.
2   Disconnect the liftgate electrical connector, then detach the wiring harness from the vehicle. Work the wiring harness through the hole in the upper part of the liftgate opening. This separates it from the body so it can be removed with the liftgate.
3   If the vehicle has a rear washer, lower the headliner and disconnect the hose.
4   While an assistant supports the liftgate, detach the gas struts.
5   Scribe marks around the hinges onto the liftgate for use during installation.

6   Remove the hinge-to-liftgate bolts and take the liftgate off. Installation is the reverse of removal.

ADJUSTMENT

7   Loosen the hinge-to-liftgate bolts just enough so the liftgate can be moved.
8   Align the liftgate with the body, then tighten the bolts.
9   With the liftgate properly aligned, remove the lower sill trim panel to expose the striker bolts.
10 Reposition the striker to obtain a flush fit between the liftgate and body, then tighten the bolts.

28 Liftgate latch and outside handle - removal and installation

1 Remove the tailgate trim panel (see Section 26).
2 Disconnect the remote control rod from the remote control.
3 Disconnect the negative cable from the battery.
4 Unbolt the latch and remove the remote control.
5 Disconnect the lock knob rod from the remote control and remove the rod from the liftgate.

6 Disconnect the lock cylinder rod from the lock cylinder.
7 Unbolt the remote control and remove it from the liftgate.
8 Remove two nuts that secure the outside handle and take it out of the liftgate.
9 Installation is the reverse of the removal steps.

29 Power liftgate actuator - removal and installation

1 Remove the liftgate trim panel (see Section 26).
2 Disconnect the actuator electrical connector.
3 If you're working on a 1996 or earlier model, remove the actuator mounting bolts and take it out. On 1997 and later models, one of the

actuator mounting bolts secures a ground wire.
4 Installation is the reverse of the removal steps. If you're working on a 1997 or later model, don't forget to reinstall the ground wire.

30 Hatchback trim panel - removal and installation

1 Remove the push-in retainers (see Section 26 for details).
2 Remove the cover from the high-mount brake light.
3 Detach the panel retaining clips and remove the panel from the hatchback.

4 Installation is the reverse of the removal steps.

31 Hatchback - removal, installation and adjustment

➡**Note: This procedure requires two people.**

REMOVAL AND INSTALLATION

◆ **Refer to illustrations 31.2 and 31.4**

1 Disconnect the package shelf cords from the hatchback and

remove the right upper quarter trim panel.
2 Separate the wiring harness from the body. Work the harness through the hole in the top of the hatchback opening (see illustration).
3 Mark the outline of the hinges on the hatchback for use during installation.
4 While an assistant supports the hatch, detach the support struts (see illustration).

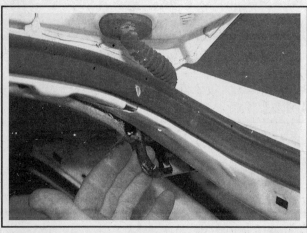

31.2 Separate the harness from the body and work it through the hole in the top of the hatchback opening

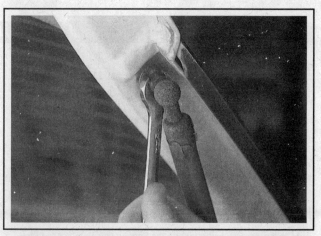

31.4 Be sure to have an assistant support the hatchback while you loosen the nuts and disconnect the gas support struts - the hatchback is quite heavy without their support

5   With the assistant still supporting the hatch, remove the hinge-to-hatchback bolts and lift the hatchback off.

6   Installation is the reverse of the removal steps.

ADJUSTMENT

▶ **Refer to illustration 31.9**

7   Loosen the hinge-to-hatchback bolts just enough so the hatchback can be moved.

8   Align the hatchback with the opening. Once it's correctly aligned, tighten the bolts.

9   With the hatchback correctly aligned, loosen the latch bolts (see illustration). Move the latch from side-to-side to align it with the striker. Move it up or down so the hatchback is flush with the body when it's closed.

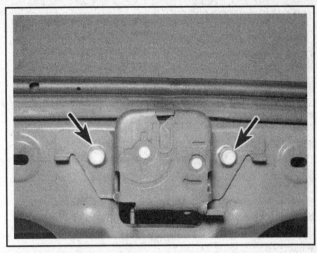

31.9 The hatchback latch is secured by two bolts (arrows)

32 Hatchback latch - removal and installation

1   Remove the trim panel from the rear end of the luggage compartment.

2   Detach the link rod from the latch.

3   Unbolt the latch and take it out (see illustration 31.9).

4   Install the latch and tighten its bolts just enough so the latch can be moved for adjustment.

5   Adjust the latch (see Section 31).

6   The remainder of installation is the reverse of the removal steps.

33 Hatchback release cable - removal and installation

1   Disconnect the negative cable from the battery.

2   Remove interior trim panels as needed to gain access to the cable.

3   Remove the latch (see Section 32).

4   Detach the release cable from the lever and release it from its clips, then take the cable out.

5   Installation is the reverse of the removal steps.

34 Hatchback lock cylinder - removal and installation

1   Remove the trim panel from the rear end of the luggage compartment.

2   Rotate the plastic clip off the lock rod and lift the rod out of the lock cylinder.

3   Pull out the lock cylinder retainer and remove the cylinder from the outside.

4   Installation is the reverse of the removal steps.

35 Bumpers - removal and installation

1991 THROUGH 1996 MODELS

Front bumper

1   Remove the splash shields.

2   Disconnect any wiring or other components that would interfere with bumper removal.

Rear bumpers

3   If you're working on a sedan or hatchback, remove the luggage

compartment rear trim panel.

4   If you're working on a station wagon, remove the rear floor trim panel.

Front and rear bumpers

5   Support the bumper with a jack or jackstand. Alternatively, have an assistant support the bumper as the bolts are removed.

6   Remove the retaining nuts and slide the bumper off the set bolts.

7   Installation is the reverse of removal.

8   Tighten the retaining nuts securely.

1997 AND LATER MODELS

Front bumper

9 If you're working on a coupe, disconnect the electrical connectors for the combination lights and for the fog lights (if equipped).

10 If you're working on a sedan or wagon, remove one screw from the underside of the bumper cover on each side of the vehicle.

11 Remove the screws and pushpins from the inner fender and move it out of the way.

12 Working inside one wheel well, remove the hidden bolts and the screw that attach the bumper cover to the fender, then remove the bolts. Do the same thing inside the other wheel well.

13 Remove two bolts and the alignment pushpin, then take off the bumper cover.

14 Remove three nuts from the bumper bracket on each side of the vehicle and remove the bumper.

15 Installation is the reverse of the removal steps.

Rear bumper

16 If you're working on a coupe equipped with stone guards at the rear edges of the rear wheel wells, remove three screws and one bolt that secure each guard and remove the guards. On all coupes, remove the two screws that secure the splash shield inside the fender and remove it.

17 If you're working on a sedan or wagon, remove the bumper cover bolt from under the rear side of the bumper on each side of the vehicle.

18 Remove the screw from the inside of each rear wheel well.

19 Remove the rear trim panel from inside the luggage compartment.

20 On each side of the vehicle, remove three nuts - one below and two above - that secure the bumper to the vehicle. Pull the bumper off. If you're working on a sedan, disconnect the electrical connector for the license plate light.

21 Installation is the reverse of the removal steps.

36 Radiator grille and opening panel reinforcement - removal and installation

▶ Refer to illustrations 36.1 and 36.2

❊❊ WARNING:

1994 and later models are equipped with airbags. Before working on or near any airbag component the system must be disarmed. To do this, disconnect the cable from the negative terminal of the battery and wait one minute for the backup power supply to discharge. See Chapter 12 for more information.

RADIATOR GRILLE (1991 THROUGH 1996 MODELS)

1 Squeeze the prongs of the retainer at the top center of the grille (see illustration) and separate it from the body.

2 Unlatch the grille retainers (see illustration). Lift the grille off.

3 Installation is the reverse of the removal steps.

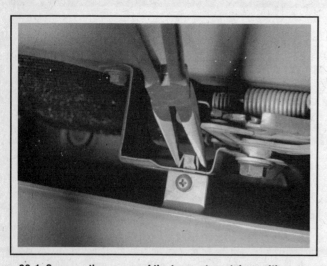

36.1 Squeeze the prongs of the top center retainer with needle nose pliers

36.2 Release the remaining clips with a screwdriver and lift the grille off

GRILLE OPENING PANEL REINFORCEMENT (1997 AND LATER MODELS)

4 Remove the front bumper cover (Section 35). It isn't necessary to remove the bumper.

5 Disconnect the headlight electrical connector on each side of the vehicle.

6 At the top of the panel, remove two nuts and two bolts on each side of the vehicle (one above the headlight opening and one nearer the center).

7 Remove one bolt from the underside of the panel on each side of the vehicle.

8 The remaining fasteners are two nuts, one on each side of the vehicle. Reach into the wheel wells to remove these, then take the panel off.

9 Installation is the reverse of the removal steps.

37 Front fender - removal and installation

1991 THROUGH 1996 MODELS

1 Raise the vehicle, support it securely on jackstands and remove the front wheel.

2 Disconnect the antenna and all light bulb wiring harness connectors and other components that would interfere with fender removal.

3 Remove the fender mounting bolts and nut.

4 Detach the fender. It is a good idea to have an assistant support the fender while it's being moved away from the vehicle to prevent damage to the surrounding body panels.

5 Installation is the reverse of removal.

6 Tighten all nuts, bolts and screws securely.

1997 AND LATER MODELS

7 If there's a stone guard on the trailing edge of the wheel well, remove the clip from its lower edge, remove the screw and pushpins and take the stone guard off.

8 Remove the screws and pushpins that secure the inner fender and take it out of the wheel well.

9 Remove the radiator grille opening panel reinforcement (see Section 36).

10 Remove the bolts along the lower edge of the fender in front of the behind the wheel opening. Remove one nut at the front of the fender.

11 Remove the bolts along the top of the fender and take it off the vehicle.

12 Installation is the reverse of the removal steps.

38 Seats - removal and installation

FRONT SEATS

▶ **Refer to illustrations 38.1, 38.2a, 38.2b and 38.3**

1 Slide the seat rearward and unbolt the front ends of the seat tracks from the floor (see illustration).

2 Slide the seat forward. Remove the trim piece that covers the rear end of each seat track (1996 and earlier models only), then unbolt the track from the floor (see illustrations).

38.1 Unbolt the forward end of each seat track from the floor

38.2a On 1996 and earlier models, remove the screw that secures the trim piece at the rear of the seat tracks . . .

38.2b . . . then remove the track mounting bolts

3   Disconnect the seat electrical connector (see illustration) and take the seat out.

4   Installation is the reverse of the removal steps.

REAR SEATS

♦ **Refer to illustrations 38.5, 38.6 and 38.7**

5   Raise the leading edge of the seat cushion slightly. Reach into the gap and press the push button to release the clip (see illustration). Do the same thing on the other side of the cushion, then lift the cushion out.

6   Unbolt the outer edge of the seat back from the body (see illustration).

7   Slide the inner edge of the seatback off the pivot pin (see illustration). Lift the seat back out.

8   Installation is the reverse of the removal steps.

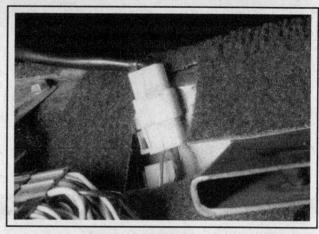

38.3 Disconnect the electrical connector to free the seat

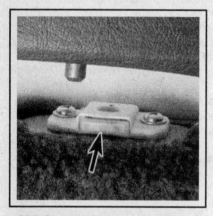

38.5 Press the button on the clip (arrow) and lift the cushion away from the clip

38.6 Unbolt the hinge at the outer edge of the seat back from the body . . .

38.7 . . . and slide the inner end off the pivot

39 Seat belt check

1   Check the seat belts, buckles, latch plates and guide loops for obvious damage and signs of wear.

2   Check that the seat belt reminder light comes on when the key is turned to the Run or Start positions. A chime should also sound.

3   The seat belts are designed to lock up during a sudden stop or impact, yet allow free movement during normal driving. Check that the retractors return the belt against your chest while driving and rewind the belt fully when the buckle is unlatched.

4   If any of the above checks reveal problems with the seat belt system, replace parts as necessary.

40 Glove compartment - removal and installation

✳ WARNING:

1994 and later models are equipped with airbags. Before working on or near any airbag component the system must be disarmed. To do this, disconnect the cable from the negative terminal of the battery and wait one minute for the backup power supply to discharge. See Chapter 12 for more information.

1991 THROUGH 1996 MODELS

♦ **Refer to illustrations 40.1, 40.2, 40.3 and 40.4**

1   Carefully pry the right dash trim panel free of the dash (see illustration). Remove the screw that secures the side of the right lower dash trim panel.

2 Remove the screws that secure the lower edge of the trim panel (see illustration) and the screws that secure the right side of the glove compartment (see illustration).

3 Remove the screws that secure the left side of the glove compartment (see illustration).

4 Remove the glove compartment and right lower trim panel (see illustration).

5 Installation is the reverse of the removal steps.

1997 AND LATER MODELS

◆ **Refer to illustrations 40.6 and 40.7**

6 Open the glove compartment and release the latch on each side by pushing in (see illustration).

7 Let the glove compartment hang down and remove the mounting screws (see illustration).

8 Installation is the reverse of the removal steps.

40.1 The right dash trim panel is secured by clips (arrows)

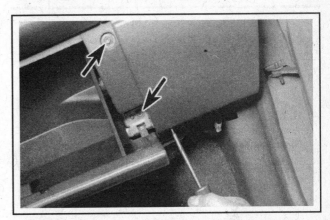

40.2 Remove the screws from the underside of the trim panel and the right side of the glove compartment

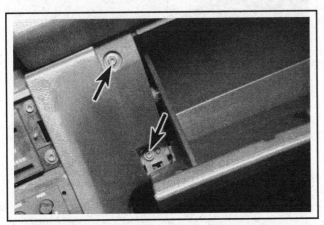

40.3 Remove the screws from the left side of the glove compartment

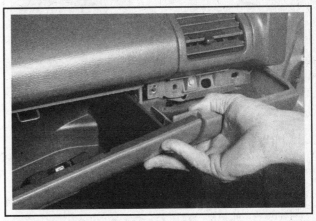

40.4 Lower the glove compartment and trim panel away from the dash

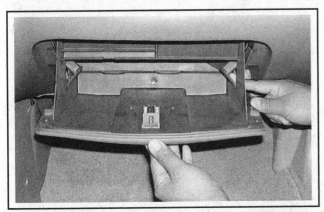

40.6 Lower the glove compartment and push the latches in to release them . . .

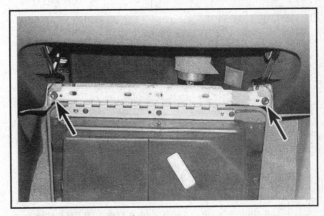

40.7 . . . then remove the screws

41 Console - removal and installation

1991 THROUGH 1996 MODELS

▶ **Refer to illustrations 41.1a, 41.1b and 41.3**

1   Remove the screws that secure the handbrake console (see illustrations).

2   Feed the seat belts through the slots in the handbrake console and lift the console out.

3   Remove the screws that secure the shift console (see illustration). Tilt the console forward, rotate it to clear the shift lever and lift it out.

4   Installation is the reverse of the removal steps.

1997 AND LATER MODELS

▶ **Refer to illustration 41.10**

5   Remove the screws that secure the shift lever console to the instrument panel.

6   Remove the two pushpins from each side of the console near its front edge.

7   If you're working on a vehicle with manual transmission, remove the knob from the shift lever.

8   If you're working on a vehicle with automatic transmission, set the parking brake and pull the shift lever back to Low.

9   Lift the cup holder up and out of the console, then lift the rear end of the console and pull it off the shift lever.

10 To remove the handbrake console, slide both seats all the way forward. Remove one screw from each side of the console and lift it off (see illustration).

11 Installation is the reverse of the removal steps.

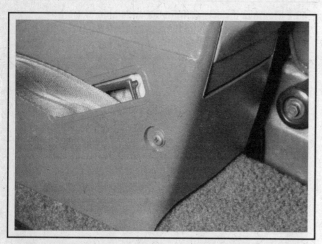

41.1a The handbrake console is secured by a screw on each side at the rear . . .

41.1b . . . and a screw on each side at the front

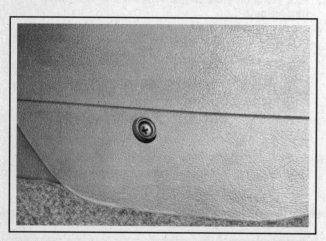

41.3 The shift console is secured by a screw on each side

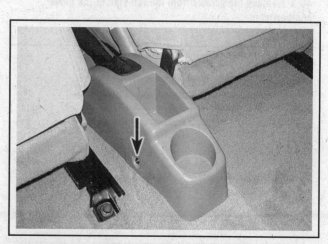

41.10 Remove one screw (arrow) from each side of the console

42 Instrument panel - removal and installation

✳✳ WARNING:

1994 and later models are equipped with airbags. Before working on or near any airbag component the system must be disarmed. To do this, disconnect the cable from the negative terminal of the battery and wait one minute for the backup power supply to discharge. See Chapter 12 for more information.

1991 THROUGH 1996 MODELS

1   Disconnect the cable from the negative battery terminal.

2   Remove the instrument cluster (see Chapter 12).

3   Remove the hood release cable from the lower left dash panel. Using a small screwdriver to release the retaining tabs, carefully remove both end panels from the dash.

4   Remove the retaining screws and detach the left and right lower dash panels. Disconnect the necessary electrical connectors.

5   Remove the glove compartment (see Section 40). Remove the ash tray.

6   Remove the heater control assembly (see Chapter 3).

7   Remove the retaining screws to the center accessory console. Disconnect the radio antenna, the electrical connectors to the radio and cigarette lighter and remove the accessory console.

8   Remove the steering column mounting bracket. Lower and support the steering column away from the instrument panel.

9   Remove the retaining screws, the defroster grille at the base of the windshield, and the defroster ducts at each end of the panel.

10   Remove the upper and lower instrument panel mounting bolts at each end of the panel. Remove the panel frame to floor pan bolts at the center. Finally, remove the mounting bolts that attach the instrument panel to the cowl at the base of the windshield.

11   Pull the instrument panel back and disconnect all electrical connectors that are connected to it. Carefully remove the instrument panel through the door opening.

12   Installation is the reverse of removal. Tighten all instrument panel mounting bolts securely. Tighten the steering column-to-dash bolts to 80 to 124 in-lbs.

1997 AND LATER MODELS

Refer to illustrations 42.17, 42.25, 42.26, 42.29a, 42.29b, 42.30 and 42.31

13   Remove the console (see Section 41).

14   Remove the screws and detach the center trim panels. If you're working on a coupe, pull the panels straight out to remove them.

15   If the vehicle has an auxiliary power socket, reach behind it and disconnect its wires.

16   Remove the center trim panel from the instrument panel. Remove the side cover from each side of the control box (each one is secured by a pushpin).

17   Free the radio antenna lead from the clip at the left side of the instrument panel center brace near the floor, then disconnect the antenna lead at the connector (see illustration). Also disconnect the multi-terminal electrical connector located near the antenna lead.

18   If you're working on a vehicle with an automatic transaxle, remove the four mounting screws that secure the PRNDL indicator. Rotate the PRNDL indicator around the shift lever 1/4-turn from its installed position to position it out of the way.

19   Remove the powertrain control module (PCM) (see Chapter 6).

20   Set the temperature switch at Cool and disconnect the temperature cable (see Chapter 3).

21   Remove the steering wheel (see Chapter 10).

22   Detach the hood release cable from the instrument panel and lower it out of the way (see illustration 9.5).

23   If you're working on a coupe, disconnect the electrical connector for the interior light dimmer switch. If you're working on a sedan or wagon, disconnect the electrical connector for the deck lid opener switch.

24   Remove the instrument panel steering column cover. Remove the screws from the underside of the steering column shroud and remove the upper and lower halves of the shroud.

25   Unbolt the steering column from the dash and lower it clear (see illustration).

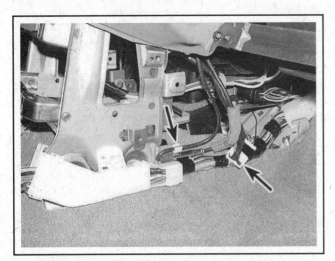

42.17 Free the antenna lead from the clip (left arrow) and disconnect the electrical connector (right arrow)

42.25 Remove the steering column mounting bolts (arrows) and lower the column

26 Remove the screws and detach the scuff plate from each front door sill. Remove the pushpins from the cowl trim panel on each side and remove the panels (see illustration).

27 Remove the passenger air bag module (see Chapter 12).

28 Disconnect the vacuum harness connector, the electrical connector on the left side of the lower instrument panel brace and the electrical connector for the blower motor resistor.

29 Free both of the instrument panel end panels from their clips and remove them (see illustration). Remove the panel bolts located beneath the trim panels (see illustration).

30 Pry up the cover to expose the bolt at the top center of the instrument panel, then remove the bolt (see illustration).

31 Unbolt the lower panel brace on each side (see illustration).

32 Pull the instrument panel out to expose the main electrical connectors, disconnect them and remove the panel.

33 Installation is the reverse of the removal steps. When installing the steering column-to-dash bolts, tighten them to 80 to 124 in-lbs.

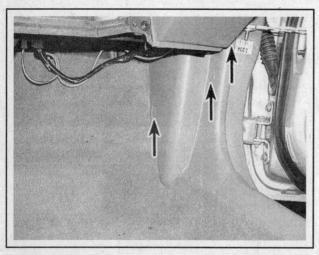

42.26 Remove the pushpins (arrows; upper pushpin hidden) and the cowl side trim panels

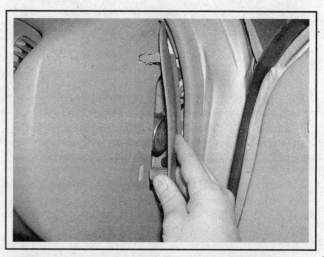

42.29a Pull the end panel clips out and remove the panel . . .

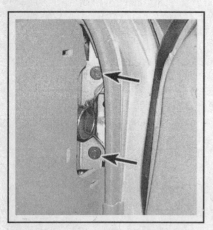

42.29b . . . and unscrew the bolts, then do the same thing on the other side

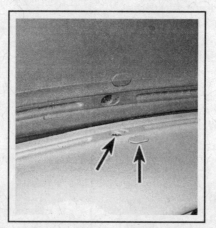

42.30 Pry out the cover (right arrow) to expose the bolt (left arrow); then remove the bolt

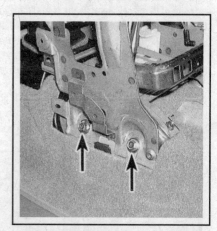

42.31 Unbolt the lower panel bolts (arrows) on each side (left side shown)

Section

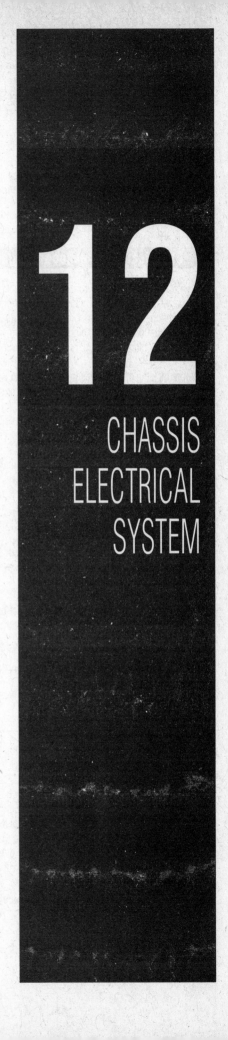

12

CHASSIS ELECTRICAL SYSTEM

1   General information

The electrical system is a 12-volt, negative ground type. Power for the lights and all electrical accessories is supplied by a lead/acid-type battery which is charged by the alternator.

This Chapter covers repair and service procedures for the various electrical components not associated with the engine. Information on the battery, alternator, ignition system and starter motor can be found in Chapter 5.

It should be noted that when portions of the electrical system are serviced, the negative battery cable should be disconnected from the battery to prevent electrical shorts and/or fires.

2   Electrical troubleshooting - general information

A typical electrical circuit consists of an electrical component, any switches, relays, motors, fuses, fusible links or circuit breakers related to that component and the wiring and connectors that link the component to both the battery and the chassis. To help you pinpoint an electrical circuit problem, wiring diagrams are included at the end of this book.

Before tackling any troublesome electrical circuit, first study the appropriate wiring diagrams to get a complete understanding of what makes up that individual circuit. Trouble spots, for instance, can often be narrowed down by noting if other components related to the circuit are operating properly. If several components or circuits fail at one time, chances are the problem is in a fuse or ground connection, because several circuits are often routed through the same fuse and ground connections.

Electrical problems usually stem from simple causes, such as loose or corroded connections, a blown fuse, a melted fusible link or a bad relay. Visually inspect the condition of all fuses, wires and connections in a problem circuit before troubleshooting it.

If testing instruments are going to be utilized, use the diagrams to plan ahead of time where you will make the necessary connections in order to accurately pinpoint the trouble spot.

The basic tools needed for electrical troubleshooting include a circuit tester or voltmeter (a 12-volt bulb with a set of test leads can also be used), a continuity tester, which includes a bulb, battery and set of test leads, and a jumper wire, preferably with a circuit breaker incorporated, which can be used to bypass electrical components. Before attempting to locate a problem with test instruments, use the wiring diagram(s) to decide where to make the connections.

VOLTAGE CHECKS

Voltage checks should be performed if a circuit is not functioning properly. Connect one lead of a circuit tester to either the negative battery terminal or a known good ground. Connect the other lead to a connector in the circuit being tested, preferably nearest to the battery or fuse. If the bulb of the tester lights, voltage is present, which means that the part of the circuit between the connector and the battery is problem free. Continue checking the rest of the circuit in the same fashion. When you reach a point at which no voltage is present, the problem lies between that point and the last test point with voltage. Most of the time the problem can be traced to a loose connection.

➡Note: Keep in mind that some circuits receive voltage only when the ignition key is in the Accessory or Run position.

FINDING A SHORT

One method of finding shorts in a circuit is to remove the fuse and connect a test light or voltmeter in its place to the fuse terminals. There should be no voltage present in the circuit. Move the wiring harness from side-to-side while watching the test light. If the bulb goes on, there is a short to ground somewhere in that area, probably where the insulation has rubbed through. The same test can be performed on each component in the circuit, even a switch.

GROUND CHECK

Perform a ground test to check whether a component is properly grounded. Disconnect the battery and connect one lead of a self-powered test light, known as a continuity tester, to a known good ground. Connect the other lead to the wire or ground connection being tested. If the bulb goes on, the ground is good. If the bulb does not go on, the ground is not good.

CONTINUITY CHECK

A continuity check is done to determine if there are any breaks in a circuit - if it is passing electricity properly. With the circuit off (no power in the circuit), a self-powered continuity tester can be used to check the circuit. Connect the test leads to both ends of the circuit (or to the "power" end and a good ground), and if the test light comes on the circuit is passing current properly. If the light doesn't come on, there is a break somewhere in the circuit. The same procedure can be used to test a switch, by connecting the continuity tester to the switch terminals. With the switch turned On, the test light should come on.

FINDING AN OPEN CIRCUIT

When diagnosing for possible open circuits, it is often difficult to locate them by sight because oxidation or terminal misalignment are hidden by the connectors. Merely wiggling a connector on a sensor or in the wiring harness may correct the open circuit condition. Remember this when an open circuit is indicated when troubleshooting a circuit. Intermittent problems may also be caused by oxidized or loose connections.

Electrical troubleshooting is simple if you keep in mind that all electrical circuits are basically electricity running from the battery, through the wires, switches, relays, fuses and fusible links to each electrical component (light bulb, motor, etc.) and to ground, from which it is passed back to the battery. Any electrical problem is an interruption in the flow of electricity to and from the battery.

3 Fuses - general information

▶ **Refer to illustrations 3.1a through 3.1f**

The electrical circuits of the vehicle are protected by a combination of fuses, cartridge-type fuse links and a circuit breaker. The fuse panel is located under the instrument panel on the left side of the dashboard and the fuse block is located in the engine compartment (see illustrations).

Each of the fuses is designed to protect a specific circuit, and the various circuits are identified on the fuse panel itself.

Miniaturized fuses are employed in the fuse panel and block. These compact fuses, with blade terminal design, allow fingertip removal and replacement. If an electrical component fails, always check the fuse first. A blown fuse is easily identified through the clear plastic body. Visu-

ally inspect the element for evidence of damage. If a continuity check is called for, the blade terminal tips are exposed in the fuse body.

Be sure to replace blown fuses with the correct type. Fuses of different ratings are physically interchangeable, but only fuses of the proper rating should be used. Replacing a fuse with one of a higher or lower value than specified is not recommended. Each electrical circuit needs a specific amount of protection. The amperage value of each fuse is molded into the fuse body.

If the replacement fuse immediately fails, don't replace it again until the cause of the problem is isolated and corrected. In most cases, the cause will be a short circuit in the wiring caused by a broken or deteriorated wire.

3.1a The fuse block is located under this cover on the driver's side of the engine compartment; the cover lists functions and capacities for the fuses and fusible links . . .

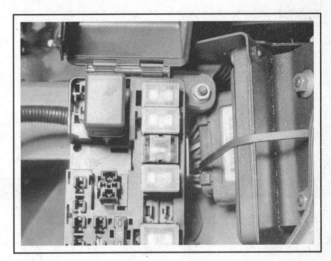

3.1b . . . which can be reached by lifting the cover off

3.1c The fuse panel cover in the passenger compartment lists fuse functions and capacities

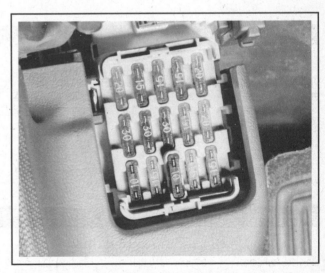

3.1d The miniaturized fuses are beneath the cover

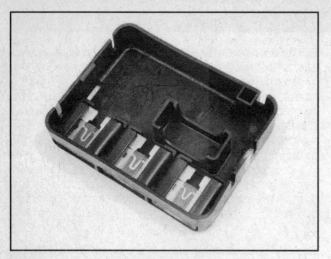

3.1e **Spare fuses are mounted in the cover**

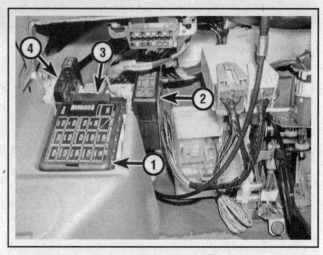

3.1f **Passenger compartment fuses and circuit breaker location - 1997 and later models**

1 *Fuse panel*
2 *Relay panel*
3 *Circuit breaker (power windows)*
4 *Circuit breaker (heater)*

4 Fusible links - general information

Some circuits are protected by cartridge-type fuse links located in the engine compartment fuse block (see illustrations 3.1a and 3.1b).

Cartridge-type fuse links cannot be repaired, but are replaced in the same manner as fuses.

➡**Note: The main fuse link is secured by two screws.**

5 Circuit breaker - general information

Various circuits are protected by a circuit breaker located above the fuses on the fuse panel in the passenger compartment. On 1991 through 1996 models, the circuit breaker protects the heater circuit and can be reset by pushing the reset button. On 1997 and later models, two circuit breakers are used, one circuit breaker protects the power window circuit and the other protects the heater (see illustration 3.1f).

If a circuit breaker trips more than once, check the circuit for a short, referring to the wiring diagrams at the end of this Chapter.

6 Relays - general information

Several electrical accessories in the vehicle use relays to transmit the electrical signal to the component. If the relay is defective, that component will not operate properly.

The various relays are grouped together in several locations.

If a faulty relay is suspected, it can be removed and tested by a dealer service department or a repair shop. Defective relays must be replaced as a unit.

7 Turn signal and hazard flasher - check and replacement

1 A single electronic flasher operates both the turn indicators and the hazard flashers.

2 If both turn signals fail to blink, the problem may be due to a blown fuse, a faulty flasher unit, a broken switch or a loose or open connection. If a quick check of the fuse box indicates that the turn signal fuse has blown, check the wiring for a short before installing a new fuse.

3 To test the flasher, locate it on the relay bracket under the driver's side of the instrument panel.

   a) Measure resistance between the flasher black wire and ground with an ohmmeter. If it's 5 ohms or more, repair or replace the wire.

   b) Disconnect the flasher unit and ground the black wire terminal. Apply 12 volts to the dark green/yellow terminal and connect a 12-volt test light between the dark green/red wire terminal and ground. If the test light flashes, the flasher is good. If not, replace it.

4 Make sure that the replacement unit is identical to the original. Compare the old one to the new one before installing it.

5 Installation is the reverse of removal.

8 Front side marker and turn signal bulb - replacement

1991 THROUGH 1996 MODELS

▶ **Refer to illustrations 8.1, 8.2, 8.3 and 8.4**

1 Remove the upper screw that secures the light assembly to the vehicle (see illustration).

2 Remove the side retaining screw and take the light assembly off (see illustration).

3 Twist the bulb socket counterclockwise and separate it from the housing (see illustration).

4 Press the bulb into the socket and turn counterclockwise to remove it (see illustration).

5 Installation is the reverse of the removal steps. Note that one of the retaining tangs on the bulb fits deeper into the socket than the other one. Be sure to place the tangs in the correct slots.

8.1 Remove the upper screw . . .

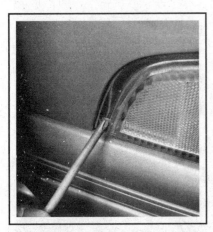

8.2 . . . and the side screw to detach the lens from the body

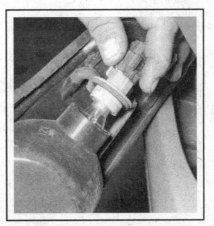

8.3 Twist the bulb socket counterclockwise and take it out of the light body

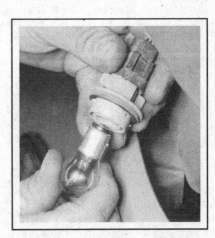

8.4 Press the bulb into the socket and turn it counterclockwise to remove it

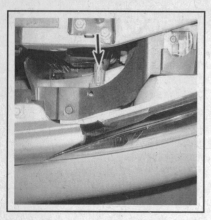

8.6a Turn signal lamp location (arrow) - 1997 and later models

8.6b Front side marker lamp location (arrow) - 1997 and later models

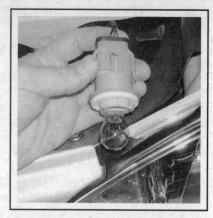

8.7 Remove the bulb socket from the housing and remove the bulb from the socket

1997 AND LATER MODELS

Refer to illustrations 8.6a, 8.6b and 8.7

6 Disconnect the electrical connector from the bulb socket (see Illustrations).

7 Twist the bulb socket counterclockwise and remove it from the housing (see Illustration).
8 Remove the bulb from the socket.
9 Installation is the reverse of removal.

9 Headlights - removal and installation

1 Disconnect the negative cable from the battery.

BULB REPLACEMENT

◆ Refer to illustrations 9.2 and 9.3

✳✳ WARNING:

Halogen gas filled bulbs are under pressure and may shatter if the surface is scratched or the bulb is dropped. Wear eye protection and handle the bulbs carefully, grasping only the base whenever possible. Do not touch the surface of the bulb with your fingers because the oil from your skin could cause it to overheat and fail prematurely. If you do touch the bulb surface, clean it with rubbing alcohol.

2 Reach behind the headlight assembly, grasp the bulb holder and turn it 1/4 turn counterclockwise to remove it (see illustration). Lift the holder assembly out for access to the bulb.
3 Squeeze the connector and disconnect it from the bulb and holder assembly (see illustration).
4 Connect a new bulb and holder assembly to the electrical connector.
5 Install the bulb holder in the headlight assembly.

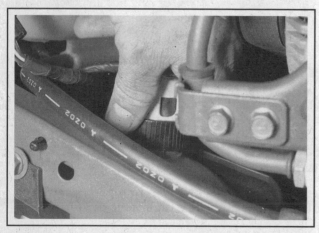

9.2 Twist the bulb holder 1/4-turn counterclockwise and take it out of the light assembly

9.3 Disconnect the electrical connector from the bulb and holder assembly

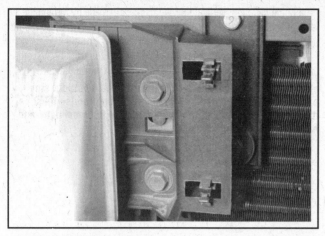

9.9a Remove the inner bolts . . .

9.9b . . . the outer bolts . . .

HEADLIGHT ASSEMBLY REMOVAL AND INSTALLATION

1991 through 1996 models

▶ Refer to illustrations 9.9a, 9.9b and 9.9c

6   Remove the parking/turn signal light assembly (see Section 8).

7   Remove the grille (see Chapter 11).

8   Remove the headlight bulb (see Steps 1 through 3).

9   Remove the inner attaching bolts, outer attaching bolts and upper attaching bolt (see illustrations). Lift the headlight assembly out.

10   Installation is the reverse of the removal steps.

11   Connect the negative battery cable.

1997 and later models

12   Disconnect the electrical connectors from the turn signal bulb, headlight bulb and side marker light bulb.

13   Remove the front bumper cover (see Chapter 11).

14   Remove the headlight housing mounting nuts/bolts and remove the housing.

15   Installation is the reverse of removal.

9.9c . . . and one upper bolt to detach the headlight assembly from the vehicle

10 Headlights - adjustment

▶ Refer to illustration 10.1

➡Note: The headlights must be aimed correctly. If adjusted incorrectly they could blind the driver of an oncoming vehicle and cause a serious accident or seriously reduce your ability to see the road. The headlights should be checked for proper aim every 12 months and any time a new headlight is installed or front end body work is performed. It should be emphasized that the following procedure is only an interim step which will provide temporary adjustment until the headlights can be adjusted by a properly equipped shop.

1   Headlights have two spring-loaded adjusting screws, both accessible from the top of the headlight (see illustration). The inner adjuster controls horizontal aim and the outer adjuster controls vertical aim.

2   There are several methods of adjusting the headlights. The simplest method requires a blank wall 25 feet in front of the vehicle and a level floor.

10.1 Headlight adjuster screw locations - 1997 and later models

3   Position masking tape vertically on the wall in reference to the vehicle centerline and the centerlines of both headlights.

4   Position a horizontal tape line in reference to the centerline of all the headlights.

➡**Note: It may be easier to position the tape on the wall with the vehicle parked only a few inches away.**

5   Adjustment should be made with the vehicle sitting level, the gas tank half-full, no load in the vehicle except the jack and spare tire and the tires inflated to the correct pressure.

6   Starting with the low beam adjustment, position the high intensity zone so it is two inches below the horizontal line and two inches to the right of the headlight vertical line. Adjustment is made by turning the vertical aim adjusting screw. The horizontal aim adjusting screw should be used in the same manner to move the beam left or right.

7   With the high beams on, the high intensity zone should be vertically centered with the exact center just below the horizontal line.

➡**Note: It may not be possible to position the headlight aim exactly for both high and low beams. If a compromise must be made, keep in mind that the low beams are the most used and have the greatest effect on driver safety.**

8   Have the headlights adjusted by a dealer service department or service station at the earliest opportunity.

11 Bulb replacement

➡**Note: Refer to Section 8 for front side marker/turn signal bulb replacement.**

REAR COMBINATION LIGHT BULB REPLACEMENT

1991 through 1996 models
▶ **Refer to illustrations 11.1, 11.4 and 11.5**

1   If you're working on a hatchback, remove the access cover in the rear of the cargo area (see illustration).

2   If you're working on a sedan, remove the trunk rear trim panel.

3   If you're working on a wagon, remove the screws and take off the light assembly.

4   Twist the bulb socket counterclockwise and remove it from the light (see illustration).

5   Press the bulb into the socket and turn it counterclockwise to remove (see illustration).

6   Installation is the reverse of the removal steps.

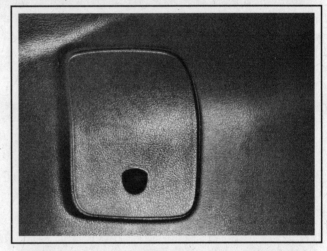

11.1 The rear bulbs on hatchback models are behind these access panels in the rear of the cargo area

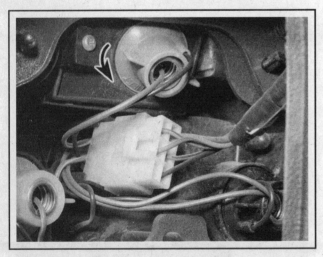

11.4 Twist the bulb socket counterclockwise and take it out of the light body

11.5 Press the bulb into its socket and turn it counterclockwise to remove it

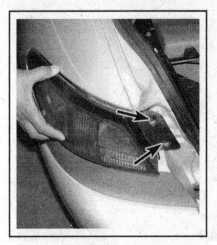

11.7a Remove the screws (arrows) and take out the lamp housing . . .

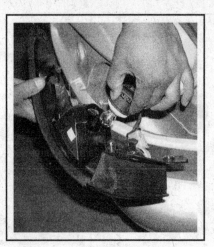

11.7b . . . detach the socket from the housing and remove the bulb

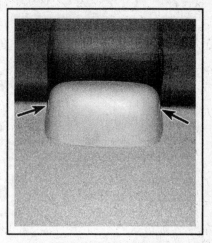

11.23 Remove the two push-pins (arrows) and remove the cover - 1997 and later models (sedan shown, wagon similar)

1997 and later models

▶ **Refer to illustrations 11.7a and 11.7b**

7 If you're working on a coupe or sedan, remove the lamp housing screws and take the housing off (see illustration). Pull the socket out of the lamp housing, then remove the bulb (see illustration).

8 If you're working on a wagon, remove the lamp screws and take the housing off. Pull out the socket(s), then remove the bulb(s).

9 Installation is the reverse of the removal steps.

FOG LIGHTS

10 Reach beneath the bumper and remove the light retaining screws (and the pushpin on 1998 and later models).

11 Take the light assembly out.

12 Twist the bulb socket and remove it from the light.

13 Remove the bulb and install a new one.

14 Installation is the reverse of the removal steps.

HIGH-MOUNT BRAKE LIGHT

1996 and earlier models without spoiler

15 Remove the push-in retainers that secure the light cover and take the cover off.

16 Disconnect the electrical connector, then rotate the socket counterclockwise to remove it from the housing.

17 Remove the bulb and install a new one.

18 Installation is the reverse of the removal steps.

1996 and earlier hatchback with spoiler

19 Remove the lens retaining screws and take the lens off.

20 Detach the bulb socket from the housing by rotating it counterclockwise.

21 Remove the bulb from the socket and install a new one.

22 Installation is the reverse of the removal steps.

1997 and later models

▶ **Refer to illustrations 11.23 and 11.24**

23 Remove the push-in retainers and remove the cover (see illustration).

24 Disconnect the electrical connector and remove the bulb socket from the hosing by rotating it counterclockwise (see illustration).

25 Remove the bulb from the bulb socket.

26 Installation is the reverse of removal.

INSTRUMENT PANEL BULBS

▶ **Refer to illustration 11.28**

27 To gain access to the instrument panel lights, the instrument cluster will have to be removed first (see Section 15).

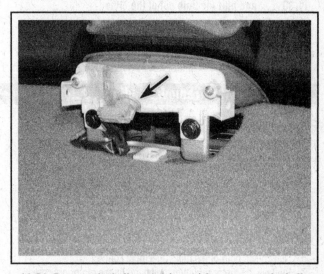

11.24 Remove the bulb socket (arrow) for access to the bulb

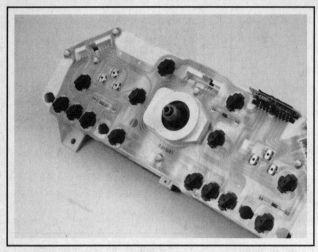

11.28 The instrument cluster bulbs are accessible from the back of the cluster once the cluster is removed

11.29 Pull off the dome light lens . . .

11.30 . . . and pull the bulb out of the clips

28 To replace a bulb, rotate its small, black-plastic socket counterclockwise and separate it from the back of the cluster. Remove the bulb from the socket and replace it (see illustration).

DOME LIGHT

▶ **Refer to illustrations 11.29 and 11.30**

29 Carefully pull the lens off the dome light (see illustration).
30 Pull the bulb out of its clips (see illustration).
31 Push a new bulb into the clips and install the lens.

REAR SIDE MARKER LIGHT (1997 AND LATER WAGON MODELS)

32 Remove the access cover and disconnect the electrical connector from the lamp.
33 Pull out the bulb socket and remove the bulb.
34 Installation is the reverse of the removal steps.

12 Wiper motor - removal and installation

FRONT WIPER MOTOR

▶ **Refer to illustration 12.7**

1 Make sure the wiper motor is in the parked position.
2 Disconnect the negative cable from the battery.
3 Remove the cowl grille.
4 Pry up four clips that secure the baffle trim and remove the trim.
5 Remove the linkage clip and detach the linkage from the motor.
6 Disconnect both of the motor electrical connectors.
7 Remove the motor mounting bolts and lift the motor out (see illustration).
8 Make sure the motor is in the parked position before you install it.
9 The remainder of installation is the reverse of the removal steps.

REAR WIPER MOTOR (STATION WAGON MODELS)

▶ **Refer to illustration 12.10**

10 Lift the cover from the wiper arm nut and remove the nut (see illustration).
11 Work the wiper arm off the motor shaft.
12 Remove the shaft seal, outer bushing nut and outer bushing.
13 Remove the trim panel from the liftgate.
14 Disconnect the electrical connector from the motor.
15 Remove the motor mounting bolts and take the motor off.
16 Installation is the reverse of the removal steps.

12.7 The wiper motor is secured by three mounting bolts (one is hidden below the motor)

12.10 Lift the cover to expose the wiper arm nut, remove the nut and take the wiper arm off

13 Windshield washer reservoir and motor - removal and installation

FRONT RESERVOIR (1.9L AND 2.0L ENGINE MODELS)

1 Remove the reservoir bolts and nuts.
2 Disconnect the motor electrical connector.
3 Detach the fluid hose from the reservoir and take the reservoir out.
4 Installation is the reverse of the removal steps.

FRONT RESERVOIR (1.8L ENGINE MODELS)

5 Unbolt the power steering fluid reservoir and position it out of the way without disconnecting any hoses (see Chapter 10).
6 Unbolt the cruise control servo bracket (if equipped) and set the bracket to one side.
7 Remove the washer reservoir mounting bolts.
8 Disconnect the motor electrical connector.
9 Detach the fluid hose from the reservoir and take the reservoir out.

10 Installation is the reverse of the removal steps.

REAR RESERVOIR (STATION WAGON MODELS)

11 Remove the trim panel from the right rear of the cargo area.
12 Remove the washer reservoir mounting bolts.
13 Disconnect the motor electrical connector.
14 Detach the fluid hose from the reservoir and take the reservoir out.
15 Installation is the reverse of the removal steps.

WASHER MOTOR

16 Remove the reservoir as described in this Section.
17 Carefully pry the motor out of the grommet in the reservoir.
18 Installation is the reverse of the removal steps.

14 Steering column switches - removal and installation

❊❊ WARNING:

1994 and later models are equipped with airbags. Before working on or near any airbag component the system must be disarmed. To do this, disconnect the cable from the negative terminal of the battery and wait one minute for the backup power supply to discharge. See Section 24 for more information.

1 Steering column switches include the ignition switch, the cruise control switch (if equipped), and the multi-function switch (which controls the lights, turn signals and wipers).

CRUISE CONTROL SWITCH

1991 through 1996 models

2 Remove the steering wheel cover and disconnect the horn electrical connector (see Chapter 10).
3 Disconnect the electrical connectors for the cruise control switch.
4 Remove the switch bracket retaining screws and remove the switch together with the bracket.
5 Installation is the reverse of the removal steps.

14.11a The multi-function switch connectors are accessible through the steering column shell opening . . .

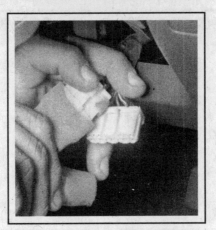

14.11b . . . don't damage the foam wrapping when you disconnect them

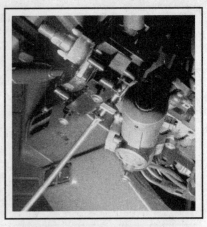

14.12 Remove the screw that secures the switch to the steering column

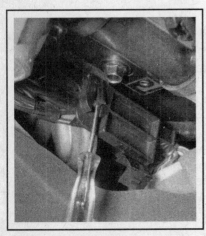

14.13a Carefully pry up the tab on the harness retainer . . .

14.13b . . . and slide it down off the bracket

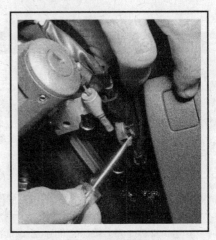

14.13c . . . then do the same thing with the other harness retainer

1997 and later models

6   Remove the driver's side air bag module and the steering wheel (see Chapter 10).

7   Remove the trim screws from the back side of the steering wheel, then take off the trim piece.

8   Remove the screws for the two cruise control switches and take the switches off the steering wheel.

9   Installation is the reverse of the removal steps.

MULTI-FUNCTION SWITCH

1991 through 1996 models

▶ Refer to illustrations 14.11a, 14.11b, 14.12, 14.13a, 14.13b, 14.13c and 14.14

10 Remove the steering wheel and the upper and lower steering col-

umn covers (see Chapter 10).

11 Locate the three multi-function switch connectors behind the instrument panel and disconnect them (see illustrations).

12 Remove the screw that secures the switch to the steering column (see illustration).

13 Carefully pry up the tab that secures the switch harness retainer to the bracket on either side (see illustrations). Pull the retainers off the brackets.

14 Remove the multi-function switch from the steering column (see illustration).

1997 and later models

▶ Refer to illustrations 14.16a and 14.16b

15 Remove the upper and lower steering column covers (see Chapter 10).

16 The wiper switch and the turn signal/headlight switch can be

14.14 Take the multi-function switch off the steering column (1996 and earlier models)

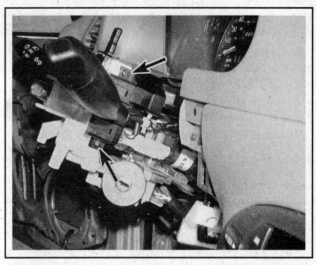

14.16a Remove the screws (arrows) and detach the wiper switch from the multi-function switch body (1997 and later models)

14.16b Remove the screws (arrows) and detach the headlight/turn signal switch from the multi-function switch body (1997 and later models)

14.19 Disconnect the ignition switch electrical connector (early model shown; later model similar)

removed separately from the switch body. To remove either switch, disconnect its electrical connector, then remove the mounting screws and take the switch off (see illustrations).

17 If necessary, remove the switch body mounting screws and take it off the steering column.

IGNITION SWITCH

▶ **Refer to illustration 14.19**

18 On 1996 and earlier models, remove the multi-function switch as described in this section. On 1997 and later models, remove the steering column covers.

19 Disconnect the ignition switch electrical connector (see illustration).

20 Remove the two screws from the ignition key reminder switch.

21 Remove the ignition switch mounting screws and remove the switch.

22 Installation is the reverse of the removal steps.

15 Instrument cluster - removal and installation

▶ Refer to illustrations 15.2a, 15.2b, 15.3, 15.4, 15.5a, 15.5b, 15.6, 15.7 and 15.8

❋❋ WARNING:

1994 and later models are equipped with airbags. Before working on or near any airbag component the system must be disarmed. To do this, disconnect the cable from the negative terminal of the battery and wait one minute for the backup power supply to discharge. See Section 24 for more information.

1   Disconnect the negative cable from the battery. Remove the steering wheel and column covers (see Chapter 10).
2   If the vehicle is equipped with a cable-operated speedometer, pull out the clip that secures the speedometer cable to the top of the transaxle, then pull the cable out (see illustrations).

3   Remove the accessory switches from the lower part of the cluster trim panel (or, if you're working on a vehicle without the accessories, remove the switch hole covers) (see illustration).
4   Disconnect the switch electrical connectors (the connectors are installed, even if the accessory switches aren't) (see illustration).
5   Remove the screws that secure the instrument cluster trim panel, then pull the panel away from the dash (see illustrations).
6   Remove the cluster fasteners (see illustration).
7   Pull the cluster out far enough so you can reach the electrical connector. Squeeze the tab and disconnect the connector (see illustration).
8   If the vehicle is equipped with a cable-operated speedometer, squeeze the tab on the speedometer cable and separate it from the speedometer (see illustration).
9   Take the cluster out of the instrument panel.
10 Installation is the reverse of the removal steps.

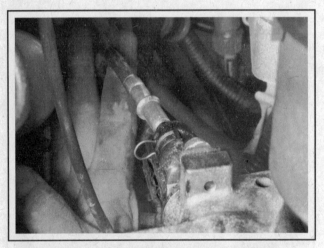

15.2a If the vehicle is equipped with a cable-operated speedometer, use a screwdriver to pry the speedometer cable retaining clip out of its slot . . .

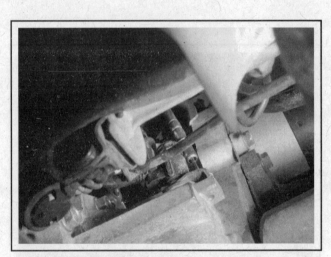

15.2b . . . then pull the cable out of the transaxle

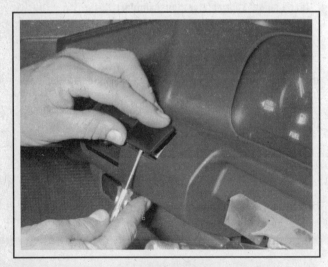

15.3 Remove the accessory switches (or pry out the cover plates if the switches aren't installed) . . .

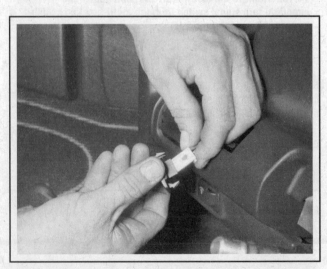

15.4 . . . and disconnect the switch electrical connectors, which are installed even if the switches aren't

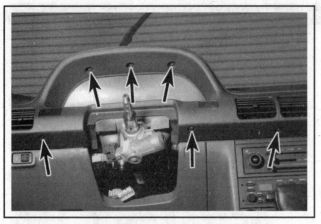

15.5a Remove the cluster trim screws with a Torx bit . . .

15.5b . . . and work the trim loose from the cluster

15.6 Remove the Torx screws and bolts that secure the cluster . . .

15.7 . . . pull the cluster out and disconnect the electrical connector . . .

15.8 . . . and disconnect the speedometer cable to free the cluster

16 Speedometer cable - removal and installation

▶ **Refer to illustrations 16.2 and 16.3**

1   Perform Steps 1 through 8 of Section 15.
2   If you're replacing just the inner cable, pull it out of the housing (see illustration).

3   Feed a new inner cable into the housing, coating it with multipurpose grease (see illustration).
4   If you're replacing the housing, detach it from its clips and pull it through the firewall.
5   Installation is the reverse of the removal steps.

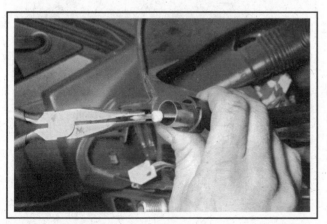

16.2 To replace the inner cable, pull it out of the housing

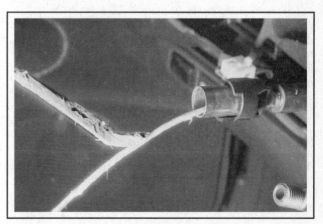

16.3 Coat a new inner cable with white grease as you install it

17 Horn - removal and installation

▶ **Refer to illustration 17.1**

1   There are one or two horns located behind the front bumper (see illustration).

2   Remove the grille (see Chapter 11).

3   Remove the headlight assembly from the side on which the horn is being removed (see Section 9).

4   Disconnect the horn electrical connector.

5   Remove the mounting bolt and take the horn out.

6   Installation is the reverse of the removal steps.

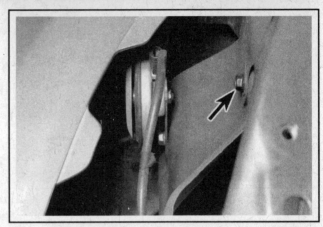

17.1 The horn (two horns if equipped) is secured by a single mounting bolt (arrow)

18 Radio and tape/CD player - removal and installation

▶ **Refer to illustration 18.3**

❈❈ WARNING:

1994 and later models are equipped with airbags. Before working on or near any airbag component the system must be disarmed. To do this, disconnect the cable from the negative terminal of the battery and wait one minute for the backup power supply to discharge. See Section 24 for more information.

1   For theft protection, the radio receiver/CD player is retained in the instrument panel by special clips. Releasing these clips requires the use of two special removal tools (available at most auto parts stores) or two short lengths of coat wire bent into U-shapes. Insert the tools into the holes at the corners of the radio/CD player until you feel the internal clips release.

2   Disconnect the negative cable from the battery.

3   Insert the special tool into the removal holes (see illustration).

4   Slip the radio out far enough to disconnect the antenna lead and electrical connectors. Lift the radio out.

5   Installation is the reverse of the removal steps.

18.3 A special tool, or its equivalent, is required to remove the radio

19 Antenna - removal and installation

▶ **Refer to illustration 19.7**

1   The old antenna cable will be attached to the new cable to pull it through the mounting hole and into position. Do not pull the old cable all the way out when the antenna is first detached.

2   Remove the instrument cluster (see Section 15).

3   Remove the radio (see Section 18).

4   Reach through the cluster hole and detach the antenna lead from the clips.

5   Disconnect the antenna cable from the radio and detach it from the heater box and remaining clip.

6   Remove two screws that secure the base of the antenna to the windshield pillar.

7   Pull up on the antenna just far enough to expose the tape (see illustration).

8   Cut the old antenna cable at the base and tape it to the radio end of the new one.

9   Remove the old antenna base and insulating tube.

10 Guide the new antenna cable into place with the old one and install the new antenna base and tube.

11 Make sure the end of the antenna drain tube fits into its hole, then attach the antenna to the windshield pillar with the screws.

12 Position the antenna lead in its clips.

13 The remainder of installation is the reverse of the removal steps.

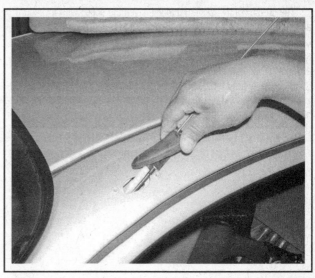

19.7 Pull the antenna up, but don't pull it all the way out until you've attached the old antenna cable to the new one

20 Radio speakers - removal and installation

DOOR SPEAKERS

▶ **Refer to illustration 20.2**

1   Remove the door trim panel (see Chapter 11).

2   Remove the speaker mounting screws (see illustration).

3   Lift the speaker out, disconnect its electrical connector and remove it.

4   Installation is the reverse of the removal steps.

REAR SPEAKERS (SEDAN)

5   Remove the retainers from the high-mount brake light cover and lift off the cover.

6   Move the package tray out of the way.

7   Remove the speaker mounting screws.

8   Lift the speaker out, disconnect its electrical connector and remove it.

9   Installation is the reverse of the removal steps.

REAR SPEAKERS (HATCHBACK AND WAGON)

10 Remove the speaker grille screws.

11 Lift the speaker and grille. Disconnect the speaker electrical connector.

12 Lift out the speaker and grille. Remove the nuts to separate the speaker from the grille.

13 Installation is the reverse of the removal steps.

20.2 The front speakers are secured to the doors by screws

21   Cruise control system - description and check

The cruise control system maintains vehicle speed with a vacuum actuated servo motor located in the engine compartment, which is connected to the throttle linkage by a cable. The system consists of the servo motor, clutch switch, brake switch, control switches, a relay and associated vacuum hoses.

Because of the complexity of the cruise control system and the special tools and techniques required for diagnosis, repair should be left to a dealer service department or a repair shop. However, it is possible for the home mechanic to make simple checks of the wiring and vacuum connections for minor faults which can be easily repaired. These include:

a) *Inspect the cruise control actuating switches for broken wires and loose connections.*

b) *Check the cruise control fuse.*

c) *The cruise control system is operated by vacuum so it's critical that all vacuum switches, hoses and connections are secure. Check the hoses in the engine compartment for tight connections, cracks and obvious vacuum leaks.*

22   Power window system - description and check

The power window system operates the electric motors mounted in the doors which lower and raise the windows. The system consists of the control switches, the motors (regulators), glass mechanisms and associated wiring. Diagnosis can usually be limited to simple checks of the wiring connections and motors for minor faults which can be easily repaired. These include:

a) *Inspect the power window actuating switches for broken wires and loose connections.*

b) *Check the power window fuse/and or circuit breaker.*

c) *Remove the door panel(s) and check the power window motor wires to see if they're loose or damaged. Inspect the glass mechanisms for damage which could cause binding.*

23   Power door lock system - description and check

The power door lock system operates the door lock actuators mounted in each door. The system consists of the switches, actuators and associated wiring. Removal and installation procedures for the actuators are provided in Chapter 11. Diagnosis can usually be limited to simple checks of the wiring connections and actuators for minor faults which can be easily repaired. These include:

a) *Check the system fuse and/or circuit breaker.*

b) *Check the switch wires for damage and loose connections. Check the switches for continuity.*

c) *Remove the door panel(s) and check the actuator wiring connections to see if they're loose or damaged. Inspect the actuator rods (if equipped) to make sure they aren't bent or damaged. Inspect the actuator wiring for damaged or loose connections. The actuator can be checked by applying battery power momentarily. A discernible click indicates that the solenoid is operating properly.*

24 Airbag - general information

1 Later models are equipped with a Supplemental Inflatable System (SIR), more commonly known as an airbag. This system is designed to protect the driver, and on some models, front seat passenger, from serious injury in the event of a head-on or frontal collision. It consists of an airbag module in the center of the steering wheel and, on 1995 models, the right side of the instrument panel, two crash sensors mounted at the front of the vehicle, a safing sensor mounted behind the left side kick panel and a diagnostic monitor which also contains a backup power supply located under the center console.

AIRBAG MODULE

Drivers-side airbag

2 The drivers-side airbag inflator module contains a housing incorporating the cushion (airbag) and inflator unit, mounted in the center of the steering wheel The inflator assembly is mounted on the back of the housing over a hole through which gas is expelled, inflating the bag almost instantaneously when an electrical signal is sent from the system. A coil assembly on the steering column under the module carries this signal to the module. This coil assembly can transmit an electrical signal regardless of steering wheel position. The igniter in the air bag converts the electrical signal to heat and ignites the sodium azide/copper oxide powder, producing nitrogen gas, which inflates the bag.

Passenger-side airbag

3 The passenger-side airbag is mounted above the glove compartment and designated by the letters SRS (Supplemental Restraint System). It consists of an inflator containing an igniter, a bag assembly, a reaction housing and a trim cover. The air bag is considerably larger that the steering wheel-mounted unit and is supported by the steel reaction housing. The trim cover is textured and colored to match the instrument panel and has a molded seam which splits when the bag inflates. As with the steering-wheel-mounted air bag, the igniter electrical signal converts to heat, converting sodium azide/iron oxide powder to nitrogen gas, inflating the bag.

Sensors

4 The system has three sensors: two forward sensors at the front of the vehicle and a safing sensor under the left side kick panel in the driver's compartment. The forward and passenger compartment sensors are basically pressure sensitive switches that complete an electrical circuit during an impact of sufficient G force. The electrical signal from these sensors is what triggers the airbag(s).

ELECTRONIC DIAGNOSTIC MONITOR

5 The electronic diagnostic monitor supplies the current to the airbag system in the event of the collision if battery power is cut off. It also checks the system every time the vehicle is started, causing the "AIR BAG" light to go on then off, if the system is operating properly. If there is a fault in the system, the light will go on and stay on, flash, or the dash will make a beeping sound. If this happens, the vehicle should be taken to your dealer immediately for service.

DISABLING THE SYSTEM

6 Whenever working in the vicinity of the steering wheel, steering column or near other components of the airbag system, the system should be disarmed. To do this, perform the following steps:

a) *Turn the ignition switch to Off.*
b) *Detach the cable from the negative battery terminal and wait at least one minute for the backup power supply in the electronic diagnostic monitor to be depleted.*

ENABLING THE SYSTEM

7 To enable the airbag system, perform the following steps:

a) *Make sure the ignition switch is in the Off position.*
b) *Connect the negative cable to the battery, start the engine and make sure the AIRBAG light on the instrument panel goes off, indicating that all is well with the system.*

REMOVAL AND INSTALLATION

⁂ WARNING:

Use extreme care when handling an airbag module. Always carry the module with the trim side facing away from your body. Store the airbag module in a safe location with the trim side facing up, DO NOT place the trim side down on the floor, a bench or other surface.

Driver's side airbag

➧ Refer to illustration 24.11

8 Disable the system as described above.
9 Remove the steering wheel trim (see Chapter 10).
10 Unscrew the airbag mounting bolts, one from each side of the steering wheel.
11 Lift the airbag away from the steering wheel and disconnect its electrical connector (see illustration).
12 Installation is the reverse of the removal steps.

24.11 Lift the airbag module away from the steering wheel and disconnect its electrical connector

Passenger's side airbag

▶ **Refer to illustration 24.15**

13 Disable the system as described above.

14 Remove the glove compartment (see Chapter 11).

15 Remove the airbag mounting bolts (see illustration). Lift the airbag out and disconnect its electrical connector.

16 Installation is the reverse of the removal steps. Tighten the airbag mounting bolts to 70 to 103 inch-lbs.

24.15 Remove the four mounting bolts (arrows) and remove the airbag module from the instrument panel

25 Wiring diagrams - general information

Since it isn't possible to include all wiring diagrams for every year covered by this manual, the following diagrams are those that are typical and most commonly needed.

Prior to troubleshooting any circuits, check the fuse and circuit breakers (if equipped) to make sure they're in good condition. Make sure the battery is properly charged and check the cable connections (see Chapter 1).

When checking a circuit, make sure that all connectors are clean, with no broken or loose terminals. When unplugging a connector, do not pull on the wires. Pull only on the connector housings themselves.

SAMPLE DIAGRAM: HOW TO READ & INTERPRET WIRING DIAGRAMS

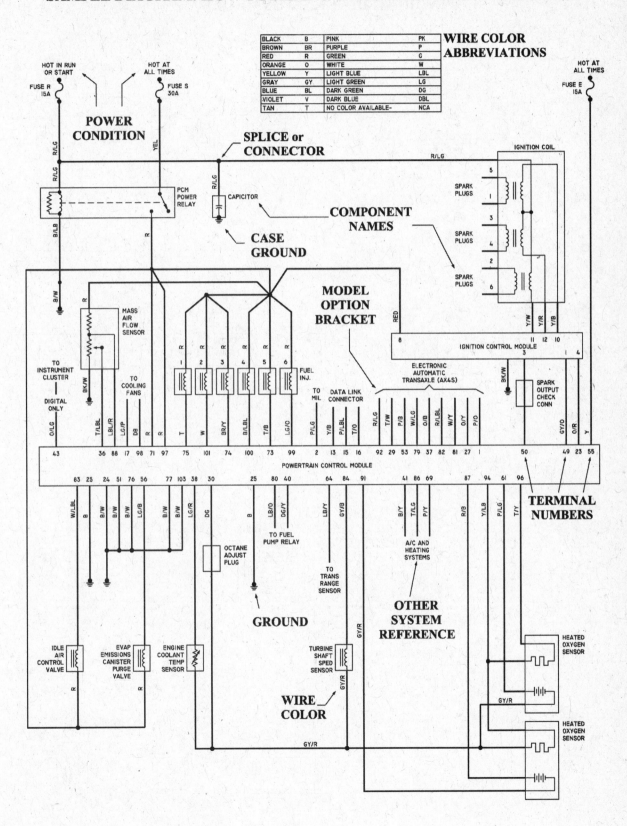

WIRING DIAGRAM SYMBOLS

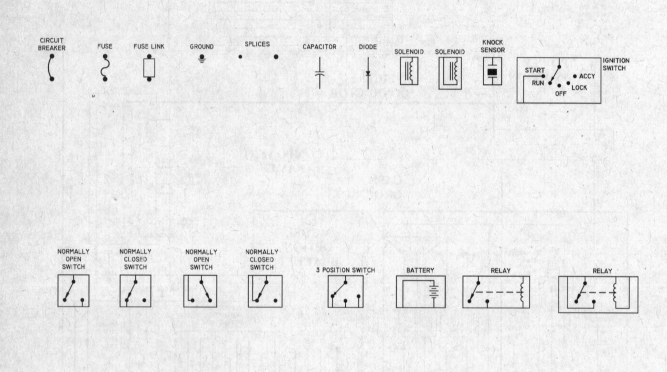

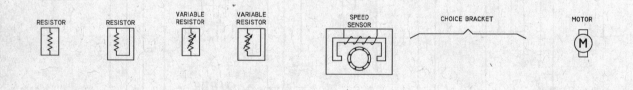

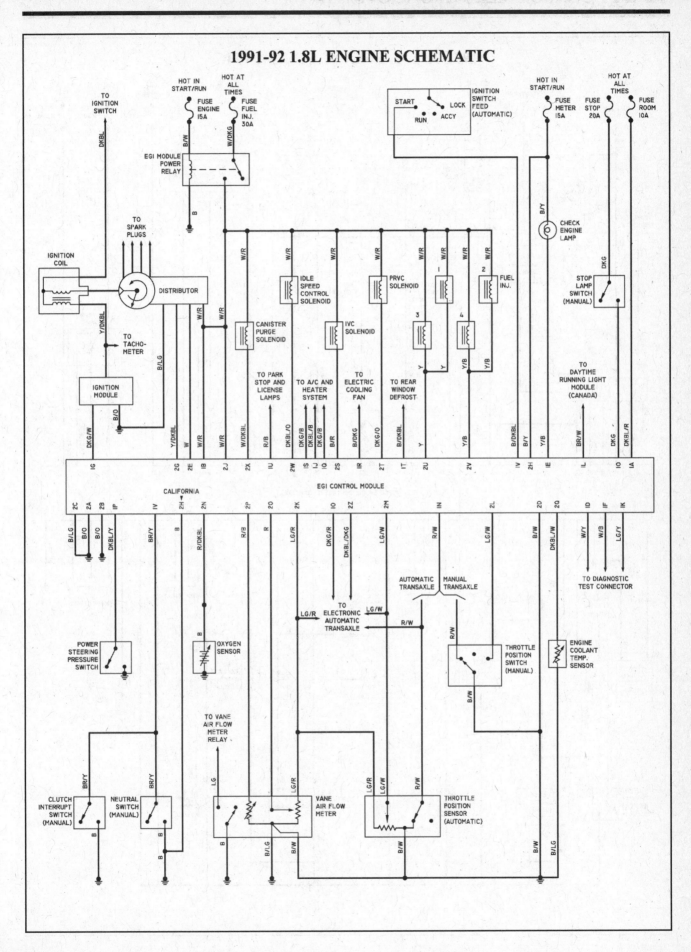

1991-92 1.8L ENGINE SCHEMATIC

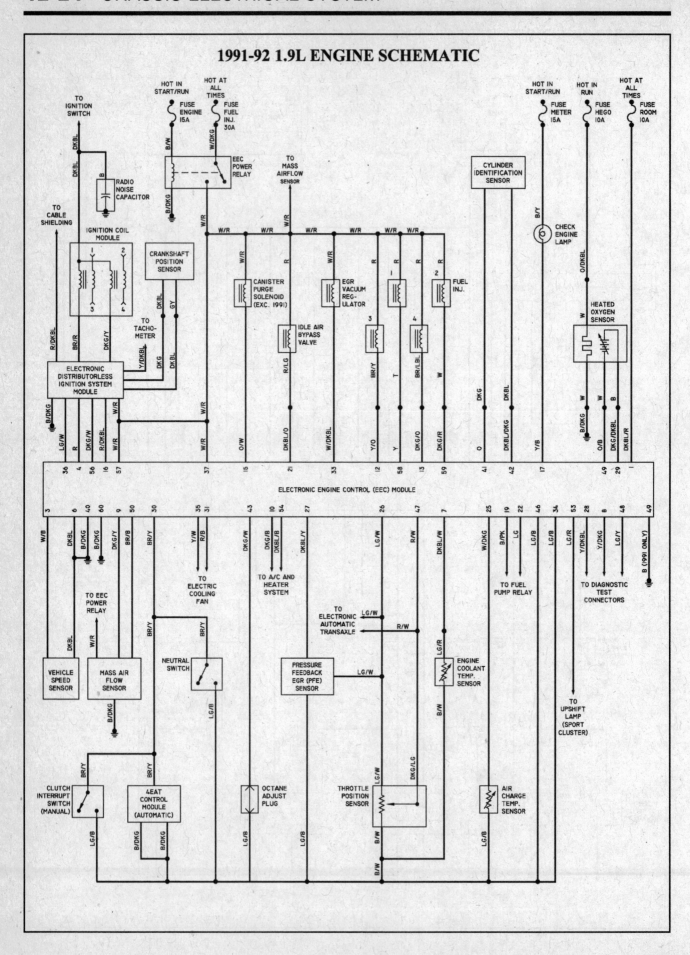

1991-92 1.9L ENGINE SCHEMATIC

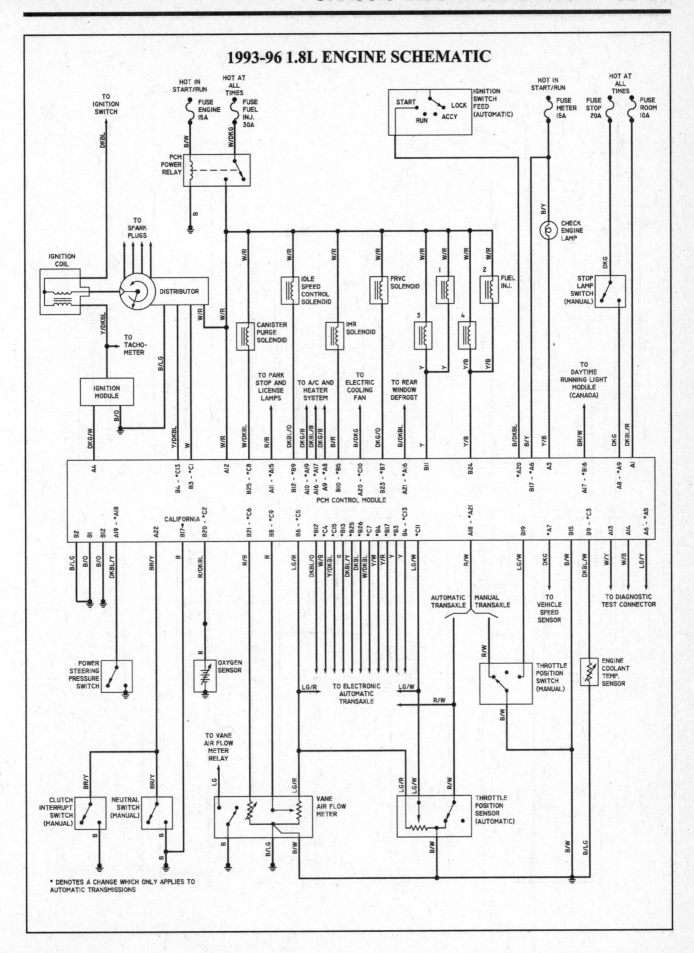

1993-96 1.8L ENGINE SCHEMATIC

1993-96 1.9L ENGINE SCHEMATIC

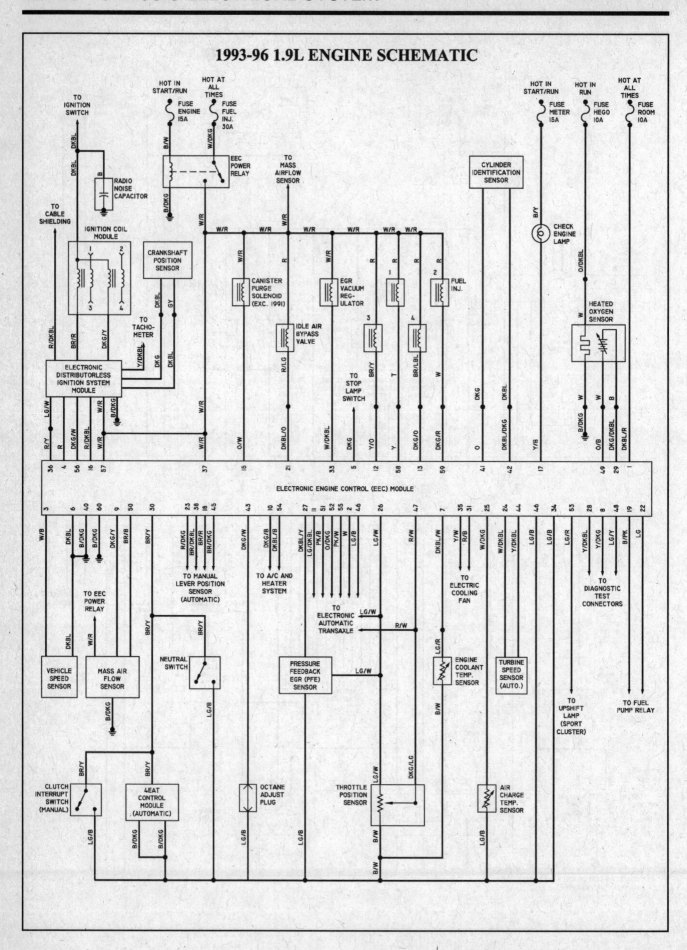

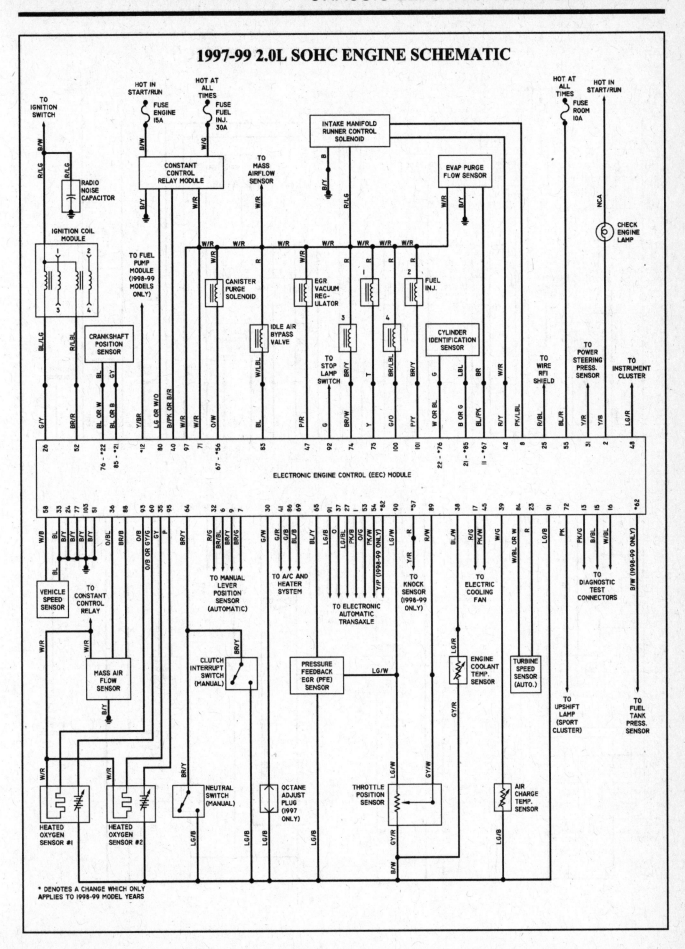

1997-99 2.0L SOHC ENGINE SCHEMATIC

1998-99 2.0L DOHC ENGINE SCHEMATIC

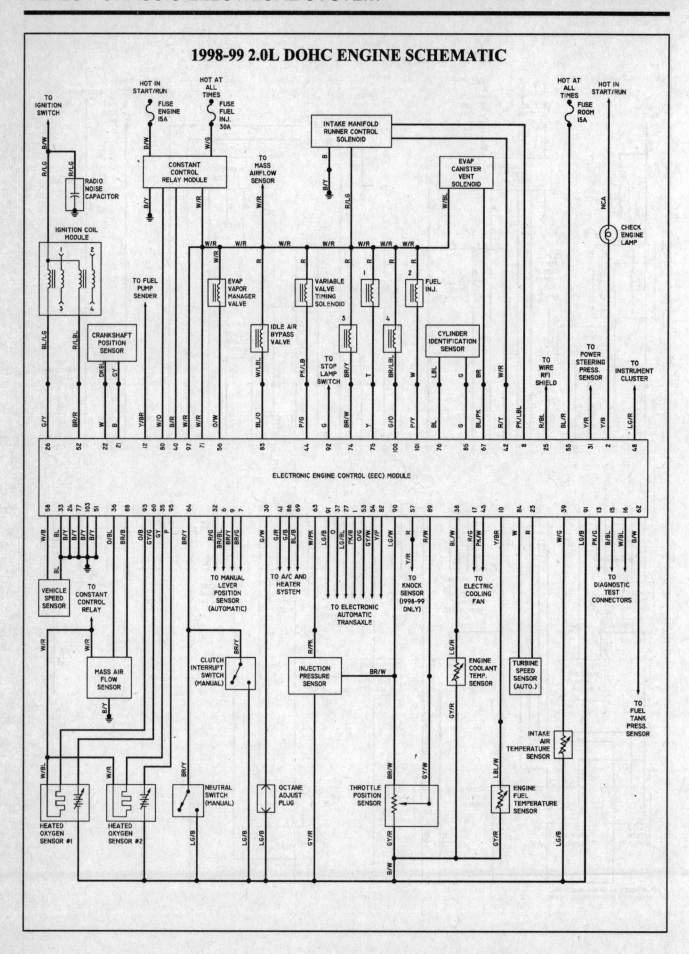

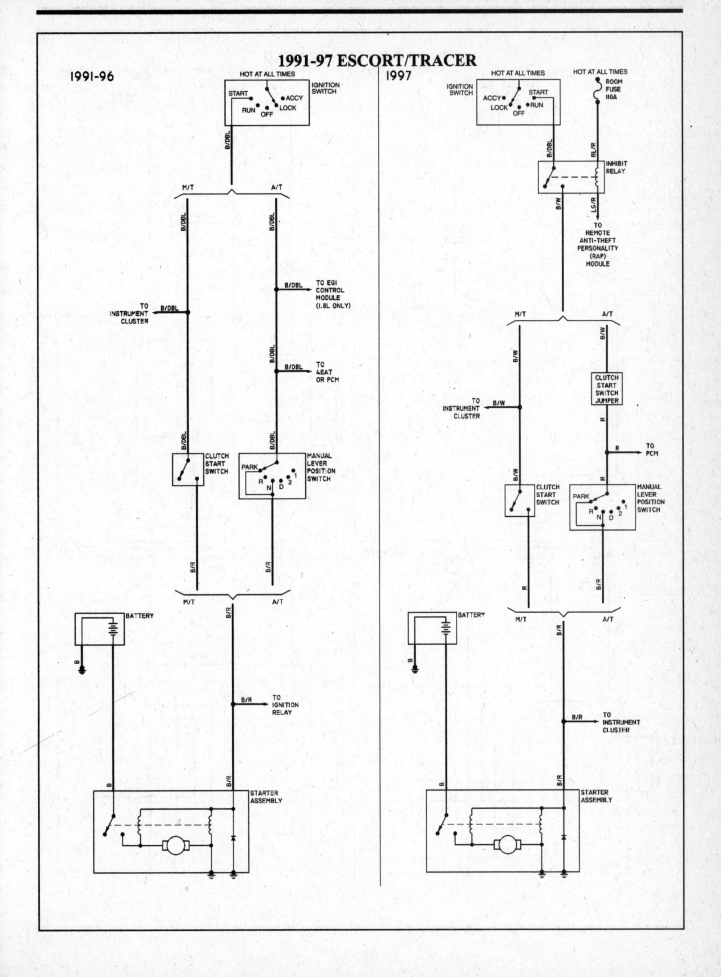

1991-97 ESCORT/TRACER

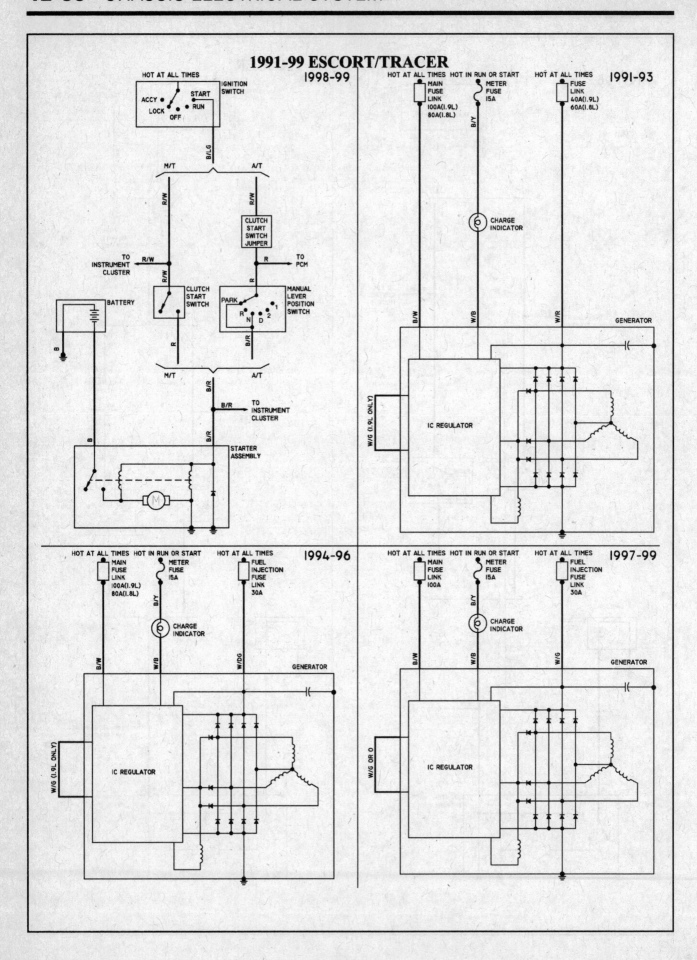

1991-99 ESCORT/TRACER

1991-97 ESCORT/TRACER

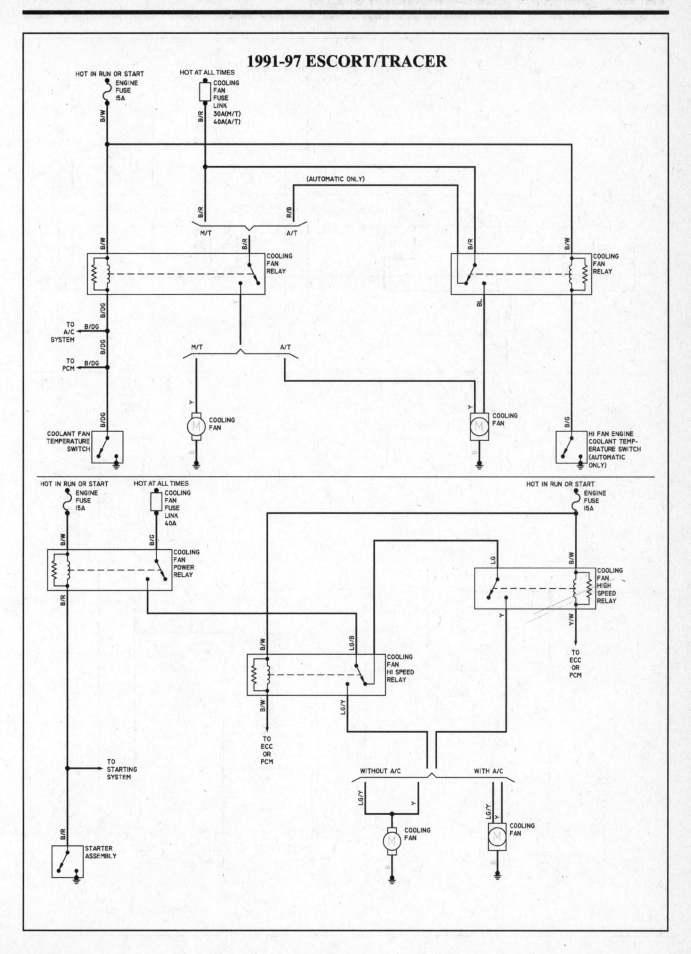

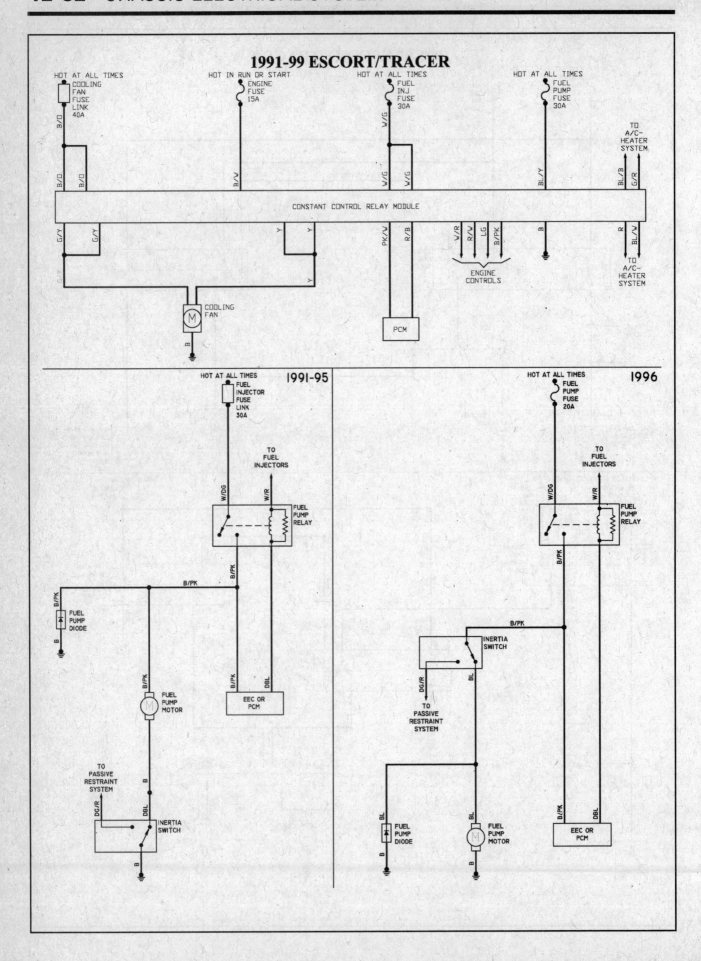

1991-99 ESCORT/TRACER

1991-99 ESCORT/TRACER

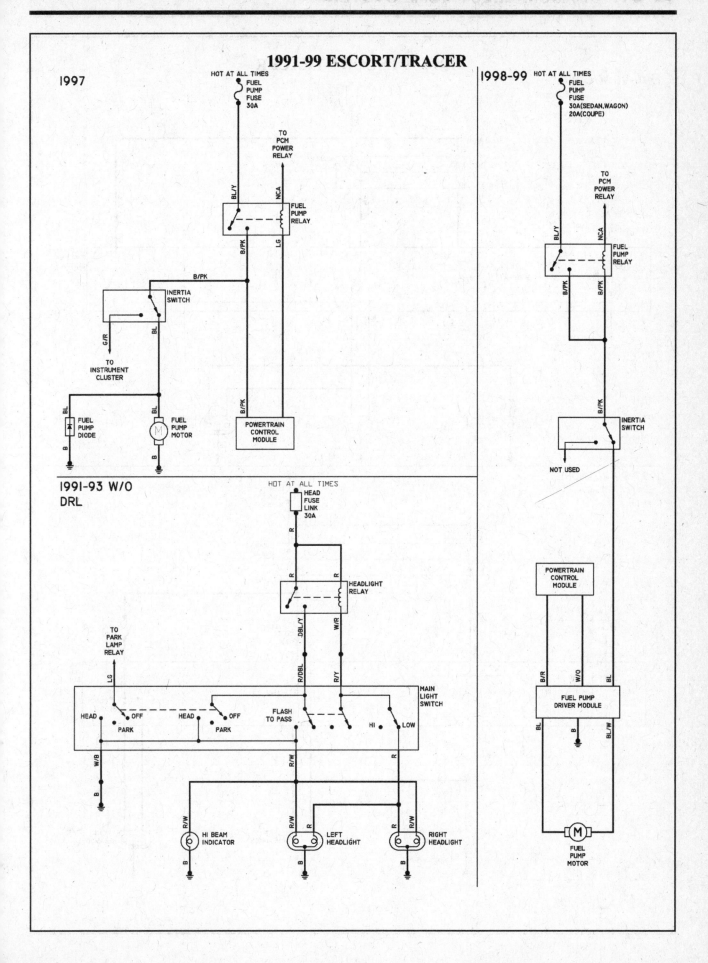

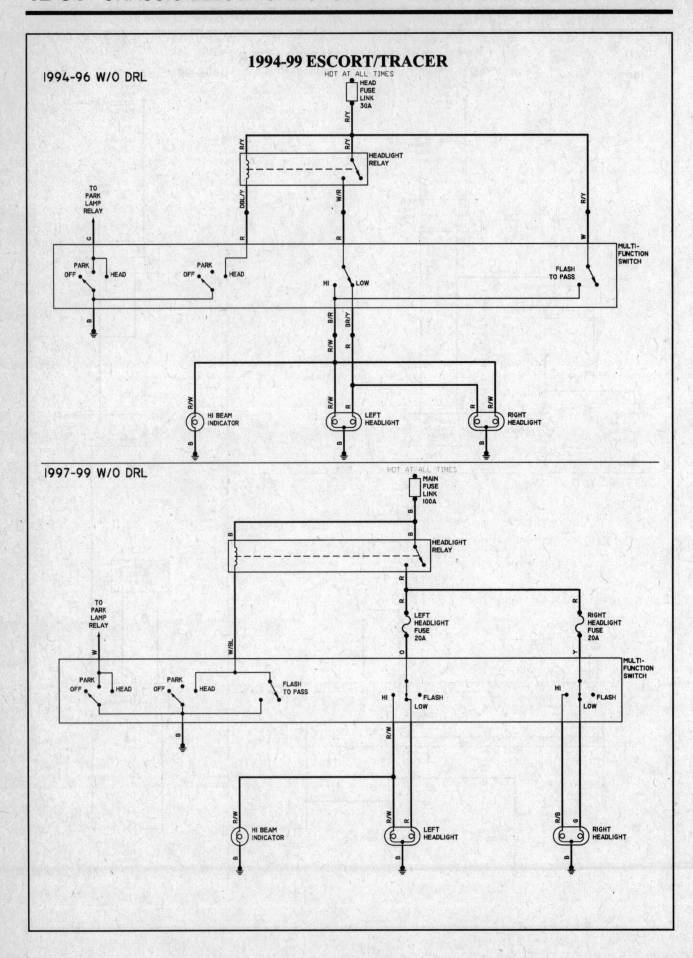

1994-99 ESCORT/TRACER

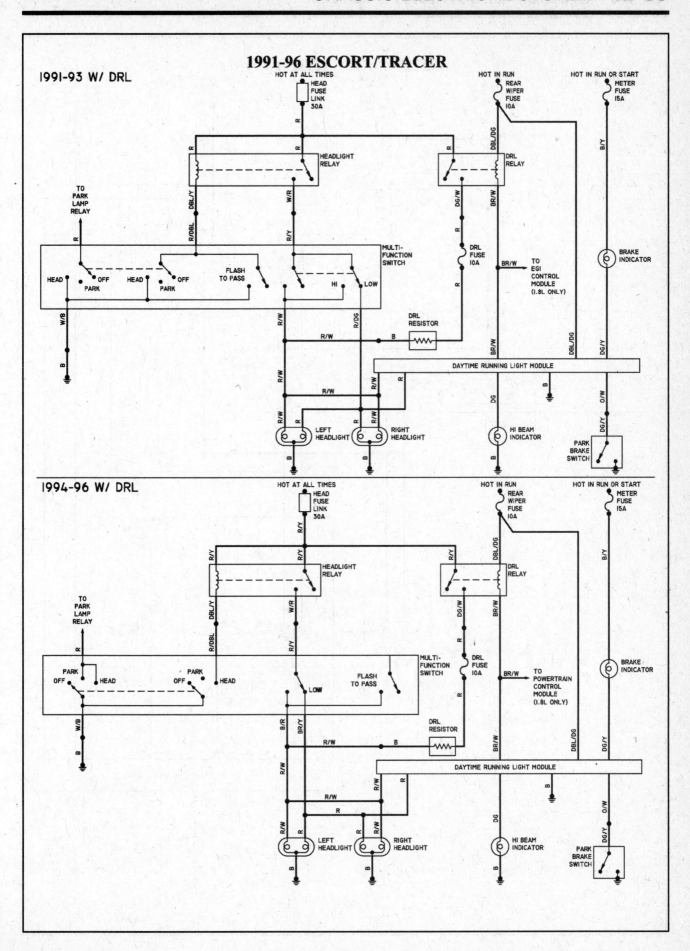

1991-96 ESCORT/TRACER

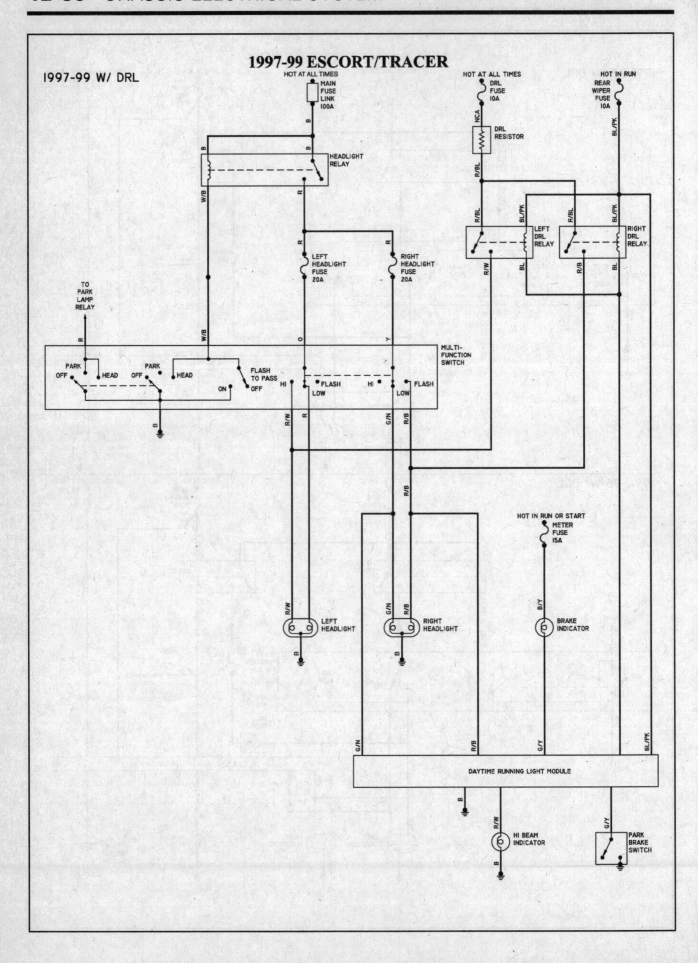

1997-99 ESCORT/TRACER

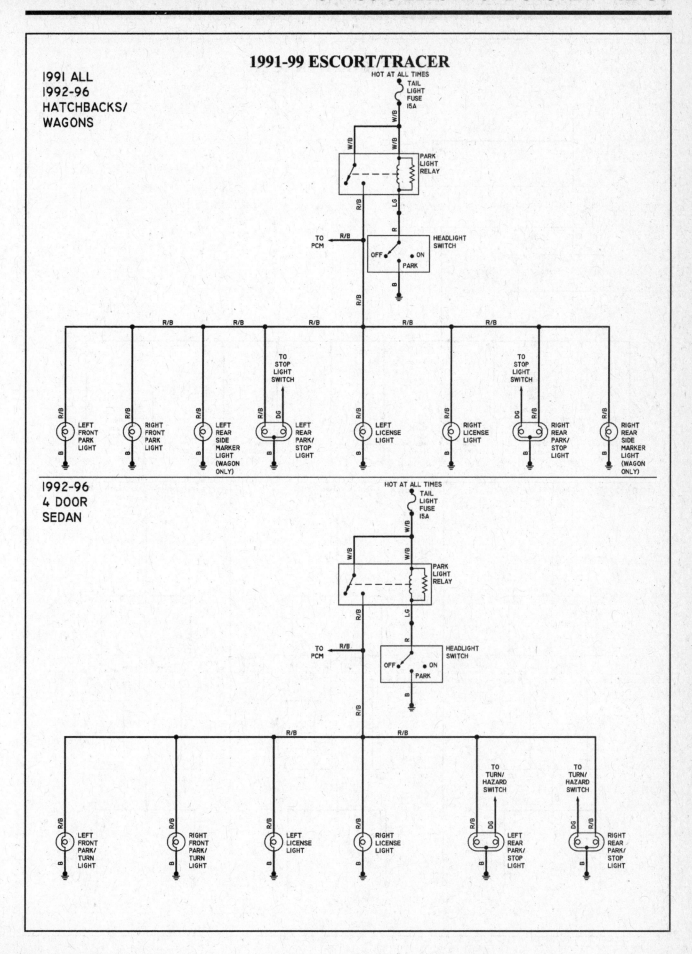

1991-99 ESCORT/TRACER

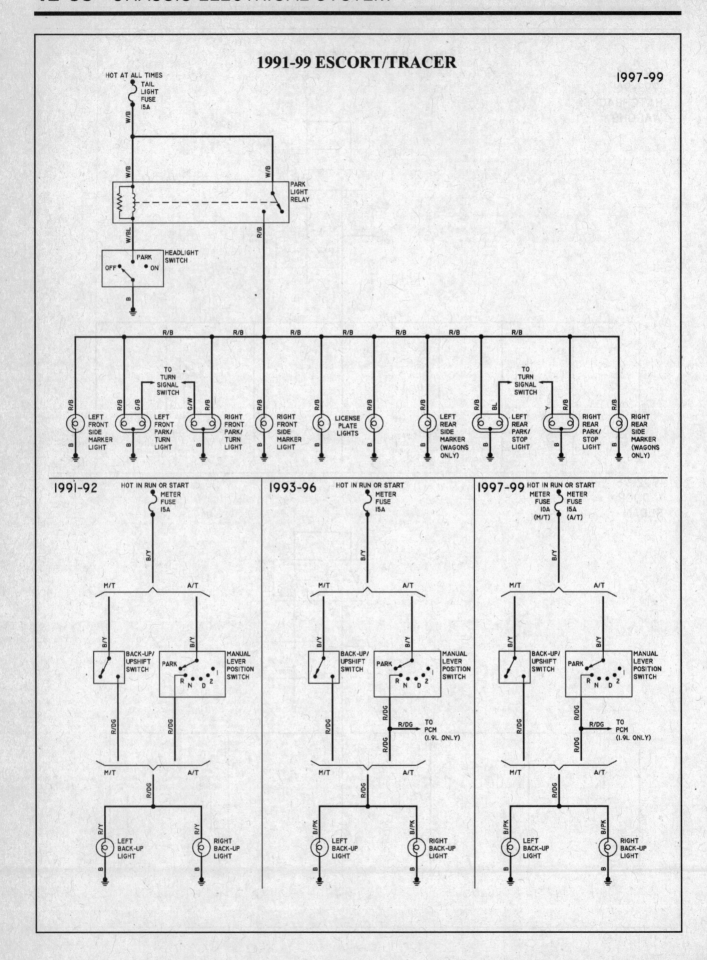

1991-99 ESCORT/TRACER

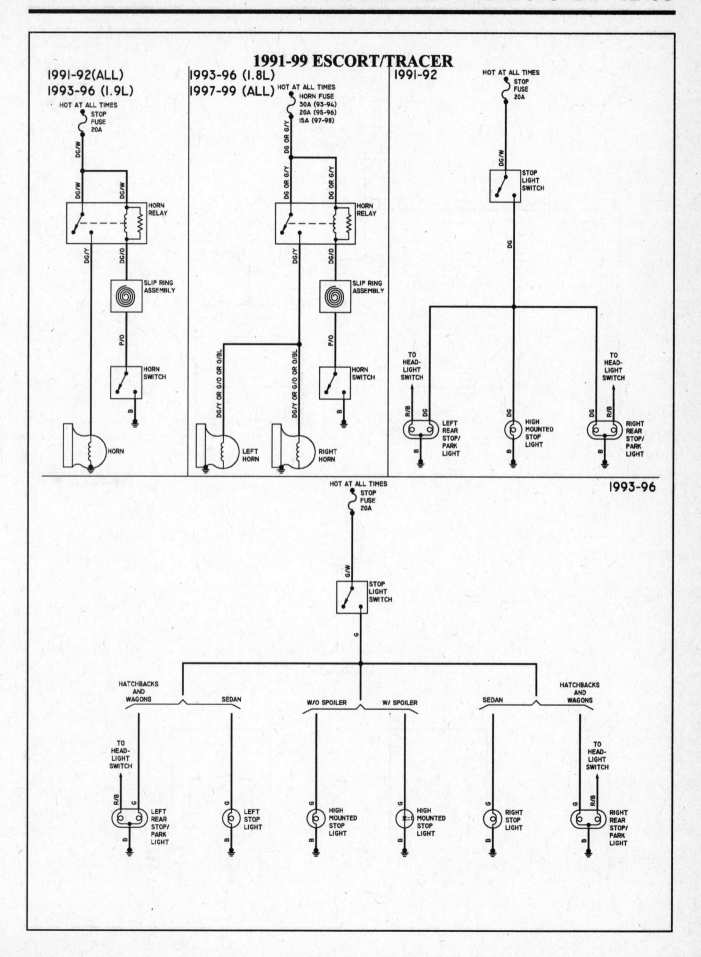

1991-99 ESCORT/TRACER

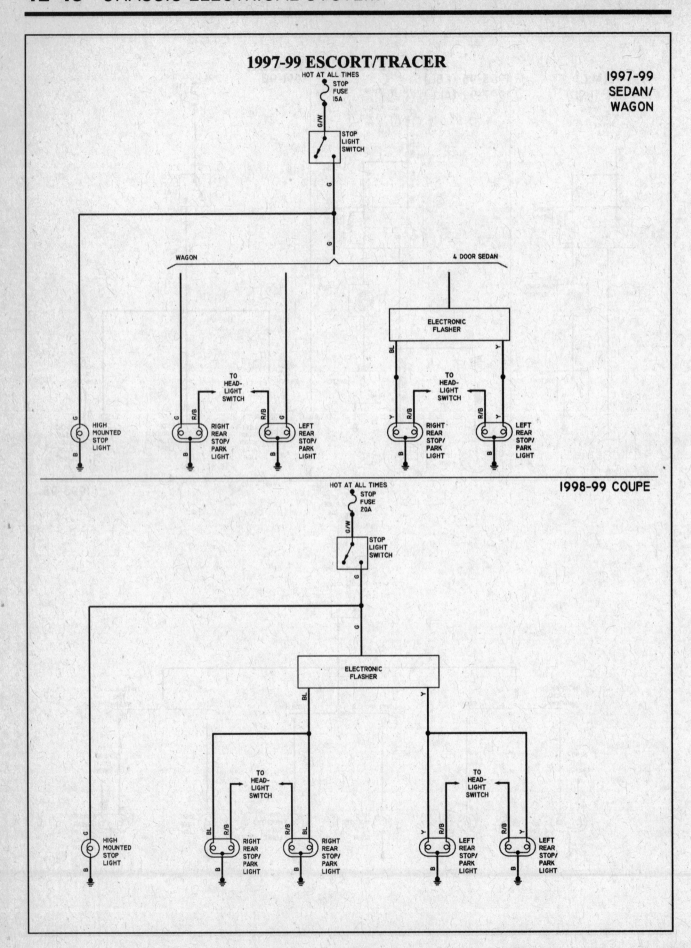

1997-99 ESCORT/TRACER

1997-99 SEDAN/WAGON

1998-99 COUPE

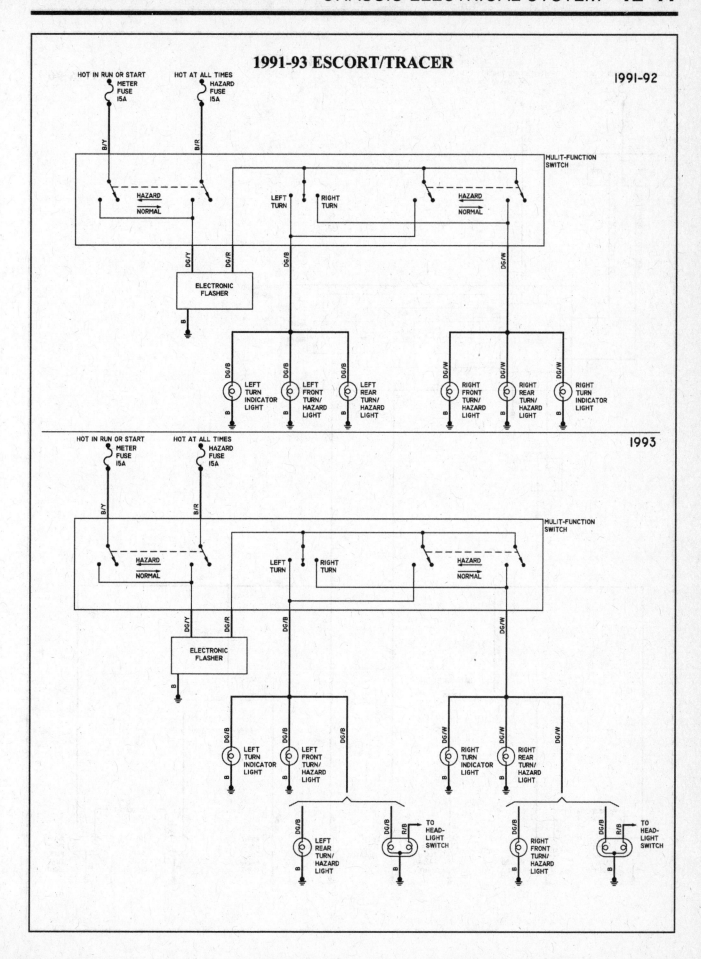

1991-93 ESCORT/TRACER

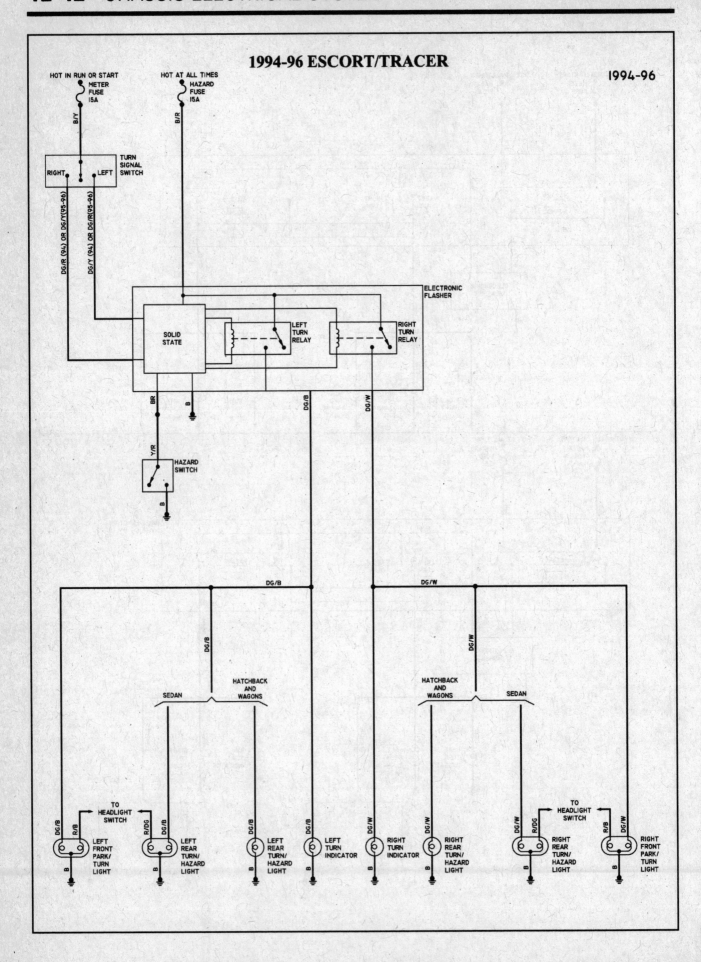

1994-96 ESCORT/TRACER

1994-96

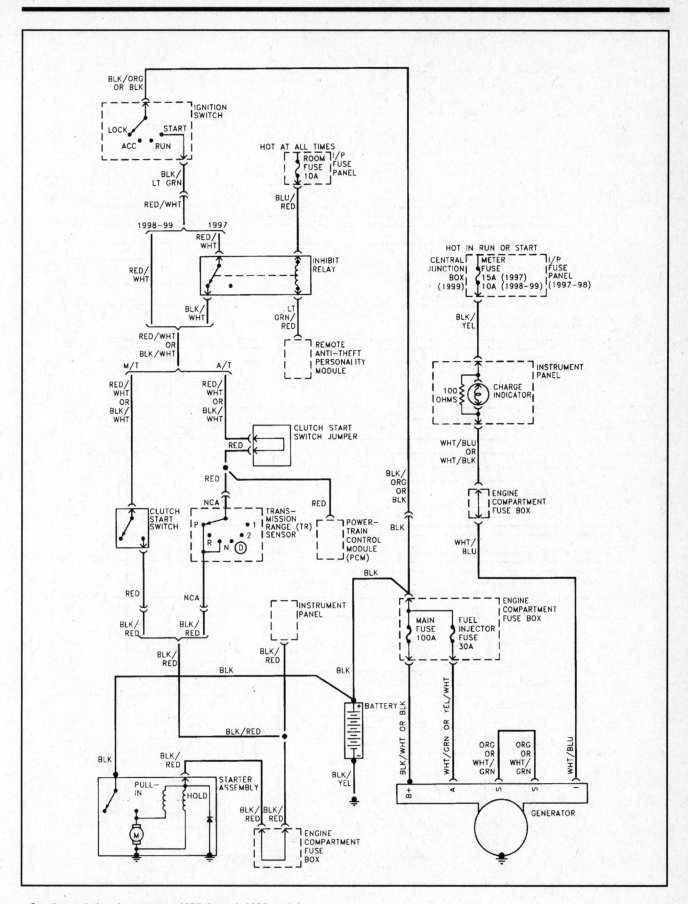

Starting and charging system - 1997 through 2000 models

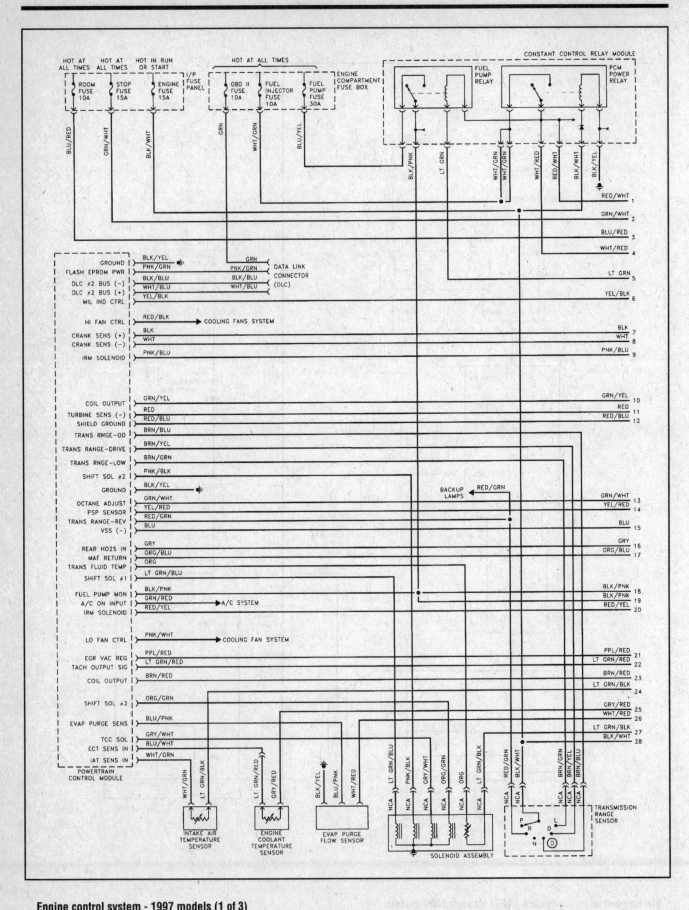

Engine control system - 1997 models (1 of 3)

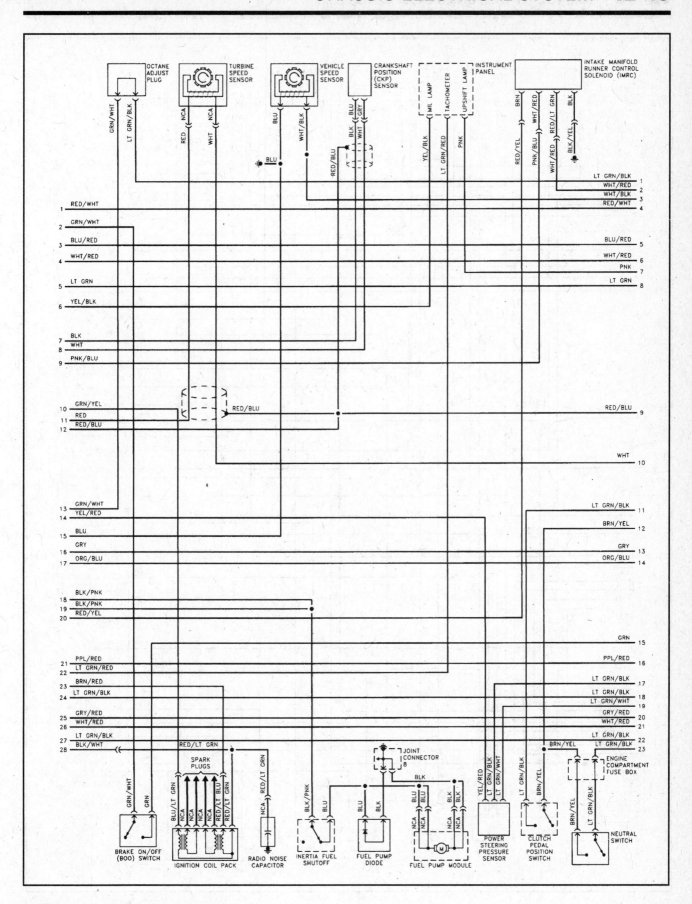

Engine control system - 1997 models (2 of 3)

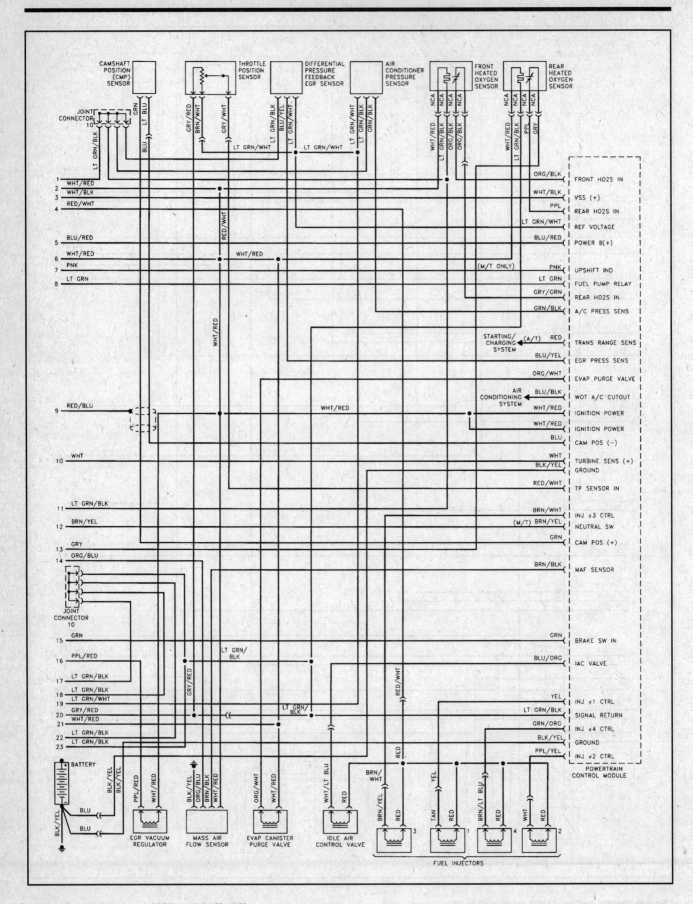

Engine control system - 1997 models (3 of 3)

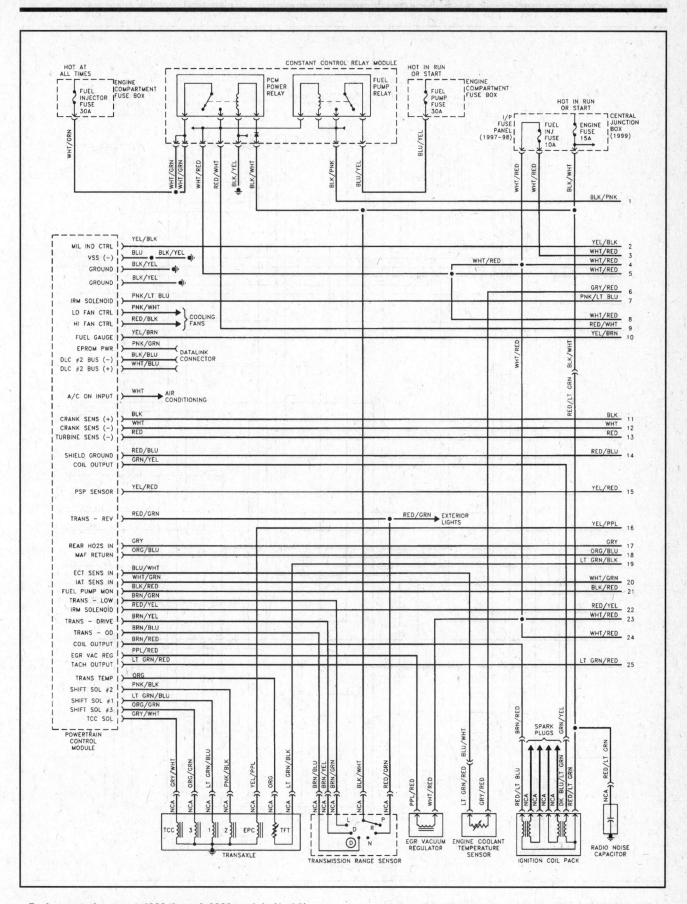

Engine control system - 1998 through 2000 models (1 of 3)

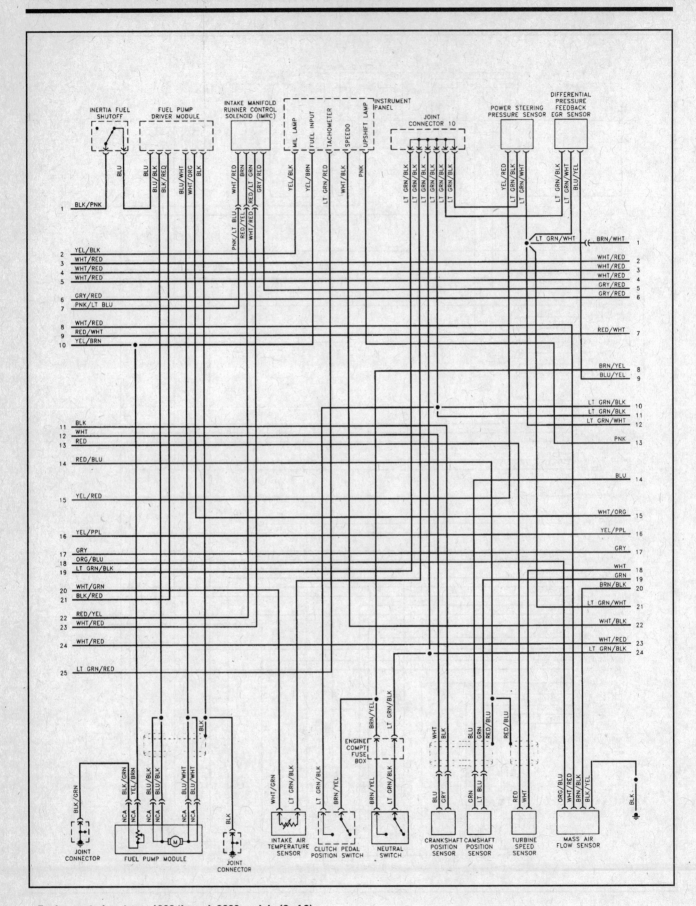

Engine control system - 1998 through 2000 models (2 of 3)

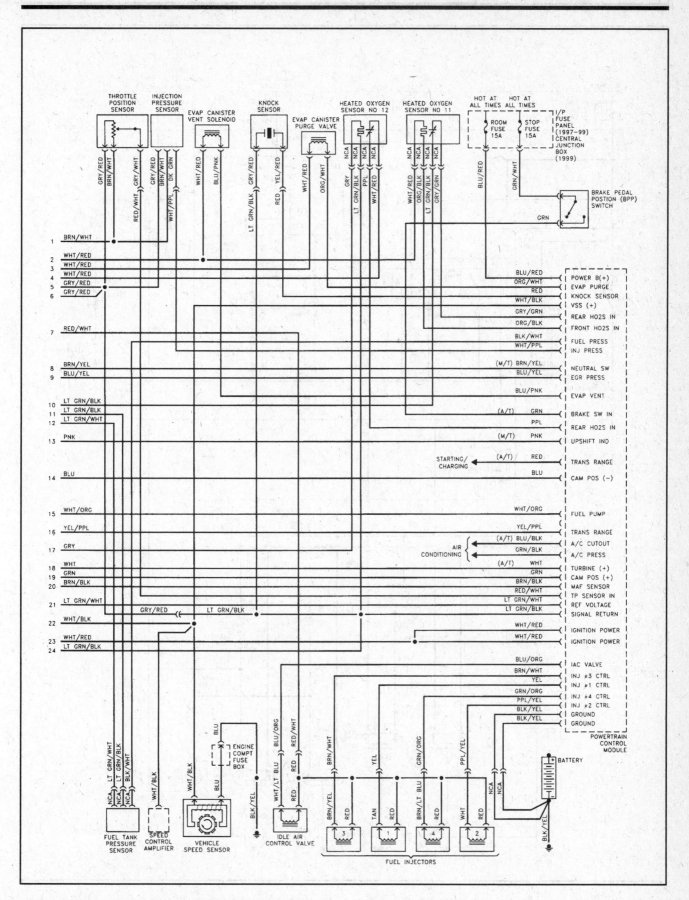

Engine control system - 1998 through 2000 models (3 of 3)

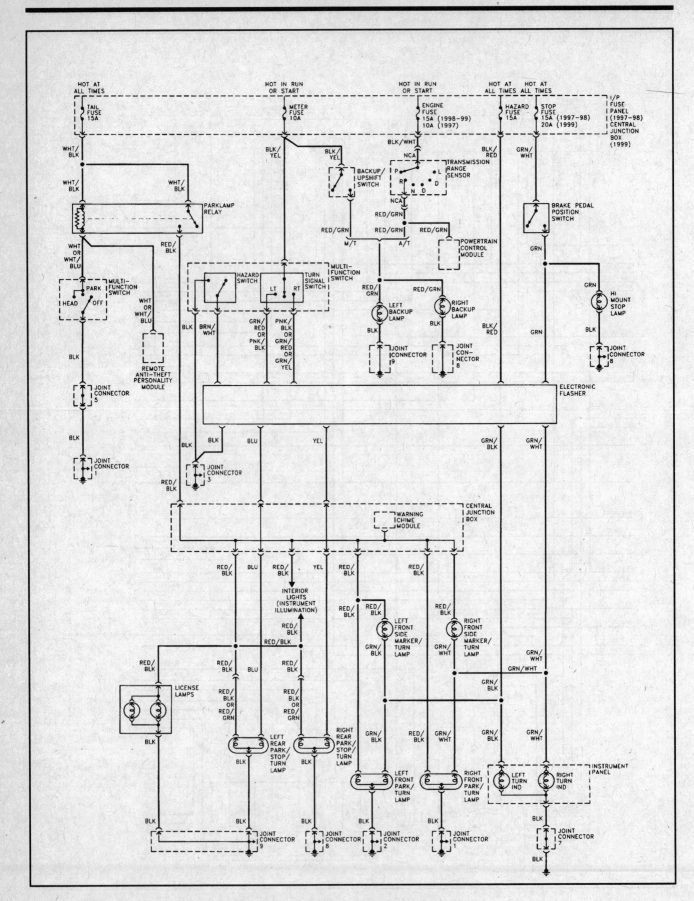

Exterior lighting system (except headlights) - 1997 through 2000 Coupe and Sedan models

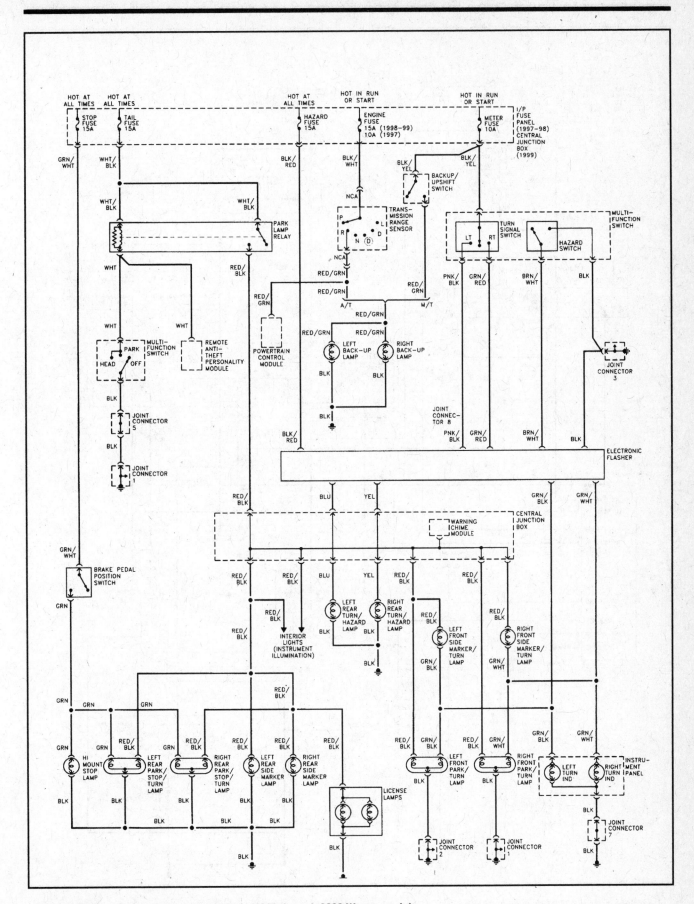

Exterior lighting system (except headlights) - 1997 through 2000 Wagon models

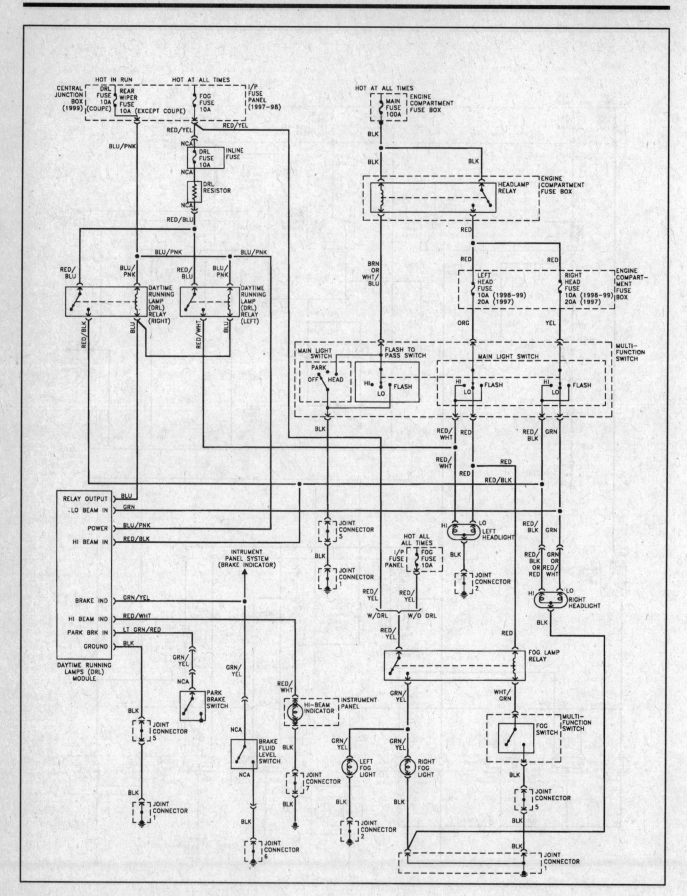

Headlight system - 1997 through 2000 models

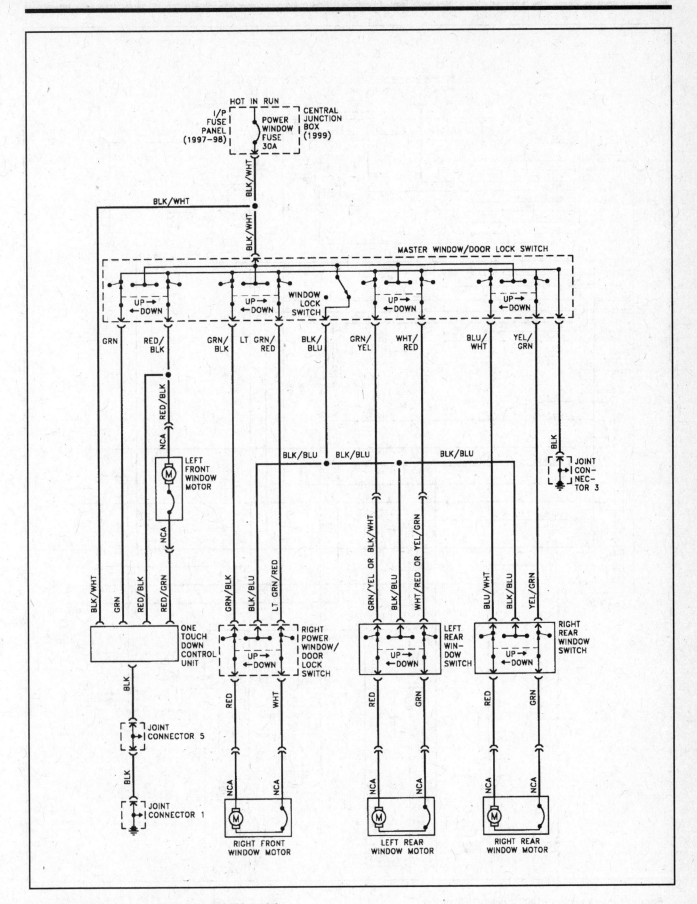

Power window system - 1997 through 2000 models

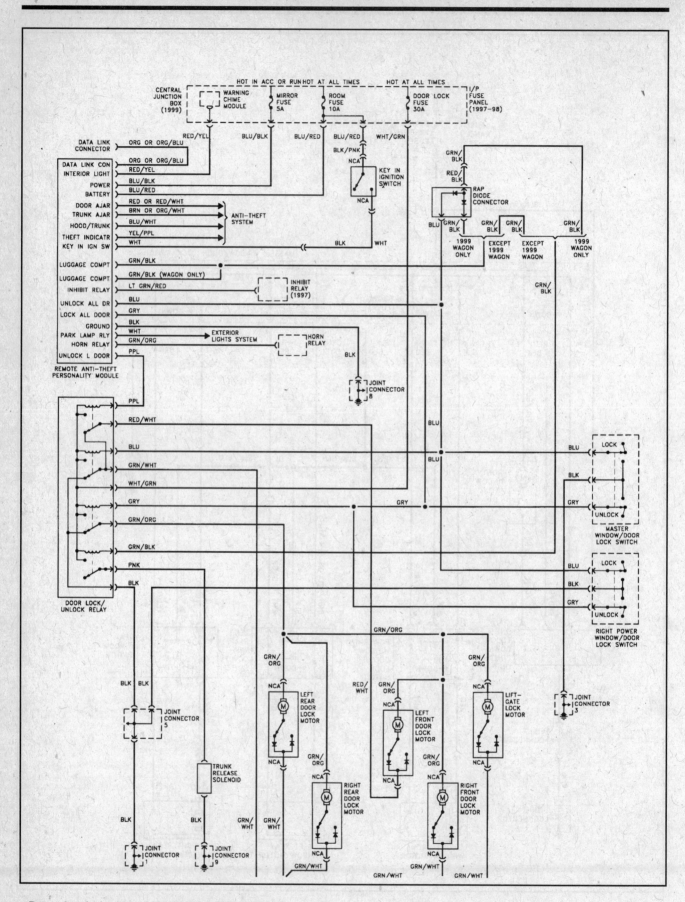

Power door lock system - 1997 through 2000 models

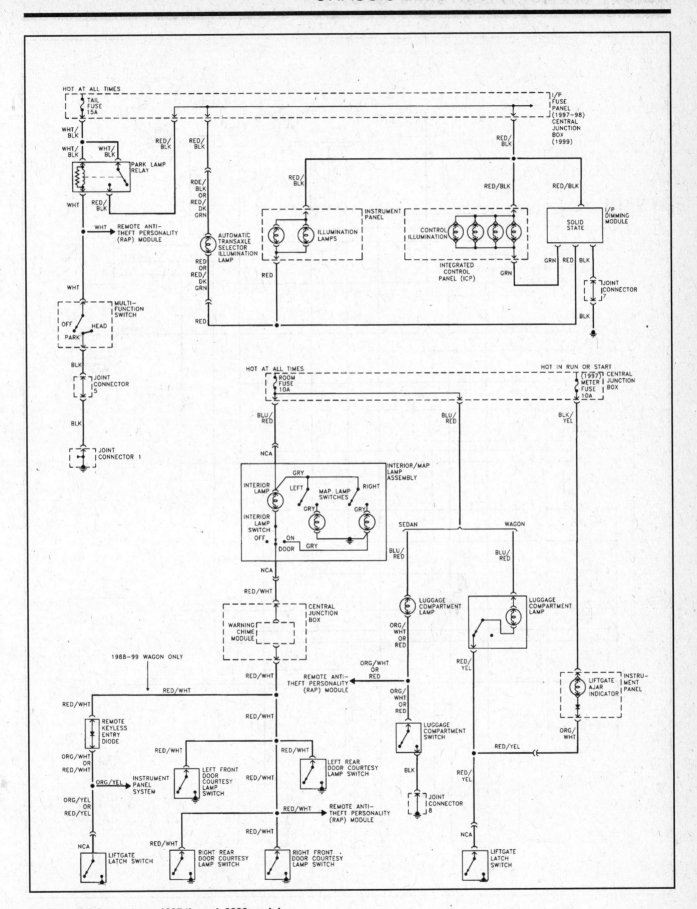

Interior lighting system - 1997 through 2000 models

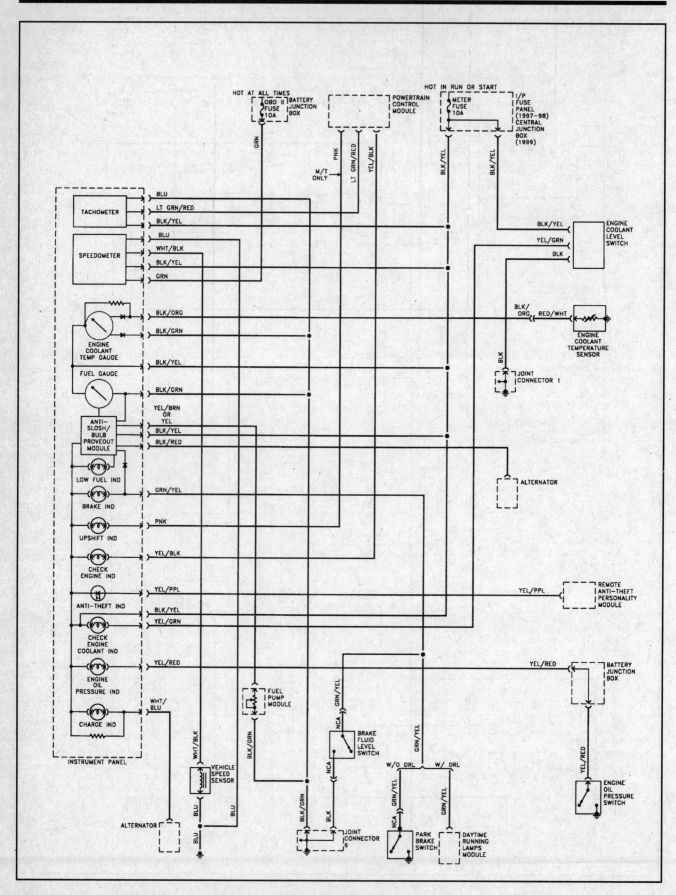

Instrument panel gauges and warning light system - 1997 through 2000 models

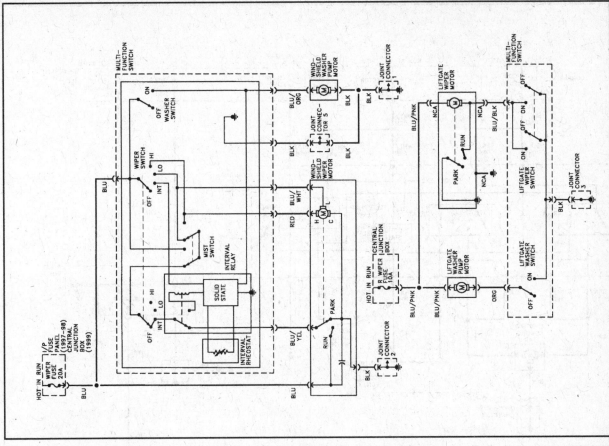

Windshield wiper and washer system - 1997 through 2000 models

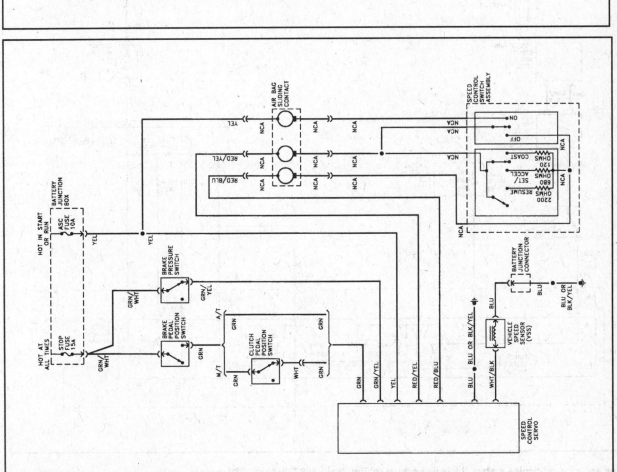

Cruise control system - 1997 through 2000 models

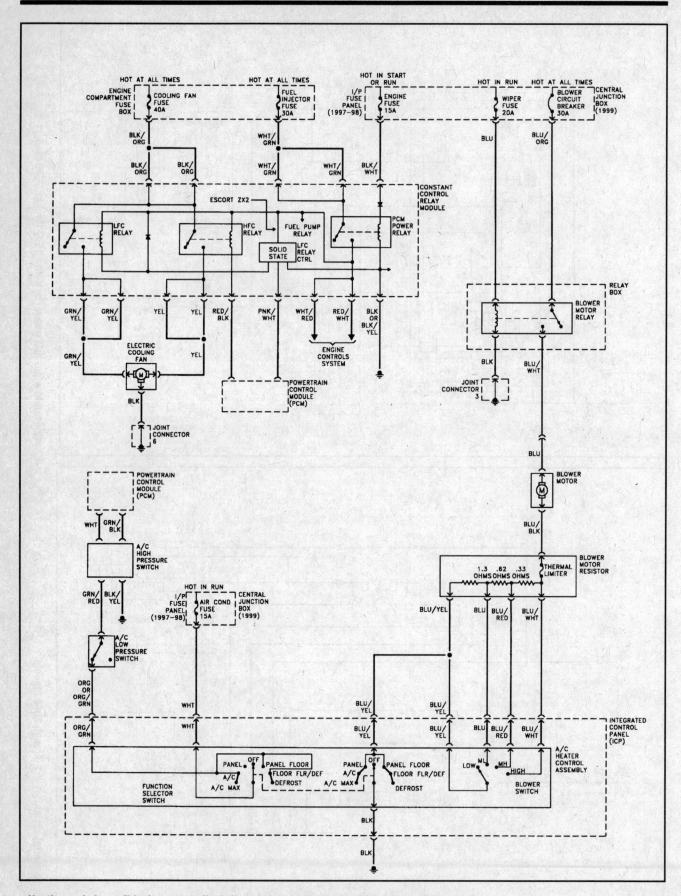

Heating and air conditioning system (including engine cooling fan) - 1997 through 2000 models

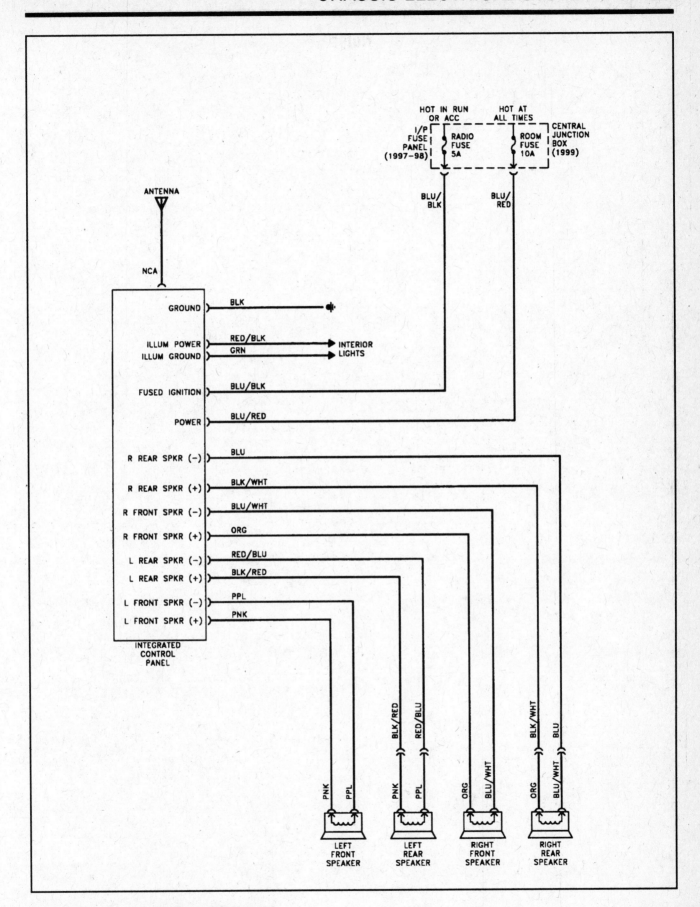

Typical stereo system - 1997 through 2000 models

Notes

GLOSSARY

AIR/FUEL RATIO: The ratio of air-to-gasoline by weight in the fuel mixture drawn into the engine.

AIR INJECTION: One method of reducing harmful exhaust emissions by injecting air into each of the exhaust ports of an engine. The fresh air entering the hot exhaust manifold causes any remaining fuel to be burned before it can exit the tailpipe.

ALTERNATOR: A device used for converting mechanical energy into electrical energy.

AMMETER: An instrument, calibrated in amperes, used to measure the flow of an electrical current in a circuit. Ammeters are always connected in series with the circuit being tested.

AMPERE: The rate of flow of electrical current present when one volt of electrical pressure is applied against one ohm of electrical resistance.

ANALOG COMPUTER: Any microprocessor that uses similar (analogous) electrical signals to make its calculations.

ARMATURE: A laminated, soft iron core wrapped by a wire that converts electrical energy to mechanical energy as in a motor or relay. When rotated in a magnetic field, it changes mechanical energy into electrical energy as in a generator.

ATMOSPHERIC PRESSURE: The pressure on the Earth's surface caused by the weight of the air in the atmosphere. At sea level, this pressure is 14.7 psi at 32°F (101 kPa at 0°C).

ATOMIZATION: The breaking down of a liquid into a fine mist that can be suspended in air.

AXIAL PLAY: Movement parallel to a shaft or bearing bore.

BACKFIRE: The sudden combustion of gases in the intake or exhaust system that results in a loud explosion.

BACKLASH: The clearance or play between two parts, such as meshed gears.

BACKPRESSURE: Restrictions in the exhaust system that slow the exit of exhaust gases from the combustion chamber.

BAKELITE: A heat resistant, plastic insulator material commonly used in printed circuit boards and transistorized components.

BALL BEARING: A bearing made up of hardened inner and outer races between which hardened steel balls roll.

BALLAST RESISTOR: A resistor in the primary ignition circuit that lowers voltage after the engine is started to reduce wear on ignition components.

BEARING: A friction reducing, supportive device usually located between a stationary part and a moving part.

BIMETAL TEMPERATURE SENSOR: Any sensor or switch made of two dissimilar types of metal that bend when heated or cooled due to the different expansion rates of the alloys. These types of sensors usually function as an on/off switch.

BLOWBY: Combustion gases, composed of water vapor and unburned fuel, that leak past the piston rings into the crankcase during normal engine operation. These gases are removed by the PCV system to prevent the buildup of harmful acids in the crankcase.

BRAKE PAD: A brake shoe and lining assembly used with disc brakes.

BRAKE SHOE: The backing for the brake lining. The term is, however, usually applied to the assembly of the brake backing and lining.

BUSHING: A liner, usually removable, for a bearing; an anti-friction liner used in place of a bearing.

CALIPER: A hydraulically activated device in a disc brake system, which is mounted straddling the brake rotor (disc). The caliper contains at least one piston and two brake pads. Hydraulic pressure on the piston(s) forces the pads against the rotor.

CAMSHAFT: A shaft in the engine on which are the lobes (cams) which operate the valves. The camshaft is driven by the crankshaft, via a belt, chain or gears, at one half the crankshaft speed.

CAPACITOR: A device which stores an electrical charge.

CARBON MONOXIDE (CO): A colorless, odorless gas given off as a normal byproduct of combustion. It is poisonous and extremely dangerous in confined areas, building up slowly to toxic levels without warning if adequate ventilation is not available.

CARBURETOR: A device, usually mounted on the intake manifold of an engine, which mixes the air and fuel in the proper proportion to allow even combustion.

CATALYTIC CONVERTER: A device installed in the exhaust system, like a muffler, that converts harmful byproducts of combustion into carbon dioxide and water vapor by means of a heat-producing chemical reaction.

CENTRIFUGAL ADVANCE: A mechanical method of advancing the spark timing by using flyweights in the distributor that react to centrifugal force generated by the distributor shaft rotation.

CHECK VALVE: Any one-way valve installed to permit the flow of air, fuel or vacuum in one direction only.

CHOKE: A device, usually a moveable valve, placed in the intake path of a carburetor to restrict the flow of air.

CIRCUIT: Any unbroken path through which an electrical current can flow. Also used to describe fuel flow in some instances.

CIRCUIT BREAKER: A switch which protects an electrical circuit from overload by opening the circuit when the current flow exceeds a predetermined level. Some circuit breakers must be reset manually, while most reset automatically.

COIL (IGNITION): A transformer in the ignition circuit which steps up the voltage provided to the spark plugs.

COMBINATION MANIFOLD: An assembly which includes both the intake and exhaust manifolds in one casting.

COMBINATION VALVE: A device used in some fuel systems that routes fuel vapors to a charcoal storage canister instead of venting them into the atmosphere. The valve relieves fuel tank pressure and allows fresh air into the tank as the fuel level drops to prevent a vapor lock situation.

COMPRESSION RATIO: The comparison of the total volume of the cylinder and combustion chamber with the piston at BDC and the piston at TDC.

CONDENSER: 1. An electrical device which acts to store an electrical charge, preventing voltage surges. 2. A radiator-like device in the air conditioning system in which refrigerant gas condenses into a liquid, giving off heat.

CONDUCTOR: Any material through which an electrical current can be transmitted easily.

CONTINUITY: Continuous or complete circuit. Can be checked with an ohmmeter.

COUNTERSHAFT: An intermediate shaft which is rotated by a mainshaft and transmits, in turn, that rotation to a working part.

CRANKCASE: The lower part of an engine in which the crankshaft and related parts operate.

CRANKSHAFT: The main driving shaft of an engine which receives reciprocating motion from the pistons and converts it to rotary motion.

CYLINDER: In an engine, the round hole in the engine block in which the piston(s) ride.

CYLINDER BLOCK: The main structural member of an engine in which is found the cylinders, crankshaft and other principal parts.

CYLINDER HEAD: The detachable portion of the engine, usually fastened to the top of the cylinder block and containing all or most of the combustion chambers. On overhead valve engines, it contains the valves and their operating parts. On overhead cam engines, it contains the camshaft as well.

DEAD CENTER: The extreme top or bottom of the piston stroke.

DETONATION: An unwanted explosion of the air/fuel mixture in the combustion chamber caused by excess heat and compression, advanced timing, or an overly lean mixture. Also referred to as "ping".

DIAPHRAGM: A thin, flexible wall separating two cavities, such as in a vacuum advance unit.

DIESELING: A condition in which hot spots in the combustion chamber cause the engine to run on after the key is turned off.

DIFFERENTIAL: A geared assembly which allows the transmission of motion between drive axles, giving one axle the ability to turn faster than the other.

DIODE: An electrical device that will allow current to flow in one direction only.

DISC BRAKE: A hydraulic braking assembly consisting of a brake disc, or rotor, mounted on an axle, and a caliper assembly containing, usually two brake pads which are activated by hydraulic pressure. The pads are forced against the sides of the disc, creating friction which slows the vehicle.

DISTRIBUTOR: A mechanically driven device on an engine which is responsible for electrically firing the spark plug at a predetermined point of the piston stroke.

DOWEL PIN: A pin, inserted in mating holes in two different parts allowing those parts to maintain a fixed relationship.

DRUM BRAKE: A braking system which consists of two brake shoes and one or two wheel cylinders, mounted on a fixed backing plate, and a brake drum, mounted on an axle, which revolves around the assembly.

DWELL: The rate, measured in degrees of shaft rotation, at which an electrical circuit cycles on and off.

ELECTRONIC CONTROL UNIT (ECU): Ignition module, module, amplifier or igniter. See Module for definition.

ELECTRONIC IGNITION: A system in which the timing and firing of the spark plugs is controlled by an electronic control unit, usually called a module. These systems have no points or condenser.

END-PLAY: The measured amount of axial movement in a shaft.

ENGINE: A device that converts heat into mechanical energy.

EXHAUST MANIFOLD: A set of cast passages or pipes which conduct exhaust gases from the engine.

FEELER GAUGE: A blade, usually metal, or precisely predetermined thickness, used to measure the clearance between two parts.

FIRING ORDER: The order in which combustion occurs in the cylinders of an engine. Also the order in which spark is distributed to the plugs by the distributor.

FLOODING: The presence of too much fuel in the intake manifold and combustion chamber which prevents the air/fuel mixture from firing, thereby causing a no-start situation.

FLYWHEEL: A disc shaped part bolted to the rear end of the crankshaft. Around the outer perimeter is affixed the ring gear. The starter drive engages the ring gear, turning the flywheel, which rotates the crankshaft, imparting the initial starting motion to the engine.

FOOT POUND (ft. lbs. or sometimes, ft.lb.): The amount of energy or work needed to raise an item weighing one pound, a distance of one foot.

FUSE: A protective device in a circuit which prevents circuit overload by breaking the circuit when a specific amperage is present. The device is constructed around a strip or wire of a lower amperage rating than the circuit it is designed to protect. When an amperage higher than that stamped on the fuse is present in the circuit, the strip or wire melts, opening the circuit.

GEAR RATIO: The ratio between the number of teeth on meshing gears.

GENERATOR: A device which converts mechanical energy into electrical energy.

HEAT RANGE: The measure of a spark plug's ability to dissipate heat from its firing end. The higher the heat range, the hotter the plug fires.

HUB: The center part of a wheel or gear.

HYDROCARBON (HC): Any chemical compound made up of hydrogen and carbon. A major pollutant formed by the engine as a byproduct of combustion.

HYDROMETER: An instrument used to measure the specific gravity of a solution.

INCH POUND (inch lbs.; sometimes in.lb. or in. lbs.): One twelfth of a foot pound.

INDUCTION: A means of transferring electrical energy in the form of a magnetic field. Principle used in the ignition coil to increase voltage.

INJECTOR: A device which receives metered fuel under relatively low pressure and is activated to inject the fuel into the engine under relatively high pressure at a predetermined time.

INPUT SHAFT: The shaft to which torque is applied, usually carrying the driving gear or gears.

INTAKE MANIFOLD: A casting of passages or pipes used to conduct air or a fuel/air mixture to the cylinders.

JOURNAL: The bearing surface within which a shaft operates.

KEY: A small block usually fitted in a notch between a shaft and a hub to prevent slippage of the two parts.

MANIFOLD: A casting of passages or set of pipes which connect the cylinders to an inlet or outlet source.

MANIFOLD VACUUM: Low pressure in an engine intake manifold formed just below the throttle plates. Manifold vacuum is highest at idle and drops under acceleration.

MASTER CYLINDER: The primary fluid pressurizing device in a hydraulic system. In automotive use, it is found in brake and hydraulic clutch systems and is pedal activated, either directly or, in a power brake system, through the power booster.

MODULE: Electronic control unit, amplifier or igniter of solid state or integrated design which controls the current flow in the ignition primary circuit based on input from the pick-up coil. When the module opens the primary circuit, high secondary voltage is induced in the coil.

NEEDLE BEARING: A bearing which consists of a number (usually a large number) of long, thin rollers.

OHM: (Ω) The unit used to measure the resistance of conductor-to-electrical flow. One ohm is the amount of resistance that limits current flow to one ampere in a circuit with one volt of pressure.

OHMMETER: An instrument used for measuring the resistance, in ohms, in an electrical circuit.

OUTPUT SHAFT: The shaft which transmits torque from a device, such as a transmission.

OVERDRIVE: A gear assembly which produces more shaft revolutions than that transmitted to it.

OVERHEAD CAMSHAFT (OHC): An engine configuration in which the camshaft is mounted on top of the cylinder head and operates the valve either directly or by means of rocker arms.

OVERHEAD VALVE (OHV): An engine configuration in which all of the valves are located in the cylinder head and the camshaft is located in the cylinder block. The camshaft operates the valves via lifters and pushrods.

OXIDES OF NITROGEN (NOx): Chemical compounds of nitrogen produced as a byproduct of combustion. They combine with hydrocarbons to produce smog.

OXYGEN SENSOR: Use with the feedback system to sense the presence of oxygen in the exhaust gas and signal the computer which can reference the voltage signal to an air/fuel ratio.

PINION: The smaller of two meshing gears.

PISTON RING: An open-ended ring with fits into a groove on the outer diameter of the piston. Its chief function is to form a seal between the piston and cylinder wall. Most automotive pistons have three rings: two for compression sealing; one for oil sealing.

PRELOAD: A predetermined load placed on a bearing during assembly or by adjustment.

PRIMARY CIRCUIT: the low voltage side of the ignition system which consists of the ignition switch, ballast resistor or resistance wire, bypass, coil, electronic control unit and pick-up coil as well as the connecting wires and harnesses.

PRESS FIT: The mating of two parts under pressure, due to the inner diameter of one being smaller than the outer diameter of the other, or vice versa; an interference fit.

RACE: The surface on the inner or outer ring of a bearing on which the balls, needles or rollers move.

REGULATOR: A device which maintains the amperage and/or voltage levels of a circuit at predetermined values.

RELAY: A switch which automatically opens and/or closes a circuit.

RESISTANCE: The opposition to the flow of current through a circuit or electrical device, and is measured in ohms. Resistance is equal to the voltage divided by the amperage.

RESISTOR: A device, usually made of wire, which offers a preset amount of resistance in an electrical circuit.

RING GEAR: The name given to a ring-shaped gear attached to a differential case, or affixed to a flywheel or as part of a planetary gear set.

ROLLER BEARING: A bearing made up of hardened inner and outer races between which hardened steel rollers move.

ROTOR: 1. The disc-shaped part of a disc brake assembly, upon which the brake pads bear; also called, brake disc. 2. The device mounted atop the distributor shaft, which passes current to the distributor cap tower contacts.

SECONDARY CIRCUIT: The high voltage side of the ignition system, usually above 20,000 volts. The secondary includes the ignition coil, coil wire, distributor cap and rotor, spark plug wires and spark plugs.

SENDING UNIT: A mechanical, electrical, hydraulic or electromagnetic device which transmits information to a gauge.

SENSOR: Any device designed to measure engine operating conditions or ambient pressures and temperatures. Usually electronic in nature and designed to send a voltage signal to an on-board computer, some sensors may operate as a simple on/off switch or they may provide a variable voltage signal (like a potentiometer) as conditions or measured parameters change.

SHIM: Spacers of precise, predetermined thickness used between parts to establish a proper working relationship.

SLAVE CYLINDER: In automotive use, a device in the hydraulic clutch system which is activated by hydraulic force, disengaging the clutch.

SOLENOID: A coil used to produce a magnetic field, the effect of which is to produce work.

SPARK PLUG: A device screwed into the combustion chamber of a spark ignition engine. The basic construction is a conductive core inside of a ceramic insulator, mounted in an outer conductive base. An electrical charge from the spark plug wire travels along the conductive core and jumps a preset air gap to a grounding point or points at the end of the conductive base. The resultant spark ignites the fuel/air mixture in the combustion chamber.

SPLINES: Ridges machined or cast onto the outer diameter of a shaft or inner diameter of a bore to enable parts to mate without rotation.

TACHOMETER: A device used to measure the rotary speed of an engine, shaft, gear, etc., usually in rotations per minute.

THERMOSTAT: A valve, located in the cooling system of an engine, which is closed when cold and opens gradually in response to engine heating, controlling the temperature of the coolant and rate of coolant flow.

TOP DEAD CENTER (TDC): The point at which the piston reaches the top of its travel on the compression stroke.

TORQUE: The twisting force applied to an object.

TORQUE CONVERTER: A turbine used to transmit power from a driving member to a driven member via hydraulic action, providing changes in drive ratio and torque. In automotive use, it links the driveplate at the rear of the engine to the automatic transmission.

TRANSDUCER: A device used to change a force into an electrical signal.

TRANSISTOR: A semi-conductor component which can be actuated by a small voltage to perform an electrical switching function.

TUNE-UP: A regular maintenance function, usually associated with the replacement and adjustment of parts and components in the electrical and fuel systems of a vehicle for the purpose of attaining optimum performance.

TURBOCHARGER: An exhaust driven pump which compresses intake air and forces it into the combustion chambers at higher than atmospheric pressures. The increased air pressure allows more fuel to be burned and results in increased horsepower being produced.

VACUUM ADVANCE: A device which advances the ignition timing in response to increased engine vacuum.

VACUUM GAUGE: An instrument used to measure the presence of vacuum in a chamber.

VALVE: A device which control the pressure, direction of flow or rate of flow of a liquid or gas.

VALVE CLEARANCE: The measured gap between the end of the valve stem and the rocker arm, cam lobe or follower that activates the valve.

VISCOSITY: The rating of a liquid's internal resistance to flow.

VOLTMETER: An instrument used for measuring electrical force in units called volts. Voltmeters are always connected parallel with the circuit being tested.

WHEEL CYLINDER: Found in the automotive drum brake assembly, it is a device, actuated by hydraulic pressure, which, through internal pistons, pushes the brake shoes outward against the drums.

Notes

A

B